Human Rights and Civil Liberties

Human Rights and Civil Liberties

Howard Davis

Routledge
Taylor & Francis Group

LONDON AND NEW YORK

First published by Willan Publishing 2003
This edition published by Routledge 2013
2 Park Square, Milton Park, Abingdon, Oxon OX14 4RN
711 Third Avenue, New York, NY 10017 (8th Floor)

Routledge is an imprint of the Taylor & Francis Group, an informa business

ISBN 978 1 84392 008 3

British Library Cataloguing-in-Publication Data
A catalogue record for this book is available from the British Library

Typeset by TW Typesetting, Plymouth, Devon.

Contents

Part III Freedom of expression and the media

Part IV Political freedom

Preface

This book is a general survey of the law of civil liberties. It aims to identify and examine the legal rules, the common law and the statutes which relate to the field of civil liberties. But civil liberties is a subject that deals in controversial, politically charged matters. Rules of law produced by Parliament or the courts may be controversial in terms, for example, of the background principles they presuppose, the coherence and consistency of the rules one to another or the social and political consequences of their application. The book aims to describe and discuss the main terms of the arguments on such issues and to demonstrate their influence on the developing law.

The Human Rights Act 1998 is having a great impact on many areas of law, an impact which is pervasive and by no means confined to public law and civil liberties. Its influence on the latter is very great indeed. In Chapter 1 it is suggested that much of civil liberties law relates to problems about the scope and significance of democracy and privacy. Both these ideas, the freedom to participate in determining public goals and the ability to preserve an area of personal autonomy, are especially touched by human rights considerations. The approach in this book is to demonstrate, so far as it is possible, human rights law as integrated with domestic law, albeit in a way which challenges many of its rules and assumptions.

The end of the twentieth century and the beginning of the twenty-first has been a period of major constitutional reform and much of this touches and affects civil liberties. In particular there have been major statutory reforms, in areas such as surveillance, protection of personal data and freedom of information, which are of great importance and fully covered in this work. Another important issue is the rise of 'terrorism' and the question of how the government should respond. The significance of this matter has warranted the inclusion of a separate chapter.

The book is in five parts. Part I looks at democracy, privacy and human rights as values underlying civil liberties law and which inform its development and are the terms of its controversies. Part I also introduces the legal framework in which the law operates. The traditional approach in England and Wales is described and contrasted to the system under the European Convention on Human Rights as it is given further effect through the Human Rights Act 1998. Part II deals with those aspects of civil liberties law which are predominantly to do with the powers and duties of state agencies, particularly the police and security services, in respect of actions they may take which affect people's liberty and privacy. Principal duties of the state include the provision of fair trials and the proper treatment of prisoners. Both of these have been influenced by human rights law and are given separate chapters. Part III deals with a range of matters involving the law of freedom of expression. The focus of Part III is on the law as it bears on the media, whose importance in the communication of the knowledge and ideas necessary for an effective democracy is recognised. Part IV deals with a number of topics involving the law in so far as it can restrict those who are acting for political reasons. This includes chapters on public order and terrorism. Aspects of privacy, the freedom people have to decide for themselves how to live their lives for themselves, is the subject of Part V. It is here that some of the most profound and controversial matters with which the law has to deal, matters of life and death, are discussed.

I would like to thank a number of colleagues, especially Professor Barry Hough and Dr Mike Bennett, who have made particular contributions to my understanding of the law. All errors are my own. My family, as ever, have tolerated my absences while writing this book.

The book is dedicated to my mother and to the memory of my father.

Table of cases

Table of Acts of Parliament

Table of Statutory Instruments

Table of Command, parliamentary and other official papers

Annan, Lord (1977) *Report of the Committee on the Future of Broadcasting*, Cm 6753. London: HMSO, 193

Calcutt, Sir David (1990) *Report of the Committee on Privacy and Related Matters*, Cm 1102. London: HMSO, 187

Calcutt, Sir David (1992) *Review of Press Self Regulation*, Cm 2135. London: HMSO, 129, 187

Chancellor of the Duchy of Lancaster (1993) *Open Government*, Cm 2290. London: HMSO, 262, 266–77

Department of Health (2000) *Protecting Children, Supporting Parents*. London: Department of Health, 372

Franks, Lord (Chairman) (1972) *Departmental Committee on Section 2 of the Official Secrets Act 1911*, Cm 5104, 283

Home Office (1985) *Review of Public Order* (White Paper), Cm 9510, 299

Home Office (1997) *Code of Practice on Access to Government Information*, 2nd edn; revised 1998. London: HMSO; also available at http://www.homeoffice.gov.uk/foi/ogcode981.htm, 266–77

Home Office (2000) *Setting the Boundaries: Reforming the Law on Sex Offences*. London: Home Office, 387–8

Home Office and Northern Ireland Office (1998) *Legislation Against Terrorism: A Consultation Paper*, Cm 4178, 332

Intelligence and Security Committee (2000) The Mitrokhin Inquiry Report, Cri. 4764. London: Stationery Office, 80

Interception of Communications in the United Kingdom (1999), Cm 4368, 129

Law Commission (1981/85) *Criminal Law: Offences against Religion and Public Worship*, Working Paper 79 (1981); Report 145 (1985), 421

Lord Chancellor's Department (1993) *Infringement of Privacy*, Consultation Paper. London: HMSO, 187

Lord Lloyd of Berwick (1996) *Legislation Against Terrorism*, Cm 3420, 332

Lord Neill of Bladen, QC (Chairman), Committee on Standards in Public Life (1998) *The Funding of Political Parties in the United Kingdom*, Fifth Report, Volume 1: Report, Cm 4057-I; Volume II: Evidence, Cm 4057-II, 240, 248–9

MacPherson, Sir William (1999) *The Stephen Lawrence Inquiry*, Report, Cm 4262-I. London: Stationery Office, 66

National Heritage Select Committee (1993) *Fourth Report: Privacy and Media Intrusion*. HC 294-I, 187

Abbreviations

Ap.	Application number (to the European Court of Human Rights)
A-TC&S	Anti-terrorism, Crime and Security Act 2001
BBC	British Broadcasting Corporation
BSC	Broadcasting Standards Commission
CLJ	*Cambridge Law Journal*
Crim LR	*Criminal Law Review*
DC	Divisional Court
DPP	Director of Public Prosecutions
ECHR	European Convention on Human Rights
EctHR	European Court of Human Rights
HL	House of Lords
HRLJ	*Human Rights Law Journal*
ICCPR	International Covenant on Civil and Political Rights
ITC	Independent Television Commission
ITV	Independent Television
LQR	*Law Quarterly Review*
MLR	*Modern Law Review.*
NLJ	*New Law Journal*
OJLS	*Oxford Journal of Legal Studies*
PACE	Police and Criminal Evidence Act 1984
PCC	Press Complaints Commission
PL	*Public Law*
RA	Radio Authority
RIPA	Regulation of Investigatory Powers Act 2000
Sched.	Schedule
SI	Statutory Instrument
SIAC	Special Immigration Appeals Commission
PPERA	Political Parties, Elections and Referendums Act 2000

Neutral citation

Neutral citation is given where possible. The date of the decision is followed by an abbreviation for the court and then the number of the case, not the page number. Cases are published with numbered paragraphs. This system has been adopted for the superior courts with jurisdiction in England and Wales and also by the European Human Rights Reports series.

PC	Privy Council
UKHL	United Kingdom House of Lords

EWCA Civ — England and Wales, Court of Appeal, Civil Division
EWCA Crim — England and Wales, Court of Appeal, Criminal Division
EWHC [case number] Admin/ QB/Ch/Fam — High Court, Administrative Court, Queen's Bench, Chancery Division, Family Division.

Law Reports

AC — Appeal Cases
Admin LR — Administrative Law Reports
All ER — All England Law Reports
Atk — Atkin's Quarter Sessions cases
BHRC — Butterworth's Human Rights Cases
BMLR — Butterworth's Medical Law Reports
Black. W — Sir William Blackstone's Reports
Bos and P — Bosanquet and Pullar's Common Pleas Reports
C & P — Carrington and Payne's Nisi Prius Reports
C of D — Collections of Decisions (European Commission of Human Rights)
CMLR — Common Market Law Reports
COD — Crown Office Digest
Ch — Chancery Division
Cox CC — Cox's Criminal Cases
Cr Ap Rep — Criminal Appeal Reports
D&R — Decisions and Reports (European Commission of Human Rights)
De G & Sm — De Gex and Smiles Chancery Reports
DLR — Dominion Law Reports
E & B — Ellis and Blackburn's Queen's Bench Reports
ECR — European Court Reports
EHRLR — European Human Rights Law Reports
EHRR CD — European Human Rights Reports, Commission Digest
EHRR — European Human Rights Reports
EMLR — Entertainment and Media Law Reports
ER — English Reports
FCR — Family Court Reporter
FLR — Family Law Reports
Fam — Family Division
Hare — Hare's Chancery Reports
ICR — Industrial Cases Reports
IRLR — Industrial Relations Law Reports
JP — Justice of the Peace reports
KB — Kings Bench
LGR — Local Government Reports
LR — Law Reports
LT — Law Times
Med LR — Medical Law Reports
NI — Northern Ireland Law Reports
QB — Queen's Bench
QBD — Queen's Bench Divisional Court

RTR	Road Traffic Reports
SA	South African Law Reports
SC	Session Cases
SLT	Scots Law Times
SR (NSW)	New South Wales State Reports
St Tr	State Trials
TLR	The Times Law Reports
WLR	Weekly Law Reports
YB	Yearbook of the European Convention on Human Rights

Part I
Values and institutions

1

Introduction and underlying values

1.1 Introduction

A group of political demonstrators are arrested when they hold a meeting on a public road, a desperately ill man wishes to choose the time of his death, a journalist with an important story about an alleged terrorist group is faced with prison for not disclosing her source. These are examples of issues about civil liberties law. In this chapter the values that underlie civil liberties law are introduced as are the broad constitutional theories, the theories of state power, which give the law its legitimacy in relation to those values. Finally, the idea of human rights is introduced since it is in relation to that idea that civil liberties law is being restated. A principal aim of this book is to integrate human rights law into the common law and statutory rules which make up the subject.

1.2 Values: democracy and privacy

Civil liberties law is to do with the relationship between citizens and the state in so far as this relationship affects two features of social life presumed to be valuable. These two 'features' are, first, 'democracy' or the good of political participation. Civil liberties law is concerned with identifying the reasonable scope of the freedom of people to participate in political processes and seek to change or maintain the laws, government policies or public opinion. The second 'feature' is the idea of privacy. Civil liberties law is concerned with the reasonable scope of the claim that there is a significant part of a person's life that should be determined by that person alone and in respect of which the state, through its laws, should have no say. From this perspective, the state also has duties, through its laws, to preserve the private part of a person's life from improper intrusion from others, such as neighbours or the media.

The current law, which is stated in this book, represents the rules and principles on these issues which have emerged from the exercise of state power in the imperfect democracy that is the United Kingdom. Their reasonableness is the subject of the arguments that surround these rules and principles. Through these arguments, the strengths and weaknesses, the reasons for supporting, for tolerating or for rejecting the current rules can be assessed.

For some writers, democracy and privacy are so independent of each other, so much dealing with distinct and unrelated matters, that they are incapable of uniting together into a single subject called 'civil liberties'.[1] The position, which is presumed in this book, is that civil liberties law engages with political activity and privacy in so far as they are affected by the law and by state power exercised under the law. From that position, privacy and democracy are interrelated. There is an essential aspect of 'privacy' underlying political activity. Political activity flows from the conceptions that individuals hold about what is good and valuable in life and what ought to be promoted or restricted in society. Such 'conceptions of the good' will, as a matter of fact, usually reflect the cultural traditions and the collective ways of life of the society; most people assert views that exist within a fairly narrow range of opinions and possibilities. Marxists, for example, and other cultural sociologists will explain such conformity in terms of a broadly deterministic relationship between the basic way of life in society, particularly the system of wealth production, and the values and ideas that people hold. Even if it is possible to explain in such deterministic ways why it is that people hold the views they do, it remains the case that those views are essentially theirs. A person's views on religion, on the justification of war or peace, on the best constitutional and economic system, on the kinds of people to befriend or love and so on are important in any understanding we may have of them as persons. We can use the word 'autonomy' to express the idea that such views are attached to them as an important part of their personality. Our assumption about what it means to be a person is that, unlike, we believe, an animal or an object, persons have the capacity to reflect upon, choose and promote their sense of what is worthwhile and worth pursuing in life, usually for themselves, sometimes for others. This 'autonomy' may be true or it may be a fiction. In either event we presume it to be true. It is the presumption at the heart of moral discourse, ethics, the criminal law and, also, of the basic idea that some conception of democracy is a good the law should promote. Civil liberties law, therefore, is about the scope and dimensions of the freedom people have to seek to get their own sense of what is worthwhile adopted by society as purposes the law is to serve.

'Democracy' and 'privacy' are also linked because the claims of privacy can be the subject matter of some of the most controversial and testing political issues. People may claim that what they read or watch, how and with whom they make love, how they treat their body and so on are matters entirely for them and there is no social or political interest that justifies the intervention of the state. Similarly they may claim that information about these and other matters, such as their income, is personal and only to be used or disclosed by others under conditions that the person controls. But these claims can be contradicted by laws relating to obscenity, sexual offences, suicide and so on, and a significant degree of democratic politics involves struggles, conducted in Parliament, the courts or on the streets, about the scope of privacy that the law should recognise.

---

[1] Ewing, K. and Gearty, C. (2000) *The Struggle for Civil Liberties.* Oxford: Oxford University Press, chapter 1.

1.2.1 Democracy

Democracy is a highly contested concept.[2] No political theory can claim to be 'democratic' which does not value at least some rights to a degree of political participation.[3] However, it is clear that there is significant disagreement as to the point and core extent of such rights. There are two standard views on why political participation is valued. One view values political participation and democratic principles instrumentally. It is a means of enabling people to obtain things they want for themselves or for others in society. An alternative view sees the point of participative politics not in achieving private goods but as an important part of the full expression of mankind's social and public personality. Through political activity we not only advance personal interests but, more importantly, we express the public aspect of our nature without which we are incomplete and unfulfilled.

Whatever the purposes, there is also disagreement about the core extent of democratic participation. Political participation is valued to different degrees and to different extents. One view asserts that society as a whole is likely to be richer, more peaceful and generally more successful if decisions about the public good are taken by educated and skilled specialists in the arts of government – by political elites of one general political orientation or another. The focus is on representative institutions and practices, above all, the institutions of elections and Parliaments and the political parties that support them. The people go about their private daily lives and are for most of the time politically disengaged and passive. The core requirement for democratic participation is regular elections to choose the elites who will then govern and be the central actors of political life.[4] Democracy as a politically passive population governed by elites recruited through representative institutions is defended not only on grounds of efficiency but also as the version of democracy that best describes the situation of political disengagement that characterises modern capitalist societies. It is interesting to note that the European Convention on Human Rights does not contain any general right of participation in public affairs but only a duty on governments to hold regular elections for the country's legislature.[5]

For many, representative democracy, in some version or other, is inadequate.[6] The representatives become too detached from the people they represent and too engaged with their own independent agenda and way of life. People are unable effectively to pursue their interests through the representative scheme. Furthermore, political passivity and withdrawal is seen as incompatible with the idea of full self-development and with a healthy and progressive society. On this view, a properly democratic society is one which

[2] See, for example: Weale, A. (1999) *Democracy*. London: Macmillan; Lakoff, S. (1996) *Democracy. History, Theory and Practice*. Oxford: Westview Press; Carter, A. and Stokes, G. (1998) *Liberal Democracy and Its Critics*. Cambridge: Polity Press; Arblaster, A. (1994) *Democracy*, 2nd edn. Buckingham: Buckingham University Press.

[3] Lively, J. (1975) *Democracy*. Oxford: Blackwell.

[4] On representative democracy see: Schumpeter, J. (1982) *Capitalism, Socialism and Democracy*. London: Routledge.

[5] See Chapter 13.

[6] Hirst, P. (1994) *Associative Democracy*. London: Polity Press.

values and gives institutional support to direct democracy. People should be able to decide directly, without the intervention of representative institutions, the issues which affect them. People should also be encouraged to develop 'extra-Parliamentary' forms of political action such as public campaigning, demonstrating and, if necessary, peaceful acts of civil disobedience. Such activities are not contrary to democracy but embody its spirit and purpose.[7] Other conceptions of democracy, which also flow from a sense of dissatisfaction with simple representative politics, value and wish to expand the role of self-governing associations in governing as many aspects of our social life as possible.[8]

Disagreements about democracy can also turn on whether or not democracy requires 'majority rule'. Majoritarian democracy authorises the law to pursue whatever ends are chosen by a majority for the time being.[9] More usual is for 'democracy' to limit majorities in terms of fundamental rights of individuals, particularly individuals in minority groups of various kinds. Fundamental rights, at least to equal concern and respect,[10] need to be protected. Minorities cannot be merely ignored or treated as a means to the ends of the majority.

These are all complicated matters that warrant more detailed treatment than is possible here. To say that civil liberties law deals with the reasonable scope of rights of political participation raises questions about what 'democracy' requires. Arguments about the law may reflect deeper arguments about the best, the most appropriate, conception of democracy that the law ought to advance. Judges faced, for example, with a prosecution of political demonstrators under public order legislation may need, perhaps, to evaluate the reasonableness of the demonstrators' use of the highway and the reasonableness of the steps taken by the police to ensure that political protests can go ahead when measured against the freedom of the public to go about their private lives unhindered. Such evaluations will reflect the particular conception of democracy that is adhered to, consciously or by inference, by the court.

1.2.2 Privacy

The second value that partially defines the scope and nature of civil liberties law is privacy. The general idea is of some inviolable area that is, and should remain, within the control of the individual person.[11] This requirement derives from the broad, cultural, sense of what it means to be a person. It is the argument from 'autonomy'. A being all of whose actions and decisions can be

---

[7] Barber, B. (1994) *Strong Democracy: Participatory Politics for a New Age.* Berkeley, CA: University of California Press.

[8] Hirst, *op. cit.*

[9] Lively, *op. cit.*, chapter 2.

[10] Dworkin, R. (1977) *Taking Rights Seriously.* London: Duckworth, chapter 6.

[11] See J.S. Mill's much quoted definition: '. . . a circle around every individual human being which no government ought to be permitted to overstep . . . there is, or ought to be some space in human existence thus entrenched around and sacred from authoritative intrusion' (*Principles of Political Economy* (1848; 1909) Longman, Green & Co., book V, chapter 9, 2). See also: Wacks, R. (1995) *Privacy and Press Freedom.* London: Blackstone Press, chapter 1; Paul, E.F. *et al.* (2000) *The Right to Privacy.* Cambridge: Cambridge University Press; Markesinis, B. (ed.) (1999) *Protecting Privacy.* Oxford: Oxford University Press.

interfered with, who has no sphere of thought, decision and actions which cannot be so interfered with, fails the test of personhood. States must respect this and so ensure that privacy is protected in law.

In civil liberties law, privacy acts in one of two ways. One is as a kind of 'trump' argument. Privacy is a claim that the state should keep out of regulating a particular matter and leave it to the individuals involved. The obvious examples relate to family life and to sexual life. It is for parents, and not the state or the community as a whole, to bring up their children and lead them towards reasonable and fruitful lives. This claim is held by few, if any, in an absolute sense. There is no compelling reason why violence against spouses, usually wives, or against children is to any degree excused because they are private matters. On the other hand, there is a continuing argument on whether the state, through law, is entitled to distribute its liberties and resources in such a way as to promote particular ways of life or forms of family existence. Should the state, for example, promote heterosexual marriage over other forms of family life? Such an issue can be raised in a legal context such as the law of adoption.

A second purpose that a claim to privacy may have is that the lawfulness, the right of the state to intervene and regulate, depends on whether the action in question takes place in public or private. Sexual conduct is often seen in this way. A sexual act in 'private' may be thought harmless and hence permitted while the exact same act in 'public' (however defined) may be prohibited. Some sexual moralists, on the contrary, argue that certain kinds of sexual conduct are so revolting in themselves that they can be prohibited, the claim to privacy not withstanding. This issue is discussed in Chapter 22

Like 'democracy', the meaning and significance of 'privacy' is endlessly contested.[12] For example, there is an ongoing argument on whether private property is necessary to any reasonable conception of privacy. On some accounts, the ownership of goods and land is an expression of personality which the state must respect in its dealings. An alternative view is that property is a collective product, reflecting the activities of all, and its unequal distribution is an exercise of social power which it is perfectly proper for the state to regulate and control. Similar controversies relate to the 'family'. Family has traditionally been seen as the institutional embodiment of privacy; the state, through its law, must respect its boundaries. From other perspectives, however, the family is the particular form in which patriarchal social relations are asserted and women generally subordinated to men and marginalised in economic life and civil society. On that view, the family is not 'private' but a social institution, the focus of political struggle and legal regulation. The claim of privacy becomes its opposite: a claim to exercise power at the expense of women and children free from state and legal interferences. Even the most intimate acts, acts of sexual expression, can raise controversial political arguments about the right of the state to forbid or promote certain forms of sexual expression rather than others.

---

[12] For example, Ryan, A. (1986) *Property and Political Theory*. Oxford: Blackwell.

1.3 Constitutional and political theory

The implication of the above is that the 'values' underlying civil liberties law, the values of 'democracy' and 'privacy', are the subject of ongoing argument and disagreement as to their meaning and implications. Part of that argument involves the question of to what regard and to what extent these values should be promoted and protected by the law. An argument, say by judges, about what the law should be in any particular instance is likely to reflect, even if unwittingly, a more general constitutional theory about the place of law and the values inherent in it.[13]

Some general political theories would, for example, simply deny any recognisable claim to democracy or privacy. The concept of a totalitarian state (linked to Stalinism or fascism) is that the state is in principle unrestrained in its right not only to control the conduct of politics but also to identify and enforce a particular conception of how individuals should conduct their lives, the values they should adopt and the sacrifices they should make. The absence of a sense of 'the private' makes it hard to see how any reasonable conception of civil liberties can exist in the public discourse of state and law.

A broadly conservative political disposition values the traditions of the established order. It supports and promotes conventional political activity and gradual change. It is, however, also amenable to strong state action against any kind of ideological, radical politics which can be seen as a threat to gradual, ordered change. Such action can appear oppressive and in need of special justification in the context, say, of public order law or police powers. A conservative political outlook underlying the law is also likely to accept that the state need not be 'neutral' as between different views of what makes a good and worthwhile life. Supporting the traditions of the public order can involve allowing the selection and promotion of certain 'goods' as being inherent in the society and what it stands for. Thus a conservative may, through the law, wish to promote and protect particular social institutions and values such as the established church or the preference for marriage as the proper form of family life. The argument in favour of such protection and promotion does not depend upon a reasoned justification from first principles but, rather, on a factual claim about the central place of such institutions in the historical and cultural identity of society.[14]

Liberal theory provides the strongest defence for a wide conception of civil liberties to be enshrined in constitutional principles and positive law. Liberalism starts with a strong conception of private life: that individuals are the best judges of what is in their own interest and of what is a valuable and worthwhile life. The state should only intervene in so far as a person's activities restrict the equal rights and freedoms of others. Liberalism claims to be based on first principles: a political value is good because our reason tells us so rather than because of long acceptance as part of the traditions of society.

---

[13] Craig, P.P. (1990) *Public Law and Democracy in the United Kingdom and the United States of America.* Oxford: Clarendon Press; Loughlin, M. (1992) *Public Law and Political Theory.* Oxford: Oxford University Press.

[14] For example, Oakeshott, M. (1991) *Rationalism in Politics and Other Essays.* Indianapolis, Indianapolis: Liberty Press; Scrutton, R. (2000) *The Meaning of Conservatism,* 3rd edn. Basingstoke: Palgrave.

The strongest modern defence of liberalism argues for a constitutional and legal system which provides the greatest amount of personal, social and political freedom for individuals in so far as this can be equally available to all. This aim is justified in abstract terms, not dependent on the facts of any particular history or culture, as a choice that would be made if people could choose under fair and equal conditions. Such fair and equal conditions of choice are that people know that they are choosing a legal and constitutional system which must produce laws which are fair to all whatever their wealth, religion, race or personal character might be. The choice is justified in so far as it is the system that would be chosen by morally reasonable people seeking to base a political system on fair principles but who do not know how they, personally, would be benefited.[15] Other versions of liberalism suggest that activities should be only restricted by law and state not because they are worthless, trashy or revolting but solely because they are harmful to others. Liberalism also supports a strong conception of political rights such as freedom of expression and freedom of association. This is predominantly as an instrumental means by which individuals can pursue their self-interest through political and public means, though for many liberals, political activity is also an embodiment of the kind of active, socially aware, person the theory (in some of its versions) seeks to promote.

The broad liberal defence of state power is criticised on many grounds. In particular, it is alleged that liberalism misunderstands and undervalues the extent to which individuals have identities which are rooted in communities and cultures and which determine, or at least strongly influence, the choices of values and ways of life available to individuals or which they claim to be their own.[16] Partly this is an argument leading to the kinds of conservative political assumptions outlined above. However, it is also the basis of more progressive criticism. Liberal perfectionism, for example, asserts that it is reasonable for the state to wish to restrict or denigrate certain pointless conditions of life, like drug addiction, for example, because they are incompatible with autonomy. They close off the possibility of future choices. Conversely the state may advance forms of life which promote the possibility of useful and fruitful choices. Feminist politics is a different example of the kind of communitarian and identity-based criticism aimed at the liberal tradition. On this view, the liberal focus on individual freedom and the realm of the private, protected from state intervention, can hide oppression from the reach of the law. The example of family life and its place in the public or private world has been given above.

1.4 Human rights

The suggestion in this chapter is that civil liberties law revolves around the related values of democracy and privacy, that these values are, in themselves,

---

[15] Rawls, J. (1972) *A Theory of Justice*. Oxford: Oxford University Press; see also Barry, B. (1995) *Justice as Impartiality*. Oxford: Clarendon Press.

[16] For example, Sandel, M.J. (1996) *Liberalism and the Limits of Justice*, 2nd edn. Cambridge: Cambridge University Press; Mulhall, S. and Swift, A. (1996) *Liberals and Communitarians*, 2nd edn. Oxford: Blackwell.

controversial and argued about and that underlying these arguments are different general conceptions of law and constitutions such as those which were briefly sketched above.

Questions about civil liberties law, about giving effect to democracy and privacy, are now overlaid with the concept of human rights. In Chapter 2 we discuss the way in which human rights law is being integrated with, or even taking over from, the traditional approaches of English law to these questions, and the process is illustrated in the rest of the book.

1.4.1 The concept of human rights

The concept of 'human rights' relates to the idea of certain freedoms, understood as entitlements, which are to be enjoyed by all persons on a basis of equality, i.e. for the sufficient reason that they are persons.[17] These entitlements or 'rights' are fundamental in the sense that they should be protected by the law even if those in power, or a majority of the population or other significant interests, wish them to be removed generally or from individuals or groups. In other words they should be protected even against strong arguments that the common good, the collective interest, would be benefited were they removed. Human rights, therefore, embody entitlements and values inherent in a kind of superior law, a law which conditions and must be taken into account by the processes of making and putting the ordinary, positive, law into effect.

1.4.2 Issues and difficulties

Rights and other political claims
At the theoretical level, the notion of human rights is controversial. There is, for example, a strong objection to the very idea of values that trump the common good. It might be said that human rights are undemocratic: they are restrictions on majority rule. This is not a strong argument since it depends upon an unconvincing account of democracy as being solely and on all matters majority decision making. The argument can, however, be more complicated. Defenders of human rights accept that rights are seldom, if ever, absolute. In great emergencies, for example, it is often accepted that at least some rights can be moderated or 'derogated' from. There is, in principle, always a need to weigh human rights against the common good, albeit the former 'trumps' the latter in all but extreme situations. Even in non-extreme situations, one claimed right may need to be weighed against some other (free speech against privacy, for example). Given this need to 'weigh' rights against the common good or other rights, a human rights claim looks, to critics, increasingly like any other political claim that might be made and everything turns on how these judgments of weight and significance are made.[18] Defenders of human rights respond by asserting that some rights are indeed absolute, or by claiming that the results of such 'weighings', even in emergency situations, will be different, and better, if done in the terms of a human rights culture.

[17] Jones, P. (1994) *Rights*. London: Macmillan.
[18] For example, Griffith, J.A.G. (1979) 'The Political Constitution', 42 1 *MLR* 1.

The derivation of human rights

There are difficulties with the derivation of human rights, with how such fundamental entitlements are identified. Various possibilities can be canvassed. A natural law approach, for example, suggests that an interrogation of our natures as human beings will disclose a conception of personhood and the circumstances under which persons can flourish, and that these conceptions, to make sense, must include the basic idea of (some) human rights.[19] Social contract theorists, concerned with the origin and legitimation of government, conclude that legitimate government is based on the consent of the people and this would not be given unless persons were secure in their basic rights.

For critics, the point is that any account of the derivation of human rights is dependent upon a prior acceptance of a particular, contested, theoretical point of view such as natural law or social contract theory. The argument for human rights is, therefore, only as good as the general political theory which supports it – human rights, like any other value system, are not given but are disclosed through a contested theoretical exercise.

The enforcement of human rights and judicial politics

Human rights involves the identification of fundamental entitlements which are supposed to be binding even on legislatures and governments. Characteristically they are given ultimate effect through the courts rather than Parliament. In a democracy, albeit an imperfect one, this can be seen as transferring ultimate decision making about important social questions, to unelected and unrecallable judges. The developing human rights 'agenda', on this account, involves the continuous narrowing of the range and type of matters that an elected assembly can decide and a demonstration of increasing distrust of the people's representatives. Some who make this criticism still accept the idea of fundamental rights but not as matters 'above' ordinary politics and reserved for judges to decide.[20] In fact, many constitutional approaches to human rights (including in the United Kingdom) still reserve to the Parliament the ultimate authority to enact laws even if they unambiguously violate 'human rights'. Defenders of human rights accept the political role for the judges. They argue that a human rights culture involves a consideration of the limits to what democratic governments and majorities can do, that this involves a careful and reasoned consideration of the principles involved and for this the courts are, indeed, most suited.

The content of human rights

Accepting a particular argument about the way in which human rights are derived does not mean that there is agreement about the content of those rights, about the identity of those entitlements which are so fundamental they must be protected even against strong arguments of the common good to the contrary. The classic statements of rights, such as found in the United Nations Declaration or in the European Convention on Human Rights, list the so-called 'great rights'. These are civil and political rights involving, for example,

---

[19] See Finnis, J. (1980) *Natural Law and Natural Rights*. Oxford: Oxford University Press.
[20] Waldron, J. (1993) 'A Right-Based Critique of Constitutional Rights', 13 *OJLS* 18.

freedom from oppressive state actions such as torture or unlawful detention, rights of privacy and rights to associate and to speak, particularly in a political context. These rights are predominantly 'negative'. They describe actions barred to state authorities. They are occasionally 'positive' but only in the sense of imposing a duty on the state to ensure that certain actions are barred to companies, families or individuals.

Critics argue that this classic conception of human rights fails to express the full range of fundamental human needs. There is little reference to social rights, such as rights to housing or to education, in the classic human rights documents yet, for many people, the right to an adequate home may be far more significant than, say, a right to freedom of speech. Similarly the classic human rights agenda has little to say on protecting the environment even though it is hard to think of a more fundamental interest that individuals can have than to live in a sustainable environment. A different version of the argument about the content of human rights is that the classic rights instruments have little to say on the 'worth' of rights. The poor and disadvantaged may have little effective opportunity to exercise their 'great' rights to freedom of expression, for example. The argument is, then, that the state should take positive steps to give access to the media through requiring community broadcasting or through rights of reply and so on.[21] Defenders of the classic human rights perspective argue that social and environmental goals are likely to involve large state expenditures and need careful evaluation against a range of issues and interests. As such these matters are unsuitable for 'hard', obligatory, human rights law enforced by judges, and should be, indeed, the meat of normal representative, democratic politics and the subject of no more than 'soft', merely aspirational, international law. It is now clear that there are significant developments in which social and environmental issues are high on the agenda of international law. There is a developing range of both 'hard' and 'soft' international obligations on matters such as the environment, economic development and the situation of children.

Rights and individualism

Critics of human rights observe that the language of rights can counterpoise the individual against the community. It is a language of entitlements for oneself rather than of duties towards others, of individual interests asserted against the claims of the common good. Rights-talk, the argument goes, reinforces these tensions and establishes them as conflicts in which the individual is likely to be victorious rather than as social dilemmas needing compromise and settlement. The argument is used, for example, by those who wish to stress the value of community decision taking which aims at a reasonable, consensus-based solution to social problems. On such a view, rights-based arguments will claim to trump the consensus view and, as such, are an unwelcome and unfair distortion of the political process. The argument is also put by those who see rights claims as being a weapon in the armoury

---

[21] For example, Campbell, T. (1983) *The Left and Rights: A Conceptual Analysis of the Idea of Socialist Rights*. London: Routledge.

of the powerful.[22] Companies, including huge commercial conglomerates, enjoy at least some 'human' rights and these can be used to inhibit the development and enforcement of the general consensus that emerges from representative politics. The obvious example is the partial successes that tobacco companies have had in claiming that their rights to freedom of expression protect them from significant bans on advertising.

1.4.3 Positive law

The matters discussed above have focused on whether the human rights perspective is the best way to deal with important issues such as how to give effect to reasonable conditions of democracy and privacy in society. This focus is necessary because, throughout the rest of the book, the validity of a human rights approach is taken for granted. The point is that in the United Kingdom, as in most of the rest of the world, there is now an instrument of positive law, the Human Rights Act 1998, which aims, in its own particular way, to establish human rights and a culture of human rights in the law. The detail of this, and its integration with conventional common law and statute, form the substance of the following chapters.

---

[22] For example, Ewing, K. (1996) 'Human Rights, Social Democracy and Constitutional Reform,' and other essays, in Gearty, C. and Tomkins, A. (eds), *Understanding Human Rights*. London: Mansell.

2

The institutional setting

2.1 The traditional approach in England and Wales

2.1.1 Parliament and the common law

The traditional approach to the protection of rights and liberties in the United Kingdom involves the interrelation of common law principles with the specific interventions, through legislation, of a supreme Parliament. It has its *locus classicus* in the account of the rule of law found in A.V. Dicey's *Introduction to the Study of the Law of the Constitution*[1] which described the late Victorian constitution but which continues to be highly influential on the way the fundamentals of the current constitutional arrangements are understood. On this account, the primary background principle of the common law is 'negative freedom'. This is the sense that a person's freedom to do as he or she wills is the natural state, it is not derived from any law or act of a sovereign. Given this, there is an assumption of lawfulness: anything is permitted unless it has been clearly forbidden by law. Dicey believed this was likely to provide effective protection for personal and political freedom because any restrictions on freedom needed to be based on judge-declared or statutory rules which needed to be identified with sufficient precision in order to defeat the presumption of lawfulness.

A consideration of the effectiveness of both the common law and Parliament in protecting personal and political freedoms involves a balanced judgment. Parliament and the common law have both been capable of establishing important protections for civil liberties; they have both also been responsible for significant inroads into civil liberties as well.

2.1.2 Parliament

In Dicey's classic definition of Parliamentary supremacy, Parliament can make or unmake any law, there is no higher legislative authority and no court can invalidate an Act of Parliament.[2] Implicit in this is the absence of any full 'bill of rights', a constitutional recognition of personal or political freedoms, expressed as rights, entrenched and immune from legislative change.

---

[1] Dicey, A.V. (1885) *Introduction to the Study of the Law of the Constitution*. Indianapolis, IN.: Liberty Classics, part II, chapter IV.
[2] Dicey, *op. cit.*, part I, chapters I and II.

The strength of Parliament, as regards its suitability to protect the political and personal liberties of the people, is that it represents the will of the people as expressed through the electoral system. The government is responsible to Parliament and so the power of the electorate to change the majority party in Parliament, and hence the government, was, for Dicey, a defence for freedom since no government could oppress the people for long without risk of being voted out of office.[3] The weakness of Parliament in this regard is that Parliament represents the majority interest and a Parliament which represents the majority and which has unlimited powers is, in principle, not the best way of protecting the rights and liberties of minorities and individuals. In the United Kingdom this problem is made significantly worse by the fact that the electoral system for national elections can produce massive Parliamentary majorities on the votes of under half of those who vote and, given that only about two-thirds of those who are entitled to vote do so, the Parliamentary majority may represent quite a small percentage of the adult population.

Parliament is also the principal forum in which the government, the executive, is made to account for its actions. However, the modern Parliament, through the party system and ministerial patronage, is dominated by the executive. Ministerial accountability is generally regarded as weak and, as a consequence, government policy, including that which impacts on civil liberties, may be inadequately scrutinised.[4] There have, however, been significant improvements in the power of Parliamentary scrutiny over the last decades. In particular, the development of the departmental select committees (now called Scrutiny Committees) since 1979 has been much commented upon. Generalisations about the weakness of ministerial accountability are unlikely to do justice to the complex range of devices and institutions by which Parliament directly as a whole or through its committees, or indirectly through its establishing of various agencies such as ombudsmen, examines legislation and scrutinises the executive.

No clear judgment can be made on whether or not Parliament really has promoted civil liberties where possible and protected them where necessary. It is clear that many of the most important human rights and liberties have been established by Parliament and not by the courts. The extension of the franchise to women, the establishment of anti-discrimination law in respect of race, gender and disability and the legalisation of trade unions are examples of major developments in civil liberties law done by Parliament often against the hostility, indifference or conceptual incomprehension of the common law. Yet, driven by the executive, Parliament has also enacted legislation which has severely restricted civil freedom in a number of ways. Draconian legislation has been rushed through Parliament with little interest shown in its impact on civil liberties. The Official Secrets Act 1911 and the Prevention of Terrorism (Temporary Provisions) Act 1973 are examples. Other legislation has openly violated rights, such as the removal of citizenship and rights of residency from

---

[3] See Craig, P.P. (1994) *Adminstrative Law*. London: Sweet & Maxwell, chapter 1, section 2.
[4] Turpin, C. (1989) 'Ministerial Responsibility – Myth or Reality', in Jowell, J. and Oliver, D. (eds), (1989) *The Changing Constitution*, 2nd edn. Oxford: Oxford University Press.

East African Asians,[5] or has increased the power of the police. Most recently Parliament has given the Home Secretary a power to detain certain foreigners without trial with appeal only to a special court.[6] The record is ambiguous as would be expected from an institution that must react to the endless flow of circumstances and changes of public opinion.[7]

2.1.3 Common law

Common law is judge made and is the underlying law which is presumed by Parliament and which, in theory, is available to cover every possible situation. The common law is subordinate to Parliament which may, and sometimes does, overturn with legislation the legal rule on which a judgment is based. Many of the absolutely basic propositions of civil liberties law have their origins in decisions of the courts. Declaring the incompatibility of slavery with the law in England[8] and holding that the government was not above the ordinary law and could be sued for trespass, its assertion of the public good notwithstanding,[9] are well known examples. Usually, however, the strength of the common law lies in the specificity and detail of its judgments, the underlying principles of law they infer and with the link with remedies rather than it does with promoting major social developments.

As with Parliament, the common law record is two-sided. For every great case in the cause of liberty there have been cases in which the courts have failed to rise to the challenge of protecting liberties.[10] In particular, the common law, by speaking the language of negative liberty, has been unable to develop positive rights in the civil liberties field, such as in respect of the law relating to political demonstrations. The fundamental values the common law has traditionally dealt with are property, the enforcement of agreements, reputation and fair procedures.[11] As is clear from the chapters that follow, such matters can have a significant impact on civil liberties, but it has also meant that the common law has found it difficult to make the law reach international standards in certain significant areas. The inability of the courts to fashion, until recently, an adequately sophisticated right to privacy is the most obvious example.[12]

The common law has undergone a great revival during the second half of the twentieth century. The view that the judges pursue a conservative agenda

---

[5] Commonwealth Immigrants Act 1962; see Lord Lester of Herne Hill (2002) 'Thirty Years on: the East African Asians Case Revisited', *Public Law* 52, Spring.

[6] Anti-terrorism, Crime and Security Act 2001 – see Chapter 19.

[7] See Klug, F., Starmer, K. and Weir, S. (1996) *The Three Pillars of Liberty*. London: Routledge for an analysis, prior to the coming into force of the Human Rights Act 1998, of the extent to which United Kingdom law met international human rights standards.

[8] *Somersett* v *Stewart* (1772) 20 St Tr 1.

[9] *Entick* v *Carrington* (1765) 2 Wils 275 (1765) 19 St Tr 1029.

[10] Late eighteenth-century persecutions of political radicals and the legal refusal to enable trade unions to flourish or permit votes for women in the late nineteenth century are examples. Again, it is in the detail of judicial judgments that the true devil lies. See Klug, Starmer and Weir, *op. cit.* for contemporary analysis.

[11] Noted in *ibid*.

[12] For example, *Kaye* v *Robertson* [1991] FSR 62. Such a right is now being developed as the common law adapts itself to the culture of human rights; see, for example, *Douglas* v *Hello!* [2001] 2 All ER 289.

in the way they develop the law and exercised their discretion within it[13] is much harder to sustain today although allegations that the courts are too 'executive minded' may resurface in the context of the judicial response to terrorism after the attacks in the United States on 11 September 2001. In particular, the last decade or so has seen the courts become significantly more 'human rights aware' in their judgments. This reflects cultural change but also the 'flowing in' of international law, above all European Human Rights, into the law. The bringing into effect of the Human Rights Act 1998 enhances and specifies this process. It makes a huge difference to the language and the approach of the courts but will not necessarily bring about radical differences in outcome. The 'rights awareness' by the judges can be found in the way statutes are interpreted (see the next section), on the development of judicial review (discussed in Chapter 3) and in the way in which the common law has been developed in areas such as defamation (see Chapter 11).

2.1.4 Statute and common law: the interpretation of statutes

Acts of Parliament, in all their detail, are often central to the way that fundamental rights and freedoms are recognised in the law of the United Kingdom. Statutes must be interpreted and it is the job of the courts to do this as they apply the general words of an Act to the particular circumstances of a case. The traditional approach of the courts is to recognise Parliamentary supremacy by giving effect to an Act even if, for example, it involves a severe restriction on fundamental rights and freedoms. The words of Lord Reid in *Madzimbamuto* v *Lardner-Burke* (1969) illustrate this approach and indicate the difficulty from a civil liberties point of view:

> It is often said that it would be unconstitutional for the United Kingdom Parliament to do certain things, meaning that the moral, political and other reasons against doing them are so strong that most people would regard it as highly improper if Parliament did these things. But that does not mean that it is beyond the power of Parliament to do such things. If Parliament chooses to do any of them, the courts could not hold the Act of Parliament invalid.[14]

Furthermore, the recognition of Parliamentary supremacy means it is impossible to entrench or establish an Act which protects fundamental rights against express repeal. The courts have accepted the idea of implied repeal whereby, in the absence of express words of repeal, an inconsistency between an earlier and a later statute is resolved by the implied repeal of the earlier statute[15] or by disregarding it to the extent that is necessary to give effect to the later statute.[16]

---

[13] Early edition of J.A.G. Griffith's *The Politics of the Judiciary* contain the clearest statements of this position (for example, 2nd edn (1981) London: Fontana).

[14] [1969] AC 645, 723.

[15] *Vauxhall Estates Ltd* [1932] 1 KB 733; *Ellen Street Estates Ltd* [1934] 1 KB 590.

[16] *Goodwin* v *Phillips* [1908] 7 CLR 1, accepted as representing the law of England by the Divisional Court in *Thorburn* v *Sunderland City Council* [2002] EWHC Admin 195 [2002] 4 All ER 156.

However, a significant development in the interpretation of Acts of Parliament can now be discerned. Unless an Act of Parliament is express and unambiguous on the point, it will not be interpreted as authorising a serious interference with fundamental rights and freedoms which are recogised by the common law or by international law. This trend, which pre-dates the Human Rights Act 1998, can be seen in the way the discretionary powers of public officials, derived from statute, are given effect and also from the way in which subordinate legislation is interpreted.[17] The courts are also beginning to recognise the existence of 'constitutional statutes', taken to be more fundamental than others, which cannot be impliedly repealed by later statutes. Examples of such statutes are Magna Carta, the Bill of Rights 1688, the Representation of the People Acts and the Human Rights Act.[18] The courts will require express and unambiguous words in primary legislation before the fundamental rights found in such statutes can be repealed.[19]

Common law recognition of fundamental values can also be found in the presumptions that are brought to bear on the interpretation of statutes. Presumptions are matters that the courts assume to be the case in the absence of express word to the contrary. Many presumptions are important in civil liberties law, such as that the Crown is not bound by legislation unless the Act expressly says so and that recognised rights cannot be removed other than by express words. Of particular importance in the civil liberties context is the presumption that Parliament intends to legislate in a manner that is compatible with the international obligations of the United Kingdom. This is discussed in the next section.

2.2 International law

The United Kingdom is a signatory to many international agreements which bear upon civil liberties issues. Traditionally, treaties and other international agreements dealt with diplomatic matters and the high politics of the relations between states. Economic and technological development and globalisation, however, are creating circumstances in which mutual interdependence between states is becoming increasingly necessary. Treaties are increasingly dealing with issues which are not only at the heart of the political agenda but which also have as their purpose the creation of rights for individuals. The World Trade Organisation is an obvious example of the former and the United Nations Convention of the Rights of the Child is an example of the second. In the United Kingdom international law cannot create rights directly enforceable by the courts unless the provisions of the treaty are enacted in an Act of

---

[17] See a powerful statement of the view in *R* v *Secretary of State for Social Services ex parte Joint Council for the Welfare of Immigrants* [1996] 4 All ER 385, 402 (maintaining the worth of the right to claim political asylum). The general principle is accepted by the House of Lords in *R* v *Secretary of State for the Home Dept ex parte Simms and another* [1999] 3 All ER 400 (the free speech rights of prisoners); see also *R* v *Lord Chancellor ex parte Witham* [1997] 2 All ER 779 (the right of access to the court). A warning that the courts should not be too ready to discover fundamental rights is in *R* v *Lord Chancellor ex parte Lightfoot* [1998] 4 All ER 764.
[18] *Ibid.*
[19] *Thorburn* v *Sunderland City Council* [2002] EWHC Admin 195 [2002] 4 All ER 156.

Parliament. The obvious example is the EC Treaty, some of which creates individual rights, and which is enforceable in the United Kingdom's courts only through the provisions of the European Communities Act 1972. In contrast the provisions of the European Convention on Human Rights have not been directly enforceable in the courts because of the absence of any such Act.

Though the courts have no authority directly to enforce treaty provisions unless these provisions have been incorporated into the law by Act of Parliament,[20] they do accept that treaties can have a persuasive influence on the way the law develops and statutes are interpreted. The courts presume a Parliamentary intention to legislate in a manner that is consistent with the international obligations of the United Kingdom and an Act of Parliament passed after a treaty has been entered into and dealing with its subject matter is to be construed, if it can reasonably bear the meaning, so as to carry out the treaty obligation.[21] However, the courts will also give effect to the clear and unambiguous words of an Act of Parliament even if those words are incompatible with, or involve a breach of, international law.[22]

2.2.1 United Nations and the International Covenant on Civil and Political Rights

The United Kingdom is a signatory to a number of highly important international agreements founded on the United Nations Declaration of Human Rights 1948 which is itself a reflection of the United Nations Charter. These emanations of the United Nations have done more than anything else to establish the language of human rights as the principal form of discourse in whose terms civil liberties issues, such as political freedom and privacy, are now given legal effect. The main instrument dealing directly with the civil liberties agenda is the International Covenant on Civil and Political Rights (ICCPR). The ICCPR identifies a range of rights. It contains an obligation on states to protect these rights within their borders, a requirement of non-discrimination in respect of the enjoyment of the rights, a power of derogation in times of emergency from all but the most fundamental of the rights and a prohibition on anyone using their Covenant freedoms in order to restrict the freedoms of others. The fundamental rights and freedoms it identifies are: the right to life, the prohibition of torture, the prohibition of slavery and forced labour, the right to liberty, the dignified treatment of prisoners, the prohibition of imprisonment for breach of contract, the right to freedom of movement, the rights of aliens, the right to fair trials, a ban on retrospective offences, the right to legal status, the rights to privacy, freedom of thought, conscience, religion and expression, a ban on propaganda for war, the right to peaceful assembly and to association, the right to marry, rights of children, the right to take part in public affairs, the right to the equal protection of the laws without discrimination and the rights of minorities. The Covenant permits states to

---

[20] See, for example, *Rayner (Mincing Lane) Ltd v Department of Trade* [1990] 2 AC 418.
[21] *Garland v British Rail Engineering Ltd* [1983] 2 AC 751, 771 per Lord Diplock.
[22] *R v Secretary of State for the Home Department ex parte Brind* [1991] 1 AC 696.

restrict the exercise of some of the rights and freedoms enumerated but only in so far as these restrictions are based on law, are confined to the pursuit of certain enumerated purposes and meet a threshold of necessity.

The principal enforcement mechanism under the ICCPR is through the Human Rights Committee established by the Covenant. States produce a quinquennial report to the Committee. The Committee may comment on the report on the basis of discussions with representatives of the states and observations from others, in particular non-governmental organisations. The Committee's comments are publicised and it is the fear of adverse publicity that is the main sanction behind the Covenant. The Human Rights Committee may, under Article 40(4) of the Covenant, make general comments on the requirements for the different articles.[23] There is an Optional Protocol to the Covenant by which individuals may petition the Committee with an allegation of a violation. The United Kingdom has not acceded to this Protocol.

The Committee has, in its last few reviews, expressed serious reservations about aspects of the protection of human rights in the United Kingdom. The situation, in its eyes, is much improved by the coming into force of the Human Rights Act 1998; nevertheless certain concerns remain. The 2001 Report expressed concern over such matters as anti-terrorism legislation, racial discrimination, the treatment of asylum seekers, killings by security forces in Northern Ireland, the absence of a public interest defence under the Official Secrets Act 1989, racial violence and the under-representation of ethnic minorities in public life.[24]

2.3 European Union law

The directly effective law of the European Community is integrated into the law of the United Kingdom and has supremacy over incompatible or inconsistent provisions of the domestic law. Similarly, the United Kingdom government is obliged to put other Community obligations into legal effect which, under the European Communities Act 1972, it may do by either primary or subordinate legislation. Obligations under Community law are enforced in the national courts but also through the institutions of the European Union, the Commission in particular. European Community law, although focused on the development of the single market, clearly bears upon civil liberties issues in many ways, as do the other pillars, on Common Foreign and Security Policy and on Police and Judicial Cooperation in Criminal Matters, on which the Union is founded. This bearing of Community law and Union policy on civil liberties matters is made all the more significant given the expansion of the legal basis of community action following the Treaty of Amsterdam. Civil liberties issues can be raised both in respect of the way national governments give effect to Community law and the way the

---

[23] For example, on Article 25 (right to participate in public affairs): General Comment 25, discussed in Davis, H. (2000) *Political Freedom*. London: Continuum, chapter 2.

[24] Fottrell, D. (2001) 'Developing Human Rights Protection beyond the Human Rights Act', 151 7008 *NLJ* 1688.

institutions of the Union act.[25] The use of search powers in enforcing competition law, restrictions on the movement of persons and fair trials are examples of such issues.

The problem has been that the original treaties on which the development of the European Community was based did not in any direct way impose legally enforceable obligations on both states and Community institutions to adhere to human and fundamental rights when giving effect to Community law. Specifically, there was no requirement to act compatibly with the European Convention on Human Rights,[26] nor, under those treaties, could the Union accede, like a signatory state, to the Convention.[27] The position is unchanged by the Treaties of Amsterdam and Nice.

In some matters bearing on civil liberties, like sex and other discrimination, the Court of Justice has full, Treaty-based jurisdiction to develop fundamental rights. Otherwise, the European Court of Justice has, after initial reluctance, developed a jurisprudence of 'general principles of law', which underlie and constrain the specific measures of Community law. These general principles include a doctrine of fundamental rights and are intended to have priority over even the fundamental constitutional rights of member states.[28] The European Court of Justice has developed an independent doctrine of fundamental rights which involves more than just the adaptation of the European Convention on Human Rights (which remains highly influential[29]). The Court is also guided by the constitutional traditions of member states[30] and by international treaties dealing with human rights of which the member states are signatories. Fundamental rights have been asserted by the Court of Justice against, first, European institutions, particularly the Commission. Examples are rights of religion,[31] privacy,[32] property[33] and to fair trials.[34] More controversially the Court will also uphold fundamental rights against member states, but only where they, the member states, are acting in the field of Community law, not where they are pursuing independent national objectives.[35] In this context rights to freedom of expression,[36] to private life[37] and to access to the courts[38] are examples of fundamental rights whose relevance and applicability have been considered.

There are problems with the adequacy of protection for fundamental rights in the European Union. In particular, the Court of Justice's approach is conditioned by the need to ensure that the overall objectives of the Community, such as a common market and economic integration, are fulfilled. These policy objectives influence the way in which the meaning and scope of

---

[25] Betten, L. and Grief, N. (1998) *EU Law and Human Rights*. London: Longman.
[26] An emanation of the Council of Europe, not the European Community and Union.
[27] *Opinion 2/94* [1996] ECR I-1759
[28] Betten and Grief, *op. cit.*
[29] For example, *Hauer v Land Rheinland-Pfalz* (1981) 3 EHRR 140 ECJ.
[30] *Nold v Commission* [1974] ECR 491.
[31] *Prais v Council* [1976] ECR 1185.
[32] For example, *National Panasonic (UK) Ltd v Commission* [1980] ECR 2033.
[33] For example, *Hauer v Land Rheinland-Pfalz* (1981) 3 EHRR 140 ECJ.
[34] For example, *Musique Diffusion Française v Commission* [1983] ECR 1825.
[35] For example, *SPUC (Ireland) v Grogan* [1991] 3 CMLR 849.
[36] *Ibid.*
[37] For example, *Rutli v Minister of the Interior* [1975] ECR 1219.
[38] For example, *Johnston v Chief Constable of the RUC* [1986] ECR 1651.

fundamental rights are interpreted[39] and the concern is that the protection of fundamental rights in a European context may thereby be affected. The answer has been to develop a full and properly grounded European conception of rights. First, there has been the gradual development and specification in the Treaties of a commitment by the European Community and the European Union to the upholding of fundamental rights.[40] The principal provision is Article 6 of the EU Treaty, originally inserted by the Maastricht Treaty. It asserts that the European Union is 'founded on' principles of liberty, democracy, respect for human rights and fundamental freedoms and the rule of law. Article 46 brings these principles within the jurisdiction of the Court of Justice. Article 6(2) incorporates support for the fundamental rights found in the ECHR. Article 7 introduces a sanctions procedure for serious violations of human rights by member states. The European Union Treaty also includes recognition of a range of fundamental social rights such as those found in the European Social Charter. Most importantly, there is now a detailed Charter of Fundamental Rights which has been adopted by the Union. The Charter is not part of the directly effective law of the Community but will have influence on the Court of Justice and hence on the national courts which must follow the European Court's rulings on European law. The Charter is too new for its impact to be assessed.

2.4 The European Convention on Human Rights

2.4.1 Introduction

The bringing into force of the Human Rights Act 1998 is the most important development bearing on civil liberties since the end of the Second World War. The Act gives further effect to the European Convention on Human Rights in English law. Its full impact on the substance of English law remains to be seen. What is clear is that it has brought into prominence a body of law, the European Convention on Human Rights and the case law (the jurisprudence) associated with it, and has made it widely effective throughout the law of the United Kingdom, so that it must be referred to in English law as setting standards which English statute and case law must normally meet. Above all it has affirmed that the terms in which civil liberties issues are to be dealt with by the courts is in the language of rights.

Prior to the Act, the Convention and the Court of Human Rights was already available to the people of Britain and of considerable influence on the law; nothing in the Act alters this. In what follows we discuss, first, the European Convention and its enforcement through the institutions of the Council of Europe and, second, the particular way in which the Human Rights Act 1998 (an Act of the United Kingdom Parliament) operates. Finally, we outline the Convention rights to which the Human Rights Act refers. The Human Rights

---

[39] For example, on the need to interpret the right to property in the light of the fundamental objectives of the Community: *Nold* v *Commission* [1974] ECR 491.

[40] There was, in 1977, a joint declaration by Commission, Council and Parliament of an intention to uphold fundamental rights ([1977] OJC 103(1)). Other statements to similar effect followed.

Act 1998 gives the Convention rights a pervasive and integrated influence on English law and so, in this book, the detail of what the Convention rights require is dealt with within the separate chapters.

2.4.2 The general scheme

The European Convention on Human Rights[41] (ECHR) is a principal creation of the Council of Europe, not produced by the European Union. The Council of Europe was created in 1949 and has always had a much larger membership than the European Union. Until the early 1990s its membership was broadly of western European countries but now has expanded to include Russia and other eastern European countries that used to be in the Soviet bloc.

While economic cooperation between Germany and France was the original basis of what has now become the European Union, the Council of Europe sought to establish a system for the protection of rights and freedoms at the European level based on the United Nations Declaration of Human Rights. The idea was to have a statement of rights and freedoms which would broadly reflect the terms of the UN Declaration and the political culture of European states and, above all, to establish a court-based system through which violations of such rights by the state parties could be dealt with.

It was not expected that there would be a huge number of cases and it was assumed that the cases that would be brought would relate to gross and systematic violations of rights, as is the point of international law. The signatory states would be democracies, albeit imperfect ones, and most issues would be properly dealt with by the national courts. The institutions enforcing the Convention (the Commission and the Court of Human Rights) were part-time. They took some time to organise and it was not until 1961 that the Court of Human Rights pronounced its first judgment.

An important feature of the Convention system is the right of individual petition by which an individual, company or other organisation can bring a case against their own government alleging a violation of the Convention. This feature, unusual in international law, is the primary explanation for the development and expansion of the Convention. From the 1980s onwards the number of applications increased dramatically leading, in 1998, to the remodelling of the institutions on the basis of a full-time court. The expansion of the work was added to by the enlargement of the Council of Europe after the end of the Cold War.

It is fair to say that what began as an attempt to establish fundamental rights in the context of the fear of totalitarianism has developed into a form of European constitutional court against which the reasonableness of the measures of more or less democratic societies, by no means under threat from totalitarian forces, are measured. Critics of the system have seen this as an unwelcome development that threatens the ability of democratic countries to determine the detail of their own laws.[42] Defenders of the system have approved the way in which, through the Convention system, international

---

[41] The European Convention for the Protection of Human Rights and Fundamental Freedoms.
[42] For example, in *Markcx v Belgium* (1979) 2 EHRR 330.

standards of human rights can be generally applied and high standards maintained. For the defenders, an adequate conception of democracy cannot be reduced to majority rule but must protect individual entitlements to participate in public affairs or to maintain their privacy against even the wishes of a majority.

2.4.3 The Convention

The Convention has been added to and amended by a series of Protocols. Protocol 11, which came into force on 1 November 1998, brought about a major reorganisation of the system and a consequential renumbering of some of the main procedural and institutional provisions.

The general obligation

The Convention is signed by the governments of the states and signature creates an obligation on the states (the 'High Contracting Parties') to 'secure to everyone within their jurisdiction the rights and freedoms defined in Section I of the Convention'.[43] The rights and freedoms are, therefore, to be secured for everyone, not just a particular class such as citizens. States cannot deny rights to a group by withdrawing citizenship and so remove them from the protection of the Convention.

The substantive rights

Section I includes a statement of particular rights and freedoms which are contained in 12 Articles. These substantive rights have been added to by a number of Protocols. These substantive rights are the Convention rights which are scheduled to and given effect by the Human Rights Act 1998 and they are identified later in the chapter. Substantive rights in the Fourth and Seventh Protocols have not been scheduled to the Act. These are, in the Fourth Protocol, 'Prohibition of imprisonment for debt', the right to 'Freedom of movement', 'Prohibition of expulsion of nationals' and 'Prohibition of collective expulsion of aliens'; the Seventh Protocol guarantees 'Procedural safeguards relating to the expulsion of aliens', the 'Right of appeal in criminal matters', 'Compensation for wrongful conviction', the 'Right not to be punished twice' and 'Equality between spouses'.

The ancillary rights

Section I, Articles 13 to 18 contain rights which are ancillary to the substantive rights. Article 13 places an obligation of the signatory states to ensure that a remedy is available from national courts for a violation of a substantive right or freedom; Article 14 requires that the substantive rights must be secured without discrimination; Article 15 allows a state party to 'derogate' from most but not all provisions of the Convention 'in time of war or other public emergency threatening the life of the nation'; Article 16 permits the states to limit certain freedoms in order to place 'restrictions on the political activity of aliens'; Article 17 denies the protection of the Convention to any state, group

---

[43] Article 1 ECHR.

or person who wishes to use a right or freedom guaranteed by the Convention in order to destroy the rights and freedoms of others, and Article 18 limits the powers enjoyed by states to restrict rights and freedoms under the Convention. These rights are considered in greater detail in the section below dealing with the Convention rights and freedoms which have been scheduled to the Human Rights Act 1998. It should be noted that Articles 13 and 15 are not so scheduled.

Non-signature, reservation and denunciations
Not all the states which signed the original Convention are signatories to all the Protocols and if they have not signed they are not bound. Similarly, states may, when agreeing to the Convention or a Protocol, enter a specific 'reservation', under Article 57. The effect is that the state is not bound to the extent of the reservation. Reservations must be specific to a particular provision. States may be responsible for the foreign affairs of other territories and must take specific measures to bring the Convention into effect in those territories. The United Kingdom has such responsibilities for the Isle of Man, the Channel Islands and Gibraltar. A state can cease to be bound by the Convention if it either leaves the Council of Europe or if it takes steps to 'denounce' the Convention. Denunciation cannot take place within the first five years following signature.[44]

2.4.4 The Strasbourg institutions and procedure

The great strength of the European Convention is its system for adjudication and enforcement. Originally there was a tripartite system. The European Commission of Human Rights, assisted by the Secretariat, would receive applications, decide on admissibility, seek facts, explanations and responses from the parties, in particular the states, and give an opinion on whether, in respect of admissible cases, there had been a violation of the Convention. The Commission could then bring a case to the Court of Human Rights and this institution would then make the final ruling on whether there had been a violation. The Committee of Ministers of the Council of Europe could make judgments on cases which the Commission had not referred to the Court and it also acted as a body through which enforcement of judgments, by diplomatic and political means, could be pursued.

Protocol 11, which was brought into effect in November 1998, changed the structure. The Commission was abolished and its role taken over by an enlarged, full-time Court assisted by the Registry and secretaries. The role of the Committee of Ministers is unchanged. Although abolished, the decisions and reports of the Commission on admissibility and substance remain an important source of Convention law.

The Court
The modern Court is established under Section II of the Convention. The full court has as many judges as there are High Contracting Parties to the

---

[44] Article 58 ECHR.

Convention and, generally, each Party supplies one judge. Judges must be of high moral character and qualified for high judicial office. They sit as independent individuals and not as representatives of their countries. They are elected by the Parliamentary Assembly from a list of three supplied by each Party. They are elected for a period of six years and cannot be dismissed other than by a vote of two-thirds of the other judges.[45]

A Plenary Court of all the judges elects the President of the Court and has other organisational functions. The work of the Court is done by Committees of three judges, Chambers of seven judges or a Grand Chamber of 17 judges.

Admissibility

Cases can be brought to the Court either by a state party alleging a violation by another state party or by 'any person, non-governmental organisation or group of individuals claiming to be the victim of a violation . . .'[46] No case can be heard unless it is admissible. The admissibility of inter-state applications is decided by a Chamber of the Court. Admissibility of individual applications, which form virtually all applications, is decided by either a Committee or a Chamber if a Committee is not unanimous.

The main rules of admissibility are in Article 35. Unless circumstances justify otherwise, an applicant needs to exhaust domestic remedies. Usually this means that the applicant must have obtained a ruling from the appropriate highest court in their country before approaching Strasbourg. An application must be made within six months of the final decision on the matter being taken. The Court cannot deal with individual applications which are anonymous or which raise issues substantially the same as issues already dealt with by the Court or by other systems of international law and adjudication. Finally, the Court must reject as inadmissible applications which are 'incompatible with the provisions of the Convention or the Protocols thereto, manifestly ill-founded, or an abuse of the right of application'.

Applications may be incompatible with the Convention for a number of reasons including, for example, that they allege a violation of a right or freedom the Convention does not protect. An application may also be incompatible with the Convention because the individual applicant does not have standing or is not a 'victim of a violation' as that term is understood by the Court. This is an important issue that is discussed below in the context of the Human Rights Act 1998.

Friendly settlement

If a case is admissible, the Court will seek information and explanation from the parties. In particular the Court may try to achieve a friendly settlement which means that the case is struck out and only a brief statement of facts and the solution is given. The danger is that state parties may be able to strike bargains with individuals, perhaps by paying compensation or dealing with specific issues, and hence avoid public responsibility for what may have been a serious or is a continuing violation of human rights.

---

[45] Article 24 ECHR.
[46] Article 34 ECHR.

Hearings, judgment and remedies

Admissible cases then proceed to a full consideration of the merits. This is normally by a Chamber of the Court. Difficult cases can be referred to the Grand Chamber. The decision of a Chamber is final although, under Article 43, there is the possibility of the Grand Chamber accepting difficult cases for reconsideration. The Court gives reasons for its decisions. Financial compensation in the form of 'just satisfaction' as well as costs may be awarded against the state Party. The High Contracting Parties have agreed to abide by the judgment. The judgment is transmitted to the Committee of Ministers which supervises its execution through the political and diplomatic means available to it.

2.4.5 The impact of the Convention on English law

Prior to the coming into effect of the Human Rights Act 1998, the European Convention on Human Rights had already had a major impact on the law of the United Kingdom. The impact can be discerned, first, in the changes to the law or to administrative practices that were made necessary by adverse rulings from Strasbourg. The statutory regime that deals with telephone tapping and surveillance, now under the Regulation of Investigatory Powers Act 2000, is based on a response to such adverse rulings.[47] There are many other examples and they are described in more detail throughout the book. Second, the Convention has influenced the way in which the courts have developed the common law and the interpretation of statutes. Well before the coming into effect of the Human Rights Act 1998 it had been common for the Convention to be cited in court and for judges to be asked to seek compatibility with the Convention in their judgment.[48] The response was not to incorporate the Convention through the back door but to develop the principles of statutory interpretation, administrative law and the common law generally, in ways which recognised 'fundamental rights'. In the cases the judges can be found sometimes referring to the Convention and at other times referring to 'fundamental rights' which are inherent in the common law. It is commonplace to find judges expressing the view that there are few, if any, significant differences between Convention rights and the common law. For example, it has been accepted that ambiguity in statutes can be resolved by reference to the Convention[49] or to a presumption that Parliament, in the absence of express words to the contrary, intends to legislate in a manner compatible with the United Kingdom's international obligations.[50] Prior to the Human Rights Act 1998, the courts were already prepared to invalidate secondary legislation on grounds of incompatibility with fundamental rights.[51] In the area of judicial review of administrative action, the same recognition of fundamental rights, mirroring Convention rights, can be found in relation to the legal test for the

---

[47] For example, *Malone v United Kingdom* (1984) 7 EHRR 14; *Halford v United Kingdom* (1997) 24 EHRR 523.

[48] See Hunt, M. (1997) *Using Human Rights Law in English Courts.* Oxford: Hart Publishing.

[49] *R v Secretary of State for the Home Department ex parte Brind* [1991] 2 WLR 588 (HL).

[50] *Garland v British Rail Engineering Ltd* [1982] 2 All ER 402, 415, per Lord Diplock.

[51] *R v Secretary of State for the Home Department ex parte Simms and another* [1999] 3 All ER 400 HL, per Lord Hoffman, 412.

reasonableness of the discretionary actions of ministers and other public officials. Ministers had already been expected to be meeting Convention standards,[52] or at least to give a fully reasoned explanation, indicating that all relevant matters pertaining to Convention rights had been taken into account. In the end, though, the Court would not substitute its own view of what the Convention required for that of the minister.[53] Finally, although the Convention's primary influence has been on the 'vertical' relationship of state and citizen, it has also had an impact on the way the common law, including ordinary private law, has developed. Even prior to the coming into force of the Act, the law on matters such as defamation and breach of confidence was influenced by the common law's developing sense of fundamental rights.[54]

2.5 The Human Rights Act 1998

2.5.1 The background

Throughout the last quarter of the twentieth century there was a developing sense of dissatisfaction with the effectiveness of the institutions of Parliament and the common law in providing protection for political and civil freedom in the United Kingdom. This arose partly from constitutional lawyers and theorists for whom the arguments were predominantly institutional, focusing on the various alleged weaknesses of the political and conventional unwritten constitution, of Parliament and of the common law such as discussed earlier in this chapter. The arguments were reinforced by reference to various political events, such as the miners' strike or the peace movement, and to the response by the state they engendered. For critics these matters, coupled with the institutional weaknesses of Parliament and the courts, created a sense of civil and political freedom being under threat.[55]

Those dissatisfied with the situation also recognised that in a number of situations United Kingdom law seemed to be falling behind international and regional standards as set, for example, through the United Nations or the Council of Europe. This point weighed heavily with a number of senior judges who contributed significantly to the debate.[56] In particular it was seen as increasingly indefensible that although the United Kingdom was a signatory

---

[52] For example, regarding decisions affecting life sentence prisoners: *R v Secretary of State for the Home Department and the Parole Board ex parte Norney* (1995) 7 Admin LR 861 [1996] COD 81.

[53] *R v Ministry of Defence ex parte Smith* [1996] 1 All ER 257, CA; *R v Lord Saville and others ex parte A and others* [1999] 4 All ER 860, CA.

[54] For examples *Derbyshire County Council v Times Newspapers Ltd* [1993] 1 All ER 1011 (HL) (defamation); *Douglass v Hello!* [2001] 2 All ER 289 (breach of confidence).

[55] See, for example, Ewing, K. and Gearty, C. (1990) *Freedom under Thatcher. Civil Liberties in Modern Britain*. Oxford: Clarendon Press. A concern for civil liberties did not, as this book illustrates, necessarily imply the desirability of some form of a bill of rights. Cf. Dworkin, R. (1990) *A Bill of Rights for Britain*. London: Chatto & Windus.

[56] See, for example, the contributions of the following judges to the debate: Lord Bingham (1993) 'The European Convention on Human Rights: Time to Incorporate', 109 *LQR* 390; Lord Browne-Wilkinson (1992) 'The Infiltration of a Bill of Rights', *PL* 397; Lord Woolf (1995) 'Droit Public – English Style', *PL* 57; Lord Steyn (1997) 'The Weakest and Least Dangerous Department of Government', PL 84. The debate about a bill of rights was, in many ways, started by Lord Scarman's 1974 lecture *English Law – the New Dimension*. London: Stevens.

to the European Convention on Human Rights, the rights and freedoms it protected were not directly protected by the courts. It was embarrassing that the courts might, because of a rule of English law, have to deny a remedy to a party in the full knowledge that the Convention was being violated and that the party would have to pursue a long and expensive remedy before the Strasbourg institutions.

Arguments for a bill of rights

The solution for many lay in the enactment of some type of 'bill or rights' – a written, legally based form of human rights protection that could be enforced in the courts. Such an approach would bring greater certainty to the question of what were the fundamental rights that all were to enjoy, it would provide a mechanism for the direct and explicit enforcement of such rights, it would require the state to take proper and appropriate steps, as necessary, to protect such rights and it would be a means for enhancing the compatibility of United Kingdom law with international and regional standards.

Arguments against a bill of rights

It is important to stress that, by no means, was there a clear consensus in public opinion in favour of some form of bill of rights. Important arguments, still of general importance, were mounted against the proposal. Opponents of a bill of rights were (are) not against improving methods for recognising and protecting political and civil freedoms; rather they argue that such protection should be given effect through the general political processes of a democratic polity rather than by relying on the courts and some more or less entrenched legal instrument.[57] The essence of the argument is that legal-rights talk fails fully to recognise the controversial nature of the freedoms expressed as human rights. Justice, as embodied in human rights, is not a general community value but a contested value whose content is disputed by a range of different social and political interests. There is no agreement over the content of rights except, perhaps, at the most abstract level. Given the different interests at stake, it is a mistake (it is undemocratic) to leave the working out of such arguments to the judges. Claims of rights are like any other political claim and should be decided through the general political system of pressure groups, parties, Parliaments and protest; the democratic process should not be foreshortened by recourse to the court.

Supporters of a bill of rights will, of course, answer these charges. Some freedoms, such as freedom from torture, are, indeed, alleged as fundamental and absolute; bill of rights supporters must accept, to mention the old example, that torturing the bomber to make him disclose the whereabouts of the bomb and thus, perhaps, save many lives, is impermissible. Other claimed rights, to freedom of speech, for example, are, indeed, controversial in their scope and meaning. Bill of rights supporters will argue that such controversies are properly resolved in court. First, the court is open to a more careful and principled consideration of the issues than are the party political processes

---

[57] See Ewing and Gearty *op. cit.*; Griffith, J.A.G. (1979) 'The Political Constitution', 42 1 MLR 1; McClusky, J.H. (Lord) (1986) *Law, Justice and Democracy*. London: Sweet & Maxwell.

where interests, irrelevant to the issue in hand, may be decisive. Second, democracy does not reduce to majority rule. The right may relate to the interests of a minority or an individual and there is no reason to have confidence in the majority, through the institutions they control, dealing fairly with the matter.

The argument continues at an abstract level. From the perspective of civil liberties law in modern Britain it is now resolved, as a matter of policy, by the enactment of the Human Rights Act 1998.

2.6 The main terms of the Human Rights Act 1998

2.6.1 Convention rights, section 1

The point of the Human Rights Act 1998 is to give further effect in the law of the United Kingdom to the main, substantive rights found in the European Convention of Human Rights. Section 1 of the Act identifies the 'Convention Rights' involved which are found in Schedule 1 to the Act. These are the substantive rights (first, the rights found in Articles 2 to 12, Article 1-3 of the First Protocol and Article 1-2 of the Sixth Protocol) as read in the light of the ancillary rights (Article 14, Article 16, Article 17 and Article 18). Reservations and derogations made by the United Kingdom are identified and have effect in respect of the Act.[58] Sections 14, 15 and 16 permit the introduction of new derogations and reservations and the withdrawal or amendment of existing ones.[59] Since the Act introduces an extensive remedy for violations of Convention rights, Article 13 ECHR (Right to an effective remedy) is excluded from the scheduled rights.

2.6.2 Consistency with the Strasbourg jurisprudence, section 2

Section 2 of the 1998 Act requires United Kingdom courts to 'take into account' the way in which the Strasbourg institutions, including the now defunct Commission, have interpreted the Convention and the rights and freedoms it describes. United Kingdom courts are not, however, bound to follow the Strasbourg view and, therefore, it is possible for a distinct 'British' approach to human rights to develop. Too much divergence between the British view and Strasbourg would be undesirable, at least if the divergence was in a state-friendly direction, since then the problem the Human Rights Act 1998 was designed to prevent, of people having to go through the long and expensive business of an application to Strasbourg to obtain their rights under

---

[58] Section 1(2) and ss. 14, 15 and 16 with Schedule 3, HRA 1998. The United Kingdom has reserved its position in respect of part of the right to education under Article 2 of the First Protocol. At the time of enactment the United Kingdom had derogated from part of Article 5 in respect of the length of time terrorist suspects could be detained without having the legality of detention tested before a judge. That derogation was removed by reference to the Terrorism Act 2000.

[59] The Anti-terrorism Crime and Security Act 2001, passed after the attacks of 11 September 2001 in the United States, provides for a new derogation in respect of the power of detention without trial.

the Convention, would be reinvigorated.[60] The view of the House of Lords is that section 2 requires the courts to follow the Strasbourg interpretation and approach unless there are special circumstances prevailing.[61] Adopting the Strasbourg approach to the Convention means taking on the interpretative style of the Strasbourg Court.[62]

An evolving document
The Convention is a constitutional, human rights document which should be read as such rather than be subject to the narrow, literal approach which, perhaps, is typical of the way Acts of Parliament are read. The Strasbourg Court, for example, takes an 'evolutive' approach to the Convention. The legislative history of the Convention can be referred to and past decisions will often be followed. However, the Court is not bound by a strict rule of precedent and may depart from its earlier decisions if the justice of the case so requires. Convention standards evolve in line with common European standards and these may change over time. The evolutive approach has its dangers. It is understood as a progressive doctrine which expands the rights and freedoms enjoyed as European political culture, in a post-Cold War world, becomes more liberal. If this liberal political, social and cultural tendency was to go into reverse, however, then, on the evolutive approach, the interpretation of the Convention ought to mean that the rights and freedoms the Convention protects should be given a more restrictive, state-friendly, scope. At the very least, the core of the rights and freedoms, their 'essence', as the Court says, need to be upheld whatever the political, social or cultural developments may be.

Legality
One of the most important concepts accepted by the courts is that the Convention embodies the principles of the rule of law or legality. The underlying idea is that the state should only act in ways which restrict human rights on the basis of promulgated rules, and that these rules should be sufficiently precise to enable a person to foresee the circumstances in which the state may act restrictively against him or her. This is a principle of great practical importance and is discussed at various places later in the book.

Positive duties
The court also recognises that, in order to protect and give effect to the rights and freedoms it identifies, the Convention requires states to take positive steps rather than merely desist from a practice. These positive duties are identified at appropriate places in the text. They include not only the idea that the state must adopt certain practices in its own behaviour but also may be required to

---

[60] The right of individual petition to Strasbourg is not limited by the Act. States have no right to 'appeal' to Strasbourg in order to try and reverse a decision of their national courts on a Convention matter.

[61] *R (on the application of Alconbury Developments Ltd) v Secretary of State for the Environment, Transport and the Regions* [2001] 2 All ER 929 HL, 969 per Lord Slynn.

[62] Pannick, D. (1998) 'Principles of Interpretation of Convention Rights under the Human Rights Act and the Discretionary Area of Judgment', *PL* 545 (Winter), pp. 546–8.

change the law in order to regulate the behaviour of others including individuals and companies pursuing their private interests. In this way the Convention develops its 'horizontal' effects on 'private law'.

The margin of appreciation

As an international court, the European Court of Human Rights allows an area of discretion to the national courts and authorities over the standards and norms by which the rights and freedoms in the Convention are protected. This is known as the 'margin of appreciation'. Thus the nature and scope of, for example, the voting system or laws against pornography[63] may vary from country to country without the Convention being violated. Despite such a tolerance of different standards, the Court insists that the essence of the right must be maintained and over this the Court has the final word.[64] The margin of appreciation is applied differently in respect of different Articles. It is most pronounced in respect of rights, such as the right to freedom of expression under Article 10, which expressly allow restrictions for certain purposes and if the restriction can be shown to be 'necessary in a democratic society', while other Articles, such as Article 3, are treated as absolute and no margin of appreciation is allowed.

The virtue of the doctrine is its recognition that reasonable differences can apply between countries with different cultures, traditions and social problems and that the national courts and institutions are best placed to have the measure of this. The vice in the doctrine is that it permits restrictions on individual freedoms based on cultural and social grounds. This may lead to the tolerance of various forms of restriction on personal and political freedom which are incompatible with liberal autonomy; it may tolerate state restrictions based on moral disapproval of what are otherwise harmless actions. Such grounds of restriction are broader than those expressly permitted by the Convention.[65] The margin of appreciation doctrine may also justify the Court in accepting lower standards of rights protection in circumstances of emergency, such as political violence, when, arguably, that is precisely the circumstance in which important human rights are most likely to be threatened.[66]

Deference and national courts

The margin of appreciation is a rule of international law. The equivalent for a domestic court, deciding cases dealing with Convention rights, is to develop a

---

[63] *Handyside* v *United Kingdom* (1979–80) 1 EHRR 737, paragraphs 48–9. For a discussion see *Brown* v *Stott (Procurator Fiscal, Dunfermline) and another* [2001] 2 All ER 97, 121, per Lord Steyn. See also Lester of Heme Hill, Lord and Pannick, D. (eds) (1999) *Human Rights Law and Practice.* London: Butterworths, p. 74, paragraph 3.21.

[64] For example, over the right to vote inferred from Article 3 of the First Protocol: *Mathieu-Mohin and Clerfayt* v *Belgium* (1987) 10 EHRR 1, paragraph 52; the issue is the related one of the reasonable restrictions that states may impose on the right to vote.

[65] Jones, T.H. (1995) 'The Devaluation of Human Rights Under the European Convention', *Public Law* 430.

[66] The Court recognises the need for special powers in the context of the state response to political violence although it also imposes limits especially in respect of the need for judicial supervision. See, for example, *O'Hara* v *United Kingdom* [2001] NLJ 1884, Ap. 37555/97.

conception of the proper deference to be shown by the judges to the executive or legislature. This is a difficult matter. An over-deferential court will be failing in its duty to make its own, independent assessment of what the Convention requires; an under-deferential court will be undermining the proper role of democratically accountable authorities in ways that weaken the very commitment to democratic politics inherent in the Convention.[67] Deference becomes highly controversial if the courts defer merely because of the nature of the issue rather than on the basis of a careful analysis of a structured human rights claim.[68] The obvious issue, particularly in the 'anti-terrorist' context, is national security and the fear that courts will defer to the state simply because national security is in issue rather than on the basis of a close analysis of the human rights issues involved. Deference, as with the margin of appreciation doctrine, must not undermine the essence of the right. If the executive's judgment strikes at the very core of what is being protected, the courts should not defer.

Appropriate deference depends upon context and circumstances. Various issues will determine the willingness of the courts to defer to the judgement of the executive or legislature on a matter. In particular, where, as under Article 3, a right is express and fundamental within the Convention system, the court will be justified in making its own, independent assessment of the matter. Where, on the other hand, specific rights are implied (e.g. under Article 6) or where they are subject to lawful and proportionate restriction (e.g. under Articles 8–11), then the courts may, properly, be more willing to defer to the views of the executive or legislature. Deference, in the latter contexts, should be confined to those balancing judgments about the need to restrict a freedom in order to meet a significant social need and will vary in accordance with the nature of the issue.[69]

Proportionality
Of all human rights concepts, proportionality is having the most significant impact on the law of the United Kingdom. Proportionality expresses the need to achieve a fair balance between the achievement of legitimate collective goals and the burden such achievement may impose on individuals. It involves the requirement that public authorities should achieve their collective goals by methods which have the minimum (or close to the minimum) impact on the freedoms of individuals who are affected. Examples of the operation of this principle can be found throughout this book. It is for the court to decide whether or not an action is properly proportionate. In coming to a judgment the court may consider whether 'relevant and sufficient' reasons have been advanced by the public authority, whether a less restrictive option existed, whether the decision-taking process resulting in the actions under consideration was fair to those affected and whether safeguards against abuse exist. A

---

[67] Mowbray, A. (1999) 'The Role of the European Court of Human Rights in the Promotion of Democracy', *Public Law* 703.

[68] I am grateful to Richard Edwards for this and other points on deference.

[69] On deference see *R v DPP ex parte Kebilene and others* [1999] 4 All ER 801, 842–3. For examples and further discussion see *International Transport Roth GmbH and others v Secretary of State for the Home Department* [2002] EWCA Civ 158; *R (on the application of Alconbury Developments Ltd) v Secretary of State for the Environment, Transport and the Regions)* [2001] 2 All ER 929.

restriction which undermined the very essence of the right in question would be disproportionate.[70] On the assessment of these issues, the courts may have grounds, as indicated above, to defer to the national authorities. However, the mere fact that the public authority has, carefully and fully, made its own judgment of proportionality will not avail it if, in the view of the court, that judgment is wrong.

2.6.3 The impact on legislation: sections 3, 4, 10, 11 and 19

Section 3 of the Human Rights Act 1998 requires United Kingdom courts to interpret legislation, as far as possible, for compatibility with the scheduled Convention rights. It applies not only to legislation in force when the Act was brought into effect but to all future legislation. It imposes an interpretive obligation on all courts including inferior courts such as magistrates courts and tribunals.

3. Interpretation of legislation
(1) So far as it is possible to do so, primary legislation and subordinate legislation must be read and given effect in a way which is compatible with the Convention rights.
(2) This section –
    (a) applies to primary legislation and subordinate legislation whenever enacted;
    (b) does not affect the validity, continuing operation or enforcement of any incompatible primary legislation; and
    (c) does not affect the validity, continuing operation or enforcement of any incompatible subordinate legislation if (disregarding any possibility of revocation) primary legislation prevents removal of the incompatibility.

Section 3 does not, therefore, permit a court to hold legislation to be invalid, no matter how incompatible with the Convention rights it may be. Section 3 was explicitly designed to maintain the principle of Parliamentary supremacy. It requires Parliament to be unambiguous and clear if it is enacting legislation which is incompatible with the Convention although the validity of any such legislation does not depend, subject to section 19 which is discussed below, on Parliament expressly acknowledging incompatibility.

Subordinate legislation
Subordinate legislation is affected differently from primary legislation. Although the Act does not expressly say so, section 3(2)(c) is taken to mean that subordinate legislation which, on interpretation, is incompatible with the Convention, must be held to be invalid and not applied by the courts.[71] The exception is if primary legislation prevents the removal of incompatibility as where, for example, primary legislation stipulates an incompatible state of affairs which the subordinate legislation is to achieve.

---

[70] From Starmer, K. (1999) *European Human Rights Law*. London: LAG, pp. 169–76.
[71] For example, Feldman, D. (2002) *Civil Liberties and Human Rights in England and Wales*, 2nd edn. Oxford: Oxford University Press, p. 89.

Declaration of incompatibility

If a court decides that primary legislation cannot be interpreted and given effect in a manner which is compatible with the Convention, then section 4 of the Act can come into effect. A superior court can make a 'declaration of incompatibility' (a statement that the legislation is incompatible with Convention rights) in respect of primary legislation and also in respect of incompatible subordinate legislation where primary legislation prevents the removal of the incompatibility. Only superior courts, such as the High Court and above, can make such declarations; they cannot, for example, be made by magistrates courts, the Crown Court or tribunals.[72] Such declarations are, therefore, possible consequences of an appeal from an inferior court or tribunal. A declaration of incompatibility does not change the fact that the incompatible legislation remains valid and should be given effect. It is, however, clearly a challenge to the government and to Parliament to change the law to achieve compatibility. The government is entitled not to change but there is nothing to stop a disappointed litigant from pursuing his or her case before the Court of Human Rights in Strasbourg and, if they were successful, the United Kingdom would be under an international obligation to change the law.

Remedial orders

The significant point about a declaration of incompatibility is that, in certain circumstances, it triggers a ministerial power to remedy the situation by amending the incompatible legislation and to do so by Order rather than by a full Act of Parliament. The power applies when either a court in the United Kingdom has made a declaration of incompatibility or incompatibility has arisen from a decision of the Court of Human Rights made after the Human Rights Act 1998 came into force.[73]

10. Power to take remedial action

(2) If a Minister of the Crown considers that there are compelling reasons for proceeding under this section, he may by order make such amendments to the legislation as he considers necessary to remove the incompatibility.

Remedial action may also be taken to amend any primary legislation which is preventing incompatible subordinate legislation from being declared invalid. Section 10 gives a minister discretion to amend or repeal all or part of incompatible primary legislation, or extend the application of some other Act to meet the incompatibility, without having to seek an amending Act of

---

[72] A situation which can be compared to the power of inferior courts or tribunals, dealing with European Community law, to set aside national law which is incompatible with directly effective Community law. Since Community law embodies human rights in its general principles of law, an inferior tribunal, perhaps, could disapply United Kingdom legislation, bearing on Community matters, which was incompatible with human rights (including Convention rights) thus having more power than the House of Lords on purely national human rights issues.

[73] For example, the Mental Health Act 1983 placed the burden of proof on applicants to Mental Health Review Tribunals. The court declared this to be incompatible with Article 5 ECHR (*R (H) v Mental Health Review Tribunal N&E London Region* [2001] EWCA Civ 415). The rules of procedure were then changed by the Mental Health Act 1983 (Remedial) Order 2001, SI 2001/3712.

Parliament. The minister must believe there are 'compelling reasons' for such action. Urgency and, perhaps, technical complexity are examples of the kinds of reasons a minister might have. In most situations the courts will not be able to grant judicial review of the exercise or refusal to exercise the power.[74] Conventions will, perhaps, arise dealing with the kinds of issues which are suitable for such 'fast-track' amendment.

Remedial orders are a controversial feature of the Act since they permit significant changes to primary legislation to be made by ministerial order and without the full Parliamentary consideration that would be given to a bill. There is a procedure for a degree of Parliamentary scrutiny of any proposed remedial order found in Schedule 2 of the Act. It should be remembered that Parliament does not always give close scrutiny to the ordinary bills it is enacting and it may be that the procedures under Schedule 2 for dealing with remedial orders could, if properly developed, provide an opportunity for focused and intensive scrutiny of the proposed amendments.[75]

The courts and section 3
Section 3 comes into effect if, following an interpretation of the legislation on ordinary principles (the literal rule etc.), there appears to be incompatibility with one or more of the scheduled Convention rights. There is some judicial disagreement about the circumstances in which a declaration of incompatibility should be issued. One view is that the court should do all it can to avoid a declaration of incompatibility and this includes being prepared to 'strain' the statutory language in order to achieve that effect. 'Straining' can include implying words into an Act. Thus in *R* v *A* (2000)[76] some Law Lords read into legislation that imposed wide limits on the ability of a rape defendant to cross examine the victim on her sexual history a general condition that this was subject to the right of a fair trial under Article 6.[77] The alternative view, argued, for example, by Lord Woolf in the Court of Appeal,[78] stresses that section 3 only permits the courts to interpret and not to legislate or write in new provisions to Acts of Parliament. A need radically to alter the effect of legislation, including by writing in words such as 'reasonably', will suggest that something more than interpretation is required for compatibility, and so a declaration should be considered. At the moment both views are current.

2.6.4 Public authorities

The second principal requirement of the Human Rights Act 1998 is to place a duty on 'public authorities' to act in accordance with Convention rights unless statute requires them to act otherwise.

---

[74] Section 6(6), HRA 1998 clarifies that it is not unlawful to refuse to make a remedial order.
[75] See Miers, D. (1999) 'Deregulation Procedure: An Expanding Role', *Public Law* 477.
[76] [2001] UKHL 25; [2001] 3 All ER 1.
[77] See, in particular, the speech of Lord Steyn.
[78] *Poplar Housing and Regeneration Community Association Ltd* v *Donoghue* [2001] EWCA Civ 595; [2001] 4 All ER 604.

6. Acts of public authorities
(1) It is unlawful for a public authority to act in a way which is incompatible with a Convention right.
(2) Subsection (1) does not apply if –
    (a) as the result of one or more provisions of primary legislation, the authority could not have acted differently; or
    (b) in the case of one or more provisions of, or made under, primary legislation which cannot be read or given effect in a way which is compatible with the Convention rights, the authority was acting so as to give effect to or enforce those provisions.

Definition of a public authority: the courts
There is no general definition of a public authority. Parliament is expressly excluded since, as indicated above, it is clearly envisaged that legislation that is unambiguously incompatible with the Convention can still be enacted and, in any case, it is hard to know what remedies might be effective.

Any 'court or tribunal', including the House of Lords in its judicial capacity, is a public authority for the purposes of the Act[79] and so is bound to act compatibly with the Convention. Thus the rules of evidence and procedure must now comply with, for instance, Article 6 ECHR. The importance of this provision is also that it may provide the basis for the so-called 'horizontal effect' of Convention rights. This means that the courts and tribunals may choose to develop private legal relations, such as defamation or employment law, in ways which give effect to the underlying values in the Convention, despite the fact that the Convention is, on its face, predominantly dealing with the relationship between the state and citizens.

Definition of a public authority: bodies exercising public functions
Section 6(3)(b) of the Act includes within the definition of a public authority 'any person certain of whose functions are functions of a public nature' but, under section 6(5), the Act states that 'in relation to a particular act, a person is not a public authority by virtue only of subsection (3)(b) if the nature of the Act is private'. Under this subsection a huge range of bodies of various kinds and to varying degrees of remoteness from government may be subject to the enforceable duty to act compatibly with Convention rights when they are performing public functions. The Act says nothing on how these bodies are to be identified. The courts will, no doubt, proceed on a case-by-case basis and of particular importance will be how to categorise the huge, variable range of non-governmental bodies which are so typical of modern public administration. The first cases have involved organisations, specifically housing associations, which are providing services on behalf of a government agency under contract.[80]

The case for a wide and inclusive approach to the problem is that the border between 'public' and 'private' is now very unclear and organisations, of

---

[79] Human Rights Act 1998. s. 6(3).
[80] *Poplar Housing and Regeneration Community Association Ltd* v *Donoghue* [2001] EWCA Civ 595; [2001] 4 All ER 604, that a housing association was sufficiently close with a local authority discharging statutory duties to be a public authority; *R (Heather)* v *Cheshire Homes* [2002] EWCA Civ 366; [2002] 2 All ER 936, a charity providing homes for the disabled partly on behalf of a local authority was not exercising public functions.

whatever type and to whatever degree of public funding or government control, whose actions and decisions affect the human rights and freedoms of people should be subject to the remedies the Human Rights Act provides. Some writers, however, argue for a much narrower approach. In particular it is suggested that bodies designated public authorities may be prevented themselves from bringing human rights cases against the government. A broadcasting organisation, for example, might want to challenge a law or administrative practice on freedom of speech grounds; if it is designated a public authority and itself vulnerable to human rights claims (about privacy for example) it may not be able to mount such a challenge.[81]

There are, therefore, three possibilities. The first is that a body is, without argument, an ordinary public authority and is clearly part of the state apparatus of government: a government department, a police force or a local authority are examples. Such bodies have no private side and are, it seems, bound by the Act in everything they do. Secondly, there are bodies which have important similarities with government bodies and which are arguably public authorities of the first kind, with no private side. NHS trusts or the Health and Safety Executive, bodies which are fully funded by the state, subject to public appointment and entirely bound by legislation, might be examples. Whether a body is in the second category will be a matter of interpretation and argument. Third there is the category mentioned above of any person, group or body exercising public functions. Only the third category has a private side not directly reached by the Act.

Legal proceedings and 'victims'

Where a person believes that a public authority has acted unlawfully by acting incompatibly with the Convention, he or she may bring a case directly against the public authority. This will normally be by exercising a right of appeal or by judicial review. Alternatively they may rely on the alleged unlawful act by the authority in any legal proceedings that may be brought against them.[82] Thus the defendant in a criminal case, for example, may offer a breach of a Convention right by the police or the prosecuting authority as part of their defence. In both situations, however, the persons alleging the breach of a Convention right must demonstrate that they are 'victims' of the breach, and the test for being a victim is that under Article 34 ECHR.[83]

Article 34

The Court may receive applications from any person, non-governmental organisation or group of individuals claiming to be victims of a violation by one of the High Contracting Parties of the rights set forth in the Convention or the protocols thereto. The High Contracting Parties undertake not to hinder in anyway the effective exercise of this right.

---

[81] Oliver, D. (2000) 'The Frontiers of the State: Public Authorities and Public Functions under the Human Rights Act 1998', *Public Law* 476.

[82] Section 7(1)(a) and (b), HRA 1998.

[83] Section 7(1) and (7), HRA 1998. As was pointed out in the Parliamentary debates, this rule introduces some uncertainty. Breaches of the European Convention can be argued in ordinary judicial review proceedings and in proceedings involving European Community law; both have different rules of standing from each other and from s. 7, HRA 1998.

The Convention test for being a 'victim' is that the person is directly affected by the act or omission in issue.[84] This is in some respects a more restrictive test than the 'sufficient interest' test under domestic judicial review. First it appears to exclude many public bodies which cannot show they are 'non-government-al'. Some public bodies, such as the Equal Opportunities Commission, for example, are able, under domestic law, to seek judicial review of government decisions which they think are unlawfully affecting their concerns. However, if such bodies are thought of as governmental bodies they will not, in their own name, be able to bring human rights cases in respect of government decisions.[85] Second, the Strasbourg test for 'victim' tends to exclude an *actio populationis*, in which one person, perhaps a pressure group, brings an action on behalf of the public generally or a particular group of persons or an interest which will not otherwise be represented, such as poor and deprived persons or an environmental interest. The 'sufficient interest test' in English judicial review is flexible enough to allow something close to such actions.[86] The Article 34 test excludes *actio popularis*. However, there is flexibility in Article 34. In particular there is no need to prove that there as been a 'specific measure of implementation' affecting the applicant. Thus any woman of child-bearing age can bring an application in respect of laws involving abortion because she might be restricted by them even though that has not actually happened.[87] Article 34 also permits a representative action, so long as those being represented can be individually identified and give their consent, and it also permits groups, such as companies, political parties or trade unions, to bring cases in respect of issues which affect them as organisations, though not if it is only their members' interests which are affected.[88]

A court dealing with a case brought under the Act can grant whatever remedy it thinks fit. The traditional judicial review remedies, by which decisions are quashed, proposed unlawful actions stopped, officials ordered to perform their duties, or the law declared on the assumption that a public body will obey it, are available. Damages can be awarded so long as the case is brought before a court with the power to award damages. The determination of an award must be based on the principles of 'just satisfaction' developed by the Court of Human Rights under Article 41.

2.6.5 Parliament

As the representative assembly of a liberal and democratic state, Parliament ought not to be bypassed in the processes of human rights protection. It is Parliament that enacts legislation and which is the prime mover, directly or through the agency of others, in securing the scrutiny of executive action.

---

[84] *Eckle* v *Germany* (1982) 5 EHRR 1; see also *Zentralrat DSRR* v *Germany* (1997) 23 EHRR 7 CD 209.
[85] The BBC is another such organisation with, perhaps, an ambiguous status. The Human Rights Commission refused to decide whether or not the Corporation was capable, in its own name, of being a victim: *BBC* v *United Kingdom* (1996) 21 EHRR CD 93.
[86] For example, *R* v *Secretary of State for Foreign and Commonwealth Affairs ex parte World Development Movement* [1995] 1 All ER 611.
[87] *Open Door Counselling and Well Woman* v *Ireland* (1992) 15 EHRR 244.
[88] For example, a political party can bring a case over a law or practice affecting political parties but not over the individual rights of their members.

Legislation is now enacted in the knowledge that it will be interpreted for compatibility with Convention rights. Section 19 requires the minister who is in charge of a government bill to make a written statement to Parliament that the bill is or is not compatible with Convention rights. The form that such statements take is left to the minister and the danger is that a brief statement of compatibility, with no argument or analysis, will be accepted by Parliament without any proper consideration.[89] Such statements are also made prior to the introduction of any amendments to the bill.

Of greater importance is the establishment, by the Lords and Commons, of a Joint Committee on Human Rights.[90] This Committee will report to Parliament on the compatibility of legislative proposals in a detailed and informed manner.

2.6.6 Freedom of speech and religion

Sections 12 and 13 of the Human Rights Act 1998 impose special requirements on the courts when they are dealing with freedom of expression and religious freedom. Whether these provisions have much impact is doubtful.

2.7 The scheduled Convention rights

The substantive rights, the 'Scheduled Convention rights' to which the Human Rights Act 1998 applies, are in Schedule 1 to the Act. They are the main substantive rights found in the European Convention on Human Rights. With a few exceptions, dealt with here, they are discussed in detail as appropriate in the different chapters of this book.

2.7.1 The preface

The Convention has a preface which is not a scheduled Convention right. Nevertheless it has some significance for the way in which the Strasbourg court, and hence United Kingdom courts, may interpret Convention rights. First, the preface refers to the United Nation's commitment to human rights and hence is a basis for reference to the provisions and case law of instruments such the International Covenant on Civil and Political Rights, mentioned above.

The fifth paragraph refers to 'democracy':

> Reaffirming their profound belief in those fundamental freedoms which are the foundation of justice and peace in the world and are best maintained on the one hand by an effective political democracy and on the other by a common understanding and observance of the human rights upon which they depend;

---

[89] Wadham, J. (2001) 'The Human Rights Act: Sufficient Protection?', *NLJ* 1411.

[90] It was first appointed shortly before the 2001 election; it was reconstituted after that election and began effective working in the 2001–02 session. Its reports can be accessed through its website: http://parliament.uk/commons/selcom/hrhome.htm. See Feldman, D. (2002) 'Parliamentary Scrutiny of Legislation and Human Rights', *Public Law* 323.

Justice and peace depend upon a combination of an effective democracy and the observance of human rights. The Convention, therefore, envisages that democracy and human rights complement each other. Democracy, by implication, involves the recognition that a just and free society is one in which all can contribute to the identification and pursuit of the common good and this is compatible with the protection of fundamental rights. The Convention conception of democracy, therefore, cannot be reduced to unrestrained majority rule.[91] The protection of rights, in the name of democracy, limit what those who control the state apparatus can do even if they have the authority of the wishes and votes of the majority behind them. The preface also has strong words on European unity and a common heritage of 'political traditions, ideals, freedoms and the rule of law'. It also, however, refers to the universality of human rights in the United Nations Declaration and so leaves open the question whether rights are universal or culturally determined.

2.7.2 Article 1

Article 1 Obligation to respect human rights
The High Contracting Parties shall secure to everyone within their jurisdiction the rights and freedoms defined in Section I of this Convention.

The point of the Human Rights Act 1998 is to provide the means by which Article 1 can be given effect and hence the latter is not a scheduled Convention right. Article 1 contains the basic obligation on states to ensure that their law and administrative practices are compatible with the Convention and to change them if not. A particular point to note about Article 1 is that it requires that the rights of 'everyone' be secured. This must include non-citizens and persons who are illegally in the country. States cannot, under the Convention, simply redefine citizenship or illegal entry so as to exclude some group from the protection of Convention rights.[92]

2.7.3 Articles 2–7

These Articles are scheduled Convention rights under the Human Rights Act 1998.

Article 2 Right to life
(1) Everyone's right to life shall be protected by law. No one shall be deprived of his life intentionally save in the execution of a sentence of a court following his conviction of a crime for which the penalty is provided by law.
(2) Deprivation of life shall not be regarded as inflicted in contravention of this Article when it results from the use of force which is no more than absolutely necessary –

---

[91] Mowbray, A. (1999) 'The Role of the European Court of Human Rights in the Promotion of Democracy', *Public Law* 703.
[92] Article 14 reinforces the point by prohibiting discrimination on, for example, racial or national grounds, in the way Convention rights and freedoms are secured. Article 16, however, does permit some degree of restriction on the political activity of aliens.

(a) in defence of any person from unlawful violence;
(b) in order to effect a lawful arrest or to prevent the escape of a person lawfully detained;
(c) in action lawfully taken for the purpose of quelling a riot or insurrection.

The right to life is seen as one of the most fundamental rights the Convention protects. Most of it is immune from derogation under Article 15. Further discussion can be found in Chapter 4, on the general powers of state agents, Chapter 9, prisoners' rights, and Chapter 20, the right to bodily integrity.

Article 3 Prohibition of torture
No one shall be subjected to torture or to inhuman or degrading treatment or punishment.

Article 3 is also one of the most fundamental rights the Convention protects. It describes an absolute right in the sense that it cannot be subject to derogation under Article 15 nor is the evil of torture or inhuman treatment to be balanced against a judgment of the public interest. The significance of Article 3 is discussed in Chapter 4, on the coercive powers of the police and other state agents; it is also considered in Chapter 20, bodily integrity.

Article 4 Prohibition of slavery and forced labour
(1) No one shall be held in slavery or servitude.
(2) No one shall be required to perform forced or compulsory labour.
(3) For the purpose of this article the term 'forced or compulsory labour' shall not include:
    (a) any work required to be done in the ordinary course of detention imposed according to the provisions of Article 5 of this Convention or during conditional release from such detention;
    (b) any service of a military character or, in case of conscientious objectors in countries where they are recognised, service exacted instead of compulsory military service;
    (c) any service exacted in case of an emergency or calamity threatening the life or well-being of the community;
    (d) any work or service which forms part of normal civic obligation.

Even in time of war or other public emergency it is not possible for a state, by derogation from Article 4(1), to use slavery; but states at such times may use forced or compulsory labour by derogating from Article 4(2). Slavery is understood in relation to status. Forced or compulsory labour relates to work exacted under the threat of some kind of penalty[93] and invokes the idea of a person subject to punishment rather than, for example, an obligation to work in certain places or at certain times in exchange for training which is beneficial but which must be undergone.

If some requirement is within the definition of forced or compulsory labour, the question then arises whether any of the exemptions within Article 4(3) apply.

---

[93] Starmer, *op. cit.*, p. 93.

Article 5 Right to liberty and security

(1) Everyone has the right to liberty and security of person. No one shall be deprived of his liberty save in the following cases and in accordance with a procedure prescribed by law:

   (a) the lawful detention of a person after conviction by a competent court;

   (b) the lawful arrest or detention of a person for non-compliance with the lawful order of a court or in order to secure the fulfilment of any obligation prescribed by law;

   (c) the lawful arrest or detention of a person effected for the purpose of bringing him before the competent legal authority on reasonable suspicion of having committed an offence or when it is reasonably considered necessary to prevent his committing an offence or fleeing after having done so;

   (d) the detention of a minor by lawful order for the purpose of educational supervision or his lawful detention for the purpose of bringing him before the competent legal authority;

   (e) the lawful detention of persons for the prevention of the spreading of infectious diseases, of persons of unsound mind, alcoholics or drug addicts or vagrants;

   (f) the lawful arrest or detention of a person to prevent his effecting unauthorised entry into the country or of a person against whom action is being taken with a view to deportation or extradition.

(2) Everyone who is arrested shall be informed promptly, in a language which he understands, of the reasons for his arrest and of any charge against him.

(3) Everyone arrested or detained in accordance with the provisions of paragraph 1(c) of this article shall be brought promptly before a judge or other officer authorised by law to exercise judicial power and shall be entitled to trial within a reasonable time or to release pending trial. Release may be conditioned by guarantees to appear for trial.

(4) Everyone who is deprived of his liberty by arrest or detention shall be entitled to take proceedings by which the lawfulness of his detention shall be decided speedily by a court and his release ordered if the detention is not lawful.

(5) Everyone who has been the victim of arrest or detention in contravention of the provisions of this article shall have an enforceable right to compensation.

Article 5 is of great practical importance. Article 5(1) asserts a fundamental right to liberty and security of the person and then, in sub-paragraphs (a)–(f), identifies the only circumstances in which people can, compatibly with the Convention, be deprived of their liberty. It is, therefore, of great significance in relation to the activities of the courts, the police and other state agents such as customs and excise and immigration officers who exercise powers to detain people against their will. It is further discussed in Chapter 5 on the powers of the police in respect of arrest and detention. Article 5(2)–(5) contains further conditions that apply to the treatment of persons who have been arrested or otherwise deprived of their liberty. They are further discussed in Chapter 8 on the right to a fair trial. Article 5 can be derogated from in time of war or national emergency under the terms in Article 15 and is significant in the context of emergency powers and anti-terrorism legislation.[94]

---

[94] The United Kingdom's derogations under anti-terrorism legislation are discussed in Chapter 18.

Article 6 Right to a fair trial

(1) In the determination of his civil rights and obligations or of any criminal charge against him, everyone is entitled to a fair and public hearing within a reasonable time by an independent and impartial tribunal established by law. Judgment shall be pronounced publicly but the press and public may be excluded from all or part of the trial in the interests of morals, public order or national security in a democratic society, where the interests of juveniles or the protection of the private life of the parties so requires, or to the extent strictly necessary in the opinion of the court in special circumstances where publicity would prejudice the interests of justice.

(2) Everyone charged with a criminal offence shall be presumed innocent until proved guilty according to law.

(3) Everyone charged with a criminal offence has the following minimum rights:

    (a) to be informed promptly, in a language which he understands and in detail, of the nature and cause of the accusation against him;

    (b) to have adequate time and facilities for the preparation of his defence;

    (c) to defend himself in person or through legal assistance of his own choosing or, if he has not sufficient means to pay for legal assistance, to be given it free when the interests of justice so require;

    (d) to examine or have examined witnesses against him and to obtain the attendance and examination of witnesses on his behalf under the same conditions as witnesses against him;

    (e) to have the free assistance of an interpreter if he cannot understand or speak the language used in court.

Article 6 is the most cited Article and a high proportion of cases taken to Strasbourg are based totally or in part on alleged violations of this Article. It is given a full discussion in Chapter 8 of this book.

Article 7 No punishment without law

(1) No one shall be held guilty of any criminal offence on account of any act or omission which did not constitute a criminal offence under national or international law at the time when it was committed. Nor shall a heavier penalty be imposed that the one that was applicable at the time the criminal offence was committed.

(2) This article shall not prejudice the trial and punishment of any person for any act or omission which, at the time when it was committed, was criminal according to the general principles of law recognised by civilised nations.

Article 7 embodies the principle that no one shall be punished other than on the basis of law and that criminal liability should not be extended retrospectively to make unlawful something which, at the time, was not unlawful. Common law offences, when first declared and applied, may raise a difficulty under this provision unless there has been a gradual process of change in the law being signalled by the courts from which the new offence or development can be predicted.[95] Article 7 also requires that a person should not be given a more severe punishment than that which could have been imposed at the time the crime was committed.

---

[95] For example, the acceptance by the House of Lords that a husband could be convicted on the rape of his wife: *R v R (Rape: Marital exemption)* [1992] 1 AC 599.

Article 7 does permit an exception in respect of acts which, when committed, were recognised as criminal by the civilised part of the international community. This probably extends to the developing law on war crimes and inhibits any defence of illegality put forward by the accused.

Articles 8, 9, 10 and 11 and Article 12

Articles 8, 9, 10 and 11 are grouped together. They have a similar format. The first paragraph of each Article identifies a fundamental right or freedom. The second paragraph identifies the exclusive circumstances in which the national law can restrict the exercise of the right or freedom. Such restrictions must meet general criteria which are repeated in each of the four articles.

First, a restriction must meet the Convention test of 'legality' by being 'in accordance with the law' (Article 8) or 'prescribed by law' (Articles 9, 10 and 11). Any restriction of a fundamental right or freedom should, first, have a clear basis in law, that is to say it is possible to identify the authority of the restriction in an officially promulgated rule. An Act of Parliament clearly meets this test as do rules of common law if declared with sufficient precision. Second, a restriction meets the Convention standard for legality if, given the basis of law, the likelihood of restriction or interference is predictable or foreseeable. The precision of what is required will depend on circumstances. The degree of forseeability required in respect of phone tapping or other forms of surveillance, for example, is high.[96]

Second, any restriction must be 'necessary in a democratic society'. This term has been interpreted to mean that the restriction meets a 'pressing social need'. It requires the courts to make a judgment of 'proportionality' concerning the balance between the achievement of a necessary social goal and the burden imposed upon individuals by the means chosen to achieve the goal. Proportionality, which is pervasive through most of the Convention, has been discussed above (page 33).

Finally, any restriction of a right or freedom guaranteed under Articles 8 to 11 can only be for one of the purposes listed in the second paragraphs of the Articles.[97] The lists have common features (all rights and freedoms in Article 8 to 11 can be restricted in order to protect the rights of others) but are also significantly different. Some differences reflect the nature of the particular freedom in question, thus freedom of expression under Article 10 can be restricted to prevent the disclosure of information obtained in confidence and the reputation and impartiality of the judiciary. Others are not so easily explained and, perhaps, reflect historical circumstances. The right to respect for private and family life under Article 8 can be restricted in the interests of the 'economic well-being of the country'.[98]

---

[96] See Chapter 7.

[97] See also Article 18 which prohibits the application of a restriction of a right or freedom to any other purpose than those permitted.

[98] The provision may have been inserted at the insistence of the British government anxious to uphold a planned economy: Wicks, E. (2000) 'The United Kingdom Government's Perception of the European Convention on Human Rights at the Time of Entry', *Public Law* 438 (Autumn), 438.

Article 8 Right to respect for private and family life

(1) Everyone has the right to respect for his private and family life, his home and his correspondence.

(2) There shall be no interference by a public authority with the exercise of this right except such as is in accordance with the law and is necessary in a democratic society in the interests of national security, public safety or the economic well-being of the country, for the prevention of disorder or crime, for the protection of health or morals, or for the protection of the rights and freedoms of others.

The lack of a clear and direct concept of privacy in English law makes this one of the most important of the scheduled Convention rights in terms of impact on English law. It is discussed generally in Chapter 20; the right is fully engaged in respect of powers of entry and search and of surveillance (Chapters 6 and 7). The tension between the right of private life and freedom of expression, as enjoyed in particular by the press, is considered in Chapters 10 and 11.

Article 9 Freedom of thought, conscience and religion

(1) Everyone has the right to freedom of thought, conscience and religion; this right includes freedom to change his religion or belief and freedom, either alone or in community with others and in public or private, to manifest his religion or belief, in worship, teaching, practice and observance.

(2) Freedom to manifest one's religion or beliefs shall be subject only to such limitations as are prescribed by law and are necessary in a democratic society in the interests of public safety, for the protection of public order, health or morals, or for the protection of the rights and freedoms of others.

Article 9 is fully discussed in Chapter 23.

Article 10 Freedom of expression

(1) Everyone has the right to freedom of expression. This right shall include freedom to hold opinions and to receive and impart information and ideas without interference by public authority and regardless of frontiers. This article shall not prevent states from requiring the licensing of broadcasting, television or cinema enterprises.

(2) The exercise of these freedoms, since it carries with it duties and responsibilities, may be subject to such formalities, conditions, restrictions or penalties as are prescribed by law and are necessary in a democratic society, in the interests of national security, territorial integrity or public safety, for the prevention of disorder or crime, for the protection of health or morals, for the protection of the reputation or rights of others, for preventing the disclosure of information received in confidence, or for maintaining the authority and impartiality of the judiciary.

Freedom of expression is fundamental to a democratic society. It is discussed in general terms in Chapter 10. It is of significance in a number of specific areas such as press and media freedom (Chapter 11), contempt of court (Chapter 12), offences connected to politically motivated speech (Chapter 14), freedom of information (Chapter 15) and offences connected to national security (Chapter 16).

Article 11 Freedom of assembly and association
(1) Everyone has the right to freedom of peaceful assembly and to freedom of association with others, including the right to form and to join trade unions for the protection of his interests.
(2) No restrictions shall be placed on the exercise of these rights other than such as are prescribed by law and are necessary in a democratic society in the interests of national security or public safety, for the prevention of disorder or crime, for the protection of health or morals, for the protection of the reputation or rights of others. This article shall not prevent the imposition of lawful restrictions on the exercise of these rights by members of the armed forces, of the police or of the administration of the state.

Article 11 provides for a right to peaceful assembly. This relates, in particular, to political actions, to marches, meetings, protests and demonstrations, and is fully discussed in Chapter 17. It also provides for freedom of association, including for political purposes, and this is discussed in Chapter 13; there is also a right to form and join trade unions.

Article 12 Right to marry
Men and women of marriageable age have the right to marry and to found a family, according to the national laws governing the exercise of this right.

Article 12 is discussed in the context of sexual freedom in Chapter 21.

2.7.5 Protocols

Articles 1 to 3 of the First Protocol and Articles 1 and 2 of the Sixth Protocol are Scheduled Convention rights. Section 1(4) of the Act empowers the Secretary of State, by order, to identify other protocols and give them effect through the Act by making any amendments to it that he or she considers appropriate. There are other substantive Protocols (listed earlier) which have not been given further effect by the Act.

The First Protocol
Article 1 Protection of property
Every natural or legal person is entitled to the peaceful enjoyment of his possessions. No one shall be deprived of his possessions except in the public interest and subject to the conditions provided for by law and by the general principles of international law. The preceding provisions shall not, however, in any way impair the right of a state to enforce such laws as it deems necessary to control the use of property in accordance with the general interest or to secure the payment of taxes or other contributions or penalties.

The late acceptance of Article 1 related to a deep dispute about the extent to which property is a fundamental right reflecting an important aspect of the personality or whether it is more of a social fact embodying particular distributions of economic, political and social power which can be legitimately altered by the state. The Court has analysed the text in terms of three rules. The first provides a general right to peaceful enjoyment of possessions; the second identifies the general conditions on which the state may seek to deprive a person of his or her possessions and the third deals with the general conditions on which the state may seek to limit the use people may make of their possessions. The third rule is apparently expressed in a way which is highly permissive of state action. Nevertheless it, along with the other two, has been interpreted by the Court on the basis of general principles of Convention law. In particular the requirements of legality and proportionality are standards against which state actions are measured, although the Court allows a wide margin of appreciation in appropriate circumstances. Article 1 does not provide a simple power of veto by property owners to prevent redistributions of wealth, for legitimate social purposes, through policies such as nationalisation, leasehold reform or rent reform. The main effect of the Article has been, linked to Article 6, to require fair and timeous procedures over planning matters and to prevent retrospective legislation aimed at overturning court judgments affecting property interests. Nevertheless Article 1 does provide an important right that companies, as well as individuals, are able to assert to protect their property interests.

The First Protocol
Article 2 Right to education
No person shall be denied the right to education. In the exercise of any functions which it assumes in relation to education and to teaching, the State shall respect the right of parents to ensure such education and teaching in conformity with their own religious and philosophical convictions.

This Article does not require state education; to the contrary, its main point is to restrict state interference with education and might be a barrier to any state which wished to abolish private education. Any fundamental right to education will invoke major disputes about the purposes of education, the proper role of the state therein and the extent to which there can be positive duties to make major expenditures on social purposes. These explain the late adoption of a reference to education in the Convention. At the heart of the provision is the need for the state to respect the religious and philosophical convictions of parents over the education of their children. This right can tie in with religious freedom (Chapter 23) and it has been accepted as including parental views on punishment (Chapter 20). The United Kingdom has made a reservation in respect of Article 2 to the extent that 'the principle affirmed in the second sentence of article 2 is accepted by the United Kingdom only in so far as it is compatible with the provision of efficient instruction and training, and the avoidance of unreasonable public expenditure'. This reservation is maintained under the terms of the Human Rights Act 1998.

The First Protocol
Article 3 Right to free elections
The High Contracting Parties undertake to hold free elections at reasonable intervals by secret ballot, under conditions which will ensure the free expression of the opinion of the people in the choice of the legislature.

Article 3 is discussed in Chapter 13.

The Sixth Protocol
Article 1 Abolition of the death penalty
The death penalty shall be abolished. No one shall be condemned to such penalty or executed.

Article 2 Death penalty in time of war
A state may make provision in its law for the death penalty in respect of acts committed in time of war or of imminent threat of war; such penalty shall be applied only in the instances laid down in the law and in accordance with its provisions. The State shall communicate to the Secretary General of the Council of Europe the relevant provisions of that law.

The abolition of the death penalty is discussed in Chapter 20.

The ancillary rights
The scope and meaning of the substantive rights must be interpreted by United Kingdom courts dealing with applications under the Act in the light of these ancillary provisions.

Article 13 Right to an effective remedy
Everyone whose rights and freedoms as set forth in this Convention are violated shall have an effective remedy before a national authority notwithstanding that the violation has been committed by persons acting in an official capacity.

Article 13 places an obligation on the signatory states to ensure that a remedy is available from national courts for a violation of a substantive right or freedom. It is arguable that, at least until the coming into effect of the Human Rights Act 1998, the United Kingdom was in breach of this provision since Convention rights could not be directly, and in terms, enforced in the courts.

Article 13 is not included in the scheduled rights in the Human Rights Act 1998. The reason given by the government for this is that Article 13 places a positive duty on the states to provide an effective remedy from the national courts for violations of Convention rights and that the Human Rights Act 1998 is, itself, the complete means of meeting Article 13. Critics were concerned that this left unchanged the difficulty of obtaining effective remedies against, for example, the secret services where, as we shall see, special tribunals may be established but where access to the ordinary courts for the administration of public justice is prevented.

Article 14 Prohibition of discrimination
The enjoyment of the rights and freedoms set forth in this Convention shall be secured without discrimination on any ground such as sex, race, colour, language, religion, political or other opinion, national or social origin, association with a national minority, property, birth or other status.

Article 14 requires that the substantive rights must be secured without discrimination. The grounds of discrimination are broadly defined and the phrase 'other status' means that they can be added to – sexual orientation is the obvious example. Article 14 only requires non-discrimination in the way in which Convention rights and freedoms are secured; it does not involve a general right not to be discriminated against on matters which fall outside the scope of the Convention.[99] The Twelfth Protocol is currently open for signing and this, if brought into effect, will provide a more general, anti-discrimination provision. The United Kingdom has not as yet chosen to sign this Protocol.

Article 15 Derogation in time of emergency

(1) In time of war or other public emergency threatening the life of the nation any High Contracting Party may take measures derogating from its obligations under this Convention to the extent strictly required by the exigencies of the situation, provided that such measures are not inconsistent with its other obligations under international law.

(2) No derogation from Article 2, except in respect of deaths resulting from lawful acts of war, or from Articles 3, 4 (paragraph 1) and 7 shall be made under this paragraph.

(3) Any High Contracting Party availing itself of this right of derogation shall keep the Secretary General of the Council of Europe fully informed of the measures which it has taken and the reasons therefor. It shall also inform the Secretary General of the Council of Europe when such measures have ceased to operate and the provisions of the Convention are again being fully executed.

Article 15 is a controversial provision which allows a state party to 'derogate' from most, but not all, of the Convention 'in time of war or other public emergency threatening the life of the nation'. The provisions which cannot be derogated from are in paragraph 2. Significant derogations have been made by the United Kingdom in respect of anti-terrorism legislation and these are discussed in Chapter 18. Article 15 is not among the scheduled Convention Rights but the Human Rights Act provides for the identification, effectiveness and repeal of existing derogations as well as for the introduction of new ones.

Article 16 Restrictions on political activity of aliens

Nothing in Articles 10, 11 and 14 shall be regarded as preventing the High Contracting Parties from imposing restrictions on the political activity of aliens.

Article 16 permits the states to limit freedom of expression or freedom of assembly and association, or to discriminate in the way the other substantive rights and freedoms are secured, in order to place 'restrictions on the political activity of aliens'. This provision has not been widely invoked by the states, though it may have relevance in the 'war against terrorism'. It does not seem compatible with the general obligation under Article 1 though it must be stressed that nothing in Article 16 permits states to restrict other Convention rights and freedoms of aliens to a greater extent than is permitted to non-aliens.

Article 17 Prohibition of abuse of rights

Nothing in this Convention may be interpreted as implying for any state, group or person any right to engage in any activity or perform any act aimed at the destruction of any of the rights and freedoms set forth herein or at their limitation to a greater extent than is provided for in the Convention.

---

[99] Much stronger non-discrimination protection is available in European Community law in the field of employment.

Article 17 denies the protection of the Convention to any state, group or person who wishes to use a right or freedom guaranteed by the Convention in order to destroy the rights and freedoms of others. Hate speech or the advocacy of anti-democratic politics or of political violence are the kinds of matters with which the Article deals. It means that those involved are unable to resist restriction on their activities on the grounds that, for instance, their right under the Convention to speech or to association has been violated. The Article also prevents states from using their powers, recognised under the Convention, to restrict freedom in proportionate ways and for certain purposes in order to restrict the Convention rights of others.

Article 18 Limitation on use of restrictions on rights
The restrictions permitted under this Convention to the said rights and freedoms shall not be applied for any purpose other than those for which they have been prescribed.

Article 18 limits the powers enjoyed by the states to restrict rights and freedoms under the Convention. Many of the substantive Articles, either expressly or by implication, permit the states to limit the exercise of rights and freedoms in order to achieve certain purposes, such as protecting the rights of others. Article 18, 'Limitation on use of restrictions on rights', restricts the scope of any such restriction to the particular purposes allowed under the Convention; a power to restrict rights and freedoms cannot be used for other purposes.

Part II
General powers and duties of the state

3

Public authorities

3.1 The public sector

Civil liberties law is dominated by the relationship of public bodies with citizens. There are specific legal rules and concepts which apply to those exercising public authority and these will be considered in this chapter. There is no legal or constitutional definition of a public body. What is referred to is the exercise of authority in order to promote a particular, probably contested, conception of the public good rather than to promote an individual or private interest. What is of importance is to understand the institutional complexity of what is meant by public bodies or the public sector and to realise that this has undergone massive transformation in recent years

There is, first, the traditional state apparatus of ministers, the Civil Service, the military, the police, the security services, Custom and Excise and local government. This sector has been subject to great change. The Civil Service is now predominantly devolved to relatively autonomous agencies headed by a chief executive, and some of its traditional functions have been further devolved to private commercial or charitable organisations (the prison system is an example[1]). These private bodies are, to some extent, exercising public functions and to that degree can be thought of as within the public domain, but are also commercial or charitable with powers determined by contract. A similar situation exists with respect to local government. A commonly recognised difficulty with such devolution is that it diminishes the effectiveness of ministerial accountability to Parliament both because of the relative autonomy of the agency and also because of the claim to commercial confidentiality that a company exercising public responsibilities can make.

Second, much regulation and acts of governance in the public interest are done by bodies which are outside the traditional boundaries of the state but can be thought of as public authorities for one or more of a combination of reasons, such as the fact that their authority is based on an Act of Parliament, they are completely or partially funded from public funds or their directing board is wholly or partially appointed by the government. Such bodies, rather vaguely called quangos or non-departmental government organisations, characteristically perform a range of functions including the provision of services to individuals (e.g. the NHS), the promotion of particular interests (e.g. the

---

[1] See Livingstone, S. and Owen, T. (1999) *Prison Law*, 2nd edn. Oxford: Oxford University Press, chapter 1. See also Chapter 9 below.

Equal Opportunities Commission), the supervision of the activities of others (e.g. the Health and Safety at Work Commission), the distribution of public funds (e.g. the Higher Education Funding Councils) and the regulation of the activities or others by producing rules and guidance and adjudicating on disputes (e.g. the Independent Television Commission). They are likely, of course, to be exercising more than one such function. The important factor from the legal point of view is that each such body is constituted, organised, funded, appointed and empowered in different ways and they enjoy vastly different degrees of independence from the government department to which they relate.

Thirdly, it is apparent that regulatory and governing activities, in which the public interest is an important motive, can be performed by 'private' bodies. These are bodies which are commercially funded or whose authority is based on the voluntary agreement of those regulated. Some such bodies have authority which is partially statutory, the professional bodies in law and medicine being good examples. Other such bodies have little, if any, statutory authority for what they do (though they may operate under the threat of statutory regulation) yet may take decisions which can have an effect on the lives of millions. Examples include some media regulators such as the Press Complaints Commission and the Advertising Standards Authority, sporting regulators such as the Football Association, or religious organisations (excepting, perhaps, the Church of England).

3.2 Legal definitions of public bodies

There is no single legal definition of a public body. There are different approaches depending on the particular legal context. The Human Rights Act 1998, as we have seen, provides no definition of a public authority but includes within the definition any person in so far as they are exercising a public function. The Data Protection Act 1998, the Freedom of Information Act 2000 and the Race Relations (Amendment) Act 2000 adopt the approach of listing all the particular bodies or types of bodies that come within the authority of the Act (though, as with the Freedom of Information Act 2000, the Secretary of State may have the power to include any person exercising 'public functions'). The Parliamentary Commissioner Act 1967, which establishes the Parliamentary Ombudsman, lists the bodies subject to the Commissioner's investigations but allows a body to be added to the list if it is established under the authority of an Act of Parliament or the Royal prerogative or by a minister exercising some other common law power, if at least half its funding comes from public funds or is based on a compulsory levy and if it is wholly or partly appointed by the Crown or the government.[2] Under common law, for the purposes of identifying bodies amenable to judicial review, the courts have developed a test which focuses on the source of authority (whether predominantly contractual or statutory) and whether functions are being performed which would otherwise be undertaken by the government. Most of the bodies

---

[2] Parliamentary Commissioner Act 1967, s. 4(3).

mentioned above are amenable to judicial review apart from sporting regulators and religious bodies.[3]

3.3 The legal authority of public bodies and officials

The identity, general authority and powers of public bodies are matters of law. The main institutions of traditional state power, such as ministers and civil servants, the army, the secret security services and the police, characteristically take their authority from a combination of the Royal Prerogative, other general powers recognised by the common law (such as entering into contracts or issuing publicity) and from Acts of Parliament. Most other bodies which are outside the scope of traditional state power, including local government, derive their existence and powers from Acts of Parliament; a few, the BBC, some professional bodies, some universities for example, derive their powers in part from Royal Charters granted under the Prerogative. Thus identifying the particular powers of public bodies and their officials will depend upon interpreting the Acts of Parliament in issue and identifying the scope of the Royal Prerogative and other common law powers as recognised by the courts. The powers of the police, for example, are looked at in detail in many of the following chapters.

3.3.1 The ordinary law

It is of the utmost importance to realise, however, that public bodies and their officials are subject to the general principles of law which apply to the public domain.

The fundamental requirement is that officials must have legal authority, in statute, prerogative or other common rule, for their actions. Without legal authority they are liable under the ordinary law for any crimes, torts or other unlawful actions they may commit. *Entick* v *Carrington* (1765) remains of great importance.[4]

> King's Messengers entered and ransacked a publisher's premises in the execution of a purported general warrant obtained from the Secretary of State.
> HELD: such a general warrant was unlawful. The King's Messengers did not have any other legal authority and, in particular, they enjoyed no privileged position just because they represented the Crown. Like anyone else, they were liable in trespass.
> *Entick* v *Carrington* (1765) 19 St Tr 1030

Entick v *Carrington* (1765) can be a little misleading. First, there remain areas in which the Crown is outside the general law. These have been largely reduced by Parliament and the courts[5] though the rule that the Crown is not bound by an Act of Parliament unless the Act expressly says so remains.

---

[3] The basic cases on the point include *R* v *Panel on Take-Overs and Mergers ex parte Datafin* [1987] 1 QB 74 and *R* v *Disciplinary Committee of the Jockey Club ex parte Aga Khan* [1992] 2 All ER 853.
[4] Its importance has recently been recognised in *R* v *Central Criminal Court ex parte Bright* [2001] 2 All ER 244.
[5] For example, Crown Proceedings Act 1947; *M* v *Home Office* [1994] 1 AC 377.

Secondly, all *Entick* v *Carrington* (1765) requires is that officials should have legal authority. As is clear from the chapters that follow, statute and common law can confer very wide powers and extensive discretion on officials. The police and above all the security services enjoy such wide discretion under the law. In some instances statute may also grant certain kinds of freedom from normal legal and judicial processes; again this can apply to the security services.[6] Thirdly, the converse of *Entick* v *Carrington* (1765) is that public officials enjoy the same negative liberty as private citizens. They may do anything that is not forbidden by law. This is convenient and it permits public bodies and their officials a whole range of ancillary powers, such as entering into contracts or publicising policies. The difficulty is when this negative freedom can also permit the state to impinge upon significant background rights or otherwise exercise coercive power without specific legal authority.

> M challenged the lawfulness of the tapping of his telephone by the police. The tapping was prior to the Interception of Communications Act 1985.
>   HELD: no legal rule authorised telephone tapping; no legal rule prohibited telephone tapping. As with a citizen, so with the state, that which was not prohibited was permitted.
>   *Malone* v *Metropolitan Police Commissioner* [1979] Ch 344

This 'negative liberty' approach is, in the human rights field, probably incompatible with the principle of 'legality' which pervades the Convention rights scheduled to the Human Rights Act 1998.[7]

3.3.2 Judicial review of administrative action

Whatever else they may be, police, security officers, customs officials, prison officers, social workers, etc. are public officials whose actions are capable of scrutiny by the administrative court on the general principles of administrative law. The court has the power to quash a decision, prevent an action going ahead, declare it unlawful or order an official to exercise his or her duty. This is not the place to outline these powers in any detail.[8] A person with a 'sufficient interest' in the matter may challenge the action of public officials on the grounds that they have acted outside their powers, that they have treated an individual unfairly particularly by violating rules of 'natural justice', or that they have departed, without proper justification, from a proposed course of action on which others have relied.[9] Though judicial review is important it must always be remembered that other methods of redress may be more effective. These may be a civil action for damages available if a tort or breach of contract has been committed; alternatively Parliament may have established a tribunal system to decide disputes or hear appeals.

---

[6] The security services are not subject to the supervisory powers of the High Court but of a special tribunal – see Chapter 7.

[7] The *Malone* case was held to be incompatible with Article 8 ECHR in *Malone* v *United Kingdom* (1984) 7 EHRR 14.

[8] Wade, H.W.R. and Forsyth, C. (2000) *Administrative Law*, 8th edn. Oxford: Oxford University Press; Craig, P. (1999) *Administrative Law*, 4th edn. London: Sweet & Maxwell.

[9] For a survey see Administrative Court Practice Statement [2002] 1 All ER 633.

One of the grounds of judicial review that is often of importance in a civil liberties context is that an official or public authority has acted 'unreasonably'. The meaning of this term is not always clear. The ground is usually known as '*Wednesbury* unreasonableness' after the leading case.[10] It includes the idea that a public body has exercised its discretion for a purpose that is irrelevant in the sense of not being explained by the principles and purposes of the Act of Parliament in question.[11] It can also mean that, although an official action would appear to be in furtherance of the Act in question and that all relevant matters had been taken into account and irrelevant matters excluded, nevertheless the decision was an improper use, or an abuse, of power. This principle has, in the past, lead to some highly controversial overturning by the courts of the decisions of elected bodies. However, the *Wednesbury* principles are also thought to be too government friendly since having to prove an abuse of power ('irrationality') places too heavy a burden on an applicant.

This issue has come to a head in the context of human rights. The notions of unreasonableness, abuse of power and irrationality are giving way to the test of 'proportionality'.[12] No matter how wide the discretion appears to be in an Act of Parliament, any particular discretionary action by a minister or official must be proportionate, based on a proper balance between the benefit to the public that it produces and the burden it places on an individual. Proportionality is thought to be somewhat more demanding of ministers and officials than the *Wednesbury* approach.[13] The *Wednesbury* test often only required the official to take certain matters into account and, if so, the court would accept his or her assessment of the situation. Under the doctrine of proportionality, it is the courts, not the official, who claim the last word on whether the balance of individual and collective interests has been properly made.[14]

3.3.3 The Human Rights Act 1998

As we have seen, public bodies and their officials are subject to the Human Rights Act 1998. As we have seen, the legislation under which they act is to be interpreted as far as possible for compatibility with the scheduled Convention rights, and public authorities act unlawfully if they violate the Convention. Section 7 provides for access to the court, by judicial review or in any proceedings, for victims of such violations to obtain a remedy. The issues, including the difficult question of identifying 'public authorities' for the purpose of the Act, have been discussed in Chapter 2.

3.3.4 Redress of grievances

Public bodies of various kinds are also likely to be subject to various general or specific systems for dealing with individual complaints and problems. For

---

[10] *Associated Provincial Picture Houses* v *Wednesbury Corporation* [1948] 1 KB 223.

[11] For example, *Padfield* v *Minister of Agriculture, Fisheries and Food* [1968] AC 997.

[12] *R* v *Secretary of State for the Home Department ex parte Daly* [2001] UKHL 26; [2001] 3 All ER 433. The House of Lords appears to apply proportionality to all or at least many administrative decisions, not just those involving human rights.

[13] For example, *R* v *Shayler* [2002] UKHL 11; [2002] 2 All ER 477 HL.

[14] *R* v *Secretary of State for the Home Department ex parte Daly* [2001] UKHL 26; [2001] 3 All ER 433. But 'context in all': the courts defer to the executive on national security matters, see *A, X and Y* v *Secretary of State for the Home Department* [2002] EWCA Civ 1502.

example, they may be within the jurisdiction of the Parliamentary Ombuds-man[15] or some other ombudsman system,[16] or subject to a particular system of financial control,[17] or subject to the jurisdiction of a tribunal established specifically to deal with disputes,[18] or there may be a regulatory agency which lays down rules or guidelines and investigates complaints,[19] or there may be an internal complaints system established.[20] Dating from the 1990s, the Citizens' Charter has spawned a range of specific charters which create guidelines dealing with the relationship between many public bodies and the people they deal with[21] and so on. The kinds of devices just mentioned are often available as alternatives to the courts and they play an important role in the public law relating to public bodies, including when the activities of public bodies affect civil liberties.

3.3.5 General and specific legislation

Subject to the general proviso that the Crown is not bound by legislation unless the Act expressly says so, ordinary legislation which affects civil liberties will be binding on public officials. However, much of such general legislation may have provisions which expressly or implicitly limit the responsibilities of some public bodies under the Act. The exemptions under the Data Protection Act 1998, discussed in Chapter 19, are examples.

Much legislation is specifically directed at public bodies. Some of it aims to establish basic principles of good practice and to create some effective rights of citizens. The Freedom of Information Act 2000, for example, imposes a duty on listed public authorities to disclose information to the public subject to a range of exemptions. Discrimination legislation, relating to the grounds of sex, race and disability, is normally binding on all persons and public bodies are not exempted. It has tended to focus on employment and the provision of commercial services. The exercise of public functions by public bodies has sometimes been outside the scope of the legislation and generally the legislation has not required public bodies to promote good race relations. The Race Relations (Amendment) Act 2000 now imposes a general duty not to discriminate on all public authorities and persons exercising public functions.[22] It goes further and lists a large number of public authorities, to which the Secretary of State can add, which are required positively to promote good race relations in their activities (this duty was already required of local councils under section 77 of the Race Relations Act 1976). The duty is exercised by reference to codes of practice issued by the government.

---

[15] The Parliamentary Commissioner Act 1967, s. 4 and Schedule 2.
[16] For example, local councils are subject to the reports and investigations of the Local Commissioners; prisoners may complain to a Prisons Ombudsman.
[17] For example, the audit system for local councils supervised by the Audit Commission.
[18] See Chapter 7 for the tribunals dealing with surveillance.
[19] For example, the Independent Television Commission – see Chapter 11.
[20] For example, under the Children Act 1989.
[21] For analysis of the position in 2002 see: Drewry, G. (2002) 'What Happened to the Citizen's Charter?', *Public Law* 9 (Autumn).
[22] With some exceptions such as the security services.

4

The police and security services

4.1 Introduction

Civil liberties law focuses attention on those agencies, such as the police and the security services, which exercise the coercive, ultimately forceful, authority of the state directly against persons or indirectly through overt or covert surveillance and investigation. In this chapter we look at the general legal position of, in particular, the police but also the security services. The details of their powers are discussed in later chapters.

Police and security services are, by any definition, public authorities performing public functions. The general constitutional and legal principles, outlined in Chapter 3, apply. Police and security officers are bound by the general law, have powers authorised by statute but can also exercise the ordinary freedoms enjoyed by private citizens. They exercise wide discretion but this is subject to the principle of 'legality' and any discretionary action may be subject to judicial review and measured against the idea of proportionality. In particular, section 6 the Human Rights Act 1998 means that actions which are incompatible with the scheduled Convention rights are unlawful unless required by the clear words of a statute.

4.2 The police

4.2.1 The police function

The coercive power of the state, particularly powers over personal liberty such as the power to require people to move on, to stop, to be searched, to be arrested and then detained and so on, are exercised predominantly by the police. The term 'police' applies to range of forces and organisations which exercise the police function generally or in specific contexts for specific purposes. The police function is concerned with the maintenance of the peace, the protection of the public and the prevention and investigation, but not the prosecution, of criminal offences. Included in this is a significant role in promoting the security of the state, a role that is shared with the security services. Unless there is a threat to the peace, the police do not have a direct role in enforcing the civil law. Other organisations, such as the security services and Customs and Excise, also perform aspects of the police function and in recent years there has been a major expansion of commercial businesses offering policing services particularly over private land such as shopping malls and leisure complexes to which the public frequently go.

4.2.2 The organisation of the police

In Britain the general police forces are organised 'locally', broadly speaking on county and metropolitan county areas. There are also police forces with specific and limited jurisdiction. In particular the Ministry of Defence Police has general police powers over any person on certain Crown land. The force is under the ultimate authority of the Secretary of State for Defence and the Defence Council who nominate its chief constable. Officers have the same 'powers and privileges of constables', found in common law and statute, that the general police enjoy. They have jurisdiction over military bases and other land occupied by the Ministry of Defence and over defence personnel anywhere in the United Kingdom.[1] In respect of Ministry of Defence land, their powers are exercisable against anyone, including, for example, anti-war demonstrators, and are not confined to forces personnel. Other forces with general police powers exercisable within defined places include the British Transport Police,[2] the UK Atomic Energy Constabulary and the Royal Parks Police. There are a number of forces which are part of the military and only have powers over military personnel[3] although these powers are extensive and can be exercised in public places.[4]

4.2.3 National or local police?

The so-called local dimension to policing in Britain is felt to be better able to establish consensual, community-based policing and it also is a barrier to the threats to liberty that a strong, centralised force might bring about. On the other hand there have always been strong arguments in favour of a national force in particular in order to give effect to a police force whose organisation and capabilities can match the organisation and capability of criminals.[5]

Though local links are maintained through, for example, community liaison and other initiatives, there is clearly a strong centralising tendency in modern policing. Apart from the position of the Home Secretary, which is discussed below, there are important institutions through which national and international policies can be advanced and promoted. The Association of Chief Police Officers meets to discuss policing issues and coordinate responses to particular

---

[1] Ministry of Defence Police Act 1987, s. 2.
[2] Others connected with transport are the Ports of Tilbury and Liverpool forces and the Airport Police.
[3] Including the Royal Navy Regulating Branch, the Royal Military Police, the Royal Air Force Police and the Royal Marines Police. See Army Act 1955, Air Force Act 1955 and Naval Discipline Act 1957. The Armed Forces Act 2001, Part 1 keeps these Acts in force and amends and increases the police powers to which they relate.
[4] See, for example, Part 2 of the Armed Forces Act 2001 over powers to stop and search.
[5] For discussion see the Royal Commission on the Police (1962), Cm 1728, chapter 5. The Commission rejected the idea of a national force. A.L. Goodhart wrote a dissenting opinion arguing for a 'centrally controlled police force, administered on a regional basis'.

issues; the Police Act 1996 allows police forces to assist each other[6] and this support can reflect national priorities through the way it is coordinated by the Mutual Aid Coordination Centre;[7] there are national police resources such as the police computer and police training is becoming increasingly centralised with the establishment, under Part 4 of the Criminal Justice and Police Act 2001, of a Central Police Training and Development Authority. Crime does not recognise county boundaries and the National Crime Squad, which developed out of the regional crime squad system, has a national role in respect of the investigation of serious crime. Similarly, intelligence gathering is increasingly organised on a national basis through the National Criminal Intelligence Service, which had a non-statutory existence until 1997. Both of these organisations have now been given a statutory structure under the Police Act 1997 and are responsible to their respective service authorities. British police are also fully involved in various international arrangements such as under Interpol, through bilateral agreements with other forces or through agreements made under the third pillar of the European Union on police and judicial cooperation on criminal matters.

4.2.4 The organisation and control of the police force

Control of the 'ordinary' police forces in England and Wales is exerted through the interrelation of three organisations, the police authorities, chief constables and the Home Secretary. The broad structure is found in the Police Act 1996 which will be supplemented by the Police Reform Act 2002 (not in force at the time of writing).

Police authorities
There is one police authority for each police force area[8] made up of a balance of local councillors, magistrates and independent members appointed by the other members from a list approved by Home Secretary.[9] It is through the police authority that the views of elected local councillors can be made known. Their main function is the 'maintenance of an efficient and effective force for its area' and much of it is to do with the provision of resources. They are also involved in determining police policy by the drawing up, in consultation with the chief constable and in the light of Home Office objectives, of a policing plan and the setting of policing objectives. Authorities also have reporting responsibilities to the public and the Home Secretary. Subject to Home Office approval, they appoint and may dismiss the chief constable and the assistant and deputy chief constables.[10]

---

[6] Section 24, Police Act 1996.
[7] The predecessor, the National Reporting Centre, played a crucial role in the suppression of the miners' strike 1984–85; Loveday, B. (1986) 'Central Co-ordination, Police Authorities and the Miners' Strike', 60 *PQ* 68.
[8] Section 1–4, Police Act 1996. Until the establishment of the Greater London Authority, the Home Secretary was the police authority in the London metropolitan area. Section 310, Greater London Authority Act 1999 establishes a police authority for London.
[9] Section 4, Police Act 1996 and Schedule 2.
[10] Section 11, Police Act 1996. For the earlier position see *Ridge v Baldwin* [1964] AC 40.

Chief constables

Chief constables have primary responsibility for the 'direction and control' of their force.[11] It is under their authority, not that of the police authority, that distribution of resources is determined, short- and medium-term priorities set and officers promoted and disciplined. As a 'constable' the chief constable is an 'officer of the peace' and is legally and constitutionally independent of both Home Secretary and police authority. Neither of the latter have the power to instruct a chief constable unless statute says otherwise. Decisions taken by or under the authority of a chief constable can be politically charged and highly controversial. Decisions about the policing of demonstrations or policies on domestic violence or drug enforcement are examples of this.

The Home Secretary

The Home Secretary has significant statutory powers and duties over the police forces of Great Britain.[12] Home Secretaries can set national policing objectives and produce codes of practice and guidance of various kinds which police forces must take into account. The Home Secretary has wide ranging statutory powers over establishment matters such as pay and uniform[13] and he or she must approve appointments and dismissals of chief constables. They receive both regular and ad hoc reports on policing matters which they can bring to Parliament. The Home Secretary's influence is assured by the fact that up to 50 per cent of a police force's funding comes from a grant that he or she authorises and which is made subject to conditions and to an inspection by the Inspector of Constabulary.[14] It seems that the Home Secretary has a residual prerogative power of supplying chief constables with the equipment they seek but which their police authority has denied them.[15] The powers of the Home Secretary to require inspections and resulting action from police authorities, and to issue guidance to police authorities, have been enhanced by the Police Reform Act 2002. The Act will also lay a duty on the Home Secretary to produce a national policing plan which sets out policing priorities in respect of which the Home Secretary will exercise his or her powers.

4.2.5 Police officers

At common law a police officer is an independent officer of the peace and considered to be a servant of the law.[16] Officers are not employees or agents

---

[11] Section 10, Police Act 1996.

[12] In particular: Police Act 1996, Part II Central Supervision, Direction and Facilities, as amended by Part I the Police Reform Act 2002.

[13] These powers usually need the approval of statutory consultation bodies, in particular the Police Negotiating Board and the Police Advisory Board.

[14] Inspectors of Constabulary are appointed by the Crown (in effect the Home Secretary) and inspect and report on the police forces.

[15] *R v Home Secretary ex parte Northumbria Police Authority* [1987] 2 WLR 98: the police authority refused to meet the chief constable's request for funds for riot equipment; the request was met by the Home Secretary.

[16] A police officer can be referred to as a servant of the Crown and is a 'Crown servant' for the purposes of the Official Secrets Acts: s. 12(1)(e), 1989 Act; however, police actions are not attributable to the Crown for the purposes of liability under the Crown Proceedings Act 1947.

of their chief constable, the police authority or the Home Office.[17] In law a police officer can be expected and permitted to exercise independent judgment over the matters that he or she deals with. The reality, of course, is that police officers are part of an organised force led by the chief constable and disobedience of orders is likely to be a disciplinary matter. Police independence is of practical significance in respect of the most senior officers who are entitled to have the decisive say particularly over operational matters free from local or central government control.

Police officers are distinguished from ordinary citizens in terms of various restraints imposed upon them. They are subject to a disciplinary regime which is based on regulations produced by the Secretary of State and administered through the office of the Chief Constable. They are not permitted to join an independent trade union,[18] though the Police Federation is created by statute to represent officers on matters affecting their welfare and efficiency;[19] a strike would be contrary to the disciplinary regulations and organising a strike probably an offence of 'causing disaffection'.[20] There are also wide ranging restrictions on the right of a police officer to take part in local and national politics in so far as such activity would seem to interfere with the impartial discharge of his or her duties.[21] This point is taken up in Chapter 13.

4.2.6 Political accountability

In relation to both the policies they pursue and their own behaviour, the police forces can be the subject of great political controversy. The last thirty years has seen widespread and continuing concern over police corruption, racism and relations with ethnic minority groups, the policing of political demonstrations and the police's role in bringing about miscarriages of justice including public interest corruption[22] and the handling of complaints. These are all matters of intense public interest and the legitimate concern of national and local representative institutions. However, political accountability, to Parliament and local authorities, is problematic. The issue is how to uphold proper police independence and avoid not only corrupt, self-serving political influence and control over the enforcement of the criminal law in particular cases but also local special pleading which may be incompatible with the duty to treat like cases alike. At the same time it is important, in a democracy, to allow an effective representative voice over 'police policies in matters which vitally concern the public interest'.[23]

Chief constables, as we have seen, must report to their police authority and the latter have increased responsibilities for plans and general policies. Police

---

[17] For example, *Fisher* v *Oldham Corporation* [1930] 2 KB 364.
[18] Section 64, Police Act 1996, though officers can remain in trade unions they were members of when they joined.
[19] Section 59, Police Act 1996. Under s. 64(5) the Superintendents' Association is recognised as representing higher ranks.
[20] An offence under s. 91, Police Act 1996.
[21] Police Regulations 1995, Part 9, Schedule 2. See Davis, H. (2000) *Political Freedom*. London: Continuum, pp. 260–2.
[22] That is, in which persons the police believe to be criminals are convicted on false evidence produced by the police.
[23] Royal Commission on the Police (1962), Cm 1728, paragraph 90.

authorities have members from elected local councils. However, the Police Act 1996 weakened the influence of local councils by increasing the proportion of independent members appointed from a Home Office approved list on police authorities. Local councils retain a power to question police authorities.[24] As indicated above, there is a significant rise in the amount of 'national policing' and bodies such as the National Crime Squad are remote from individual local authorities.

The Home Secretary is accountable to Parliament for those policing matters which are within his or her responsibility. The effectiveness of Parliamentary accountability and scrutiny is questionable and, in any case, Home Secretaries do not have direct responsibility for police policies.

The major developments in accountability in recent times are focused on direct community liaison. Police are under a statutory duty to establish community liaison groups.[25] 'Institutional racism' was found to exist by the Macpherson Report[26] into the investigation of the murder of Stephen Lawrence, a black teenager, and this has led to a range of initiatives and changes in practice as regards police treatment of ethnic minorities, a process which is advanced by the provisions of the Race Relations (Amendment) Act 2000.[27]

4.2.7 Legal control of the police

The Human Rights Act 1998
The police service, as a 'public authority', is required to act compatibly with the scheduled Convention rights in the Human Rights Act 1998. The impact of the Convention rights on the use of force by the police is discussed later in this chapter.

Judicial review
The fact that police are public officials also means that the lawfulness of their actions can be challenged in ordinary judicial review proceedings, which may or may not be linked to a human rights issue. In practice the courts recognise that chief constables enjoy a wide discretion with which the courts are reluctant to interfere,[28] though the courts might take action if a chief constable persisted with a policy of not enforcing certain laws, such as drug laws.

> Section 32(1), Betting Gaming and Lotteries Act 1963 required certain gambling games to have equal chances between the punter and the bank. The police, as a matter of policy, decided not to enforce this provision. B sought mandamus (now called a mandatory order) to require the police to reverse this policy and enforce the law. The application was refused. The police then changed the policy. B appealed to the Court of Appeal.

[24] Section 20, Police Act 1996.
[25] Section 106, Police and Criminal Evidence Act 1984.
[26] Macpherson of Cluny, Sir William (1999) *The Stephen Lawrence Inquiry. Report*, Cm 4262-I. London: Stationery Office, chapter 6, paragraphs 6.39 and 6.45.
[27] See Chapter 3.
[28] *R v Chief Constable of Devon and Cornwall ex parte Central Electricity Generating Board* [1982] 1 QB 458; *R v Oxford ex parte Levey* (1986) *The Times*, 1 November; *R v Chief Constable of Sussex ex parte International Trader's Ferry Ltd* [1999] 2 AC 418.

HELD: although the police have wide discretionary powers over policy, the discretion is not absolute. The CPM owed a duty to the public to enforce the law and he could, by mandamus, be compelled to perform this duty. In this case, given the change in policy, the courts would not interfere.

R v *Commissioner of Police of the Metropolis ex parte Blackburn* [1968] 2 QB 118

It is always important to remember that even though an officer has the legal power to act in a certain way, the reasonableness and proportionality of any particular exercise of that power can be tested in the court.

Civil liability

Police may also be liable for civil actions and claims for compensation. Individual officers can be liable if their actions constitute a tort. Actions for false imprisonment, assault and battery, or trespass to land are not uncommon; actions for misfeasance in public office are also known.[29] The chief constable, though the employer of an officer, is vicariously liable for such torts and is the defendant for such actions. Damages can be paid out of the police fund by the police authority.[30] The attractiveness of such actions, as an alternative to using the complaints procedure, has been limited by the Court of Appeal giving guidelines to juries assessing damages to be awarded against the police for unlawful conduct. An award of exemplary damages is subject to a maximum of £50,000 in exceptional cases involving senior officers.[31] Police officers can also be liable for the negligent performance of their duties. It is, however, difficult to establish that claimants, other than those under the direct and immediate control of the police, are owed a duty of care.[32] At one time it was thought that such public policies were incompatible with the right of access to the court under Article 6 ECHR but that view is no longer being followed.[33]

Complaints against the police

Civil action, though it may result in damages, is expensive and time-consuming. The alternative is to use the police complaints process which involves the investigation of a complaint and the publication of a report and links with the discipline process applied to officers. The system of complaints has been reformed under the provisions of the Police Reform Act 2002.

Under the current system, found in the Police Act 1996, complaints against senior officers are dealt with by the police authority; other complaints are dealt with by the chief constable. In both cases the more serious complaints are likely to be investigated by officers from another force. If criminal conduct is disclosed by an investigation the matter will be forwarded to the Director of

---

[29] For example, *Elliott* v *Chief Constable of Wiltshire* (1996) *The Times*, 5 December.

[30] The Police Act 1996, s. 88. This provision does not apply to damages against the chief constable him or herself. It should also be remembered that a really serious, self-motivated assault by a police officer on a member of the public may be outside the scope of duty and thus not establish vicarious liability: *Makanjuola* v *Commissioner of Police of the Metropolis* [1992] 3 All ER 617 CA.

[31] *Thompson* v *Commissioner of Police of the Metropolis, Hsu* v *Commissioner of Police of the Metropolis* [1997] 2 All ER 762.

[32] *Hill* v *Chief Constable of West Yorkshire* [1989] AC 53. Cf. *Alexandrou* v *Oxford* [1993] 4 All ER 328; *Swinney* v *Chief Constable of Northampton Police* [1997] QB 464 CA.

[33] *Z and others* v *United Kingdom*, Ap. 29392/95; cf. *Osman* v *United Kingdom* (1998) 29 EHRR 245.

Public Prosecutions who will decide whether to bring charges. In other cases the police authority, for senior officers, or the chief constable, for junior officers, may decide to instigate disciplinary action under the disciplinary regulations or to take no action.

The fundamental problem has always been the lack of an independent element in the investigation of complaints. Under the 1996 Act the Police Complaints Authority (PCA) exercises a supervisory and reporting role over investigations, particularly of the more serious or complex complaints. This has been central to improving the credibility of the complaints system. The Police Reform Act 2002 will, for the first time, introduce a provision for independent investigation. When brought into effect, the Act will introduce a new system of handling complaints. The Police Complaints Authority is to be replaced by the Independent Police Complaints Commission.[34] The Commission will have a more extensive jurisdiction than the Authority which includes a general duty to ensure public confidence in the system of handling complaints. The Secretary of State will be able to make regulations authorising the use of covert surveillance in police complaints investigations. The most important change is that the Commission will have more extensive powers over the investigation and handling of complaints. There are four types of investigation: by the police authority, supervised by the Commission, 'managed' by the Commission and, for the most serious offences, a power to investigate a complaint itself using its own staff. The Act introduces, for the most serious and complex cases, the independent investigatory element that has been missing from the system.

4.2.8 The general powers of the police

Citizens in uniform

The general powers of the police include those that are enjoyed by ordinary citizens such as making summary arrests for 'arrestable offences',[35] detaining persons for breach of the peace[36] or entering private property under a duty of necessity to prevent murder[37] or other serious harms.[38] Police officers enjoy the same freedoms as private citizens to go on the highway or other places, like shops, car parks or shopping malls, where the public are likely to have express or implied permission to enter. Where, however, the police are claiming to be acting in the exercise of their duty they may, unlike the general public, need a reason related to that duty to be on the property.[39] There are, of course, many other reasons why the citizen in uniform idea is unrealistic including the fact that the police are part of a disciplined force and also because, on the basis of their office, they enjoy a wide range of particular powers and are subject to particular duties.

---

[34] The Police Reform Act 2002, Part 2; Schedule 2 establishes the Commission; Schedule 3 details its investigatory powers. See further, Zander, M. (2002) 'The Police Reform Act 2002' part 2, 152 7048 *NLJ* 1387.

[35] The power of citizen's arrest is retained by s. 24(4), PACE 1984; its limits are discussed in Chapter 5.

[36] *Albert* v. *Lavin* [1982] AC 547. Breach of the peace is discussed in Chapter 17.

[37] *Handcock* v *Baker* (1800) 2 Bos & O 260.

[38] For example, to put out fires: *Cope* v *Sharpe* (2) [1912] 1 KB 496 CA.

[39] See Chapter 6.

Keeping the peace

At common law a police officer, a constable, is under a general duty to 'be a keeper of the peace and to take all necessary steps with that in mind'.[40]

> Two police officers were summoned to a boys club and requested, by the leader of the club, to ensure that S and H left the club before a 'disco' began. The officers did not suspect that S and H had committed criminal offences. S and H left; then S returned and struck one of the officers. There ensued a struggle which was joined by H. S and H were charged with assaulting a constable in the execution of his duty. S and H alleged that the presence of the police officers in the club was not in the execution of a duty.
> HELD (QBDC): the police were under a general duty to keep the peace which they were exercising in entering the boys club.
> *Coffin* v *Smith* (1980) 71 Cr Ap Rep 221

Private citizens are not under a similar duty.[41] The common law accepts there is a duty to investigate crime[42] and to take other actions, such as dealing with breaches of the peace. Even if off-duty a police officer may be still under a duty to act to maintain the peace. At best private citizens may do these things voluntarily on the basis of an imperfect moral duty.[43] The language of 'duty' must be used with care. Any legal duty that officers have to protect the peace must be put in the context, first, of their individual discretion and, second, the law-enforcement policies of the force to which they belong.

The consequence of the peace-keeping 'duty' is that the police have discretionary power to take actions, including stopping, detaining, arresting persons and bringing them before magistrates for actual or anticipated breaches of the peace. They may also enter private property to deal with breaches of the peace. The law on this matter is examined in Chapter 17, on public order.

Obstruction, assault and cooperation

It is an offence, in section 89 of the Police Act 1996, to assault or to resist or wilfully obstruct a constable, or a person assisting a constable, where the constable is acting 'in the execution of his duty'.[44] There is no direct power of summary arrest for the section 89 offence[45] but arrest can usually be justified either by a threatened breach of the peace, for which there is a power of arrest, or under the general arrest conditions under section 25, PACE 1984.[46]

The investigation of offences is a part of police duty. There is, however, no equivalent legal obligation on citizens to cooperate with the police, be civil or answer their questions.[47] This both exemplifies the liberty of the subject but it

---

[40] *Coffin* v *Smith* (1980) 71 Cr Ap Rep 221.
[41] See *R* v *Dytham* [1979] 3 WLR 467.
[42] *Davis* v *Lisle* [1936] 2 KB 434.
[43] In *Albert* v *Lavin* [1982] AC 547, Lord Diplock described the citizen's duty to deal with breaches of the peace as a 'duty of imperfect obligation' and contrasted the duty with that of a constable.
[44] See also *Lewis* v *Cox* [1985] QB 509.
[45] *Wershof* v *Metropolitan Police Commissioner* [1978] 3 All ER 540; Feldman, D. (2002) *Civil Liberties and Human Rights in England and Wales*, 2nd edn. Oxford: Oxford University Press, p. 328.
[46] See Chapter 5.
[47] *Rice* v *Connolly* [1966] 2 All ER 649.

is also justified in terms of a person's right not to be compelled to answer self-incriminating questions. The use of force to compel a person to stop in order to ask them questions, where the police are not intending or have no grounds for an arrest and are not exercising some other statutory power such as stop and search,[48] is likely to be both outside their duty and an actionable trespass. The person stopped may use reasonable force to resist and escape and will not be assaulting or obstructing the officers in the exercise of their duty.[49] Touching by a police officer to attract attention is not outside the scope of duty.[50] If the person who was unlawfully stopped uses disproportionate force he or she, while not committing the section 89 offence, may be committing some other offence against the person.

Similarly there is no duty on citizens to report crime or disclose information to the police. Exceptions to this principle can be found in special legislation such as that dealing with terrorism[51] and with company dealings and city takeovers. In so far as a person is placed under a criminal penalty to produce information which can then be used to secure their conviction for an offence, such provisions are likely to violate Article 6 ECHR and the rule against self-incrimination.[52]

The Police and Criminal Evidence Act 1984
Outside of actions dealing with breach of the peace, the powers of the police are predominantly statutory. The core powers of stop and search, arrest, detention and entry, search and seizure are found and defined in the Police and Criminal Evidence Act 1984 (PACE 1984). The Act unifies police powers which, previously, had often been based on local Acts and varied from place to place. In important areas, particularly the treatment of suspects in police stations, the Act provides a statutory regime for what had previously been discretionary and based on judicial guidelines.

Police powers are also found in a host of other statutes that permit the exercise of such powers in various circumstances or under certain conditions. Often the powers in these other statutes can be exercised only on the basis of general conditions established in PACE 1984. The powers in PACE 1984 are additional to the common law powers mentioned above. Sometimes PACE 1984 expressly abolishes one-time common law powers;[53] in other circumstances, such as the power to enter property to deal with a breach of the peace, the Act expressly adopts the common law.[54] Where PACE 1984 does not expressly or by implication abolish a common law power, the power can still be exercised by the police.[55]

The Act is supplemented by detailed guidance found in Codes of Practice produced by the Home Office under section 66 of the Act. These relate to the

---

[48] See Chapter 5.
[49] *Kenlin* v *Gardner* [1966] 3 All ER 931; *Bentley* v *Brodzinskki* (1982) 75 Cr App Rep 217.
[50] *Donnelly* v *Jackman* [1970] 1 All ER 987.
[51] For example, under the Terrorism Act 2000 , discussed in Chapter 18.
[52] *Saunders* v *United Kingdom* (1997) 23 EHRR 313 – a controversial case which has been both followed and criticised. The issue is discussed further in Chapter 5.
[53] Section 17(5), PACE 1984 abolishes common law powers to enter property.
[54] Section 17(6), PACE 1984.
[55] For example, a common law power of seizure of property in *Cowan* v *Commissioners of Police of the Metropolis* [2000] 1 All ER 504, 511–10 (see Chapter 6).

exercise of the power to stop and search under Part I of the Act (Code A), to the power to search premises and to seize property (Code B), and to the detention, treatment and questioning of persons by the police (Code C). Police powers exercised under other statutes are often also subject to these Codes. The Codes can be amended or reissued in the light of changes in the law or policy and annexes can be introduced to deal with particular matters. The Act also empowers the Home Secretary to produce a code of practice to deal with tape recording of interviews. Revised codes are in force from April 2003.[56]

Enforcement

Breach of a provision of PACE 1984 is not in itself a criminal offence nor does the Act establish legal duties whose breach, in itself, is an actionable tort. There are provisions in the Act which provide important protection for a suspect, or which are expressed in mandatory terms or which say that contravention renders an action 'unlawful'.[57] Breach of such provisions is likely to mean that the police cannot claim, unless they have other authority, to be acting within the scope of their duty and so the offence of obstruction or assault under section 89, Police Act 1996 cannot be made out.[58] The victim of such unlawful action can use reasonable force to avoid its consequences and may also be able to bring civil proceedings for damages. Some of the provisions of PACE 1984 give effect in English law to Convention rights, for example a detainee's right of access to legal advice. Breach of the Act in this respect can be the basis of an action under section 7, Human Rights Act 1998.[59]

Breach of the Codes, like breach of the Act, is not of itself either a criminal offence or a civil wrong.[60] The Codes are admissible in all criminal or civil proceedings,[61] including under section 7, Human Rights Act 1998, and any breach which is relevant to the proceeding must be taken into account by the court. Breach of a Code can also be a significant factor in disciplinary actions taken against police officers, though a mere breach is not a disciplinary matter.

There is no general principle in English law requiring the automatic exclusion of unlawfully obtained evidence, though it is often argued that such a rule would deter breaches of the Act and the Codes by the police. Sections 76 to 78, PACE 1984 permit a court to exclude evidence. Confessions made by 'oppression' or which, in consequence of anything said or done are likely to be 'unreliable', must be excluded by the court unless the prosecution proves the contrary.[62] Confessions by mentally handicapped persons require special caution by jury or magistrates.[63] Under section 78 the court has a discretion to exclude unfairly obtained evidence if its admission 'would have such an adverse effect on the fairness of the proceedings that the courts ought not to

---

[56] Zander, M. (2002) 'The Revised PACE Codes', 152 7039 *NLJ* 1035.
[57] For example, s. 16, PACE 1984 regarding the execution of a warrant.
[58] For example, *Osman* v *Southwark Crown Court* (1999) CO/2318/98 (Smith Bernal).
[59] Adhering to the Act might, in principle, also be incompatible with the Convention, in which case a declaration of incompatibility can be issued.
[60] Section 67(10), PACE 1984.
[61] Section 67(11), PACE 1984.
[62] Section 76, PACE 1984. See, on oppression. *R* v *Fulling* [1987] QB 426; on reliability: *R* v *Delaney* [1989] Crim LR 139.
[63] Section 77, PACE 1984.

admit it'. Section 78, on the other hand, is concerned with the overall fairness of the proceedings and if, notwithstanding unlawfulness in the way evidence was obtained, a conviction would still be safe, the courts may still exercise their discretion and admit.[64] There is a potential conflict here with a suspect's Convention rights. Article 6 ECHR provides certain fair trial rights, some of which are in PACE 1984 and which the state must safeguard. Setting aside these Convention rights on the grounds that their violation is unlikely to result in a wrongful conviction may not be compatible with the Convention.

4.2.9 General principles governing the exercise of police powers

The specific powers of the police are the subject matter of many of the chapters that follow. There are, however, a number of general concepts that govern the exercise of police powers.

Reasonable suspicion
Police action can usually only be authorised on the basis that there is a reasonable suspicion, on the part of the officer, that a state of affairs exists which is needed to trigger the action. Reasonableness and proportionality is, in any case, a general requirement for all official actions. In some circumstances the law offers little guidance; in others, such as the stop and search power under Part 1 of the Police and Criminal Evidence Act 1984, the Code of Practice Code A, gives detailed guidance as to the factors which can or cannot be the basis of a decision to exercise the power. The general idea of a reasonable suspicion is that there is an objective basis to grounds on which an officer decides to act. There must, first, be an honest belief in the existence of triggering facts. But honesty is not enough. The belief must be well grounded in the sense that facts exist on which the honest belief could be based even if the belief turns out to have been mistaken. A mere hunch is not enough.[65]

Reasonable 'suspicion' is not a high standard. It does not mean that the officer already possesses evidence which, if confirmed, would be sufficient to convict or otherwise demonstrate forbidden behaviour. There can be a reasonable 'suspicion' even though, on investigation, what was suspected turns out not to be true. In *Castorina v Chief Constable of Surrey* (1988),[66] the Court of Appeal rejected, as being too demanding, the view that the grounds of suspicion need to be the existence of reasons which would lead 'an ordinary cautious man to the conclusion that the person arrested was guilty of an offence'. A lesser basis of suspicion can be 'reasonable' and further investigation is not required before action based on 'reasonable suspicion', such as an arrest, can be taken.

---

[64] The following are included in the matters which have justified not admitting unlawfully obtained evidence: denial of access to a solicitor; a defendant not being advised on his right to legal advice; the police not keeping proper records of their actions; plea bargaining; no proper caution being administered; and the evidence of a minor interviewed without an appropriate adult – cited in Bailey, S.H., Harris, D.J. and Jones, B.L. (1995) *Civil Liberties Cases and Materials*, 4th edn. London: Butterworths, p. 160.

[65] See, in particular, Code A, discussed in Chapter 5.

[66] [1988] NLJR 180.

Reasonable suspicion is firmly entrenched in the European Convention on Human Rights. Article 5(1) permits detention on 'reasonable suspicion of having committed an offence'. The leading case is *Fox, Campbell and Hartley* v *United Kingdom* (1991)[67] in which it was said: '. . . a "reasonable suspicion" presupposes the existence of facts or information which would satisfy an objective observer that the person concerned may have committed the offence in question'. Honest belief is not enough. The factual basis need only justify a belief that the person 'may' have committed the offence. In *Murray and others* v *United Kingdom* (1995)[68] the court said: '. . . facts which raise a suspicion need not be of the same level as those necessary to justify a conviction or even the bringing of a charge, which comes at the next stage of the process of criminal investigation'. These cases are terrorist cases and the court implies that it takes a more tolerant attitude towards the police in such circumstances.[69] Nevertheless it is likely that the courts in Britain will have little difficulty in making the 'reasonable suspicion' criteria in United Kingdom statutes compatible with the Convention.

Serious arrestable offence

A number of police powers, especially those that involve the greatest interference with liberty, are triggered by the fact that a person is suspected of a 'serious arrestable offence', for example the power to delay a detained person's right to inform a person or to have access to independent legal advice. An arrestable offence is an offence for which the power of summary arrest is available. It is defined by section 24, PACE 1984 and is discussed in Chapter 5. It relates to offences such as murder for which the sentence is fixed by law, offences for which a sentence of five years' imprisonment is available for a first offender and any other offence listed in section 24(2). A 'serious' arrestable offence is defined in section 116, PACE 1984. Some offences are always 'serious' no matter what the circumstances and they are either identified in section 116 or listed in Schedule 5. These include offences such as murder, manslaughter and rape which have a common law basis and also other, specified, statutory offences.[70] Any arrestable offence, even though it is not listed in schedule 5, can become 'serious' if its commission led or was intended to lead to certain consequences.

116 Meaning of 'serious arrestable offence'

. . .

(6) The consequences mentioned in subsections (3) and (4) above are –
   (a) serious harm to the security of the State or to public order;
   (b) serious interference with the administration of justice or with the investigation of offences or of a particular offence;
   (c) the death of any person;
   (d) serious injury to any person;
   (e) substantial financial gain to any person; and
   (f) serious financial loss to any person.

---

[67] (1991) 13 EHRR 157.
[68] (1995) 19 EHRR 193.
[69] Starmer, K. (1999) *European Human Rights Law*. London: LAG, 15.60–15.63.
[70] The full list is in Schedule 5, Parts 1 and 2. The list can, of course, be added to.

4.3 The use of force

The use of force is unlawful unless authorised by law. The general position is described in section 3 of the Criminal Law Act 1967.

> **3 Use of force in making arrest, etc.**
> (1) A person may use such force as is reasonable in the circumstances in the prevention of crime, or in effecting or assisting in the lawful arrest of offenders or suspected offenders or of persons unlawfully at large.

This provision replaced common law rules existing at the time which related to the use of force for the purposes given in section 3. It applies to all persons, police, military, other officials or citizens. Other Acts expressly authorise the use of force to assist in achieving their purposes but this authorisation is normally confined to a police officer or other person with constabulary powers.[71] Section 117, PACE 1984 applies to the police when exercising their powers under the Act.

> **Section 117 Power of constable to use reasonable force**
> Where any provision of this Act –
> (a) confers a power on a constable; and
> (b) does not provide that the power may only be exercised with the consent of some person, other than a police officer,
> the officer may use reasonable force, if necessary, in the exercise of the power.

This power will authorise, for example, the use of force to execute a search warrant issued under section 8 of the Act.

Common law permits the use of reasonable force for other purposes than those found in section 3 of the 1967 Act. The use of reasonable force to remove trespassers from land or to resist unlawful detention by the police are recognised, as is the use of reasonable force in self-defence.[72] Such force must be proportionate and reasonable. The fact that a person uses force to escape unlawful detention by the police may enable them to avoid prosecution for assault of a constable in the execution of his duty but will not prevent a prosecution for an offence against the person, including murder, if the force used is disproportionate.[73]

4.3.1 The use of force and Convention rights

The use of force by the police, military and others for whom the state has responsibility is subject to the European Convention on Human Rights. Under section 6 of the Human Rights Act 1998, such 'public authorities' act unlawfully if they act incompatibly with the Convention. The two main

---

[71] For example, section 2(5) of the Public Order Act 1936 authorises the use of force to execute a search warrant to give effect to the prohibition on quasi-military organisations; s. 114, Terrorism Act 2000 permits the use of reasonable force by a constable 'if necessary' for the purpose of exercising most of the powers in the Act.

[72] *R v Clegg* [1995] 1 AC 482.

[73] For example, *Osman v Southwark Crown Court* (1999) CO/2318/98 (Smith Bernal), per Sedley LJ.

Convention rights in issue are the right to life under Article 2, and the prohibition of torture and inhuman or degrading treatment or punishment under Article 3.

Article 3[74]

Torture, inhuman treatment or punishment and degrading treatment or punishment are separate concepts which are distinguished in terms of severity.[75] Torture denotes the special stigma that international law places on 'deliberate inhuman treatment causing very serious and cruel suffering'.[76] Inhuman treatment or punishment 'causes intense physical and mental suffering' and degrading treatment or punishment 'arouses in the victim a feeling of fear, anguish and inferiority capable of humiliating and debasing the victim and possibly breaking his or her physical or moral resistance'.[77]

Inhuman and degrading treatment requires a threshold of severity. Lawful punishment, for example, brings with it its own humiliation and for Article 3 to be engaged something more than that must be alleged.[78] Methods of policing may raise Article 3 issues. A police beating of a suspect will be a violation[79] and may even be classified as torture if the point is to extract information from a suspect.[80] 'Techniques' employed by British security forces against Irish republicans were, in the end, only classified as inhuman treatment.[81] There is no evidence that, in respect of Article 3, the Convention permits lower standards to be applied in the context of opposing terrorism.

There is a question whether the common law concept of 'reasonable force' can guarantee that Convention standards are met. It may give a jury or court too much discretion so that behaviour which a jury accepts as reasonable may, in fact, be too severe or otherwise not permitted under the Convention.[82]

Article 2, the use of lethal force

Every year a number of people are killed by armed police.[83] The use of lethal force is governed by Article 2 of the Convention.[84] In *McCann* v *United Kingdom* the Court of Human Rights, in a case concerned with the use of lethal force by the United Kingdom's armed forces, identified some of the general principles underlying Article 2.

> Members of a suspected Provisional IRA active service unit, believed to be planning an attack, were followed into Gibraltar. The SAS were sent to assist the Gibraltar

---

[74] For text see Chapter 2.
[75] *Ireland* v *United Kingdom* (1979–80) 2 EHRR 25.
[76] *Ireland* v *United Kingdom* (1979–80) 2 EHRR 25, paragraph 167.
[77] Starmer, *op. cit.*, p. 91.
[78] See Chapter 9.
[79] *Ribitsch* v *Austria* (1996) 21 EHRR 573. 'In respect of a person deprived of his liberty, any recourse to physical force which has not been made strictly necessary by his own conduct diminishes human dignity and is in principle an infringement of the right set forth in Article 3 of the Convention' (paragraph 38). Starmer, *op. cit.*, paragraphs 15.81–15.87.
[80] *Aksoy* v *Turkey* (1997) 23 EHRR 553.
[81] Suspects were made to stand for hours in uncomfortable postures, hooded, deprived of sleep, subjected to disorientating noise and deprived of food and drink.
[82] *A* v *United Kingdom* (1999) 27 EHRR 611.
[83] The organisation Inquest provides some information – see http://www.inquest.org.uk/.
[84] For full text see Chapter 2.

authorities and they subsequently shot and killed the IRA suspects. Relatives of the dead claimed that the killings violated Article 2.

HELD (ECHR): that the actions of the soldiers did not in themselves violate the Convention. However, by a majority of 10 to 9, it was held that aspects of the planning and control of the operation violated Article 2. In particular, the decision to allow the suspects to enter Gibraltar rather than to arrest them at the border, the fact that assumptions made by the planners, such as that the suspects had remote control means of detonation, were communicated to the soldiers as certainties rather than possibilities and the policy of the SAS of only shooting to kill, together meant that the decision to use force was more than was absolutely necessary.

McCann and others v *United Kingdom* (1996) 21 EHRR 97

In the course of its judgment the Court recognised the fundamental nature of the right to life. It held that Article 2 should be interpreted in order to give practical and effective protection to people. Thus Article 2(2) is not confined to intentional killing but includes situations where there is a use of force that may result in unintended death. Such force can only be used compatibly with the Convention in so far as its use is confined to the achievement of one of the purposes listed in Article 2(2) (defence of any person from unlawful violence, to effect a lawful arrest, to prevent an escape from lawful custody or to quell a riot or insurrection) and is no more than is absolutely necessary in the particular circumstances. The test of whether force is no more than absolutely necessary is more rigorous than the test for whether a restriction is 'necessary in a democratic society'; lethal force is not justified merely because it meets a pressing social need. The use of force must, in the circumstances, have been strictly proportionate and is to be subjected, by the court, to the most careful scrutiny. As was clear from *McCann*, such scrutiny can include examining the decisions made in the course of the planning and control of the operation.

The Court in *McCann* held that the reasonableness test in section 3 of the Criminal Law Act 1967 could be compatible with the Convention. The implication of this is that domestic courts should ensure that, in the circumstances of a particular case, the effect of the reasonableness test is not more accommodating of the use of lethal force by the authorities than is the test of absolute necessity under Article 2.

Article 2 also requires states to take positive steps to ensure that some form of adequate investigation of deaths is undertaken. The investigation must be thorough and independent but need not take any particular form[85] nor need it be in public.[86] There have been strong criticisms of the inadequacies of the investigations of killings by the police and into deaths in custody[87] in United Kingdom prisons and young offender institutions. The influence of Article 2,

---

[85] A thorough coroner's inquest in the Gibraltar killings case was sufficient.

[86] In *Taylor* v *United Kingdom* (1994) 79-A D&R 127, the Commission found no breach of Article 2 when killings by a hospital nurse where investigated by an independent panel sitting in private.

[87] For example, the case of Zahid Mubarak, a British Asian prisoner detained in a young offender's institution and killed by his known racist cell mate. An independent investigation was ordered by the High Court on 6 October 2001. The Crown Prosecution Service is to re-examine its decision in the case of Christopher Alder who died while in police custody: *The Independent*, 25 September 2001. See: *R (Amin)* v *Secretary of State for the Home Department* [2002] EWCA Civ 390.

with what are arguably its higher and more demanding standards, ought to be significant in this area. Article 2 may also require that a state's laws enable persons affected by the use of lethal force to bring civil proceedings. In the United Kingdom, for example, any rule by which negligence actions in such circumstances are ruled out on public policy grounds may possibly be inconsistent with positive duties under Article 2.[88]

4.4 Security and intelligence services

The security and intelligence services were established, originally, under the general prerogative power of the Crown, recognised by the common law, to organise its activities as it will. The services have now been put on a statutory footing which both, to a limited degree, advances the general cause of openness in government and helps to establish the legal basis of any activities of the secret services that interfere with individuals' Convention rights.

The main agencies are the Security Service (MI5), the Secret Intelligence Service (MI6) and the General Communications Headquarters. These are now publicly acknowledged. A civil service committee, the Joint Intelligence Committee, identifies and reviews the main intelligence needs of the country and the agencies work to those policies. There is, however, a wider 'intelligence community' going beyond these agencies. The Defence Intelligence Staff serves the Ministry of Defence, some other government departments and the armed forces. It is part of a larger network of undisclosed intelligence-gathering organisations for which the Ministry of Defence, through the Chief of Defence Intelligence, has overall responsibility and for which he or she is accountable to the Secretary of State and the Prime Minister.[89]

4.4.1 The Security Service

The Security Service was established in 1909 and became known as MI5 in 1916. Its main concern is with threats to national security that manifest themselves within the United Kingdom. Its powers are now based on the Security Service Act 1989, as amended by the Security Service Act 1996. The Act defines the functions of the Service and establishes a Director-General who is appointed by the Secretary of State. He or she is responsible for the general efficiency of the Service and has a few other statutory duties. The Director-General reports to the Prime Minister and the Secretary of State. Compared with the statutory regime governing the police forces the provisions of the 1989 Act are paltry.

The functions of the Security Service are defined in section 1.

---

[88] The issue would be one of providing a proper remedy for the breach of a Convention right.
[89] Though the Defence Intelligence Staff is publicly acknowledged, the existence of the undisclosed network of intelligence agencies is inferred from the defence budget, Bradley, A. and Ewing, K. *Constitutional and Administrative Law*, 12th edn. London: Longmans, p. 637.

The Security Service

(1) . . .

(2) The function of the Service shall be the protection of national security and, in particular, its protection against threats from espionage, terrorism and sabotage, from the activities of agents of foreign powers and from actions intended to overthrow or undermine parliamentary democracy by political, industrial or violent means.

(3) It shall also be the function of the Service to safeguard the economic well-being of the United Kingdom against threats posed by the action or intentions of persons outside the British Islands.

(4) It shall also be the function of the Service to act in support of police forces, the National Criminal Intelligence Service, the National Crime Squad and other law enforcement agencies in the prevention and detection of serious crime.

The scope of these powers is considerable. The civil libertarian issue is whether the powers authorise the Security Service to interfere with legitimate political activity in a manner that is not justified by a potential threat. The 'undermining of Parliamentary democracy by political, industrial or violent means' authorises a possible role for the Security Service against radical opposition groups and trade unions organising strikes that perhaps should be the concern of the police. Subsection 4 was added by the Security Service Act 1996 and reflects the need for the security services to redefine their role after the end of the Cold War. It increases the concern that the Security Service may be used against legitimate civil disobedience since 'serious crime' is defined, in part, by reference to non-serious crime being conducted by persons acting in a group such as, for example, peace activists undertaking civil disobedience.

4.4.2 Special Branch

Intelligence-gathering and the taking of action against internal 'subversion' is also undertaken by the Special Branch which was formed in 1883 to act against Irish republican bombing campaigns. Since 1945 each police force has its own Special Branch. The Special Branch is integrated with the police forces and has no distinct statutory role. Home Office Guidelines identify its function as primarily concerned with intelligence-gathering and assessment in respect of national security and to assist the Security Service.[90] The role of the special branches may be less significant as the risk of internal subversion has been downgraded after the Cold War, the lead intelligence-gathering group on anti-terrorism is the Security Service and general criminal intelligence is increasingly focused on the nationally organised National Criminal Intelligence Service.

4.4.3 Secret Intelligence Service

Spying for Britain is undertaken by the Secret Intelligence Service. Like the Security Service, it was established under the prerogative but has now been

---

[90] Home Office (1994) *Guidelines on Special Branch Work in Great Britain*, reproduced at http://www.scotland.gov.uk/hmic/docs/fpeo-12.asp.

placed on a statutory footing by the Intelligence Services Act 1994. Its functions are limited to obtaining information about the activities of persons outside the British Islands. The Service is led by the Chief of the Intelligence Service who is appointed by the Secretary of State and who reports to the Prime Minister and the Secretary of State. The Intelligence Services Act 1994 also gives statutory authorisation to the Government Communications Headquarters which is under the control of a Director appointed by the Secretary of State.

4.4.4 General powers

The Acts of Parliament that provide a statutory basis for the security and intelligence services say little about their general powers. There is nothing equivalent to the Police and Criminal Evidence Act 1984 to give security and intelligence agents specific powers and to subject them to specific duties. They are public authorities and, under the Human Rights Act 1998, they act unlawfully if they fail to respect Convention rights in their dealings. There is likely to be an obvious problem of evidence and, in any case, in respect of surveillance, it is not the courts but a special tribunal, the Security Tribunal, which will adjudicate a Human Rights Act 1998 claim. Their powers are, therefore, mainly those of ordinary citizens. Other than Special Branch, security agents do not enjoy the powers and privileges (and duties) of constables. Much intelligence-gathering can be done by lawful activities; however, if either the criminal law or the civil law is broken, there is no legally recognised exemption for security officials though the courts have sometimes seemed to turn a blind eye to various forms of covert breaking and entering undertaken by the Security Service.[91] The major exception to this lack of legal regulation relates to those surveillance activities which may involve unlawful activity such as trespass. Here the Intelligence Services Act 1994 and the Regulation of Investigatory Powers Act 2000 provide a power to apply for warrants to undertake surveillance activities, although certain restrictions are attached to the power and through the work of a Commissioner and a Tribunal there is a process for supervision and the handling of complaints. These matters are described in Chapter 7.

4.4.5 Scrutiny and accountability

The distribution of functions between the police and security and the intelligence services involves a political judgment on whether a matter is subversive or merely criminal. The secret nature of the services means that there is inadequate public accountability for that judgment as there is in respect of the covert activities of the services which interfere with both the political and private freedom of individuals and associations.

The basic responsibility of the services is directly to the executive, particularly to the Prime Minister. In 1964 the Security Commission was established with a brief to report to and advise the Prime Minister of security breaches, especially those located in the public service. The Commission sits

---

[91] *Attorney General* v *Guardian Newspapers (No. 2)* [1990] AC 109, per Lord Donaldson, 190.

as required and is normally chaired by a retired law lord. Its reports are published. It does not provide general, continuous oversight of the security services, and is not responsible to Parliament.

Prime Ministers have been very reluctant to permit more than rather general, informal links between the security services and Parliament. Select Committees, such as Defence and Home Affairs committees, have found it difficult to obtain the means for adequate scrutiny. Similarly the Parliamentary Ombudsman, who reports to Parliament, does not have jurisdiction over national security matters.[92] Section 10 of the Intelligence Services Act 1994 establishes the Intelligence and Security Committee which, for the first time, provides for some degree of significant Parliamentary scrutiny of the work of the security and intelligence services. The members of this committee are senior backbench Members of Parliament. There remains considerable executive influence since they are all appointed by the Prime Minister in consultation with the Leader of the Opposition. The remit of the Committee is to 'examine the expenditure, administration and policy' of the three services.[93] As such they are able to receive sensitive information, though the extent of this must rely on the mutual trust between the Committee and the services. Sensitive information can be withheld from the Committee.[94] They report in general terms to the Prime Minister and not to Parliament. They can report on particular issues particularly if invited to do so by the Secretary of State.[95] Although the Committee has consistently affirmed the high quality of the intelligence and security community in the United Kingdom, it is widely accepted to take a serious and critical approach to scrutiny and to have had a significant effect on improving the public accountability of the secret services.[96]

The surveillance activities of the secret services are reviewed and reported on by the Intelligence Services Commissioner and to the Security Tribunal which deals with complaints from the public. These matters are discussed in Chapter 7.

4.5 Other organisations

A large range of other state organisations have powers which impinge in one way or another on civil liberties and may raise human rights questions. Customs and Excise, for example, have considerable powers of investigation; they are among the bodies which, as discussed in Chapter 7, have powers to obtain various warrants and permissions under the Regulation of Investigatory Powers Act 2000.

The increasing use of private security organisations to perform police functions should be noted. In particular such private firms are used for

---

[92] Parliamentary Commissioner Act 1967, s. 5(3) and Schedule 3, e.g. paragraph 5.

[93] Section 10(1), Intelligence Services Act 1994.

[94] Intelligence Services Act 1994, Schedule 3, paragraph 3(2). The Secretary of State can withhold non-sensitive information: schedule 3, paragraph 3(4).

[95] See Intelligence and Security Committee (2000) *The Mitrokhin Inquiry Report*, Cm. 4764. London: Stationery Office.

[96] For example, Fenwick, H. (2000) *Civil Rights, New Labour Freedom and the Human Rights Act*. Harlow: Longman, pp. 333–5.

security in places which, though privately owned, are those to which the public have access such as shopping malls or leisure centres. The extent to which the general law and, in particular, the Human Rights Act 1998 might be relevant here is discussed in Chapter 17 in the context of public order. Private security companies are subject to a limited degree of regulation.

5

Police powers: stop and search, arrest and detention

5.1 Introduction

The state, acting through its agents such as the police, claims the monopoly of the exercise of legitimate force. The claim is, first, to establish the conditions in which others can use force, such as parents on their children, and, second, to exercise force directly in various circumstances such as the identification, investigation and punishment of criminal behaviour. This coercive power of the state to detain people, to make them move on, to search their person or their property is predominantly exercised by the police. One of the central issues of civil liberties law is the identification and analysis of the legal powers and duties of the police.

5.2 Police questions

As discussed in Chapter 4, the police do not have a power to stop someone simply to question them. They are under a legal duty to maintain the peace and investigate crime but citizens are not under a related duty to cooperate with the police other than in a few specifically identified circumstances.

5.3 Stop and search

Stopping and searching people in public places, when there are no or insufficient reasons to think that an arrestable offence has been committed, is one of the most controversial powers enjoyed by the police. There are two main authorities for this power. Part 1 of the Police and Criminal Evidence Act 1984 gives a power to stop and search for stolen or prohibited goods and section 60 of the Criminal Justice and Public Order Act 1994 allows stopping and searching for dangerous instruments and offensive weapons in circumstances where violence is likely. Additional powers apply in a terrorist context.

5.3.1 Part 1, Police and Criminal Evidence Act 1984

[PART 1]
[POWERS OF STOP AND SEARCH]
1. Power of constable to stop and search persons, vehicles, etc.

A constable may exercise any power conferred by this section –

(a) in any place to which at the time when he proposes to exercise the power the public or any section of the public has access, on payment or otherwise, as of right or by virtue of express or implied permission; or

(b) in any other place to which people have ready access at the time when he proposes to exercise the power but which is not a dwelling.

Subject to subsection (3) to (5) below, a constable –

(a) may search –

(i) any person or vehicle;

(ii) anything which is in or on a vehicle,

for stolen or prohibited articles or any article to which subsection (8A) below applies; and

(b) may detain a person or vehicle for the purpose of such a search.

This section does not give a constable power to search a person or vehicle or anything in or on a vehicle unless he has reasonable grounds for suspecting that he will find stolen or prohibited articles or any article to which subsection (8A) below applies. (Subsections 4 and 5 are referred to in the text below; section 8A applies to offences under section 139, Criminal Justice Act 1988 which are offences involving knives and bladed articles.)

Public places

The power to stop and search can be exercised in places to which the public have access not only as of right (such as the highway) but also places such as shops, shopping malls, leisure complexes or football stadiums which are privately owned and operated but to which the public have access on payment or on the basis of express or implied permission; it can also be exercised on any other land to which the public have access as a fact even if there is no legal entitlement (e.g. a highway being used obstructively). The power to stop and search can be exercised on 'private' land but it cannot be exercised in a dwelling house though it can used against a person on land attached to a dwelling (e.g. where a person goes from the street into the garden of a private house) but not against a person who is a resident in the dwelling or who is on the land with the permission of such a resident. Similarly vehicles cannot be searched if they are in the charge of a resident of the land they are on.[1] Part 1 of PACE does not extend the rights of the police to enter property; a constable can only exercise the power if he or she has the right to be on the land in question.

Stolen and prohibited goods

Stop and search can only be exercised in respect of stolen goods, prohibited articles or knives and other bladed articles. A prohibited article is defined, by section 1(7), as, firstly, an 'offensive weapon'. This is defined widely to include not only articles made or adapted for causing injury to persons but also any article where the immediate circumstances give rise to a reasonable suspicion that the thing is intended to cause injury. A prohibited article can also be

---

[1] Section 1(4) and (5), PACE 1984.

something made, adapted or carried in connection with theft, burglary and other offences under the Theft Act 1968.[2] Stop and search can also be used to find knives and other bladed articles as defined by section 139, Criminal Justice Act 1988. Any article which a constable reasonably believes to be stolen or prohibited etc. can, under section 1(6), be seized.

An offensive weapon is defined in terms of the police view of the context of its use. Political banners, for example, can easily become offensive weapons if the police believe that, in the context of a demonstration that is or might become disorderly or violent, a banner could be intended to cause injury to persons. There is a Human Rights Act issue here since a political banner is a form of political expression and enjoys protection under Article 10 ECHR. Article 10(2) will permit seizure to prevent disorder so long as the power is sufficiently clear and precise to meet the 'prescribed by law' test and so long as any particular act of seizure is necessary in a democratic society and proportionate in the circumstances. The stop and search power is, on its face, widely drawn and will need to be interpreted with these Convention restraints in mind. Similarly, articles with religious significance, such as ceremonial swords, will be protected under Article 9 ECHR, the freedom to manifest one's religious belief in public. The freedom can be restricted on similar grounds to freedom of expression.

The extent of the search

The nature or extent of the search permitted is limited. A search in public view cannot involve requiring the removal of clothing, other than outer clothing.[3] A more extensive search, such as requiring the removal of a T-shirt, should be conducted out of public view in a nearby police station or police van. An intimate search requires special authorisation under section 55, PACE 1984, but other than that, no further limits on the type of search that may be required are given in the Act. Nothing in the Act prevents a strip search, for example, so long as it is based on reasonable suspicion and not done in public. The Code makes various provisions aimed at minimising embarrassment.[4] A disproportionate search or one done in demeaning circumstances may be unlawful, even if only police officers are present,[5] by virtue of the Human Rights Act 1998 and Article 3 ECHR.

Reasonable suspicion

A constable must have 'reasonable grounds for suspecting that he will find prohibited articles' etc. as a result of the search. A person against whom no reasonable suspicion can lie cannot be detained in order to find grounds for reasonable suspicion.[6] Reasonable suspicion is discussed in Code A. The Code recognises that reasonable suspicion depends on the circumstances of the case

---

[2] The offences are identified by s. 1(7), Police and Criminal Evidence Act 1984.
[3] PACE 1994, s. 2(9)(a).
[4] Code A, paragraph 3.
[5] *Tyrer v United Kingdom* (1979–80) 2 EHRR 1.
[6] As observed by Code A, paragraph 2.1. See *Black v DPP*, 11 May 1995, Lexis transcript CO 877–95.

but requires an objective basis.[7] Examples of what that might be are given and include action taken on the basis of information about a crime or a suspect, or on the basis of observing a person acting 'covertly or warily'. Failure to cooperate with the police is not, in itself, the basis for reasonable suspicion.

> S, a 30-year-old black male of good character, was walking slowly home through an area in which there had been a number of burglaries. He was observed looking around by police. He was questioned without being stopped but refused to give cooperative answers. He was detained under the stop and search power. After a struggle he was arrested and detained for four hours in a police station. He brought an action for assault and false imprisonment against the police.
>
> HELD (CA): his slow speed of walking and his looking around was not an objective basis on which reasonable suspicion could be based; nor could reasonable suspicion be based on his refusal to give cooperative answers since, as a matter of law, he was entitled not to answer police questions. S's appeal against the loss of his civil action was allowed.
>
> *Samuels* v *Commissioner of Police for the Metropolis*, 3 March 1999, Lexis, Smith Bemal CA

The Code is emphatic that the objective grounds cannot be based on personal factors or stereotyped images alone, though it does not prevent such issues from contributing to the grounds for a search.

> 1.7 . . . reasonable suspicion can never be supported on the basis of personal factors alone without supporting intelligence or information. For example, a person's colour, age, hairstyle or manner of dress, or the fact that he is known to have a previous conviction for possession of an unlawful article, cannot be used alone or in combination with each other as the sole basis on which to search that person. Nor may it be founded on the basis of stereotyped images of certain persons or groups as more likely to be committing offences.

Despite this, stop and search has been highly controversial because of significant evidence of its disproportionate use against young black males in certain urban areas.[8] Controversy about the use of the power continues.

5.3.2 Stop and search under other powers

Other Acts give the police the power to stop and search. Examples[9] are searches in public places for firearms under the Firearms Act 1968, for controlled drugs under section 23(2) of the Misuse of Drugs Act 1971, and for alcoholic drinks and other articles whose possession is made unlawful under the Sporting Events (Control of Alcohol etc.) Act 1985. There are significant stop and search powers in the Terrorism Act 2000.

---

[7] See *Castorina* v *Chief Constable of Surrey* (1988) 138 NLJ Rep 180 which deals with reasonable suspicion and the power of arrest.

[8] See Bailey, S.H., Harris, D.J. and Jones, B.L. (1995) *Civil Liberties Cases and Materials*, 4th edn. London: Butterworths, p. 83.

[9] For a full list see Code A, Annex A.

5.3.3 Section 60, Criminal Justice and Public Order Act 1994

This section, as amended by the Knives Act 1997, permits a constable in uniform to stop and search people in a particular locality. A police inspector,[10] or more senior officer, must believe that incidents of 'serious violence' in the locality are likely or that persons are carrying 'dangerous instruments or offensive weapons' there. The powers under section 60 can be used for a period of 24 hours and can be extended for another 24 hours if the authorising officer believes it expedient to do so. The powers are: to stop and search any pedestrian or vehicle and its driver and passengers for offensive weapons or dangerous instruments; to require a person to remove clothing by which their identity may be hidden and to seize any offensive weapons or dangerous instruments found. It is an offence not to stop when required to do so by a constable exercising this power.

The central point is that these powers allow random stops in the sense that the police do not need to have reasonable suspicion that the person searched is in possession of an offensive weapon or dangerous instrument. There is no express power to detain and this may mean that only searches that can be conducted on the basis of a minor interference with liberty can be authorised under the Act. The powers have a place in policing political demonstrations which, in the view of the police, threaten to become violent.

5.3.4 Safeguards

Sections 2 and 3, PACE 1984 introduce safeguards which apply generally to stop and search powers including those under section 60 of the Criminal Justice and Public Order Act 1994.[11] In particular the constable making the search must identify himself and make clear the purpose of the search and why it is thought necessary. If a search is made of an unattended vehicle, a note detailing the search must be left. No one can be detained for longer than is required to permit the search to be carried out properly. Section 2 imposes express mandatory duties on the police and represents important protection for the citizen. A search conducted without, for example, the police properly identifying themselves will be unlawful and undertaken outside their duty.[12] A consequence of this is that reasonable resisting force against the police may not be a criminal obstruction or assault. Section 3 details the record of the search that must be taken.

5.3.5 Vehicle checks and road blocks

The power of the police to stop vehicles for normal road traffic purposes is found in section 163 of the Road Traffic Act 1988 which simply imposes a duty on a driver or cyclist to stop if required to do so by a constable in uniform.

---

[10] Authorisation by an inspector must be confirmed by a more senior officer.
[11] PACE 1984, s. 2(1)(b). Searches under s. 27, Aviation Security Act 1982 are expressly excluded.
[12] *Osman v Southwark Crown Court*, 1 July 1999, transcript CO/2318/98. The case involved a search without reasonable suspicion under s. 60, Criminal Justice and Public Order Act 1994 but applies also to any search covered by s. 2, PACE.

Section 163 stipulates no limiting purposes for stopping cars nor does it require that there should be reasonable suspicion of some unlawful activity. Section 163 can be used for individual stops but it can also be used to set up a general road block to warn of a danger or even, controversially, randomly to seek evidence for drink driving[13] (though not to breathalyse). Where the police want a road block in order to search for a person who is believed, on reasonable grounds, to have committed a serious arrestable offence, been a witness to such an offence, is intending to commit such an offence or is unlawfully at large, then section 4, PACE 1984 must be used. A section 4 road check requires authorisation by at least an officer of superintendent rank, unless there is a situation of urgency. A person stopped is entitled to a written explanation of the purpose of the check.

5.3.6 Stop and search and Article 5 ECHR

The compatibility of the power to stop and search with the Convention rights scheduled to the Human Rights Act 1998 raises a number of issues. As has already been mentioned the seizure of objects with political or religious significance may involve Article 10 (freedom of expression) or Article 9 (freedom of thought, conscience and religion). Any search must not be so humiliating as to violate Article 3 (which prohibits degrading treatment). If stop and search is used in a racially discriminatory fashion then Article 14, which bans discrimination in the way the other Convention rights are protected, may be involved – so long as one of the other Convention rights is also in issue.

It is not certain that Article 5,[14] which deals with a person who has been 'deprived of his liberty', is necessarily engaged by stop and search. Part 1, PACE 1984 has not been directly considered by the Strasbourg court. Whether there has been a deprivation of liberty depends upon a range of factors such as the type of interference, the duration of any detention and so on.[15] Stopping someone for a short time with the purpose of searching them may not trigger Article 5 protection. Thus in *X v Germany* (1981)[16] there was no violation, in the view of the Commission, when the applicant was questioned by police in order to obtain information under a law which gave police no power to detain; similarly in *Hojemeister v Germany* (1983)[17] a detention incidental to a lawful search was held, again by the Commission, not to raise Article 5 issues.

Section 1, PACE 1984, but not section 60 of the Criminal Justice and Public Order Act 1994, expressly permits a person to be detained for the purposes of the search. A detention for a significant period of time, especially if linked with an extensive search undertaken, perhaps, at a police station, would be likely to engage Article 5. Furthermore, there appear to be reasons for thinking that, in some circumstances, such a detention may be hard to justify under the

---

[13] *Gwent v Dash* [1986] RTR 41; *DPP v Wilson* [1991] RTR 284.
[14] Article 5 is quoted in full in Chapter 2.
[15] See *Guzzardi v Italy* (1981) EHRR 333, paragraph 92.
[16] (1981) 24 DR 158.
[17] (1983) unreported 6 July 1981, cited by Starmer, K. (1999) *European Human Rights Law*. London: LAG, p. 432.

Article. Article 5(1) identifies the exclusive reasons for which a person can be deprived of their liberty and these do not expressly accommodate the purposes of stop and search.

Article 5(1)(b) permits lawful detention 'to secure the fulfilment of any obligation prescribed by law'. But what obligation is secured through stop and search? The obligation to submit to the search is one possibility, but that rather begs the point. The Court of Human Rights requires a specific legal duty and does not accept upholding the law generally as an obligation prescribed by law.[18] An obligation not to carry articles whose possession is expressly banned by law, such as knives and other articles with blades under section 139 of the Criminal Justice Act 1988, might suffice. Whether this would extend to all prohibited articles is doubtful especially since the possession of an offensive weapon is not in itself an offence and the identity of such a weapon, since it can depend upon the police view of context, may not meet the 'prescribed by law' requirement of Article 5(1)(b).

Article 5(1)(c) permits lawful detention on reasonable suspicion of having committed an offence. This, of course, is emphatically not a necessary condition for the exercise of stop and search. Article 5(1)(c) also requires an intention of bringing the person detained before a court which, again, is not the point of stop and search. However, a stop and search might well be justified, in some circumstances, as being 'reasonably considered necessary to prevent [the person searched] from committing an offence'. This could impose a difficult evidential burden on the police. The point is that a non-trivial and lengthy stop and search will not be automatically compatible with the Convention; compatibility will depend on the likelihood that the search will disclose articles whose possession is already unlawful or whose discovery and removal is, on reasonable grounds, necessary to prevent the commission of an offence.

5.4 Arrest

5.4.1 The concept of arrest

An arrest occurs when a person is placed under the compulsory physical control of the arrester. Police officers and citizens can make arrests, although on somewhat different grounds. Arresting someone is a significant moment in the criminal justice process in which the state takes control of that person's personal freedom. Reasonable force can be used to give effect to a lawful arrest. Conversely, the arrested person may use reasonable force to resist an unlawful arrest. A police officer making an unlawful arrest will not be acting in the course of duty. The power of arrest is not confined to the criminal law and can be found in other contexts such as mental health or child protection.

An arrest can be lawfully achieved by physical restraint or by clear words. In either event the physical act or the use of the words must be calculated to bring to the arrested person's notice that he or she is now under direct coercive

---

[18] *Engel* v *Netherlands* (1979–80) 1 EHRR 647, paragraph 69; *Guzzardi* v *Italy* (1981) EHRR 333, paragraph 101, noted by Starmer, *op. cit.*, p. 441.

authority.[19] The arrested person must be aware that he or she is under compulsion and, at least for a time, submit to it. Shouting 'I arrest you' at someone who is running away from the scene of the crime, is not the making of a valid arrest.

5.4.2 Article 5 ECHR

An arrest involves the deprivation of liberty and so is within the scope of Article 5 ECHR. Article 5(1)(c) covers arrest for a criminal offence.

First, any arrest must be 'lawful'. It must be in accordance with a rule of domestic law and the law in question must have identified the grounds and procedures for arrest with sufficient clarity for them to be followed. The legal basis of the power to arrest in England and Wales is almost entirely statutory and is expressed with sufficient precision to meet the 'prescribed by law' requirement of Article 5. Such statutes must, under section 3 of the Human Rights Act 1998, be interpreted for compatibility with the Convention. Arrest for breach of the peace, still a common law matter, has been retained by virtue of section 25(6), PACE 1984 but has been sufficiently refined by the courts as to the scope and the circumstances for its use that, as a general provision, it is compatible with Article 5.[20]

Secondly, any arrest must be based on reasonable suspicion and this is clearly part of English law. Both Convention and English law require there to be an objective basis to the suspicion but accept that that basis needs to be the existence of sufficient evidence to justify a criminal charge. Nevertheless English case law has, in the past, indicated a very minimal factual basis for reasonable suspicion. In *Mohammed-Holgate* v *Duke* (1984),[21] for example, a description coupled with the fact that the plaintiff lodged in the premises from which the theft took place, was found to be sufficient to justify arrest by the judge at first instance and to be not set aside on appeal.[22] It is arguable that a higher level of suspicion is required under the Human Rights Act 1998.

Thirdly, Article 5 requires an intention by the arrester that the suspect be brought before a competent court. There must be at least the possibility of a charge at the time of the arrest. The fact that no charge ultimately materialises from the prosecuting authorities does not affect the compatibility of the arrest with the Convention. In English law it can be an unreasonable exercise of the discretion to arrest if it can be proved by the suspect that the arresting officer knew no prosecution was possible.[23] An arrest, other than for breach of the peace, in which there was no intention of pursuing the matter with the prosecuting authorities but simply aims to remove the person from the scene,

---

[19] *Alderson* v *Booth* [1969] 2 QB 216.

[20] *Steel and others* v *United Kingdom* (1988) 28 EHRR 603. The developments in English law are given the approval of the Court of Appeal in *Bibby* v *Chief Constable of Essex* (2000) 164 JP 297. Breach of the peace in a political context is discussed in Chapter 17 below. It remains the case that particular instances of arrest for breach of the peace can violate the Convention.

[21] [1984] 1 All ER 1054.

[22] See also *Ward* v *Chief Constable of Avon and Somerset Constabulary* (1986) *The Times*, 26 June, CA, and *Castorina* v *Chief Constable of Surrey* (1988) NLJ Rep 180. See, generally, *Blackstone's Criminal Practice* (1999) London: Blackstone Press, D1.5.

[23] *Plange* v *Chief Constable of South Humberside Police*, 23 March 1992, *The Times*.

would be incompatible with Convention rights, and, depending on the circumstances, be an unreasonable exercise of power and, if knowing and deliberate, could be actionable as a misfeasance in public office. However, the fact that police have additional reasons for arrest, such as removing the suspect from his home so that a surveillance device can be planted, does not render unlawful an arrest on other grounds which is lawful.[24]

Both the Convention and the ordinary principles of English administrative law require any particular arrest to be a proportionate act. The decision by a police officer to arrest is the action of a public official. This means that even if the power for arrest exists, the law also requires that the particular arrest is a proportionate exercise of discretion in the circumstances.

5.4.3 Grounds for arrest

In summary the grounds for arrest are: (1) arrest by a police officer on the authority of a warrant; (2) summary arrest (i.e. arrest without a warrant) by a police officer or private person for an 'arrestable offence' as defined by section 24, PACE 1984; (3) summary arrest only by a police officer for any criminal offence where the 'arrest conditions', in section 25, PACE 1984, apply; (4) summary arrest by a police officer (occasionally a private person) under express powers in other statutes.

Warrants
Section 1(4) of the Magistrates' Court Act 1980 permits the issue of an arrest warrant in respect of a person who has reached 17 years old, who is charged with an indictable or an imprisonable offence, or whose address, for the service of a summons, is not known. For lesser offences the issue of a summons is the proper initial course but an arrest warrant can be issued if the summons is not answered.[25] Arrest warrants can be issued in other circumstances such as in the context of extradition or where arrest powers are attached to other orders such as in the context of domestic violence injunctions. A warrant is issued to the police on the basis of a sworn statement and it is not clear how closely the grounds of reasonable suspicion are inquired into by magistrates. Under section 17, PACE 1984 the police have the power to enter premises without a warrant in order to execute an arrest warrant.

General warrants, which do not identify individually the person or persons to be arrested but, for example, purport to authorise the arrest of anyone found on certain premises or to identify a role (such as 'publisher') and leave it to the police to identify and arrest whoever that person is, are unlawful.[26]

Summary arrest
Summary arrest – arrest without a warrant – dispenses with even the somewhat minimal judicial oversight of reasonable suspicion of arrest by warrant. Summary arrest is permitted to police and citizens in relation to

---

[24] *R* v *Chalkley* [1988] 2 All ER 155.
[25] Section 13, Magistrates' Courts Act 1980.
[26] *Money and others* v *Leach* (1764) 1 Black. W 555; 96 ER 320.

'arrestable offences', to the police where they are given arrest powers in respect of other offences, to the police for any offence if the 'general arrest conditions' apply and for breach of the peace.

Section 24, PACE 1984 defines 'arrestable offences' for which summary arrest is permitted.

24 Arrest without warrant for arrestable offences

(1) The powers of summary arrest conferred by the following subsections shall apply –
   (a) to offences for which the sentence is fixed by law;
   (b) to offences for which a person of 21 years of age or over (not previously convicted) may be sentenced to imprisonment for a term of five years (or might be so sentenced but for the restrictions imposed by section 33 of the Magistrates' Courts Act 1980); and
   (c) to the offences to which subsection (2) below applies.

The main offence for which the sentence is fixed by law is murder for which a life sentence is mandatory. A range of serious offences are found in subsection 2. These can and have been added to by amendments introduced by other statutes. The power of summary arrest also applies to conspiring, attempting, inciting, abetting, counselling or procuring arrestable offences.

Summary arrest for an arrestable offence may be done by a police officer or civilian. The arrest power of the non-police officer is now a matter of considerable importance not only for store detectives but also for the burgeoning numbers of those employed in the private security industry. Pubs, clubs, leisure centres, shopping malls and many other places where the public go in large numbers are, in effect, policed by private security organisations. This is a sensitive issue which may need general regulation.[27] A long-standing restriction of the authority of private citizens to make summary arrest is retained. Police and private citizens may arrest without a warrant someone who is or is reasonably suspected of being in the act of committing an arrestable offence.[28] The police, but not a private citizen, can arrest if they have reasonable grounds to believe that an arrestable offence has taken place and they have reasonable grounds for suspecting the arrested person committed the offence.[29] Furthermore the police, but not a private person, may arrest someone where there are reasonable grounds to believe that the person is about, in the immediate future, to commit an arrestable offence.

The main point of difference, therefore, is that a private person who purports to arrest someone who they have reasonable grounds to believe committed an arrestable offence in the past lays themselves open to a tort action if it transpires that an arrestable offence was not, in fact, committed. The distinction between the powers of police and private citizen is traditional[30] and the courts have refused to dispense with it.[31]

---

[27] Parpworth, N. (2000) 'The Citizen's Power of Arrest', *Justice of the Peace*, 3 June.
[28] Section 24(4), PACE 1984.
[29] Section 24(6), PACE 1984.
[30] *Allen* v *Wright* (1835) 8 C&P 522; 173 ER 602
[31] *Walters* v *W.H. Smith* [1914] KB 595.

S was stopped by a store detective who had reasonable grounds to suspect him of theft. S assaulted the detective and ran off. A member of the public witnessed the events and gave chase and arrested S on suspicion of theft. S was later acquitted of theft.

HELD: S's conviction for assault was overturned; he successfully argued that he was entitled to resist the attempts to stop him.

R v *Self* [1992] 3 All ER 476

Where it is intended to give an arrest to other state agents, such as the army, they will only have the ordinary citizen's power of arrest and any additional powers, such as on reasonable suspicion that an arrestable offence has been or is likely to be committed, will require special statutory authorisation.

Section 25, PACE 1984 permits a police officer, though not a citizen, to make summary arrest on reasonable suspicion that any offence, including an offence which is not an arrestable offence, has been committed by the suspect. The ground of arrest under section 25 is that it appears to the officer that 'service of a summons is inpracticable or inappropriate because any of the general arrest conditions is satisfied'.

25 General arrest conditions

. . .

(3) The general arrest conditions are –

(a) that the name of the relevant person is unknown to, and cannot be readily ascertained by, the constable;

(b) that the constable has reasonable grounds for doubting whether a name furnished by the relevant person as his name is his real name;

(c) that –

(i) the relevant person has failed to furnish a satisfactory address for service; or

(ii) the constable has reasonable grounds for doubting whether an address furnished by the relevant person is a satisfactory address for service;

(d) that the constable has reasonable grounds for believing that arrest is necessary to prevent the relevant person –

(i) causing physical injury to himself or any other person;

(ii) suffering physical injury;

(iii) causing loss of or damage to property;

(iv) committing an offence against public decency; or

(v) causing an unlawful obstruction of the highway;

(e) that the constable has reasonable grounds for believing that arrest is necessary to protect a child or other vulnerable person from the relevant person.

(4) . . .

(5) Nothing in subsection (3)(d) above authorises the arrest of a person under subsection (iv) of that paragraph except where members of the public going about their normal business cannot reasonably be expected to avoid the person being arrested.

This is clearly a very broad power of arrest in respect of otherwise non-arrestable offences. Section 25(3)(d)(v), for example, can easily be used against political demonstrators who obstruct the highway or against the homeless. There is no independent judicial supervision of this ground for arrest, nor is there any Code of Practice covering the way it is put into effect by the police. When relying on section 25, a police officer must have had the powers in the section in mind as authorising the arrest at the time it was made. Section 25 cannot provide a retrospective justification for an arrest on other grounds which was unlawful or was not, but could have been, made on section 25 grounds.[32] It should be assumed, particularly regarding the Human Rights Act 1998, that the reasonableness of the belief in the need for an arrest, e.g. under subsection (3)(e), must contain an objective basis and be more than an honest hunch or a general prejudice. The honest belief, for example, that certain categories of people give a false name is insufficient to justify arrest under section 25(3)(b).[33]

Section 26, PACE 1984 repeals the power of summary arrest by police found in any Act enacted before PACE came into effect. Schedule 2, PACE 1984 contains a list of specific exceptions to this rule. Furthermore, it was held in *Gapper* v *Somerset Constabulary* (1988)[34] that summary arrest in Acts of Parliament survived the section 26 repeal where the power of summary arrest was enjoyed by police and private citizen alike and was not confined to the police. Examples of the surviving power of summary arrest are: section 6 of the Vagrancy Act 1824 in respect of various offences of begging and unlicensed peddling; and section 3 of the Theft Act 1978 which allows an arrest, while the offence is being committed, for making off without payment. The section 26 repeal obviously has no effect on powers of summary arrest enacted since 1984. A number of statutes empower usually constables, often with a requirement that they be in uniform, to make arrests. These are not arrestable offences in the strict sense of the word. Offences under the Public Order Act 1986 and the Criminal Justice and Public Order Act 1994 provide good examples.

Citizens and police may have equal powers to arrest for an occurring or imminent breach of the peace.[35] This is discussed further in Chapter 17.

5.4.4 Information when arrested

The legality of an arrest and hence of any physical resistance to that arrest may depend on whether proper information has been given to the person arrested. The person arrested must be informed of the fact that he or she is under compulsion and what the grounds of arrest are.[36] The point is now given a statutory basis by section 28 of the Police and Criminal Evidence Act 1984.[37] Similar provisions are found in Article 5(2) ECHR.

Whether sufficient information has in fact been given is a matter for the magistrate or jury[38] unless the information given was not capable of justifying

---

[32] *Edwards* v *DPP* (1993) Cr App Rep 301.
[33] *G* v *DPP* [1989] Crim LR 150.
[34] [1998] 4 All ER 248.
[35] *Albert* v *Lavin* [1982] AC 547.
[36] *Christie* v *Leachinsky* [1947] 1 All ER 567.
[37] Parpworth, N. (2000) 'Section 28 of PACE and Unlawful Arrest', *Justice of the Peace*, 1 July.
[38] Standard examples are: *Gelberg* v *Miller* [1961] 1 All ER 291 compared with *R* v *Telfer* [1976] Crim LR 562.

the arrest.[39] The information must be given at the time of arrest or as soon as practicable afterwards, it must be sufficient to enable the arrested person to know that he or she is under compulsion and it must give a general idea of the offence in issue. The word 'arrest' need not be used; 'you're nicked', for example, will probably do.[40]

> Inwood went voluntarily to a police station and submitted to questions about the possession of stolen goods and a search. He was cautioned but not charged. When he tried to leave he was restrained. Following a struggle he was charged and convicted of assault of a constable in the execution of his duty.
>   HELD (CA): the conviction would be set aside. The police had a duty to ensure that a suspect knew he or she was under compulsion.
>   *R* v *Inwood* [1973] 2 All ER 645

In *Clarke* v *Chief Constable of North Wales Police* (2000)[41] the issue was whether the statement that the suspect was arrested 'on suspicion of possession of controlled drugs' was sufficient explanation given that possession is only an arrestable offence for certain classes of controlled drugs. The majority of the Court of Appeal accepted that the arrested person would have understood that she was being arrested for a serious offence related to the possession of a controlled drug for which they had the power to arrest. For Sedley LJ, dissenting on this point, the purpose of the information requirement is to permit challenges to the legality of the arrest, therefore, given the fact that the power of arrest depended on whether or not the drugs in issue were of a particular class, further information, albeit expressed in a non-technical way, ought, perhaps, to be a requirement.

Article 5(2) ECHR has been said to require the arrested person to be told 'the essential legal and factual grounds for his or her arrest'[42] and English law seems to meet this requirement. The Strasbourg court has accepted that the discharge of the duty may depend on the circumstances, allowing more flexibility, for example, to the police in terrorist cases. Article 5(2) also requires that the arrested person should be informed of the grounds of arrest in a language he or she understands and, under the Human Rights Act 1998, this must now be a factor to be considered when assessing the legality, under section 28, PACE 1984, of the arrest of a non-English speaker.

5.5 Treatment of arrested persons

5.5.1 Search at the time of arrest

Section 32, PACE 1984 permits a person arrested away from a police station to be searched at the time of arrest. The power of the police to search in these

---

[39] *R* v *Abbassy* v *MPC* [1990] 1 WLR 385 where being arrested for 'unlawful possession' was said to be capable of justifying arrest for unlawfully taking and driving away a vehicle; whether it was sufficient in the circumstances was a matter for a jury.

[40] *Clarke* v *Chief Constable of North Wales* [2000] WL 345127, paragraph 36, quoted in Parpworth (2000), *op. cit.*

[41] *The Independent*, 22 May 2000.

[42] *Fox, Campbell and Hartley* v *United Kingdom* (1991) 13 EHRR 157, paragraph 40.

circumstances must be based on a reasonable belief that the arrested person may be a danger to him or herself, or that he or she has on them something that may assist their escape or be evidence relating to 'an offence' (i.e. not only the offence for which the arrest was made). Items relevant to the purpose of the search may be seized. Only a superficial search is permitted in public. Fuller searches, including a strip search but not an 'intimate search', could be done away from the public gaze, in the privacy of a police van, perhaps. These powers of search must be exercised in conformity with Articles 3 and 8 ECHR whose provisions in this context are discussed below.

The police may enter and search the premises in which the suspect was immediately before arrest. This can, of course, involve the search of the victim's premises. Likewise, the home or other premises which are occupied or controlled by an arrested person may be entered and searched and anything relating to the offence may be seized. These powers are only to search for and seize evidence relating to the offence. However, a police officer undertaking such searches will be lawfully on the premises and so has a power under section 19, discussed in Chapter 6, to seize anything reasonably believed to be there as a consequence of crime – any crime and not just the one for which the arrest was made.

5.5.2 Designated police stations

Perhaps the most important innovations of the Police and Criminal Evidence Act 1984 relate to the treatment of persons in police stations. There are a range of rights enjoyed by suspects and duties required of the police. In particular the Act created the role of custody officer. Custody officers must be at least of the rank of sergeant. Their basic duty is to ensure that detained persons are treated according to the provisions of the Act and the Codes of Practice it authorises. 'Designated police stations' are those properly equipped to deal with suspects under the PACE 1984 provisions. Section 30, PACE 1984 requires that an arrested person is taken to a designated police station as soon as is practicable after arrest.

5.5.3 Detention

An arrested person may be charged with an offence and released, with or without bail, or detained without being charged. Another possibility is immediate release. This would be necessary if it became obvious that the grounds for arrest no longer applied. Immediate release without there being changes in the circumstances might imply that the arrest had not been made with a view to bringing the arrested person before the courts. This would make the arrest unlawful in relation to Article 5(1)(c) ECHR.[43]

The main focus of civil liberties concern is on a decision to detain an arrested person. Article 5 ECHR requires that no one shall be deprived of their liberty other than on the basis of a 'procedure prescribed by law' and section 34(1), PACE 1984 stipulates that 'A person arrested for an offence shall not be kept in police detention except in accordance with the provisions . . .' of the Act.

---

[43] Unless the arrest was for breach of the peace.

Judicial supervision and Article 5(3) ECHR

Article 5(3) requires that anyone arrested under Article 5(1)(c) (i.e. for committing a criminal offence) must be brought promptly before a judicial officer or, alternatively, released promptly.[44] The point is that the grounds of detention should be subject to some degree of independent judicial supervision by a court which has, if necessary, the power to order the suspect's release.[45] Promptly has not been given precise definition by the Strasbourg institutions. In *Brogan and others* v *United Kingdom* (1989)[46] the shortest period of detention before the suspects were taken before a court was 4 days and 6 hours and this was held to violate Article 5(3) even in the context, in that case, of terrorism. A period of four days was too long in the context of a blackmail case in *Brincat* v *Italy* (1993).[47] The maximum period of police detention allowed under the Police and Criminal Evidence Act 1984 is 36 hours. Longer periods require authorisation by a magistrate.

Detention of suspects who are charged

When an arrested person arrives at a designated police station, a custody officer must determine whether there is or is not sufficient evidence to charge the suspect. Unless the arrest is on the basis of a warrant endorsed for bail, the suspect may be detained for that purpose.[48] If there is sufficient evidence, the suspect should be charged.[49]

If charged the suspect must be released, either with or without bail, unless certain conditions exist. The presumption in favour of 'release pending trial' in Article 5 ECHR is thus met. A charged suspect can be detained on the grounds specified in section 38(1), PACE 1984. These are, in summary, that the suspect's name and address cannot be convincingly ascertained or that the suspect may fail to answer bail, that (for a suspect charged with an imprisonable offence) detention is necessary to prevent the suspect committing further offences or (for a suspect charged with a non-imprisonable offence) causing injury to another person or damage to property or interfering with the administration of justice, or that detention is necessary for the suspect's own protection. The detention of a juvenile who has been charged can also be on the grounds that detention is necessary 'in his own interests'. The custody officer must make a written record of the reasons for the decision to detain. The detention of charged suspects must be reviewed, by the custody officer acting as a review officer, in accordance with the provisions of section 40, PACE 1984, which are discussed below.

Under Article 5 ECHR the Court of Human Rights has identified four grounds for the refusal of bail: the threat of absconding, interference with the course of justice, commission of further offences and the preservation of public order. Some of the grounds in section 38(1), PACE 1984 for not releasing

---

[44] *Brogan and others* v *United Kingdom* (1989) 11 EHRR 117, paragraph 58. See Starmer, *op. cit.*, p. 231.

[45] *Schiesser* v *Switzerland* (1979–80) 2 EHRR 417. See Starmer, *op. cit.*, p. 233.

[46] (1989) 11 EHRR 117.

[47] (1993) 16 EHRR 591.

[48] PACE 1984, s. 37(1).

[49] PACE 1984, s. 37(7).

charged suspects appear not to be compatible with the Strasbourg grounds – for example, the provision permitting refusal of release to a juvenile because it is in his or her own interests. Of course these Strasbourg grounds are general and are open to an interpretation which may include much of section 38(1). Also the principal purpose of Article 5(3) is for there to be prompt review of detention by an independent judicial officer, such as a magistrate, who can order release. Persons charged with offences must, under section 46, PACE 1984, be brought before magistrates as soon as is practicable and, in most cases, this meets the 'promptness' requirement of Article 5(3).

Detention of suspects who are not charged

If the custody officer takes the view that there is not sufficient evidence for a charge, the suspect should be released either with or without bail. The custody officer may, however, order the detention of the suspect on certain grounds.

37 Duties of custody officer before charge

(1) . . .
(2) If the custody officer determines that he does not have such evidence before him [to justify charging the suspect], the person arrested shall be released either on bail or without bail, unless the custody officer has reasonable grounds for believing that his detention without being charged is necessary to secure or preserve evidence relating to an offence for which he is under arrest or to obtain such evidence by questioning him.
(3) If the custody officer has reasonable grounds for so believing, he may authorise the person arrested to be kept in police detention.

A written record of the decision to detain must be made.

Detention for questioning in order to obtain evidence that will confirm or deny a reasonable suspicion is compatible with Article 5 ECHR: 'the object of questioning during detention under subparagraph (c) of Article 5(1) is to further the criminal investigation by way of confirming or dispelling the concrete suspicion grounding the arrest'.[50] Of course detention for questioning without that 'concrete suspicion' is incompatible with the Convention.

Detention under section 37 is for limited periods which need to be read in the light of the 'promptness' requirement under Article 5(3). The detentions are subject to regular review conducted not by the custody officer but by an officer of at least the rank of inspector and who had not been involved in the investigation. These reviews should be carried out within six hours of detention being authorised and then at nine-hour intervals. A review can be postponed on various grounds including that it would prejudice the investigation.[51] Sections 41–45 prescribe the time limits for detention. Detention on the initial authority of the custody officer is for a maximum period of 24 hours. After that the suspect should be charged or released. This period runs from the time of arrest or of arrival at the police station, whichever is the earlier.

---

[50] *Murray and others* v *United Kingdom* (1995) 19 EHRR 193, paragraph 55.
[51] PACE 1984, s. 40(4)(b)(i).

There are provisions for longer periods of detention but these can be authorised only in respect of the investigation of a 'serious arrestable offence'.[52] Section 42 permits a police officer of superintendent or above to authorise, within the initial 24-hour period, the extension of the period of detention for a further 12 hours to 36 hours from the start of the detention. This can only be done to secure or preserve evidence or to obtain evidence by questioning and the superintendent must be satisfied that the investigation is being 'conducted diligently and expeditiously'. The suspect or his or her solicitor must have the opportunity of making representations to the detaining officer or of contacting a solicitor and making a phone call if not already done.

Further extensions of detention for securing or preserving evidence or obtaining it by questioning are permissible but only on the basis of a warrant obtained from a magistrate under section 43, PACE 1984. A warrant can only be issued if there is a hearing which the suspect is entitled to attend and be legally represented at. Magistrates must be satisfied of the matters mentioned above under section 42. If so they can extend the period of detention for a maximum of a further 36 hours. Section 44 allows a second extension, by magistrates, of up to 36 hours although this is subject to a maximum period of detention, from the beginning, of 96 hours. As mentioned above since magistrates are involved after 36 hours, these provisions are likely to be compatible with Article 5(3).

5.6 The rights and treatment of detained persons

Part V, PACE 1984 deals with the questioning and treatment of persons by the police. The provisions of this Part are given effect in terms of Code C.

5.6.1 Be informed of rights

Arrested suspects must be informed of their rights by the custody officer who is required to open a 'custody record' as soon as practicable for each arrested person.[53] The record can be consulted by the suspect's representatives but not by the suspect until he or she leaves the police station. Arrested suspects have a right to consult the Codes of Practice[54] and should also be given a written statement setting out their basic rights. This is of increasing importance since the coming into effect of the Human Rights Act 1998 because a number of rights to a fair trial under Article 6 can relate to the early stages of an investigation.[55] Some rights under PACE 1984 are available only on the request of the suspect and so knowledge of the right is a necessary precursor to deciding whether or not to make the request.

---

[52] Section 116 PACE 1984. A serious arrestable offence is described in Chapter 4.
[53] Section 39 PACE 1984; Code C, 2.2.
[54] Code C, 3.1(iii), Note 3E.
[55] *Murray* v *United Kingdom* (1996) 22 EHRR 29, paragraph 62; *Imbriosca* v *Switzerland*, 24 November 1993.

5.6.2 Right to have someone informed

Section 56, PACE 1984 provides for a right to have someone informed.[56] However, this right can be delayed under certain conditions[57] for a maximum of 36 hours. Any delay requires the authority of an officer whose rank is superintendent or above and can only be authorised in respect of a serious arrestable offence. Delay can be authorised only if the authorising officer has reasonable grounds for believing that the exercise of the right will have certain effects.

> **56 Right to have someone informed when arrested**
> (1)–(5) . . .
> (5) . . .
>   (a) will lead to interference with or harm to evidence connected with a serious arrestable offence or interference with or physical injury to other persons; or
>   (b) will lead to the alerting of other persons suspected of committing such an offence but not yet arrested for it; or
>   (c) will hinder the recovery of any property obtained as the result of such an offence.

5.6.3 Right to legal advice

Section 58, PACE 1984 allows, on request, the right of a detainee to a private consultation with a solicitor.[58] Independent, free legal advice is also to be available for a suspect who requests it. From the point of view of basic fair trial rights under Article 6(3) ECHR, the right to legal assistance is the most important and is of particular significance if the statements and attitudes of the accused under questioning can be used as evidence at his or her trial.

> M, a terrorist suspect, was interviewed 12 times without legal assistance during a period of 48 hours. When he did see a solicitor he was advised to remain silent. Silence during questioning was a matter on which an adverse inference could be drawn at the trial.
>   HELD (EctHR): there had been a violation of Article 6. Where national laws attach consequences (such as the drawing of an inference of guilt) to the attitude of the suspect during interrogation 'Article 6 will normally require the accused be allowed to benefit from the assistance of a lawyer already at the initial stages of police interrogation' (paragraph 63).
>   *Murray* v *United Kingdom* (1996) 22 EHRR 29

The availability of this right and service is to be advertised by a prominently displayed poster. According to Code C an available solicitor can insist on being present while the suspect is questioned. The solicitor can only be asked to leave 'if his conduct is such that the investigating officer is unable properly to put questions to the suspect'.[59] The right to legal advice is protected under

---

[56] Code C, 5.1.
[57] See also Code C, Annex B.
[58] Code C, 6 applies to the exercise of this right and Code C, Annex B to its delay.
[59] Code C, 6.8–6.10. The provision is not in the Act itself and so it is not clear that the solicitor has a right to be present which is directly enforceable by the courts.

Article 6(3) and should be upheld by the courts even if there is no evidence that the suspect was prejudiced by its denial.[60] Nevertheless a minor failure to fulfil a matter incidental to the right may be thought, by English courts, to be illusory or theoretical and give rise to no remedy.[61]

The right to legal advice in respect of a serious arrestable offence can be delayed for up to 36 hours under similar conditions as those authorising the delay in the right to have someone informed. In *Murray v United Kingdom* (1996) the Court of Human Rights made it clear that specific rights which are inferred from the express provisions of Article 6 are subject to reasonable restriction: '[the right to a lawyer during police interrogation at least when inferences at trial can be drawn] . . . is not explicitly set out in the Convention [and it] may be subject to restrictions for good cause. The question, in each case, is whether the restriction, in the light of the entirety of the proceedings, has deprived the accused of a fair hearing'. Courts in the United Kingdom have shown themselves very receptive to the restrictable nature of the inferred rights in Article 6[62] and so it is likely that the power to delay will be thought compatible with the Convention. Of course, individual exercises of the delaying power can be challenged on the grounds that, in the individual circumstances of the case, delay is disproportionate given its likely impact on any resulting trial.

5.6.4 The right to silence

Questioning in police stations is subject to the right of silence. The basic idea is that no one can be compelled, under a criminal penalty, let alone under torture or mistreatment, to answer questions. Silence is essential to the rights of the defence and is inherent in the idea that the burden of proof be on the prosecution to prove its case without relying on statements compulsorily obtained from the accused. The right to silence may also have an important role in preventing miscarriages of justice. Statements made in the police station may have a significant and unwitting impact on a defendant, especially one who is vulnerable though age, mental incapacity or some other reason. The legal issue may be complicated and silence the simplest option for a person who may otherwise talk themselves into a guilt they do not have.

The fundamental idea is retained in English law. There are no criminal penalties for failing to answer self-incriminating questions as part of the direct investigation of a crime. Oppressive questioning violates Code C[63] and such methods would, of course, be grounds for excluding from the trial any statements made on the grounds that they represented a confession made by oppression[64] or would be evidence whose admission would have

---

[60] *Artico v Italy* (1980) 3 EHRR 1.
[61] *R (M) v Commissioner of Police for the Metropolis* (2001) 151 NLJ 1212 where M's legal consultation took place in a police cell rather than interview room and *R (LaRose) v Commissioner of Police for the Metropolis* (2001) 151 NLJ 1212 where R's telephone call to his solicitor took place in the custody suite with officers present.
[62] See, for example, summaries in *Brown v Stott (Procurator Fiscal, Dunfermline) and another* [2001] 2 ALL ER 97.
[63] Code C, 11.3.
[64] Which should be excluded under s. 76, PACE 1984.

such an adverse effect on the fairness of the proceedings that it ought to be excluded.[65]

However, in two respects, the impact of the right to silence has been significantly reduced in recent years. The first is in respect of the right of a magistrate, jury or judge as finder of fact to make an adverse inference – to infer guilt – from a defendant's silence in the police station or at trial. The second is the admissibility, as prosecution evidence, of incriminating statements obtained from the accused under special powers of inquiry and investigation backed by the threat of punishment.

Right to silence: drawing adverse inferences
Traditionally juries have been directed that the silence of defendants under police questioning or their refusal to give evidence under oath is not to be taken into account as a factor weighing against them in determining guilt or innocence. The rule has now been changed, first in respect of Northern Ireland offences[66] and, since 1994, for criminal offences in England and Wales. This has been a highly controversial change which was opposed by the Royal Commission on Criminal Procedure[67] and by the Royal Commission on Criminal Justice.[68] The argument for change is that an unqualified right to silence can be exploited by the skilful, guilty defendant to avoid conviction. In particular it was thought unreasonable that a defendant should be able to rely at trial on claims that were never made under police questioning and which could not, therefore, be tested at the time. It is also suspected that juries do infer guilt from silence and that it is better for the law to establish the circumstances in which this can properly be done.

Section 34, Criminal Justice and Public Order Act 1994 permits the jury or magistrate when determining guilt or innocence to draw any proper inference, including an inference of guilt under certain circumstances. These are, first, failure by the defendant to mention, when questioned by the police under caution, or charged, any fact which is later relied on as a defence at trial which could reasonably have been mentioned; secondly, refusal by the defendant, at the time when he or she had been arrested, to give police an explanation of objects, substances or marks in their possession or about their person which the police officer reasonably believed may have been attributable to their participation in an offence; and thirdly, refusal by the defendant, at the time when he or she had been arrested, to explain their presence at the scene of the crime where it was reasonable for a police officer to attribute their presence to participation in the offence.[69] The caution administered to suspects has been amended to warn suspects of the risks that an adverse inference may be drawn from their silence.[70]

---

[65] Under the discretion given to the court by s. 78, PACE 1984.
[66] Criminal Evidence (Northern Ireland) Order 1988.
[67] (1981) Cm 8092, paragraphs 4.32–4.67.
[68] (1993) Cm 2263, Ch. 4, paragraphs 20–25.
[69] Section 35, Criminal Justice and Public Order Act 1994 permits the jury or magistrate to draw an adverse inference from a defendant's refusal to give sworn evidence and submit to cross examination during the trial.
[70] The general caution is in Code C, 10.4; more specific cautioning, in terms indicated by the Code, is necessary if the police believe that the refusal to answer may give rise to the drawing of an adverse inference at trial.

These amendments to the right to silence are subject to important restraints, though no one knows the extent to which a jury takes them into account (any more than the extent to which the un-amended rule was followed is known). Silence remains a right and the burden of proof remains with the prosecution. In particular a finding of guilt cannot be based solely on an inference from the defendant's silence.[71] The prosecution must have established a 'case to answer' and so it is a matter for the judge whether or not there is a sufficient independent case against the defendant to permit an adverse inference to be drawn should the jury so wish.[72] An adverse inference should only be drawn by the jury or magistrate if they conclude that the reasons for the defendant's silence under police questioning are, given the circumstances at the time,[73] inadequate and that his or her silence can only be attributable to having no explanation, or an explanation which would not stand up to cross examination. The courts have refused to say that silence on legal advice is a sufficient reason for withdrawing the possibility of an adverse inference from the jury. The difficulty is that the reasons for the legal advice will be subject to legal privilege. However, where a lawyer gives a statement of the reasons for the advice this can be put before the jury and the lawyer may be subjected to cross examination, privilege will be considered to have been waived. The jury can then assess the reasons for the advice in the light of the circumstances.[74]

The right to silence is understood by the Strasbourg Court to be fundamental to the concept of a fair criminal trial under Article 6. The right is inferred from the general right to a fair trial in Article 6(1) and from the presumption of innocence in Article 6(2). The right is seen as central to the general scheme of Article 6 and as a significant contribution to the avoidance of miscarriages of justice. As an inferred right, however, it is not absolute and the Court of Human Rights has accepted that the drawing of an adverse inference does not, necessarily, violate the Convention. To base a conviction on an inference from silence would violate the Convention,[75] but there may be situations where there is a significant independent case against the defendant which establishes a situation which 'clearly calls for an explanation' by the defendant. In that circumstance the defendant's silence on the point may be taken into account when the strength of the prosecution's evidence is being assessed. As we have seen, English law is, in principle, compatible with this Convention requirement. Under the Convention the drawing of an adverse inference requires careful judicial supervision and the Strasbourg Court seems to be much more concerned when it is a jury rather than a judge who makes the inference.[76] Similarly, legal advice is an essential part of the protection offered by Article 6. It was held in *Murray v United Kingdom* (1996)[77] that its absence at the time of police questioning meant that the drawing of an adverse inference violated

---

[71] Section 38(3), Criminal Justice and Public Order Act 1994.
[72] *R v McGarry* [1999] 1 Crim Ap Rep 377.
[73] *R v Argent* [1997] Crim Ap Rep 27.
[74] *R v Bowden* [1999] 1 WLR 823; *R v Condron* [1997] 1 WLR 827. For compatibility with Convention rights see: *Condron v United Kingdom* (2000) Ap. 35718/97, Hudoc, paragraph 60.
[75] *Murray v United Kingdom* (1996) 22 EHRR 29, paragraph 47
[76] *Condron v United Kingdom* (2000) Ap. 35718/97, Hudoc.
[77] (1996) 22 EHRR 29.

Article 6. English law has now been changed so that no adverse inference can be drawn from a defendant who, at the time of the silence, had not been allowed access to a solicitor.[78]

Right to silence: statements made under penalty
A number of statutes in English law empower the authorities to undertake investigations and impose a duty, sanctioned by a criminal penalty, on various parties being investigated to answer questions. Numerous examples are found under various companies and financial services legislation. Article 6 ECHR is invoked if the answers, given under the threat of criminal sanction, are then made admissible in a subsequent criminal trial. In *Saunders v United Kingdom* (1997)[79] the applicant was convicted on the basis of evidence he had been compelled to produce. The Court of Human Rights held there was a right not to be compelled to incriminate oneself which was to be inferred from Article 6(1).[80] The use of the evidence was a violation of the Article which was not remedied by the power of the courts to exclude the evidence, on grounds of unfairness, under section 78, PACE 1984.[81] As a consequence of *Saunders* the evidence obtained by investigators under compulsory powers is no longer admissible in criminal prosecutions.[82]

5.6.5 Treatment in the police station

Section 39, PACE 1984 requires that the custody officer ensure that a suspect is treated according to the Codes and the Codes contain various provisions requiring, for example, that cells must be properly heated and that there must be proper access to toilet and washing facilities;[83] medical treatment must also be available.[84] Detained persons need to be visited regularly and reasonable force can be used to ensure compliance with reasonable instructions or to prevent escape, injury, damage to property or the destruction of evidence.

5.6.6 Interviews

Code C, paragraphs 10 and 11, cover the cautioning and interviewing of suspects. In particular, interviewing should stop once the investigating officer believes there is sufficient evidence for a prosecution. Questioning should not be oppressive. Most interviews, though not in respect of terrorist or official secrets offences, should be tape recorded.[85] An experimental scheme for the videoing of interviews has begun. Compulsory fingerprinting is normally

---

[78] Section 58, Youth Justice and Criminal Evidence Act 1999.
[79] (1997) 23 EHRR 313.
[80] As an inferred right it can be subject to reasonable exceptions. The argument that the Court of Human Rights in *Saunders v United Kingdom* accepts too absolute a version of the right against self-incrimination was taken by the Judicial Committee of the Privy Council in *Brown v Stott (Procurator Fiscal, Dunfermline) and another* [2001] 2 ALL ER 97.
[81] See also *Funke v France* (1993) 16 EHRR 297.
[82] Youth Justice and Criminal Evidence Act 1999, s. 59 and Schedule 3 – which lists the statutes affected.
[83] Code C, 8.
[84] Code C, 9.
[85] See Code E for detailed provisions and guidance.

permitted since it can be required where a senior officer believes that it will help to confirm or deny a suspected involvement in crime.[86]

Special provisions apply in respect of the detention and questioning of vulnerable persons such as juveniles and mentally disordered and mentally handicapped persons.[87] Statute requires that the person responsible for the welfare of a child be informed[88] and the Code requires such an 'appropriate adult' (a person closely associate with the care and support of the detained person) to be present when interviewing takes place.[89] The 'appropriate adult' cannot be a lawyer even though one of their main functions is to prevent the vulnerable person from making self-incriminating statements.[90] However, vulnerable detainees retain their general rights, so they must, for example, be informed of their right to independent legal advice. The power of the police to postpone the exercise of this right is retained despite the vulnerability of the detainees.

Deaf persons and non-anglophones should have the benefit of interpreters.[91]

As made clear above, the interviewing of suspects can raise issues within the scope of Articles 5 and 6 ECHR. Article 14 prohibits treating categories of people less favourably with respect to Convention rights[92] and the provisions relating to vulnerable detainees should be interpreted as far as possible to ensure this.

5.6.7 Search and samples

Personal search

As mentioned above, a suspect may be searched at the time of arrest away from the police station. A person who has been arrested and detained at a police station can only be searched if there is some additional factor, contained in PACE 1984, which authorises a personal search.[93] Personal searches must, of course, be conducted subject to Article 3 ECHR.

Section 54, PACE 1984 authorises custody officers to search detained persons in order to fulfil their duties of ascertaining and recording the personal possessions of an arrested person.[94] Clothes and personal effects can be seized if there are reasonable grounds to believe they are evidence relating to an offence or they could be used to cause physical injury to themselves or others, could cause damage to property or could assist in an escape. Section 54(6A) (introduced by the Criminal Justice and Public Order Act 1994) allows a search of detained suspects, independently of making the record, to see whether they have about them anything that could be seized by the custody officer. Items found may be seized. Police have additional powers of seizure under section 51 of the Criminal Justice and Police Act 2001.

---

[86] Section 61, PACE 1984.
[87] Section 57, PACE 1984; Code C, 3.6–3.14.
[88] Section 34, Children and Young Persons Act 1933, which was amended by s. 57, PACE 1984 and other statutes.
[89] Code C, 11.14–11.16.
[90] Note to Code C, 11B.
[91] Code C, 3.6 and 13.
[92] Though there is no need to show that a Convention right has been violated.
[93] Different rules apply under anti-terrorism legislation – see Chapter 18
[94] Section 54(1) and (6), PACE 1984.

Strip searches can be authorised under either power subject to the provisions of Code C, Annex A. These require, for example, that the search must be conducted by a member of the same sex as the person being searched.

Intimate searches (the examination of a person's body orifices other than their mouth[95]) can only be undertaken if the conditions in section 55, PACE 1984 are fulfilled. Authorisation must be by a senior officer who has reasonable grounds for believing that such a search of a detained person might disclose a Class A drug, or something that could cause physical injury to the detainee or to others and which might be used for such harmful purposes while in custody.

A properly and lawfully conducted personal search, even an intimate search, is unlikely to violate Convention rights. Article 3 ECHR requires a standard of severe degradation which such searches are unlikely to reach and the provisions of Article 8(2), which permit lawful and proportionate restrictions on private life for the prevention of crime, are likely to accommodate searches under PACE 1984. This is likely to include intimate searches.[96] If, however, a search is undertaken to humiliate or punish then it will be both unlawful under PACE and incompatible with Article 8.

Samples

Intimate samples (defined as blood, semen, urine, pubic hair or a dental impression) may be taken with the written consent of the person involved. Unreasonable refusal of consent can be the basis on which a trial court can draw an inference pointing towards guilt.[97] The rule against self-incrimination in Article 6 ECHR is confined to 'testamentary evidence' (words and writings spoken or written by the defendant concerning the offence) and do not cover intimate samples.[98] Article 3 and Article 8 would be violated if the samples were forcibly obtained.

Non-intimate samples and fingerprints can be taken, in some circumstances without consent, under powers in sections 63 and 61, PACE 1984 respectively. Even if the suspect is cleared, not prosecuted or, after questioning, not suspected of an offence, his or her fingerprints can be kept indefinitely for the purposes of the investigation of crime.[99] This interference with the privacy of innocent or at least unconvicted persons has been upheld by the Court of Appeal as being compatible with Article 8 ECHR.[100] It may be the beginning of the establishment of a national, universal DNA database. The Criminal Justice and Police Act 2001 and the Anti-terrorism Crime and Security Act 2001 have increased the powers of the police in respect of fingerprinting, photographing, requiring the removal of disguises and taking samples from suspects. In the context of terrorism, at least, the European Court of Human

---

[95] Section 65, PACE 1984.
[96] *McFeely* v *United Kingdom* (1981) 3 EHRR 161.
[97] Section 62(10), PACE 1984. Different procedures apply to breathalyser legislation.
[98] *Saunders* v *United Kingdom* (1997) 23 EHRR 313.
[99] Section 64, PACE 1984, amended by the Criminal Justice and Police Act 2001, s. 82.
[100] *R (Marper)* v *CC South Yorkshire* [2002] EWCA Civ 1275 [2002] NLJ 1483.

Rights has accepted that such powers may be necessary.[101] Their extension to non-terrorist crime by both[102] the Acts mentioned above may raise questions of proportionality.

---

[101] *McVeigh, O'Neill and Evans* v *United Kingdom* (1983) 5 EHRR 71; *Murray* v *United Kingdom* (1995) 19 EHRR 193.
[102] In the 2001 Act the fingerprinting provisions are confined to terrorist investigation; the other provisions amend the Police and Criminal Evidence Act 1984 and apply generally.

6

Police powers: entry, search and seizure

6.1 Introduction

A wide range of state officials claim authority to enter premises, to conduct searches and to arrest or seize persons or things found there without, if necessary, the consent of the party being searched. This chapter will concentrate on the powers of the police but other officials, such as VAT inspectors, Customs and Excise officers and officials from the European Commission, have some such powers available to them in the exercise of their duties, and in some cases, where ordinary discovery may be difficult, the same is true of private parties to civil proceedings. Police and the security services may exercise powers of entry covertly; this matter is considered in the next chapter.

6.2 Privacy and property

Powers of entry, search and seizure invoke the related rights of privacy and property. The idea that human dignity may have as one of its essential incidents the right to possess some personal space which is immune from the incursions of others, including the state, is deeply held and given justification in liberal political theory. It is, of course, also highly controversial because property is unequally distributed; many persons who are entitled to their human dignity nevertheless possess little if any property and, for those with large amounts of property, its possession is a means of exercising social and political power over others. In the modern world huge amounts of property are corporately owned and it is not clear that corporations are entitled to their 'dignity' in the way that human beings are. Political theorists are unable to agree whether the possession of property is, morally, a fundamental human right which the state ought to protect or whether, alternatively, it is merely an efficient means of providing personal happiness and the productive use of land which the law ought to support. In any event, the claims of property have never been absolute. The background right protects against the non-consensual, arbitrary, unreasonable and non-compensated invasion of property by others and, particularly, by the state. The prevention and detection of crime is a reason which justifies non-consensual interference with property by the state. The background right to property means that such interferences must be strictly limited to their proper purposes, proportionate and subject to proper safeguards.

6.3 Convention rights

Common law has long recognised the background assumptions in favour of the protection of property and, as we shall see, this has often found its way into the law. Entry, search and seizures by public officials such as the police is, of course, now also subject to the provisions of the Human Rights Act 1998.

Article 8 gives protection to 'private and family life ... home and ... correspondence'. It permits interference on various grounds including 'the prevention of disorder or crime'. Such interference must be 'in accordance with the law'. The purposes of, and the detail in, the Police and Criminal Evidence Act 1984 and the other legislation means that entry, search and seizure is likely to be only authorised for legitimate purposes and to meet the test of legality. Interferences, however, must also be 'necessary in a democratic society' which, increasingly, is equated with the 'proportionality' test: although the legal powers authorising a search are consistent with the Convention, any particular exercise of the power may, in the circumstances, be unnecessary and disproportionate. 'Home' is given a wide definition under the Convention. It will include domicile, including one occupied unlawfully;[1] it may also include premises used for commercial premises at least when a place is used for both residential and work-related purposes.[2] The argument of the court is that respect for private life in Article 8 protects the right to develop one's interests as a person and to foster relationships with others. Since work can be a major focus for such development the protection of Article 8 should not exclude professional or business activities. Whether such an argument can ground the right of a company in its own name to a private life to weigh against an otherwise lawful search is not clear.[3]

The power of entry, search and seizure can also raise questions under Article 1 of the First Protocol, the 'protection of property'. On its face the Article provides a general right to the peaceful enjoyment of possessions and a specific right not to be deprived of possessions 'except in the public interest and subject to the conditions provided for by law'. At the same time it appears to provide a wide scope for public authorities to control the use of property, through planning laws etc., 'in accordance with the general interest'. Despite these widely drawn words, the courts have allowed a proportionality test on interferences with, rather than just deprivations of, property. Entry, search and seizure can, therefore, be challenged under either article but, in the view of the court, similar principles apply to both. These matters will be developed more precisely in the following pages.

---

[1] *Buckley* v *United Kingdom* (1996) 23 EHRR 101.

[2] *Niemietz* v *Germany* (1993) 16 EHRR 97. See also *Chappell* v *United Kingdom* (1990) 12 EHRR 1 in which the Anton Piller search order, used exclusively in the context of commercial activity, was held to be compatible with Article 8.

[3] In *Noviflora AB* v *Sweden* (1993) 15 EHRR CD 6, it was accepted by the Commission that a company could be a victim of a violation of Article 8 in respect of the search and seizure of materials belonging to it.

Searches undertaken by the EC Commission in policing competition policy can be considered by the Court of Justice for compatability with the general principles of law that the Court upholds and which include the Convention rights.[4]

6.4 Common law

Convention rights are, in any case, broadly compatible with the underlying position in common law. The background principle in English law is that no one can lawfully enter another's premises without the other's consent, under a rule of common law or under the authority of an Act of Parliament. The weight given to rights of property by the general law means that such statutory authority will be strictly interpreted.

The absence of consent or proper lawful authority is likely to render the entry unlawful. Unlawful entry in itself (without aggravating circumstances such as the use of force or accompanying theft) is not usually a criminal offence. More likely it is the commission of a tort, particularly trespass, and this can be the basis for an action in damages or, in some cases, an injunction. It is important to recall that public officials who act unlawfully are not, by virtue of their status, immune from a tort action. They can be liable individually or may make the Crown, a higher public official or a public authority for which they work vicariously liable.

6.5 Lawful entry and search with consent

As 'citizens in uniform', the police and other public officials may enter private property with the consent of the occupier or the person in possession. An entry or search or seizure is only authorised so long as it is within the boundaries of the consent; agreement to allow the police to enter is not agreement to allow a search and if the terms of the consent are overreached an officer, from that point, is a trespasser. A police officer will, however, only be acting in the exercise of his or her duty if there is a duty-related reason for entering the property; for example, they are acting in pursuit of a reasonable suspicion of an offence.[5] As well as going on the highway, the police also have the same rights as the public to enter areas such as shopping malls, shops and car parks where express or implied permission has been granted by the occupiers. Public officials such as the police do not, without other legal authority, have any greater powers in such areas than the ordinary public.

Permission to enter private premises may be implied. The police, for example, enjoy the general implied power to approach the front door of a dwelling or otherwise enter private property to make contact with the occupier.[6] Code B, 4.4. and Notes for Guidance 4.C take matters a little further

---

[4] For example, *National Panasonic (UK)* v *Commission* (Case 136/79) [1980] ECR 2033; see generally Craig, P. and de Búrca, G. (2003) *EC Law: Text, Cases and Materials*, 3rd edn. Oxford: Oxford University Press, chapter 8.
[5] *Davis* v *Lisle* [1936] 2 KB 434.
[6] *Robson and another* v *Hallett* [1967] 2 QB 939; *Davis* v *Lisle* [1936] 2 KB 434.

and suggest that express permission to enter in order to search need not be sought if to do so would cause 'disproportionate inconvenience to the person concerned'. The paragraphs assume that innocent occupiers would be bound to agree, for example, to checks in gardens and other readily accessible parts of their land for recent fugitives or stolen goods.[7] Permission to go over the threshold and enter the dwelling house, to question occupants, for example, can be express or implied by actions. In *Faulkner* v *Willetts* (1982),[8] for example, the suspect's wife answered the door and, on seeing the police, said nothing but left the door open and withdrew into the dwelling. The court took the view that this was permission to the police to enter.

Permission, implied or express, can be withdrawn at any time. If it is withdrawn, police should take immediate steps to leave, otherwise they may become trespassers and step outside the scope of their duty. Reasonable time must be given to allow the police to leave and within that period the officers will still be within the scope of their duty and so any assault may still be a criminal offence.[9] The withdrawal of permission seems to require express words indicating that the police are now trespassers and should leave.[10] So long as that is the clear sense of the words used, they may be abusive but still effective.[11] However, merely being abusive to the police or mere assertions of possession or occupation by a person may not be enough for an implied revocation.[12] Once permission has been revoked and time to allow the police to withdraw has passed, reasonable force may be used to eject the trespassing officers. Of course, if the degree of force is disproportionate, an offence against the person may still have been committed and the fact that they are trespassers is irrelevant.[13]

Consent to enter is not the same thing as a consent to a search. For this further, express, permission is required. This view is reinforced by Code B which lays down a number of conditions for a consensual search.[14] It is proposed to give these greater emphasis in the re-drafts to the Codes put out to consultation in 2002. Subject to a practicability test, the consent should be in writing from a person properly entitled to give the consent. In particular, the person concerned should be informed of the purpose of the search and that anything seized may be used in evidence. Any search must be discontinued if the permission is withdrawn. The person should be informed if they are not suspected of an offence. Above all consent must be real in the sense that the person concerned must be informed that they are under no obligation to give consent; to the same point, any search would not be authorised if the consent was given under duress. Of course many people will agree to a search under the threat that, without their consent, a warrant can be obtained.

---

[7] See also *McArdle* v *Wallace* (1964) 108 SJ 483, DC.
[8] [1982] Crim LR 453.
[9] *Robson and another* v *Hallett* [1967] 2 QB 939.
[10] *Lambert* v *Roberts* [1981] 2 All ER 15.
[11] *Davis* v *Lisle* [1936] 2 KB 434
[12] *Snooks* v *Mannion* (1982) *The Times*, 19 March.
[13] The point was raised in *Davis* v *Lisle* [1936] 2 KB 434.
[14] *Code of Practice for the Searching of Premises by Police Officers and the Seizure of Property Found by Police Officers on Persons or Premises* (Code B), 4.

6.6 Lawful entry and search at common law

Limited powers at common law authorise police and also citizens to enter private property and seize objects found there. Section 17(5) and (6), PACE 1984 abolished all the rules of common law under which a constable had the power to enter premises without a warrant, apart from the power to enter premises to deal with or prevent a breach of the peace.[15] However, a common law power to seize the property of a person arrested for a serious criminal offence in order to assist the investigation of the offence has been recently upheld by the courts.

> The police seized a car belonging to a man arrested in respect of allegations of sexual abuse against children. The offences may have been committed in the car. The trial judge took the view that the seizure could not be authorised under PACE 1984 since the Act only authorised the seizure of items found on the premises searched. A vehicle is 'premises' for the purpose of the Act and so the power to seize things 'on the premises' could not authorise the seizure of premises themselves. The judge took the view that despite the absence of a statutory power, there remained a common law power to seize items, including vehicles, and that this survived the 1984 Act which did not expressly revoke such powers of seizure as it did in respect of powers of entry.
> HELD: the judge's view of the common law was correct, though the seizure of the car could be authorised by the Act
> *Cowan* v *Commissioners of Police of the Metropolis* [2000] 1 All ER 504.[16]

Police can also exercise those common law powers to enter the property of others which have not been revoked by the Police and Criminal Evidence Act 1984. These are powers that are available to any person and are not confined to the police. They include the power to abate a nuisance and actions authorised by the defence of necessity on tort.[17] The latter include the power to enter property to prevent murder[18] (which can also be done by the police under subsections 17(1)(b) or (e), PACE 1984) or to prevent serious damage to property from fire.[19]

6.7 Statutory powers to enter without a warrant

The police and other officials have powers under Acts of Parliament to enter premises without the consent of the occupier. Like the common law powers mentioned above, these powers are exercised on the basis of the judgment and discretion of the police and are not subject to any prior judicial supervision or authorisation.

The principal statutory authorisation for the police is at section 17, PACE 1984.

---

[15] Section 17(6), Police and Criminal Evidence Act 1984 – see Chapter 17.
[16] In *R (Rottman)* v *Commissioner of Police of the Metropolis* [2002] UKHL 20, [2002] 2 All ER 865 the House of Lords upheld a common law power to search the premises of a person arrested on the authority of an extradition warrant.
[17] See *Halsbury's Laws of England*, 4th edn, reissue vol. 45(2) 'Tort' (1999), paragraphs 361 and 372.
[18] *Handcock* v *Baker* (1800) 2 Bos & O 260.
[19] *Cope* v *Sharpe (2)* [1912] 1 KB 496 CA.

17 Entry for purpose of arrest etc.

(1) Subject to the following provisions of this section, and without prejudice to any other enactment, a constable may enter and search any premises for the purpose –

   (a) of executing –
      (i) a warrant of arrest issued in connection with or arising out of criminal proceedings; or
      (ii) a warrant of commitment issued under section 76 of the Magistrates' Courts Act 1980;

   (b) of arresting a person for an arrestable offence;

   (c) of arresting a person for an offence under –
      (i) section 1 (prohibition of uniforms in connection with political objects) of the Public Order Act 1936;
      (ii) any enactment contained in section 6 to 8 or 10 of the Criminal Law Act 1977 (offences relating to entering and remaining on property);
      (iii) section 4 of the Public Order Act 1986 (fear of provocation of violence);
      (iv) section 76 of the Criminal Justice and Public Order Act 1994 (failure to comply with interim possession order);

   (ca) of arresting, in pursuance of section 32(1A) of the Children and Young Persons Act 1969, any child or young person who has been remanded or committed to local authority accommodation under section 23(1) of that Act;

   (cb) of recapturing any person who is, or is deemed for any purpose to be, unlawfully at large while liable to be detained –
      (i) in a prison, remand centre, young offender institution or secure training centre, or
      (ii) in pursuance of section 92 of the Powers of Criminal Courts (Sentencing) Act 2000 (dealing with children and young persons guilty of grave crimes), in any other place;

   (d) of recapturing any person whatever who is unlawfully at large and whom he is pursuing; or

   (e) of saving life or limb or preventing serious damage to property.

(2)–(4) . . .

(5) Subject to subsection (6) below, all the rules of common law under which a constable has power to enter premises without a warrant are hereby abolished.

(6) Nothing in subsection (5) above affects any power of entry to deal with or prevent a breach of the peace

These powers are to enter and search for persons, not goods or property. No types of premises are excluded: the power can be used in respect of offices, shops, churches, community buildings, etc. The power to enter and search the common areas of blocks of flats, such as entrances and lifts, though not flats other than those in which the person sought is believed to be, is expressly included.[20] The scope of this power has been added to by primary legislation.

The principal safeguards for the exercise of these powers lie, first, in the requirement that the constable must have reasonable grounds for the belief that the person being sought is on the premises and that the power to search is limited by what is reasonably required to fulfil the purpose of entry. There is no authority under section 17 to search for or seize goods. However, as discussed later in this chapter, police officers who are lawfully on premises

[20] Section 17(2).

enjoy a general and extensive power of seizure of goods.[21] Code B, although it relates to searches, can be relevant to determining the proper exercise of the section 17 power.[22]

The police may use reasonable force to effect an entry authorised under section 17.[23] However, the use of force must be necessary in order to achieve section 17 purposes. The mere fact that an occupier refuses entry to the police is not sufficient to justify the use of force. The police must have section 17 grounds for entry and they are required to inform the occupier of those reasons, unless circumstances make it impossible, undesirable or impracticable, before using force to enter. If they have section 17 grounds but do not inform the occupier of those grounds any use of force to enter may be unlawful.[24]

The use of the section 17 power has not given rise to great controversy.[25] Problems have arisen over the maintenance, by section 17(6), of the common law power of entry to deal with or prevent a breach of the peace.[26] Similarly, section 17 is likely, in general terms, to be compatible with Article 8(2) of the Convention. It permits a restriction on a person's right to private life, for reasons found in Article 8(2) such as the prevention of crime and disorder. *McCleod* v *United Kingdom* (1999)[27] was concerned with entry to deal with a breach of the peace but it indicates the principal Convention issues relating to section 17.

Police assisted McCleod's ex-husband while he removed furniture from McCleod's house. The husband was trespassing since the time for McCleod to deliver the furniture to her husband under the legal settlement had not passed and McCleod, who was out of the house, had not given permission for her husband to enter. McCleod returned home and insisted the property be restored. Police refused. The court held that the police had acted lawfully under section 17(6), PACE 1984. McCleod applied to the European Court of Human Rights.

HELD (ECHR): there had been a violation of Article 8 ECHR.

McCleod v *United Kingdom* (1999) 27 EHRR 493

First, an entry under section 17 will be an interference with the freedom protected by Article 8(1). Second, such interferences must be justified under Article 8(2). In particular the interference must be 'by law' and this includes the requirement that a person can foresee with reasonable certainty the circumstances in which the power is likely to be used. In *McCleod* the court held that the power to enter to deal with or prevent a breach of the peace under section 17(6) met this requirement and it seems likely that the same can be said about the other grounds for entry in section 17. However, although the power may be compatible as a body of rules with the Convention, any particular exercise of the power must also be 'necessary in a democratic

---

[21] Section 19, PACE 1984.
[22] *O'Loughlin* v *Chief Constable of the Essex Police* [1998] 1 WLR 374, CA.
[23] Section 117, PACE 1984; see Chapter 3.
[24] *O'Loughlin* v *Chief Constable of the Essex Police* [1998] 1 WLR 374, CA.
[25] Cf. *D'Souza* v *DPP* [1992] 4 All ER 545 reading the concept of hot pursuit into s. 17(1)(d).
[26] This issue is dealt with in Chapter 17 on public order.
[27] (1999) 27 EHRR 493; see, further, Chapter 17.

society', and be proportionate to the purported social benefit. It was on this ground that there was held to be a violation of Article 8 in *McCleod*.

Section 18, PACE 1984 authorises the entry and also the search of premises occupied or controlled by a person under arrest for an arrestable offence. 'Controlled' has a wide meaning and can extend to at least some places, such as an office, in which a person works. The purpose of the search is confined to seeking evidence which 'relates' to the offence for which the arrest was made or for some other related offence. The extent of the search is confined to what is reasonable given the purpose. The search must be authorized in writing by an officer with, at least, the rank of inspector and should normally take place after the arrested person has been taken to a police station. These provisions can be temporarily dispensed with if the effective investigation of the offence requires the arrested person to be taken immediately to the place to be searched. A record of the search should be made. Matter for which the search is made can be seized. Section 32(2)(b), PACE 1984 authorises police to enter and search premises where an arrested person was at immediately before his arrest. This has been discussed in Chapter 5.

There are many other Acts of Parliament which grant a power to enter premises to search or for other purposes. The general principles under Article 8 ECHR apply to these as they apply to section 17. Examples include the Customs and Excise Management Act 1979, s. 84(5) and a range of powers enjoyed by those working for gas and electricity suppliers and by trading standards, fire and valuation officers.

6.8 Entry by warrant

In the absence of consent or statutory or common law authorisation, police and other public officials may gain entry to premises, undertake searches and seize items only on the authority of a warrant. The point about a warrant is that it requires a degree of independent judicial supervision, exercised prior to the event, of the grounds on which the power to enter, search and seize is to be exercised. Usually it is a magistrate who issues warrants and there has, certainly in the past, been criticism of the extent to which a proper scrutiny of police applications takes place.[28] As we shall see, where confidential matter is involved or journalist's materials, applications by the police must be to judges.

Warrants can only be obtained on the basis of the provisions of an Act of Parliament. There is no common law warrant; famous cases[29] establish that there is no power under the prerogative to issue warrants, particularly with general, non-specific objectives exercisable on the non-accountable discretion of officials. Statutes, the Police and Criminal Evidence Act 1984 in particular, require the specification of the type of property or the identification of the persons being sought by a search under warrant. Powers contained in some legislation, the Terrorism Act 2000 for example, seem to grant very wide

---

[28] For example, Bailey, S.H., Harris, D.J. and Jones, B.L. (1995) *Civil Liberties Cases and Materials*, 4th edn. London: Butterworths, pp. 96–7.

[29] For example, *Entick* v *Carrington* (1765) 19 St Tr 1029; *Wilkes* v *Wood* (1763) 19 St Tr 1153; *Leach* v *Money* (1765) St Tr 1002; *Wilkes* v *Lord Halifax* (1769) 19 St Tr 1406.

discretion to police and security officials which is inconsistent with the principle against general warrants. It needs also to be remembered that a warrant to search premises for persons or objects can be issued to seek evidence of an offence. No arrest need have taken place and, indeed, there need be no evidence that the persons involved have committed an offence.

6.8.1 The Police and Criminal Evidence Act 1984

The main general power for the police to seek a warrant for the purpose of investigating an ordinary offence is in section 8, PACE 1984.

8 Power of justice of the peace to authorise entry and search of premises
(1) If on an application by a constable a justice of the peace is satisfied that there are reasonable grounds for believing –
  (a) that a serious arrestable offence has been committed; and
  (b) that there is material on premises specified in the application which is likely to be of substantial value (whether by itself or together with other material) to the investigation of the offence; and
  (c) that the material is likely to be relevant evidence; and
  (d) that it does not consist of or include items subject to legal privilege, excluded material or special procedure material; and
  (e) that any of the conditions specified in subsection (3) below applies,
he may issue a warrant authorising a constable to enter and search the premises.

The conditions in subsection 3, of which at least one must apply, are:

(3) . . .
  (a) that it is not practicable to communicate with any person entitled to grant entry to the premises;
  (b) that it is practicable to communicate with a person entitled to grant entry to the premises but it is not practicable to communicate with any person entitled to grant access to the evidence;
  (c) that entry to the premises will not be granted unless a warrant is produced;
  (d) that the purpose of a search may be frustrated or seriously prejudiced unless a constable arriving at the premises can secure immediate access to them.

There are, therefore, significant conditions that must be fulfilled before a warrant can be issued: it may only be issued in respect of the investigation of serious arrestable offences,[30] in respect of material that is not only likely to be of substantial value to an investigation but also to be relevant in the sense of being admissible at a trial for the offence[31] and must exclude material subject to limitation. Furthermore, the warrant must be necessary in the sense that alternative means of obtaining the evidence are not possible for the reasons found in subsection 3. These are significant conditions. Magistrates have a duty under the law, a duty that can only be reinforced by the general principle of legality which pervades the Convention, to form an independent assessment

[30] See Chapter 4.
[31] Section 8(4), PACE 1984.

of the evidence purporting to justify the warrant; they should not, as is sometimes alleged, merely accept the police view.[32]

6.8.2 Other statutes

There are many other statutory provisions which authorise police and other officials to obtain warrants in order to enter premises to search for and seize material of various kinds. Warrants may be issued, for example, to search for stolen goods,[33] for explosives,[34] for knives whose possession is an offence under the Knives Act 1997[35] or for evidence of an offence under the Official Secrets Act 1911.[36] Similarly, there are powers under statutes such as the Theatres Act 1968 which authorise magistrates to grant a warrant to a police constable to enter a theatre and observe a performance when there is reason to believe it might be obscene and contrary to the Act or to enter licensed sex shops on suspicion that various offences may have been committed.[37]

6.8.3 Safeguards

Sections 15 and 16, PACE 1984 introduce a number of safeguards in respect of both the issuing and execution of warrants. There are further requirements in Code B, which are a gloss on the statutory terms. Such safeguards are especially necessary since warrants are issued *ex parte* and the person against whom a warrant is issued has no rights in the matter.[38] Sections 15 and 16 apply not only to warrants issued under PACE 1984 but also to the issuing and execution of warrants issued under any other enactment. Section 15 also purports to bind future Parliaments by applying its provisions to any later Act which authorises the issuing of warrants (which will be effective unless the later Act is unambiguously to the contrary). Code B applies to any entry, search and seizure undertaken on the basis of a warrant to which section 15 applies but will not apply to powers of entry that are not related to the investigation of crimes.[39] Failure to give effect to the provisions in sections 15 and 16 renders any entry and search unlawful. This would mean, for example, that the officers conducting it could be trespassers and any goods seized ordered to be returned.[40]

Thus, on applying for a warrant, the constable must state the ground and statute on which the application is made and specify the premises and, so far as is practicable, the articles or persons to be sought.[41] The application should be supported by an information in writing and the constable must answer any

---

[32] *R v Guildhall Magistrates Court ex parte Primlaks Holdings Co. (Panama) Inc.* [1990] 1 QB 261.
[33] Section 26, Theft Act 1968.
[34] Section 8, Explosive Substances Act 1883.
[35] Section 5, Knives Act 1997.
[36] Section 9, Official Secrets Act 1911.
[37] Local Government (Miscellaneous Provisions) Act 1982, Schedule 3, paragraph 25(4).
[38] Section 15(3), PACE 1984.
[39] Code B, 1.3.B.
[40] See, for example, *R v CCCt ex parte AJD Holdings Ltd* [1992] Crim LR 669; *R v CC Lancashire ex parte Parker & McGrath* [1993] Crim LR 204.
[41] Section 15(2), PACE 1984.

questions from magistrates on oath.[42] A warrant can authorise entry only on one occasion rather than for a continuous period; it must specify the name of the constable who applied for it, the date of issue and the Act under which it was issued. It must identify the premises to be searched and, again 'so far as is practicable', the articles or persons to be sought.[43]

Section 16 provides a range of protections dealing with the way in which a warrant can be executed. For example: it must be executed within a month of issue; normally it should be at a reasonable hour unless the purpose of the search would thereby be frustrated; the constable must properly identify himself to the occupier or person in charge of the premises or leave a copy of the warrant if there is no one in; the warrant should be endorsed if any goods are seized; the occupier of the premises is permitted at any time to inspect the warrant. Perhaps the central protection, inimical to the idea of a general warrant, is section 16(8): 'a search under a warrant may only be a search to the extent required for the purpose for which the warrant was issued'. A warrant for one purpose does not justify a general search of a person's premises.

6.9 Seizure

8 Power of justice of the peace to authorise entry and search of premises

. . .

(2) A constable may seize and retain anything for which a search has been authorised under subsection (1) above.

Section 8, PACE 1984 permits seizure of goods specified in the warrant. It should be recalled that the need to specify such goods in the warrant is subject to a practicability test and so the degree of protection this section gives against general seizure must depend on the extent to which circumstances permit precision on the warrant. Many other statutes which permit entry and search on the basis of a warrant also permit the seizure of relevant goods.

Section 19, PACE 1984 provides a wide-ranging power of seizure which extends well beyond items specified in a warrant. A constable (or person accompanied by a constable[44]) who, for one reason or another, is lawfully on any premises can seize an item if he or she has a reasonable belief that the item was obtained as a consequence of the commission of any offence or that it relates to such an offence. Seizure must be necessary to prevent it being concealed, lost, damaged, altered or destroyed.[45] The seizure of computerised information can include the power to have it produced in an accessible form. Seizure under section 19 can be in relation to any offence, not just an offence the constable may have been investigating. Furthermore, as indicated above, there are complementary common law powers to seize objects necessary for the investigation of an offence.[46]

---

[42] Section 15(4), PACE 1984.
[43] Section 15(5) and (6), PACE 1984.
[44] Section 56, Criminal Justice and Police Act 2001.
[45] Section 19(2) and (3), though the seizure of evidence under subsection (3) excludes the prevention of damage.
[46] *Cowan* v *Commissioner of Police for the Metropolis* [2000] 1 All ER 504.

The occupier of the premises from which an object has been seized may require a record of the seizure to be produced and this must be produced within a reasonable time. Requests to view or to make copies of things seized must be acceded to unless the officer in charge believes that this would hamper this or other investigations.[47] Seized goods can be retained for as long as is necessary for use, for example, in a trial.[48]

6.10 Material subject to limitation

The power to enter premises and search and seize material found there gives police and other state agents considerable powers. These powers may undermine the protection or exercise of other rights and freedoms. Particular concern has been in respect of rights to a fair trial, to the protection of personal and confidential matter and to the protection of journalism and a free press. These fundamental values are protected through a ban on the search for and seizure of material which is legally privileged and by the introduction of a special procedure, more demanding on the officials and giving rights to the other party to be represented, if various forms of confidential material, including journalistic material, are in issue.

6.10.1 Legal privilege

Items are subject to legal privilege if they involve communications between legal advisers and their clients, or clients' representatives, which relate to the giving of legal advice or are produced in connection with legal proceedings.[49] Such communications have long received the protection of the common law.[50] Similar protection is found under the Human Rights Act 1998. Confidentiality between legal advisor and client is not only an incident of Article 8, the right to respect for private life,[51] but it is also an important right implied from Article 6, the right to a fair trial.[52] Legal privilege is, in particular, a necessary incident in the right of access to the courts, a right upon which the vindication of all other rights and freedoms recognised by law depends.

In order to pursue their investigations of crime, the police may be pressing at the boundaries of what constitutes privileged material. Privilege does not extend to documents, such as conveyances or trust agreements, produced on the basis of legal advice, even if they are stored in a lawyer's office.[53] Furthermore, privileged items are confined to those held by lawyers 'in the

---

[47] Section 21(3)–(8), PACE 1984.
[48] Section 22, PACE 1984.
[49] Section 10(1), PACE 1984.
[50] For a recent House of Lords affirmation of the importance of privilege in common law and its close links with the related rights of access to the courts and access to legal advice, see *R v Secretary of State for the Home Department ex parte Daly* [2001] UKHL 26, [2001] 3 All ER 433.
[51] See, for example, the prisoners cases such as *Golder v UK* (1979–80) 1 EHRR 524 and *Campbell v UK* (1992) 15 EHRR 137.
[52] *Niemietz v Germany* (1993) 16 EHRR 97.
[53] For example, *Crown Prosecution Service on behalf of DPP for Australia v Holman, Fenwick and William* [1994] COD 174

legitimate course of professional conduct'[54] and this is given statutory force by section 10(2), PACE 1984 which states that 'items held with the intention of furthering a criminal purpose are not items subject to legal privilege'. Privilege does not, therefore, prevent the search of a solicitor's office for non-privileged items either because the solicitor's firm is itself suspected or is believed to be holding relevant materials. The intention with which a legal advisor is holding materials is determined by the context and not merely from the legitimate intention of lawyers to provide legal services or even the innocent intention of their clients. Police searching for evidence of purchases funded by crime, such a drug trafficking, may benefit from this.[55]

On receiving an application for a warrant under section 8, PACE 1984 magistrates or circuit judges should satisfy themselves that there is no apparent reason for thinking privileged material is included in the warrant[56] and give adequate reasons for permitting a search where privileged matter might be involved.[57] Unless it is inappropriate, because, for example, a solicitor is under suspicion, applications involving possibly privileged material should be made *inter partes*.[58] The powers of the police to remove items which might include matters of privilege is now covered by the Part 2 of the Criminal Justice and Police Act 2000 and is described below.

6.10.2 Excluded or special procedure material

As well as giving absolute protection to privileged materials, the law also gives procedural protection where matter seen as fundamental to personal privacy and dignity is sought. This procedural protection also has great importance for the freedom of the press since it also applies when 'journalistic material' is sought. Such confidential or journalistic material is either in the most fully protected category, 'excluded material', or in the lesser protected category 'special procedure material'. The courts have acknowledged the high weighting, given by Parliament, to the protection of such rights and freedoms, in one case reluctantly recognising that its impact can be a significant impediment to a police investigation of a serious crime of violence.[59]

Under section 8(1)(d), PACE 1984 a search warrant under section 8 cannot be issued in respect of excluded or 'special procedure material' and section 9(2) of the Act repeals any provision of an earlier Act in so far as it could authorise such searches.

Section 9(1) requires that if the police are seeking access to excluded or 'special procedure material' they must apply under the terms of Schedule 1 of the Act. The central point about the Schedule 1 procedure is that it involves application to a circuit judge rather than a magistrate, the application must be

---

[54] *R v Cox and Railton* (1884–85) 14 LR QBD 153.
[55] See, for example, *Francis and Francis (a firm)* v *Central Criminal Court* [1988] 3 All ER 775.
[56] *R v Guildhall Magistrates Court ex parte Primlaks Holding Co. (Panama) Inc.* [1990] 1 QB 261, following *Francis and Francis (a firm)* v *Central Criminal Court* [1988] 3 All ER 775, HL; *R v Chesterfield Justice and Another ex parte Bramley* [2000] 1 All ER 411
[57] *R v Southampton Crown Court ex parte J and P* [1993] Crim LR 962.
[58] *R v Inner London Crown Court ex parte Baines & Baines* [1988] QB 579; *R v Maidstone Crown Court ex parte Waitt* [1988] Crim LR 384.
[59] *R v Cardiff Crown Court ex parte Kellam* (1993) TLR 239 (3 May).

inter partes,[60] so giving an opportunity to the person involved to object, and the application is normally for an order requiring the person involved to produce or give the police access to the material rather than a warrant empowering the police to search. Failure to comply with an order to produce or give police access to 'special procedure material' can be dealt with by a judge as if it were a contempt of court.[61] Often, of course, such an application will be made in respect of a public authority or organisation such as a hospital from whom eventual compliance can be expected; press and broadcasting organisations, on the other hand, may feel that their highest authority is to protect the anonymity of their source and refuse to comply.[62] In certain circumstances a warrant to search, coupled with a power of seizure, can be issued.[63] Despite the protection that this procedure gives to protect excluded and special procedure material it should be noted that, unlike matters subject to legal privilege, nothing in section 18 (power to enter and search premises occupied or controlled by a person under arrest), section 19 (general power of seizure) or section 32 (power of search and seizure of premises in which a person was immediately prior to arrest) prevents the seizure of such material if the police come across it during a lawful search for other matter. Similarly the protections of section 9 are lost if a warrant from a jurisdiction that does not have such protections is validly executed in England.[64]

Excluded material
'Excluded material' is defined by sections 11, 12 and 13, PACE 1984. It refers, first, to personal records, held in confidence and acquired or created in the course of 'trade, business, profession or other occupation' or for the 'purposes of any paid or unpaid office'. A personal record is defined in section 12 as a documentary or other record 'concerning' an individual, alive or dead, who can be identified from the record. The record must be 'relating to' his or her 'physical or mental health' or 'spiritual counselling or assistance' or other counselling or assistance concerning personal welfare. Records whose content deals with other matters, e.g. administrative matters, can be included if they only exist as a consequence of the dealings with the person in relation to his or her physical or mental health or personal welfare.[65] Thus personal details of hospital patients and even, perhaps, social work records are included. 'Excluded material' also includes human tissue or tissue fluid which has been taken for medical purposes (thus blood samples taken as part of a criminal investigation, for example, are not within the definition) and are held in confidence. For both personal records and human tissue, confidentiality is

---

[60] Schedule 1, paragraph 7; *R v Maidstone Crown Court ex parte Waitt* [1988] Crim LR 384. As with matters of legal privilege the judges have a responsibility to ensure that the protections offered by Schedule 1 are upheld.

[61] Schedule 1, paragraph 15, PACE 1984.

[62] For example, *DPP v Channel 4 TV* [1993] 2 All ER 517.

[63] Schedule 1, paragraph 12, PACE 1984.

[64] In *R v Manchester Stipendiary Magistrate and another ex parte Granada Television Ltd* [2000] 1 All ER 135, the House of Lords held that a search warrant issued in Scotland could be validly executed against a television company based in England even though Scottish law does not contain the same protections for journalistic material as in England.

[65] *R v Cardiff Crown Court ex parte Kellam* (1993) TLR 239.

defined in respect of either the existence of an express or implied undertaking of confidentiality or a statutory requirement of non-disclosure or secrecy.

Thirdly, excluded material includes 'journalistic material' consisting of records or other kinds of documents which are held in confidence. The material must have been acquired or created for the purposes of journalism and be in the possession of a person who acquired or created it for that purpose. If, for example, a journalist receives confidential material through the post which is sent to be used for journalistic purposes, it is covered by the Act.[66] The power of the press to prevent police access to journalistic material may depend on whether it is confidential, as defined by the Act. It will only be confidential if the material is held by the journalist subject to an 'undertaking, restriction or obligation' of confidentiality and that it has been continuously held under the burden of confidentiality since acquired or created for journalistic purposes.[67] Journalists conventionally offer protection to their sources and are likely to be able to use that in order to bring matter within the protection of 'excluded material'.

Applications for 'excluded material' must be made under Schedule 1, paragraph 3, PACE 1984 only. This refers to the 'second set of access conditions'. A circuit judge can order a person to produce 'excluded material' or give a constable access to it only if there are reasonable grounds for believing that 'excluded material' is in the premises specified in the application and that, under previous legislation, as repealed by section 9(2) PACE 1984, a search warrant for such material both could and would have been issued. The test is historical, the Act does not change the law. There is no necessary public interest test for the issuing of the warrant though such tests were inherent in the earlier law.

Special procedure material

Special procedure material[68] is any other material (not personal records relating to physical or mental health or spiritual or welfare counselling) which is held subject to an obligation of confidentiality and which is 'acquired or created in the course of any trade, business, profession or other occupation' or for the 'purposes of any paid or unpaid office'. It includes various types of financial and property records. 'Special procedure material' also includes any journalistic material, defined as for 'excluded material' but which does not consist of documents or records or which, more importantly, is not held under an obligation of confidentiality or secrecy. This will include the notes relating to published articles unless disclosure would break a duty of confidentiality such as leading to the disclosure of a source.

A judge may order the disclosure to the police of 'special procedure material' if either the second or first set of access conditions, found in Schedule 1 of the Act, apply. As we have seen, the production of 'excluded material' can only be ordered if the second set of access conditions apply, i.e. that production could have been ordered prior to the coming into effect of PACE.

---

[66] Section 12, PACE 1984.
[67] Section 11(3), PACE 1984.
[68] Special procedure material is defined by s. 14, PACE 1984.

Special procedure material can also be ordered to be produced if it could have been so ordered prior to PACE 1984; in addition, 'special procedure material', but not excluded material, can be ordered to be produced if the first set of access conditions apply.

Police and Criminal Evidence Act 1984
Schedule 1 SPECIAL PROCEDURE

(1) If on an application made by a constable a circuit judge is satisfied that one or other of the sets of access conditions is fulfilled, he may make an order under paragraph 4 below.

(2) The first set of access conditions is fulfilled if –

    (a) there are reasonable grounds for believing –

        (i)   that a serious arrestable offence has been committed;

        (ii) that there is material which consists of special procedure material or includes special procedure material and does not also include excluded material on premises specified in the application;

        (iii) that the material is likely to be of substantial value (whether by itself or together with other material) to the investigation in connection with which the application is made; and

        (iv) the material is likely to be relevant evidence;

    (b) other methods of obtaining the material –

        (i)   have been tried without success; or

        (ii) have not been tried because it appeared that they were bound to fail; and

    (c) it is in the public interest, having regard –

        (i)   to the benefit likely to accrue to the investigation if the material is obtained; and

        (ii) to the circumstances under which the person in possession of the material holds it

    that the material should be produced or that access to it should be given.

All the grounds in paragraph 2 must be properly established by evidence, even in national security cases.[69] The judge must be satisfied on his or her own judgment that the grounds are made out and not just be satisfied that there are circumstances in which it is reasonable, in the administrative law sense, for the police to have made the application.[70]

Of particular importance from a civil liberties point of view is the impact these procedures have on freedom of the press. In *R v Bristol Crown Court ex parte Bristol Press and Picture Agency Ltd* (1987),[71] the police successfully applied for an order requiring the disclosure of photographs of riots and rioters which they believed would help in the identification of offenders. Such orders are likely to have an inhibiting effect on the reporting and investigation of crime and disorder. In particular, the availability of such orders will turn journalists into potential agents of the police and destroy whatever impartiality as observers and reporters they may have and, perhaps, jeopardise their personal safety.

---

[69] *R v Central Criminal Court ex parte Bright* [2001] 2 All ER 244, though the presence of national security issues may cause the court to take precautionary procedural steps.
[70] *Ibid.*
[71] (1987) 85 Cr App R 190, QBD.

The issue turns on the approach of the courts to the question of the public interest, to the factors that can be brought into consideration and to when in the process of reasoning the judgment is to be made. The fullest discussion is in *R* v *Central Criminal Court ex parte Bright* (2001).[72]

> Police, investigating offences under the Official Secrets Act 1989 by David Shayler sought, first, the disclosure of files, including Shayler's e-mail address, relating to a letter he sent to *The Guardian*, and, second, files relating to an article written by Bright, a journalist, and published in *The Observer*, which was based on information supplied by Shayler to Bright and which might disclose an offence committed by the latter under the Official Secrets Act 1989. At first instance the judge granted the orders, for special procedure material, that were requested by the police.
>
> HELD (QBD): the orders should be discharged except for one relating to a letter sent by Shayler to Bright.
>
> *R* v *Central Criminal Court ex parte Bright* [2001] 2 All ER 244

A judgment on the public interest arises, according to the majority, in two places. First, in respect of paragraph (c) of Schedule 1 as part of the judgment whether the access conditions have been made out. However, public interest on this point is to be treated narrowly and confined to the issues in paragraph (c). Broader questions, such as the impact of an order on freedom of the press and other fundamental or human rights, are excluded at this point. Such broader issues are relevant to a second judgment that needs to be made: whether, given that the access conditions are made out, the order should be issued. Under paragraph 1 of Schedule 1 the judge has a discretion on this matter.[73] The court stressed that placing the broader public interest here does not diminish the importance to be given to fundamental or human rights and, in particular, to freedom of the press and to the right not to be required to incriminate oneself. By relating issues of the broader public interest to the judicial discretion over whether to issue an order rather than to the judgment on whether or not the first set of access conditions are made out, it may be possible to avoid the difficulty of a finding both that the material being sought was likely to be of substantial value in the investigation of a serious arrestable offence and that, nevertheless, it was not in the public interest to order production.[74]

R v *Central Criminal Court ex parte Bright* contains strong words in support of freedom of the press.[75] In particular it is authority for the view, echoing *Bristol Press and Picture Agency*, that a production order for journalistic material should be based on compelling reasons otherwise 'investigative journalism will be discouraged, perhaps stifled'. The case was decided before the coming into effect of the Human Rights Act 1998 and the argument, especially of Judge J, is based on the congruency of the fundamental rights recognised by the common law with the human rights recognised by the Convention.[76] Since the

---

[72] [2001] 2 All ER 244.

[73] Gibbs J dissented on the point; he thought that paragraph (c)(ii) was expressed with sufficient width to include matters such as freedom of the press. In *Bristol Press Agency* freedom of the press is treated as pertaining to paragraph (c).

[74] *R* v *Crown Court at Northampton ex parte DPP* (1991) 93 Cr App R 376.

[75] Especially per Judge J; it also recognises that self-incrimination may be in issue.

[76] *R* v *Central Criminal Court ex parte Bright* [2001] 2 All ER 244, paragraph 87.

coming into effect of the Act a number of points need to be noted. Section 6 of the Act requires courts, as public authorities, to give effect to the Convention. Article 10, freedom of expression, therefore must be taken into account by the courts, though, in the light of Article 10(2), there may be little of substance between the common law and the Convention. Section 12 of the Human Rights Act 1998 reinforces the point with its requirement that courts must have 'particular regard' to the importance of freedom of expression under the Convention and, in particular, 'the extent to which . . . it is, or would be, in the public interest for the material to be published'. This underlines the positioning *ex parte Bright* that freedom of the press must be taken into account in deciding whether to issue an order even though the access conditions have been made out. A further point should be noted. In dealing with human rights cases, courts must be satisfied that any restriction of a Convention right, such as freedom of expression, is proportionate to the public benefit that will accrue. This principle is already found in paragraph 2(a)(iii) of Schedule 1 but is to be given greater prominence as a side constraint following the coming into effect of the 1998 Act.[77]

In the context of anti-terrorism, the courts may take a more executive minded approach. This issue is discussed in Chapter 18.

6.10.3 The Criminal Justice and Police Act 2001

When the police are lawfully conducting a search of premises or persons under a range of statutes including PACE 1984, they may come across material which may or may not be privileged, 'excluded' or 'special procedure material', or they may seize items which are inextricably linked with such material. Under the 2001 Act police are now[78] able to seize such material and remove it in order to ascertain whether they are or are not entitled to seize. The material must be examined as soon as is reasonably practicable and non-seizable matters must be 'secured' (not further examined) or returned. The Act thus increases or at least clarifies police powers of seizure. In balance, the Act also provides a procedure for applying, as appropriate, to the Crown Court or High Court for the return of seized items which are outside police powers to seize. The need for such a procedure clearly reflects the human rights requirement for proper judicial supervision of search and seizure powers.

6.11 Search orders

The search and seizure powers discussed above are exercisable by police and, under other statutes, by other officials and must be exercised in the public interest. Parties to civil proceedings may also be able obtain 'search orders' against the other party to proceedings.[79] The order may be wide ranging. It is

---

[77] *R* v *Secretary of State for Home Department ex parte Daly* [2001] UKHL 26 [2001] 3 All ER 433.
[78] For the common law position as regards privileged material see *R* v *Chesterfield Justice and Another ex parte Bramley* [2000] 1 All ER 411.
[79] *Anton Piller KG* v *Manufacturing Processes Ltd* [1976] 1 All ER 779 CA.

designed to supplement a normal discovery order where there is serious grounds for thinking that evidence needed by the applicant for litigation may be otherwise hidden, destroyed or removed. It is issued *ex parte* and in the private interests of the applicant. It is enforced by the applicant and his or her solicitor. Concern that the order was being issued routinely and oppressively rather than in exceptional circumstances led to a review and tightening up of the procedure including, in some cases, supervision of the execution of the order to be by an independent solicitor.[80] However, even in advance of these changes, the procedure was compatible with Convention rights.[81]

---

[80] *Universal Thermosensors Ltd* v *Hibben* [1992] 3 All ER 257.
[81] *Chappell* v *United Kingdom* (1990) 12 EHRR 1.

7

Surveillance

7.1 Surveillance

7.1.1 The point of surveillance

The core meaning of surveillance is the obtaining of information about persons and organisations by covert means. The information is obtained without the target's knowledge or consent. State agencies (secret services and, later, police forces) have from time immemorial conducted surveillance against their institutional opponents. The twentieth century saw a huge expansion in the quantity and scope of surveillance and this continues as state functions have widened and perceived threats continue. In particular, technological development continues at a fast rate and it is this more than anything that has made surveillance such an important and problematic issue. It vastly increases the opportunities for and likely effectiveness of surveillance, especially that which can be conducted remotely. Through devices such as the computer and the mobile phone it has also transformed the means of communication and thus, in parallel, the means by which such communications can be monitored.

Surveillance enables the identification of evidence which, if sought through more open means, would otherwise disappear. It enables suspicions to be confirmed to the extent that more open means can then be used to obtain evidence that is admissible in court. It can also be used to know what the opponents are doing and to take appropriate countermeasures.

7.1.2 The problem of surveillance

Surveillance involves an interference with private life. Privacy is interfered with even if the surveillance is unknown to the person involved.[1] Surveillance can also threaten other, more political, freedoms, in particular freedom of expression and freedom of association. The possibility, quite as much as the actuality, of surveillance, is an inhibition on political and other organisations and an interference with their freedom.[2] Surveillance raises a genuine tension with which the law should deal. There are clear public benefits that the practice can bring. Surveillance is used not only in respect of ordinary crime

---

[1] This mirrors the view taken by the European Court of Human Rights in one of its leading cases on surveillance: *Klass and others* v *Federal Republic of Germany* (1979) 2 EHRR 214.

[2] *Klass and others* v *Federal Republic of Germany* (1979) 2 EHRR 214, paragraph 41, a case decided on the right to privacy rather than to expression or to association.

but to counter 'subversion' and 'terrorism', both terms of very wide application. There is also the need properly to secure the private and political rights of those directly affected and to maintain an open society amenable to political dissent and a plurality of views some of which may be unpopular with those exercising state power. Surveillance sits uncomfortably with democratic values and practices as these are understood in conventional liberal and human rights discourse. Any justification for surveillance should be carefully and restrictively assessed. In particular its purposes should be limited to those which advance rather than restrict the openness of society and any authorisation must be subject to reasonable and effective safeguards aimed at protecting the private and political rights not only of those directly affected but of citizens generally.

The opportunity for state wrongdoing is clearly considerable. The fear is that the state will use surveillance to pursue improper objectives, such as the suppression of political dissent, or use it to pursue proper objectives by disproportionate means. Few governments which claim to be democratic will claim an unlimited power to use surveillance. Of great importance, therefore, is the issue of who, what kind of body, has the job, firstly, of deciding what general rules are to apply to the authorisation of surveillance, and, secondly, of supervising and enforcing those rules in particular instances. In the United Kingdom, it has not been until recently that Parliament, rather than the executive, has established the general rules governing state surveillance. The United Kingdom also tolerates executive authorisation of particular acts of surveillance and largely avoids review by the ordinary courts, preferring review by specialist officials and tribunals. This system will be discussed in greater detail in what follows.

Others, apart from state agents, may wish to use covert means to obtain information. Security firms and private investigators are examples and they, of course, will be acting for a range of commercial and private interests with any public benefits being remote. More problematic is the investigative journalist. There may be both a private interest (the reputation of the journalist and the commercial success of his or her employer) and a public interest from the publication of a story that exposes wrongdoing; alternatively there may be only the publication of a story that feeds base curiosity about the private lives of others.

7.2 Surveillance and legality

Until the mid-1980s surveillance activities, such as phone tapping, watching and following people or planting listening devices, was largely unregulated by the general law. Generally no statute permitted such activities but nor did any statute make them unlawful. If a criminal offence was committed or a civil wrong then the courts could provide a remedy. This was most likely to be the commission of a trespass, the direct interference with a person or his or her property, which could occur when property was entered to plant a device, for example. More remote forms of surveillance, such as telephone tapping or watching and following are outside the interests that trespass protects and the common law did not develop a general right to privacy which such surveillance might violate. Legal authority for surveillance lay, at that time, in the application to state officials of the general principle that what is not forbidden is permitted.[3] Guidelines were produced to govern some surveillance activities, particularly by the police.[4] 'Guidelines' are not law, they cannot make lawful that which is unlawful, and so they could not authorise what was otherwise a trespassory interference with property. Conversely, surveillance outside the guidelines would not, for that reason, be unlawful though it could, perhaps, lead to disciplinary activity within the police force. The courts, however, took a tolerant view and evidence from surveillance, even if unlawful, would not be automatically inadmissible.[5]

The absence of clear legal regulation violated the fundamental principle of legality found in the ECHR.[6] The consequence of this has been a progressive extension of statute law over a range of surveillance activities. The tapping of a public phone system was regulated by the Interception of Communications Act 1985 which made such interceptions an offence unless authorised by a warrant obtained from the Home Secretary. Police, the secret services and other public bodies could apply for such warrants. A tribunal was established to which an aggrieved person could apply and the general system was reviewed by a commissioner reporting to the Prime Minister. All other forms of surveillance were left unregulated by legal rules. The Security Service Act 1989 (amended by the Security Service Act 1996) provided legal authorisation for covert, otherwise tortious, entry onto property by the internal security service for surveillance purposes. The Intelligence Services Act 1994 took over these provisions and gave similar authorisation for GCHQ and the security services dealing with overseas threats. A similar system as under the Interception of Communications Act 1985, of needing a warrant from the Secretary of State with complaint to a tribunal and review by a commissioner was used. Legal authority for covert, otherwise tortious, interference with property by the police was only given a statutory basis by the Police Act 1997, discussed below.

Gaps in legal regulation remained and these were increased by technological developments available both to those conducting and to the targets of surveillance. The Interception of Communications Act 1985 was limited to public telephone networks and had no effect on interception of messages over private systems[7] or cordless phones[8] of various kinds. Similarly, the Security Service Act 1989, the Intelligence Services Act 1994 and the Police Act 1997 had no regulatory effect on forms of surveillance that were not tortious or otherwise unlawful. Remote surveillance techniques, which do not require tortious entry onto property, were not covered by the legislation. Technological advances of the late twentieth century significantly increased the utility of this type of surveillance for the authorities[9] and also the efficiency of methods

---

[3] *Malone* v *Metropolitan Police Commissioner* [1979] 1 Ch 344.
[4] As discussed in *R* v *Khan (Sultan)* [1997] AC 558, 573.
[5] *R* v *Khan (Sultan)* [1997] AC 558.
[6] *Malone* v *United Kingdom* (1984) 7 EHRR 14; *Halford* v *United Kingdom* (1997) 24 EHRR 523.
[7] *Halford* v *United Kingdom* (1997) 24 EHRR 523.
[8] *R* v *Effick* [1994] 3 WLR 583.

for storing and retrieving the data obtained. There were also significant problems perceived about the use of remote surveillance by the media involving sometimes gross, and by no means covert, intrusion into people's lives.[10]

The lack of legal regulation became, therefore, a matter of significance particularly after the coming into effect of the Human Rights Act 1998. Interferences with Convention rights, such as the right to private life, must be 'in accordance with the law' and mere negative freedom, the absence of express statutory regulation, fails the Strasbourg test for legality. There was a danger that, under that Act, much surveillance would become unlawful.[11] European Community law also required greater legal restraint to protect privacy in the light of technological development in the telecommunications area.[12]

Following investigation and reports[13] the government had Parliament enact the Regulation of Investigatory Powers Act 2000 which aims to provide a comprehensive legal structure for various forms of 'lawful', non-tortious, surveillance.

7.3 Interception of communications

7.3.1 The offence

Section 1, Regulation of Investigatory Powers Act 2000 (RIPA 2000) creates an offence for any person to make an unlawful interception of a communication in the course of its transmission by post or telephone.

1 Unlawful interception
(1) It shall be an offence for a person intentionally and without lawful authority to intercept in any place in the United Kingdom, any communication in the course of its transmission by means of –
  (a) a public postal service; or
  (b) a public telecommunication system.
(2) It shall be an offence for a person –
  (a) intentionally and without lawful authority, and
  (b) otherwise than in circumstances in which his conduct is excluded by subsection (6) from criminal liability under this subsection,
  to intercept, at any place in the United Kingdom, any communication in the course of its transmission by means of a private telecommunication system.

---

[9] For example, arial cameras with high magnification, night vision technology, stroboscopic cameras, automatic vehicle recognition and CCTV – Colvin, M. (1999) 'Surveillance and the Human Rights Act', in the University of Cambridge Centre for Public Law (ed.) *The Human Rights Act and the Criminal Justice Regulatory Process*. Oxford: Hart Publishing, p. 73.

[10] As early as 1992 Sir David Calcutt's *Review of Press Self Regulation*, Cm 2135, recommended the creation of both criminal and tortious actions against remote surveillance.

[11] See, for example, JUSTICE (1998) *Under Surveillance – Covert Policing and Human Rights Standards*. London: JUSTICE.

[12] Telecoms Data Protection Directive, 97/66/EC.

[13] The Act includes the legislative response to two reports: *Interception of Communications in the United Kingdom* (1999) Cm 4368; and *Promoting e-Commerce* (1999) Cm 4417.

This adopts and expands the offence under the Interception of Communications Act 1985 which is largely repealed.[14] No proceedings can be brought without the consent of the Director of Public Prosecutions.

Section 1, RIPA 2000 extends the offence of unlawful interception to private telephone systems thus going some way to remedy the problem exposed in *Halford* v *United Kingdom*.[15] A telephone tap placed on the internal telephone system of the Merseyside Police in order to monitor calls made by the applicant was held to have violated Article 8 ECHR. The Court of Human Rights held that, since the Interception of Communications Act 1985 did not apply to such non-public telephone systems, there was no legal basis for the interference with the applicant's Article 8 rights. Section 1(6), RIPA 2000 permits the interception of a private telecommunication transmission if done by or with the express or implied consent of the person with a right to control the system; employers may continue to tap their employees' work telephones without committing a criminal offence. However, section 1(3) creates a tort action, for damages or other civil remedy. The sender and receiver of a message that is intercepted with the express or implied consent of a private system controller has a cause of action against the controller. However, no tort is committed if the controller can show that he or she acted with 'lawful authority' which, in respect of businesses, is extensive.

7.3.2 Lawful authority

No crime or tort is committed if an interception is made with 'lawful authority'.[16] Lawful authority includes interceptions made with the reasonable belief that both parties had consented or made because they are necessary for the effective operation of a telephone or postal service (opening non-addressed letters, for example). Lawful authority also covers the situation in which the police are authorised under Part 2 of the Act to conduct surveillance and the non-target party has consented to this being by the interception of telephone or post;[17] interceptions in prisons and high security hospitals are lawful so long as authorised under relevant regulations such as the Prison Rules. The Act, however, provides no public interest defence that a journalist, for example, might wish to claim.

Business communications
There are wide grounds for the lawful interception of business communications and these may make it relatively easy for employers and other controllers of a private telecommunications system to make out a defence to the tort created by section 1(3), RIPA 2000. The Act empowers the Secretary of State to make regulations authorising the interception by businesses of communica-

---

[14] The provisions which remain amend the Telecommunications Act 1984 by making it an offence for those operating a public telecommunications service to make unauthorised disclosure of information obtained by an interception.

[15] (1997) 24 EHRR 523. Similarly, the use of covert listening devices in a police cell violated Article 8: *PG and JH* v *United Kingdom* Ap. 44787/98; (2001) *The Times*, 19 October.

[16] Section 1(5), RIPA 2000.

[17] Section 3, RIPA 2000.

tions made with them and their employees. There is no definition of 'business' but the term is capable of wide use and includes government departments, public authorities and office holders.[18] Establishing compliance with procedures, detecting or preventing crime, detecting the unauthorised use of telecommunications systems, monitoring help lines and, even, furthering the interests of national security are examples of the wide-ranging purposes for which the interception of business communications will be permitted. The Act requires little of the Secretary of State as regards safeguards though the regulations should stress the need for businesses to take reasonable steps to inform people that interception or monitoring is possible.

Warrants

From the civil liberties point of view, the most important and controversial form of lawful authority is on the basis of a warrant obtained under section 5, RIPA 2000. It is on this basis that, for example, the covert, non-consensual interception of communications by alleged subversives or terrorists is authorised.

The warrant is issued only by the Secretary of State or, in urgent cases, by a senior official. Warrants issued by the Secretary of State last for three months and can be renewed for a further six months or three months depending on their purpose. Warrants issued by officials last for five days only but can be renewed for a three-month period.

There is no requirement for direct judicial authorisation, by judge or magistrate, of such warrants and it may be that a Secretary of State or a senior civil servant lacks the independence and impartiality that authorisation of such a major interference with privacy and, perhaps, political freedom ought to have. The strength of this argument depends on the countervailing provisions for review, supervision and complaint and the commissioners and tribunal which are discussed later in the chapter. Only police (who apply through the National Criminal Intelligence Service), security services and the Customs and Excise, as specified in section 6, are allowed to apply for a warrant. Covert surveillance by other officials or journalists, for example, remains a crime.

The Secretary of State must believe that a warrant is necessary to achieve certain purposes which cannot be achieved in any other reasonable way and that the interception is a proportionate way of achieving the result the interception is aimed to achieve. The purposes are: 'the interests of national security', the 'preventing or detecting of serious crime' and 'safeguarding the economic well-being of the United Kingdom' where the information relates to persons or actions outside the British Isles. These provisions are clearly designed to ensure that the issuing of warrants is compatible with Convention rights, in particular Article 8(2) ECHR. Of particular concern in the civil liberties context is the concept of 'serious crime' which includes 'conduct by a large number of persons in pursuit of a common purpose' and would seem to be capable of authorising the interception of communications by political groups planning demonstrations or protests involving, for example, obstruction of the highway. The government's explanation is that the definition is

---

[18] Section 7, RIPA 2000.

aimed at organised crime and that the protection for reasonable political protest lies with the duty of those officials involved to act proportionately and otherwise compatibly with Convention rights such as Article 10, freedom of expression, and Article 11, freedom of assembly and association.

The legal regime under Part 1, Chapter 1, RIPA 2000 provides wide discretionary powers to the Secretary of State and, in reality, to the officials whose judgments on the need for an interception are likely to determine the Secretary of State's decision. There is a procedure for complaint to a tribunal by anyone who believes their communications have been intercepted, and the system is reviewed and reported on by a chief commissioner. This is discussed later in the chapter. The issuing and execution of warrants, as the actions of 'public authorities', must, under section 6 of the Human Rights Act 1998, be compatible with Convention rights and this is also discussed later in the chapter although it is worth noting that in *Christie v United Kingdom*[19] the general scheme under the Interception of Communications Act 1985 was upheld by the Commission on Human Rights though the case did not involve 'serious crime' to which more demanding standards may apply.[20]

7.4 Access to communications data

Communications organisations, such as telecommunications companies, will hold 'communications data'. This is information about the use of communications rather than about their content. It may be, for example, information on the numbers dialled from a particular telephone and the duration of a call or similar information about mobile phones including the general location of callers. Communications data can assist public authorities in the investigation of crime and other purposes and can also be of significance for journalists investigating stories.[21] Section 45(1)(b) of the Telecommunications Act 1984 makes the intentional disclosure of information about the use made of a telecommunication service an offence, unless otherwise authorised. Similarly, the provision of such information is also likely to violate the Data Protection Act 1998.

Chapter 2 of Part 1 of the Regulation of Investigatory Powers Act 2000 provides for the compulsory disclosure of communications data by 'anyone who provides a postal or telecommunications service'. Named officials within the police, Customs and Excise, the Inland Revenue and the intelligence services will have the authority to require disclosure if it is necessary in the interests of national security, the prevention or detection of crime or disorder, the economic well-being of the United Kingdom, public safety, public health, the assessment or collection of tax, and preventing serious harm, such as death an injury, in an emergency.[22] This is a much wider range of purposes than those for which a warranted interception of a communication in order to know

---

[19] (1994) Ap. 21482/93, 78-A D&R 119.

[20] Fenwick, H. (2000) *Civil Rights, New Labour, Freedom and the Human Rights Act*. Harlow: Longman, pp. 331, 365.

[21] For example, BBC's *Panorama* used mobile phone metering to chart the movements of suspects for the Omagh bomb outrage.

[22] Section 22(2), RIPA 2000.

its content can be made. Obtaining the data must be necessary and a proportionate way of obtaining the benefit that disclosure should achieve.[23] The operators of postal or telecommunications services are under a duty to do what is reasonably practicable to disclose the data. Refusal is not a crime but can give rise to a civil action by the Secretary of State for an injunction or order of specific performance. The Anti-terrorism, Crime and Security Act 2001, Part 11 authorises the Secretary of State to produce a Code of Practice and to make agreements with particular providers detailing the circumstances in which communications data should be retained to facilitate disclosures which might be required. There must be consultation with the Information Commissioner since the Code of Practice is likely to be at odds with significant data protection principles, such as those requiring the timeous destruction of data.

The Secretary of State may add to the organisations that can obtain communications data and increase the purposes for which it can be obtained. This is controversial since it enables the Secretary of State, by order, to greatly increase the ability of public authorities to obtain information about people and organisations. The statute requires Parliamentary approval and the power must be exercised in a manner compatible with Article 8 ECHR and with the Data Protection Act 1998, to the extent that it is not impliedly repealed. In July 2002 proposals to widen the list of authorities were subject to strong opposition in Parliament and from the Information Commissioner and were withdrawn. A much restricted list was re-introduced in March 2003.

7.5 Encrypted data

The Regulation of Investigatory Powers Act 2000 gives the police, Customs and Excise, defence and intelligence services power to obtain, under criminal sanction, the ability to decode encrypted material that is lawfully in their possession. The grounds for which such disclosure may be allowed are national security, the economic well-being of the United Kingdom and the prevention or detection of crime (not only serious crime). Authority to compel this disclosure will normally be, for police and Customs and Excise, from a circuit judge or, for the intelligence services, from the Secretary of State.[24] There are various safeguards against misuse. It may be that these provisions could involve the decoding of self-incriminating material since the Court of Human Rights in *Saunders* v *United Kingdom* found that the compulsory disclosure of documents, which are non-testamentary and exist independently of the will of the suspect and which can thus be distinguished from information given directly under questioning, may not violate Article 6 ECHR.

7.6 Surveillance involving interference with property

Other forms of surveillance, such as planting a listening device in someone's home, may involve entering on and interfering with property. If this is done

---

[23] Section 22(5), RIPA 2000.
[24] RIPA 2000, Schedule 2.

without the occupier's consent, the tort of trespass may have been committed. The action will not be tortious if it has lawful authority. We know from *Entick* v *Carrington* (1765) that such authority cannot be found in the mere claim of state bodies to be acting in the public interest but requires a statutory or common law rule. For most of the twentieth century no such lawful authority was available. Home Office Guidelines were issued to regulate the way such surveillance was conducted by the police. These are not 'law' and are insufficient to authorise what is otherwise a tort, though following them might protect a police officer from disciplinary action.[25] There is also some evidence that the courts would be tolerant of unlawful entry by the security services.[26] Unlawfully obtained evidence is not necessarily inadmissible in English courts.

If nothing else, this situation would seem to be incompatible with the requirement, in Article 8 ECHR, that interferences with private life, home and correspondence by public bodies must have proper lawful authority. Legislation (not RIPA 2000) now covers this matter. It is confined to certain public bodies, such as the police and security services, and is not available to, for example, a journalist pursuing a story.

7.6.1 Police and Customs and Excise

Part III of the Police Act 1997 now provides lawful authority for otherwise tortious interferences with property by police, including the National Criminal Intelligence Service and Customs officials. Any proposed trespassory surveillance can only be authorised if it is 'necessary' in the sense, both, that it is of 'substantial value in the prevention and detection of serious crime' and that the anticipated outcome 'cannot be achieved by other means'. Serious crime is defined as in RIPA 2000 and other Acts and the fear of its use against protest groups is as strong in the context of interference with property as with interception of telecommunications.

Authorisations of interference with property under Part III of the Police Act 1997 are made by the highest ranking officers (e.g. the chief constable) though senior officers of lower rank are allowed to deputise in certain circumstances.[27] Applications can only come from within the organisations and not, for example, from members of the public. The problem here is the lack of an independent, perhaps judicial, component in the authorising process. This problem led to the establishment of commissioners who are senior judges of High Court status who exercise a number of approving, reviewing and reporting functions.

In particular, 'sensitive authorisations' require the prior approval of a commissioner. Sensitive authorisations are those pertaining to property that is believed to be used wholly or mainly as a dwelling, as a hotel bedroom or as office premises, or where it is believed that knowledge of matters subject to legal privilege, confidential personal information or confidential journalistic

---

[25] *R* v *Chief Constable of West Yorkshire ex parte Govell*, 23 May 1994.
[26] See remarks by Lord Donaldson: *Attorney-General* v *Guardian Newspapers* (2) [1990] AC 109, 190.
[27] Sections 93 and 94, Police Act 1997.

information might be obtained. Prior approval by a Commissioner is not, however, required in urgent cases.[28] Non-sensitive authorisations and urgent sensitive authorisations can be given immediate effect. They then require notification to be given to a commissioner. The notified commissioner has the power to quash an authorisation because either the reasons justifying the surveillance never existed,[29] no longer apply[30] or because the commissioner's prior approval was in fact necessary because it was, contrary to the view of the authorising officer, a non-urgent sensitive authorisation.[31] The authorising officer may be able to appeal to the chief commissioner against the quashing of an authorisation by a commissioner.[32]

Complaints by members of the public are to a tribunal established under RIPA 2000 and are discussed later in the chapter.

7.6.2 The secret services

The secret services (the Security Service, the Intelligence Service and GCHQ) may obtain authorisation for otherwise unlawful surveillance involving entry on or interferences with property by virtue of section 5, Intelligence Services Act 1994. Such entry on or interferences with property will not be unlawful if undertaken on the authority of a warrant issued, on the application of one of the services, by the Secretary of State either directly or, in urgent cases, through an official with the approval of the Secretary of State. A warrant can only be issued if the Secretary of State is satisfied that the warrant is necessary for 'assisting' the services in carrying out their functions. This is a very wide term and even easier to satisfy than 'substantial value' which was the test prior to amendments made under RIPA 2000. The Secretary of State must be satisfied not only that the proposed action is necessary but also that it is a proportionate means of achieving what is sought and cannot reasonably be achieved by other means. Furthermore, the Secretary of State must be satisfied that proper arrangements are in place to ensure that any information obtained is not improperly disclosed.

The functions of the Security Service are widely defined and include protection from threats of terrorism and internal subversion. The Security Service Act 1996 extended the functions of the Service to include supporting the police in the prevention and detection of 'serious crime'. Warrants for that purpose can be issued.[33] Given this development there is a possible overlap between the targets of police surveillance and Security Service surveillance. The danger from this is that restrictions which apply to the police, in particular the requirement that 'sensitive authorisations' need the approval of an independent commissioner, do not apply to Security Service authorisations even though their surveillance can be for the same kinds of purpose and the same kinds of target. Similarly police forces act under a much more rigorous

---

[28] Section 97(3), Police Act 1997.
[29] Section 103(1), Police Act 1997.
[30] Section 103(4), Police Act 1997.
[31] Section 103(2), Police Act 1997.
[32] Section 104, Police Act 1997.
[33] Section 3B, Intelligence Services Act 1994.

statutory regime and are subject to a complaints process which does not apply to members of the Security Service.[34]

The Intelligence Service, specifically the Secret Intelligence Service and GCHQ, operates in respect of persons outside the United Kingdom.[35] The Secretary of State can authorise actions by the Intelligence Service and GCHQ abroad in pursuit of its functions and, on the basis of this authorisation, such acts cannot be unlawful under United Kingdom law. The Security Service Act 1996 permits the Secretary of State to issue warrants which authorise the Security Service to undertake surveillance inside the United Kingdom in support of the Intelligence Service in respect of targets inside the United Kingdom.[36] Such surveillance, related to activities abroad, cannot be for the purpose of preventing or detecting serious crime.

The Security Service Act 1989 and the Intelligence Services Act 1994 established complaints and supervision structures based on a tribunal and a commissioner with judicial standing. The tribunal and commissioner systems have been reconstituted under RIPA 2000 and are considered below.

7.7 Other forms of surveillance

Many forms of surveillance, such as following a suspect or using long-distance lenses or remote listening devices, are not likely to involve civil wrongs or criminal offences. They might be unlawful if, for example, they involve harassment contrary to the Protection from Harassment Act 1997 or if they involve an improper and unauthorised use of the highway. The police follow Home Office Guidelines on the issue but, though departure from these may be the basis of disciplinary action, it will not render the surveillance unlawful.

Such surveillance can, however, involve an interference with freedoms protected by Convention rights such as the rights to private life, freedom of expression or freedom of association. The United Kingdom has international obligations to uphold these rights and, in particular, section 6 of the Human Rights Act 1998 makes it unlawful for a public authority, such as the police, to act incompatibly with these rights. Any interference with such protected freedoms must, as we have seen, be compatible with the conditions found in the second paragraphs to Articles 8, 10 and 11. It must be 'in accordance with' or 'prescribed by' law and this means not only that they are in the form of officially promulgated rules but that they must also have sufficient precision so that the behaviour they allow or forbid can be reasonably predicted. The interference must be necessary in a democratic society, which means that they must be a proportionate way of meeting a pressing social need, and they must be for a specific, exclusive range of purposes given in the paragraphs.[37]

---

[34] For vigorous comment, including reference to the views of Lord Browne-Wilkinson in the House of Lords, see *Current Law Statutes* (1996) Vol. 2, ch. 35, annotations by O, Higgins, P.

[35] Section 1(1)(a), Intelligence Services Act 1994.

[36] Sections 4 and 5, Intelligence Services Act 1994.

[37] Surveillance by private persons, including journalists, will not be vulnerable to a Human Rights Act 1998 action unless a public authority or a body exercising public functions, such as the Press Complaints Commission, is held to be responsible or unless the Convention rights are given 'horizontal effect' in the way the courts apply the 1998 Act.

To meet these requirements Part II of the Regulation of Investigatory Powers Act 2000 provides lawful authority for three types of covert surveillance: 'directed' and 'intrusive' surveillance and surveillance by 'covert human sources'. The Act stipulates that other forms of surveillance are not thereby unlawful.[38]

7.7.1 Directed surveillance and surveillance involving covert human sources

Directed surveillance involves action which is planned and covert and aimed at obtaining personal information. It does not involve 'intrusive surveillance'. It might include, for example, the organised following of a person in the street.[39]

Surveillance by 'covert human sources' relates to the setting up and running, usually through a 'source', of a personal relationship with a surveillance target to obtain personal information about or disclose information to the target. It is likely to include some of the activities of police informants.

These two forms of surveillance are subject to rather loose regulation. A wide range of public authorities are listed in Schedule 1 of the Act and the Secretary of State identifies the ranks of officials within those authorities who can authorise surveillance.[40] The list is by no means confined to the police, security and defence sources. Local authorities and a range of government departments and agencies are included (though some, such as the NHS, can use directed surveillance but not covert human sources). Such surveillance can be only undertaken in the interests of national security, the prevention or detection of crime or disorder, the economic well-being of the United Kingdom, public safety, public health, the assessment or collection of tax, etc. The Secretary of State can add to these purposes by statutory instrument.[41] Any authorisation must be believed to be necessary and proportionate to what is sought to be achieved.

7.7.2 Intrusive surveillance

Intrusive surveillance is covert, carried out in relation to residential premises or private vehicles and involves either the presence of a person on the premises or in the vehicle or the use of a surveillance device.[42] The use of a remote surveillance device against residential premises is only 'intrusive' if it provides information of the same quality and detail as would be provided by a device placed on the premises. Otherwise, remote surveillance of residential property, only requires authorisation by the directed surveillance procedure.

---

[38] Section 80, RIPA 2000.

[39] The use of undercover officers in criminal investigations has been considered by the Court of Human Rights. The need for proper organisation and supervision is an important requirement: *Teixeira da Castro* v *Portugal* (1999) 28 EHRR 101.

[40] See Regulation of Investigatory Powers (Prescription of Offices, Ranks and Positions) Order 2000, SI 2000, No. 2417.

[41] See ss. 28(3) and 29(3).

[42] The use of a vehicle tracking device is not intrusive surveillance.

Intrusive surveillance overlaps with the kinds of otherwise tortious surveillance that can be authorised under the Police, Security Services and Intelligence Services Acts discussed above. These Acts will continue to authorise such surveillance.

The authorisation of 'intrusive surveillance' is subject to a tighter regime and intrusive surveillance by police and Customs is subject to a different authorisation process from that for the security services.

Intrusive surveillance by any agency can only be authorised for similar purposes as for interception warrants under section 5, RIPA 2000: the interests of national security, the prevention or detection of serious crime and the interests of the economic well-being of the United Kingdom.[43] These purposes are more restricted than for directed surveillance and surveillance involving covert human sources. It is, for example, limited to 'serious' crime and is not permitted to promote public safety or health or for the raising of taxes. Similarly, intrusive surveillance can only be authorised by a narrower range of public authorities and officials. The authorising official must believe intrusive surveillance is necessary in order to achieve certain objectives and it is proportionate to the benefit likely to be gained.[44] Whether the information could be obtained by other means is a judgment that must be made when considering the necessity of the surveillance.

Police and Customs authorisations

Police and customs authorisations can only be by chief officers, such as chief constables,[45] or, in cases of urgency, by senior officers of lower rank. Application can only come from within the force they control – this is not a service open to journalists, for example. The safeguard is similar to that for 'sensitive authorisations' under the Police Act 1997. Any authorisation must be approved by a surveillance commissioner, as appointed under the Police Act 1997, before it can be put into effect. In cases of urgency the surveillance can start on simple notification to the commissioner. The commissioner cannot approve an authorisation if, for example, the grounds for it no longer apply.[46] The authorising officer can appeal to the Chief Surveillance Commissioner, established under the 1997 Act, against a non-approval or quashing.

Security service authorisations

A 'member' of any of the intelligence services,[47] an 'official' of the Ministry of Defence, a 'member' of HM Forces and an official of any designated public authority can apply to the Secretary of State for authority to conduct intrusive surveillance. There is no restriction as to rank and seniority. The distinguishing point about these authorisations by the Secretary of State is that they do not

---

[43] Section 32(3)(a)–(c), RIPA 2000 (surveillance at the behest of a foreign country is excluded). The economic well-being of the United Kingdom is not a ground available to the Ministry of Defence or the armed forces.
[44] Section 32(2), RIPA 2000.
[45] Listed in section 32(6), RIPA 2000.
[46] Section 37, RIPA 2000.
[47] Section 81, RIPA 2000.

require notification or approval by a surveillance commissioner. The executive grants authorisation of intrusive surveillance in respect of defence and security targets on its own motion with no judicial or quasi-judicial supervision.

7.8 Supervision and control of surveillance

7.8.1 Codes of Practice

Section 71, RIPA 2000 empowers the Secretary of State to make Codes of Practice relating to different forms of surveillance under the Act, the Intelligence Services Act 1994 and the Police Act 1997. The Codes must be had 'regard to' by persons undertaking surveillance and are to be taken into account by commissioners and the tribunal when making their decisions. Breach of a Code, however, cannot in itself be the basis for either criminal or civil liability though the Codes are admissible in proceedings. Three such Codes are currently in force, on interception of communications, covert surveillance and the use of covert human sources.

7.8.2 The commissioners

The Chief Surveillance Commissioner, the Interception of Communications Commissioner and the Intelligence Services Commissioner have, in their own contexts, reporting and reviewing powers over police surveillance, the interception of communications and the surveillance activities of the intelligence services respectively. Surveillance commissioners established under the Police Act 1997 also have a role in authorising 'sensitive authorisations' and 'intrusive surveillance' by the police and Customs. Reporting is generally to the Prime Minister who has a duty to lay the annual report before Parliament[48] but who also has a power to censor prejudicial matters.

The commissioners are recruited from the senior judiciary and are able to provide some degree of independent review of surveillance authorisations which otherwise would be within the secret discretion of the executive. However, the extent to which the commissioners can provide adequate protection from the misuse of powers is limited. They have limited resources though RIPA 2000 does make provisions for the appointment of staff.[49] In particular, they have no powers over unauthorised interceptions or surveillance. For example, an allegation of non-warranted surveillance is either an allegation of a crime, a matter for the police, or it is an allegation of a trespass or other civil wrong. The wronged citizen can seek a civil remedy but can expect little help from the commissioners. Regarding their reviewing functions, they report to the executive about the practices of the executive. They do not report directly to Parliament and the Prime Minister can censor their reports before publishing them for Parliament. Successive governments have never had enough trust in the integrity of Parliament to allow direct Parliamentary supervision of the intelligence services though, since 1994, the

---

[48] Section 58(6), RIPA 2000.
[49] Sections 57(7), 59(7) and 63, RIPA 2000.

Intelligence and Security Committee contains Parliamentarians;[50] similarly governments are reluctant to allow too much direct Parliamentary supervision of the police.

7.8.3 The tribunal

The commissioners do not hear complaints about surveillance from members of the public. These are now heard by a tribunal established under Part IV, RIPA 2000. The tribunal replaces the tribunal established under the Interception of Communications Act 1985, the Security Service Act 1989 and the Intelligence Services Act 1994 and takes over the complaints jurisdiction of the surveillance commissioners under the Police Act 1997.

The tribunal's jurisdiction includes the surveillance activities of the intelligence services (including the Security Service), the police and Customs in so far as these ought to have been authorised under RIPA 2000 or the Police Act 1997, Part III. The way the jurisdiction is defined authorises the tribunal to deal with some allegations of unlawful surveillance.

The tribunal is the appropriate forum for any case brought under the Human Rights Act 1998 regarding matters within its jurisdiction. It is also a forum to hear other complaints about surveillance within its jurisdiction and to hear complaints by persons that they have been prejudiced by the ban on disclosure in court of information obtained by post and telecommunications interception. The Secretary of State can allocate other complaints, involving the intelligence services or other surveillance, to the tribunal.

The tribunal has a general power to make its own rules subject to the power of the Secretary of State to produce rules under section 69. The intelligence services, police and other public authorities involved are required to cooperate with the tribunal. Its remedies are to award compensation as it sees fit and it can quash an authorisation and order the destruction of material obtained.[51] The tribunal is not required to give reasons for its decisions, merely a statement to the complainant of whether the decision was for or against them. The Secretary of State may make rules requiring further information to be disclosed,[52] but not to order disclosure in individual cases.

There is no general right of appeal to the courts from the decisions of the tribunal.[53] Such provisions, which 'oust' the jurisdiction of the courts, have often been disregarded by the courts on the grounds that a decision that is wrong in law is likely to be a decision taken outside a tribunal's jurisdiction and therefore, as it were, not a decision of the tribunal at all and properly quashed by the court.[54] However, the 'ouster clause' in the Act, like its predecessors, expressly includes decisions of the tribunal 'as to whether they have jurisdiction'. Whether ouster is consistent with right of access to the court under Article 6 ECHR remains to be decided. Such implied rights under

---

[50] Chapter 4.
[51] Section 67(7), RIPA 2000.
[52] Section 68(4), RIPA 2000.
[53] Section 67(8), RIPA 2000.
[54] See Wade, Sir William and Forsyth, C.F. (2000) *Administrative Law*, 8th edn. Oxford: Oxford University Press.

Article 6 are subject to reasonable restriction and, in any case, the tribunal may meet the requirements of a court under Article 6. The Secretary of State is empowered to produce rules which permit appeal and is required to do so in respect of allegations of prejudice from non-disclosure in court of information obtained by surveillance.[55] Appeal on any of these matters need not necessarily be to an ordinary court. It can be to some individual or process established by the Secretary of State. If the point of allowing certain appeals is to satisfy Article 6 ECHR then any such alternative to the courts must satisfy requirements for independence etc. found in the article.

The success of this tribunal is clearly of great importance in establishing the credibility and acceptability of the surveillance regime in this 'rights aware' age. This will depend not only on the tribunal's own approach but also on the nature of the rules, if any, the Secretary of State produces, in particular in relation to the information that the tribunal is required to produce and the extent to which it is required to explain its decisions to the complainant.

7.9 Compatibility with Convention rights

7.9.1 The application of Article 8(1)

The compatability of this legal regime relating to surveillance with the Convention rights scheduled in the Human Rights Act 1998 will, no doubt, be tested in years to come.[56]

Article 8, the right to respect for private and family life, is the core right involved. The first question is whether surveillance activities are within the reach of Article 8(1). It is well established that the interception of post and telecommunications from both business and private premises[57] and the metering of telecommunications[58] are within the scope of Article 8(1). The same is true of surveillance involving an interference with property[59] including, for example, intrusive surveillance regulated in Part II, RIPA 2000. There is, however, a point at which Article 8(1) may not be engaged. The overt photographing of someone in the street, for example, has been thought by the Commission to be unprotected by Article 8[60] and so some forms of surveillance may be too remote or insufficiently covert to amount to an interference with private life. Article 8, for example, might not apply to some forms of directed surveillance and the use of covert human sources, where the targets are part of a criminal gang who might expect their activities to be observed.[61] Most importantly, the Court of Human Rights has accepted that the menace of

[55] Section 67(9), RIPA 2000.
[56] Fenwick, *op. cit.*, chapters 9 and 10.
[57] *Klass and others* v *Federal Republic of Germany*, Series A, No. 28 (1978–79) 2 EHRR 214 is the leading case. See also *Kopp* v *Switzerland* (1999) 27 EHRR 91; *Halford* v *United Kingdom* (1997) 24 EHRR 523.
[58] *Malone* v *United Kingdom* (normal business practices are excluded); *Valenzuela Contreras* v *Spain* (1999) 28 EHRR 483.
[59] For example, *Govell* v *United Kingdom* [1999] EHRLR 121, where a hole was drilled into a wall possibly to install a covert listening device.
[60] *Brüggemann and Scheuten* v *FRG* (1977) 3 EHRR 244.
[61] For example, *Ludi* v *Switzerland* Ap. 12433/86; (1993) 15 EHRR 173.

surveillance, its possibility, can, in itself, be an interference under Article 8 and so specific acts of surveillance do not need to be proved by a complainant. Surveillance used against parties, trade unions and other organisations might also raise issues under Article 10, freedom of expression, and Article 11, freedom of association, but the Convention principles in issue are likely to be the same as under Article 8.

7.9.2 Article 8(2)

Assuming that Article 8 is engaged by some act of surveillance, the issue then focuses on whether the act is allowable by virtue of Article 8(2). Article 8(2) permits interferences with rights to private and family life if they are 'in accordance with the law', 'necessary in a democratic society' and for the exclusive range of listed purposes.

Purposes
Interferences with private and family life by a public authority can be in the 'interests of national security, public safety or the economic well-being of the country, for the prevention of disorder or crime, for the protection of health or morals, or for the protection of the rights and freedoms of others'. The need for surveillance in democratic societies was recognised in *Klass and others* v *Federal Republic of Germany*[62] in so far as it was strictly necessary to protect democratic institutions. Similarly its use to prevent and detect crime has not been a problem under the Convention on the grounds that it was for an illegitimate purpose.[63]

Necessary in a democratic society and proportionality
Any use of surveillance must be proportionate to the benefit to society that will accrue. The more intrusive and covert the surveillance used, the greater the justification that is likely to be necessary. Surveillance which significantly invades privacy against minor or non-serious crime could be disproportionate. United Kingdom legislation restricts the most intrusive surveillance to the prevention and detection of 'serious crime'. There may, however, be a Convention issue in so far as the definition of serious crime extends to minor crime made serious by the fact that it is committed by many people in concert.

Proportionality requires that, in relation to crime, surveillance be used only against serious, properly defined offences, that it should be based on well-founded suspicion and not be merely exploratory and should only be used in the absence of the likely success of other methods.[64] A standard feature of the authorisation process under RIPA 2000 and the Police Act 1997 is that a consideration of the prospects for obtaining the desired information by other methods is necessary.

Proper supervision is necessary. In *Klass and others* v *Federal Republic of Germany*[65] supervision, or review, was required over the process or authorisa-

---

[62] (1979) 2 EHRR 214.
[63] For example, *Kopp* v *Switzerland* (1999) 27 EHRR 91; *Valenzuela Contreras* v *Spain* (1999) 28 EHRR 483.
[64] Starmer, K. (1999) *European Human Rights Law*. London: LAG, 15.26.
[65] (1979) 2 EHRR 214.

tion, over the conduct of the surveillance and after the surveillance was terminated. Guarantees against abuse must be adequate and effective. It is suggested in *Klass* that supervision over authorisation and conduct should be by a judge;[66] the point is that ultimate review of authorisation and conduct of surveillance should be independent, impartial and based on a proper procedure. The role of the Interception and Surveillance Commissioners under RIPA 2000 may meet this requirement. An important factor in *Christie v United Kingdom* (1994),[67] where the Commission found that the regime under the Interception of Communications Act 1985 was compatible with the Convention, was the supervisory role of the commissioners, which is maintained under the new law. However, strong doubts as to the adequacy of safeguards must lie where authorisation and review of conduct is confined to the executive, such as in respect of surveillance by the intelligence services under the Intelligence Services Act 1994. The role of the tribunal, therefore, is very important. It can undertake various supervisory roles both during and after the surveillance activity is carried out. It is likely that the tribunal will meet the requirements for independence, impartiality and proper procedure though the extent to which it is prepared to give reasons may be challengeable, probably, because of the 'ouster clause', only in Strasbourg.[68]

'In accordance with the law'

The Convention requires that any surveillance be 'in accordance with the law'. Surveillance must have a proper basis in law and unlawful surveillance or surveillance done at the discretion of the executive with no particular and positive statutory or common law authorisation will fall foul of this requirement.[69] The state is under a duty to establish a positive entitlement of its agents to conduct surveillance rather than merely accommodate it as part of the 'negative freedom' of the state. 'In accordance with the law' also means that the express legal rules must do more than simply give a wide discretion to a judge or an official or police officer.[70] The legal rules must be accessible and clear so that citizens can foresee, albeit, sometimes, with legal advice, the circumstances in which surveillance might be used and regulate their conduct accordingly.[71] Such forseeability applies to the general legal rules and also to the administrative and police practices they authorise. In *Kopp v Switzerland*[72] for example, there was an apparent contradiction between the written law which barred the interception of lawyer's communications and the surveillance practice which permitted such interceptions when lawyers were not acting in that capacity. A violation of Article 8 was based on the lack of any clear legal rules controlling when legal privilege would protect lawyers and

---

[66] (1979) 2 EHRR 214, paragraph 55.
[67] (1994) Ap. 21482/93 78-A D&R 119
[68] For the argument that the system may not be compatible with the Convention see Fenwick, *op. cit.*, p. 368.
[69] *Malone v United Kingdom* [1979] 1 Ch 344; *Halford v United Kingdom* (1997) 24 EHRR 523.
[70] For example, *Valenzuela Contreras v Spain* (1999) 28 EHRR 483, where, at the time, Spanish law gave a wide, unqualified discretion to a judge to permit interceptions: telecommunications were 'confidential unless the court decides otherwise'.
[71] *Amann v Switzerland* (2000) 30 EHRR 843.
[72] (1999) 27 EHRR 91.

when it would not. The law governing surveillance should specify, for example, the categories of person who are exposed to possible surveillance (e.g. persons contemplating serious crime), the types of offences for which surveillance is permitted, the limit on the duration of lawful surveillance, the procedure for reporting on surveillance, the procedure for the involvement of the independent supervisory agency and the circumstances for disposing of records kept if the target is acquitted.[73] The rules should also specify what is to be done in respect of those accidentally involved in a surveillance when someone else is the target.[74] These restrictions are, of course, focused on surveillance in the context of serious crime. Intelligence surveillance, presumably because it seldom finds the light of day and may be just to obtain information rather than to promote a prosecution, is not necessarily so strictly controlled. *Christie* v *United Kingdom*[75] is a case involving information-gathering through routine interception of a trade unionist's contacts with Eastern Europe. The interception satisfied the legality provision.

7.10 Admissibility of evidence

Evidence obtained from lawful or unlawful interceptions of communications is usually, though not always, inadmissible in legal proceedings.[76] Unlawfully obtained surveillance evidence can be excluded under section 78, PACE 1984. The exercise of this discretion will now need to be done in the light of the requirements in Article 6 for a fair trial. However, the Court of Human Rights, also, has made it clear that the mere fact that evidence has been obtained unlawfully does not in itself mean that it should be inadmissible. The important point from the Convention point of view is the overall fairness of the trial[77] which remains principally a matter for the national court. This returns the question to the courts exercising their section 78 discretion. The ECHR may, under Article 6, require the disclosure of evidence obtained by covert sources, for example, under the principle of equality of arms.

7.11 Closed-circuit television

Closed-circuit television (CCTV) is now the most widespread form of general surveillance. It is used by public authorities and private organisations and persons in many areas to which the public go and also on private land to which the public have no express or implied rights of access. The general justification for CCTV is the reduction of crime, the prosecution of offenders and the development of a feeling of relative safety in the public and in private landowners. The extent to which it succeeds in these objectives is disputed but it remains very popular. There is little direct legal regulation of the use of

---

[73] *Kruslin* v *France* (1990) 12 EHRR 528 and *Huvig* v *France* (1990) 12 EHRR 538, followed in *Valenzuela Contreras* v *Spain* (1999) 28 EHRR 483.
[74] *Amann* v *Switzerland* (2000) 30 EHRR 843.
[75] (1994) 78-A D&R 119.
[76] Section 17, RIPA 2000.
[77] *Schenk* v *Switzerland* (1991) 13 EHRR 242.

CCTV. Local authorities have express powers to use CCTV on any land in their area[78] and may also have implied powers in this matter. Principally, any use of CCTV must be compatible with the Data Protection Act 1998 (regarding the obtaining and disclosure of personal information) and the provisions of the Regulation of Investigatory Powers Act 2000, discussed above. The Information Commissioner, who administers the Data Protection Act, has produced a Code of Practice providing a gloss on the requirements of the 1998 Act.[79]

[78] Section 163, Criminal Justice and Public Order Act 1994.
[79] Data Protection Commissioner (2000) *Code of Practice for Users of Closed Circuit Television*. See Wadham, J. (2000) 'Remedies for Unlawful CCTV Surveillance – Part 1' *NLJ*, 4 August, 1173; '. . . Part 2', *NLJ*, 11 August, 1236.

8

The right to a fair trial

8.1 Fair trials and civil liberties issues

Without effective remedies the law is useless. At the centre of any legal system, therefore, must be a means by which legal rights can be asserted and breaches remedied through the processes of a fair trial in a court. The right to a fair trial is, itself, an important human or civil right. It pervades all those aspects of life that are covered by law and is by no means confined to the conventional subject matter of civil liberties law – in fact the bulk of fair trial issues arise in the context of ordinary criminal and civil proceedings.

Civil liberties law, with its focus on issues of privacy and political activity, raises important fair trial issues in civil, administrative and criminal contexts. Political demonstration, for example, might lead to a civil action for trespass brought by the person or organisation in possession of land used for the demonstration; the same event could lead to a judicial review in the Administrative Court against the police or some other public body in respect of their actions or inactions; likewise criminal prosecutions and trials before magistrates or the Crown Court may result. Two fair trials issues can be especially relevant in a civil liberties context. First, civil liberties disputes can often involve a complaint against a state agency such as the police or a regulatory body. At first instance this may be dealt with by some form of tribunal or internal committee which has a specific jurisdiction and which is something less than a full court. The procedures before such bodies raise issues of fairness that do not apply to the ordinary courts. Second, civil liberties disputes, relating to terrorism or surveillance for example, may involve matters involving national security or matters in respect of which a degree of secrecy may be appropriate. The extent to which the general principles on which normal fair trials are based can be abrogated in such contexts is an ongoing issue of civil liberties law.

Most of the specific issues about fair trials in a civil liberties context are dealt with in the appropriate chapters of this book as they arise. The rest of this chapter introduces the main themes on which the right to a fair trial, particularly under ECHR Article 6, is based.

8.2 Common law

The need for fair trial procedures is well recognised in the law of England and Wales. Standards, of course, change and develop over time and, from time to time, significant areas of controversy arise. The desire of the executive to demonstrate it is responding to serious crime and the threat of terrorism and the ever present drive for 'efficiency' in public services can lead to tensions with the judiciary and with some parts of public opinion. In recent years there have been arguments over matters such as the extent of jury trial,[1] the limitation on the 'right to silence'[2] and the type of trial process that is appropriate in a national security or anti-terrorism context.[3] A continuing issue involves administrative and domestic tribunals and the range of tribunals, inquiries, committees and so on which make decisions directly affecting individuals often in their relations with the state and other public bodies. These bodies are outside the main court system, though often linked to it by appeal procedures. It is important that persons affected by such bodies feel fairly treated and the need for a fair hearing applies as strongly as it does to the courts although, in the context, different rules and principles may be appropriate.[4]

There are a number of deep-rooted general principles which are part of the common law and seen as pervasive requirements of a fair procedure or trial. That the burden of proof generally lies with the prosecution in crime or claimant in civil cases, or that the standard of proof in criminal cases should be 'beyond a reasonable doubt', or that trials should normally be held in public, etc. are well established as maxims in the traditions of the law. This means that they apply generally but not absolutely. However, any departures from such principles are worthy of comment, should be convincingly justified and be clearly permitted by express legal provisions.[5]

The rules of evidence are also central to the nature and provision of a fair trial. Rules against hearsay or the admission of similar fact evidence and so on, in their complexity, exceptions and detail, embody the particular, detailed conception of fairness that applies to a trial. The duty of a court to exclude a confession obtained through oppression[6] and the discretion a court has to exclude other evidence which it would be unfair to admit, including because of the unlawful or improper way it was obtained,[7] are both of special importance in maintaining the fairness of a trial. The requirements of fairness can be highly controversial. The extent to which fairness requires a particular balance, in the detail of the matter, between defence and prosecution is a

---

[1] There has been continual pressure by governments, often in the face of independent advice, to restrict a defendant's right to choose jury trial. There are some areas, such as fraud trials, where it is suggested that juries may be incompetent and should be replaced by a more expert panel.

[2] Discussed in Chapter 4.

[3] Discussed in Chapter 18.

[4] The Tribunals and Inquiries Acts provide a statutory framework for most administrative tribunals but the detail of rules of procedure will vary. Rules need the approval of the Lord Chancellor's Department and general supervision is exercised through the Council on Tribunals. The planning system operates in terms of its own legislative regime as do tribunals set up in other contexts such as prisons, surveillance or security. Inadequacies in the statutory regime can, unless excluded, be subject to the supervisory jurisdiction of the High Court. Domestic tribunals, such as professional disciplinary bodies, can also be subject to the general fair trial requirements of the law. See Wade, Sir William and Forsyth, C.F. (2000) *Administrative Law*, 8th edn. Oxford: Oxford University Press, p. 900.

[5] Anti-terrorism law, for example, has instances of so-called 'reverse burden' defences, in which a defence requires proof of facts or intentions by a defendant. See Chapter 18.

[6] Section 76, PACE 1984.

[7] Section 78, PACE 1984.

matter of reasonable disagreement; the degree to which the complainant in a rape case can be cross examined on her recent sexual activity is an example.[8]

Requirements of fairness have also been developed by the Administrative Court and applied to a huge range of administrative bodies of various kinds.[9] The fundamental principle is that a person whose 'rights or legitimate expectations' are directly affected by the decision of a public body has a right to a fair hearing before an unbiased tribunal in respect of any dispute that may arise. To deny such a fair hearing requires exceptional justification. These rules of 'fairness', sometimes known as rules of 'natural justice', have also been applied to decisions of non-public bodies, such as trade unions or sports regulators, either as implied terms in contracts or matters of public policy. The rules of fairness are detailed, complex and context-dependent,[10] but their availability is central to the claim that fair trial procedures exist in the United Kingdom.

The concept of fair trials as a general principle brings with it the presumption that persons have access to the courts to have their claims fairly tested. English law recognises the existence of a general principle of law granting such access. This means that, normally, people should be able to argue their claim to a legal right in court and that any restrictions need to be express and ought to be carefully justified. When the Lord Chancellor, for example, produced rules of court which made it expensive for a litigant in person, not legally aided, to go to court, the High Court held the rules to be void: such restrictions would need to be expressly provided for in primary legislation.[11] Sometimes an Act of Parliament expressly states that some question decided by a body is not to be questioned in a court. The judges have generally been hostile to such provisions and have sought to oust such ouster clauses.[12] Lord Woolf, then the Master of the Rolls, has even suggested, in academic writing, that the courts might have a duty not to give effect to a statute, Parliamentary supremacy notwithstanding, if it tried to abolish judicial review generally.[13] It is now clear that if Parliament wishes to create such non-reviewable bodies, as it does seek to do in the context of the secret services, surveillance and anti-terrorism, for example, it can only do so if it uses the clearest words.[14]

8.3 Article 6 of the European Convention on Human Rights

With the coming into effect of the Human Rights Act 1998, Article 6 of the scheduled Convention rights is now an important source of law which is

---

[8] See *R v A* [2001] 3 All ER 1, which includes judicial and non-judicial references to the discussions and law on the issue.

[9] See *Ridge v Baldwin* [1964] AC 40, which may be thought to have opened the floodgates on this issue. It made clear that there was not and never had been any rule which restricted the High Court to imposing rules of fairness only on judicial bodies such as magistrates courts.

[10] For example, Wade and Forsyth, *op. cit.*, Part VI.

[11] *R v Lord Chancellor ex parte Witham* [1997] 2 All ER 779.

[12] *Anisminic Ltd v Foreign Compensation Commission* [1969] 2 AC 147. In general see Wade and Forsyth, *op. cit.*, pp. 700–14.

[13] The Rt Hon Lord Woolf of Barnes (1995) 'Droit Public – English Style', *Public Law* 57.

[14] Ouster clauses in the context of surveillance are discussed in Chapter 7; anti-terrorism in Chapter 18.

having an increasingly significant impact on domestic law. There are, however, many statements to the effect that, on issues such as fair trials, there are no significant differences between the requirements of the Convention and the common law.[15]

Article 6. Right to a fair trial

(1) In the determination of his civil rights and obligations or of any criminal charge against him, everyone is entitled to a fair and public hearing within a reasonable time by an independent and impartial tribunal established by law. Judgment shall be pronounced publicly but the press and public may be excluded from all or part of the trial in the interests of morals, public order or national security in a democratic society, where the interests of juveniles or the protection of the private life of the parties so requires, or to the extent strictly necessary in the opinion of the court in special circumstances where publicity would prejudice the interests of justice.

(2) Everyone charged with a criminal offence shall be presumed innocent until proved guilty according to law.

(3) Everyone charged with a criminal offence has the following minimum rights:

   (a) to be informed promptly, in a language which he understands and in detail, of the nature and cause of the accusation against him;

   (b) to have adequate time and facilities for the preparation of his defence;

   (c) to defend himself in person or through legal assistance of his own choosing or, if he has not sufficient means to pay for legal assistance, to be given free when the interests of justice so require;

   (d) to examine or have examined witnesses against him and to obtain the attendance and examination of witnesses on his behalf under the same conditions as witnesses against him;

   (e) to have the free assistance of an interpreter if he cannot understand or speak the language used in court.

The right to a fair trial is absolute in the sense that a trial in violation of Article 6 is unlawful. A criminal conviction, for example, should be set aside.[16] The basic guarantee is to a fair trial. What this requires involves, first, a number of express rights as identified in Article 6(1), (2) and (3). These express rights apply without any other restriction other than those, such as the exceptions to public pronouncement in Article 6(1), which are found in the article. However, the Strasbourg institutions have also identified a range of rights which can be implied from the express rights and which are manifestations of the basic guarantee to a fair trial.

An important feature of the Article 6 protection is the acceptance of the 'curative appeal' by which it is recognised that even if the procedure at first instance does not conform to Article 6 the possibility of an appeal to a court or tribunal whose procedures do so conform and which can deal with all the issues in dispute generally meets the requirements of the Article.[17]

---

[15] For example, *R v A* [2001] 3 All ER 1[54]: 'But the principles which are enshrined in [Article 6, the right to a fair trial] have for long been part of our common law', per Lord Hope.

[16] *R v Forbes* [2001] 1 All ER 686, 697 [24].

[17] For example, *R (Alconbury Developments Ltd) v Secretary of State for the Environment, Transport and the Regions* [2001] 2 All ER 929, HL; *Bryan v United Kingdom* (1995) 21 EHRR 342; *Director General of Fair Trading v Proprietary Association of Great Britain and another* [2001] NLJ 1372, CA. Cf. *Kingsley v United Kingdom* Ap. 35605/97, *The Times*, 9 January 2001.

Article 6 rights are not necessarily confined to the trial process itself. The requirement of a fair trial, particularly the need that defendants should not be disadvantaged, can mean that they are relevant to the investigation of crime. Evidence obtained by improper process may violate Article 6.[18]

8.3.1 Reasonable restrictions

The requirements of a fair trial in Article 6 can be subject to reasonable and proportionate restriction without there being a violation of the rights. The possibility of such restrictions applies especially to the implied rights. Any restriction must be for a legitimate purpose. The Court has the last word on the compatibility of restrictions with Article 6 but it gives the states a wide margin of appreciation over the need for a restriction and the means by which it is put into effect. The Court's concern is with the overall compatibility of the process with the Convention. Where restrictions have a significant effect on the rights of the defence then the Court will expect to see countervailing procedures created to minimise any detriment, and a strong conception of proportionality is applied so that if a less onerous approach could have achieved the same effect it violates the Convention not to have taken it.[19]

8.3.2 The scope of Article 6

Article 6 only applies to the determination of 'civil rights and obligations or any criminal charge'. These are 'autonomous' convention terms which are independent of how a matter is classified in domestic law. Disputes over 'civil rights and obligations', for example, exclude the determination of various political[20] and administrative rights,[21] such as the right to stand in an election, which may exist against state agencies. In respect of state benefits, such as welfare rights, the tendency in recent years has been to include disputes within the scope of Article 6. The disciplinary bodies of the professions are likely to be thought of as determining a 'civil right' rather than a criminal charge.[22] Whether 'criminal charge' is being tried will depend not just on the domestic classification of the process but also on other factors, especially the nature of the offence and the severity of any penalty.[23] Thus courts martial and the more serious forms of prison discipline have been characterised as criminal and made subject to Article 6 requirements[24] as can some so-called administrative offences.[25] Anti-social behaviour orders, however, have been held by British courts to be civil rather than criminal matters for Article 6 purposes.[26]

---

[18] *Murray* v *United Kingdom* (1996) 22 EHRR 29.
[19] For example, *Van Mechelen and others* v *The Netherlands* Ap. 21363/93; (1997) 24 EHRR 647.
[20] For example, the right to stand in an election: *Pierre-Bloch* v *France* (1998) 26 EHRR 202.
[21] For example, parental right to express a choice over schooling: *R* v *Richmond upon Thames LBC ex parte JC (a child)* (2000) *The Times*, 10 August.
[22] *R (Fleurose)* v *SFA Ltd* [2001] All ER (D) 189.
[23] *Engel* v *The Netherlands* (1976) 1 EHRR 706.
[24] For example, *Findlay* v *United Kingdom* (1997) 24 EHRR 221; *Campbell & Fell* v *United Kingdom* (1984) 7 EHRR 165.
[25] For example, traffic offences in *Mauer* v *Austria* (1998) 25 EHRR 91.
[26] *R (McCann)* v *Crown Court Manchester* [2001] 4 All ER 264.

8.3.3 Substantive rights

Delay

Significant delay, especially in criminal trials, may be a breach of the Convention. Article 5 is also involved. An arrested person is entitled to have the legality of the arrest and detention tested 'promptly' by a judicial officer such as a magistrate[27] and to be released on bail or, if not released on bail, to trial 'within a reasonable time'. A reasonable length of detention will depend on the circumstances but a delay of less than two years is unlikely to be unreasonable[28] – a much longer period than is normal under a common law system. Article 6(1), though using the same words as Article 5 and applying to both civil criminal trials, including of those on bail, nevertheless is not the governing article for those in detention and so it has been interpreted to allow longer waits for trial. Again whether there is a breach will depend upon the circumstances.[29]

Bail

Article 5(3), linked with the presumption of innocence in Article 6(2), gives rise to a strong presumption in favour of bail[30] which can only be refused on certain grounds and these must be proved by relevant evidence which will be different from the evidence on which the arrest was made. Automatic refusal of bail in respect of certain serious crimes, for example, violates the Convention. A similar presumption is found in the Bail Act 1976 but it may be that the Convention imposes a higher standard of proof of the factors on which bail can be denied.[31]

Access to the courts

To make the rights and freedoms provided for by the Convention effective, people need a right of access to the courts. Article 5(4) ECHR expressly entitles detainees to have the lawfulness of their detention speedily decided by a court which is capable of ordering their release if they have been unlawfully detained. In the United Kingdom the lawfulness of detention can be determined by a range of procedures, which include habeas corpus and, more generally, judicial review proceedings.[32]

A general right of access to the courts is implied from Article 6(1) ECHR. What is caught by this provision are administrative or legal rules which, in effect, make it impossible to go to independent courts. Similarly, Article13 ECHR requires the signatory states to provide 'effective remedies' before a

[27] Article 5(1)(3) – see Chapter 4.
[28] Starmer, K. (1999) *European Human Rights Law*. London: LAG, p. 243.
[29] For example, a delay of seven years was, in the circumstances of a complex case, acceptable in *Neumeister* v *Austria (No. 1)* (1979–80) 1 EHRR 91, while in *Robins* v *United Kingdom* (1998) 26 EHRR 527 the failure to determine a simple costs and legal aid matter within four years did amount to a breach. A nine-year delay on a civil matter was a breach in *Editions Periscope* v *France* [1992] 14 EHRR 597 as was a five-year delay on a criminal matter in *Philis* v *Greece* (1998) 25 EHRR 417.
[30] For example, *Letellier* v *France* (1991) 14 EHRR 83.
[31] Burrow, J. (2000) 'Bail and the Human Rights Act 1998–1' [2000] *NLJ* 677; '. . .–2' [2000] *NLJ* 736.
[32] For the provisions concerning detention in the context of anti-terrorism legislation see Chapter 18.

'national authority' for violations of the 'rights and freedoms set forth in this Convention'. Rules which prevent groups such as prisoners from pursuing a civil or a Convention right through legal action in the courts,[33] government rules and practices which cannot be tested in the courts on, for example, national security grounds,[34] attempts to establish tribunals whose decisions cannot be challenged in the ordinary courts and rules which restrict a right of action such as defamation on the ground that a matter is subject to absolute or qualified privilege[35] are all examples of the issues raised by the right of access to the courts. The courts to which access is an entitlement must be properly established by law and properly independent of the executive. The tribunals established to deal with surveillance, national security or anti-terrorism matters clearly raise issues in this respect.[36] Article 6 is not, however, a backdoor route to widening substantive rights. A rule of law which has the effect of exempting certain groups from an action in negligence is best seen as determining the scope of a duty of care rather than preventing access to the courts.[37]

As an implied right, access to the court is not absolute. Reasonable and proportionate restrictions may be accepted as being within a state's margin of responsibility. Some restrictions on prisoners, on minors, on adults bringing actions in respect of harms suffered as children,[38] on vexatious litigants, on persons of unsound mind and on bankrupts are examples of restrictions widely adopted by signatory states and accepted in principle by the Strasbourg institutions.[39]

Equality of arms, disclosure and public interest immunity

The principle of equality of arms requires that there should be 'fair balance' between the parties in both criminal and civil trials. This has been described as that 'each party must be afforded a reasonable opportunity to present his case – including his evidence – under conditions that do not place him at a substantial disadvantage *vis-à-vis* his opponent'.[40] Rules or procedures which have an unequal effect on one party to proceedings can be challenged on these grounds. Particular features of equality of arms include the right of parties to know and comment on the evidence of the other party and the right to disclosure of evidence by the prosecution. Equality of arms is an implied right

---

[33] *Golder* v *UK* (1979–80) 1 EHRR 524, paragraph 35; *Ashingdane* v *UK* (1985) 7 EHRR 528 (paragraph 57). One of the first declarations of incompatibility under the Human Rights Act 1998 related to provisions in the Consumer Credit Act 1974 which prevented creditor institutions from pursing their debtors in court if certain formalities had not been followed: *Wilson* v *First County Trusts Ltd* [2001] EWCA Civ 633; [2001] 3 All ER 229.

[34] For example, in a national security context, *Tinnelly & Sons* v *UK* (1998) 4 BHRC 393.

[35] *Fayed* v *United Kingdom* (1994) 18 EHRR 393.

[36] On the tribunals established to deal with surveillance matters see Chapter 7 and with anti-terrorism see Chapter 18.

[37] See *Z and others* v *United Kingdom* (2002) 34 EHRR 97 which can be contrasted with the heavily criticised *Osman* v *United Kingdom* (2000) 29 EHRR 245. In *Osman* a rule of law which prevented, on pubic policy grounds, some negligence actions against the police was considered by the Court of Human Rights to violate Article 6. In *Z* a similar rule barring negligence actions against social workers has been held not to violate Article 6.

[38] *Stubbings & others* v *United Kingdom* (1997) 23 EHRR 213.

[39] *M* v *United Kingdom* 52 D&R 269, 270.

[40] *Dombo Beheer BV* v *The Netherlands* (1994) 18 EHRR 213, paragraph 230.

and so is subject to reasonable and proportionate restrictions such as, in criminal trials, issues of national security, the protection of witnesses or secret police methods.[41] In criminal proceedings the requirement of equality of arms is reinforced by more specific rights such as, in Article 6(3)(b), the need for a defendant to have adequate time and facilities to prepare his or her defence.

The principle that the defendant should know of and be able to cross examine on the prosecution's evidence and not be denied important evidence that can assist his or her defence is important. It is, however, one which is subject to restrictions in domestic law. The restrictions that apply in a terrorist context, particularly in respect of the Special Immigration Appeals Commission, are clearly likely to be challenged in respect of Article 6 and are discussed in Chapter 18.

Parties to civil trials and defendants in criminal trials should have access to the evidence to be used in the trial. Under United Kingdom law, a civil litigant can seek an order of disclosure in order to obtain information or documents which, it is believed, will assist the case. In criminal trials the rules of disclosure are now covered by statute. The Criminal Procedure and Investigations Act 1996 places the primary duty on the prosecution to disclose any evidence which, in the opinion of the prosecution, 'might undermine the case for the prosecution against the defence'.[42] Disclosure, therefore, depends on the prosecution's discretion. The defence has a duty to disclose an outline in general terms of the defence that will be offered. There is then a secondary duty on the prosecution to disclose any further evidence which 'might be reasonably expected to assist the accused's defence' as disclosed by the defence statement.[43]

The principle of public interest immunity permits the prosecution to refuse, on public interest grounds, to disclose matters, including those which would assist the defence. This privilege applies in both a civil and a criminal context. In the past it has been highly controversial since it seemed to act as a device by which the Crown, in particular, could keep a wide a range of matters outside the scrutiny of the courts to the disadvantage of litigants. It is now accepted that it is the courts which should have the final say on the matter and that, even in the context of national security, they should not automatically accept government claims.[44] The focus, today, is on the damaging content of any document or information for which disclosure is sought and the old principle which permitted non-disclosure of types of document, such as Cabinet minutes, irrespective of whether their disclosure would actually be damaging, is now much reduced though still present.[45]

Public interest immunity is available in regard to criminal trials despite the danger of a wrongful conviction. It is justified on the grounds of the need to protect national security, police and security service procedures, informers and

---

[41] *Fitt v United Kingdom* (2000) 30 EHRR 480, 510–11; quoted in *Brown v Stott (Procurator Fiscal, Dunfermline) and others* [2001] All ER 97, 106, per Lord Bingham.

[42] Section 3, Criminal Procedure and Investigations Act 1996.

[43] Section 7, Criminal Procedure and Investigations Act 1996.

[44] *Conway v Rimmer* [1968] AC 91.

[45] *Air Canada v Secretary of State for Transport* [1983] 1 All ER 910. For a general discussion see Supperstone, M. and Coppell, J. (1997) 'A New Approach to Public Interest Immunity?', *PL* 211.

information provided in confidence. Any application for non-disclosure can be challenged by the defence[46] and the matter is determined by the trial judge. Rules of court, produced under section 19 of the Criminal Procedure and Investigations Act 1996, give the prosecution the opportunity of an *ex parte* procedure by which an application not to disclose documents or information can be made without the defence knowing what information is in issue or even knowing that an application has been made.[47]

The compatibility of public interest immunity and other restrictions on disclosure with Article 6 is complex and will depend on circumstances. Proportionate and reasonable restrictions of normal fair trial requirements are permitted if for legitimate purposes. National security or the protection of police informers may be such purposes. States have a significant margin of appreciation and it is for the domestic courts, not Strasbourg, to decide whether the grounds for non-disclosure were strictly necessary in any particular case. The job of the Court of Human Rights is to ensure that the rights of the defence to an adversarial trial in which, as far as possible, the defence case can be made on equal terms with the prosecution are maintained. The *ex parte* procedure mentioned above is clearly capable of challenge in relation to Article 6. In *Rowe and Davis* v *UK* and *Atlan* v *UK*[48] it was found to be a violation of the Convention. In these cases the lack of defence involvement at first instance was crucial. In *Fitt* v *United Kingdom* (2000)[49] on the other hand, an exercise of the *ex parte* procedure which involved the defence as far as was reasonable at first instance was held not to violate Article 6. The new procedure, in so far as it affords the defence maximum involvement, and given the acceptance in general terms of restrictions on disclosure, may be held to be compatible.[50]

Reasons
Under Article 6(1) courts should normally give reasons for their decisions.[51] Juries in criminal cases do not give reasons and it may be that, in difficult cases, some statement should be required although there is no Strasbourg reasoning to that effect. Courts and tribunals in the United Kingdom usually give reasons for their decisions;[52] however, the House of Lords has denied that there is a general principle to that effect applying to all tribunals and administrative bodies.[53] Many administrative decisions will not be within the

---

[46] Section 3(6), Criminal Procedure and Investigations Act. Disclosures which contravene provisions relating to surveillance in the Regulation of Investigatory Powers Act 2000 are also prohibited.

[47] The Crown Court (Criminal Procedure and Investigations Act 1996) (Disclosure) Rules 1997, SI 1997/698, paragraph 2.

[48] (2000) 30 EHRR 1; (2002) 34 EHRR 33 respectively.

[49] Ap. 29777/96; (2000) 30 EHRR 480.

[50] Though it should be noted that, in *Fitt* v *United Kingdom*, the Court of Human Rights divided 9 to 8. Proportionality may require that a special counsel procedure, as used in immigration cases, which allows stronger representation of the defence in *ex parte* cases, lessens the restrictions of the rights of the defence and so, on proportionality grounds, should be chosen: Enright, S. (2000) *Crime Brief NLJ*, 14 July, 1047.

[51] For example, *Hiro* v *Spain* (1995) 19 EHRR 566, paragraph 27.

[52] The Tribunals and Inquiries Act 1992 requires a large range of tribunals to give reasons on request; other statutes require reasons to be given.

[53] *R* v *Home Secretary ex parte Doody* [1994] 1 AC 531. On the duty to give reasons see Wade and Forsyth, *op. cit.*, pp. 516–20 and other places.

scope of Article 6; where, however, such bodies are determining a person's 'civil rights and obligations' or a 'criminal charge' a duty to give reasons applies. The flexibility of Article 6 may relieve bodies of this duty in certain appropriate circumstances. Reasons must be sufficient but need not involve a detailed consideration of every argument raised by the parties.[54]

Public hearing

Article 6(1) provides that civil and criminal trials should generally be in public; however, it expressly identifies a number of purposes for which it is legitimate to hold hearings in the absence of 'press and public'. Such restrictions must, however, be properly justified and proportionate. Disciplinary procedures used against prisoners, for example, can, be held in private if this is required by reason of public order or security.[55] Public hearings are fundamental to the Convention. They protect litigants from secret justice and maintain public confidence in the courts.[56] Apart from the clear cases, such as juvenile crime, hearings should be in public unless there are compelling reasons in individual cases for departing from this.

Impartiality and independence

Courts, tribunals and other bodies which determine civil rights and obligations and criminal charges need to be impartial and independent. This applies to criminal courts which should take appropriate steps if allegations of bias are made.[57] In English administrative law, the rules of fairness, or natural justice, provide appropriate remedies in respect of well founded allegations of the appearance of bias,[58] and these have been recently widened in their scope.[59] They can also apply to non-public bodies. The common law concept of bias may need adjusting for compatibility with Article 6 ECHR in order to ensure the appearance of impartiality.[60]

Independence has caused greater problems. A number of bodies and procedures have been successfully challenged on the grounds of insufficient independence from the executive and there have had to be legislative or administrative changes to remedy the problem.[61] Some major procedures, such as planning law, have avoided change only through the ultimate availability

---

[54] *Ruiz Torija v Spain* Ap. 18390/91; [1999] EHRLR 334, paragraph 29.

[55] *Campbell & Fell v United Kingdom* Ap. 7819/77; (1984) 7 EHRR 165, paragraphs 86–88

[56] *Diennet v France* Ap. 18160/91; (1996) 21 EHRR 554, paragraph 33.

[57] *Gregory v United Kingdom* (1997) 25 EHRR 577.

[58] See Wade and Forsyth, *op. cit.*, Chapter 14.

[59] See in particular *R v Bow Street Stipendiary Magistrate ex parte Pinochet Ugarte (No. 2)* [2000] 7 AC 119, which extended the types of interest which can require a judge to step down from a trial. Clarified in *Locabail (UK) Ltd v Bayfield Properties Ltd and another and other applications* [2000] 1 All ER 65 CA.

[60] *In re Medicaments and related classes of goods (2)* [2001] 1 WLR 700.

[61] For example, courts martial (*Findlay v United Kingdom* (1997) 24 EHRR 221); aspects of planning process on Guernsey (*McGonnell v United Kingdom* (2000) 8 BHRC 56); the system of temporary sheriffs in Scotland (*Starrs v Ruxton* (2000) SLT 42 HCJ); the Police Complaints Authority has been held to be insufficiently independent for the purposes of providing a remedy for unlawful police surveillance (*Khan v United Kingdom*, (2000) *The Times*, 23 May); Employment Tribunals were insufficiently independent for some disputes involving the government (*Scanfuture UK Ltd v Secretary of State for Trade and Industry* [2001] All ER (D) 296). Such rulings as these have led to statutory and administrative changes and no longer state the law.

of judicial review.[62] Tribunals, if they are too closely linked to the executive, if they follow executive guidelines or if their members' appointments need regular review, may fall foul of this requirement. The absence in England of a general administrative tribunal, with a broad jurisdiction, and the traditional preference for particular bodies with a limited jurisdiction and only partial executive autonomy, is at the root of this problem. It is in this regard that the Convention, through the Human Rights Act 1998, has had one of its most significant impacts.[63]

Criminal trials

Article 6(2) and (3) contains further express rights which relate only to criminal trials. Although express, these rights, too, are subject to reasonable and proportionate restriction. There is a huge Convention case law on the subject that specifies the rights of the defence and prosecution and the kinds of restrictions on those rights which are reasonable.[64]

The presumption of innocence in Article 6(2) is fundamental. It provides an important standard against which, for example, restrictions on the right to silence or the use of defences which appear to shift a burden of proof to the defendant are to be measured. Likewise the Court of Human Rights accepts in effect, if not in words, the criminal standard of proof beyond a reasonable doubt.[65] These matters are discussed in other places in this book.[66]

Access to a lawyer is considered to be particularly important by the Strasbourg court. This is a right inferred from Article 6(3)(b) and (c). It applies from early in a criminal investigation. In matters such as the limitations imposed on the right to silence it is the absence of a lawyer to advise that can be a major factor in the finding of a violation.[67]

A person has a right under Article 6(3)(c) of the Convention to defend him or herself. In political cases defendants may see political and financial advantages in this. This is not an absolute right and a domestic requirement for representation can be upheld.[68] The Convention does not provide an absolute right to legal aid in criminal cases; the right to legal aid is conditional on the accused's lack of means and, second, that the interests of justice require it.

---

[62] *Bryan v United Kingdom* (1995) 21 EHRR 342; *R (Alconbury Developments Ltd) v Secretary of State for the Environment, Transport and the Regions* [2001] 2 All ER 929, HL.

[63] This is predominantly a matter of administrative law and outside the scope of this book.

[64] Starmer, *op. cit.*, Part II on criminal law; Part III on civil proceedings. Harris, D., O'Boyle, M. and Warbrick, C. (1995) *Law of the European Convention on Human Rights*. London: Butterworths; see also Lester, Lord Anthony and Pannick, D. (eds) (1999) *Human Rights Law and Practice*. London: Butterworths.

[65] Starmer, *op. cit.*, p. 276.

[66] Right to silence, Chapter 4; reverse onus defences are discussed in Chapter 18.

[67] *Murray v United Kingdom* (1996) 22 EHRR 29.

[68] For example, *Croissant v Germany* (1993) 16 EHRR 135.

9

Prisoners' rights

9.1 Introduction

States claim to monopolise control over the exercise of legitimate violence and at the heart of the claim is the coerced deprivation of liberty involved in sending a convicted person to prison on the basis of law. A prisoner's civil liberty is fundamentally diminished as his or her normal freedom is restricted. The issue for civil liberties law is the extent to which restriction is necessary in order to pursue the objectives of the prison system. Different objectives may authorise different degrees of restriction. If the aim is merely to punish through detention, the necessary limitations on a prisoner's freedom within a prison may, in fact, be less than if additional purposes such as reformation, rehabilitation or, in the words of the Prison Rules for England and Wales, enabling 'a prisoner to live a useful life' are pursued. Of overriding concern for civil liberties law is that, whatever the aim of the prison system, certain basic entitlements, consistent not only with human dignity but also with the requirements of legality, are upheld for prisoners.

9.2 International law

The right of states to imprison under their laws is recognised by international law. Article 5(1)(a) ECHR legitimates the lawful deprivation of liberty for 'the lawful detention of a person after conviction by a competent court' and permits the remand in prison of persons awaiting trial in certain, limited conditions given in Article 5(1)(c). Similarly Article 9 of the International Covenant on Civil and Political Rights (ICCPR) permits deprivation of liberty 'on such grounds and in accordance with such procedure as are established by law'.[1] Neither instrument expresses restrictions on the kinds of matters for which laws can prescribe imprisonment (though both ban imprisonment merely for the non-performance of a contract) but it is obvious that states would violate their international obligations if they have laws which permit the imprisonment of a person exercising the freedoms the instruments protect.

Though permitting imprisonment, international law imposes duties on states in respect of the treatment of prisoners and the conditions under which they are detained. Article 10 ICCPR does this expressly by requiring that 'all

---

[1] Nowak, M. (1993) *U.N. Covenant on Civil and Political Rights. CCPR Commentary.* Kehl: N.P. Engel, pp. 158–82.

persons deprived of their liberty shall be treated with humanity and with respect for the inherent dignity of the human person', that the aim of any prison system should be the 'reformation and social rehabilitation of prisoners', and that, other than in exceptional circumstances, remand prisoners be segregated and treated differently from convicted prisoners and juveniles be separated from adults.[2] ECHR makes no specific reference to the treatment of prisoners but prisoners are able to seek the protection of the Convention's provisions such as those relating to inhuman and degrading treatment and punishment, freedom of expression and private life. Other international instruments also apply to the treatment of prisoners such as the United Nations Minimum Rules for the Treatment of Prisoners and, of greater direct significance for the United Kingdom, the European Committee for the Prevention of Torture and Inhuman and Degrading Treatment or Punishment[3] (a committee of the Council of Europe) and the European Prison Rules. Only the ECHR has direct effect in UK courts; the other instruments can be taken into account in the interpretation of legal obligations and can be a useful reference for prison reform campaigners.[4]

9.3 Prisons in the United Kingdom

Prisons in England and Wales[5] are under the ultimate control of the Home Secretary although, since 1993, responsibility for the day-to-day running of all prisons has been transferred to the Prison Service, an executive agency. The Home Secretary is accountable to Parliament but has only limited responsibility for matters within the control of the Prison Service. The extent to which the Home Secretary can impose policies on the Service is controversial. The Prison Service has direct responsibility for most prisons though it also has the power to contract out the running of any prison or part of a prison to a private company.[6] Each state prison is run by prison officers who are ultimately responsible to the governor who has direct statutory authority. Each prison has a Board of Visitors which has a general supervisory role in a prison and can be complained to by prisoners. Boards have been criticised for a lack of independence from the authorities and, since 1992, have lost their formal disciplinary powers. Inspections of prisons, especially in respect of treatment and conditions, are undertaken by an independent official, the Chief Inspector of Prisons.

---

[2] *Ibid.,* 183–92.

[3] Evans, M.D. and Morgan, R. (1998) *Preventing Torture: A Study of the European Convention for the Prevention of Torture and Inhuman or Degrading Treatment or Punishment.* Oxford: Oxford University Press.

[4] Livingstone, S. and Owen, T. (1999) *Prison Law,* 2nd edn. Oxford: Oxford University Press, p. 128, 3.39–3.60. On international law generally see Rodley, N.S. (1998) *The Treatment of Prisoners under International Law,* 2nd edn. Oxford: Oxford University Press.

[5] Prisons are not a reserved matter and hence are within the competence of the Scottish Parliament and executive.

[6] Under powers found in the section 84, Criminal Justice Act 1991, amended by section 96, Criminal Justice and Public Order Act 1994. Standards of treatment are contained in the contract and have been held to be confidential. Disciplinary decisions in private prisons are taken by the 'controller' who is a Crown servant and not an employee of the company. The 'director' must be approved by the Home Secretary – see Livingstone and Owen, *op. cit.,* 1.48–1.58.

Prisoners in England and Wales live lives circumscribed by rules covering most of the detail of their daily existence. The basic legal authority for the actions of the governors, the Prison Service and the private prisons is found in the Prisons Act 1952. This is, predominantly, an enabling Act and under section 47(1) the Home Secretary may issue rules, in the form of a statutory instrument, 'for the regulation and management of prisons ... and for the classification, treatment, employment, discipline and control' of prisoners. The Prison Rules are regularly updated. They also authorise the Home Secretary to make Prison Service Orders (dealing with detailed matters in the long term) and Prison Service Instructions (dealing with short-term issues). Under the purported authority of the Act, the Rules, the Orders and the Instructions and other documents, the Prison Service and governors can pursue particular policies and make particular decisions. The Prison Rules provide for a system to handle prisoners' complaints about treatment. This is predominantly by complaint to the governor or to the Board of Visitors. Prisoners also have the right to petition the Secretary of State and may complain to their MP. Following the Woolf Report a further avenue open to prisoners is to apply to the Prisons Ombudsman for an investigation, a report and an agreed remedy.

9.4 The civil rights of prisoners

Prisoners are not outlaws and are not denied civil rights and the benefit of the rule of law.

The regime outlined above is legally based and prisoners have enforceable rights.[7] The Prison Rules are made by statutory instrument and can be challenged, as a matter of public law, on the grounds that they are outside the scope of the rule-making power in section 47(1) of the Prison Act 1952.[8] The Orders and Instructions, however, are not made by statutory instrument and not directly enforceable, though it is arguable that they can in some situations create a legally enforceable legitimate expectation among prisoners.[9] They cannot increase the legal powers of the prison authorities[10] which remain based on the proper interpretation of the Act and the Rules.[11] A policy of the prison authorities on operational and management matters is open to judicial review on the grounds that it is not capable of being authorised under the proper interpretation on the Act, the Rules or other Orders and Instructions.[12]

---

[7] 'Despite the deprivation of his liberty, a prisoner remains invested with residuary rights appertaining to the nature and conduct of his incarceration': *R v Board of Visitors of Hull Prison ex parte St Germain* [1979] QB 425, 455.

[8] For example, *R v Home Department ex parte Leech* [1994] QB 198, where one of the Prison Rules authorising the censoring of prisoners' letters of inordinate length was held to be *ultra vires* the rule-making power in the Prisons Act 1952.

[9] Livingstone and Owen, *op. cit.*, p. 22.

[10] See, in general terms, *Gillick v Wisbech and West Norfolk Area Health Authority* [1986] 1 AC 112, cited Livingstone and Owen, *op. cit.*,

[11] For example, *R v Secretary of State for the Home Department ex parte Anderson* [1984] 1 QB 778, where a Standing Order preventing access to a legal advisor unless a prisoner was, at the same time, using the internal prisons complaints system was held to be *ultra vires*.

[12] *R v Deputy Governor of Parkhurst Prison and others ex parte Hague/Weldon v Home Office* [1992] 1 AC 58, 155.

In *Raymond* v *Honey* the House of Lords made it clear that prison punishment lies in the deprivation of liberty and in those restrictions which are ordinary and reasonable consequences of that deprivation. A convicted prisoner retains those civil rights which have not been expressly taken away or removed by necessary implication of the Rules etc.[13] In *R* v *Secretary of State for the Home Department ex parte Daly* (2001)[14] Lord Bingham, in the House of Lords, enumerated these as: the right of access to a court; the right of access to legal advice; and the right to communicate confidentially with a legal advisor under the seal of legal professional privilege. The courts have also recognised that prisoners retain their fundamental or human rights and this principle informs their interpretation of the Prison Rules and of the Orders and policies the Rules are capable of authorising.

> Prison authorities would only allow convicted prisoners personal access to journalists if the journalists agreed not to publish stories resulting from the meetings. This was so even though the prisoners were seeking journalistic help to pursue their case that they were unjustly convicted. The prison authorities' decision was based a policy purportedly justified by a Prison Service Standing Order made by the Home Secretary under his powers in the Prison Act 1952 and the Prison Rules.
>
> HELD (HL): in so far as the decision prevented the pursuit of claims of wrongful conviction, the policy violated the fundamental rights of prisoners which they still retained. The Standing Order was not *ultra vires* because it did not expressly authorise or require the decision. The decision was unlawful because it was not authorised by the Act, Rules or Standing Order which were to be construed to protect the fundamental rights of prisoners.
>
> *R* v *Secretary of State for the Home Department ex parte Simms and another* [1999] 3 All ER 400, HL

9.4.1 Access to the courts and privileged correspondence

A fundamental right of great importance to prisoners is the right of access to the courts. Without it prisoners would be unable to challenge both the legality of their detention in itself and also of their treatment and the conditions of detention under the rules. It is a recognised Convention right. Article 5(4) ECHR gives any one deprived of their liberty a right to have the legality of their detention speedily tested by a court. This applies to convicted prisoners pursuing their cases on appeal but it does not assist convicted prisoners who have exhausted their rights of appeal but who are pursuing a miscarriage of justice or some other legal complaint. Similarly, a right of access to the court has been inferred from Article 6 as necessary to achieve a fair trial respecting the 'determination . . . of any criminal charge'[15] but, again, it is not clear that this would apply to a claimed miscarriage of justice. If a prisoner is pursuing a 'civil right' such as an action for defamation against a prison officer,[16] then

---

[13] [1983] 1 AC 1.
[14] [2001] 3 All ER 433.
[15] *Golder* v *United Kingdom* (1979–80) 1 EHRR 524.
[16] As in *Golder* v *United Kingdom* (1979–80) 1 EHRR 524.

Article 6(1) applies and, following *Silver* v *United Kingdom* (1983)[17] this includes seeking legal advice over possible legal actions.

Linked to the right of access to the court is a prisoner's rights to correspondence under Article 8, particularly where legally privileged correspondence with legal advisors is involved. Violations of the Convention have been found where Prison Rules have permitted governors to restrict a prisoner's ability to correspond with his or her legal advisor or to write to MPs or others to complain about treatment or conditions.[18] The principle of access to the courts and the protection of the right to correspond with legal advisors has been firmly entrenched in English law.[19] The right to meet with legal advisors and pursue legal entitlements, even bypassing the official complaints system, has been upheld as a fundamental right which only clear words in primary legislation could displace.[20] Only the minimum necessary checking of correspondence to ensure it 'is in truth bona fide legal correspondence' can be authorised under the ultimate authority of the Prisons Act 1952.[21] Prisoners' correspondence can only be opened to be checked for improper enclosures or read to see whether legal privilege is being misused, if there are reasons to think that such abuse of the right to correspondence is taking place. Routine opening is unjustifiable. The policy of removing prisoners from their cells while searches and scrutiny of privileged correspondence took place was held to be illegal by the House of Lords in *R* v *Secretary of State for the Home Department ex parte Daly* (2001).[22] The impact of the Human Rights Act 1998 can be only to strengthen these protections.

9.5 Disciplinary procedures

'Legality', embodied in the Woolf Report[23] and other reforms, has meant that the system for disciplining prisoners has become less based on the discretion of prison governors and other officials. Governors have the power to punish, including by keeping a person in prison for longer than would otherwise be the case, for what, outside prison, would be ordinary crimes. Prisoners should have the same procedural protections as others when being tried for such offences. The Board of Visitors no longer has jurisdiction over formal discipline and serious alleged offences are now dealt with by the police, CPS and ordinary courts.

Under Rule 49, governors could award up to 42 'extra days' to prisoners convicted of the lesser disciplinary offences.[24] Their decisions are subject to judicial review on, for example, a failure to uphold the principles of natural

---

[17] (1983) 5 EHRR 347.
[18] For example, *Golder* v *United Kingdom* (1979–80) 1 EHRR 524; *Silver* v *United Kingdom* (1983) 5 EHRR 347; *Campbell* v *United Kingdom* (1993) 15 EHRR 137.
[19] *Raymond* v *Honey* [1983] AC 2.
[20] *R* v *Secretary of State for the Home Department ex parte Anderson* [1984] 1 QB 778.
[21] *R* v *Secretary of State for the Home Department ex parte Leech (2)* [1994] QB 198.
[22] [2001] 3 All ER 433.
[23] Woolf, LJ and Tumim, J (1991) *Prison Disturbances: April 1990*, Cm 1456. London.
[24] Prison Rules, Rule 50. The Criminal Justice Act 1992 replaced 'remission' by a system of early release. Governors' awards delay consideration of early release.

justice or fairness.[25] Many of these less serious charges will be within the definition of a 'criminal charge' as defined by Article 6 ECHR and 'natural justice' at common law will not necessarily provide the full set of entitlements required to meet Article 6. Natural justice does not, for example, grant a right to legal representation before a governor's hearing.[26] The Court of Human Rights has held that, judicial review notwithstanding, where, in effect, a governor is determining a 'criminal charge', as understood in Convention terms, Article 6 protection applies.[27] A system providing Article 6 rights to prisoners being dealt with for disciplinary offences which are also 'criminal charges' will need to be developed.

9.6 Treatment

In the past twenty years serious problems have arisen regarding the treatment regime and the conditions under which prisoners serve their sentences. Issues such as overcrowding, racism, the suicide rate, strip searching, medical facilities, facilities for disabled prisoners, limitations on educational facilities, a negative, demoralising culture and oppressive actions by prison officers have been noted by many including those with official reporting responsibilities. These include successive Chief Inspectors of Prisons who have statutory duties to report to the Home Secretary on treatment and conditions, the United Nations Human Rights Committee which has expressed serious concerns[28] and the Committee administering the European Convention on the Prevention of Torture and Inhuman or Degrading Treatment or Punishment which makes regular visits, resulting in reports, to signatory countries and which, in a series of visits to the United Kingdom, has expressed major concerns.[29]

The scope and seriousness of the Committee's concerns has diminished somewhat over the decade; similarly the Prison Service has responded to some of the Chief Inspector's criticisms. The claim at the beginning of the twenty-first century is of continuing improvement in the physical conditions under which an increasing number of prisoners serve their sentences and in the dignity they are accorded. Overcrowding remains the central problem[30] from which others flow, but this is unlikely to go away while politicians, probably with popular support, continue to encourage the use of prison punishment.

The problem is that there are few, if any, legally binding standards for prison conditions. There are none in the Prison Rules; Article 10 ICCPR, as

---

[25] *Leech* v *Deputy Governor of Parkhurst Prison/Prevot* v *Deputy Governor of Long Lartin Prison* [1988] 1 AC 533. The case followed *R* v *Board of Visitors of Hull Prison ex parte St Germain and others* [1979] 1 QB 425 which held that the decisions of Boards of Visitors were subject to judicial review and rejected the idea that there were relevant differences between Boards of Visitors and governors on the matter.

[26] *R* v *Secretary of State for the Home Department ex parte Tarrant* [1985] 1 All ER 799. (Boards of Visitors had a discretion to allow representation in certain circumstances; these principles would also apply to governors.)

[27] *Ezeh* v *United Kingdom* (2002) Ap. 39665/98; *The Times* 30 July.

[28] Klug, F., Starmer, K. and Weir, S. (1996) *The Three Pillars of Liberty*. London: Routledge, p. 307.

[29] For report of 1994 visit see: www.cpt.coe.int/en/reports; for 1997 see: www.cpt.coe.int/en/states/gbr/htm. A further visit is planned for 2001.

[30] Reports by Her Majesty's Chief Inspector of Prisons.

mentioned above, has some express requirements but these cannot be expressly enforced as legal entitlements through the courts. There are the European Prison Rules 1987 which do provide detailed minimum standards but, again, though they may be standards for adverse comment, they are not incorporated into or expressly furthered through United Kingdom law. There is reason to think that in some respects United Kingdom prison conditions fall short of these minimum standards.[31]

9.6.1 Convention rights

The Human Rights Act 1998 means that the Convention rights are now directly enforceable against the Home Department and the Prison Service. Article 3 bans 'inhuman or degrading treatment or punishment' but, until recently, has not required particularly high standards.[32] The court requires a degree of humiliation or debasement which is greater than the usual level of humiliation inherent in punishment.[33] Solitary confinement or other treatment regimes which are imposed for reasons such as security or good order and discipline are unlikely, without more, to violate Article 3.[34] The Strasbourg Court is beginning to change its position and find violations of Article 3 in the context of mentally or physically disabled prisoners and, perhaps, in respect of seriously bad treatment in overcrowded conditions.[35] Such cases do not require the applicant to prove that the state has acted in bad faith. Article 8 includes a right to develop relationships with others. However, Article 8(2) will usually justify the use of segregation regimes for proper purposes and not require the transfer of prisoners to a prison nearer home.[36] Under Article 2, the Right to Life, the state is required to take positive measures to protect the lives of prisoners and not, for example, to place persons into a treatment regime in which death is more likely than if other actions were taken;[37] also, any deaths in custody need to be properly investigated. Article 2 appears to impose a higher standard than the traditional 'reasonable care' approach found in United Kingdom law. However, the courts seem reluctant to use the Article to lay down absolute standards on matters such as whether inquiries should be in public or the degree of the involvement of relatives.[38]

9.6.2 Public law

It is hard for prisoners to challenge authorised decisions by the Prison Service as to their treatment and conditions. 'Intolerable conditions' can be challenged

---

[31] Livingstone and Owen, *op. cit.*, 3.56–3.58.
[32] For example, *Delazarus* v *UK* (1993) Ap. 17525/90.
[33] *Tyrer* v *United Kingdom* (1979–80) 2 EHRR 1
[34] For a discussion of Article 3 in relation to prison conditions and examples of case law see Starmer, K. (1999) *European Human Rights Law*. London: LAG, 16.8–16.36; Livingstone and Owen, *op. cit.*, 5.69–5.73.
[35] See Foster, S. (2001) 'Inhuman and Degrading Prison Conditions', *NLJ*, 1222, and the cases cited therein.
[36] Starmer, *op. cit.*, p. 478.
[37] *Simon-Herold* v *Austria* (1971) Ap. 4340/69.
[38] *R (Amin)* v *Secretary of State for the Home Department* [2002] EWCA Civ 390; [2002] 4 All ER 336.

through judicial review[39] though it is not clear what this standard is and whether it is more demanding than Convention standards. Neither Article 3 nor Article 8 is likely to justify a judicial challenge to good faith policy-based decisions, for example about the dispersal of a prisoner,[40] or authorised actions such as intimate bodily searches.[41] In any case the courts, in this context, could only offer a public law remedy which, although it could stop the action and declare it unlawful, will not, without more, provide compensation for harm suffered by the prisoner.

The Bill of Rights 1688 provides an entitlement not to suffer 'cruel and unusual punishment' and it has been held that this principle limits what can be done under the Prison Act 1952 and the Prison Rules.[42] A punishment needs to be both cruel and unusual.[43] Detaining a prisoner of sound mind with mentally disturbed patients might be an example.

9.6.3 Private law actions

Prisoners have pursued a range of private law remedies in the hope of more effective legal definition and protection of their rights and of better, compensatory and financial outcomes. In *R v Deputy Governor of Parkhurst and others ex parte Hague/Weldon v Home Office,*[44] Hague sought damages in respect of the deputy governor's decision to segregate him under Rule 43(1) and Weldon sought damages in respect of allegations he made of brutality by prison officers. Though the House of Lords accepted that a public law remedy was available in respect of intolerable prison conditions, a private law action for damages against the prison authorities was much harder to establish. It was necessary to establish a breach of statutory duty and the court held that nothing in either the Prison Act 1952 nor the Prison Rules was intended by Parliament to give prisoners a right of action for damages. Nor would the House of Lords sanction an action for false imprisonment in respect of authorised treatment outside the Rules. Prisoners had residual civil rights but, once lawfully imprisoned, they had no residual physical freedom which the prison authorities, so long as they acted in ways authorised by the Rules, could violate.[45] Unauthorised or unlawful action, such as the kidnapping of a prisoner by a fellow inmate, or, 'arguably', the locking of a prisoner in his cell by officers taking industrial action[46] could ground an action for false imprisonment. 'Intolerable' conditions which caused damage to the prisoner, as well as grounding a public law action, might also be the basis for an action

---

[39] *R v Deputy Governor of Parkhurst Prison and others ex parte Hague/Weldon v Home Office* [1992] 1 AC 58. The court took it to be 'sensible' that the Home Office did not challenge the court's judicial review jurisdiction to hear complaints relating to treatment of prisoners under the Prison Rules.

[40] *Togher v United Kingdom* [1998] EHRLR 627.

[41] For example, *McFeely v United Kingdom* (1981) 3 EHRR 161.

[42] *R v Secretary of State for the Home Department ex parte Herbage (No. 2)* [1987] 1 QB 1077.

[43] *Williams v Home Office (No. 2)* [1981] 1 All ER 1211.

[44] [1992] 1 AC 58.

[45] Actions by prison authorities which keep a prisoner in detention longer than the law permits can be the basis for false imprisonment: *R v Governor of Brockhill Prison, ex parte Evan (No. 2)* [2000] 4 All ER 15.

[46] *Toumia v Evans* (1999) *The Times*, April 1.

in negligence.[47] Action by a prison officer or official which is known to be unlawful or which is intended, maliciously, to harm the prisoner, could ground for an action for misfeasance in public office.[48]

9.7 Other civil and human rights

Other issues about the residual civil rights of prisoners can be briefly mentioned. These are likely to expand as the impact of the Human Rights Act 1998 is felt.

Like all patients, prisoners are owed a duty of care by medical practitioners. At one time it was accepted that the standard of care of prisoners could be lower in recognition not only of resources issues but also of the distinct purposes of the prison service.[49] Recent cases show a change in attitude so that in *Brooks* v *Home Office*,[50] for example, it was held that a pregnant prisoner was entitled to the same standard of obstetric care as if she had been at liberty. It remains unclear whether such a view is required under Article 3 ECHR where the case law is still evolving.[51]

Prisoners have the right to be married in prison.[52] A claim, involving Article 8, to found a family through artificial insemination has been rejected.[53] Prisoners have rights of religious freedom though, under Article 9 ECHR, the state may impose reasonable restrictions over both the range of services and the kinds of activities that must be permitted to a prisoner manifesting religious belief. Prisoners may have some rights of association under Article 11 such as the right not to be prevented from joining a trade union by an employer although there is no duty on the prison authorities to promote trade union membership.[54]

9.7.1 Freedom of expression

Under the Convention, prisoners have rights to freedom of expression subject to necessary and proportional restrictions under Article 10(2). Therefore absolute restrictions on, for example, access to writing materials and newspapers, and a complete ban on a prisoner sending out materials to publishers,

---

[47] *R* v *Deputy Governor of Parkhurst Prison and others ex parte Hague/Weldon* v *Home Office* [1992] 1 AC 58.

[48] For recent developments in this tort see *Three Rivers DC* v *Bank of England* [2000] 3 All ER 1, HL; for alleged malice by a police officer see *Elliott* v *Chief Constable of Wiltshire* (1996) *The Times* 5 December. The tort was said to be 'arguable' in *Toumia* v *Evans* (1999) TLR 269), mentioned above.

[49] *Knight and others* v *Home Office and another* [1990] 3 All ER 237 QBD.

[50] [1999] 2 FLR 33.

[51] Claims of inadequate medical treatment in prisons seem to be within the domain of Article 3 ECHR but must still be sufficiently serious to be a breach: *Jastrzebski* v *Poland, Commission Report*, 19 May 1998. See also *Price* v *United Kingdom* (2002) 34 EHRR 53 and *Keenan* v *United Kingdom* (2001) 33 EHRR 38.

[52] Section 1 of the Marriage Act 1983 (there is an exception for Quaker and Jewish marriages).

[53] *R (Mellor)* v *Secretary of State for the Home Department* [2001] EWCA Civ 472, [2002] QB 13.

[54] *X* v *United Kingdom* (1981) 24 D&R 57 – the prisoner was on a pre-release employment scheme; if he lost his job by anti-trade union discrimination by his employer, he would be returned to prison.

would violate Article 10. The right of prison authorities to scrutinise writings and impose restrictions on the receipt of books are, however, more likely to be capable of justification under Article 10(2).[55] Prisoners have rights, under Article 8, to correspond with journalists, subject to limited rights of the authorities to check the bona fides of such correspondence and restrictions on direct contact with the media, such as appearances on phone-in programmes, can be compatible with Article 10(2).[56] The right to pursue allegations of a miscarriage of justice by contacting journalists is protected.[57]

9.7.2 Political rights and the right to vote

Convicted prisoners are not entitled to vote. Section 3 of the Representation of the People Act 1983, as amended by the Representation of the People Act 2000, disenfranchises all convicted prisoners and those convicted of criminal offences who are detained in mental hospitals. Remand prisoners may vote and the 2000 Act facilitates this by allowing prisoners to register as resident in their prison or to declare a 'local connection' and register in respect of the place they would be living were they not detained. They can then obtain a postal vote under the more generous rules in the 2000 Act.

Denial of the right to vote might appear to be inconsistent with the basic principle that prisoners retain their civil and fundamental rights other than those necessarily implied by the deprivation of liberty. There is an issue whether the denial of votes to prisoners is compatible with Article 3 of the First Protocol ECHR. However, as discussed in Chapter 13, this right is subject to reasonable, non-arbitrary restrictions and restrictions on prisoners voting have been consistently upheld by the Commission. Early cases concerned Nazi sympathisers who had misused their political rights during the Nazi era[58] or were decided on the grounds that denying the vote to prisoners would not compromise the outcome of elections and thus the 'free expression of the opinion of the people'[59] was not undermined. Arguably these cases have weaker authority in respect of ordinary, non-political prisoners and should now be understood in the light of the Court's recognition that Article 3 guarantees individual rights to vote and stand.[60] Nevertheless an administrative refusal to allow a prisoner to vote was recently upheld in *Holland* v *Ireland* (1998)[61] and it may be hard to persuade a court to take a different view. In *R (Pearson and another)* v *Secretary of State for the Home Department*[62] the Divisional Court has held that section 3 of the Representation of the People Act 1983 is not incompatible with Article 3 of the First Protocol.[63]

---

[55] *T* v *United Kingdom* (1986) 49 D&R 5.
[56] *Bamber* v *United Kingdom* [1998] EHRLR 110.
[57] *R* v *Secretary of State for the Home Department ex parte Simms and another* [1999] 3 All ER 400, HL.
[58] For example *X* v *Netherlands* Ap. 6573/74; *X* v *Belgium* 18 D&R 250.
[59] *X* v *FRG* Ap. 2728/66 25 CofD 38; *X* v *FRG* Ap. 4984/71 43 CofD 28. In *X* v *United Kingdom* (1975) 3 D&R 165 a prisoner's claim to vote in a referendum was denied because Article 3 of the First Protocol ECHR does not cover referendum votes.
[60] *Mathieu-Mohin and Clerfayt* v *Belgium* (1987) 10 EHRR 1.
[61] *Holland* v *Ireland* (1998) Ap. 24827/94, 14 April.
[62] [2001] EWHC Admin 239 [2001] HRLR 39.
[63] 'Prisoners and the Right to Vote', *NLJ*, 20 April 2001.

9.8 Life sentences

In the United Kingdom a life sentence is mandatory for those convicted of murder and is within the discretion of judges for some other serious offences.[64] The judge may set 'the tariff', the period which must be served to meet the requirements of punishment and deterrence. The actual release date will depend upon a later judgment, not made by the judge, about whether the prisoner's release would endanger or, controversially, be unacceptable to the public. Article 5 ECHR requires that detention in prison be 'in accordance with a procedure prescribed by law' and this means that the sentence ought to be determined by independent judicial bodies acting under fair procedures.

The position of discretionary lifers was held to be incompatible with the Convention for this reason in *Weeks* v *United Kingdom*.[65] The law was changed so that the release date for discretionary lifers is determined by the Parole Board, which is independent of the Home Secretary and acts on judicial principles.

Mandatory lifers remain subject to the discretion of the Home Secretary who 'may' release a prisoner on the recommendation of the Parole Board. Release is on licence subject to recall if the conditions of the licence are broken (by committing another serious crime, for example). The obvious problem is that political and electoral considerations might influence the Home Secretary's decisions. The Home Secretary is under no obligation to release and, in the case of the most heinous crimes, may impose a 'whole life' tariff (such a case needs to be kept under review[66]). Mandatory life sentence prisoners have some rights such as to make written representations, to know the tariff period set by the trial judge and Lord Chief Justice and to be given reasons if the Home Secretary departs from that period.[67] The system remains open to challenge in Convention terms. In *Stafford* v *United Kingdom* (2002),[68] for example, the Court of Human Rights found that the system of recall violated Article 5 ECHR and the concept of the life sentence, though clearly authorised by legislation,[69] is under threat. Prisoners who were children when they committed murder are detained at Her Majesty's Pleasure. The Home Secretary has delegated his decision as to their release to the Lord Chief Justice who acts independently of the political pressures that can beset a member of the executive.

---

[64] See Livingstone and Owen, *op. cit.*, chapters 13 and 14 for a full account of the law and policy relating to the release of those serving mandatory and discretionary life sentences or who have been detained at Her Majesty's Pleasure.

[65] (1987) 10 EHRR 293.

[66] *R* v *Secretary of State for the Home Department ex parte Hindley* [1999] 2 WLR 1253. A lifelong sentence for a child offender may violate Article 3 ECHR (*Singh* v *United Kingdom* (1996) 22 EHRR 1), though is less likely to if the offender was over 18: *Ryan* v *United Kingdom* (1998) Ap. 32875/96.

[67] *R* v *Home Secretary ex parte Doody* [1994] 1 AC 531.

[68] Ap. 46295/99 (2002) 152 NLJ 880.

[69] *R (Anderson)* v *Secretary of State for the Home Department* [2001] EWCA Civ 1698, [2002] 2 WLR 1143.

Part III
Freedom of expression and
the media

10

Freedom of expression

10.1 Introduction

Freedom of expression is a recognised general principle of English law[1] and its advancement or protection can explain particular decisions or general developments in the law. It can affect the way in which the common law develops, as with defamation;[2] in interpreting statutes, the courts presume that Parliament did not intend to restrict freedom of expression more than it expressly said so, and, through judicial review, it is a principle by which the courts limit the exercise of discretion by officials.[3] The Human Rights Act 1998 turns judicial discretion into a duty. Freedom of expression, in Article 10 ECHR, is one of the scheduled Convention rights and courts must interpret Acts of Parliament, as far as possible, to achieve compatibility with it and must provide a remedy against a public authority which violates its terms. Freedom of expression is also widely found in international law such as the International Covenant on Civil and Political Rights. As well as being binding in international law, such provisions are part of the underlying influences on English courts as they develop and apply the law.

10.2 Freedom of expression as a value[4]

10.2.1 Autonomy

The concept of individual autonomy provides the most generally applicable defence of freedom of expression. Autonomous persons are ends in themselves existing for their own good and not merely as instruments for the ends and happiness of others. Autonomy requires freedom of expression because individuals are entitled to choose for themselves their goals, values and their

---

[1] Boyle, A. (1983) 'Freedom of expression as a public interest in English law', *Public Law*, 574. For a recent instance see *R v Shayler* [2002] UKHL 11; [2002] 2 All ER 477 HL, for cases justified by the 'democratic society' defence of free speech.

[2] For example, *Derbyshire County Council v Times Newspapers* [1993] AC 534. The issue is discussed in Chapter 15.

[3] In *R v Secretary of State for the Home Department ex parte Simms and another* [1999] 3 WLR 328 HL, for example, the House of Lords denied, on freedom of expression grounds, the right of the Prison Service to restrict access to journalists by prisoners who were pursuing a case of wrongful conviction.

[4] Schauer, F. (1982) *Freedom of Speech: A Philosophical Inquiry*. Cambridge: Cambridge University Press, Part 1; Barendt, E. (1987) *Freedom of Speech*. Oxford: Clarendon Press, chapter 1.

reasons for acting. The free expression of others is necessary to allow the range of possibilities to be available for persons to make their choices. It is not open to the state to restrict this choice.[5]

Such an argument justifies freedom of expression from the point of view of the hearer. Autonomy also justifies expression from the point of view of the speaker since the expression of views and opinions is an important way of asserting individual and social being. The same can be said of expressive acts which have no other purpose than delight or fun.[6] A problem with this justification is that the needs of an autonomous person extend well beyond expression. Other things such as food, warmth, housing, education and so on are necessary incidents of autonomy. Autonomy is not, therefore, a good 'speaker's interest' defence of freedom of expression. It cannot show why expression should be singled out as being of particular value, greater than other things, and needing the special protection of the law.

10.2.2 Democracy

If self-government, government based on consent and at least minimal forms of participation, is valued, then so too should be freedom of expression.[7] In a 'democratic' society the people must be able to know the arguments of those seeking power, be able to challenge those in power and be able to seek power themselves. This implies freedom of expression. It also gives reasons for valuing freedom of expression highly, since self-government means little if those currently in power can prevent the expression of contrary opinions and prejudge and limit the range of reasons and purposes relating to the common good that the people may have. Free expression justified by democracy is about maintaining the flow of information and argument on which the people can make their choices for the future development of the common good of society. It is a particular form of the hearers' interests aspect of the argument from autonomy. It is also a speakers' interests argument since free expression is a necessary incident in persons' rights of political participation.

The argument from democracy to free expression is open to objections. It must, for example, be part of a general set of arguments in favour of democracy itself rather than showing the particular worth of free expression. Otherwise, peculiarly, it would have no weight in a non-democratic society where the populace would have no grounds for arguing for a right to free expression.

Secondly, it appears to be incompatible with majority rule. If democracy means government based on the views of the majority, the majority should be able to hinder speech it finds offensive or otherwise unpalatable. The answer, of course, is that all the different conceptions of democracy, including majoritiarianism, require limits to what governments can do in the name of the people, and these limits must involve respect for free expression as an underlying principle. Different conceptions of democracy will provide different

---

[5] For example, Scanlon, T. (1972) 'A Theory of Freedom of Expression', in R. Dworkin (1977) *The Philosophy of Law*. Oxford: Oxford University Press.

[6] For example, Feldman, D. (2002) *Civil Liberties and Human Rights in England and Wales*, 2nd edn. Oxford: Oxford University Press.

[7] Meiklejohn, A. (1961) 'The First Amendment is an absolute', *Supreme Court Review*, 245.

explanations of why freedom of expression is valuable and what its core sense is. A majoritarian approach will require free speech in order that the views of the majority are regularly identified; a liberal approach will value freedom of expression as one of a parcel of fundamental rights necessary for just, limited government. Utilitarians, who justify government on the sole criteria that policies will be chosen which maximise aggregate happiness in society, must support equal rights of voting and expression if, in the calculation of aggregate happiness, each person's preference is to count the same as anybody else's. Participative conceptions of democracy support social institutions in so far as they enable self-government through providing means for people to participate in decision making. More quietist, representative theories see democracy as satisfied by regular elections in which political elites compete for votes but are otherwise free to govern as they see best. Participative and quietist views will justify and explain different views of the purpose and the scope of the kinds of expressive acts which an overriding right to free expression protects.[8]

10.2.3 Truth

The truth, whatever it is, is an absolute. The common good, the majority's will, the will of the powerful, tradition, authority and so on are not sufficient reasons to justify restricting the expression of the truth. Only freedom of expression will allow orthodoxies to be challenged, hypotheses to be asserted and tested and provisional truths, accepted until falsified, to emerge. For J.S. Mill, with whom this argument is associated,[9] freedom of speech is the condition of a robust, dynamic and progressive society in which individuals can flourish. Societies in which religious, moral, historical and scientific orthodoxies cannot be challenged are likely to be despotic and subject to decline.

The truth of the argument from truth is open to challenge. The point of the argument is to deny that the truth derives from authority (e.g. from the Bible) or is expressed in orthodoxy. The alternative is that the truth emerges from a 'marketplace of ideas' through the processes of argument and doubt. We have no reason to think that the truth emerges in this way than in any other. The argument locates the truth in those ideas and propositions which survive, for the time being, in the marketplace, yet the truth of that location is itself a mere assertion.

10.3 Free expression problems

10.3.1 Balancing

Arguments about the value of free expression are, in a legal and constitutional context, about the justification for a general background right to freedom of expression. There are a number of characteristic problems about adjudication

---

[8] See Chapter 1.
[9] Mill, J.S. (1968) 'On Liberty', in Mill, John Stuart, *Utilitarianism, Liberty and Representative Government*. London: Dent. Everyman, especially chapter 2.

of free expression issues with which the courts have to deal. The extent to which the different justifications for free expression assist the legal solution to these problems is debatable. A judicial solution to a free speech problem may presuppose a particular view of why free speech should be asserted as a fundamental value.

Typically the courts must weigh freedom of expression against other interests or claims. The latter may be either claims about the needs of the common good or claims that free expression must be balanced against some other right. The law of contempt of court[10] exemplifies both. The right to express oneself on matters that are before the courts is restricted both by the common good (protecting the integrity of the legal system) and by the rights of others (individual's rights to a fair trial). Similarly, one of the strongest dilemmas involving free expression is how to balance the right of expression with another person's right to privacy. The answers to these 'balancing' problems can be politically controversial and reflect different conceptions of the value and point of free speech. Liberals, who value individual rights and freedoms highly, will come to different answers from, say, communitarians for whom a meaningful life is dependent on being part of a community and who may, therefore, give greater weight than liberals to the protection of common interests and identities from hostile forms of expression; Conservatives, who value order and continuity in social life, may reach different conclusions as to what speech is acceptable from radicals; and so on. The courts, of course, will claim to be neutral on such matters and merely be giving effect to a positive right to free expression adopted by the community.

10.3.2 The scope of free expression

Constitutional protection may refer to 'speech' or 'expression'. 'Freedom of expression' includes more than words. It includes conduct, such as taking part in political demonstrations, and it can extend to the wearing of clothes and to expenditures of money on persuasion. It will normally include the visual arts such as painting, sculpture and film. All of these can be ways of expressing a truth or a political view and neither the argument from 'democracy' or from 'truth' will justify confining constitutional protection to words. The argument from 'autonomy' suggests an even wider scope to include any self-expressive conduct such as the visible consumption of goods. It is highly doubtful that such expressive activities need the protection of a strong right.

10.3.3 Hearers' or speakers' interests?

The question may arise whether the central point of the legal or constitutional protection of free expression is to protect the rights of the persons expressing themselves or the rights of the hearers or witnesses. Issues such as whether commercial organisations have free speech rights in respect of advertising, for example, can turn on the point. The arguments from democracy and from truth are focused on the benefit to the hearer or witness and so are tolerant of

---

[10] See Chapter 12.

commercial speech which may communicate information on which choices can be based. Justifications for free expression based on self-expression have fewer reasons to treat commercial expression like that of individuals.

10.3.4 Expression and harm

The most pressing and controversial problems relate to the balance between the right to freedom of expression and a range of community or society-based claims that certain general interests are too significant to be abused by speech and other expressive acts. Most would agree that speech which causes harm to others, by a direct and proximate incitement to violence or other harmful action, for example, can be suppressed. Similarly the suppression of noise nuisance may not be controversial so long as it is not merely an excuse for censorship.

'Harm' is a concept of uncertain proportions and a narrow conception is necessary to prevent it being used to justify widespread restriction on expression. Any alleged 'harm' needs to be proximate, in terms of time, and direct, in terms of causation, to the harms they are alleged to bring about. The advocacy of unlawful action, for example, should be tolerated at least in so far as it aims to produce reasons for doing the, perhaps harmful, unlawful action. It is for others to decide whether to accept the reasons given and to act; the advocacy is thus too remote from the harm for prosecution.

The 'harm' alleged against speech should be limited to harm to the interests of those harmed in the sense that the expressive act prevents those harmed from living their life as they will. This is an important point because it withdraws justification from the suppression of speech or other expression merely because others find what is said or done to be offensive or disgusting or that the state claims the right to enforce a particular conception of morality. It is a point that comes up in a number of free expression contexts such as racist speech, blasphemy, obscenity and laws restricting the full range of consensual sexual acts between adults.

10.3.5 Free expression and private interests

A general problem about freedom of expression is whether it is confined to protection from public authorities or whether it also extends to the exercise of private power. The fact is that the restrictions on freedom of expression most likely to have an impact on ordinary lives are those restraints that might be exerted by private employers through, for example, the contract of employment. The extent to which such restrictions can be tested against the common law's recognition of freedom of expression as a fundamental principle is unclear. The 'horizontal' effects of the Human Rights Act 1998 may mean that speech-restricting clauses in contracts will be judged against Article 10 ECHR requirements.

10.3.6 Free expression and a free press

The general arguments for freedom of expression may also be applied to justify a free media. The principle arguments for a free media are discussed in

Chapter 11. It is just worth noting that the general arguments for free expression do not necessarily justify a free media. In particular, as the courts have noted, the media exercise economic and social power and they have commercial interests which may be relevant when evaluating the public interest in a publication.

10.3.7 Free expression and positive duties

Most people have no effective means of exercising their 'right' to freedom of expression, especially in respect of speech acts aimed at influencing others. There is a general argument, sometimes found from a 'left' political stand-point, which asserts a positive duty on the state to enhance the access persons have to the media by, for example, distributing broadcast licences to reflect the diversity of political opinion or allowing a right of reply to those who oppose a position adopted in a broadcast or an article. There is little general support for this view found in the general law.

10.4 Freedom of expression and English law

The background right to freedom of expression is raised in a number of legal contexts. Decisions made in these areas indicate the strength and the limits to the recognition of freedom of expression in English law.

10.4.1 Prior restraint

Injunctions
Legal restrictions on freedom of expression can be either aimed at preventing the expression in the first place or at visiting punitive or redressive consequences on the person responsible after the event. The general policy of the law, in defamation for example, is against prior restraint. The values of freedom of expression are better served if the publication goes ahead even if it is then the subject of a legal remedy.

Remedies of prior restraint are available to protect an interest which would be irreversibly damaged if publication went ahead. Injunctions to prevent publication can be issued, if the public interest requires, to protect relation-ships of confidentiality such as between the government and its officials on national security matters,[11] to protect legal proceedings that are to decide on confidentiality and, perhaps, on simple privacy,[12] to protect a person's medical history or a company's commercial secrets, etc. The protection of rights to a fair trial and the integrity of the judicial process can also ground a prior restraint on the basis of the principles of a contempt of court.[13]

Much of the law on these matters has involved temporary injunctions which prevent publication until the final injunction is decided. A temporary

---

[11] See Chapter 16.
[12] See *Douglas* v *Hello!* [2001] 2 All ER 289, discussed in Chapter 11. Doubt has been cast on the point by a differently constituted Court of Appeal in *A* v *B Plc* [2002] 2 All ER 545.
[13] See Chapter 12.

injunction is not decided on the issue of the applicant's rights but on the degree of harm that either party will suffer if they have to wait, until after full trial, to do what they have a legal right to do. Where the issue at full trial is to be confidentiality, a temporary injunction will normally be issued. The problem is that a temporary injunction is often sufficient to make it impractical for publication to take place at all. Section 12(3) of the Human Rights Act 1998 now requires that the likelihood of winning at full trial, and hence the issues of right on which that would be decided, must be taken into account by the courts issuing temporary injunctions.[14]

Censorship and regulation

Censorship involves the submitting of intended publications to an official for approval. It has little formal existence in the United Kingdom and has been abolished for the theatre though it is retained in a limited way in respect of film since cinemas need to be licensed by local authorities and local authorities require (a matter of practice not law) that films be classified by a voluntary body, the British Board of Film Classification.[15]

Regulation of speech, on the other hand, is found as the principal form of control of the content of broadcasting in the United Kingdom. A regulatory body, under statute, lays down guidance in the form a code. The broadcasting organisations have primary responsibility to ensure the quality of the programmes and they must meet the statutory and regulatory standards laid down by the regulator.[16] The regulator deals with significant violations of the code after the event.

Seizure

Prior restraint can be effected through powers of seizure. Police and Customs officials have powers to seize indecent and obscene publications in order to prevent their distribution in the United Kingdom.[17]

10.4.2 Civil liability for publication

The law will grant a civil remedy, usually damages, in respect of a publication which is defamatory or involves a breach of legally recognised confidence and, perhaps, the invasion of privacy.[18]

10.4.3 Criminal liability for publication

The criminal law is used to punish certain forms of speech and expression. State punishment of speech acts challenges the core instance of freedom of expression and so the use of the criminal law in such areas tends to be controversial. Politically motivated speech which incites violence against the state or hate against certain social groups can involve offences such as sedition

[14] See, further, Chapter 16.
[15] See Chapter 22.
[16] See Chapter 11.
[17] See Chapter 22.
[18] See Chapter 11 on the defamation of politicians and public bodies.

or incitement to racial hatred.[19] Police discretion exercised over political demonstrations is limited by the need to recognise freedom of expression.[20] The criminal law is still available, in controversial circumstances, to protect Christianity from blasphemous abuse[21] or to protect society from indecent or obscene publications.[22] Finally the criminal law is used to uphold the authority of the judiciary and the fairness of trial through the law on contempt of court.[23]

10.4.4 Absolute or qualified privilege

Sometimes the point of the law is to protect speech or other expression from what would otherwise be civil or criminal liability. Expression thus protected is 'privileged'.

Absolute privilege is where no form of legal liability, criminal or civil, can result from the expression and the words cannot be considered by a law court. The primary examples are the absolute privilege enjoyed by Members of Parliament in so far as they are participating in debates or involved in 'proceedings in Parliament', the privilege accorded to communications between client and lawyer and the words spoken by judges in their judicial capacity.

Qualified privilege gives limited immunity from an action for defamation where the courts accept that there is a duty to publish. Qualified privilege is lost if the court finds that the publication was motivated by malice. It applies predominantly to the media.[24]

10.4.5 Promotion of free expression

Rarely there is a legal duty to provide a positive entitlement and practical opportunities to speak. This is confined to the right of election candidates to address the electors or of political parties to broadcast.[25]

10.4.6 Limits to political expression by public bodies

Impartiality is seen as an important virtue in some areas of social life. The freedom of certain persons and organisations to promote political purposes is restricted. The regulated broadcasting organisations, for example, are not allowed to editorialise and are required to exercise due impartiality.[26] Many civil servants, local government officers and police officers are severely restricted in their political actions and expressions. Publicly funded schools must be impartial in the way they deal with politically controversial matters.[27] Further and higher education institutions are under a different legal duty to uphold the principles of freedom of speech.[28]

[19] See Chapter 14.
[20] See Chapter 17.
[21] See Chapter 23.
[22] See Chapter 22.
[23] See Chapter 12.
[24] See Chapter 11.
[25] See Chapter 17.
[26] See Chapter 11.
[27] See Chapter 13.

10.5 The Human Rights Act 1998 and Article 10

Article 10 ECHR 'Freedom of expression' is a scheduled Convention right of the Human Rights Act 1998.[29] Article 10(1) prescribes a fundamental right to freedom of expression. The term is broadly defined to include some non-verbal forms of expression including pictures and dramatic displays. Commercial, artistic or pornographic[30] expressions are within its scope. Freedom of expression generally is protected as are, specifically, the freedoms to hold opinions and to receive and impart information and ideas. Article 10(1) is expressly concerned with interference by 'public authorities' and it does not, therefore, bear directly on private interferences by employers, for example. Under Article 10 states may license media organisations, even with conditions which restrict content such as political impartiality.[31] Although there is a 'right to receive ... information and ideas', the Court has not turned this into positive duties on the states to disclose information or to require media organisations, for example, to give rights of access to the public.[32]

Freedom of expression can be restricted in a manner that is compatible with Article 10(2). Article 10(2) recognises, uniquely among the Convention rights, that the exercise of the freedom involves duties and responsibilities. This understanding justifies lawful, necessary and proportionate restraints on speech for a range of purposes listed in the paragraph.[33] 'National security' and 'public safety' are relevant to the compatibility of the Convention with, for example, official secrets law;[34] the 'prevention of disorder or crime' can be relevant to surveillance[35] and public order law[36] and 'protection of health or morals' to the law on obscenity,[37] for example. 'Protecting the rights and freedoms of others' has a wide potential effect. Such purposes are also found in connection with the other Articles; Article 10(2) also includes restrictions on expression aimed at protecting the reputation of others, protecting information obtained in confidence and maintaining the authority and impartiality of the judiciary.[38]

Any restrictions must have a proper basis in law and be 'necessary in a democratic society'. The test of necessity and proportionality is very important. By use of the doctrine of margin of appreciation, the Court of Human Rights gives different degrees of protection to the different purposes of expression. Political expression, broadly defined to include general matters of public interest, is given the highest European protection against a state's restrictions; it is an essential incident in the Convention conception of a democratic society as open and tolerant. Only the most pressing social

---

[28] Section 47, Education Act (2) 1986.
[29] Article 10 is given in full in Chapter 2.
[30] See Chapter 22.
[31] See Chapter 11.
[32] See Chapter 15.
[33] See Chapter 2 for a general discussion of these terms.
[34] See Chapter 16.
[35] See Chapter 7.
[36] See Chapter 17.
[37] See Chapter 22.
[38] For a general discussion of Article 10 by the House of Lords, see *R v Shayler* [2002] UKHL 11; [2002] 2 All ER 477 HL.

necessities can justify its restriction,[39] though that may include suppression of racist speech.[40] Artistic and commercial speech are given relatively lower degrees of protection.

Though fundamental and pervasive, the right to freedom of expression is capable of being derogated from under the terms of Article 15.

Section 12 of the Human Rights Act 1998 requires the courts to give proper weight to freedom of expression when granting remedies involving freedom of expression. In particular it requires courts to consider the likely final outcome of a case before granting an interim injunction. The section does not give absolute priority to freedom of expression when weighted against other rights such as privacy[41] and it may do no more than state what is already a duty on the courts under the Act.

---

[39] See Chapter 14.
[40] See Chapter 14.
[41] *Douglas* v *Hello!* [2001] 2 All ER 289, discussed in Chapter 11.

11

The media

11.1 Introduction

'Media' refers to the different means and different types of organisation through which information and ideas about the world are made available to the public. The term includes publishers and distributors of books, magazines, journals and the daily and weekly national and local newspapers; it includes the broadcasting organisations, both public and commercially owned, who deliver their programmes by terrestrial means, or by cable or satellite. It also includes those involved with theatre, film and video and, of increasing importance, the providers of information and services on the Internet.

Generalisations about the impact of the media need to be made with great caution. From the civil liberties perspective there are three principal areas of concern. First: it is through the media that most people are likely to obtain the information and ideas about the public world, the world outside their direct experience, on which their political understanding, their intentions on voting and other forms of political activity will be grounded. This may occur directly through the content of programmes and stories, or less directly by means, for example, of the formal properties of the media (television emphasises visual experience) or through the hidden presumptions behind the selection and prioritising of material. The whole range of stories and programmes, not just news and documentaries, can affect our understanding of the world in both these direct and indirect ways. These are matters for media sociology and not for a textbook on civil liberties. The nature and extent of media influence on political understanding and behaviour is controversial and disputed. Nevertheless the media, especially the press, television and the Internet, is believed to be, actually or potentially, of great influence and for this reason, at least in the case of broadcasting, subject to regulation.

Second, is concern about media intrusions into privacy. Technological advances enables the media, especially press, magazines and television, to find out and disclose personal and intimate details about individuals and this may be inconsistent with their fundamental autonomy and right to be left alone. On the other hand the protection of privacy may be used to protect the powerful from proper investigation. The tension between privacy and freedom of expression is one of the themes of legal regulation.

Third is the issue of offensiveness. The portrayal, in particular, of sexual and violent scenes may offend against community notions of taste and decency. This matter is raised in more detail in Chapter 22, nevertheless it should not be forgotten that the portrayal of sex and violence may be making a general political point about the restraints of social morality or be a metaphor for real social or political violence.

The complexity of the concept of 'the media' is added to by the fact that, in its major forms, it is conducted by huge, often global organisations for whom a story or a representation of the world is a commodity and whose function is to make money out of selling these productions or the advertising that surrounds them. The balance between the special concern that should be given to the legal protection for political speech in the broadest sense and the fact that, thereby, special protection is given to one form of commercial commodity which is not given to others is another theme to be taken into account when considering the issues underlying media regulation. These issues will be pursued a little further in the different contexts of the law.

11.2 The media and the general law

The media is subject both to the general law and to specific forms of regulation.[1] Press and broadcasters enjoy no special exemption from the ordinary criminal law and editors, journalists, proprietors and, indeed, media corporations, can be prosecuted, if the appropriate *mens rea* is established for criminal offences such as sedition, blasphemy, incitement to racial hatred, etc., as much as any ordinary person.[2] Similarly, the media may be liable, on the same grounds as others, in civil action for breach of contract or in torts such as defamation.

Conversely, some general legislation is likely to bear most heavily on the media. The Obscene Publication Acts 1959 and 1964, for example, create offences relating to publication of obscene matter and 'publication' is wide enough to include press, broadcasting, cinema, video and, it seems, the Internet.[3] Similarly the laws on contempt of court, such as the Contempt of Court Act 1981, which create a strict liability offence for publications which are likely seriously to prejudice the outcome of trials, bear most heavily on media organisations.[4]

Although not exempted from the ordinary law the public interest in a free press is recognised. In numerous cases freedom of expression, exemplified in press freedom, has weight as a background value of the common law. In *Derbyshire County Council* v *Times Newspapers* (1993),[5] for example, the House of Lords held that an elected political body could not, in its own name, protect its reputation by an action for defamation against the media or, indeed, any person. The Lord's decision was a clear assertion of the value in a democracy, established in the common law, of free speech and a free press.[6] But while

---

[1] For more detailed discussion see, for example, Robertson, G. and Nicol, A. (1992) *Media Law*, 3rd edn. Harmondsworth: Penguin; Gibbons, T. (1998) *Regulating the Media*, 2nd edn. London: Sweet & Maxwell.
[2] See Chapter 14.
[3] See Chapter 22.
[4] See Chapter 12.
[5] [1993] AC 534.
[6] The Court of Appeal, in coming to the same conclusion, had relied more on Article 10 ECHR.

freedom of speech may be a value supporting the development of the law, the claims of the press are unlikely to support special treatment.[7] Some recent cases on qualified privilege, discussed below, show the courts acknowledging that, whatever else they may be, the media consists of ordinary commercial organisations pursing ordinary commercial objectives.[8]

11.3 The Human Rights Act 1998, Article 10 and a free media

11.3.1 Media freedom

Under the Human Rights Act 1998, media freedom may be pursued by the English courts on the basis of Article 10 ECHR, taking the Strasbourg court's jurisprudence into account. There is likely to be little difference between Article 10 and the common law.[9] Journalists and also their media companies have standing as 'victims' to bring Convention cases to Strasbourg alleging interference with their freedom of expression by public authorities.

The value of a free media is clearly recognised by the Court of Human Rights when measuring interferences against Article 10(2). The value is particularly strong in the context of political speech, broadly defined.

In *Lingens* v *Austria* (1986)[10] the press was held to be under, almost, a duty ('it is . . . incumbent on it') to impart not only information in the narrow sense but also ideas. The case dealt with political criticism of a leading politician and the importance of the press is that it 'affords the public one of the best means of discovering and forming an opinion of the ideas and attitudes of political leaders' and so can promote the kind of open political debate which is 'at the very core of the concept of a democratic society which prevails throughout the Convention'. It is, in particular, a channel of communication with politicians. Press freedom extends beyond political matters to 'other areas of public interest'.[11]

Conflict between freedom of the press and other Convention values such as privacy and fair trials are also recognised. The Court gives heavy weighting but not absolute priority to freedom of the press. In *De Haes and Gijsels* v *Belgium* (1998),[12] articles had been published in a Belgium magazine alleging bias against members of the judiciary involved in child custody cases. The Court upheld freedom of the press in so far as the matters discussed were in the public interest but would not have given Convention protection, had it been severable from the totality, to allegations about the political allegiance of one of the applicant judge's father. This was unacceptable and interfered with a legitimate right to privacy.

---

[7] *Francome* v *Mirror Group Newspapers Ltd* [1984] 1 WLR 892, 897 per Lord Donaldson, quoted Wacks, R. (1995) *Privacy and Press Freedom*, London: Blackstone Press, p. 33.
[8] *Grobbelaar* v *News Group Newspapers Ltd and another* [2001] EWCA Civ 33; [2001] 2 All ER 437.
[9] On Article 10 generally see Chapter 10.
[10] (1986) 8 EHRR 407.
[11] *Lingens* v *Austria* (1986) 8 EHRR 407, paragraphs 41 and 42. See also *Castells* v *Spain* (1992) 14 EHRR 445, paragraph 43.
[12] (1998) 25 EHRR 1

11.3.2 The media and section 6, HRA 1998

Section 6 of the Human Rights Act 1998 applies to public authorities (not defined) and to any person in so far as they are performing a 'public function'.[13] The press and television, with the exception of the BBC, is privately owned and controlled and so is unlikely to come within the definition of a public authority. It is possible to suggest that the media is performing a 'public function' in so far as it is advancing the cause of open debate in a democracy and so is within section 6(3) and directly bound by Convention rights.

As regards the BBC, the Commission of Human Rights has, in its time, never found it necessary to rule on the status of the Corporation as a public body;[14] however, the regulatory bodies, such as the Independent Television Commission, the Radio Authority and the Broadcasting Standards Commission, which are established by statute, could come within a broad definition of 'public authority'. The self-regulatory bodies such as the Advertising Standards Authority and the Press Complaints Commission are not established by statute but may come within the section 6(3) definition because they self-consciously perform a public function of regulating media content on public interest principles.

There is a danger, particularly, of designating media organisations or regulators as public authorities but also of accepting they are performing 'public functions' under the Act. Only a 'victim', as defined by Article 34 ECHR, may bring a human rights case under the HRA 1998, and Article 34 excludes public bodies. 'Public authorities' and, perhaps, persons in so far as they are exercising public functions, may be thus excluded.[15] There are strong public interest grounds for allowing media organisations to protect their freedom of expression by action in the courts and the provisions of the Act should not prohibit this.

The courts, as noted in Chapter 2, are public authorities for the purposes of HRA 1998 and so, even if the newspapers and broadcasters are not directly bound by the Convention rights, the statutes and the common law rules which do apply, such as defamation, are developed by the courts in such a way as to give some form of 'horizontal effect' to Convention rights. The early case law under the Act suggests that this is happening.[16]

Section 12 of the Human Rights Act 1998 purports in a number of ways to give added weight to freedom of expression and freedom of the press. Whether the section adds anything to the judgments that judges already are required to make is doubtful.

---

[13] See Chapter 2.

[14] See, for example, *British Broadcasting Corportion* v *United Kingdom* Ap. 25798/94; (1996) 21 EHRR CD 93; *British Broadcasting Corporation Scotland and others* v *United Kingdom* (1997) Ap. 00034324/96.

[15] The argument is developed in Oliver, D. (2000) 'The Frontiers of the State: Public Authorities and Public Functions under the Human Rights Act 1998', *Public Law*, 476.

[16] For example, *A* v *B Plc* [2002] 2 All ER 545.

11.4 The press

11.4.1 Ownership

The national and local press is owned by a relatively small number of private companies. There is no public publisher which mirrors, for example, the BBC in broadcasting. During the General Strike in 1926 the government did produce the *British Gazette* but it has been generally regarded as a pro-government propaganda sheet which vividly demonstrated the vice inherent in the public ownership of the press.

The argument for private ownership lies in the claim that anyone can establish a newspaper to promote their ideas and view of the world, and that, in a free, competitive market, no one organisation, and therefore no one view of the world, can dominate. Such assertions can be challenged on the grounds both of the huge expense involved in establishing a national newspaper and on the tendency of markets to move towards an oligopolistic or even monopolistic condition dominated by a small number of companies. British national newspapers are all commercial organisations which can only survive either by making a profit greater than the prevailing rate of interest or by being owned by very rich individuals who are prepared, for a time, to accept losses in order to promote their ideas. New entrants into the market have found it exceptionally difficult to survive and there has been a clear tendency towards monopoly. This has involved not only different newspapers being owned by the same company but also a pressure for cross-media ownership in which a media corporation owns both press and broadcasting organisations. Legislation exists to limit both mergers and cross-media ownership.[17] New legislation is proposed.[18] The rules inhibiting newspaper mergers, which are based on requiring the Secretary of State's permission if the publications of the resulting company would dominate their sector, are broadly to be retained. The ban on cross-media ownership will be retained in so far as it prevents any newspaper company from owning more than 20 per cent of an ITV 3 company but much greater freedom is proposed for media companies to buy into radio stations and Channel 5. The government believes that, in this way, it can obtain the competitive advantage from deregulation in the fast growing media world but also preserve adequate plurality in the dissemination of ideas, information and entertainment. These proposals are controversial and likely to be opposed.[19]

11.4.2 Press regulation

The principal control over press content is exercised by proprietors and editors but also, increasingly, by the directors of major corporations who need to ensure a proper level of profit from sales and advertising. There is no reason to think that a free, competitive market will necessarily produce a plural and critical press presenting the full range of reasonable ideas about the world to

---

[17] See the Fair Trading Act 1973 and the Broadcasting Acts 1990 and 1996.
[18] Department of Trade and Industry/Department of Culture, Media and Sport, Draft Communications Bill, www.communicationsbill.gov.uk – for passage through Parliament.
[19] DTI/DCMS, Draft Communications Bill, www.communicationsbill.gov.uk, chapter 9.

the reading public rather than a preponderance of broadly right-wing, non-socialist, views which will not seek to undermine either the predilections of 'press barons' or the needs of media corporations to promote consumer capitalism. A free market is also likely to cause newspapers to promote sensational stories and features which, though popular with readers, raise serious doubts about whether the press, taken as a whole, really is worth defending on the grounds of the virtues of free speech. Proponents of a free market argue, on the contrary, that only a free market can prevent media companies from all competing for the ideologically unified centre ground, thereby stifling pluralism. Some newspapers seek to protect their identity through the device of a trust which may make them less vulnerable to take-over; such newspapers can also benefit from the anti-monopoly controls that competition policy provides.[20]

Political impartiality

The press is not bound by any requirement of political impartiality and is suspected of having, from time to time, a significant influence on political issues, such as the anti-Labour Party campaigns of the 1980s, although the full extent of such influence is controversial. Content-based political restriction on the press would be hard to justify. There is no consensus on there being a major human interest or right to receive unbiased political information and any such attempt would be vulnerable to challenge under the Human Rights Act 1998 and Article 10 ECHR. No such scruples stand in the way of impartiality restrictions on the regulated broadcasting media and it is not clear why the two media should be treated so differently. The answer presumably lies on the technical limits of broadcasting, in particular the small number of wavelengths which require state distribution and hence justify licensing[21] and in the alleged greater psychological impact of broadcasting over the printed media. These justifications are weakened by the huge widening of broadcast capacity brought about by digital television and by the familiarity derived from the sheer pervasiveness of television. These, of course, are arguments for weakening the impartiality requirement on broadcasters rather than for imposing the same on the press.

Privacy

Privacy is different.[22] Here there is a generally recognised human interest and background right. Throughout the twentieth century the unregulated press has published stories which have intruded into the private lives of both public and private persons. The response of the press to concern on this matter has always been self-regulation and in 1953 the Press Council was established. It could do little in the face of the expansion of tabloid journalism. From the 1970s onwards, a continuous range of stories, often involving the Royal Family, led to a number of investigations and proposals. A range of issues have to be dealt with such as whether different standards apply as between private persons

---

[20] These points are best developed in the context of media theory and history; see, for example, Curran, J. and Seaton, J. (1997) *Power without Responsibility*, 5th edn. London: Routledge.
[21] Article 10 ECHR permits restrictions on freedom of expression by virtue of licensing broadcasting, television and cinema.
[22] Generally see Wacks, R. (1995) *Privacy and Press Freedom*, London: Blackstone Press.

and those in the public eye who may use the media to advance their interests, or the question of the extent to which the public interest can justify exposure of private life and how and by whom public interest is identified. The underlying issue is whether the press should be regulated by an independent statutory public authority or whether self-regulation remains the answer. The idea that those affected should have a civil remedy against intrusive invasions of privacy such as the use of surveillance devices was proposed by the Younger Committee[23] as far back as 1972 and, later in the 1990s, by other inquiries reporting in the light of significant technological developments.[24] Journalists can now be liable for offences under the Regulation of Investigatory Powers Act 2000 and be subject to civil action under the Protection from Harassment Act 1998.[25]

Concern at what was, for many, a contemptuous attitude towards the privacy of others shown by the press led to the investigation and report of a Departmental Committee, set up by the government and chaired by Sir David Calcutt QC. His first report in 1990[26] concluded that the Press Council needed to be replaced by a more powerful, but still self-regulating, body administering a Code of Practice produced by a committee of national and regional newspaper editors. Self-regulation was to be given one more chance. The Commission was established and its working reviewed in 1993, after a series of sensational Royal Family stories, by Calcutt in his second report.[27] Calcutt concluded that self-regulation was not working and that a statutory regulatory body, with powers to award damages and impose fines, should be established. Parliament and the government[28] preferred to stick with enhanced self-regulation. In 1997 the Code of Practice was strengthened and the Commission appointed a Privacy Commissioner to deal specifically with privacy issues. Some national newspapers also appointed their own ombudsman.

Press Complaints Commission
The Press Complaints Commission adjudicates on complaints that the press have published a story which violates the Code of Practice. Complaints can be from anyone who feels they have suffered from a breach of the Code. There is no need for complainants to give up any other legal rights they might have. The Commission has a chairman and 15 other members, a minority of whom are directly involved in newspaper and magazine publishing. The Code has sections on accuracy, privacy, harassment, discrimination and other matters concerning journalists' conduct. There is a 'public interest' provision which can justify stories which would otherwise breach the Code. The privacy provision, for example, says:

[23] *Report of the Committee on Privacy*, Cm 5012, 1972
[24] For example, National Heritage Select Committee *Fourth Report, Privacy and Media Intrusion*, July 1993; Lord Chancellor's Department Consultation Paper, Infringement of Privacy, 1993.
[25] See below.
[26] Calcutt, Sir David, QC (1990) *Report of the Committee on Privacy and Related Matters*, Cm 1102.
[27] Calcutt, Sir David, QC (1993) *Review of Press Regulation*, Cm 2135
[28] The National Heritage Select Committee, *Fourth Report, Privacy and Media Intrusion*, July 1993, recommended a reformed self-regulatory system overseen by a statutory press ombudsman; the government's response (17 July 1995, Secretary of State for the Department of National Heritage) was that the PCC should continue its work and seek to strengthen its position.

Press Complaints Commission, Code of Practice
(4) Intrusions and enquiries into an individual's private life without his or her consent, including the use of long-lens photography to take pictures of people on private property without their consent, are not generally acceptable and publication can only be justified when in the public interest . . .
(18) *The Public Interest* . . .
    (i)   detecting or exposing crime or a serious misdemeanour;
    (ii) protection of public health and safety;
    (iii) preventing the public from being misled by some statement or action of an individual or organisation
[or the newspaper to provide] full explanation . . . seeking to demonstrate how the public interest was served.

The benefits claimed for self-regulation are that the regulator has a better understanding of the workings of the press and of the significance of the stories they publish and that the press will be happier to conform to the rulings of their peers to which they have voluntarily consented rather than those of some statutory body imposed upon them. The difficulty is that the regulator will be too sensitive to the interests of the press at the expense of the complainant. Particular concerns with the Press Complaints Commission relate to the weakness of the remedies they can impose: their principle power is to require a newspaper to publish its adjudication in a suitably prominent place. Though they can give general advice and warnings, the Commission are unable to act in advance on individual cases to prevent publication, a matter that can be relevant where privacy and confidentiality are in issue. This weakness has been noted by the courts[29] who may issue an injunction. The grounds for an injunction are much more limited than breach of the Code and going to court a more complicated and potentially expensive business than a complaint to the PCC.

The Press Complaints Commission's decisions are amenable to judicial review in principle and the Commission and courts accept that it is arguably a public authority for the purposes of section 6 of the Human Rights Act 1998 and so directly bound by Articles 8 and 10 of Schedule 1.[30] However, the principle of deference[31] applies in that the courts recognise the Commission is best placed to decide what the Code requires and whether it has been breached in a particular case. An application for judicial review, including on human rights grounds, is likely to be refused other than in exceptional cases[32] so applicants who are disappointed by Commission decisions are unlikely to get much help from the courts unless clear violations of legal rights are in issue.

---

[29] *Venables and another v News Group Newspapers Ltd and others* [2001] 1 All ER 908, paragraph 96. The claimants, who, as children, had murdered a small child and had been subject to a controversially early release, succeeded in obtaining an injunction preventing their identification by the press on the grounds that the injunction was necessary to protect their right to life.

[30] *R (Ford) v Press Complaints Commission* [2001] EWHC Admin 683; [2002] EMLR 5, following *R v Press Complaints Commission ex parte Stewart-Brady* [1997] EMLR 185. See Crown, G. (1997) 'Judicial Review and Press Complaints', 147 *NLJ* 8.

[31] See Chapter 2.

[32] *R (Ford) v Press Complaints Commission* [2001] EWHC Admin 683; [2002] EMLR 5. A similar deference to the Commission and the sense that the role of the Court is to police the boundaries can be found in *A v B Plc* [2002] 2 All ER 545.

The ability of the Press Complaints Commission to secure acceptable standards, particularly regarding the protection of privacy, remains controversial and contingent on the Commission's response to particular stories as they arise. Pressure for a statutory body has, by the early twenty-first century, diminished and the political influence of the press is such that any government is unlikely to antagonise it by setting one up. An issue of continuing importance is the need to restrain the press from sensational reporting of serious crimes which may prejudice the outcome of resulting criminal trials. Press treatment of the murder of two children in Cambridgeshire in August 2002 led to critical comments from the coroner. Payments to witnesses is another serious issue, though the government has left this with the Commission.

11.4.3 Press advertising

Press advertising is regulated by another voluntary body, the Advertising Standards Authority[33] which administers a Code of Practice. Advertisements must be 'legal, decent, honest and truthful'. There are no direct restraints on political advertising in the press by, for example, political parties, companies or trade unions seeking to influence elections or political controversies. This is in stark contrast with broadcasting. The Authority exempts party political advertising, such as poster campaigns during elections, from the provisions of the Code.[34] However, politically controversial advertisements by pressure groups may be banned by the Authority on the grounds, for example, that they are misleading. The decisions of the Authority are subject to judicial review and the authority is arguably a public authority under the Human Rights Act 1998, but, as with the Press Complaints Commission, the Administrative Court is likely to defer to decisions clearly within the Commission's jurisdiction and which do not affect recognised legal rights. Advertisers making a political point, however, may be able to invoke not only rights under the Human Rights Act 1998 but also a fundamental common law right to be protected from censorship on, in particular, 'decency' grounds. In *R (Pro-Life Alliance)* v *British Broadcasting Corporation* (2002)[35] the Court of Appeal gave a strongly worded defence of freedom of speech against the BBC's refusal to show a party political broadcast on taste and decency grounds.[36] Though the context is different for press and poster advertisement, this decision is likely to influence the Authority and be a weapon for those whose advertisements are banned.

---

[33] Lawson, R. (2001) 'Challenging the Advertising Standards Authority', *NLJ*, 13 April, 526–7.
[34] That is, advertising whose principal function 'is to influence voters in local, regional, national or international elections or referendums'; public service advertisements are still covered by the Code: *The British Codes of Advertising and Sales Promotion*, paragraphs 12.1 and 12.2.
[35] [2002] EWCA Civ 297; [2002] 2 All ER 756.
[36] See Chapter 13.

11.5 Broadcasting

11.5.1 Licensing and regulation

Broadcasting is treated very differently from the press. It is subject to state licensing and regulation, including content regulation. Licensing derives from the restricted availability of wavelengths which requires the distribution among broadcasters on principles ultimately derived from international agreement. It also reflects a deep-seated belief in the power of the medium as a purveyor of information and meaning about the political and social world and from its unmediated, visible and audible, presence in people's homes. The 'digital revolution' and other technological developments such as international satellite broadcasting and the Internet may mean that both the point of licensing and the ability to give it effect may be lost and that states will have to rely more and more on international agreements which may limit the terms that states can impose on broadcasters. Article 10 ECHR expressly permits states to restrict broadcasting opportunities by licensing[37] and, at times, the Court of Human Rights has seemed to accept questionable content restrictions on the grounds that they are reasonable licence terms.[38]

BBC

The British Broadcasting Corporation provides a comprehensive television and radio service throughout the United Kingdom with significant regional and national variations. Its formal claim to independence is based on its being constituted by Royal Charter rather than Act of Parliament. It broadcasts under a licence granted by the government and an agreement is attached to the licence which contains various terms and conditions. The BBC may also, from time to time, set out its own self-denying conditions such as its original commitment to political impartiality.[39] The BBC is both regulator and broadcaster. The Board of Governors have ultimate, supervisory responsibility for the public service the Corporation provides. Primary control over content, however, rests with the Director General and the managers and producers employed directly or by contract with the Corporation.

ITV

Independent, commercial broadcasting in the United Kingdom is regulated by the Independent Television Commission (ITC), the Welsh Authority[40] and the Radio Authority (RA). The Commission and Radio Authority are established by the Broadcasting Act 1990. They allocate broadcasting franchises to broadcasting companies. The ITC allocates the franchises to the Independent Television companies who enjoy a monopoly of commercial terrestrial broadcasting in their area; it also regulates cable television and those satellite stations which are rebroadcast or receive material from the United Kingdom.

---

[37] *Groppera Radio AG* v *Switzerland* (1990) 12 EHRR 321.
[38] See: *Autronic* v *AG* v *Switzerland* (1990) 12 EHRR 485.
[39] First expressly given in a letter from the Chairman of the Board of Governors to the Postmaster General, then as a resolution of the Board of Governors (Boyle, A.E. (1986) 'Political Broadcasting, Fairness and Administrative Law', *Public Law*, 562, 567, n. 24.)
[40] Which regulates SC4 Wales.

Digital terrestrial broadcasting by commercial companies is also within the Commission's remit.[41]

The ITC and RA have duties to regulate the content of programmes. This is a supervisory duty to 'do all that they can to secure' compliance with the provisions as to content, such as good taste, decency and due impartiality, in the Broadcasting Act 1990. The duty also relates to television advertising. The Commission has produced a Programme Code with reference to which complaints about programmes can be adjudicated. Broadcasters who permit serious breaches of the Code can suffer various penalties such as being required to provide on-screen corrections; only in extreme cases will the Commission revoke a licence.

Some foreign-based satellite broadcasting and, of course, the Internet, are not subject to formal regulation by the ITC. Regulation will need to be based on international agreement. The United Kingdom is bound by the European Union Directive on Transfrontier Television (89/552/EEC) for a service licensed by another EU state, and UK law must not discriminate against such services.

Ofcom
The government intends to introduce a single regulator, the Office of Communications (Ofcom), for the media and communications industries.[42] It will have a limited role in regulating the BBC thus bringing that organisation closer into line with commercial broadcasters. Ofcom will take over the functions of the Independent Television Commission, the Radio Authority, the Broadcasting Standards Commission, the Office of Telecommunications and the Radio Communications Agency. The new body will be independent but will work closely with both the Department of Trade and Industry and the Department of Culture, Media and Sport. A 'light touch' regime is promised with a greater emphasis on self-regulation. However, basic programme standards will be applied to all broadcasters through the production of Codes and these are likely to retain the current commitment to accurate and impartial news services, overall political impartiality in programme making and the ban on political advertising.[43]

11.5.2 Content

Direct control by government
The institutions of the BBC and ITC have, as one of their principal aims, the establishment of independence and the distancing of broadcasters from government. In a liberal society the idea of the direct control of broadcasting by government is anathema and a major sign of an authoritarian society. Nevertheless section 10(3) of the Broadcasting Act 1990, with a similar provision in the Licence and Agreement with the BBC,[44] empowers a government minister to prevent certain matters from being broadcast.

---

[41] By virtue of the Broadcasting Act 1996.
[42] It may begin work in 2003.
[43] DTI/DCMS, *Draft Communications Bill*, www.communicationsbill.gov.uk, chapter 8, also chapters 3 and 5. The bill was introduced in session 2002–3.
[44] BBC Agreement, section 8.2.

Broadcasting Act 1990

10 (3) The Secretary of State may at any time by notice require the Commission to direct the holders of any licences specified in the notice to refrain from including in the programmes included in their licensed services any matter or classes of matter specified in the notice; and it shall be the duty of the Commission to comply with the notice.

This apparently unfettered power has been used sparingly. Its most controversial exercise was the banning of the broadcast of direct speech by members or representatives of various political groups in Northern Ireland identified by the government as promoters or defenders of terrorist violence. The ban was challenged in the courts but the House of Lords[45] was only prepared to review a minister's decision for irrationality, a severe test, which would not apply if the minister had considered relevant issues and had proper public interest grounds for the order. Section 6 of the Human Rights Act 1998 will require the courts to measure any ministerial notice, as the act of a public authority, against Schedule 1, Article 10.

Programme standards

Government clearly retains a close interest in broadcasting but, apart from the provision just mentioned, can only control content indirectly. The government, through legislation and the BBC Licence and Agreement, sets the context and basic conditions under which the broadcasters operate; it also appoints the Board of Governors of the BBC and the members of the Independent Television Commission, and it exercises informal influences and pressures.[46]

Primary control over content lies with the broadcasters. Section 6 of the Broadcasting Act 1990 requires the ITC (similar provisions apply to the BBC through the Licence and Agreement) to do all it can to ensure that programmes do not 'offend against good taste or decency', 'encourage or incite to crime or ... lead to disorder or to be offensive to public feeling'; proper care must be taken to protect the religious susceptibilities of viewers. Of special significance in a civil liberties context is the requirement that 'due impartiality is preserved on the part of the person providing the service as respects matters of political or industrial controversy or relating to current public policy'.[47] Section 6 of the Broadcasting Act 1990 is intended for repeal by the draft Communications Bill, though some sense of underlying programme standards is to be retained, and so the value of 'due impartiality', other than in news broadcasting, will depend on Ofcom. Impartiality in news programmes provided by the main broadcasters will still, it seems, be a direct legal requirement.[48]

Programme standards are potentially controversial matters. Good taste, decency and offensiveness involve culturally specific judgments which are

---

[45] *R v Home Secretary ex parte Brind* [1991] 1 AC 696.

[46] Ministers who directly comment on programmes are likely to be criticised in the press, as were various ministers who, in 2001, made critical comments on a *Brass Tacks* programme satirising the media's treatment of 'paedaphilia'.

[47] Section 6(1)(c), Broadcasting Act 1990. The news must be presented with 'due accuracy and impartiality' (s.6(1)(b)) and s.6(5) and (6) contain further legal requirements about how the Commission should deal with due impartiality).

[48] See DTI/DCMS, *Draft Communications Bill*, www.communicationsbill.gov.uk, chapter 8, 8.2.9.2.

likely to leave some sections of the viewing public unsatisfied and complaining. Freedom of expression, as a Convention right, extends to unpopular and offensive ideas, though, on moral (sexual) matters, as distinct from political and public issues, the Convention has been interpreted in a way which is tolerant of state restriction.

Political impartiality

'Due impartiality' has engendered a wide-ranging debate.[49] Supporters argue that it is necessary to the public service remit of television and an antidote to the political partiality of the press. At its strongest due impartiality does not mean a bland neutrality on all issues but it embodies a positive, democratic, value in favour of seeking out and bringing issues in a changing world before the public and so encouraging an informed and engaged citizenry.[50] This conception of impartiality aims to prevent the domination of the political agenda by economically powerful forces and to provide a full range of reasons for actions that citizens may choose between. Opponents of due impartiality believe that political choice and openness is best obtained by allowing a plurality of broadcasters to put forward their messages uninfluenced by the state thus leaving viewers to choose the station most amenable to their political taste. The state, by this critical account, is necessarily over-paternalistic and its broadcasters become the definers and guardians of the limits of what can count as reasonable ideas for citizens to hold. Impartiality, for the critics, is inconsistent with the diversity of conceptions of the good and of forms of political activity found in a modern multicultural society and becomes no more than the defence of the established order.[51] There is always criticism, both from academics and politicians, of media bias, both about the angle of particular stories or about more systematic, general orientation towards an issue.[52] Such criticisms do not necessarily oppose, but may seek to uphold, the notion of impartiality.

An element of due impartiality is that a number of types of organisation are expressly disqualified from holding a television licence from the ITC.[53] These include political parties, religious bodies (subject to special exemption), local authorities and (for general broadcasting) many other public authorities. The new legislation is likely to end or at least moderate some of these restrictions.

---

[49] See, for example, Gibbons, T. (1998) *Regulating the Media*, 2nd edn. London: Sweet & Maxwell, pp. 94–125; Barendt, E. (1998) 'Judging the Media: Impartiality and Broadcasting', in Sector, J. (ed.), *Politics and the Media Harlots and Prerogatives at the Turn of the Millenium*. London: Blackwell; Davis, H. (2000) *Political Freedom* London: Continuum, ch. 10, esp. pp. 269–73.

[50] Annan, Lord (1977) *Report of the Committee on the Future of Broadcasting*, Cm 6753. London: HMSO, section 17.

[51] See, for example, Goldberg, D., Prosser, T. and Verhulst, S. (eds) (1998) *Regulating the Changing Media: A Comparative Study*. Oxford: Clarendon Press, p. 16. The Annan Report, *op. cit.*, reinforced this view by seeming to suggest that part of the duty of impartiality was for broadcasters to uphold Parliamentary democracy and give a best case defence to government and establishment views: Annan Report, 17.9.

[52] For example, the criticisms of the Glasgow Media Group about the presentation of economic news in the 1980s. For criticism see McNair, B. (1996) *News and Journalism in the UK*, 2nd edn. London: Routledge. Politicians' criticisms can be found on the ITC website. For other examples see Davis, *op. cit.*, p. 290, n. 18.

[53] Broadcasting Act 1990, Schedule 2, Part II 1(1)(d) and (e)–(j); see also s. 143, Broadcasting Act 1996.

Neither the BBC nor broadcasters regulated by the ITC are able to editorialise in the sense of promoting a particular point of view on political matters.[54] Ultimate responsibility lies with the Governors of the BBC and the Commission, though primary responsibility is with the broadcasters. There have been times when the BBC governors have intervened prior to a broadcast such as preventing the broadcast of a documentary on the lives of some of Northern Ireland's paramilitary leaders. This was highly controversial and, for critics, the Governors' concept of impartiality seemed to be rather close to the censorious views of the government.

Due impartiality expressly does not mean that the broadcasters need be neutral on fundamental values[55] and these might include a preference for democratic procedures over authoritarian societies or opposition to racism. The BBC has stated that it is not 'neutral as between truth and untruth, justice and injustice, freedom and slavery, compassion and cruelty, tolerance and intolerance'.[56] There is, of course, little consensus, other than at a very general, truistic, level, of what counts as fundamental values and the danger of this position is that it may inhibit the reasonable discussion of fundamental values and the proper reporting and understanding of 'extreme' or radical politics.[57]

Programme standards, including due impartiality, are given their most precise effect by means of guidance codes that both the BBC and the ITC are required to produce.[58] These codes will be taken over by Ofcom under the terms of the proposed legislation. The BBC's Producer Guidelines is a code to be followed by its producers and programme-makers. The ITC Programme Code is both guidance to the broadcasters the Commission regulates and a set of standards for the adjudication of complaints. Both the Guidelines and Code have significant sections devoted to due impartiality much of which embody specific provisions in the Licence and Agreement and the current Act. It is accepted that due impartiality in news and current affairs does not require the mechanical reporting of every known view on a controversial subject but can explore an issue in a selective way if the context permits. Due impartiality is not required in every programme but can be achieved over a series of programmes. Serious political controversy does require the presentation of all principal viewpoints in each programme, however.[59] The Guidelines in particular warn broadcasters against the possibility of pressure being exerted on them by politicians.

Judicial review
Complaints about due impartiality, from political parties for example, are made in the first place, to the broadcasters. The BBC deals with such complaints through its own internal procedures. Complaints about indepen-

---

[54] BBC Licence and Agreement, Cl. 5.1(c); s.6(4), Broadcasting Act 1990.
[55] Section 6(6) Broadcasting Act 1990; BBC Licence and Agreement, Cl. 5.5(d)(ii).
[56] BBC, *Annual Report and Handbook 1989*. London: BBC, p. 184. On institutional opposition to political violence see comments by Lord Donaldson and McCowan LJ in *R v Home Secretary ex parte Brind* [1990] 1 All ER 469, 481, 488.
[57] As may have happened in the BBC's reporting of the troubles in Northern Ireland during the 1970s; see Annan, Lord (1977) *Report of the Committee on the Future of Broadcasting*, Cm 6753. London: HMSO, section 17.12.
[58] For example, s. 6(1)(b), Broadcasting Act 1990 (proposed for repeal).
[59] For a full discussion see Gibbons, *op. cit.*, chapter 3, E.

dent television can also be sent to the ITC which will adjudicate. Dissatisfaction with the results may involve the courts, but there are great difficulties facing a complainant. Politicians or members of the public will normally only be able to challenge a broadcasting decision by way of judicial review. This is not available against private companies such as the ITV companies but is available against the Commission, a public authority exercising statutory powers. Despite early doubts,[60] the BBC now takes the view that it is legally bound by the duty of due impartiality.[61]

The standing of a complainant to bring judicial review can be a difficulty, although English law takes a permissive approach to any applicant with a well founded case and sufficient resources to present it effectively.

There are also significant difficulties of substance in trying to challenge a broadcast regulator in the courts. First, the duty, at least that imposed by the Act on the ITC, is only to 'do all they can to secure' that the broadcasters are kept in line and breach of such a subjective duty may be hard to show. Secondly, 'due impartiality' (the same applies to taste and decency) is so contestable a value that the courts are likely to find it a non-justiciable matter requiring deference to the broadcaster.[62] There have been occasional successes in the Scottish courts. For instance, an interim injunction was obtained to prevent the broadcasting in Scotland of a UK-wide interview with the Prime Minister, three days before Scottish local elections.[63] As suggested below, the courts find it easier to adjudicate in the context of election broadcasting.

Political broadcasting

The influence of broadcasting, especially television, on political opinions and voting habits is thought to be considerable although the claim that an election can be won on political advertising alone is subject to some major examples to the contrary. The danger with political advertising is that rich and powerful individuals or groups can, by buying airtime, have a major effect on the political agenda and undermine the competition between the major parties. The argument is that political parties, assuming they are broadly democratic and that they are open to all to join and influence, should be protected as the dominant players in elections. The broad position in the United Kingdom is that political parties cannot advertise on television or radio but enjoy rights to free airtime: party election or party political broadcasts. These matters are fully discussed in Chapter 13.

[60] *R* v *Lynch* [1983] NI 193.
[61] This was accepted by the BBC in *Houston* v *BBC* (1995) SLT 1305.
[62] See Munro, C. (1996) '*SNP* v *BBC* round two, 146 NLJ 1433; *SNP* v *Scottish Television and Grampian TV* (1997) 147 NLJ 528. The ITC's predecessor, the Independent Broadcasting Authority was successfully challenged on the taste and decency issue but only to require a viewing by the Authority, so that it would exercise its judgment. The power to preview programmes is not enjoyed by the ITC: *Attorney General ex rel McWhirter* v *IBA* [1973] 1 QB 629; cf *R* v *IBA ex parte Whitehouse* (1985) *The Times*, 4 April.
[63] *Houston* v *BBC* (1995) SLT 1305 (Munro, C. (1996) 'The Banned Broadcasting Corporation', 146 NLJ 1433). See also *Wilson* v *IBA* [1979] SC 351 where an interim injunction was issued on the grounds of an arguable breach of the impartiality requirement when the coverage given to the referendum debate in Scotland would have given the No campaign three times as much coverage as the Yes.

11.5.3 Broadcasting complaints

Broadcasting Standards Commission

Individuals and organisations may wish to complain about their treatment by a broadcaster or about broadcast standards, particularly the portrayal of sex and violence. The Broadcasting Act 1996 established the Broadcasting Standards Commission by merging the Broadcasting Standards Council which had advised on standards and the Broadcasting Complaints Commission which had adjudicated on complaints about individual treatment. The possibility for overlap with the content-orientated regulatory activities of the ITC is one of the reasons why the draft Communications Bill 2002 proposes that the work of the BSC , along with the ITC and other regulators, should be taken over by Ofcom.

In its adjudicative role, the Broadcasting Standards Commission deals with complaints about 'unjust or unfair' treatment. Any complaints must be based on the breach of one of the Codes the Commission has produced, one of which relates to fairness and privacy, the other to standards. Complaints are usually about an individual's treatment in a single programme. The Commission adjudicates on such complaints and, in relation to a successful complaint of a breach of the Fairness and Privacy Code, can compel the broadcasting of a summary of both the complaint and the adjudication. Fairness and privacy in this context are not legal rights and so the Commission is able to provide a remedy where an action in the courts would not be appropriate.

If the Commission acts outside its jurisdiction, an application for judicial review is possible. Complaints aimed at general broadcasting policy rather than individual treatment have raised jurisdictional issues.

> David Owen, one the leaders of the SDP/Liberal Alliance, complained to the Broadcasting Complaints Commission that it was receiving less coverage in news and current affairs programmes than was warranted by its level of support in the country. The Commission declined jurisdiction to hear such a general complaint because it related to broadcasting policy rather than individual treatment. On judicial review of this decision, the Court of Appeal held that the Commission did have jurisdiction to hear such a complaint. However, the Court also supported the Commission's statement that, even if it did have jurisdiction, it would decline the case because it was ill equipped to decide between different conceptions of political fairness and impartiality. This was a matter for broadcasters. In the Court's view a direct challenge to the statutory duty of the broadcasters was the proper procedure.
> *R* v *Broadcasting Complaints Commission ex parte Owen* [1985] 2 All ER 522

Public interest groups or political parties may also have difficulties in establishing that they have standing to bring a complaint to the Commission.

> The National Council for One Parent Families complained successfully to the Commission about the portrayal of single mothers on benefit by a BBC programme. The BSC found that the programme was unfair and unjust on several points but this judgment was set aside on judicial review. The courts, largely on freedom of the press grounds, agreed with the BBC that the National Council did not have sufficient standing to bring a complaint to the BSC.
> *R* v *BCC ex parte BBC* (1995) 7 Admin LR 575

The BSC is, presumably, a public authority under the Human Rights Act 1998 and so will need to adhere to Convention standards of privacy and freedom of expression. Both these Convention rights are, of course, restrictable. The doctrine of deference, applied by the courts to Commission decisions, is likely to apply as it does to the Press Complaints Commission and it will be only in the rarest of cases that the courts will substitute their view for that of the Commission.

Prior to the Human Rights Act 1998 the courts have tended to accept the Commission's own conception of privacy.[64] The point is that this may be more intense than the background, legal, conception of privacy required by the Convention.

> D. Co. Ltd complained that covert filming by BBC TV was an 'unwarranted infringement of privacy' in terms of s.110(1), Broadcasting Act 1996. The Broadcasting Standards Commission upheld the complaint. On judicial review, sought by the BBC, the judge held that the privacy provision in the Act did not apply to companies and that the surreptitious filming of an event in public, such as sales in a shop, could not be an invasion of privacy. The Commission appealed. (The Human Rights Act 1998 was not in force at the time.)
>
> HELD: the Broadcasting Act 1996 did apply to companies and the Commission's approach was well within its discretion. Privacy in the context of the Broadcasting Act 1996 (i.e. in the Commission's Codes) was not necessarily the same as under Article 8 ECHR.
>
> *R v BSC ex parte BBC (Liberty intervening)* [2000] 3 All ER 989

In the case, the Convention view on the rights of companies to privacy (a matter on which there is doubt) could not be used to reduce the protection for privacy offered under the Broadcasting Act 1996, not withstanding the coming into force of the Human Rights Act 1998. Lord Woolf MR (as he then was) suggested that where greater protection to privacy is available under domestic legislation, that fact implies that the legislation 'may well be compatible with ECHR rights'. Lord Woolf's suggestion must depend, however, on context. The domestic law may, for example, give too much weight to one value, say privacy, at the expense of another, say freedom of expression. If the Convention gives a different weighting to these values than under domestic law, then a legal challenge under the Act is appropriate and the courts would be wrong simply to uphold the domestic law. Similar issues may arise on the question of standing. In the National Council for One Parent Families case, mentioned above, the court departed from the more generous position of the BSC. One reason accepted by the court was that it was bound to apply the more restrictive approach to standing found under the Convention, where the 'victim' test makes it harder for pressure groups to bring cases. Lord Wolfe's suggestion provides an argument for the Commission's more generous approach to standing to be permitted in cases brought under the Broadcasting Act.

---

[64] *R v BCC ex parte Granada TV Ltd* [1995] COD 207.

11.6 Free media and the law

The law recognises the public interest in a free media in a number of legal contexts. These are considered in detail in the chapters to which they relate. For example, the media enjoys limited protection from prosecution in respect of the publication of information obtained in breach of the Official Secrets Act 1989,[65] 'journalistic material' can only be compulsorily disclosed under the provisions of the Police and Criminal Evidence Act 1984 on the basis of a hearing before a judge rather than the *ex parte* issuing of a warrant from a magistrate,[66] and journalistic material also enjoys certain exemptions under data protection legislation.[67]

In other legal contexts, however, no special protection is allowed to journalists. For example, journalists have no special, public interest defence in respect of an unlawful telephone interception or unlawful acts of surveillance under the Regulation of Investigatory Powers Act 2000, even though disclosures genuinely in the public interest might result. This is, perhaps, hardly surprising since journalists are not subject to the general controls and disciplined structures that may be essential if there are to be adequate protection for surveillance targets as required by the ECHR.

11.6.1 Privacy and breach of confidence

The availability, nature and scope of a legal remedy may require a judgment by the courts of the weight to be given to the public interest in a free media weighed against a person's interest in protecting their privacy. If, for example, a civil action is taken against a journalist for trespass, any discretionary elements in the remedy, such as whether to grant an injunction, will have to give proper weight to media freedom. Section 12(4) of the Human Rights Act 1998 emphasises this. Journalistic freedom is not a 'trump' outweighing all other considerations. The Protection from Harassment Act 1998, which creates both a right of action and criminal penalties for persistent behaviour amounting to 'harassment', has, at least once, been used against the press for running campaigns against an individual.[68] The Act provides a defence of reasonableness in which the public interest inherent in the story can be raised before the court.

Injunctions, temporary and permanent
The weighing of free expression and media freedom with individuals' interests in their privacy is found most clearly in respect of breach of confidence. A permanent or temporary injunction can be available to prevent the disclosure of information obtained by a breach of a relationship of confidentiality. This

---

[65] See Chapter 16.
[66] See Chapter 6.
[67] See Chapter 19.
[68] *Esther Thomas* v *Newsgroup Newspapers* (2001) NLJ 1221 CA where the Court of Appeal refused to strike out a claim under the Act brought by a civilian police worker who had made well founded allegations of racist behaviour against police officers and who, consequently, had been the subject of a number of hostile articles and letters in *The Sun*.

remedy is available not only against the person in direct breach of trust but also against those, such as in the media, who are responsible for further dissemination.[69]

A temporary injunction is, predominantly, decided on the basis of a balance of convenience (who has most to lose if, at the temporary stage, they are prevented from doing what, at the full stage, it turns out they have a right to do); a claimant seeking to protect confidentiality is likely to be able, temporarily, to prevent publication on those grounds. This can sometimes resolve the issue permanently since media interest may be dissipated. However, under the common law and now under section 12 of the 1998 Act, the likelihood of a full injunction being issued (i.e. the final issue of right) must be taken into account when considering a temporary injunction. Section 12 also requires the court to have 'particular regard' to the importance of freedom of expression in the Convention scheme, and, in relation to journalistic, literary or artistic material, to have particular regard to whether the material is or is about to be available to the public or whether its publication would be in the public interest. Courts are also required to have particular regard to any relevant privacy code.[70]

Confidentiality and privacy

There must be a relationship of confidentiality recognised by the law which is about to be breached. Such relationships have been upheld by the courts in contexts such as: employer and employee and other business relationships in order to protect trade secrets and commercially sensitive documents;[71] employer and employee in the context of domestic service;[72] medical confidentiality.[73] Information about matrimonial[74] and sexual life[75] and the lives of children[76] can also be protected by injunctions. The use of such injunctions in the political sphere is discussed in Chapter 16. The independent development of the common law and, in particular, the influence of Article 8 ECHR, has meant that such an action may be based upon an alleged invasion of privacy. This was accepted in *Douglas and others* v *Hello! Ltd* (2001)[77] where it was suggested that an action could be based on persons 'simply find[ing] themselves subjected to an unwarranted intrusion into their private life . . . The law no longer needs to construct an artificial relationship of confidentiality between intruder and victim: it can recognise privacy itself as a legal principle drawn from the fundamental value of personal autonomy',[78] though the point has been doubted.[79]

---

[69] For example, *Prince Albert* v *Strange* (1842) 2 De G & Sm 652; 64 ER 293.
[70] See *Douglas and another* v *Hello!* [2003] 2 All ER 289 for discussion of the relationship between freedom of expression (Article 10) and privacy (Article 8) in the light of s. 12.
[71] For example, *Morison* v *Moat* (1851) 9 Hare 241; 68 ER 492, and numerous other cases.
[72] Most famously *Prince Albert* v *Strange* (1842) 2 De G & Sm 652; 64 ER 293; in March 2000 the Prime Minister, Tony Blair, and his wife obtained an injunction to prevent the publication of a former nanny's memoirs.
[73] For example, *X* v *Y* [1988] 2 All ER 648.
[74] *Duchess of Argyll* v *Duke of Argyll and others* [1964] 1 Ch 302.
[75] *Stephens* v *Avery* [1988] Ch 449.
[76] *Re Z (a minor) (freedom of Publication)* [1995] 4 All ER 961
[77] [2001] 2 All ER 289
[78] *Douglas and others* v *Hello! Ltd* [2001] 2 All ER 289, paragraph 126, per Sedley LJ.

Public interest in disclosure

The central point of argument over the issue of an injunction, especially a temporary one, relates to the question whether there is an overriding public interest in favour of disclosure. The court is then a forum of principle in which the public interest in effective investigative journalism can be considered. The courts accept that an injunction should not be available if its impact is to prevent the disclosure of information that ought to be disclosed to the public. Such information might, for example, point to crime or other misconduct[80] or be necessary to counteract factual inaccuracy.[81] In *Lion Laboratories Ltd v Evans and others* (1984)[82] it was held that matters for consideration by the court include: distinguishing between what the public are interested in and what is in the public interest (mere curiosity or sensation-seeking is not enough), and, secondly, that the private interest of the media in profiting from extra sales needs to be taken into account.[83] The availability of other effective avenues of complaint also needs to be weighed in the judgment. The courts require something more than a mere assertion; the allegations need to have, at least on the face of it, some substance.[84] The claim that there is a public interest in the disclosure of the information involved is not a side constraint but a factor to be weighed in deciding whether or not there is a public interest in publication which outweighs the interest in maintaining confidentiality. Thus, even if the courts accepted that, for example, an allegation of wrongdoing had, subject to further investigation, some substance, it would not follow that an injunction would be refused. The public interest in confidentiality might still outweigh the reasons for disclosure. This position will be all the stronger if other proper channels are thought to exist through which disclosure could be made even if using these channels maintains the confidentiality of the information.

In *A v B Plc* (2002) a Premier League footballer sought an injunction to prevent a Sunday newspaper from publishing details of his extra-marital affairs. A temporary injunction was discharged by the Court of Appeal. The judgment lays down guidelines for dealing with the increased number of privacy cases brought by celebrities since the coming into effect of the Human Rights Act 1998. The judgment gives strong weight to freedom of the press. Instead of placing the burden on the press to show why the public interest demands protection from a claim to privacy, the burden is on the applicant seeking an injunction to show why the assumption in favour of a free press should be overborne. The press is entitled to publish stories which interest the public; they are not required to show that there is a significant public interest in favour of publication which is sufficiently important to override a general 'right' to privacy. The press is not, however, free to publish anything at all about celebrities and injunctions can still be issued to protect personal

---

[79] *A v B Plc* [2002] 2 All ER. 545.

[80] For example, *Initial Services Ltd v Putterill and another* [1967] 3 All ER 145.

[81] For example, evidence of the unreliability of a widely used breathalyser machine in *Lion Laboratories Ltd v Evans and others* [1984] 2 All ER 417.

[82] [1984] 2 All ER 417

[83] These strictures may not survive the more media friendly approach in *A v B Plc* (2002) 2 All ER 545.

[84] *Attorney General v Guardian Newspapers and others (No. 2)* [1988] 3 All ER 545

information the law has traditionally protected such as medical data and, perhaps, matrimonial confidences.[85]

11.6.2 Defamation and media freedom

Defamation provides a remedy in damages to a claimant who can prove that words written or spoken and received by others have the effect of lowering his or her reputation in the eyes of right thinking people. If the claimant can satisfy the court that the words have that effect, damages will be awarded unless the defendant can establish one of a number of defences. This can be that the words are true or that, being judgments about the claimant rather than statements of fact, they amount to fair comment on a matter of public interest.

Qualified privilege
A defence can also be founded on the existence of a qualified privilege. A qualified privilege exists where, as a matter of law, the courts accept that statements can be made without threat of proceedings for defamation so long as they are not made with the intention of harming the person concerned. The media may enjoy qualified privilege. If so, the burden of the case shifts to the complainant to prove that a newspaper or broadcaster told falsehoods with the intention of causing him or her harm.

Qualified privilege requires both an interest or a duty to publish and a reciprocal interest or duty to receive the publication.[86] In the cases the major issue is whether the courts think that the media have a duty to publish. The media cannot claim qualified privilege merely because they believe a story is in the public interest.[87] In *Reynolds* v *Times Newspapers Ltd and others* (1999)[88] Lord Nicholls identified a number of factors to be considered by a court in deciding whether there was a duty on the press to publish sufficient to establish a qualified privilege. These included matters such as the seriousness of the allegation, the steps made by the media to verify the story and, also, the tone of the article, especially whether it adopted allegations as if they were statements of fact. In *Grobbelaar* v *News Group Newspapers Ltd* (2001)[89] the question of 'tone' was particularly important with the court stressing that a sensational approach which assumed a person had acted infamously made it less likely that there would be a duty to publish. Qualified privilege requires satisfying the court that the journalism has been 'responsible' and careful with the truth. However, it places the threshold too high if qualified privilege is only allowed if statements made are actually true; factual inaccuracy, in good faith, does not prevent privilege.[90]

---

[85] Cf. *Campbell* v *Mirror Group Newspapers* [2002] EWCA Civ 1373 where the Court of Appeal denied damages, on breach of confidence grounds, to Naomi Campbell. In the Court's view, given that her drug addiction was not a matter of confidentiality, there could be no legally recognised confidentiality in ancillary stories and pictures of her treatment for it. The judgment in *A* v *B Plc* (2002) suggests that the courts may give greater weight to protecting the confidences relating to long-term relationships.

[86] *Adam* v *Ward* [1917] AC 309.

[87] *Loutchansky* v *Times Newspapers* [2001] 4 All ER 115.

[88] [1999] 4 All ER 609.

[89] [2001] EWCA Civ 33; [2001] 2 All ER 437 (the decision has been overturned on other grounds).

Political libels

As well as qualified privilege the English courts have, in recent times, come to impose a barrier on various public bodies preventing them from being able to defend their reputations in proceedings for defamation. Originally public bodies, like commercial corporations, has been able to defend their reputations from fierce criticism alleging corruption and inefficiency.[91]

In the United States the courts took a different view and put a bar on the right not only of political bodies but also politicians and officials to use the courts to defend their reputations from political attack. A similar, though not so far reaching, position has now been developed in English law.

> Corruption and inefficiency was alleged against Derbyshire County Council by the defendant newspapers.
>   HELD (HL): in the absence of proof of malice, a political body could not defend its reputation by instituting defamation proceedings. Freedom of speech is protected by the common law, Convention rights notwithstanding.
>   *Derbyshire County Council* v *Times Newspapers Ltd* [1993] AC 534

The justification for this decision was that without it there would be a 'chilling' effect on freedom of speech and legitimate political criticism would be inhibited. The common law gave considerable weight to freedom of speech which needed to be recognised even in a private law context such as defamation.[92]

It is not clear that the position as identified in *Derbyshire* is satisfactory.[93] The argument is rooted in the requirements of a democratic society: citizens and the press must be free to criticise the government without having to prove the truth of their claims. Public bodies can be powerful organisations with the resources that enable them to protect their position from criticism by using the courts. It is not clear what bodies are contained within the *Derbyshire* rule. It may be confined to elected bodies, though there is clearly a case for the rule to apply more widely.[94] The public interest in free speech applies to public issues broadly defined.

There is, however, a contrary argument that it is undemocratic to permit unrestrained criticism of public bodies. Entirely unfair and malicious stories can be published which may distort the requirements of a reasonable democracy, play into the hands of powerful, private interests and, above all, deter ordinary well intentioned people from going into politics which becomes the preserve of a thick-skinned elite. In fact *Derbyshire* v *Times Newspapers* applies specifically to governmental bodies and does not extend to individual politicians or officials. Such individuals can still protect themselves through an action for defamation.

[90] *Loutchansky* v *Times Newspapers Ltd (No. 2)* [2001] EWCA Civ 1805; [2002] 1 All ER 652.
[91] *Bognor Regis UDC* v *Campion* [1972] 2 QB 169.
[92] Such a view was probably not open to the Court of Appeal which was bound by its own earlier decisions. The Court of Appeal came to a similar conclusion as the House of Lords, but based its judgment on reception of the European Convention of Human Rights.
[93] See Loveland, I. (ed.) (1988) *Importing the First Amendment*. Oxford: Hart Publishing.
[94] See, for example, the striking out of an action brought by British Coal against the National Union of Miners: *British Coal Corporation* v *NUM*, 28 June 1996, QBD.

Under the European Convention, free speech is recognised as fundamental to a democratic society and clearly involves robust criticism. The highest protection is given to political speech including that by the press.[95] Political speech is broadly defined to include all matters of public interest. A legal requirement that critics must prove the truth of their claims about politicians is likely to be incompatible with Article 10. The protection extends to attacks not just on governmental institutions but to individual politicians and officials including the police.[96] The test as laid down in *Derbyshire*, in so far as it excludes individuals and is, perhaps, confined to governmental bodies and not a fuller range of public bodies, may be too narrowly described and the law will need to develop more broadly.

As a general rule, a restraint on freedom of speech under the Convention can be justified in order to advance democracy and so, under Article 10(2), the kinds of arguments pressing for restraints in order to encourage participation in the democratic process can be made. In particular, the Convention expressly permits restrictions on speech in order to protect privacy. Politicians and public figures clearly have rights of privacy and these can be upheld against the press at least when they have no appreciable bearing on the public matter in issue.[97] Prying intrusion into the private lives of politicians threatens political participation. The Convention can help to provide a protection from this which can be properly balanced with the right to freedom of speech.

11.6.3 Protection of sources

The law permits a degree of protection for journalists who wish to protect their sources from legal action by an aggrieved party. The protection of sources is a matter of great concern to the media; in particular it enables them to receive stories from sources who would otherwise not volunteer or sell the information. It is essential to the trust that journalists need to enjoy and protects them from being unwilling police informers, a role in which the reporting of controversial events would be impossible. The public interest in a free media, to have knowledge of public affairs on which political judgment can be based, requires the protection of sources.

A court order requiring a journalist to disclose his or her sources can be required as part of other proceedings, such as an action for breach of confidence when the order is sought to identify the person responsible for the breach or where the police seek an order for the disclosure of journalistic material under PACE 1984. There is no requirement that the journalist or media organisation should, themselves, have committed a wrong, just they have got 'involved in' in another's wrong doing.[98] Orders requiring the disclosure of sources cannot be made unless they come within the exceptions found in section 10 of the Contempt of Court Act 1981.[99]

---

[95] *Lingens* v *Austria* (1986) 8 EHRR 407; *Castells* v *Spain* (1992) 14 EHRR 445; *Oberschlick* v *Austria* (1998) 25 EHRR 357.

[96] For example, *Thorgiersen* v *Iceland* (1992) 14 EHRR 843.

[97] For example, *De Haes and Gijsels* v *Belgium* (1998) 25 EHRR 1.

[98] *Ashworth Security Hospital* v *MGN Ltd* [2002] UKHL 29; [2002] 1 WLR 2033, commenting on the jurisdiction first developed in *Norwich Pharmacal Co.* v *Customs and Excise Commissioners* [1973] 2 All ER 943.

10 Sources of information

No court may require a person to disclose, nor is any person guilty of contempt of court for refusing to disclose, the source of information contained in a publication for which he is responsible, unless it be established to the satisfaction of the court that disclosure is necessary in the interests of justice or national security or for the prevention of disorder or crime

The courts have recognised that the necessity test means that the interests of a free press are to be given a significant weighting but it is one that can, nevertheless, give way if the interests of justice etc. are 'preponderating'.[100]

The 'interests of justice', for example, has been used to justify ordering disclosure in order to identify a disloyal employee who had communicated confidential and sensitive company information to a journalist. 'Interests of justice' was given a wide meaning to enable persons, including companies, 'to exercise important legal rights and to protect themselves from serious legal wrongs'.[101] This approach has continued after the coming into effect of the Human Rights Act 1998.[102] The section has also been used to require the disclosure of sources where medical confidentiality has been breached.[103] Disclosure might be ordered where there is an indication that the source has breached legal privilege, but this is not necessarily the case.[104]

The prevention of crime exception in section 10 has been used to require disclosure in the context of company fraud investigations which might (not would) result in criminal cases even where there was no need for the party seeking disclosure to identify the particular crime in issue.[105]

The national security provision has been used to order disclosure in order to identify a potentially disloyal civil servant.[106]

The ability of journalists to protect their sources is recognised by the European Court of Human Rights as being an important aspect of freedom of expression and the public good inherent in freedom of the press. In *Goodwin v United Kingdom* (1996),[107] the court asserted the importance of protection and argued that any order for disclosure must be justified by 'an overriding requirement in the public interest'. The court's view of the particular case was that the disclosure of sources was disproportionate.[108] United Kingdom courts take the view that the basic structure of section 10 of the Contempt of Court Act 1981 is compatible with the Convention. In *Ashworth Security Hospital* v

---

[99] Website operators do not enjoy the s. 10 defence to an order for disclosure: *Totalise Plc* v *Motley Fool Ltd* (2001) *The Times*, 15 March.

[100] *X* v *Morgan Grampian* [1990] 2 All ER 1 (HL)

[101] *X* v *Morgan Grampian* [1990] 2 All ER 1 (HL); see also *Camelot Group* v *Centaur Communications* [1998] 1 All ER 251.

[102] *Interbrew SA* v *Financial Times* [2002] EWCA Civ 274.

[103] *Ashworth Security Hospital* v *MGN Ltd* [2002] UKHL 29; [2002] 1 WLR 2033.

[104] Compare *Saunders* v *Punch Ltd (trading as Liberty Publishing)* [1998] 1 All ER 234 and *John and others* v *Express Newspapers plc and others* [2000] 3 All ER 257 CA.

[105] *Re an Inquiry under the Company Securities (Insider Dealing) Act 1985* [1988] AC 660.

[106] *Secretary of State for Defence* v *Guardian Newspapers Ltd* [1984] 2 WLR 268

[107] (1996) 22 EHRR 123

[108] See also *K* v *Austria* A/255-B (1993) Com Rep; *Fressoz and Roire* v *France* [1999] EHRLR 399, cited in Starmer, K. (1999) *European Human Rights Law*. London: LAG, 24.42.

MGN Ltd (2002)[109] the House of Lords stressed that there must be a strong case requiring disclosure which was proportionate in each particular case. Even so critics of these disclosure cases take the view that insufficient weight is given to the public interest in a free media when the courts exercise their discretion.

---

[109] [2002] UKHL 29; [2002] 1 WLR 2033.

12

Contempt of court

Freedom of expression, particularly freedom of the media, can be restricted in order to preserve the integrity of the judicial system and the fairness of trials. The law on contempt of court creates criminal penalties for those who interfere directly or indirectly with the progress or integrity of court proceedings.

The behaviour capable of being contemptuous was first categorised in the eighteenth century.[1] The law has gone through considerable development and the modern law was summarised, by the Phillimore Committee in 1974,[2] as including:

> 'Contempt in the face of the court', for example, throwing missiles at the judge, insulting persons in court, demonstrating in court.
> (a) Contempt out of court: (i) reprisals against witnesses after the conclusion of proceedings; (ii) 'scandalising the court', for example, abusing a judge *qua* judge or attacking his impartiality or integrity, (iii) disobedience to a court order, (iv) conduct, whether intentional or not, liable to interfere with the course of justice in particular proceedings' . . .

It is clear from the list that the law of contempt of court can create tensions between fair trials and free expression, especially of the media. These issues are dealt with both under the common law which requires intention to attack the integrity of court proceedings and, under the Contempt of Court Act 1981, in respect of publications that have the unintended consequence of prejudicing the outcome of a trial.

12.1 Fair trials and media freedom

12.1.1 Open justice

In any society that values the rule of law there is a strong, legitimate, public interest in maintaining the openness of the judicial system. The law expresses the will of society and so society has an interest in understanding how it is given effect. Through the legal process, punishment may be sanctioned, property disposed of, families separated and so on. Such coercive acts should be done publicly and openly. Secret justice that cannot be challenged or

---

[1] *Roach v Garvan* (1742) 2 Atk 469.
[2] Philimore Committee (1974) *Contempt of Court*, Cm 5794.

commented upon is, without some overriding justification, an abuse or, at the least, a condition under which abuse is likely. The public nature of the administration of justice lessens distrust of the judicial system, provides a strong incentive for judges, lawyers and other practitioners to maintain a full commitment to impartiality and to the other virtues of the rule of law, and makes it harder for improper or abusive practices to develop.

As well as in the general process, there can be an equally strong public interest in the personnel or the subject matter of particular trials. Famous people, about whose deeds the public like to know, may be accused of crime or may be pursuing a legal right through the civil courts; a trial may be dealing with a shocking crime or with a matter of great social concern, or may be part of an ongoing political controversy or seem like an attempt by the government to silence its opponents.

There is also the individual interest of defendant or litigant that the trial process should be open. A strong sense of grievance and enhanced powerlessness is likely from someone imprisoned, fined, made to pay damages and so on through a secret process of which there is little or no public knowledge. This argument, of course, is contingent on the circumstances. There can be equally strong reasons why an individual defendant or litigant would prefer the matter to be decided quietly and privately behind closed doors. Personal shame and the protection of confidential matters are two obvious reasons. There is no 'right' to open justice in the sense of an entitlement capable of being waived in favour of secrecy. The public interest controls the matter.

It is not enough to discharge the legitimate public interest and the litigant's contingent interest in open justice merely by allowing the public to attend a trial. The most effective ways of providing the public with the knowledge they are entitled to should be used, and this implies media freedom to report and comment on the legal system and the trial process.

12.1.2 Fair trials

The problem is that openness and media freedom can sometimes conflict with the public and individual interest in fair trials. Publicity and media comment can, for example, undermine the effect of the rules of evidence on which a trial is conducted. These rules protect against trials being decided on the basis of irrelevant but prejudicial information about the matters in issue or the persons involved and this requires significant media restraint. Similarly there are good reasons, reflected in public policy, why certain categories of defendant or litigant should be protected from public scrutiny. Children and young persons, the mentally handicapped, divorcing spouses, rape complainants and others are entitled to varying degrees of confidentiality in the legal and trial process which the public and the media must respect. Media comment may also have the effect of influencing the outcome of a trial by commenting not only the trial itself but also on underlying issues. A further threat derived from open justice is that comment may undermine respect for and the integrity of the judicial system which, again, may be detrimental to the public interest.

12.1.3 Priority to fair trials

Clearly, therefore, there needs to be a recognition in the law of these two significant public and individual interests: open justice and fair trials. However, the metaphor of 'weighing' these interests is not necessarily appropriate. It is strongly arguable that the requirements of a fair trial should be met before those of open justice and freedom of the media. The public interest in, for example, knowing that the defendant in a high-profile trial has a long list of earlier convictions is not to be put into the balance with the rules of evidence which prohibit publication of such information. Openness requires that the restraints on media freedom should be no more than is necessary for a fair trial, a different exercise from balancing the two interests. Few would disagree with this as regards protecting the rules of evidence and the integrity of the trial process. Problems of 'weighing' the different interests do still arise in respect of media comment on the underlying issues of a trial or on the general integrity of the judicial system.

The issues are, first, to identify restraints on freedom of the media that are necessary to protect the integrity of the trial process and, second, how to give proper weight to a free media, fair trials and the integrity of the legal system in the context of comment on issues. It should be noted that these serious public interests are open to abuse and litigants' invocations of fair trials or media freedom may sometimes reflect private interests that the law need not reflect. Prominent persons may, for example, seek to silence media criticism by commencing legal proceedings; conversely the media's interest in a matter before the court may be, in reality, no more than a commercial desire to increase sales by sensation or distortion.[3]

12.2 Convention rights

12.2.1 Article 6, fair trial

English courts recognise that HRA 1998, Schedule 1, Article 6 provides a 'right to a fair trial' and they have made it clear that the right, once established, is absolute.[4] What the right entails, however, is far from clear. There is no express reference to contempt in the Convention, but in so far as the law of contempt is necessary to maintain the rules of evidence and the fairness of the trial process, it is likely to be required by Article 6.

Article 6(1) grants a right to a '. . . public' hearing and this certainly permits media coverage of trials. If this was an individual right it would be capable of being waived by a litigant. However, publicity also reflects the public interest in open justice and the Convention would not justify a litigant's request for privacy.[5]

---

[3] See *Grobbelaar v News Group Newspapers Ltd and another* [2001] EWCA Civ 33; [2001] 2 All ER 437 for judicial awareness of the point in the context of the qualified privilege of the media.

[4] *R v A* [2001] 3 All ER 1.

[5] See *Axen v Germany* (1984) 6 EHRR 195: publicity assists the aim of a fair trial by protecting litigants and defendant from secret justice and helps maintain public confidence in the courts. The detail of the rules on publicity depend on the circumstances of the case.

In certain circumstances Article 6 expressly allows the media and public to be excluded from trials. These are for reasons that are widely recognised as justifying confidentiality in the trial process: 'the interests of morals, public order or national security in a democratic society, where the interests of juveniles or the protection of the private life of the parties so require . . .' The Convention language makes it at least arguable that states have a duty to exclude the public and media in clear cases. Publicity can also be restricted 'to the extent strictly necessary in the opinion of the court in special circumstances where publicity would prejudice the interests of justice'.

12.2.2 Article 10, freedom of expression

Such restrictions on publicity or media reporting of trials will need to be compatible with Article 10. The compatibility of the common law contempt with the 'prescribed by law' requirement of Article 10, which includes the requirement that the circumstances in which contempt will be invoked must be reasonably foreseeable, was accepted in *Sunday Times* v *UK* (1979–80).[6] The case is referred to at a number of points in this chapter.

The Sunday Times sought to publish articles critical of a drug company which, in the view of the newspaper, was refusing to make a generous settlement to victims of the thalidomide tragedy and, as a potential defendant, was using its legal rights to hinder the victim's actions for compensation.

HELD: the proposed articles could be contemptuous. It involved prejudgment of the trial.

Attorney General v *Times Newspapers* [1974] AC 273

Times Newspapers took the case to the Court of Human Rights.

HELD: the ban on the articles was a disproportionate restriction on freedom of expression and violated Article 10.

Sunday Times v *United Kingdom* (1979) 2 EHRR 245

Though the United Kingdom lost the case on the proportionality point, some important aspects of the contempt law were upheld.

Compatibility with Article 10 requires that contempt restrictions must be for one of the legitimate aims listed in Article 10(2). The Strasbourg case law has dealt with contempt as involving restrictions on expression which aim at 'maintaining the authority and impartiality of the judiciary'. This phrase has been held to include the matters covered by the English law on contempt.[7] The phrase covers not only matters relating to the machinery of justice, the judiciary and the trial process but, importantly, it extends to include the individual rights of litigants to a fair trial.[8] The general approach has been recently discussed by the Court.

---

[6] (1979–80) 2 EHRR 245. See also 'A significant body of case law on the applicability and content of contempt law have been developed so as to make it "reasonably accessible and foreseeable" ': *C Ltd* v *United Kingdom* (1989) Ap. 14132/88.

[7] *Sunday Times* v *United Kingdom* (1979–80) 2 EHRR 245, paragraph 55.

[8] *Sunday Times* v *United Kingdom* (1979–80) 2 EHRR 245, paragraphs 55 and 56.

> W, a journalist, wrote a critical article about a senior Austrian politician who was on trial. The article implied the politician's guilt and was published before the court gave its verdict. W was convicted under a contempt law that prohibited publications which influenced the outcome of judicial proceedings.
>   HELD (EctHR): there had been no violation of Article 10.
>   *Worm* v *Austria* (1998) 25 EHRR 454

Legal restrictions aiming to prevent publications which may lead to prejudgment of trials will, in general terms, be compatible with the Convention. The Court's discussion makes it clear that states may restrict publications in order to protect the administration of justice generally – contempt need not be confined to the particular circumstances of an individual trial. Penalties for making serious allegations against court officials have been found to be compatible with the Convention[9] as have criminal penalties for making unfounded, destructive attacks on the judiciary.[10]

At the same time, in *Worm* v *Austria*, the Court insisted on proper recognition for freedom of expression. Freedom of expression protects vigorous discussion of 'public affairs' and this can clearly include the judiciary, the court system generally and also matters that are the subject matter of trials. Prior or contemporaneous discussion of general issues that come before the courts should be permitted. Freedom of expression can only be restricted to the minimum extent necessary to uphold the authority and impartiality of the courts and it may be that the Court is signalling a slightly greater tolerance of attacks on the judiciary. In *De Haes and Gijsels* v *Belgium* (1998),[11] successful defamation proceedings against journalists who had made serious allegations of bias against judges involved in child abuse cases were held to be a violation of Article 10. The allegations did not involve prejudgment of cases and they were found by the court to be well researched.[12] The Court in *Worm* v *Austria* also expressed concern about a threat of psuedo trials or trial by media and, generally, the Strasbourg authorities have not found reason to object to bans on media re-enactments of trials while they are going on.[13]

Article 10 requires restrictions on freedom of expression to be 'necessary in a democratic society' in the sense of being a proportionate response to a pressing social need. The facts and circumstances of individual cases are important. The fact, for example, that attacks on the judiciary are well researched or only likely to have a minimal prejudgment effect will be relevant to the decision. In *Worm* v *Austria* evidence of an intention to influence the outcome of proceedings indicated that the penalty was proportionate. In *Sunday Times* v *United Kingdom* the issue was whether the risk of prejudgment of a future civil action for negligence could prevent the publication of a well researched article dealing with responsibility for a major drugs tragedy

---

[9] *Prince* v *United Kingdom* (1986) Ap. 11456/85; 46 D&R 222.
[10] *Prager and Obserschlick* v *Austria* (1995) 21 EHRR 1; *Barfod* v *Denmark* (1989) Ap. 11508/85.
[11] (1998) 25 EHRR 1.
[12] The attacks can be compared to the unfounded allegations made in *Prager* and *Barfod*, mentioned above. Attacks on the private lives of judges could, however, be legitimately dealt with by law.
[13] *C Ltd* v *United Kingdom* (1989) Ap. 14132/88; *Hodgson, Woolf Productions, NUJ and Channel Four TV* v *United Kingdom* (1988) EHRR 503.

involving hundreds of people. The Court found against the United Kingdom on proportionality grounds: in the circumstances British courts had not given enough weight to freedom of speech, the litigation was dormant, there were substantial public interests dealt with by the article, the article had a moderate tone and the terms of the order restraining publication were too wide.[14] The Court of Human Rights recognises that states have a margin of appreciation over the nature and extent of their contempt rules.[15] However, that margin is quite narrow and the Court is capable of detailed scrutiny of particular cases to ensure that these two important Convention values, fair trials and freedom of expression, are properly upheld.

12.3 The courts to which contempt law applies

Section 19 of the Contempt of Court Act 1981 applies the contempt jurisdiction to any tribunal or body which is exercising the 'the judicial power of the state' and this has been accepted as also applying to contempt at common law.[16] The 'superior courts' (the House of Lords in its appellate jurisdiction, the Court of Appeal, the High Court and courts with High Court status, the Crown Court and the Courts-Martial Appeal Court[17]) which are unambiguously part of the judicial system are subject to the contempt jurisdiction as are the magistrates' courts.[18] Administrative tribunals which can make coercive orders affecting the rights of individuals, such as local valuation courts,[19] employment tribunals[20] and, given their power to order a patient's release, mental health review tribunals,[21] are also within the scope of the contempt jurisdiction. The disciplinary panels of the professions, however, are not considered to be part of the 'judicial power of the state' and, despite the impact of their decisions, are not able to protect their proceedings by means of contempt of court.[22]

12.4 Civil and criminal contempt

Contempt is criminal in nature in the sense that it involves punishment and the criminal standard of proof is required. The conventional language is to distinguish 'civil' from 'criminal' contempt. A 'civil' contempt involves punishment for breach of a court order; 'criminal' contempt refers to the other forms of interference with the judicial process covered by the concept of contempt. Civil contempts are predominantly matters for the parties; other contempts are usually raised by the Attorney General.[23]

---

[14] *Sunday Times* v *United Kingdom* (1979) 2 EHRR 245, paragraphs 62–7.
[15] For example, *Sunday Times* v *United Kingdom* (1979) 2 EHRR 245, 268; *Prager and Obserschlick* v *Austria* (1995) 21 EHRR 1, paragraph 35.
[16] *Pickering* v *Associated Newspapers Holdings Plc* [1991] 2 AC 370, 380 per Lord Donaldson. The point was not commented upon by the House of Lords.
[17] Defined in s. 19, Contempt of Court Act 1981.
[18] The Contempt of Court Act 1981, s. 12, expressly gives magistrates power to deal with persons who wilfully insult the court or wilfully interrupt proceedings.
[19] *Attorney General* v *BBC* [1981] AC 303.
[20] *Peach Grey & Co (a firm)* v *Sommers* [1995] 2 All ER 513 ('industrial tribunals').
[21] *Pickering* v *Associated Newspapers Holdings Plc* [1991] 2 AC 370.
[22] *General Medical Council* v *British Broadcasting Corporation* [1998] TLR 372.

12.5 Penalties for contempt

Criminal contempt is tried summarily by the High Court in the absence of a jury. Magistrates can punish for their own contempts. A fine, imprisonment up to two years[24] and in some cases an injunction to stop repeated contempts are available. Civil contempts can be punished in the same way though committal to prison should be very rare and the court has an additional power to order sequestration of property. Cases involving a strong public interest can be brought by the Attorney General. The hearing for contempt is independent from the proceedings to which the contempt relates and is governed by particular rules of court. Fair trial provisions, including Article 6 rights, must, of course apply.

In exceptional circumstances, such as (but not confined to) where the contempt is in the face of the court, it may be dealt with summarily and immediately by the judge. Whether a judge in such circumstances can be thought of as properly independent must be doubted. This power of immediate committal was retained by the courts in *Balogh* v *St Albans Crown Court* (1975)[25] but recognised as being 'rough justice' and 'arbitrary, contrary to natural justice, and far removed from the ordinary processes of the law' and so should only be invoked in the most pressing circumstances where no other course is available. Compatibility with Article 6 ECHR provides further strength to this proviso.

A judge trying a criminal case may feel that media comment on the trial is so prejudicial that the trial should be stopped. That itself does not establish a contempt. In such cases the judge will normally refer the matter to the Attorney General who will decide whether or not to bring contempt proceedings before the High Court. The High Court then decides whether there has been a contempt and, if so, the appropriate punishment. The fact that, in the end, the courts decide there has not been a contempt of court does not mean that the judge was wrong to have stopped the trial.[26]

12.6 Civil contempt

The punishment of a person for disobedience to a court order is known as a 'civil contempt'.[27] This is largely a matter dealing with the effective operation of the legal system and the general effectiveness of the rule of law[28] and is outside the scope of this book.[29]

A person may break a court order for broadly political reasons. Such a reason is not a defence to a civil contempt even if it is argued that the order

---

[23] *Attorney General* v *Newspaper Publishing plc* [1988] Ch 333, from a passage (p. 362) in which Lord Donaldson doubted the usefulness of the civil/criminal distinction.

[24] Contempt of Court Act 1981, s. 14.

[25] [1975] 1 QB 73.

[26] For example, *Attorney General* v *MGN Ltd and others* [1997] 1 All ER 456.

[27] Though see the doubts expressed by Lord Donaldson in *Attorney General* v *Newspaper Publishing plc* [1988] Ch 333, 362.

[28] See, especially, *M* v *Home Office* [1994] 1 AC 377 for the application of civil contempt to a minister of the Crown acting in his official capacity.

[29] See, for example, *Halsbury's Laws of England*, 4th edn, reissue vol. 9(1) 'Contempt of Court' (1998), paragraphs 458–90.

ought not to have been made because the judge misstated the law or because the judge was motivated by socio-political bias or some other political fault. Disobedience will be a contempt.[30] Similarly, media freedom and freedom of expression generally does not outweigh the determination of the court to maintain the integrity of judicial proceedings. The issue arises if publications are made allegedly in breach of a court order. When a solicitor in a prisons case gave to a journalist documents relating to special regimes in prisons, she was held to be in contempt of court. The documents had been subject to an order of disclosure and the solicitor had broken a rule that documents disclosed in that way should not be used for any other purpose, including a political one. The case, *Harman* v *Secretary of State for the Home Department* (1982)[31] was highly controversial because the information in the documents had been disclosed in open court and, in any case, it seemed that the government was trying to keep details of the treatment of prisoners secret. A majority of the judges declined to see the importance of freedom of expression. In *Weber* v *Switzerland* (1990)[32] the punishment of a journalist for disclosing a confidential matter was held to breach Article 10 by the Court of Human Rights. The matter in issue had ceased to be confidential before the journalist made his disclosure. In England and Wales the Civil Procedure Rules now permit greater scope for the use of disclosed material which has been referred to in public hearings though court orders preventing wider disclosure are still possible.[33]

Recent cases show that human rights, specifically freedom of expression, has an impact on the way in which both the *actus reus* and *mens rea* of civil contempt[34] is understood.

> The Attorney General obtained a court order restraining S from disclosing information he received while acting as a British intelligence officer. S then wrote articles for the magazine *Punch*. The Attorney General, on the basis of the order, sought amendments to one of the articles but not all these amendments were included in the published article.
>
> HELD: the original court order aimed at protecting confidential information and the publication of an article which destroyed such confidentiality satisfied the *actus reus* of civil contempt. Publication of material already in the public domain did not offend against such an injunction protecting confidentiality though publishing new material in breach of confidence did. On the facts of the case there was no contempt because the Attorney General had not made out the *mens rea* of contempt by showing that the editor knew that the intention to protect confidentiality would be interfered with.
>
> *Attorney General* v *Punch Ltd and another* [2001] EWCA Civ 403; [2001] 2 All ER 655

---

[30] *M* v *Home Office* [1994] 1 AC 377; *R* v *Socialist Worker Printers and Publishers Ltd and another ex parte Attorney General* [1975] 1 QB 637.

[31] [1982] 2 WLR 338.

[32] (1990) 12 EHRR 508.

[33] Rule 31.22(1), Civil Procedure Rules.

[34] The language of a criminal offence is used by Lord Phillips MR in *Attorney General* v *Punch Ltd* [2001] 2 All ER 655, for example.

This judgment, in line with Article 10 ECHR, insists that a court order designed to protect confidentiality can only be enforced to protect information which has retained its confidential nature. If a court order has a different purpose, to protect the overall integrity of the security service perhaps, then enforcement can be in respect of a wider, appropriate range of information. Article 10 ECHR may be in issue here since the need for such an injunction may be difficult to justify under the Convention. In *The Observer and the Guardian* v *United Kingdom* (1992)[35] an injunction partly intended to protect the integrity of the security service was only compatible with the Convention so long as it protected genuinely confidential information; once confidentiality was lost the injunction violated Article 10 despite its other purpose.[36]

12.7 Criminal contempt: intention and strict liability

The term 'criminal contempt' describes various forms of serious interference with the course of justice generally and legal proceedings in particular. These are common law offences and, as such, it is necessary to prove *mens rea*, that the defendant intended so to interfere with the course of justice. An action for contempt will fail, therefore, if the Attorney General cannot establish intention. However, the common law used to recognise some of these contempts as capable, also, of being committed on the basis of strict liability. Certain forms of interference with the course of justice were offences irrespective of whether or not an interference was intended. In *Sunday Times* v *United Kingdom* (1979)[37] the compatibility of common law, strict liability contempt with Article 10 ECHR (freedom of expression) was questioned. Subsequently, the Contempt of Court Act 1981 was enacted. Its effect is that a prosecution for contempt requires proof of intention unless the contempt can be brought within the terms of the Act. In summary, strict liability is confined to 'publications' which create a 'substantial risk' that the course of justice of particular proceedings will be 'seriously impeded or prejudiced'. Contemptuous acts which are not 'publications' or which do not interfere with particular proceedings but only with the judicial system generally can only be prosecuted on the basis of proof of intention. Conversely, a publication which creates a substantial risk that the course of justice of particular proceedings will be seriously impeded or prejudiced can be prosecuted, without having to prove intention, only so long as the requirements of the Act are met. If, for example, the prejudice from a publication occurs before proceedings are 'active' and within the effect of the Act, it will still be necessary to prove intention. Similarly certain defences are only available if the contempt is within the terms of the Act; of particular importance is the defence that the interference was merely an 'incidental' effect of a good faith discussion of public affairs.

---

[35] (1992) 14 EHRR 153.
[36] *The Observer and the Guardian* v *United Kingdom* (1992) 14 EHRR 153, paragraph 68.
[37] (1979) 2 EHRR 245.

12.8 The main forms of criminal contempt

12.8.1 Contempt in the face of the court

This form of contempt involves, usually, physical acts that interfere directly with court proceedings. The use of violence against judges, parties, witnesses and other court personnel or interrupting proceedings and making speeches or allegations are the kinds of things covered by this category of contempt.[38] Intention to interfere with the course of justice is likely to be easy to prove and, in any case, such actions are unlikely to come within the terms of the Contempt of Court Act 1981.

Interrupting court proceedings can be part of a political campaign.

> Welsh students, protesting about the lack of official status for the Welsh language in Wales, interrupted a libel case by shouting slogans, scattering pamphlets and singing songs. The trial judge had them committed instantly to prison for contempt.
> HELD (CA): their punishment for contempt was lawful; their good faith justified a lesser degree of punishment.
> *Morris & others* v *Crown Office* [1970] 2 QB 114

Making such a protest speech in court is now likely to be a 'publication' for the purposes of the Contempt of Court Act 1981;[39] however, defendants who intend to disrupt proceedings would not have the benefit of the 'public interest' defence,[40] available to those prosecuted under the Act because it only applies to where the interference is 'incidental' which is not the case with a politically inspired interruption.[41] Such protestors have rights under Article 10 (freedom of expression) and 11 (freedom of assembly and association) ECHR. However, protecting the integrity and effectiveness of the trial process is, certainly under Article 10 and, arguably, under Article 11, a legitimate purpose which justifies states in imposing proportionate restrictions on the exercise of these freedoms.

12.8.2 Indirect interference with court proceedings and access to court

Actions taken outside the court which interfere with particular trials or with the judicial process generally can be punished for contempt. This, typically, involves bribing, threatening or punishing witnesses or litigants so as to deter them and perhaps others from the court. Usually such actions will be outside the scope of the Contempt of Court Act 1981 because they do not involve 'publication'. Often proving intention is not likely to be a problem.

---

[38] For examples see *Halsbury's Laws of England*, 4th edn, reissue vol. 9(1) 'Contempt of Court' (1998), paragraph 407.
[39] Section 2(1), Contempt of Court Act 1981 includes within the definition of 'publication' any 'speech . . . which is addressed to the public at large or any section of the public'.
[40] Section 5, Contempt of Court Act 1981 which is discussed below.
[41] See also *Bodden* v *Commissioner of Police for the Metropolis* [1989] 3 All ER 833, which involved a protest rally about one trial which could be heard in and interfered with another trial. Continuing the rally could be a contempt.

Groups and associations which take action against their members, officers or those in their power for going to court or being witnesses can be liable for this kind of contempt even when their motive is mixed.[42]

Payments to witnesses by the media, for example, might also be a contempt. Despite a number of alleged scandals, the Lord Chancellor decided in August 2002 that the matter should, for the time being, be left to the self-regulatory power of the Press Council.

Interferences with the course of justice can stem from publications and raise issues of freedom of speech. Articles in newspapers or journals, for example, may amount to pressure on a witness not give evidence or on a litigant not to pursue a cause in court.[43] The issue was discussed in the *Sunday Times* thalidomide case[44] where the House of Lords defended the principle of access to the courts and granted an injunction, on contempt grounds, to prevent improper pressure being put on witnesses or litigants. The Lords accepted, however, that there was nothing unlawful in reasoned argument which aimed to dissuade a person from exercising his or her legal rights. Lord Cross said: 'To seek to dissuade a litigant from prosecuting or defending proceedings by threats of unlawful action, by abuse, by misrepresentation of the nature of the proceedings or the circumstances out of which they arose or such like, is no doubt a contempt of court; but if the writer states the facts fairly and accurately, and expresses his view in temperate language the fact that the publication may bring pressure – possibly great pressure – to bear on the litigant should not make it a contempt of court'.[45] There was no discussion of this 'access to court' point when the case was before the Court of Human Rights. Given the importance the Strasbourg court places on protecting access to the courts, it can be suggested that legal rules punishing improper pressure being placed on potential litigants may be positive duties required of states. Such restrictions on expression will need to be balanced with the requirements of Article 10 ECHR and this defends journalists' rights to make vigorous comments on matters in the public interest. Lord Cross's distinction between persuasion on the basis of reasons relevant to the issue in hand and trying to force, by threats or other forms of pressure, a person to renounce their legal rights would seem to be the principled basis for reconciling the two rights, access to courts and freedom of expression. Of course any particular restraint on a journalist will need to be proportionate in the circumstances.

Since this type is contempt by publication, the Contempt of Court Act 1981 may well be relevant. If an intention to interfere with a witness or litigant cannot be proven, the Attorney General may still proceed though only under the terms of the Act. If he does so, the defendant has the benefit of the defences

---

[42] *Attorney General v Butterworth and another* [1963] 1 QB 696, where a trade union was in contempt for taking prejudicial action against an official who had given evidence against the union interest in the Restrictive Practices Court. Action by the Prison Officers Association to deny visits to mental patients and so deter them from pursuing complaints in the courts, as reported, could also amount to a contempt.

[43] See, for example, *Attorney General v Hislop and another* [1991] 1 QB 514, where *Private Eye* published derogatory articles about the wife of a serial killer in order to deter her from pursuing a libel action against them.

[44] *Attorney General v Times Newspapers Ltd* [1974] AC 274; see above.

[45] *Attorney General v Times Newspapers Ltd* [1974] AC 274, 326C, per Lord Cross.

available. Where there is evidence of an intention to interfere with the course of justice, the Attorney General seems to have a choice of how to proceed.[46]

12.8.3 Scandalising the court

'Scandalising the court' was defined in *R v Gray* (1900)[47] as 'any act done or writing published calculated to bring a court or a judge of the court into contempt, or to lower his authority'. Abuse of judges or allegations of bias and prejudice, indicating that a person had not had a fair trial, have been held to be contempt on this ground.[48] The offence involves an attack on the institution of the judiciary or on individual judges and does not necessarily involve an interference with particular proceedings; the Contempt of Court Act 1981 will not, therefore, apply and so an intention to act contemptuously will need to be proved.

Important issues of freedom of speech are raised and these have usually been recognised by the courts. In *R v Commissioner of Police of the Metropolis ex parte Blackburn (No. 2)* (1968)[49] it was said that 'no criticism of a judgment, however vigorous, can amount to contempt of court, providing it keeps within the limits of reasonable courtesy and good faith'.[50] Courteous criticism is lawful. There could still be a prosecution in respect of disrespectful and bad faith allegations of bias which, therefore, may still be in contempt of court.

Any prosecution on such grounds would need to be compatible with Article 10 ECHR.

> Belgian journalists published strong and personal attacks on judges alleging that they had been biased and cowardly in the way they handled a number of child abuse cases. They were convicted of a criminal libel under Belgian law.
>
> HELD (ECHR): the law must balance the protection of the integrity of the judiciary with freedom of expression on public affairs. Apart from a particular attack on the family of one of the judges, the conviction was, in the circumstances, disproportionate and a violation of Article 10.
>
> *De Haes and Gijsels v Belgium* (1998) 25 EHRR 1

In the case, the Court of Human Rights recognised that the courts should enjoy public confidence and that judges can be protected by law from unfounded and destructive attacks including allegations of bias; this was especially so since judges would normally be unable to respond to such charges. The states had a limited margin of appreciation concerning the specifics of the laws by which the protection was achieved. Equally, however, it had to be recognised that the courts were important public institutions often dealing with matters of great public concern and the media and the public should be able to speak out about them. Article 10 protects speech which is aggressive, opinionated

---

[46] *Attorney General v Hislop and another* [1991] 1 QB 514 is an example of a contempt which was both common law and statutory.

[47] [1900] 2 QB 36.

[48] *R v Gray* [1900] 2 QB 36; *R v Editor of the New Statesman ex parte DPP* (1927–28) xliv TLR 301.

[49] [1968] 2 QB 150.

[50] See also *Ambard v Attorney General for Trinidad and Tobago* [1936] AC 322, 335, Lord Atkin.

and which may offend, shock and disturb; comment may involve exaggeration and provocative language.

12.8.4 Contempt by prejudgment

Publications which involved the prejudgment of issues before the courts could be prosecuted as a common law offence of strict liability without the need to prove an intention to interfere with the administration of justice. This was confirmed by the House of Lords in the *Sunday Times* thalidomide case. The articles in issue, in the understanding of the court, clearly implied the drug company's legal responsibility for what had happened even though this responsibility was the central issue with which legal proceedings were concerned. The court held that any such prejudging of an issue was capable of being a contempt, notwithstanding the publisher's intention. Whether a case would be brought was within the discretion of the Attorney General. Contempt by prejudgment at common law did not depend on whether the publication is actually likely to prejudice the outcome of particular proceedings. The policy of the law is against trial by media and the contempt jurisdiction can punish prejudgment in order to prevent any tendency towards this.

Contempt by prejudgment is, in principle, compatible with Convention rights, particularly Article 10 (freedom of expression). A litigant's right to a fair trial under Article 6 justifies such restrictions on freedom of expression and they serve the legitimate purpose of 'maintaining the authority and impartiality of the judiciary'. *Worm v Austria* (1998) acknowledges that laws may enforce the principle of the courts, not the media, being the proper forum for determining disputes over civil rights and obligations and criminal charges[51] and that this can be done by restrictions which go further than just stopping interferences with particular proceedings.

Despite its general acceptance of the principle of contempt by prejudgment, the European Court of Human Rights nevertheless found, in the *Sunday Times* case, that the potential width of common law contempt could, and did on the facts, violate Article 10 ECHR.[52] This led to the enactment of the Contempt of Court Act 1981 whose impact is discussed below.

12.8.5 Prejudicing the jury

Trials should be determined solely on the basis of evidence presented in court. This is fundamental to the common law and is implicit in the right to a fair trial, Article 6 ECHR and the principle of equality of arms. To publish information, which is not part of the evidence before the court, which might, intentionally or not, affect, in one way or another, the eventual outcome of a trial can be punished as a contempt of court. Judges will normally consider themselves immune from any influence such publication may exert and so the

---

[51] *Worm v Austria* (1998) 25 EHRR 454, paragraph 40.
[52] *Sunday Times v United Kingdom* (1979) 2 EHRR 245.

principal burden of this form of contempt relates to publications which may prejudice a jury.

The existence of prejudicial publications might be, first, grounds on which a judge stops a trial from continuing, second, grounds for appeal if, for example, the trial judge merely directed the jury to disregard comments rather than stopped the trial, and, third, grounds for the Attorney General to bring proceedings for contempt. The stopping of a trial does not necessarily mean that there was a contempt of court; conversely, the fact that the Attorney General does not bring proceedings for contempt or that such proceedings fail does not mean that the judge was wrong to stop the trial.[53]

The kinds of press coverage that can persuade judges to stop trials or the Attorney General to bring proceedings include: authoritative statements by officials directly or indirectly indicating the guilt of defendants[54] (this is likely to include assertions by police that they have caught the guilty person); revealing information such as previous convictions about a defendant;[55] and asserting the existence of some matter which has been expressly denied by the court:[56]

> Famous footballers were on trial for an attack on an Asian student. The judge had told the jury that there was no evidence of a racist aspect to the attack. Late in the trial the newspaper published an article by the victim's father in which he alleged that the attack was, indeed, motivated by race hatred. The trial was stopped and the Attorney General brought contempt proceedings.
>
> HELD: the newspaper was in contempt. It was fined £75,000 and made to pay the Attorney General's costs of £54,000. The costs of the retrial were very much greater.
>
> *Attorney General* v *MGN Ltd* [2002] EWHC 907 Admin QBD

Sensational press coverage of events or of trials involving famous personalities has raised difficult issues. The Attorney General has shown reluctance to bring proceedings against the popular press even though the trial was stopped or convictions set aside on appeal.[57] Celebrities who are already given sensationalist treatment in the press may find it difficult to convince a court that additional stories, though relating to a trial, have increased whatever prejudice there already exists.

> A soap opera star and an alleged East End villain, already the subject of major, sensationalist tabloid interest, were involved in a criminal trial. While the judicial process was under way sensational stories were published about the personalities and circumstances before the court and the trial was halted. Proceedings for contempt were brought by the Attorney General.
>
> HELD: there was no contempt. The articles about the trial, in the circumstances, did not create any greater prejudice than already existed.
>
> *Attorney General* v *MGN Ltd & others* [1997] 1 All ER 456

---

[53] *Attorney General* v *MGN Ltd and others* [1997] 1 All ER 456; *Attorney General* v *Birmingham Post* [1998] 4 All ER 49.

[54] *R* v *McCann and others* (1991) 92 Cr App R 239.

[55] *Attorney General* v *Times Newspapers Ltd* (1983) *The Times*, 12 February.

[56] *Attorney General* v *MGN Ltd* [2002] EWHC 907 Admin QBD.

[57] *R* v *Taylor and Taylor* (1994) 98 Cr Ap Rpts 361.

Proceedings such as the examples given here, will normally be based on strict liability rule and so must meet the requirements of the Contempt of Court Act 1981.

12.8.6 Frustrating, thwarting or subverting the purpose of a court order made against others

It is a fundamental principle that a court order is binding only on the parties and is not a restriction on the world in general, including the media. A third party can be liable if he or she aids and abets one of the parties in breach of the order. More controversially, however, a third party can be liable for contempt of court if, without aiding and abetting a party, they nevertheless do something which they know has the effect of defeating the purpose for which the court order was made.

This form of contempt of court is potentially a burden on the media since it may prevent discussion of matters which are subject to a court order. It arose expressly in the context of the so-called *Spycatcher* litigation in which, in the mid-1980s, the United Kingdom embarked on a long and complicated series of court cases in order to prevent the publication of a book of memoirs by Peter Wright, a retired security service agent, and, also, of commentary and extracts in the national press. The government was concerned that the disclosure of confidential matter obtained by a security agent would harm national security. The media, on the other hand, believed there was a strong public interest which justified publication: the book contained, *inter alia*, allegations of subversive[58] and unlawful activities by the security services.[59]

In one of the cases the House of Lords held that it could be contempt of court for a newspaper to knowingly publish an article which had the effect of defeating the point of an injunction made against another paper.[60] This decision has recently been analysed in *Attorney General* v *Punch Ltd* (2001), the facts of which are described above.

The courts seek to maintain the well established principles that only the parties are directly bound by an injunction although there is liability for aiding and abetting a party to breach an injunction. The point of the *Spycatcher* injunction is that a third party can be liable, not for breaching the terms of the injunction as such, but for the taking of an action which destroys the purpose the court had in making the original injunction. In *Attorney General* v *Punch*, for example, the order against S was made to prevent the disclosure of confidential information which might damage national security. A third party would not be in contempt if it published material that was in the public domain or which would not damage national security, even if such a publication broke the terms of the injunction. The third party is not liable unless what it has done renders the point of the injunction obsolete. A third party, for example, must respect an injunction whose point is to protect confidentiality only so long as the material remains confidential.

---

[58] Specifically, gathering intelligence on members of the government.
[59] For further details see Chapter 16.
[60] *Attorney General* v *Newspaper Publishing Plc and others* [1987] 3 All ER 276.

This is a strict liability form of contempt. It must be proved that the person in contempt knew that they were destroying the effect of an injunction made against others and that this would destroy the point of the injunction. Strict liability contempt, as we shall see, has a public interest defence in section 5 of the Contempt of Court Act 1981. Furthermore, the courts, as public authorities, are bound to act consistently with the Convention and, by section 12(4) of the Human Rights Act 1998, they must have 'particular regard' to freedom of expression and to the extent it is in the public interest for journalistic material to be published. Whether these provisions will have any additional impact on the way the courts handle such injunctions remains to be seen.[61]

12.9 Strict liability and the Contempt of Court Act 1981

At common law contempt based on inhibiting litigants and witnesses from their access to the court, contempt by prejudgment and contempt by prejudicing a jury can all be offences of strict liability and can be prosecuted even if there is no evidence of an intention to interfere with the course of justice. The other forms of contempt, such as contempt in the face of the court, indirect interference with court proceedings, scandalising the court or frustrating the purpose of a court order normally require proof of an intention to interfere with the course of justice or at least proof that actions continued after the defendant obtained knowledge that such interference was likely.

In relation to the former, contempt in which the common law accepts strict liability, if intention cannot be proved, then a prosecution, on the basis of strict liability, is only possible under the terms of the Contempt of Court Act 1981. If those terms cannot be met, any prosecution must prove intentional contempt. There is no requirement that these types of contempt can only be prosecuted under the terms of the Act. It seems the Attorney General has a choice between proving intention and avoiding the restrictions and defences found in the Act or not having to prove intention but accepting these restrictions and defences.

Proving 'intent' may not be difficult. In *Attorney General* v *Times Newspapers Ltd* (1992) the Court of Appeal held that the intention could be inferred from the circumstances and, in particular, could be grounded on the fact that impeding or prejudicing the administration of justice could be foreseen even if such an interference was not desired and the person involved had other intentions and motives. The court added that the 'more obvious the interference ... the more readily will the required intent be inferred'.[62] Thus the fact that a newspaper is motivated by the public interest, to tell a good story or to make profit, will not enable it to escape liability if it foresees or has knowledge of the likely prejudice to the administration of justice that will result.

---

[61] In *Attorney General* v *Punch* [2001] EWCA Civ 403; [2001] 2 All ER 655 the requirement in the original order that the consent of the Attorney General should be obtained before publication was held, on free speech grounds, not to restrict third parties.

[62] [1992] 1 AC 191. The text says 'referred'.

12.9.1 The Human Rights Act 1998

An action for contempt of court based upon strict liability is subject to the terms of the Contempt of Court Act 1981. Following the bringing into force of the Human Rights Act 1998, the 1981 Act must be interpreted, so far as possible, for compatibility with the scheduled Convention rights and prosecution decisions by public authorities must be consistent with those rights. The two rights principally involved are Article 10 and Article 6 ECHR and, as we have seen, the Convention permits proportionate restrictions on freedom of expression in order to maintain the fairness of trials and the integrity of the judicial system. As we shall see, the 1981 Act permits restrictions on freedom of expression only if there is a 'substantial risk that the course of justice in the proceedings in question will be seriously impeded or prejudiced' and, in general terms, this is likely to be compatible with the Strasbourg jurisprudence.[63] Of course, the necessity in a democratic society, the proportionality, of any restriction on expression in order to maintain the fairness of a trial will also need to be assessed by the court.[64]

12.9.2 Publications

The Contempt of Court Act 1981 restricts a prosecution based on strict liability to where the interference with the course of justice is by 'publication'. This term is widely defined to include speech, writing, broadcast programmes and any 'other communication in whatever form, which is addressed to the public at large or any section of the public'. As said above, this can clearly cover a demonstration inside or outside the court, though intention in such cases is usually easy to prove and not in issue.

12.9.3 '... in the proceedings in question ...'

Section 2 of the Contempt of Court Act makes it clear that strict liability contempt can only apply to publications that interfere with the course of specific proceedings. Generalised attacks on the judiciary, on a particular judge or on the legal process cannot be punished for contempt without proof of intention. In any case, as is indicated by the discussion of 'scandalising the court' above, this form of contempt is now very restricted to the most extreme situations.

12.9.4 Proceeding must be active

The question of when the process of justice begins and hence restraints on the media should begin has been a problem in the common law. The general test is that proceedings must be 'imminent' or 'pending', but these are vague phrases open to some width of interpretation which may go to a time before some formal stage, such as an arrest or the institution of proceedings, has taken place.

---

[63] *Worm v Austria* (1998) 25 EHRR 454 discussed above; *Attorney General v Guardian Newspapers Ltd* [1999] EMLR 904, 918 per Collins J.
[64] *Attorney General v Guardian Newspapers Ltd* [1999] EMLR 904, 923 per Sedley LJ.

The Sun, with the intention of succeeding in a private prosecution of a man accused of child rape, published prejudicial articles. At the time of publication no proceedings were active. The man was acquitted, and the Attorney General brought proceedings for contempt.

HELD: common law contempt proceedings could be brought when proceedings were 'imminent', as, it was accepted, they were in this case. In some circumstances contempt proceedings could be brought even if proceedings were not imminent if there was an overwhelming requirement to protect the administration of justice.

Attorney General v *News Group Newspapers Plc* [1989] QB 110

The case contains strong words on the need to 'curb' the excesses of the press in order to protect the right to a fair trial.[65] This view, that where there was an overwhelming need, contempt could be brought in respect of acts done before proceedings were 'imminent', was followed but doubted in *Attorney General* v *Sport Newspapers Ltd and others* (1992).[66] It was held, however, that where proceedings were not at least 'imminent', it would be hard to prove the necessary degree of intention. There would need to be a very high degree of probability that the foreseen interference with justice would in fact occur.[67]

Strict liability contempt only becomes possible once proceedings are 'active'[68] and this is more precisely defined than the common law test. 'Active' is defined in Schedule 1 to the Contempt of Court Act 1981. The schedule is detailed. Criminal proceedings are 'active' once 'initial steps' have been taken such as an arrest without a warrant or the issue of an arrest warrant. They remain active until 'concluded' by, for example, acquittal or sentence. Civil proceedings are 'active', for example, from the 'time when arrangements for the hearing are made' such as the setting down for trial in the High Court or the setting of a date for a trial or hearing, and so on. The rules have the virtue of considerable precision which is helpful to the press commenting on criminal matters. There are still problems. A person who voluntarily assists the police and who is subsequently arrested and charged with an offence may, prior to arrest, be subject to highly prejudicial reporting which is not subject to strict liability contempt (though it could come within common law, intentional contempt).[69]

12.9.5 '. . . substantial risk that the course of justice in the proceedings will be seriously impeded or prejudiced'

Strict liability contempt should only be used in serious cases. The Act gives statutory force and attempted precision to what has always been the intention of the common law. Only a publication which 'creates a substantial risk that the course of justice in the proceedings will be seriously impeded or prejudiced'

---

[65] *Attorney General* v *News Group Newspapers Plc* [1989] QB 110, 134 per Watkins LJ.

[66] [1992] 1 All ER 503.

[67] This would seem to be compatible with *News Group* anyway: where there is a strong desire by the media, for example, to obtain a particular result from the judicial system and they are prepared to perform prejudicial or other contemptuous acts in order to achieve it, it is reasonable for the contempt jurisdiction to be flexible enough to meet this challenge.

[68] Section 2(3), Contempt of Court Act 1981.

[69] The issue was raised by press treatment of Ian Huntley and Maxine Carr who were eventually charged, with different offences, in connection with the murder of two children in Cambridgeshire in 2002.

can be the subject of strict liability contempt. This term was discussed in *Attorney General* v *English* (1983).[70] 'Substantial risk' means a likelihood, to a degree that need not be huge but is more than remote and not merely minimal, that the course of justice in particular proceedings will be impeded or prejudiced. It requires consideration of the factors, such as timing and geographical scope, which may indicate this. 'Seriously impeded or prejudiced' relates to the degree of impediment or prejudice which will result if such a 'substantial risk' materialises. 'Seriously' has its ordinary meaning which is left to the court. The complete expression excludes a publication which only creates a remote risk of interference.[71] Both the substantial risk and the serious prejudice must be present. The factors by which they are identified are likely to overlap.[72]

Cases will be decided on their individual merits. If contempt is alleged against a number of publications, each publication must be looked at separately, the law does not recognise contempt based on the accumulation of publications where each one, in itself, is not contemptuous.[73] Similarly, it is the likely impact of the publication at the time it was published which must be considered.

Various factors have been identified as needing consideration.[74] Of particular importance is whether the proceedings involve a jury. Proceedings which are determined by judges alone, most civil proceedings and appeal hearings, are assumed to be professionally incapable of influence by media reporting[75] and so contempt proceedings are unlikely.

Whether the risk of impediment or prejudice is 'substantial' may depend upon a range of matters. For example, the likelihood that the publication in issue will come to the attention of the jurors or still be in their mind at the time of the proceedings is important. The place of trial as compared with the area of circulation of the publication[76] is relevant here as is the degree of prominence and sensational treatment that is given.[77] The length of time between publication and the proceedings at risk is important. In one case a three-month gap was a major reason for finding that there was no substantial risk of prejudice while in another the fact of a six-month period between publication and trial did not prevent a substantial risk.[78] These various factors must be weighed. A remote risk of serious prejudice cannot ground strict liability contempt.

Two Irishmen were arrested for murder. ITN news and, later, local London papers in their first editions identified the men as escaped IRA prisoners. Their trial took place nine months after the stories were published. The Attorney General brought contempt proceedings.

---

[70] [1983] 1 AC 116.
[71] *Attorney General* v *English* [1983] 1 AC 116, 142, per Lord Diplock.
[72] *Attorney General* v *BBC* [1997] EMLR 76, 81.
[73] *Attorney General* v *MGN Ltd and others* [1997] 1 All ER 456.
[74] See, in particular, the ten principles identified in *Attorney General* v *MGN Ltd and others* [1997] 1 All ER 456.
[75] See *R* v *Lonrho* [1989] 2 All ER 1100.
[76] For example, *Attorney General* v *Birmingham Post and Mail Ltd* [1998] 4 All ER 49.
[77] For example, *R* v *Taylor and Taylor* (1994) 98 Cr Ap Rpts 361.
[78] Contrast *Attorney General* v *News Group Newspapers Ltd* [1986] 2 All ER 833.

HELD (QBD): the stories, if remembered by jurors at the trial, would have been highly prejudicial. Nevertheless, the Attorney General had not proved that there was a 'substantial risk' of this happening. Because of the brevity and ephemeral nature of a news item and the small circulation of the first edition of the papers and, in particular, the time gap of nine months between publication and trial, the risk of serious prejudice was remote, not substantial.

Attorney General v *Independent Television News Ltd and others* [1995] 2 All ER 370

Different kinds of factors relate to whether the substantial risk will 'seriously' prejudice or impede the course of justice in the proceedings. It is, predominantly, the impact on the notional juror in the case which needs to be considered. The jury will hear the case as a whole and, in particular, the judge's directions to them. The ability of a jury self-consciously to be impartial should not be underestimated. These matters can be taken into account in contempt proceedings.[79] It is the likely impact of the publication at the time it was published that is in issue; actual prejudice does not need to be proved and the lack of actual prejudice may be a factor in deciding that the prejudice was not serious.[80] The fact that a judge found it necessary to stay proceedings, discharge a jury and order a retrial is not of itself conclusive evidence that the trial has been seriously impeded or prejudiced, though it is a matter of great weight. Whether there should be a stay and whether there has been contempt are different questions with contempt indicating a lesser degree of prejudice than required for a stay.[81]

The degree of seriousness of any prejudice can depend on whether the stories in issue add anything to whatever existing prejudice there might be. Celebrities who are already subject to media attention may find it hard to show that stories about a trial they are involved in have added to popular prejudice about them that already exists.[82] Where, however, a jury may already have some prejudicial knowledge, stories which add to and expand upon this may be in contempt.

Six IRA prisoners escaped from Whitemoor Prison. They were recaptured and put on trial for escaping. The escapes had a great deal of media attention at the time and it was accepted that, while the jury should not be told the nature and context of their original offences, the jury would be presumed to realise that the original offences were serious, might be connected with IRA activities and might relate to the well known escape from Whitemoor. However, during the trial and despite the discharge of the first jury, the *Evening Standard* published particular details of three of the defendants and of serious allegations of prison officer complicity in the escape.

HELD (QBD): the *Evening Standard* story added significantly to the knowledge a notional juror might already have. The story seriously prejudiced the defence in a way that judicial direction could not redress. This was a serious contempt.

Attorney General v *Associated Newspapers Ltd and another* [1998] EMLR 711

---

[79] *Attorney General* v *MGN Ltd and others* [1997] 1 All ER 456.
[80] The difference between contempt and appeals on the grounds of an unsafe conviction because of media prejudice is exposed here. A trial is not likely to be unsafe if there was no actual prejudice: *Attorney General* v *Birmingham Post and Mail* [1999] 4 All ER 49, 57 per Simon Brown LJ.
[81] *Attorney General* v *Birmingham Post and Mail* [1999] 4 All ER 49, 59 per Simon Brown LJ.
[82] *Attorney General* v *MGN Ltd and others* [1997] 1 All ER 456.

Seriousness may depend upon the detailed content and nature of the publication in issue. A sensational, misleading treatment of a defendant may be more prejudicial than a serious treatment,[83] though the seriousness of an article can be a factor in finding that prejudgment has occurred.[84] Publications which disclose previous offences are likely to be seriously prejudicial.[85] Stories that make claims a jury is likely to find authoritative, made by ministers or senior judges, for example, are also likely to be looked at seriously.[86] The fact that a prejudicial statement is made in the obvious context of a humourous, satirical programme does not in itself exclude contempt.[87]

The factors introduced in the previous paragraphs are not rules of law but rather the kinds of issue that will be weighed and considered in deciding whether there has been a contempt that can be punished on the basis of strict liability.

12.10 Defences that apply to strict liability contempt

12.10.1 Innocent publication

The Contempt of Court Act 1981 permits a number of defences. Publishers and distributors may be able to defend themselves against strict liability contempt on the grounds that, despite taking reasonable care, they did not know that the proceedings in question where 'active' or (distributors only) that the material published was contemptuous.

12.10.2 Contemporaneous reports

A person, usually a newspaper or broadcaster, can defend themselves from strict liability contempt on the grounds that the publication in issue was a 'fair and accurate report of legal proceedings held in public, published contemporaneously and in good faith'.[88]

The courts have the power to postpone such contemporaneous reports if it appears necessary so to do in order to avoid 'a substantial risk of prejudice to the administration of justice in those proceedings'. Clearly there is a potential conflict between the public interest in trials, expressed in the media's need for topicality,[89] and the dangers that contemporaneous reports may undermine the fairness of trials by prejudicing juries, adding to the pressure on defendants and witnesses or by creating an atmosphere in which witnesses, defendants and even the judge[90] sensationalise and over-dramatise proceedings in order

---

[83] The reporting in *R v Taylor and Taylor* (1994) 98 Cr Ap Rep 361 (although the Attorney General chose not to bring contempt proceedings) was 'unremitting, extensive, sensational, inaccurate and misleading'.

[84] *Attorney General v Times Newspapers Ltd* [1974] AC 274.

[85] *Attorney General v Times Newspapers Ltd* (1983) *The Times*, 12 February.

[86] *R v McCann and others* (1991) 92 Cr App R 239.

[87] *Attorney General v BBC; Attorney General v Hat Trick Productions Ltd* (1996) TLR 460.

[88] Section 4, Contempt of Court Act 1981.

[89] *Attorney General v Times Newspapers* [2001] EMLR 19.

[90] Allegations of that kind were made in respect of the 'O.J. Simpson' trial.

to meet a media agenda. A particular problem is where reporting of one trial may prejudice a later prosecution on different but related matters.[91]

The approach of the courts to postponement orders under section 4 of the Contempt of Court Act 1981 has been recently summarised in *R v Telegraph Group* (2002),[92] where the Court of Appeal upheld a postponement order relating to the reporting of a murder trial involving police officers who had shot an unarmed man; the reports would have prejudiced future trials involving the same incident. It is a judgment that identifies the relevant factors he courts should consider and takes the Human Rights Act 1998 fully into account, specifically the need to ensure that fair trial rights under Article 6 are properly protected and not merely 'weighed' against the public's interest.[93]

Restrictions on contemporaneous court reporting are likely to be compatible with scheduled Convention rights, specifically Article 10(2) ECHR. The Contempt of Court Act 1981 gives a sufficient basis in law and the orders under section 4(2) are clearly to maintain the 'authority and impartiality of the judiciary'. The courts are clearly sensitive to the needs of a democratic society and the issue of proportionality when deciding whether or not an order should be made. The Strasbourg institutions have not found that particular orders have breached the Convention.[94]

12.10.3 '. . . discussion in good faith of a matter of public affairs or other matters of general public interest . . .': section 5

From the civil liberties perspective the most important defence is that based on the public interest in allowing the discussion of issues which may underlie a trial.

The thalidomide case, *Attorney General v Times Newspapers* (1974),[95] seemed to many, including the Court of Human Rights, to permit judges to make orders which had the effect of preventing legitimate discussion by the media of important public issues. As we have seen, the Contempt of Court Act 1981 was enacted, in part, to attempt to redress the balance somewhat in favour of freedom of expression. Section 5 is one of the main ways in which this is attempted.

5. Discussion of public affairs
A publication made as part of a discussion in good faith of a matter of public affairs or other matters of general public interest is not to be treated as a contempt of court under the strict liability rule if the risk of impediment or prejudice to particular legal proceedings is merely incidental to the discussion.

This 'public interest' defence is restricted to unintended contempt. It should not be taken to mean that the public interest in free expression has no place in

---

[91] *R v Beck ex parte Daily Telegraph* [1993] 2 All ER 177.
[92] [2002] EMLR 10.
[93] See also *MGN Pension Trustees Ltd v Bank of America and others* [1995] 2 All ER 355, a case decided before the coming into effect of the Human Rights Act 1998.
[94] For example, *Hodgson, Woolf Productions, NUJ and Channel Four TV v United Kingdom* (1988) EHRR 503 (the trial of Clive Ponting); *C Ltd v United Kingdom* (1989) Ap. 14132/88 (the release of the Birmingham Six).
[95] [1974] AC 274.

cases of intentional contempt. The circumstances are likely to be very different but, in principle, the Human Rights Act 1998 requires the courts, as public authorities, to give proper effect to Article 10, freedom of expression, when considering whether an action is contemptuous and this duty is enhanced by section 12, Human Rights Act 1998. However, the common law does not require freedom of speech to 'trump' fair trial rights as is, perhaps, the case under statute.

Section 5 of the Contempt of Court Act 1981 was considered in *Attorney General* v *English*.

> E, editor of the *Daily Mail*, published an article supporting the position of a 'pro-life' parliamentary candidate who expressly opposed euthanasia type actions by doctors. The article was published at the time of a high-profile trial of Dr A on euthanasia type charges. The Attorney General brought contempt proceedings after Dr A's acquittal.
> HELD: the article involved a substantial risk of prejudice to the proceedings but was within the s.5 defence. The Attorney General could not show that the risk was more than incidental to the publication.
> *Attorney General* v *English* [1983] 1 AC 116

Once the defence is raised and it is accepted that the article was a good faith discussion of a public matter, the burden of proof is on the Attorney General to show that the effect of the publication was more than incidental. In *English* Lord Diplock said that the prejudicial effect of the publication had to be no more than an 'incidental consequence of expounding its main theme'. In the article there had been, for example, no mention of the trial. Whether or not a prejudicial effect is 'incidental' is likely to be 'a matter of impression'.[96] The closer the main subject matter of a publication is to the subject matter in a trial, the easier it will be for the Attorney General to prove its non-incidental character.[97]

> The *Mail on Sunday* published an article about Michael Fagan, who had broken into the Queen's bedroom. The article alleged a homosexual relationship between Fagan and one of the Queen's bodyguards and described him as a 'rootless neurotic'. It was held that, although the articles created serious prejudice, the section 5 defence applied: the main point of the article had been security failures at Buckingham Palace.
> *Attorney General* v *Times Newspapers* (1983) *The Times* 12 February[98]

This case can be compared with other in which the section 5 defence has been denied.

> An artist was prosecuted for the theft of body parts from a mortuary; the body parts were used to make moulds for sculptures. The issue in the trial was whether the artist had acted honestly. *The Observer* published a story implying that the artist was a necrophile and had a perverted personality.
> HELD: on balance the story did not create a substantial risk of serious prejudice to the artist's trial. If it had done, however, the section 5 defence would not have been

---

[96] *Attorney General* v *Guardian Newspapers Ltd and another* [1992] 3 All ER 38 QBD.
[97] *Attorney General* v *TVS TV* (1989) *The Times*, 7 July.
[98] The case involved contempt proceedings brought in respect of a number of articles.

available. Though, as in the first Fagan article, the trial dealt with a matter of public interest, the main focus of the article in question was on the artist and his activities and so was not incidental to the trial. Here there was no independent issue, such as Royal safety, that existed independently of the issues in the trial.

Attorney General v *Guardian Newspapers Ltd* [1999] EMLR 904

It needs to be clear what it is that section 5 permits. It is a defence which only comes into issue once it is accepted that the publication creates a 'substantial risk that the course of justice in the proceedings will be seriously impeded or prejudiced'. It allows to go unpunished by contempt an article that may have prevented a person from getting a fair trial. Of course the judge in the trial may have stayed proceedings and discharged the jury or given sufficiently compensating directions to the jury, but this is not necessarily so and, in any case, without the force of the law of contempt, there is nothing to stop the same kind of prejudicial publication at the time of re-trial. The common law position, which section 5 replaced, recognised that contempt of court should not punish discussions of public affairs just because they had, as 'an incidental but not intended by product . . . some likelihood of prejudice' to a litigant or defendant.[99] The Contempt of Court Act 1981, however, goes further and removes the protection of the contempt laws even where there is a non-trivial risk of serious prejudice to a trial. The 'mischief' of the common law position that the 1981 Act aimed to remedy was that there needed to be a better balance between fair trials and freedom of expression, not that freedom of expression, in certain circumstances, could 'trump' a fair trial. There is clearly an argument to be made that section 3 of the Human Rights Act 1998 requires the interpretation of section 5 of the Contempt of Court Act 1981 to be limited by a person's right to a fair trial under Article 6(1) ECHR. On this argument, section 5 would, by interpretation, not provide a defence for a publication which created an incidental but substantial risk of serious prejudice, where the prejudice involved a risk to a fair trial as defined by Article 6 ECHR. This would, perhaps, involve a 'strained' interpretation of section 5 but, in relation to protecting Article 6 rights in the context of a criminal trial, the House of Lords has expressed a willingness to do this. The alternative would be a declaration of incompatibility under section 4 of the Human Rights Act 1998.[100]

12.11 Orders preventing or restricting the publication of trials

The general principle is that trials should be open to the public and may be reported in full in the press.[101] To the same effect, Article 6(1) ECHR states: 'In the determination of his civil rights and obligations or of any criminal charge against him, everyone is entitled to a fair and public hearing . . .' However, both English law and the Convention accept there are reasons justifying the exclusion of press and public from proceedings and allowing limits to be

---

[99] Quoted by Lord Reid in *Attorney General* v *Times Newspapers* [1974] AC 274 from *Re Truth and Sportsmen Ltd* (1937) SR (NSW) 242, 249–50.
[100] See the discussion in *R* v *A* [2001] UKHL 25 [2001] 3 All ER 1.
[101] *Scott* v *Scott* [1913] AC 417 HL.

placed on the detailed reporting of a trial. Article 6(1) allows this to be done in the interests of morals, public order or national security; to protect juveniles; to protect the private life of parties if this is necessary; 'or to the extent strictly necessary in the opinion of the court in special circumstances where publicity would prejudice the interests of justice'. Even when media and public are excluded from the trial, judgment should be expressed publicly.

Statute can require or may permit part or all of some trials to be held in private. Many matrimonial proceedings, trials in Youth Courts and hearings before Mental Health Review Tribunals are examples. A prosecution under the Official Secrets Act is an example of a trial that may be *in camera* if the judge so rules.[102] There is also discretion at common law for judges to exclude public and media if the interests of justice so require. This can be done, for example, where the confidentiality of material is the central issue in the proceedings. Any such exclusions must now be compatible with Article 6. There are similar duties or powers respecting particular information which must or can be withheld even though a trial is otherwise held in public. Thus the identity of a rape victim cannot be disclosed in court[103] and, under the Children and Young Persons Act 1933, the court may order the anonymity of any child who is a party or witness to any proceedings.[104]

At common law judges have considerable discretion to make aspects of public trials secret; in particular they may order that a defendant, a party or a witness should be anonymous. This power must be used only when necessary for the administration of justice[105] and not for the avoidance of embarrassment[106] or the simple protection of privacy.[107] Protection from blackmail[108] or to protect the security services[109] are acceptable reasons. The protection of the right to life of a witness or defendant or, equally, their right not to be tortured or suffer inhuman or degrading treatment may require an order to be made. Unpopular defendants and witnesses are entitled to protection of their fundamental human rights and the principle of open justice must give way to this.[110]

Such orders as these can be given effect through section 11 of the Contempt of Court Act 1981 which allows a court to issue orders prohibiting the publication, particularly in the media, of matters such as those mentioned above. Such orders can be highly controversial and should be used sparingly. In making such orders the courts are required to balance the administration of justice with freedom of the press and the rights of persons to free expression under common law and HRA 1998, Schedule 1, Article 10.[111]

---

[102] Section 8(4), Official Secrets Act 1920.
[103] Section 4, Sexual Offences (Amendment) Act 1976.
[104] Confined to non-criminal proceedings.
[105] *R v Evesham Justices ex parte McDonagh and Berrows Newspapers Ltd* [1988] 1 QB 553.
[106] *R v Malvern Justice ex parte Evans and Berrows Newspapers Ltd* [1988] 1 QB 540.
[107] *R v Westminster City Council ex parte Castelli* (1995) 7 Admin LR 840.
[108] *R v Socialist Worker Printers and Publishers Ltd ex parte Attorney General* [1975] QB 637.
[109] *Attorney General v Leveller Magazine Ltd* [1979] AC 440.
[110] *R v Lord Saville and others ex parte A and others* [1999] 4 All ER 860, in which the Court of Appeal allowed the applicants, soldier witnesses, to retain their anonymity for the purpose of the 'Bloody Sunday' inquiry. See also *Venables and another v News Group Newspapers* [2001] 1 All ER 908.
[111] *Clibbery v Allan* [2002] 1 All ER 865.

12.12 Jury secrets

Section 8 of the Contempt of Court Act 1981 makes it a criminal contempt for a disclosure to be made of what is said by jurors in the course of their deliberations. The disclosure need not come from the jury themselves.[112] The jury is at the heart of the criminal justice system; juries both represent the principle of freedom from state control but, at the same time, have been implicated in all the miscarriages of justice that have beset the criminal justice system since the 1970s. No one knows whether their deliberations are careful and rational or whether they are based on bigotry and a world view found in the mass media. Section 8 prevents any of this information from being considered, even on the basis of careful research. Most importantly section 8 seems to be a barrier to an effective examination in court of any inadequacies of a jury's decision. Yet a jury's decision that is, for example, tainted by racism[113] or irrationality[114] ought to be set aside and may, in any case, be incompatible with a person's right to a fair trial. In so far as section 8 prevents the proper testing in court of the fairness of a trial, it is arguably incompatible with Article 6 ECHR.

---

[112] *Attorney General* v *Associated Newspapers* [1994] 1 All ER 556.
[113] *Sander* v *United Kingdom* (2001) EHRR 44; cf. *Gregory* v *United Kingdom* (1998) 25 EHRR 577.
[114] *R* v *Young* [1995] QB 324.

Part IV
Political freedom

13

Political participation and electoral politics

13.1 Political participation

The right of people to participate in public affairs is fundamental to a reasonable democracy. For most people it is predominantly through the processes and institutions of representative politics that such participation takes place. Voting in elections for the House of Commons, the European Parliament, for one of the devolved legislative bodies or for a local council is a fundamental, though in many ways, minimal means of participation. For those who are or wish to be politically active, there should also be in a democracy the freedom to be a candidate in elections and, if successful, a member of the representative body to which elected. Similarly the politically active should not be denied, by arbitrary or unreasonable laws, the right, if properly selected, to be a member of the government or a local council or a devolved executive.

As indicated in Chapter 3, public life in the United Kingdom is conducted by a large range of organisations of various kinds and of various degrees of independence from central government. Appointment to such bodies is normally within the patronage of a minister or the discretion of a professional body, for example, though they may be supervised by an appointments commission. Few such bodies are in any way directly or even indirectly elected. They may have to consult with the public but are not in any direct way subject to public censure or recall. While fundamental rights to vote and to stand for representative bodies are widely recognised, rights of wider participation are much less clear.

13.1.1 International law

International law recognises the value of political activity in an effective, pluralist democracy. Predominantly such activity is protected by fundamental rights of expression and political association and assembly. A wider, rather abstract right to political participation is also recognised. Article 25 of the International Covenant on Civil and Political Rights establishes rights not only to vote and be elected and to have equal access to public service but also declares that 'every citizen shall have the right and the opportunity . . . to take part in the conduct of public affairs, directly or through freely chosen representatives'. A broad conception of public affairs is meant which includes the exercise of legislative, executive and administrative power and includes all aspects of public administration.[1] However, it seems that little that is specific is required under the Article. No particular political system is required, there is no attempt to identify the kinds of public body that ought to be elected and, in any case, this part of Article 25 is understood to be 'programmatic', merely identifying aspirations,[2] rather than laying down specific duties.

13.1.2 Freedom of association

Effective participation in the public and political life of the country is likely to be in concert with others and so the extent and limits of freedom of association are of great importance. Liberal political theory upholds a wide ranging freedom for political associations. At the heart of liberal theory is the assertion that human beings differ in their views of what is worthwhile and it follows that fundamental rights to associate and organise to further these conceptions of the good, including having them adopted as community purposes, would be accepted by the kind of rational, morally sensitive being that liberal theory predicates good constitutional law making on.

Convention rights
Rights of political association are asserted in international law and, indeed, they are central to the conception of a democratic state that is made explicit in international human rights instruments or jurisprudence.[3] In particular the European Court of Human Rights has made it clear that political parties are essential to the proper functioning of a democracy and that democratic practices are of great importance in maintaining the rights and freedoms the Convention upholds.[4]

Rights to establish political parties and other types of political association derive from Article 11 ECHR.[5] As well as providing for freedom of assembly, the Article seeks to protect freedom of association, and includes the right to form and to join trade unions. It permits restrictions on these freedoms which are 'prescribed by law and are necessary in a democratic society' and the purposes of such restrictions are confined to: 'the interests of national security

---

[1] United Nations Human Rights Committee, General Comment 25: UN Doc. CCPR/C/21/Rev/ Add7, paragraph 5.
[2] Steiner, H. (1988) 'Political Participation as a Human Right', 1, *Harvard Human Rights Yearbook*, 77. The right to vote and to be elected and the right to equal access to public office are likely to generate harder, more specific, rights.
[3] For example, the strong statement in favour of political pluralism and independent political parties in *Document of the Copenhagen Meeting of the Conference on the Human Dimension of the Conference on Security and Cooperation in Europe*, in Brownlie, I. (ed.) (1992) *Basic Documents on Human Rights*, 3rd edn. Oxford: Clarendon Press.
[4] *United Communist Party of Turkey and others v Turkey* (1998) 26 EHRR 121. On the conception of democracy inherent in the Convention see Mowbray, A. (1999) 'The Role of the European Court of Human Rights in the Promotion of Democracy', *Public Law*, 703.
[5] Quoted in Chapter 2. See also Article 22 ICCPR discussed in Nowak, M. (1993) *UN Covenant on Civil and Political Rights. CCPR Commentary*. Kehl: N.P. Engel, pp. 384–400. The right is expressed in similar terms to Article 11 ECHR except the political restrictions relating to public service are confined to the armed forces and the police and so do not necessarily include civil servants.

or public safety, for the prevention of disorder or crime, for the protection of health or morals, for the protection of the reputation or rights of others'. It expressly permits restrictions on freedom of association by members of the armed forces, the police and by government officials.

Other Articles of particular relevance to political parties and associations include Article 10, freedom of expression, and Article 3 of the First Protocol, which provides for elections and implies the rights of individuals to vote and to stand in elections. Political parties and other associations have standing to bring cases before the Court, under Article 34, if they are directly affected by legislation or state action which restricts Convention freedoms. They are much less likely to have standing if their complaint relates, for example, to some aspect of the election system or other policy that affects members and citizens generally and not the party as such, although it is unlikely to be difficult to find individual applicants who can adopt the party's arguments as their own.[6] The same standing rules will apply if cases are brought under section 7 of the Human Rights Act 1998.

English law

English law recognises freedom of association as a general principle.[7] The value of political association is often expressed by the courts in terms of freedom of expression rather than association. An interesting example is the upholding by the courts of a contract entered into by the National Front (a forerunner of the British National Party) with a local authority for the hire of a hall for a general, private meeting of the party. The council, on changing its party balance, tried to resile from the contract on grounds that, in the court's opinion, related to opposition to the views likely to be expressed. The court ordered specific performance of the contract exercising its discretion as to remedies in order to further the freedoms of expression and, in effect, of association.[8]

Freedom of association to pursue political ends is restricted in respect of some types of organisation which aim to advance their non-political principal purposes by political means. This involves areas of law which are outside the main concerns of this chapter.[9] Trade unions, for example, can only support political parties on the basis of a regular ballot of members and exclusively with money from a political fund held separately from the general funds and to which members may choose not to contribute.[10] Commercial companies must obtain shareholder consent and disclose their political donations. Charitable organisations are prohibited from having political purposes or supporting political parties but may pursue non-political objectives by other, restrained political means.

---

[6] Discussed in *Liberal Party* v *United Kingdom* (1982) 4 EHRR 106.
[7] See for the philosophical basis, for a comparison with US law and for a consideration of specific issues including the political purposes of trade unions: Leader, S. (1992) *Freedom of Association*. New Haven, CT: Yale University Press.
[8] *Verrall* v *Great Yarmouth* [1981] 1 QB 202.
[9] Davis, H. (2000) *Political Freedom*. London: Continuum, chapters 4–7.
[10] Trade Union and Labour Relations (Consolidation) Act (1992), Part I, Chapter VI. See, for example, Pitt, G. (2000) *Employment Law*, 4th edn. London: Sweet & Maxwell, ch. 11, pp. 350–5.

13.1.3 Political restriction

The major exception found in United Kingdom law regarding freedom of political association relates to the many thousands of public officials of one kind or another who are 'politically restricted'. The contracts of employment of many local government officers are required, by statute, to contain terms restricting the officers' political activities. The restriction applies to those occupying specified senior posts or who are paid over a certain point on the salary scale or who, though paid below that point, give advice or speak on behalf of the council.[11] Local government officers, especially those whose restriction is solely based on salary, may seek exemption from the ban. Many civil servants are similarly restricted. The Civil Service Management Code, produced ultimately under the Prerogative, imposes both general restraints of style and behaviour on all civil servants and specific political restrictions on significant numbers. Senior civil servants are politically restricted by virtue of their office, a very large middle group are restricted but may obtain exemption (which can derive from a block exemption), and industrial and non-office staff are under no restrictions except in relation to becoming a Member of Parliament or other, non-local representative assembly.

The restrictions that such groups are under relate, first, to a ban on membership of and candidature for the House of Commons, the European Parliament and the devolved Parliament and Assemblies. Restricted local government officials, but not civil servants (though some may need permission), are banned from being local councillors. Second, those who are politically restricted are banned from taking managing roles in political parties and from canvassing. Simple membership and limited participation is not banned. Third, there are restrictions on freedom of speech, in public meetings or through publications of various kinds, where a main aim of the speech is to effect support for a political party. These are very significant but perhaps not total bans on political activity. Subject to general behavioural restraints, especially on civil servants, it is at least arguable that political restriction does not apply to non-party political activity such as supporting organisations pursing aims which are not the focus of the party political battleground. Environmental issues may be examples of this. They may be highly controversial but, so long as proper 'reserve' is maintained and so long as political masters are not embarrassed, may be pursued by politically restricted officials. Nothing in the political restriction provisions should inhibit trade union activity in the public sector.

Police officers are under much wider restriction even than civil servants or local government officers. They are prohibited from 'any active part in politics', a ban which would appear to include the pursuit of any controversial cause whether or not it is a matter of concern to the political parties. The ban on politics is not a ban on public service such as school governorship.[12]

Political restriction is justified on two general grounds. The first is that it is necessary in order to maintain the integrity and effective functioning of

---

[11] Sections 1–3, Local Government and Housing Act 1989. There are various statutory instruments. Local Government Officers (Political Restrictions) Regulations 1990 SI 1990 No. 851 defines political activities.
[12] *Champion v Chief Constable of the Gwent Constabulary* [1990] 1 WLR 1.

representative institutions. The scrutiny of the executive, for example, would be compromised if conducted by the very officials whose decisions were being examined. The second justification is that official impartiality, or at least its appearance, is necessary to the effectiveness and proper administration of government and the public services. Few dispute these aims; however, whether the system of political restriction is a reasonable way of achieving them is open to argument. In particular it is suggested that banning officials from representative assemblies may deny the assembly certain sorts of experience which, overall, would enhance its effectiveness; restriction means that citizens have limits placed upon their choice of representative; most importantly it is observed that these restrictions are major interferences with many people's political freedom, particularly in the sense that private life is restricted because of the job a person does.[13] It is doubted whether the scale of the restrictions are necessary in order to achieve an effective public service. Nevertheless, the European Court of Human Rights, in *Ahmed* v *United Kingdom* (2000),[14] has refused to find that, in many of its respects, political restriction (here in respect of local government officers) violates Convention Rights, in particular Articles 10 and 11 and Article 3 of the First Protocol. The public interest in an impartial public service is of overriding importance. Strong dissents by a minority of judges were made to the effect that such widespread restriction of political freedom is not necessary in a democratic society and the aims of impartiality in the public sector can be achieved by an approach which is more focused on particular roles and only brings in the law when there are particular abuses which are dealt with through the disciplinary process.

13.2 Political parties

The major way in which people seek to participate directly in political affairs is through political parties and, in a democracy, their work is focused on elections.

In the United Kingdom people may (they are not prevented) form and join political parties without state approval or regulation and those parties and associations are permitted to pursue their general activities bound only by the general law and not by specific, restrictive laws. There is, however, an increasing body of regulative law which relates to parties and elections.

13.2.1 Banning political parties and organisations

The essence of freedom of association is the independence of political parties and associations from the state. The state may, however, have legitimate

---

[13] Morris, G.S. (1998a) 'Political Activities of Public Servants and Freedom of Expression', in Loveland I. (ed.), *Incorporating the First Amendment*. Oxford: Hart Publishing; Morris G.S. (1998b) 'Local Government Workers and Rights of Political Participation: Time for a Change', *Public Law* 25; Morris, G. (1999) 'The Political Activities of Local Government Workers and the European Convention on Human Rights', *Public Law* 211.

[14] (2000) 29 EHRR 1. Greek provisions preventing broadcasting officials from Parliamentary candidature were upheld in *Gitonas* v *Greece* (1997) 27 EHRR 417.

grounds for seeking to ban political organisations which are compatible with the rights to freedom of association. The modern law in the United Kingdom relates to terrorism and is discussed in Chapter 17.

13.2.2 The registration of political parties

The state may also seek to exercise control over political parties through registration. In the United Kingdom, registration provisions and other restriction have been introduced under the Political Parties, Elections and Referendums Act 2000.[15] Political parties who wish to field candidates in their name or wish, as themselves, to stand under a party-list system of proportional representation[16] can only do so if they are registered with the Electoral Commission, a body created under the Act. The point of registration is to enable certain kinds of proportional representation to be possible and also to permit various restrictions as to funding and campaign spending to be imposed. The aim of such restrictions is to limit the ability of rich and powerful organisations and individuals to have a disproportionate impact on the agenda of elections and on the policies that parties choose to pursue. To do this, the freedom of parties to finance themselves and spend as they will is curtailed.

The impetus to these reforms was a major review of the funding of political parties undertaken by the Parliamentary Committee on Standards in Public Life.[17] The context in which the Committee wrote was widespread concern about large, undisclosed donations made to parties and the possibility that they may influence policy or provide access to ministers for the donors. Also there was a long-standing though, for the time being, diminishing concern at what was believed to be a funding imbalance between major parties with the Conservatives being funded by private companies to a higher level than Labour who were more reliant on donations from trade unions.[18] There was also a concern that current electoral law could not effectively prevent misleading practices.

Background constitutional and human rights theory discloses two principal approaches. One gives prominence to freedom of expression over other democratic values and so opposes the notion of restraining donations and, perhaps, limiting party expenditures.[19] This somewhat absolutist promotion of free speech is associated with some constitutional courts.[20] The other approach is that the freedom of donors and parties can be properly circumscribed in the

---

[15] Which adopts and expands provisions first introduced by the Registration of Political Parties Act 1998.

[16] As has been used in elections for the European Parliament and is part of the election system for the devolved Parliament and Assemblies.

[17] Lord Neill of Bladen, QC (Chairman), Committee on Standards in Public Life (1998) *Fifth Report: The Funding of Political Parties in the United Kingdom*, Volume I: Report and Volume II: Evidence. Cm 4057-I, Cm 4057-II.

[18] By the General Election of 1997 this imbalance had been significantly reduced.

[19] In the USA it is harder to make restrictions on donations compatible with the constitution than restrictions on campaign expenditure.

[20] For example, in Australia as discussed in Ewing, K. (1993) 'New Constitutional Constraints in Australia', *Public Law* 256.

name of creating election conditions under which the competition for votes can be conducted reasonably free of the desires of the party sponsors and the general influence of the socially powerful. The second view is the one adopted under the new Act. The evidence from the European Court of Human Rights is that proportionate restrictions on freedom of expression, whose purpose is fair elections, is compatible with the Convention.[21]

Under the Act, political parties that seek registration have to adopt a certain organisational structure. The main parties must have a leader, a nominating officer and a treasurer, and they may have a campaigns officer.[22] They also need a system for arranging the financial affairs of the party. The Electoral Commission must register a party which meets these requirements unless the party is proposing to campaign under a name which might, by being associated with another party, confuse voters. Registration may also be refused if the proposed name is more than six words, is obscene or offensive, includes words which would be likely to amount to the commission of an offence, includes non-Roman script or includes any word banned by the Secretary of State under powers in the Act.[23] As well as registering names, parties may register political emblems. Only registered political parties are permitted to have party political broadcasts.[24] As well as registration, the Act imposes significant duties of accounting onto the party treasurers, including an annual statement of accounts and audit.[25] Criminal offences can be committed if these provisions are not adhered to without proper excuse.

Registration and Convention rights

Legal restraint on political parties through registration by a state body seems to be consistent with Convention Rights. Article 3 of the First Protocol has been raised by political parties objecting to the application to them of various registration provisions. Article 3 is construed as creating an individual right to stand in elections and also a recognition that, if the will of the people in the choice of the legislature is to be given effect, political parties must be free to put forward candidates and campaign. The Court of Human Rights, in the principal case, recognised that these rights and freedoms can be subject to reasonable restriction.[26] These can include, for example, registrations which require a small number of signatures as a measure of public support,[27] or which must be in an official language.[28] Given that individuals retain the right to stand in elections without registration, and given the exceptions from some of the more onerous organisational requirements enjoyed by small parties, there would seem to be a strong case that the restrictions on the electoral

---

[21] For example, *Bowman* v *United Kingdom* (1998) 26 1 EHRR 1 which dealt with limits on expenditure by third parties in constituency campaigns.

[22] There are some provisions which make it easier for small parties or parties which resist heirarchical organisation still to register: see section 34, PPERA 2000. There are provisions for the Electoral Commission to assist parties in meeting the requirements of the Act.

[23] PPERA 2000, s. 28.

[24] PPERA 2000, s. 37.

[25] PPERA 2000, Part III.

[26] *Mathieu-Mohin and Clerfayt* v *Belgium* (1987) 10 EHRR 1, see paragraph 52.

[27] For example, *X* v *Austria* (1976) 6 D&R 120.

[28] *Andecha Astur* v *Spain* (1997) 90-B D&R 172.

freedom of political parties are likely to be reasonable and compatible with the Convention.

The point of registration in United Kingdom law is to facilitate mechanisms for protecting the integrity of the election process. Proportionate restrictions on freedom of expression, made in pursuit of this end, have been accepted by the Court[29] and the same argument would be likely to justify proportionate restrictions on freedom of association. The Court would otherwise have to display a strict, absolutist preference for freedom of speech over all other legitimate election concerns for it to find that the restrictions on the right to stand inherent in the Political Parties, Elections and Referendums Act 2000 are incompatible with Article 3 of the First Protocol.

It does not seem possible to refuse registration on content-specific grounds under the 2000 Act since the grounds on which the Commission may refuse registration could be easily avoided by any party. Thus the Electoral Commission would appear to have no option but to register an out-and-out racist party, assuming that its name does not amount to the commission of a criminal offence. The Court of Human Rights, however, might well accept a refusal to register, for election purposes, parties, such as racist parties, who, by campaigning let alone by winning, might violate the rights of others. The provision in Article 17, that the exercise of Convention Rights cannot be used to violate the rights and freedoms of others, has been held, by the Commission, to apply to political parties seeking election registration.[30]

13.3 Elections and the law

13.3.1 Convention rights: Article 3 of the First Protocol

Surprisingly, for an instrument committed to democracy as the most effective means of protecting human rights, the European Convention on Human Rights provides little by way of direct promotion of political participation. Of course that goal is implicit in the protection of freedom of expression, assembly and association. The only explicit reference to participation in the political process is Article 3 of the First Protocol.

Article 3 Right to free elections
The High Contracting Parties undertake to hold free elections at reasonable intervals by secret ballot, under conditions which will ensure the free expression of the opinion of the people in the choice of the legislature.

Despite the importance of 'democracy' in the Convention system a provision relating to voting was one of the hardest to obtain agreement on, and this explains why it is contained in a Protocol. The United Kingdom, in particular, was anxious to avoid an overly prescriptive approach to what was required by a political system and needed a form of words which would recognise the different systems in Europe. The United Kingdom, in particular, sought to

---

[29] *Bowman v United Kingdom* (1998) 26 1 EHRR 1.
[30] *Glimmerveen and Hagenbeek v Netherlands* (1979) 18 D&R 187.

avoid any requirement, express or implied, for a system of proportional representation or for a wholly elected system which would have compromised the hereditary House of Lords. What emerged was, apparently, no more than an agreement by the states to hold fair elections for the national legislature. Nevertheless, the Court of Human Rights has read into Article 3 an individual right to vote and stand in elections, albeit a right subject to reasonable restrictions.[31] Restrictions on the franchise as to age, period of residence, language, imprisonment and membership of foreign legislatures have been accepted by the Commission and Court of Human Rights. No particular system of voting is required, there is no requirement that votes should be equally weighted, that the legislature should be proportionately representative[32] or that national, racial or other minorities should be specially represented.[33] The Court does, however, have the final say on voting restrictions and any which strike at the very essence of the right would violate the Convention.

The scope of Article 3 of the First Protocol is very narrow and apparently narrower than Article 25 ICCPR. The duty on states and the rights of individuals to stand and to vote are confined to the 'legislature'. This is an autonomous Convention term that has been defined by reference to those bodies which can enact the primary, supreme law of a country and it can be a complex entity. In the United Kingdom it will include the House of Commons, the European Parliament[34] and, perhaps, the Scottish Parliament, the Northern Ireland Legislative Assembly but not the National Assembly of Wales since the latter cannot enact primary legislation.[35] The reference to 'the legislature', however, means that a great deal of the public life of the country is outside the scope of Article 3. In particular elections for parish councils, principal local authorities, mayoral elections and elections for regional assemblies should they develop are not covered; nor are referendums, increasingly important in United Kingdom politics, required to meet the standards of Article 3. Nor is there any requirement that other public bodies, even if they are rule-making, should be even elected; nothing in Article 3 promotes wider participation in public life.

13.3.2 The United Kingdom electoral system

The electoral system of the United Kingdom appears to meet the minimum standards under the Convention.[36] A first-past-the-post, winner-take-all system is used for the House of Commons and local, including mayoral, elections and this is not incompatible with the Convention. Elections for the European Parliament and for the devolved assemblies combine this system with a form of proportional representation. It is worth noting that the voting system is

---

[31] *Mathieu-Mohin and Clerfayt v Belgium* (1987) 10 EHRR 1.
[32] *Liberal Party v United Kingdom* (1982) 4 EHRR 106.
[33] *Lindsay v United Kingdom* (1979) 1 D&R 247.
[34] *Matthews v United Kingdom* (1999) 28 EHRR 361.
[35] Davis, H. (1999) 'Constitutional Reform in the United Kingdom and the Right to Free and Fair Elections, *EHRLR* 4, 411.
[36] For a more detailed description see, for example, Ewing, K. and Bradley, A. (2002) *Constitutional and Adminstrative Law*. London: Pearson Longman, chapter 9.

decided by the government of the day and enacted as ordinary legislation; the voting system enjoys no particular constitutional protection. The Electoral Commission has been given an important advisory role on such matters. Constituency boundaries are agreed by Parliament on the basis of ten-yearly reports by the Boundary Commission, a task which will, under the Political Parties, Elections and Referendums Act 2000, be reassigned to the Electoral Commission. Persons are not compelled to vote. There is increasing concern with voter apathy and the government is cautiously experimenting, mainly in local elections, with new methods of voting such as extensive postal voting and voting on-line or by using touch tone telephones.

13.3.3 The franchise

The franchise is declared in the Representation of the People Act 1983, as amended, particularly by the Representation of the People Act 2000. A person is entitled to vote if he or she is on the register of electors for the constituency for which they are voting, is not under any legal incapacity to vote, is a Commonwealth citizen (including, of course, a British citizen) or a citizen of the Republic of Ireland, and is over 18 years of age.

Registration provisions have, in the past, been a significant barrier to the exercise of the franchise by some otherwise qualified persons. The Representation of the People Act 2000 makes registration easier. An otherwise qualified person is entitled to be registered if he or she is resident in the constituency in which they wish to vote at the time they seek registration. Residency is no longer defined by reference to a particular date. A person residing illegally (e.g. a trespasser) is not disenfranchised[37] though illegal entrants under the Immigration Acts are not entitled to be registered. Homeless people may now obtain registration by showing a 'local connection' to the constituency. Those with more than one home in which they reside (e.g. students in halls of residence) may register in more than one place, though they may only vote once.[38] Both prisoners on remand and persons detained for treatment under mental health legislation are entitled to vote but, in the past, have found it difficult to establish residency. The Representation of the People Act 2000 has facilitated arrangements for both these classes.[39] Merchant seamen may vote[40] and members of the armed forces serving overseas, along with their families, may establish a 'service connection' and be registered.[41] British citizens resident overseas for, in some cases, as long as 15 years, may be entitled to vote if they are able to make and do make an 'overseas elector's declaration'.[42]

The law identifies certain persons as under a legal incapacity and they are not entitled to be registered and to vote. Peers of the realm, but only if they are entitled to sit in the House of Lords, including the Lords Spiritual and the Law Lords, may not vote.[43] Irish peers and hereditary peers of the United

---

[37] *Hipperson* v *Newbury Electoral Officer* [1985] QB 1060.
[38] *Fox* v *Stirk; Ricketts* v *Cambridge City Electoral Registration Officer* [1970] 2 QB 463.
[39] Representation of the People Act 1983, s. 7A.
[40] Under the terms of s. 6, Representation of the People Act 1983.
[41] Under the terms of ss. 14–17, Representation of the People Act 1983.
[42] Representation of the People Act 1985, ss. 1–4.

Kingdom who are, under the House of Lords Act 1999, not entitled to sit in the House of Lords can vote in elections and sit in the House of Commons. Convicted prisoners who are detained in prison or offenders detained in mental hospital are not entitled to vote.[44] Persons convicted of illegal practices in elections are disenfranchised for five years.

Only citizens of the Commonwealth (including British citizens) or of the Republic of Ireland may be registered and vote in general elections. The exclusion of non-Commonwealth resident foreigners, even though they have lived in the country for many years, is compatible with common practice and allowed under Article 18 ECHR and is accepted as a reasonable restriction on the franchise compatible with Article 3 of the First Protocol. As a matter of general European Union law, resident citizens of the European Union are not entitled to vote in general elections but they may be registered for local elections and elections for devolved assemblies.

13.3.4 Candidature in the United Kingdom

Wider participation can be through candidature in elections and membership of elected bodies such as the House of Commons and local councils. To be a Member of Parliament a person must be over 21, must be a British citizen or a citizen of a Commonwealth country or the Republic of Ireland, and must not be legally disqualified. Disqualification can be either in respect of candidature or because membership of the body concerned is barred. Peers and peeresses who are entitled to sit in the House of Lords are barred from the House of Commons. Persons convicted of treason are disqualified as are convicted prisoners serving a sentence of at least one year. Undischarged bankrupts may not be MPs and persons convicted of corrupt or illegal election practices are barred for five years. The mentally ill may also be ineligible for membership. The bar on the clergy being MPs has now been lifted.[45] In quantitative terms, the largest number of people prevented from being Members of Parliament are those officials (office holders and employees) who are prohibited by the House of Commons Disqualification Act 1975. Judges, civil servants, members of the armed forces and police officers are, by section 1, disqualified from membership of the House of Commons. Parts 2 and 3 of Schedule 1 specify a large number of public offices whose holders are likewise barred from Parliament. Schedule 1 can be added to by Order in Council made after a resolution of the House of Commons. In the case of civil servants, the police and local government officers, this ban is part of a wider series of political restrictions which have been described above.

13.3.5 Campaigning

Donations and disclosure
Some of the most significant provisions of the Political Parties, Elections and Referendums Act 2000 impose duties on registered political parties in relation

---

[43] House of Lords Act 1999.
[44] Sections 3 and 3A, Representation of the People Act 1983. See Chapter 9.
[45] House of Commons (Removal of Clergy Disqualification) Act 2001.

to donations by supporters. 'Donation' is broadly defined to include, for example, the provision of services to the party on other than commercial terms.[46] The Act restricts donations to those which come from a 'permissible' source. Permissible donors are individuals, companies, trade unions and various other organisations who might want to pursue their activities by party political means.[47] Most public authorities (including local councils) are prevented by law from being donors. Charities, as unincorporated associations, are not excluded by the Act but are banned, certainly in the view of the Charity Commissioners, from such donations. The main thrust of the definition of a permissible donor is to exclude anonymous donations and individuals, companies and organisations from outside the United Kingdom (or, if a company registered in the European Union, carrying on business in the United Kingdom). Seeking to avoid these restrictions can be a criminal offence.

In relation to permissible donations the Act then imposes duties of disclosure onto political parties. In particular parties must, on a regular basis, disclose donations from individual permissible sources which, individually or by aggregation, come to over £5,000 and additional donations from the same source aggregating to £1,000.[48] Donations of less than £200 do not need to be disclosed by the party but need to be disclosed by the donor if they aggregate to more than £5,000 in a year. During general election periods the reports must be made on a weekly basis.[49] These disclosures of donations are made to the Electoral Commission. Failure to make proper disclosure to the Commission can be an offence if done without reasonable excuse.[50] The Act imposes no limit on the amount of a donation and to that extent the problem of the influence of large donations and the influence over or access to government that it may or may not buy, remains.

Campaign expenditure
The traditional approach under the Representation of the People Act 1983 and its predecessors has been to impose strict, low limits on the amount that can be spent on encouraging people to vote or not to vote for particular candidates, and to require that only candidates and their agents can make such expenditures. Third parties in constituencies have been prevented, subject to minimal limits, from spending money. National campaigns, on the other hand have been, subject to broadcasting restraints discussed below, unlimited as to expenditure.

For the reasons given earlier in this chapter, the situation has been changed under the Political Parties, Elections and Referendums Act 2000. Rather than limit donations the Act limits direct and 'notional'[51] campaign expenditures by and on behalf of political parties during election periods. The limits for General Election spending were, at the time of enactment in 2000, £30,000 for each constituency in Great Britain in which the party fields candidates. This means that a party campaigning throughout the United Kingdom[52] could

---

[46] Sections 50–53, PPERA 2000.
[47] Section 54, PPERA 2000.
[48] Section 62, PPERA 2000.
[49] Section 63, PPERA 2000.
[50] Section 65, PPERA 2000.
[51] For example, the advantageous transfer of property to a party: s. 73, PPERA 2000.

spend an amount approaching £20m.[53] In Northern Ireland the limit is £30,000 for each constituency without an overall limit for small parties. Different amounts apply in respect of the European Parliament and the devolved legislatures. The treasurer, or someone he or she appoints, is responsible for campaign expenditure and they can commit an offence if they knowingly authorise expenditure outside the limits. Anyone who incurs campaign expenditure for a party without the consent of the Treasurer or her or his appointee may also commit an offence. Campaign expenditures must be reported to the Electoral Commission. Similar restrictions apply, taking into account necessary differences, to referendum campaigns. Similarly the Act limits the amount that third parties such as individuals, trade unions, commercial companies or pressure groups can spend on supporting or opposing parties or candidates at elections nationally. Expenditures of around £500 are now permitted in individual constituencies.

Election meetings
The extent to which the state has the duty to take positive steps to promote political life is unclear. As has been mentioned above, there are currently steps being taken to encourage voters to cast their ballot by introducing easier forms of voting. A positive duty is imposed on local authorities to provide suitable rooms for candidates to hold public meetings in support of their candidature during Parliamentary and local elections.[54] The rooms, which may be in maintained schools, must be provided free of charge though candidates must defray any expenses and pay for any damage caused. In *Webster* v *Southwark London Borough Council*[55] the court held that a local authority has no discretion to refuse to provide a room, particularly on political grounds, since only Parliament, and not a local council, could, in effect, proscribe a political party. Threats to public order are the concern of the police. Once it is established that the request for an election room has come from a bona fide candidate, no further public law judgments are involved and the candidate has a private law right to a room.[56] In fact, the issue can, at times, give rise to controversies over whether the meeting is open to the public rather than being confined to ticket-holding members or, in the case of some National Front candidates in the 1980s, whether the meeting is in furtherance of the candidature rather than aimed at intimidation of the local community.[57]

13.3.6 Political broadcasting

Advertising
In the United Kingdom, election law bans broadcast advertising by individuals, candidates or parties but, in exchange, creates a system of party political

---

[52] PPERA 2000, Schedule 9. The Conservative and Labour Parties do not campaign in Northern Ireland.
[53] The relevant provisions came into force on 16 February 2001 though lower amounts were stipulated in transitional provisions for the General Election of May 2001.
[54] Currently ss. 95 and 96, Representation of the People Act 1983.
[55] [1983] 1 QB 698.
[56] *Ettridge* v *Morrell* (1987) 85 LGR 100 CA.
[57] See Rawlings, H.F. (1988) *Law and the Electoral Process*. London: Sweet & Maxwell, pp. 189–5.

broadcasts which, at election time, become party election broadcasts.[58] Press and poster advertising is permitted but such campaigns are subject to the expenditure limits on constituency and national campaigns.[59] Clearly this general scheme involves a restriction on the freedom of expression of individuals and groups wishing to advertise and, in some countries, it has been found to violate fundamental rights.[60] The ban on political advertising, as a licence condition, has been accepted by the European Commission on Human Rights[61] and the purpose of severe restrictions on election spending in order to maintain the fairness of elections has been accepted in principle, subject to the proportionality of individual bans, by the Court of Human Rights.[62]

The BBC is, of course, not allowed to carry any advertisements, including political ones, and the Broadcasting Act 1990 bans television and radio stations licensed by the Independent Television Commission and Radio Authority respectively from broadcasting political advertising. The ban is embodied in the ITC's Code of Advertising Standards and Practice.[63] In November 2001, for example, a proposed advertisement by the RSPCA which detailed the lives of broiler chickens was banned from television broadcasting.[64] The ban on political advertising will continue under the proposed reforms to broadcasting law.[65] 'Political' is not defined but the regulators' views, that it extends beyond party political activity, has been accepted by the courts. In *R v Radio Authority ex parte Bull* (1995)[66] the courts upheld a ban by the Radio Authority on advertising by Amnesty International relating to atrocities in Rwanda. Pressure groups, as much as political parties, can pursue controversial objectives. The argument for groups such as Amnesty International is that their objective is one which is recognised and valued in international law, it does not involve seeking a change or to resist a change in the law but merely to prevent governments and others from breaking the law and to hold them to fundamental and humane practices and, as a matter of the United Kingdom's domestic politics, it is not controversial as between the major parties. As yet the courts do not distinguish between the pursuit of human rights standards and other forms of political activity in this context.[67]

Party political broadcasts

The BBC has agreed, as part of its public service remit, to provide airtime for the political parties, particularly at election time. Section 36 of the Broadcasting

---

[58] The Neill Committee recommended that the system continue: Lord Neill of Bladen, QC (Chairman), Committee on Standards in Public Life (1998) *Fifth Report: The Funding of Political Parties in the United Kingdom*, Volume I, Cm 4057–I, 13.1–13.12 and R.94.

[59] See above.

[60] As in Australia, see Ewing, K. (1993) 'New Constitutional Constraints in Australia', *Public Law* 256.

[61] *X and the Association of Z v United Kingdom* (1971) 38 CD 862.

[62] *Bowman v United Kingdom* (1998) 26 1 EHRR 1; for comment see Davis, H. (1998) '*Bowman v United Kingdom* – a Case for the Human Rights Act?', *Public Law* 592.

[63] The broadcasters are advised by the British Advertising Clearance Centre.

[64] *The Independent*, 23.11.01; the advertisement could be shown in cinemas.

[65] See Chapter 11.

[66] [1995] 4 All ER 481.

[67] Stevens, J. and Feldman, D. (1997) 'Broadcasting Advertisements by Bodies with Political Objectives, Judicial Review and the Influence of Charities Law', *Public Law* 615.

Act 1990 requires the ITC to include provision for party political broadcasts in the licences it issues and other broadcasters, such as Sky TV, have transmitted such broadcasts on a voluntary basis. The distribution of airtime is made on the basis of a formula agreed between political parties and broadcasters. With the coming into effect of the Political Parties, Elections and Referendums Act 2000, only registered political parties will be able to make broadcasts and the view of the registering body, the Electoral Commission, must be taken into account in agreeing the formula. In 2002 the Electoral Commission published a consultation paper on the future of party broadcasts proposing to ensure that the regime was compatible with the Human Rights Act 1998 and suggesting a possible extension of the system to a wider range of broadcasters.[68]

Inevitably, perhaps, some parties have been aggrieved by the formulas produced. Small parties and new arrivals tend to think that too much emphasis is placed on the results at the last elections while nationalist parties tend to think that United Kingdom parties are over-represented in the broadcasts received in Scotland and Wales. These arguments have sometimes gone to the courts on the grounds that the distribution of airtime has violated the due impartiality principle. The courts have generally been reluctant to intervene. So long as the interests of small parties, new entrants and nationalist parties etc. are taken into account in the formula, the specific way in which the competing claims are balanced is unlikely to be a justiciable matter.[69] In a Scottish referendum case the Scottish courts did provide a remedy on the grounds that referendums should be subject to different principles than elections and that the tendency should be towards equal airtime for the yes and no camps.[70]

The content of party political and election broadcasts is a matter for the parties. The broadcasters have duties to prevent programmes which, for example, are libellous or which offend against taste and decency. However, in *R (Pro-Life Alliance)* v *British Broadcasting Corporation* (2002)[71] there was a strongly worded judgment upholding freedom of expression, especially by political parties at election time. For the Court, preventing broadcasts on taste and decency grounds could only be done in the most extreme circumstances and would otherwise be thought as censorship incompatible with the common law, let alone Article 10.[72] Racist parties may have a right to a broadcast if the formula so dictates and the view of the ITC is that the broadcasts are acceptable so long as they do not themselves contain racist content.[73]

---

[68] Electoral Commission (2002) *Party Political Broadcasts Consultation Paper*, building on Electoral Commission Discussion Paper (2001) *Party Political Broadcasting Review*.

[69] *R* v *BBC ex parte Referendum Party* [1997] *The Times*, 29 April, regarding a new entrant; *Wilson* v *IBA (2)* (1988) SLT 276, regarding a nationalist party.

[70] *Wilson* v *IBA* (1979) SC 351.

[71] [2002] EWCA Civ 297; [2002] 2 All ER 756.

[72] In December 1999 the ITC upheld a complaint that a Liberal Democrat broadcast, in the form of a mock news bulletin, breached the due impartiality provision.

[73] A complaint in May 1999 against the British National Party was rejected by the ITC on these grounds. See ITC website: www.itc.org.uk/.

14
Political offences

14.1 Introduction

Crimes committed for political reasons are predominantly dealt with through the law of public order and are discussed in Chapter 17. A political motive will rarely justify what is otherwise an offence, although it may affect defences based on reasonableness and it may influence the penalty imposed. There are, however, some circumstances in which a political reason for action, proof of a desire to act or speak in order to further an effect on the law, government policy or public opinion, is the particular focus of the definition of an offence: the offence exists as a distinct offence because of the political content of what has been done, written or spoken. A new range of offences, those dealing with 'terrorism', come within this notion but, because of their seriousness and currency, are dealt with separately.

Political speech enjoys a particularly strong protection under the European Convention on Human Rights. Under the Human Rights Act 1998, any prosecution which restricts political expression will need careful scrutiny by reference to Article 10(2), whose general features have been discussed in Chapter 10. The Court of Human Rights has long recognised that a democratic society is one of the most effective means of upholding Convention rights. Freedom of political speech, including the freedom to shock and offend, is one of the central pillars of the Convention conception of democracy.

14.2 Treason

Treason is an ancient offence which, until 1998, attracted the death penalty.[1] It is defined by the Treason Act 1351 and involves plotting or carrying out acts against the person of the monarch or close members of the Royal family, fighting with or giving support to the Crown's enemies and killing certain senior ministers and judges while sitting in court.

Treason Act 1351
Declaration what offences shall be adjudged treason
... that is to say; when a man doth compass or imagine the death of our lord the King, or of our lady his Queen or of their eldest son and heir; or if a man do violate

---

[1] Section 36(4) and (5), Crime and Disorder Act 1998 abolished the death penalty for treason and aggravated piracy.

the King's companion or the King's eldest daughter unmarried, or the wife [sic] the King's eldest son and heir; or if a man do levy war against our lord the King in his realm, or be adherent to the King's enemies in his realm, giving to them aid and comfort in the realm, or elsewhere, and thereof be probably attainted of open deed by the people of their condition . . . and if a man slea the chancellor, treasurer and the King's justices of the one bench or the other, justices in the eyre, or justices of the assise, and all other justices assigned to hear and determine, being in their places, doing their offices . . .

It has not been used in modern times other than as offence by means of which the death penalty could be imposed on British subjects[2] or on aliens with an alleged loyalty to the Crown,[3] for assisting the enemy in war time. Allegiance to the Crown is a necessary component of the offence. Natural born or naturalised subjects may find it hard to show they have cast off this duty of allegiance. An alien, while in the United Kingdom, owes allegiance to the Crown and, it seems, the possession of a British passport may be enough to continue the allegiance until some express act of renunciation is performed. Treason can be committed abroad. Giving aid and comfort to the King's enemies can include various forms of speech such as broadcasting enemy propaganda.[4] It has recently been suggested that British Muslims fighting for the Taliban and Al Q'aida in the Afghan War 2001 have, by being apparently 'adherant to the [Queen's] enemies', committed treason. The justice of imprisoning or executing the defeated enemy is questionable, particularly since it is based on an allegiance they have done all they can to renounce. In modern times it may be that evidence of 'war crimes' or 'terrorism' is a surer footing for any prosecution that wishes to avoid the claim of victor's justice.[5]

The Treason Felony Act 1848 lists a somewhat more specific range of offences which involve actions taken with the purpose of deposing the monarch; using war-like force, inside the United Kingdom, in order to force a change of policy; to use force so as to intimidate Parliament, or to encourage a foreign invasion. It is made expressly clear that these offences can be committed by utterances and by publication of any printing or writing.[6] On conviction the penalty can be life imprisonment.[7]

Both treason and treason felony can, in some of their forms, be committed by speech alone – by, for example, enemy propagandists or advocates of revolutionary violence. They are both confined to speech or actions advocating serious violence to overthrow or undermine state institutions.

---

[2] *R v Casement* [1917] 1 KB 98. Casement's real loyalty was, of course, to an Irish state.
[3] *Joyce v DPP* [1946] AC 347.
[4] The points in the sentences preceding this footnote are derived from *Joyce v DPP* [1946] AC 347.
[5] 'Treason doth never prosper, what's the reason? If it prosper, none dare call it Treason' (Sir John Harrington (1977) *Epigrams* [1618]. New York. Octagon, Book 4, No. 5).
[6] Section 3, Treason Felony Act 1848.
[7] Originally transportation for life.

14.3 Seditious libel

14.3.1 The nature of the offence

There is a common law offence of publishing words with a 'seditious intent'. The offence involves words that are published with the intention of promoting a violent attack on the authority of state institutions.

In *R* v *Burns* (1886)[8] four prominent socialists were prosecuted, and acquitted, for the offence of seditious libel. The offence was defined as words said or published with a seditious intention, and these are words intended to bring the Crown into 'hatred or contempt'; or to 'excite disaffection' against the Crown, Parliament, government or the courts; or to excite Her Majesty's subjects to attempt by unlawful means to alter any matter 'in Church or law established'; or to 'to raise discontent or disaffection amongst Her Majesty's subjects'; or to 'promote feelings of ill-will and hostility between different classes of such subjects'.[9]

R v *Burns* (1886) is too broad in its statement of the law. Recently it has been accepted that the burden of a seditious intention is confined to attacks on the state, on 'constituted authority', and does not include attacks by one group of citizens on another.

> The Chief Metropolitan Stipendiary Magistrate refused to issue a summons against the publishers of *The Satanic Verses* by Salman Rushdie which, it was alleged, was a book published with seditious intent because it raised widespread 'discontent or disaffection amongst Her Majesty's subjects'. The applicants sought judicial review of the magistrate's refusal.
>
> HELD: the law was correctly stated in a Canadian case, *Boucher* v *R* (1951) 2 DLR 369. The magistrate was correct; essential to a seditious intention was an intention to attack 'constituted authority', specifically the sovereign or the institutions of government.
>
> *R* v *Chief Metropolitan Stipendiary Magistrate ex parte Choudhury* [1991] 1 All ER 306

The refusal by the House of Lords to hear an appeal suggests that the latter, modern case correctly gives the law. If so, sedition focuses on attacks on 'constituted authority' and excludes attacks on social groups, corporate enterprises, religions, other forms of social power and, perhaps, the social and economic system generally. It does not, however, involve a rigid division between public and private authority. Rather the issue is whether there is an attack on the performance of a public function. The court in *Choudhury* said: 'By "constituted authority" what is meant is some person or body holding public office or discharging some public function of the state'. Thus an attack on a private body exercising a public function could be within the ambit of sedition.[10]

A seditious intention must involve an intention that the attack on constituted authority be pressed by violence or disorder. The mere utterance of

---

[8] (1886) XVI Cox CC 355.
[9] Sir James Stephen (1883) *A History of the Criminal Law*. London: Macmillan, vol. 2, p. 298 was the main source of this definition.
[10] The point is now echoed in the Human Rights Act 1998.

strong criticism is not enough. The extent to which the defendant must be proved to have sought a violent reaction from the audience is unclear. The speaker's or writer's intentions are not to be based on what he or she sought but are to be construed, as a matter of fact, from all the circumstances of the case. Matters such as the type of audience addressed, the state of public feeling at the time and the place and mode of publication are all relevant. In *R v Aldred* (1909)[11] a journalist was convicted who had written approvingly of the recent assassination of a British Indian official and who advocated further assassinations as a means to Indian independence. It was implied that words with a tendency to incite others to violence could be seditious whatever the intentions or motives of the speaker.[12] This approach to intention permits the 'opposition veto', the conviction of a person on the basis of on an unintended, unsought but violent audience reaction. As such it raises issues under the Convention right to freedom of expression. The matter has arisen in recent cases relating to arrest for breach of the peace and is discussed in that context in Chapter 17.

14.3.2 Freedom of expression

Seditious libel raises important issues of political freedom, free speech and freedom of the press. The offence cannot be grounded just on robust or radical criticism of the government. In a passage quoted in *R v Burns* (1886) Stephen's definition continues: 'An intention to show that Her Majesty has been misled or mistaken in her measures, or to point out errors or defects in the government or constitution as by law established, with a view to their reformation, or to excite Her Majesty's subjects to attempt by lawful means the alteration of any matter in Church or State by law established, [or to incite any person to commit any crime in disturbance of the peace] or to point out, in order to their removal, matters which are producing, or have a tendency to produce, feelings of hatred and ill will between classes of Her Majesty's subjects, is not a seditious intention'.[13] In the cases the judges have stressed the duty of the jury to decide in a manner that protects freedom of the press.[14]

Uncompromising political criticism is protected by Article 10 ECHR. A court, would, under section 6 of the Human Rights Act 1998, act unlawfully if it permitted the kinds of political speech protected by the Convention to be the basis of a conviction. Nor, it can be suggested, is it enough to lay down the test for a seditious intention and then leave particular instances to a jury. The law should not permit a jury to convict in breach of Convention rights.[15]

There is little scope under the Convention for a state to restrict political speech. Protected speech includes expressions that may 'offend, shock or

---

[11] *R v Aldred* (1909) XXII Cox CC 1.

[12] See also *R v Caunt*, 17 November 1947, unreported, Liverpool Assizes, commented upon by Wade, E.C.S. (!948) 'Seditious Libel and the Press', 64 *LQR* 203.

[13] The part in square brackets is found in the fourth edition.

[14] For example, in *R v Burns* the jury were told they were the 'guardians of the liberties of the press, and whilst you will check its abuse, you will preserve its freedom'.

[15] For example, the law on 'reasonable chastisement' of a child by a parent is incompatible with the Convention if it allows a jury to acquit on facts which, nevertheless, disclose a breach of Article 3; see *A v United Kingdom* (1999) 27 EHRR 611.

disturb the State or any sector of the population'.[16] It also includes speech aimed at constitutional change including the break up of the state through forms of separatism;[17] though the Court of Human Rights has accepted that a democratic state is entitled to take proportionate steps to protect the institutions necessary to its democracy.[18] A state may also take action against incitements to violence, although under strict Strasbourg supervision.[19] Within this framework, a conception of seditious libel which confines itself to protecting democratic institutions by punishing the advocacy of political violence may still be compatible with the Convention.

Article 10(2) permits restrictions on speech for various purposes including 'the prevention of disorder or crime'. Any prosecution would have to show that the law on sedition is sufficiently accessible and followable to be 'prescribed by law'. The common law basis of sedition, uncertainty surrounding its use, uncertainty over whether it is confined to attacks on public institutions alone and uncertainty on the required state of mind of the defendant are all issues that raise significant questions regarding the compatibility of the offence with Convention rights. Similarly any prosecution would have to meet a pressing social need and be, in each individual case, a proportionate response by the state.

Sedition has rarely been invoked in recent times. Governments have preferred to use public order legislation or, these days, anti-terrorist powers derived from emergency legislation. Regulations produced during the Second World War, for example, permitted prosecutions for expressions which had the effect of 'corrupting public morale', of newspapers for 'fermenting opposition' or of publications which caused 'alarm and despondency'.[20] It is hard to accept that, absent a derogation under Article 15, such provisions could be compatible with the Convention. Sedition was used in the 1920s in an attempt to destroy the Communist Party of Great Britain.[21] Whether such actions would be compatible with the Convention is a matter of speculation. During the 'cold war' the Commission of Human Rights, in *KPD* v *Federal Republic of Germany* (1957)[22] upheld the German government's proscription of the German Communist Party by using Article 17 to prevent a challenge to the ban by the party. With the end of the 'cold war' a more tolerant approach has been adopted in Strasbourg. The general political circumstances in which a sedition trial takes place may, therefore, be important in determining its compatibility with the Convention. The 'war against terrorism'[23] may mean we have returned to a situation in which the courts are able, consistently with

---

[16] Much repeated words derived from *Handyside* v *United Kingdom* (1979–80) 1 EHRR 737. On political speech see *Lingens* v *Austria* (1986) 8 EHRR 407; *Castells* v *Spain* (1992) 14 EHRR 445; *Oberschlick* v *Austria* (1998) 25 EHRR 357.

[17] *United Communist Party of Turkey and others* v *Turkey* (1998) 26 EHRR 121; the case refers to Article 11 on freedom of association (see Chapter 18) but is relevant to the scope of free expression, too.

[18] *United Communist Party of Turkey and others* v *Turkey* (1998) 26 EHRR 121, 32.

[19] *Sener* v *Turkey* [2000] 11 HRCD 399.

[20] Ewing, K. and Gearty, C. (2000) *The Struggle for Civil Liberties.* Oxford: Oxford University Press.

[21] *Ibid.*, pp. 136–44.

[22] (1957) Ap. 250/57, 1 Yearbook 222.

[23] See Chapter 18.

human rights, to accept different standards when a terrorist context is alleged. Advocacy of terrorist activity could, conceivably, be seditious though the government has preferred to adopt detailed anti-terrorist statutes rather attempt to use seditious libel.

14.4 Incitement to disaffection

If the United Kingdom is involved in war against another state, or if there is violent disorder within the country such as, for example, in Northern Ireland or during the miners' strike 1984–85, a possible strategy for those in opposition to government policy is to encourage members of the armed forces or the police not to carry out their orders. Such a strategy is in danger of involving criminal activity. Armed forces legislation creates a range of military offences relating to mutiny and other forms of refusal of duty which apply to military personnel but also civilians subject to military law. The death penalty can no longer be imposed for such offences even when committed in the face of the enemy.[24] Civilian political activists seeking to persuade members of the armed forces to refuse to undertake certain duties can face prosecutions for incitement.

Incitement to Disaffection Act 1934
(1) If any person maliciously and advisedly endeavours to seduce any members of His Majesty's forces from his duty or allegiance to His Majesty, he shall be guilty of an offence under this Act.

The Act includes attempts to incite from 'duty' or from 'allegiance'; members of the armed forces, like anyone in the United Kingdom, owe allegiance to the Crown.[25] Possession of documents which could have the seductive effect identified in section 1 is an offence. There are powers for the police to obtain warrants to enter and search premises, to seize material[26] and to destroy documents found.[27] The consent of the DPP is needed for any prosecution.

Since acts of seducing involve expression, an Article 10 ECHR issue is raised.[28] However, the Commission has found that prosecutions can be justified under Article 10(2).

> A had been prosecuted under the Incitement to Disaffection Act 1934 for distributing leaflets in army bases which suggested that soldiers should leave the army or desert rather than serve in Northern Ireland. The leaflets gave information on how this could be done. The prosecution was upheld by the Court of Appeal.
> HELD (Commission of Human Rights): the Act provided a sufficient basis in law for the prosecution; the Act restricted freedom of expression in the interests of national security; the Act was proportionate in that it did not make the mere expression of opinion a criminal offence but required an intention to incite, and the prosecution was necessary in that, from previous actions, the applicant intended to continue unless prosecuted.
> *Arrowsmith* v *United Kingdom* (1978) D&R 19/5

---

[24] The Human Rights Act 1998, s. 21(5).
[25] *R* v *Arrowsmith* [1975] QB 678.
[26] Incitement to Disaffection Act 1934, s. 2.
[27] Incitement to Disaffection Act 1934, s. 3(4).
[28] *Arrowsmith* v *United Kingdom*. Admissibility: D&R 8/123; report: D&R 19/5.

There is a similar offence relating to the police, currently found in section 91 of the Police Act 1996. It makes it an offence to cause disaffection among the police or to induce a member of the force to withhold his services. This offence was first introduced in 1919 after a police strike and its impact is linked to the prohibition on police officers striking as much as on politically motivated actions.

It is compatible with the interests of a democratic society to insist that the political views of state officials (such as the military, the police, civil servants, etc.) should not be allowed to interfere with the achievement of the collective goals of society as chosen by the elected and accountable government.[29] State agents have the same vote as everybody else and should not be able to use their position to prevent a properly chosen policy from being put into effect. To give state agents a veto over policy is to give them hugely unequal weight in the political process. This is one of the reasons why the political freedom of officials is often restricted and the restriction accepted, in general terms, by the Court of Human Rights.[30] The laws against incitement serve, indirectly, the same goal. They can be thought of as proportionate limits on speech that further the interests of a democratic society by being designed to limit the likelihood of a politically motivated breach of duty by state officials. Of course this argument will always be vulnerable to a well-founded argument that the policy being opposed is itself incompatible with any reasonable conception of democracy, or at least of that conception which characterises the general constitutional arrangements. That, of course, is a very hard argument to establish generally and, in particular, before the courts.

14.5 Incitement to racial hatred

14.5.1 Part III of the Public Order Act 1986

Speech and actions which involve racial discrimination can be unlawful and lead to various civil penalties in contexts such as employment and the provision of services to the public.[31] Some criminal offences are considered to be made worse when committed with a racist motive and are subject to a higher penalty.[32] This principle has been extended to offences committed with religious hatred.[33]

Incitement to racial hatred is, in various forms, a criminal offence. The offences are presented in a public order context, as Part III of the Public Order Act 1986. Much racism that black and Asian people experience in the course of their everyday lives consists either of acts of discrimination or of personal

---

[29] For example, on political strikes, MacFarlane, L.J. (1981) *The Right to Strike*. Harmondsworth: Penguin, 158–65.

[30] See Chapter 13. The main justification for imposing political restrictions on civil servants and others is the maintenance of the appearance of impartiality.

[31] For example, the Race Relations Act 1976, whose provisions have been extended to the services of many public authorities, including the police, by the Race Relations (Amendment) Act 2000.

[32] Crime and Disorder Act 1998, Part II.

[33] Anti-terrorism Crime and Security Act 2001, Part V.

abuse and insult expressed in racial terms. The hate crimes in Part III provide a context for dealing with the more serious forms of the latter. Of course 'ordinary' public order offences can be committed by racist behaviour.[34] These can include, for example, words or actions that create the fear of violence (section 4, Public Order Act 1986) or words or action that cause harassment, alarm or distress (section 5, Public Order Act 1986). The 'hate crimes' in Part III of the Act do not require proof of likely violence and they provide for more severe punishment, including the possibility of prison, than is available under section 5 of the Public Order Act 1986.

Racist speech and action can be political. They can be expressions of opinions about how society should be and they can be linked to the programmes of organisations or parties which are trying to obtain governmental power or seeking changes to the law, government policy or public opinion. Racist speech creates a difficulty in a society that values the political freedoms of expression and of association. People should be able to hold and express whatever political ideas they wish and the state should not try to close off in advance particular ways in which society may develop in the future. So long as society remains democratic, all views should be given equal protection of the law, no matter how unpopular or offensive, since none can triumph without majority acceptance. Against this is the view that anti-racist laws, as well as protecting individual members of ethnic minority groups from kinds of abuse and insult that the white majority does not frequently experience,[35] are also necessary to protect a democratic society. The promotion of racial hatred is inconsistent with the fundamental dignity which all should be accorded in a society and with the right of everyone to equal concern and respect. Racist hatred is incompatible with the procedural equality which is necessary for any reasonable conception of democracy and, therefore, a democratic society can, without contradiction, take steps to suppress it.

The essence of the offences in Part III of the Public Order Act 1986 is behaviour or the use of words which is 'threatening, abusive or insulting' and which is intended to 'stir up racial hatred' or which, in the circumstances, is likely to have the effect of stirring up racial hatred. Behaviour or the use of words with this intention or effect is an offence in the following situations: where a person uses 'words or behaviour or displays any written material' (section 18); where a person 'publishes or distributes written material' (section 19); where a person 'presents or directs' the public performance of a play (section 20); where a person 'distributes, or shows or plays, a recording of visual images or sounds (section 21); or where a person provides, produces or directs a broadcast, or where a person uses racially offensive words or behaviour during a broadcast (section 22). These offences can be committed by individuals or companies, including, for example, media companies. Someone who places material which incites racial hatred on the Internet is, presumably, 'using' words and therefore could be caught by section 18. An Internet Service

---

[34] See Chapter 17. Ongoing racist abuse which amounted to a course of conduct aimed at an individual could also be an offence under the Protection from Harassment Act 1997.

[35] White people can be the victims of racist abuse and are, of course, equally protected by Part III as are members of ethnic minorities.

Provider will be caught if it can be said that they are either publishing or distributing written material but, in so far as they have no control over what is placed on the Internet, this may be difficult to establish.

The concept of race in the offence is identified by section 17. It refers to any 'group of persons defined by reference to colour, race, nationality (including citizenship) or ethnic or national origins'. 'Hatred' or the unusually colloquial 'stirring up' are not further defined. It is no longer necessary for the persons subject to the hatred to be in Great Britian.[36]

These offences do not require proof that racial hatred was, in fact, 'stirred up'. The offence can be committed if, in the circumstances, the stirring up of race hatred is likely. What might be called 'intellectual racism', the expression of racist political theory or of science which suggests patterns of racial superiority and inferiority, may stir up racial hatred but be outside the scope of the offences because the words are not 'threatening, abusive or insulting'. These statutory terms are not defined but have their ordinary meaning and are to be left to the jury or magistrate.[37] A work of science done in good faith, or a serious novel such as *The Satanic Verses* by Salman Rushdie, could be held to be insulting and be thought likely to stir up racial hatred in the circumstances. This would raise serious issues of freedom of expression. The problem is that the offences permit the so-called 'opposition veto': an offence can be brought into existence by the behaviour and reaction of those who oppose what is being said and choose to create the circumstances in which racial hatred is likely to be stirred up. Where the charge is based upon the circumstances in which the words were spoken, but not where the prosecution is trying to prove an intention to stir up racial hatred, the Act permits a defence. This is to the effect that the defendant did not intend and was not aware that the words etc. might be threatening, abusive or insulting. This defence implies that a writer etc. should desist from publication if he or she is aware that what they are doing might be insulting. In the, perhaps rare, circumstances of a serious and good faith discussion of matters impinging on race which are taken by others to be insulting, the defence implies that it is the writer who should hold back in the face of attack and this may be incompatible with freedom of speech. If the offence is ever extended from race to religion,[38] the importance of this issue will be much greater since religion is more likely to be the subject of attack;[39] religious authorities take up controversial positions on moral questions, for example, and these can lead to attacks which others might find offensive.

The section 18 offence, using threatening, abusive or insulting words to stir up racial hatred, can be committed in both 'public' and 'private' places. Meetings by racist political parties in private halls, for example, are not exempt from the reach of the Act, nor if such statements were to be made in party offices. However, no offence is committed if the racist expressions are confined to people's dwellings.

---

[36] The Act was amended by the Anti-terrorism, Crime and Security Act 2001.

[37] *Brutus* v *Cozens* [1973] AC 854 HL; discussed in Chapter 19.

[38] As was the unfulfilled intention of the government in 2001.

[39] In so far as some ethnic groups are already coterminous with religion, such as Sikhs and, perhaps, Jews (see Chapter 21) the Act may already apply to religious attacks.

The section 19 offence, publishing or distributing written material, is an arrestable offence as defined by section 24, PACE 1984. By section 17(1)(b) of PACE, private premises may be entered without a warrant in order to make an arrest. Police may arrest for a section 18 offence but it is not 'arrestable' under section 24, PACE 1984; there is, therefore, no power of the police to enter private premises to make an arrest in the absence of an anticipated breach of the peace or unless they have some other lawful basis to be on the premises. The absence of an express power to enter theatres and cinemas etc. can also present difficulties of evidence-gathering in relation to those offences relating to the public performance of a play or the distribution etc. of recordings.

Section 23 of the Public Order Act 1986 creates an offence of the possession of racially inflammatory material. This can be written or recorded material in written or visual form. It must be threatening, abusive or insulting and the offence is based on the intention to stir up racial hatred. The defence of no intention to stir up racial hatred or the absence of a reason to think that the expression was abusive etc. is available. Under section 24 police may obtain a search warrant to search for and seize material which is believed to contravene section 23. Section 25 of the Act gives magistrates the power to order forfeiture of any material that relates to the offences under sections 18, 19, 21 or 23.

Racist chants and other forms of expression can also be the basis of criminal offences under section 3 of the Football (Offences) Act 1991. These are not likely to raise significant problems regarding the freedom of political speech.

14.5.2 Convention rights and hate speech

'Hate crimes' can involve restrictions on political speech and raise significant issues under Article 10 ECHR. Political speech is the most strongly protected form of speech under Article 10 and so, if restrictions are permissible under the Convention, it is all the more likely that non-political forms of racist expression can also be suppressed without violating Convention rights.[40]

Racist speech invokes at least two different issues under the Convention. The first is whether the state, by law, is permitted to restrict racist speech, particularly political speech. Bans on political freedom based on race hatred are, it seems, likely, in principle, to be within Article 10(2) as being to protect the 'rights and freedoms of others'.[41] Any particular restriction will need to meet the general tests of the Article and be proportionate. The second issue is whether racists themselves and their organisations are entitled to use the Convention to uphold their freedom of action. This raises Article 17 ECHR which prevents any 'state, group or person' from using their Convention rights to enable them to engage in activities aimed at the destruction or limitation of the Convention rights and freedoms of others. The Strasbourg institutions have also accepted that attempts by racist organisations or individuals to assert

[40] See Starmer, K. (1999) *European Human Rights Law*. London: LAG, 24.48–24.51.
[41] See *Jersild v Denmark* (1994) 19 EHRR 1, which accepted the previous practice of the Commission on the intentional propagation of race hatred. See also Harris, D.J., O'Boyle, M. and Warbrick, C. (1995) *Law of the European Convention on Human Rights*. London: Butterworths, p. 374, n. 14.

Convention rights may fail because of this.[42] Article 17, it should be remembered, only applies to an attempt to uphold Convention rights which, if exercised in the manner envisaged, would lead to violations of the rights of others. It does not permit the withdrawal of other Convention rights, such as the right not to be tortured or detained without trial etc. to persons just because they are racist.

Racism raises issues of great public importance and is a fit matter for good faith public interest broadcasting. Attempts to prevent such programmes from broadcasting the words and opinions of racists may, in all the circumstances, be disproportionate restrictions.

> Danish journalist were prosecuted for aiding and abetting race hatred by broadcasting the views of racists in a current affairs programme. The Danish courts upheld the conviction.
>
> HELD (ECHT): the underlying motive of the programme was anti-racist. There was an attempt at a balanced and serious programme aimed at informing an audience. In the circumstances the prosecution was disproportionate.
>
> *Jersild* v *Denmark* (1994) 19 EHRR 1

In English law, section 18(6) says that the offence of using threatening etc. words to stir up racial hatred does not apply to words etc. said solely for use in a broadcast. However, section 22, which relates to broadcasting, does seem to be more restrictive of what can be contained in a broadcast than, perhaps, is permitted by *Jersild* v *Denmark* (1994). The persons responsible for a broadcast can be guilty of an offence if, though they themselves do not intend to stir up racial hatred, hatred may, in all the circumstances, be stirred up. A broadcaster's defence can be that there was no reason to suspect that the offending material would be in the broadcast and, given the circumstances of the broadcast, it was not possible to remove the offending material. This clearly does not protect the kind of programme in *Jersild* in which the producers seem to have deliberately set out to give a public airing to the views and sentiments of racists albeit with a view to encouraging rejection by most people.

---

[42] *Glimmerveen and Hagenbeek* v *Netherlands* (1979) 18 DR 187 in which the Commission advised that a restriction on the ability of convicted racists to stand for election could not, because of Article 17, be challenged as a violation of Article 10 or Article 3 of the First Protocol. See also *Kühnen* v *FRG* (1988) Ap. 12194/86.

15

Access to public information

Effective political participation requires knowledge and information in order to challenge or defend the activities of government, yet British government and administration has, in the past, been notorious for the secrecy with which it has conducted it affairs. There has been a widespread reluctance to permit the disclosure of information held by the government and a corresponding reluctance to grant rights of access to information to members of the public.

15.1 The argument for secrecy

The defence of secrecy is, first, that certain matters, most obviously those involving national security, defence and diplomatic relations, should be kept secret in the public interest. As a general principle this is widely accepted: operational matters connected with the defence of the nation from genuine threats to its stability or sovereignty coming from overseas or by internal subversion can legitimately be kept secret. Other governmental functions, for example the investigation of crime, are in the same category. Personal information, matters received in confidence, and, perhaps, certain types of exploitable economic information are also properly invested with secrecy.

It is the scope and consequences of this need for secrecy that is disputed. The principle which justifies secrecy in certain areas is capable of such a broad and discretionary application by the government that it can include all sorts of matters for which there are strong, countervailing public interests which justify, permit or excuse disclosure or access. Secrecy, on this view, has been disproportionately valued at the expense of, for example, the ability of citizens effectively to participate in the political process.

A second defence of secrecy is that it is necessary for the effective functioning of government and public services generally. In particular it is alleged that civil servants and other officials will be unwilling to give full and unfettered advice to ministers or to make judgments about the best interests of individuals, such as patients or children in care, if they know that such advice or judgments will become both public knowledge and also the personal knowledge of those directly affected. Officials may fear political or personal criticism or even legal action resulting from their best efforts. This argument for secrecy is easily derided as wrongly implying a general weakness of character among civil servants,[1] and, regarding personal information, assumes

---

[1] For example, Robertson, G. (1993) *Freedom, the Individual and the Law*, 7th edn. Harmondsworth: Penguin, p. 174.

a now unacceptable form of paternalism towards individuals directly affected by the decisions and actions of public authorities. Yet the argument has a reasonable core. First, it may be necessary for maintaining the appearance of an impartial and professional civil service who advise ministers under the condition that it is the ministers who are accountable for the policies and actions that result. This argument holds in so far as such a civil service is valued and still reflects the structure and conduct of the public sector. A second related point is that secrecy is needed to enable ministers, officials and others to consider the range of facts and policy proposals without being faced with criticism just for considering options they are unlikely to put into effect.

Arguments for secrecy elide into arguments against giving the public general access to official information. First, it is argued that freedom of information is costly. This is undoubtedly true but the cost will be born predominantly by the taxpayer which is a factor influencing all government decisions on any matter and is not special to policy on freedom of information. Secondly, it is argued that access to information by the public undermines the Parliamentary system in the United Kingdom by which ministers are accountable to Parliament. This argument simply fails to take into account the weaknesses of ministerial accountability by which not only can ministers avoid giving account for a range of reasons but, as a matter of principle, it leaves the decisions on what information to give and what to retain within the exclusive discretion of ministers who can only be challenged by a House of Commons the majority of whose members are ultimately sympathetic to the government's cause and concerned to avoid matters embarrassing to the government from being made public.

15.2 The legal basis of secrecy: official secrets and public records

There are two great legal monuments to secrecy.

First is the criminalisation, dating from the second half of the nineteenth century, of unauthorised disclosures of official information. This is dealt with in Chapter 16.

The second legal monument to secrecy is the law relating to public records which denies public access to public records for 30 years or longer. Section 5(1) of the Public Records Act 1958, amended in 1967, prevents public access to records which have not been in existence for 30 years.[2] Furthermore, the government can impose longer (or shorter) bans and, under section 3(4) of the Act, permit departments to retain records for longer periods, such as 100 years, or with the intention that they are never to be disclosed.[3]

The Freedom of Information Act 2000, which will be brought into force by 2005, replaces section 5(1) of the Public Records Act 1958. It permits retention

---

[2] The system is detailed in the open government White Paper: Chancellor of the Duchy of Lancaster (1993) *Open Government*, Cm 2290. London: HMSO, chapter 9. Thirty miles of records are, apparently, reduced to 4.5 miles after five years and, in the end, only about 1 mile of records are selected for preservation.

[3] In the appendix to their *The Struggle for Civil Liberties* (Oxford: Oxford University Press, 2000) K. Ewing and C. Gearty list a number of records which were retained for 100 years and suggest that a provision in the Code relating to the '*unreasonable* [emphasis in the Code] diversion of resources' may make it impossible for historians to challenge existing closures.

beyond 30 years on terms which are compatible with the structure of the 2000 Act. As we shall see, the Act imposes a duty on public authorities either to publish or disclose on demand information and documents in their possession. Many categories of information and documents are 'exempted' from this duty. Under the Act, material which is not exempted can be made available to the public before 30 years have passed. Material which is exempted from the duty to disclose can be retained for 30 years at least and in some cases held for longer.[4] Whether the new Act will make much difference remains to be seen since, just as under sections 5(2) (repealed) and 3(4) (retained in force) of the Public Records Act 1958, many important records, including those pertaining to national security and sensitive commercial information, will be able to be closed to the public for as long as the government wishes. The matter is complex and a Code of Practice can be issued.

15.3 Justifications for openness

The White Paper of Open Government and the Freedom of Information Act 2000 are evidence of significant moves towards greater openness. The case for greater openness has been strongly put and has been accepted, with qualifications, by successive governments.

Openness serves the ideal of citizenship. It is necessary for voters to be able to make informed choices, for political parties, pressure groups and other political associations to be able to pursue their particular interests or their conceptions of the public good effectively, for individuals, companies and associations to pursue their self-interest by political means, and so on. Effective political activity requires access to public information. This justification extends to political representatives who do not necessarily have any greater access to official information than the public. It extends to the media through which most people obtain their understanding of public life, and also to contemporary historians. This justification for openness extends to access to the facts on which government policies and decisions are made. There is, however, an interesting distinction to be made. Government has, particularly in the twentieth century, become increasingly involved in the provision of services to the population: health, education and welfare being the most obvious examples. As a consequence public authorities hold significant amounts of information about social and environmental policies which can affect individuals directly. Two models of the participant citizen emerge. One is the traditional democratic citizen, seeking the common good with no special personal advantage to be gained. The other, more modern, is the citizen as the 'consumer' of government services who requires, as it were, market information about those services in order the better to choose between alternatives and the better to know their rights and entitlements. Requiring the publication of information to the 'consumers' of public services is an important theme of open government.

Openness also serves the ideal of personal autonomy. It is simply the right of persons to have access to and to control the use of the personal information

---

[4] Sections 62 and 63, Freedom of Information Act 2000.

that others have about them – and government and public authorities, these days, hold huge amounts of personal data. The law on personal information is discussed in Chapter 19.

Openness is also involved in accountability. Both help to make for better, more careful government and administration. They act as internal restraints on officials but also as conditions under which maladministration or the abuse of power become clearer to citizens who are better placed to take remedial action.

Another justification relates to commercial needs. Public services are increasingly being privatised or contracted out to commercial companies. The government is also the producer of much factual information and the generator of policies which may suggest new market needs which companies can meet. Given that this interrelation of the public and private sector is a fact of modern society, information to assist it should be available.[5]

The move to greater openness can also be explained by important contextual changes. First, the role of modern government in the provision of a vast range of services which are way beyond its so-called traditional role of maintaining the rule of law, upholding order and sound money and dealing with defence and foreign policy has been noted above. It not only creates pressure for access to information on services, it also weakens the defences for secrecy since these have their greatest weight in respect of matters involving, for example, national security, but much less weight regarding, for example, housing policy. A second context is the 'new' technology, particularly the Internet. It means, first, that it is much harder to maintain secrecy especially in respect of information available overseas. It also means that it is much easier for the government and public authorities to make information available relatively cheaply and with ease of access.

15.4 Convention rights

The European Convention on Human Rights, directly or through the Human Rights Act 1998, has not been a major explanatory factor behind the move to greater openness. Article 10, freedom of expression, includes the right to receive information. However, in *Leander* v *Sweden* (1987),[6] followed in *Gaskin* v *United Kingdom* (1990),[7] it was said that 'the right to receive information basically prohibits a government from restricting a person from receiving information that others wish or may be willing to impart to him'. The Strasbourg view[8] is that Article 10 'is primarily a freedom of access to general sources of information which may not be restricted by positive action of the authorities'.[9] Article 10 cannot mean that, for example, an official body can be forced to divulge information it is unwilling to give. It provides for freedom

---

[5] See Stanley, P. (2000) 'Freedom of Information Act 2000', annotations to *Current Law Statutes*, 2000 Vol. 2, c.36. London. Sweet & Maxwell, pp. 36–3, introductory and general note.
[6] (1987) 9 EHRR 433.
[7] (1990) 12 EHRR 36.
[8] Harris, D.J., O'Boyle, M. and Warbrick, C. (1995) *Law of the European Convention on Human Rights*. London: Butterworth, pp. 379–80.
[9] *Z* v *Austria* (1988) 56 DR 13.

of expression, not forced expression.[10] This view of Article 10 was endorsed as regards English law in *R (Persey)* v *Secretary of State for the Environment, Food and Rural Affairs* (2000)[11] involving an unsuccessful challenge to the government's decision not to hold the inquiries into the foot and mouth crisis of 2001 in public.

The Strasbourg view of Article 10 is logically strong but depends on treating the state and its agencies as being in the same position as citizens and journalists. Alternatively, the particular position of the state, as the monopoly controller of much public information and bound by convention, law and morality to act in the public interest, could found an argument for a properly qualified duty of disclosure, particularly since the distinction between the state authorities and the rights of persons within their jurisdiction is at the heart of the Convention system.[12]

The Convention may grant rights of access to information under Article 8. But this is to personal data which has particular significance for the applicant's private life[13] rather than general information to facilitate political participation. The Court has asserted positive obligations, under Article 8, on states to provide information in respect of environmental issues[14] and in respect of health fears arising out of nuclear testing.[15] Such information is needed to enable a person to assess the risks to their private and family life and so the duty is to provide the information necessary to consider Convention claims. There may also be rights of access to information by the defence in criminal and civil trials on the principle of equality of arms. In certain circumstances, to the contrary, the Convention may require non-disclosure, such as where secrecy is necessary to protect the right to life.

15.5 Freedom of information: the Code of Practice and the Freedom of Information Act 2000

The arguments for openness have been increasingly accepted during the last quarter of the twentieth century and limited statutory developments have occurred.[16] Most of these developments have been in respect of personal information held by government agencies and is looked at in more detail in Chapter 19. There have also been significant developments regarding access to non-personal information about public matters. In local government, for example, the Local Government (Access to Information) Act 1985 provides a public right of access to meetings, reports and documents subject to a range of powers to restrict access on confidentiality and other grounds. The Local Government Finance Act 1982 included a right of access to the audited

---

[10] Barendt, E. (1987) *Freedom of Speech*. Oxford: Clarendon Press, pp. 107–13.

[11] [2000] EWHC 371; [2002] 3 WLR 704.

[12] See Bayne, P. (1994) 'Freedom of Information and Political Free Speech', in T. Campbell and W. Sadurski (eds), *Freedom of Communication*. Aldershot: Dartmouth, ch. 1, cited by Stanley, *op. cit.*

[13] *Gaskin* v *UK* (1989). 12 EHRR 36. See also *Guerra* v *Italy* (1995) 20 EHRR 277.

[14] *Guerra* v *Italy* (1995) 20 EHRR 277; *Lopez Ostra* v *Spain* (1998) 26 EHRR 357.

[15] *McGinley and Egan* v *United Kingdom* (1999) 27 EHRR 1.

[16] For the position prior to 1990 see Birkinshaw, P. (1990) *Government and Information: The Law Relating to Access, Disclosure and Regulation*. London: Butterworths.

accounts of a local authority;[17] the right continues in section 14 of the Audit Commission Act 1998. Public registers of enforcement notices in certain environmental areas were established under the Environment and Safety Information Act 1988. A range of administrative measures, in the Health Service, for example, have also taken place during the late twentieth century.[18]

Despite such provisions strong criticism continued to the effect that there was no general right of access to public information and what rights existed were too discretionary and contained too many exempting provisions. In 1993 the Conservative government produced a White Paper on open government[19] to which was appended a Code of Practice. The Code, now in its second edition, has been continued and revised[20] by the Labour government. A Code of Practice does not create a legal right to government information. It remains the basis of open government but will be supplanted by the provisions of the Freedom of Information Act 2000 whose preparatory provisions are already in force and whose substantive provisions will be gradually brought into force before 2005. Section 45 of the Freedom of Information Act 2000 requires the Secretary of State to issue a new Code of Practice which will replace the current one.

In what follows in this chapter, the current Code and the requirements of the new Act will be compared. Both cover very similar ground but the Act gives greater detail, particularly of the grounds upon which exemption can be claimed. It should not be forgotten, however, that the Code was supported by detailed guidance issued from time to time. The crucial distinction is that the Act gives a right, which is ultimately enforceable in the courts, to the disclosure of information.

15.5.1 Public authorities

The Code of 1993/1998 applies to all government departments and public authorities under the jurisdiction of the Parliamentary Commissioner for Administration, the Ombudsman. It is the Ombudsman who enforces the Code. Section 4 and Schedule 2 of the Parliamentary Commissioner Act 1967 (as amended by the Parliamentary and Health Service Commissioners Act 1987) identify and list the bodies subject to the jurisdiction. Government departments and a large range of public authorities are included. Many areas are not included, such as educational establishments. Similarly there are, in Schedule 3, a number of governmental functions from which the Ombudsman is excluded such as the prerogative of mercy and commercial transactions.

The Act has a wider range than the Code. It identifies the specific public authorities to which it applies. (An approach that can be contrasted with the

---

[17] Bailey, S.H. (1997) *Cross on Principles of Local Government Law*, 2nd edn. London: Sweet & Maxwell, pp. 13–45.

[18] Chapter 2 of the Open Government White Paper identifies, for the period prior to 1993, some of these measures which relate to both personal and policy information in specific areas of government activity.

[19] Chancellor of the Duchy of Lancaster (1993) *Open Government*, Cm 2290. London: HMSO.

[20] Latest at time of writing: Home Office (1997) *Code of Practice on Access to Government Information*, 2nd edn, revised 1998. London: HMSO (available at http://www.homeoffice.gov.uk/foi/ogcode981.htm).

Human Rights Act 1998 which refers to 'public authorities' and, with some exceptions, leaves it to the courts to identify which bodies are included in the term). Schedule 1 of the 2000 Act includes all government departments, the House of Commons and the House of Lords, the Northern Ireland Assembly and the National Assembly of Wales, the armed forces (but not 'special forces'), local authorities (including parish councils) and local or regional boards and committees. The National Health Service, maintained educational institutions at all levels, police forces and a vast range of public authorities and any companies they wholly own, are also included. Section 15 of the Act, reminiscent of section 6(3) of the Human Rights Act 1998, permits the Secretary of State, by order, to add to the list any person exercising 'public functions' such as, for example, the providers of private prisons. By section 4 the Secretary of State, by order, can add other public authorities to the Schedule.

15.5.2 Publication

The Code and Act place a requirement on public authorities voluntarily to publish information; they are not just concerned with disclosure on request. The Code describes information which the government will volunteer and publish.[21] This includes, for example, 'the facts and analysis of the facts which the government considers relevant and important in framing major policy proposals and decisions' and 'explanatory material on departments' dealings with the public'; reasons for decisions should also be given.[22] A significant amount of information is now in the public domain through, for example, the open government website.

Under the Act public authorities must publish 'publication schemes' which specify the type of information they intend to publish. Schemes should assist the 'consumers' of public services in making rational decisions. Publication, of course, is within the control of the departments and there is a danger that, in some circumstances, information can be extracted from its original form and given a gloss aimed at promoting departmental interests rather than providing information. These schemes must be approved by the Information Commissioner. The White Paper and Code of Practice require the departments to publicise their procedures for open government and for putting the Code into effect.

15.5.3 Disclosure

The Code gave a government commitment:

Part 1 v
... to release, in response to specific requests, information relating to their policies, actions and decisions and other matters related to their areas of responsibility.

---

[21] Chancellor of the Duchy of Lancaster (1993) *Open Government*, Cm 2290. London: HMSO, paragraph 4.6.
[22] Home Office (1997) *Code of Practice on Access to Government Information*, 2nd edn, revised 1998. London: HMSO, Part 1, 3(i)(ii)(iii).

In contrast, the Act creates an entitlement, a legal right with a correlating duty, to know whether a public authority has information and, if so, to the disclosure of that information.

> **Freedom of Information Act 2000**
> 1(1) Any person making a request for information to a public authority is entitled –
>   (a) to be informed in writing by the public authority whether it holds information of the description specified in the request, and
>   (b) if that is the case, to have that information communicated to him.

15.5.4 Enforcement

Enforcement of the Code
Under the Code, enforcement is, first, by complaint to the department or public authority involved, and, if that fails, a further complaint to the Parliamentary Ombudsman.[23] The Ombudsman has significant powers of investigation, including a power to call for departmental papers and records. The investigation can then be the basis of a report and the report can make recommendations of action, including the making of *ex gratia* payments, to be taken by the authority. The Ombudsman's recommendations are 'almost invariably'[24] accepted. The problem with this method of enforcement is that the Ombudsman cannot be contacted directly but only though a Member of Parliament and that the Ombudsman has no power to make binding orders and so, ultimately, there is no legal sanction if any recommendations are not followed, though a Parliamentary investigation by Departmental Scrutiny Committee might follow. There is no statutory right of appeal, for complainant or public authority, although judicial review of an Ombudsman's decision has been allowed.

Enforcement of the Act
The central innovation of the Act is that it creates a duty of disclosure which is ultimately enforceable by a court order disobedience to which can be punished as a contempt of court. However, primary enforcement is not by the courts but through the offices of the Information Commissioner and the Information Tribunal.

If a public authority refuses a request for information, the person making the request is expected to pursue any complaints or appeals process that are open to them under the authority's open government procedures. These procedures will be produced in conformity to the Code of Practice made under section 45. If unsuccessful the complainant may then apply to the Information Commissioner.[25] The Data Protection Commissioner is renamed the Information Commissioner and the jurisdiction of the office has been extended to include all freedom of information complaints. The Commissioner's jurisdic-

---

[23] *Ibid.* Part 1, 11.
[24] White Paper 4.20. The initial refusal to compensate investors in the failed company Barlow Clowes and the issue of planning blight along the route of the Channel Tunnel rail link are two examples where recommendations were not accepted.
[25] Freedom of Information Act 2000, s. 50.

tion is to decide whether a request for information has been properly dealt with under the Act.

The Commissioner may issue an 'information notice'. By this notice the public authority involved must disclose information to the Commissioner who can then determine whether there is a duty under the Act to disclose the information to the applicant. The Commissioner, for example, can judge whether or not a claimed exemption really exists. Under section 55 and Schedule 3 the Commissioner has powers of entry and inspection if there are reasonable grounds for suspecting that a public authority is not complying with the Act. These powers are exercised on the basis of a warrant issued by a circuit judge; there are various exemptions such as in respect of national security and the security and intelligence services.

Following investigation, the Commissioner has two principal powers. The first is to issue a 'decision notice' under section 50(3)–(6). This is the decision in respect of a particular complaint and it lays down the steps the public authority needs to take in the case. The second is an 'enforcement notice' which can be issued if the Commissioner is satisfied that a public authority has failed to comply with the Act. An 'enforcement notice' does not require a complaint. The Commissioner can take legally enforceable steps, on his or her own initiative, to promote freedom of information in respect of particular authorities.

The public authority and the complainant enjoy rights of appeal in respect of a 'decision notice' while public authorities may appeal in respect of an 'information notice' or an 'enforcement notice'. Appeal is to the Information Tribunal: the Data Protection Tribunal renamed and given an extended jurisdiction.[26] The grounds of appeal are wide: that the Commissioner has made an error of law or that the Commissioner 'ought to have exercised his discretion differently'.[27] It is an appeal and not a review of the Commissioner and, therefore, the Tribunal can consider the issues, including findings of fact, anew. The Tribunal may dismiss the appeal, quash the notice or substitute its own notice for the Commissioner's.[28] The Tribunal's decisions can be appealed against, though only on a point of law, to the High Court.[29]

Information notices, decision notices and enforcement notices have the status of court orders. If a public authority, after exercising its rights of appeal, fails to comply adequately, the Commissioner can certify this to the High Court. The High Court can make inquiries and, after hearing representations, can deal with the failure to comply with the notices as if the public authority had committed a contempt of court.[30]

[26] Freedom of Information Act 2000, s. 18.
[27] Freedom of Information Act 2000, s. 58(1).
[28] Freedom of Information Act 2000, s. 58(1).
[29] Freedom of Information Act 2000, s. 59.
[30] Freedom of Information Act 2000, s. 54.

Section 53

A major loophole is created by section 53 of the 2000 Act. In some important instances, the government will be able to substitute its views for that of the Commissioner on whether it has a duty to disclose. This loophole does not apply to all public authorities but it does apply to government departments, the National Assembly of Wales and any other public authority the Secretary of State, by order requiring the affirmative resolution of Parliament, decides to designate. Section 53 applies when a public authority to which it relates claims an exemption from disclosure and it is an exemption involving a judgment that, on balance, the public interest favours secrecy rather than openness.[31] On the public interest issue the view of the public authority, through its 'accountable person', overrides that of the Commissioner or the Tribunal. A section 53 certificate must be laid before Parliament. Other than that there is no right of appeal by an applicant and, given the clear statutory basis of the power, judicial review of the accountable person's decision is likely to be difficult. Until the Act has been in effect for some time it will be unclear how great a departure from the principle of an enforceable duty to disclose section 53 creates. Given the authorities to which it applies, section 53 is likely to have its greatest impact on the 'active citizen' seeking access to general policy information rather than the citizen as consumer of services.

15.5.5 Exemptions

The value of both Code and Act depends upon the exemptions and the extent to which they undermine the value of the commitment to or the duty of disclosure. The more discretionary and open textured the grounds for exemption, the more it is that the value of the commitment to openness and citizens' right to disclosure under the Act is diminished. The exemptions in Code and Act cover, broadly speaking, the same ground. The Act is, at times, a little more specific.

Types of exemption

The Code distinguishes between exemptions that do and those that do not depend upon a judgment of harm or prejudice. Exemptions that do not expressly require identifiable resulting harm or prejudice are class exemptions. These apply to any information in a particular class. The scope of the exemptions is given further gloss in Guidance issued under the Code. In the absence of legal enforcement, the final decision on exemption lies within government discretion.

The Act creates a more complex position. It distinguishes between 'absolute' exemptions and other exemptions. An 'absolute' exemption cannot be overridden even if, on balance, the public interest would be served by disclosure. For example, absolute exemptions apply to information which must be disclosed under the provisions of other Acts. Whether an exemption is absolute or not depends solely on its statutory classification given in section 2(3). Other, non-absolute, exemptions apply in respect of stipulated subject matter. The

---

[31] Freedom of Information Act 2000, s. 53(1)(b).

exemption is not absolute because information relating to that subject matter should still be disclosed unless 'in all the circumstances of the case the public interest in maintaining the exemption outweighs the public interest in disclosing the information'.[32] Thus, in respect of non-absolute exemptions, the presumption in favour of disclosure still applies though it can be outweighed by the weight of the reasons for maintaining secrecy. The public authority will make the initial judgment of the public interest but its view can be overridden by the Commissioner or, on appeal, the Tribunal (unless section 53 applies)

Under both Code and Act, each exemption is distinct in terms of its structure and conditions. Some of the non-absolute exemptions specify the need for harm or prejudice of various kinds; others identify a class or general subject matter of information and an exemption can be claimed in respect of any information in that class. Even so, class-based exemption is not 'absolute'. Disclosure may still be in the public interest, under section 2(2), if the public benefit of any particular disclosure outweighs the general arguments for non-disclosure of the class of documents. However, these general arguments for secrecy of the class are likely to be weighty, all the more so because they have been specifically endorsed by the identification of the class in the Act. Arguments for disclosure are likely to be hard to formulate.

The exemptions under the Act apply to both the information itself and whether it exists or not.

The specific exemptions
In what follows, the exemptions, which are all different, are listed and summarised in terms of subject matter.

1 Exemptions and disclosure or non-disclosure under other Acts
Both Code and Act preserve the scope and jurisdiction of other Acts of Parliament dealing with access to information. The non-statutory nature of the Code means that it cannot override statutory provisions which allow for, or prohibit, disclosure. The White Paper, on which the 1993 Code is based, identified about 200 statutes which prohibited or limited disclosure of information.

Section 21 of the 2000 Act gives absolute exemption in respect of information which is reasonably accessible by other means, such as under other Acts. Section 78 makes it clear that nothing in the Act can limit existing powers of disclosure. Section 44 confers absolute exemption where disclosure is already prohibited by an existing statute, under Community law or where it would be a contempt of court. Section 75, however, gives a wide power to the Secretary of State to repeal or amend primary or secondary legislation which prevents the disclosure of information which would otherwise be disclosed under the Act.

1(a) Personal information
Code and Act preserve the Data Protection Act 1998 as the proper statutory regime under which disclosure and control of personal information held by

---

[32] See Code of Practice, Part II; Freedom of Information Act 2000, s. 2(2)(b).

public authorities is dealt with.[33] The 2000 Act widens the protection given to personal information by giving absolute exemption under its terms to some personal information which is outside the scope of the 1998 Act, such as personal data whose disclosure to a third party would violate data protection principles.[34]

1(b) Environmental information

The Code recognises and keeps in place existing rights of access to environmental information. The Code also exempts information which, if disclosed, might endanger the environment or rare or endangered species.[35]

Under section 74 of the Freedom of Information Act 2000 existing environmental regulations will be replaced by new regulations implementing the Aarhus Convention[36] and these, not the 2000 Act, will govern access to information of environmental matters. This is not an absolute exemption and so a public interest disclosure under the 2000 Act, where, for example, the environmental regulations do not permit disclosure, remains a possibility in any particular case.

2 Exemption where there is an existing intention to publish

The Code and the Act both exempt information which the government already intends to publish.

Under section 22 of the Act, the mere intention to publish does not create an absolute exemption. Strong public interest arguments could justify an order for earlier publication but will be unlikely to do so if the public authority sticks to its publication scheme.

3 Exemption regarding research

The Code has specific provision exempting incomplete research where disclosure might be misleading or might deprive the researcher of commercial advantage.[37]

The Act does not have such specific provisions. Research intended for publication can be withheld until publication under section 22, above, or, depending on its subject matter, under the other exemptions.

4 Administrative exemptions

Under the Code 'voluminous or vexatious requests' for information can be denied. This includes requests that are 'manifestly unreasonable' or formulated in too general a manner or which, to answer, would require 'unreasonable diversion of resources'.[38]

---

[33] Freedom of Information Act 2000, s. 40(1). This is an absolute exemption.
[34] Freedom of Information Act 2000, s. 40(2).
[35] Code of Practice, Part 2, paragraph 5.
[36] United Nations Economic Commission for Europe Convention on Access to Information, Public Participation in Decision-making and Access to Justice in Environmental Matters, 1998. Section 74 was brought into force with Royal Assent on 30 November 2000.
[37] Code of Practice, Part 2, paragraph 11.
[38] Code of Practice, Part 2, paragraph 9.

Similar provisions are found in the Act though they are expressed as qualifications on the general duty of disclosure rather than exemptions.[39] Section 12 allows an authority to refuse to disclose on cost grounds.

5 Information supplied in confidence

The Code exempts confidential information such as where it was given under a statutory guarantee of confidentiality[40] or information affecting the privacy of a third party.[41]

Section 41 of the Act gives absolute exemption to information disclosure of which would be actionable as a breach of confidence. The absoluteness of the exemption is qualified by the fact that a breach of confidence, at common law, may only be actionable if, on balance, the public interest dictates secrecy. This exemption will cover the kinds of family, medical and commercial matters which the law protects on confidentiality grounds but it can also extend into the political realm including Cabinet secrets and national security matters.[42]

6 Privilege: Parliamentary and legal

Code and Act both exempt information disclosure of which would violate either Parliamentary or legal privilege.[43] A certificate from the Speaker or the Clerk of the Parliaments that Parliamentary privilege is engaged is conclusive evidence that the exemption applies. Parliamentary privilege creates an absolute exemption; legal privilege does not. However, a third party's legal privilege would be absolutely protected, under section 41, as information whose disclosure could be actionable as a breach of confidence.

7 Commercial secrets

Code and Act exempt commercial confidences from disclosure. Specifically these are trade secrets and information disclosure of which would harm a person's competitive or commercial position.[44] Under the Code disclosure of commercial information can also be avoided since such matters may be outside the jurisdiction of the Parliamentary Commissioner.[45]

These provisions are of great importance given increasing 'privatisation' of government under which more and more public services are performed by profit-making companies under contract with public agencies. The commercial terms of such a contract may disclose policy choices and practices which it is in the public interest to disclose. The exemption under the Act is non-absolute and so such matters could be disclosed if the public interest in favour of disclosure outweighs the public interest in maintaining commercial confidentiality.

---

[39] Freedom of Information Act 2000, s. 14.
[40] Code of Practice, Part 2, paragraph 14.
[41] Code of Practice, Part 2, paragraph 12.
[42] See Chapter 16.
[43] Code of Practice, Part 2, paragraph 4 expressly exempts legal privilege and paragraph 15 exempts parliamentary privilege; s. 42 of the Freedom of Information Act 2000 exempts information covered by legal professional privilege and s. 34 exempts parliamentary privilege.
[44] Code of Practice, Part 2, paragraph 13. Freedom of Information Act 2000, s. 43.
[45] Parliamentary Commissioner Act 1967, s. 4(6) and Schedule 3(9). The restriction applies to 'predominantly' commercial activity.

8 Policy-making

The most controversial areas of exemption, under both Code and Act, relate to the policy and decision processes of public authorities. As Guidance on the Code makes clear: the 'emphasis is on assisting understanding, consideration and analysis of *existing* and proposed policy. The Code does not provide access to the details of the process underlying the Government's preparation of proposals . . .'[46] Of great importance, in the context of civil liberties and the ideal of the active citizen, is the Code's exempting of 'internal discussion and advice'.[47] It establishes a general exemption for 'information whose disclosure would harm the frankness and candour of internal discussion' and, specifically, this is said to include: 'proceedings of Cabinet and Cabinet Committees; internal opinion, advice, recommendation, consultation and deliberation; projections and assumptions relating to internal policy analysis; analysis of alternative policy options and information relating to rejected policy options; confidential communications between departments or public authorities including regulatory bodies.' Although subject to a harm test, this class of exemption continues to seal off the workings of government from public gaze and does so on the challengeable assumption that 'frankness and candour' of policy advice would otherwise be compromised. The public may have access to the final proposals but not to the alternatives and the arguments by which they were rejected.

Sections 35 and 36 of the Act produce a similar outcome. Section 35 only applies to government departments and the National Assembly of Wales. It gives class exemption to information relating to the formulation or development of government policy, including ministerial communications, Law Officers' advice and the operation of a minister's private office. Section 35 does not create absolute exemptions but, as class exemptions, the government does not need to show that any specific disclosure would be damaging; only the most pressing public interests, sufficient to outweigh the general reasons supporting non-disclosure of the class, would justify disclosure. The 'loophole' under section 53, by which the government can override the views of the Commissioner or Tribunal that the public interest justifies disclosure, is likely to be significant on these matters. It should be noted that section 35(4) says that regard should be given to the public interest in the disclosure of factual information which has informed policy-making and this may make it easier for a court to resist the arguments for non-disclosure. The general reasons for non-disclosure of this class of documents relate to the protection of collective responsibility. Decisions should be taken by processes through which policy is collectively agreed. Policy-making institutions, it is thought, cannot operate if these working are open to public exposure since the position of those who opposed a measure that, by collective responsibility they must now accept, would be untenable. Section 35, however, creates a very wide exemption which has no necessary relationship to the content of the information in issue. By including all ministerial communications, whatever they are about, the

---

[46] *Code of Practice on Access to Government Information, Guidance on Interpretation*, 2nd edn (1997), paragraph 3.
[47] Code of Practice, Part 2, paragraph 2.

exemption seems to go far wider than is necessary to protect the processes of policy formulation.

Section 36 builds on these exemptions. Unlike section 35, it applies to all public authorities and establishes a harm or prejudice-based exemption rather than, as under section 35, a class exemption. The matters specifically referred to are: prejudicing the maintenance of the convention of collective responsibility, prejudicing the work of the Executive Committee of the Northern Ireland Assembly and the National Assembly of Wales, inhibiting the free or frank provision of advice or the exchange of views or information which would otherwise prejudice 'the effective conduct of public affairs'. The test for whether such disclosure would be harmful is that of 'the reasonable opinion of a qualified person' as designated in a list of offices in section 36(5).

9 The functioning of the public service and the audit

A number of other exemptions apply in respect of disclosures which might harm the effective and efficient functioning of the public service.

Under the Code disclosures which would harm the 'proper and efficient conduct of the operations' of a public authority are exempt.[48]

This is a very open-textured exemption which is not reproduced in the Act which relies on sections 35 and 36. Under section 33 of the Act, however, there is a specific non-absolute exemption relating to disclosures which would prejudice the exercise by a public authority of its audit function. There is no such specific exemption in the Code.

10 Relations within the United Kingdom

Section 28 of the Act introduces a category of exemption not found in the Code, that disclosure would prejudice relations between different administrations in the United Kingdom, such as between the United Kingdom government and the Scottish Executive or the Scottish Executive and the Executive Committee of the Northern Ireland Legislative Assembly. Although non-absolute and harm-based rather than class-based, this exemption may apply to prevent disclosure of some very controversial and highly charged matters relating to the various jurisdictions of the different administrations.

11 International relations and the economy

In both Code and Act information relating to international relations and the economy are exempt from disclosure.[49] These exemptions are non-absolute and so require proof of harm. Both Code and Act exempt information which would prejudice the economy. Such prejudice, however, need not be serious, though the Commissioner or Tribunal might accept arguments for disclosure in the public interest that outweigh a low degree of harm.

12 National security and defence

Part II, paragraph 1 of the Code produces a harm test: 'information whose disclosure would harm national security and defence'.

---

[48] Code of Practice, Part 2, paragraph 7.
[49] Code of Practice, Part II, paragraph 1.

The Act, on the other hand, takes a more complex approach. Section 23 creates an exemption which is not only class-based but also absolute (i.e. good against even the strongest of public interests favouring disclosure) in respect of information supplied by, or relating to, the main security bodies as identified by the Act. It applies not only to the security services but also to 'the special forces' and the surveillance tribunals established under the Regulation of Investigatory Powers Act 2000 and other legislation. A certificate from a Cabinet minister or the Attorney General is conclusive proof that the information is within the section.[50] If the effect of such a certificate is to prevent access to information that a person needs in order to defend a criminal charge or to uphold a civil right in the courts, an Article 6 ECHR issue is raised.[51]

Section 24 allows such a certificate to be produced in respect of other information not covered by section 23 which, nevertheless, relates to national security. The exemption created by section 24 is class-based but is non-absolute and so national security information, not within section 23, could be disclosed on a balance of public interests.

On defence matters the Act, like the Code, establishes a prejudice test. Information can be exempt if its disclosure would be likely to prejudice the defence of the British Islands or any colony, or likely to prejudice the capability, effectiveness or security of the armed forces.[52]

13 Law enforcement and investigations

Complex provisions relate to law enforcement.

The Code establishes a prejudice test.[53] Under the Act, non-absolute class-based exemptions apply to certain types of law enforcement such as information about criminal investigations, decisions about criminal proceedings and on the use of confidential sources such as informers.[54] Other law enforcement matters are subject to a prejudice test, for example that disclosure would prejudice the prevention or detection of crime.[55]

14 Others

Other exemptions relate to court records or disclosures which would be contempt of court,[56] communications with the Royal Household[57] and in relation to honours[58] and disclosures which would endanger health and safety.[59] Public safety and disclosures relating to immigration are in the Code but not specifically exempt under the Act.

---

[50] Freedom of Information Act 2000, s. 23(2).
[51] *Tinnelley & Sons* v *UK* (1998) 4 BHRC 393.
[52] Freedom of Information Act 2000, ss. 26 and 44.
[53] Code of Practice, Part II, paragraph 4.
[54] Freedom of Information Act 2000, s. 30.
[55] Freedom of Information Act 2000, s. 31.
[56] Freedom of Information Act 2000, s. 32.
[57] Code of Practice, Part II, paragraph 3; Freedom of Information Act 2000, s. 37.
[58] Code of Practice, Part II, paragraph 8; Freedom of Information Act 2000, s. 37.
[59] Code of Practice, Part II paragraph 4; Freedom of Information Act 2000, s. 38.

15.6 Conclusion

Time will tell how effective the Freedom of Information Act will be. It is most likely that the provision of information to the consumer of public services will improve as will the ease of public access, particularly through the Internet, to policy and legislative proposals. What can, and may still, be kept from public view are not only national security matters but also the documents by which policy options are understood and selected. In this sense, the 'active citizen' has less to gain from the new openness than the 'citizen as consumer'.

16

National security

16.1 National security

It is widely accepted that states can properly pursue and protect their security by means of armed forces and by employing police and secret services to gather and interpret information. They also undertake various forms of more or less covert action. The security of the state can also be legitimately protected by legal measures which aim to maintain the secrecy of information pertaining to state security, in particular information about the operations of the defence and secret services. It is the scope of the activities justified by national security that raises the hard questions.

'National security' is not defined with any precision and its accepted application is broad.[1] It includes matters relating to war and defence,[2] including the disposition of armed forces[3] and nuclear weapons.[4] The activities of the security and intelligence services are also included.[5] These involve not only military and political threats from overseas but also internal subversion. Subversion involves threats to the safety or well-being of the state and activities which are 'intended to undermine or overthrow Parliamentary democracy by political, industrial or violent means'.[6] The functions of the security and intelligence services also include combating 'serious crime' (a term which can include minor crime committed by groups, including political protestors) and also matters relating to the economic well-being of the United Kingdom. Action against terrorism is likely to be within the remit of the security and intelligence services.[7]

The breadth of the definition of national security raises controversy. The government may use it to try and justify secrecy over a wide range of activities where others believe that openness to the public or its representatives is proper and consistent with adequate security. Secondly, most of the categories of national security mentioned above can include opposition political activity, especially of a radical kind. Such activity ought to be legitimate in an open democracy, subject only to the ordinary criminal law rather than to the special measures available in respect of designated threats to national security.

---

[1] Stone, R. (2000) *Textbook on Civil Liberties*. London: Blackstone Press, p. 172, citing the cases given in the following sentence.
[2] *The Zamora* [1916] 2 AC 77.
[3] *Chandler* v *DPP* [1964] AC 763.
[4] *Secretary of State of State for Defence* v *Guardian Newpapers* [1984] 3 All ER 601.
[5] *Attorney General* v *Guardian (No. 2)* [1988] 3 All ER 545.
[6] For example, section 1, Security Service Act 1989.
[7] See Chapter 18.

Arguments about this borderline are ongoing. The consent of the Attorney General is often needed for prosecutions though that office's apparent lack of independence from the executive and the width of the discretion to be exercised may raise a Convention point.

The courts used to be reluctant to test government claims that serious national security issues justified the imposition of some penalty or restriction on a person.[8] From the later 1980s, however, there was evidence of the courts requiring the government to explain why national security is involved.[9] The 'war on terrorism' may, however, lead the courts back to a general acceptance that a ministerial assertion of a need based on national security is sufficient.[10]

National security, in its various forms, is protected both through the criminal law and on the basis of civil actions against, for example, the press.

16.2 The Official Secrets Act 1911, section 1

The protection of military and related secrets from 'spies' is widely accepted as a legitimate function for the criminal law. The core instance is to protect such secrets from being communicated directly or indirectly to an actual or possible enemy. Section 1 of the Official Secrets Act 1911 (as amended in 1920) creates a large number of offences, any one of which is subject to a maximum sentence of 14 years imprisonment,[11] and which are described as 'penalties for spying'.

1. Penalties for spying
(1) If any person for any purpose prejudicial to the safety or interests of the state –
  (a) approaches, inspects, passes over or is in the neighbourhood of, or enters any prohibited place within the meaning of this Act; or
  (b) makes any sketch, plan, model, or note which is calculated to be or might be or is intended to be directly or indirectly useful to an enemy; or
  (c) obtains, collects, records, or publishes, or communicates to any other person any secret official code word or pass word, or any sketch, plan, model, article, or note, or other document or information which is calculated to be or might be or is intended to be directly or indirectly useful to an enemy;
  he shall be guilty of a felony.

A prejudicial purpose can be established on the basis of 'the circumstances of the case', the defendant's 'conduct' or 'his known character as proved'.[12]

[8] For example, *R v Secretary of State for the Home Department ex parte Hosenball* [1977] 3 All ER 452. See Griffith, J.A.G. (1985) 'Judicial Decision-Making in the Law', *Public Law* 564 for a general argument that the courts are too uncritical in their acceptance of government claims.

[9] For example, *R v Secretary of State for the Home Department ex parte Ruddock* [1987] 2 All ER 518. But see the reluctant acceptance of Sedley J (as he then was) that, in the context of Prevention of Terrorism (Temporary Provisions) Act 1989, there was binding authority requiring the courts to accept the government's claim that national security was involved without inquiring into the reasonableness of the claim: *R v Secretary of State for the Home Department ex parte McQuillan* [1995] 4 All ER 400.

[10] See *Secretary of State for the Home Department v Rehman* [2001] UKHL 47; [2002] 1 All ER 122, especially Lord Hoffman, paragraph 62. See also [2002] EWCA Civ 1502.

[11] Fourteen years was introduced by the Official Secrets Act 1920 and represented a doubling of the maximum sentence introduced in 1911.

[12] The latter, in particular, seems to allow previous convictions and similar fact evidence to be put before a jury and may not be consistent with the fair trial provisions of Article 6 ECHR.

Similarly, the doing, without lawful authority, of any of the actions listed in section 1(1)(b) or (c) sets up a presumption of a prejudicial purpose 'unless the contrary is proved'. This is a 'reverse onus' provision which may not be compatible with the presumption of innocence in Article 6(2) ECHR.[13] If any of the actions described in section 1(1)(a) are in issue, it is the prosecution who must prove the prejudicial purpose. In *Chandler* v *DPP* (1964)[14] the defendants sought to have the issue of prejudicial purpose treated as an open question subject to argument and cross examination and to be decided, in the end, by the jury. The House of Lords did not accept this but nor did it accept that the issue of prejudice was entirely for the government of the day to determine. The 'state' does not mean 'the government' but refers to a general collective entity which Lord Reid called 'the organised community'. The possibility of disputing the government's view on what is or is not prejudicial to the state remains theoretical. In *Chandler* the issue was defence policy, which has always been an exclusive matter for the Crown. On such an issue, a defendant cannot dispute the government's or the military's views of the existence of prejudice to the safety and interests of the state. The courts not only recognise the Royal prerogative but also accept that any challenge to defence policy would raise political questions of a kind inappropriate for courts to determine.

Subsections 1(1)(b) and (c) create offences on the basis of actions which are useful to an enemy. The section is broadly defined. The information in issue need not be secret, almost any information is likely to be in some way useful, and there is no requirement that the defendant knowingly or intentionally communicated to an enemy. 'Enemy' can include a potential enemy[15] and so is not confined to wartime and, perhaps, could include a terrorist organisation. The government's designation of a country or an organisation as a potential enemy is hard to challenge in court.

The offences in section 1(1)(a) are committed in relation to a 'prohibited place'. This is defined in section 3 and includes a variety of military establishments whether or not under the direct control of the Crown. Other places, such as those connected with means of communication, the public utilities, shipyards and arms factories, even if under private ownership, can also be declared to be 'prohibited places' by order of the Secretary of State. Some nuclear installations, for example, are declared to be prohibited places under the Act.[16]

Section 7 of the Official Secrets Act 1920 makes acts which are 'preparatory' to the commission of a section 1 offence into crimes. A preparatory act may be more remote than an incitement and could include, for example, planning protests and demonstrations which eventually lead to offences being committed.[17]

---

[13] See *R* v *DPP ex parte Kebilene* [1999] 4 All ER 801 for conflicting judicial views on how the compatibility with Article 6(2) ECHR of reverse onus provisions in the definition of national security (terrorism) offences should be assessed.

[14] [1964] AC 763.

[15] *R* v *Parrott* (1913) 8 Cr App Rep 186, CCA.

[16] For example, some nuclear installations: Official Secrets (Prohibited Places) Order 1994, SI 1994 No. 968.

[17] See *R* v *Bingham* [1973] QB 870; Stone, *op. cit.*, pp. 177–8.

The Act is not confined to deliberate spying.[18] In *Chandler* v *DPP*[19] section 1 was used against peace demonstrators intending, temporarily, to inhibit the workings of a military airbase but who had no intention to assist an enemy, and, in the trial of Aubrey, Berry and Campbell, against a serviceman and two journalists who were concerned with a highly controversial deportation of an American journalist on national security grounds. Although, in this 'ABC trial', the judge accepted that section 1 was not confined to spying and sabotage, he did declare that it should only be used in the most serious cases.[20] The safeguard against oppression is said to be that prosecutions (but not arrests and remands[21]) require the consent of the Attorney General. Activists may also be vulnerable to prosecution under section 3 of the Official Secrets Act 1920 for actions such as interfering with police or military personnel engaged in guard or similar duties at a prohibited place.[22]

Section 9 of the Official Secrets Act 1911 authorises search warrants (or in emergency cases searches by the police without a warrant). It is the potential use of these powers against political activists and, in particular, against journalists which is controversial and will now raise points of proportionality under Articles 10 and 11 ECHR. The power was used against BBC Scotland in the 'Zircon affair', involving a television programme, made but not shown, giving information about a spy satellite whose existence and cost had not been disclosed to Parliament.[23]

16.3 The disclosure of information

Official secrets legislation also creates criminal offences relating to the unauthorised disclosure of information concerning national security. In addition, national security has both absolute and harm-based exemption from disclosure under the provisions of the Freedom of Information Act 2000 (see Chapter 15).

Given the scope of 'national security' it is clear that official secrets legislation can prevent the bringing into the public domain of knowledge of government affairs which may be highly significant for voters and for activists seeking to make well-informed political choices. Political expression is in issue. Under the Human Rights Act 1998 such expression is highly weighted. National security is accepted as a legitimate purpose for restriction under Article 10(2), but any particular limitation must be necessary for and proportionate to a pressing social need. Of particular concern is whether, as a matter of proportionality, the law allows an unauthorised disclosure to be defended on public interest grounds.

---

[18] Recent prosecutions, however, have been in respect of spying against defence contractors.

[19] [1964] AC 733.

[20] The s. 1 offences were dropped. The defendants were eventually convicted by a politically vetted jury for offences under s. 2 of the Official Secrets Act 1911 but punished with low sentences. See Nicol, A. (1979) 'Official Secrets and Jury Vetting', *Crim LR* 284.

[21] Official Secrets Act 1911, s. 8.

[22] *Alder* v *George* [1964] 2 QB 7.

[23] See Bailey, S.H., Harris, D.J. and Jones, B.L. (1995) *Civil Liberties Cases and Materials*. London: Butterworths, pp. 454–5; Ewing, K. and Gearty, C. (1990) *Freedom under Thatcher*. Oxford: Clarendon Press, pp. 147–52.

Section 2 of the Official Secrets Act 1911 was very widely drawn and fell into disrepute. It was too inclusive, it caught the trivial as well as the important,[24] and the Attorney General's discretion over prosecutions could be exercised for purposes which, in the eyes of many, were aimed at the avoidance of government embarrassment or to keep infamy hidden even from the people's representatives. The government seemed to lose confidence in the legislation, preferring not to prosecute and to depend instead on civil proceedings based on confidentiality provisions in civil servant's contracts. Various attempts at reform, including government bills, foundered on the difficulty of formulating the terms of a replacement statute. Eventually the Official Secrets Act 1989 was enacted. It repealed section 2 (but not section 1) of the 1911 Act and substituted new provisions.

16.4 The Official Secrets Act 1989

The 1989 Official Secrets Act remains in force. In the early years of the twenty-first century, however, there is a very different political context from the late 1980s. The sense of a stable threat from the Soviet Union has been replaced, not by a sense of security, indeed, but by a sense of shifting threats from a range of different sources.[25] Since 11 September 2001 these are now focused on the fear of terrorist attack from organisations and from alleged terrorist states. On the other hand, there remains, as discussed in Chapter 15, a policy of greater openness in government though it hardly extends to national security. The Freedom of Information Act 2000, for example, contains exceptions for national security and the secret services. The Public Interest Disclosure Act 1998 provides some protection from legal action for 'whistleblowers'. It is, however, of little assistance to a civil servant or security officer making a disclosure in breach of the Official Secrets Act 1989 since security officers are and other Crown servants may be excluded from the Act and, in any case, its protection is lost 'if the person making the disclosure commits an offence by making it'.[26]

The Official Secrets Act 1989 continues to be used. David Shayler, an ex-security service officer, was convicted in 2002 in respect of the publication of his experiences in which official wrongdoing was alleged. However, the Act has not deterred members of the security services from publishing[27] and it may permit restrictions on freedom of political expression to a disproportionate degree. In 2001 the Intelligence and Security Committee has recommended that the Act be reformed.

---

[24] *R v Crisp and Homewood* (1919) 83 JP 121, involving disclosure of the details of officer's uniforms.
[25] See, for example, introductory remarks to the reports of the Intelligence and Security Committee, August 2000 and 1999.
[26] Section 43B(3), Employment Rights Act 1996, inserted by s. 1, Public Interest Disclosure Act 1998.
[27] Richard Tomlinson was convicted and imprisoned under the Act in 1995. In 2001, he intended to publish a book on his experiences. The government sought an injunction to prevent publication in the United Kingdom: 'Britain tries to stop MI6 spy's "revenge" book', *The Times*, 15 January 2001, p. 9.

16.4.1 The scheme of the Act

The Act replaces the catch-all provisions of section 2 of the Official Secrets Act 1911 with a system that identifies specific subject categories of information, disclosure of which is an offence. The categories are: security and intelligence, defence, international relations, information obtained in confidence from another state and crime. Unauthorised disclosure of other matters, sensitive economic information[28] for example, may result in civil action but is not the basis of a criminal offence. With one major exception (members of the security and intelligence services disclosing security information), no offence is committed unless the disclosure is proved to be damaging in ways the Act specifies; mere disclosure is not enough.

The power to issue search warrants under section 9(1) of the Official Secrets Act 1911 is extended to include offences under the 1989 Act. Prosecutions require the Attorney General's consent; the main offences are arrestable offences and the maximum penalty is two years' imprisonment.

Application
The Act applies to security and intelligence officers and to other 'Crown servants and government contractors'. These terms are defined by section 12 of the Act and include ministers, members of the Scottish Executive, civil servants, members of the armed forces and police officers and civilian police employees. The list can be expanded by order of the Secretary of State.[29] Members of Parliament are not Crown Servants. Government contractors are persons who are not Crown servants but who provide goods or services for government purposes. This is a large category of persons operating in the public sector.

Defences
The Act provides a general defence to any defendant if they can prove a belief that disclosure was lawfully authorised and there was no reasonable cause to believe otherwise.[30] A second defence is that the defendant can prove that he or she neither knew, nor had reasonable grounds to believe, that the information related to a forbidden category of information (e.g. security or intelligence or defence[31]). Where the offence requires proof that the disclosure was damaging it is also a defence for the person charged to prove that he or she did not know nor had reasonable grounds to believe that the disclosure would be damaging in the way identified by the Act. The fact that information is already in the public domain is not expressly mentioned in the Act but might be covered by this defence. The prosecution of an army officer for disclosing information about army operations in Northern Ireland to a journalist was dropped after it was discovered that allegedly secret matters had already been published.[32]

---

[28] The Franks Committee would have included information relating to the currency generally and to the reserves in particular within the reach of the criminal law, as it would any matter found in a Cabinet document: Cm 5104 paragraph 275.
[29] Section 12(1)(f)(g), Official Secrets Act 1989.
[30] Section 7(4), Official Secrets Act 1989.
[31] For example, s. 1, Official Secrets Act 1989.
[32] 'Official secrets trial of army officer collapses', *The Times* 2 November 2000, p. 9.

No public interest defence

What is not available is a public interest defence in which the disclosure, though otherwise within the terms of the Act, is said to be justified because it discloses apparent government wrongdoing which would otherwise be unknown to the public or its representatives.[33] The old section 2 of the 1911 Act had a form of public interest defence if it could be shown that official information had been communicated to 'a person to whom it is in the interests of the State his [i.e. the communicator's] duty to communicate it'. The scope of the defence was drastically limited in *R* v *Ponting* (1985)[34] where it was held that the communicator's 'duty' was his or her official, rather than moral, duty and that the 'interests of the state' were as determined exclusively by the government. The government rejected the idea of a public interest defence for the 1989 Act because it would render the law uncertain and because damaging disclosures for whatever purpose were not justifiable.[35]

The trouble with a public interest defence is that it is not clear what the test for the public interest should be. A policy disagreement or a disagreement on a matter of conscience are insufficient justifications for a security officer or civil servant to make an unauthorised disclosure, particularly if it is damaging. No civil servant can claim to be unjustly treated who is required to subordinate his or her judgment on such matters to that of the government. Unauthorised disclosure of serious crime[36] or seriously unconstitutional activity by the government, such as the abuse of Parliament, might justify a public interest disclosure since, in those respects, the public interest standard is likely to be clear. Even then it is not obvious that a damaging disclosure would be justified. One of the most delicate and exacting arguments about the public interest relates to the extent to which there can be a general social benefit from the 'dirty hands' of the secret service and, though such activity cannot be publicly justified, to condemn it, having received its benefit, is a form of moral free-riding.

Under the Human Rights Act 1998, restrictions on freedom of expression must be justified under Article 10(2) ECHR. In an argument about the necessity and proportionality of a restriction, say on the publication of a book by a member of the security service, a court could balance the pressing social need which justifies the restriction with the public interest going to justify publication. That this balancing could be done was a reason for the Strasbourg court's finding of a general compatibility with the Convention of the law relating to breach of confidence injunctions.[37] There is no statutory basis for doing such balancing under the Official Secrets Act 1989 and so, arguably, a declaration of incompatibility might be necessary. Conscientious disclosure by members of the security and intelligence services has been a matter of

---

[33] The absence of such a defence is a matter of concern for the United Nations Human Rights Committee: 2001 Report of the United Kingdom of Great Britain and Northern Ireland: http://www.un-hchr/ch/tbs/doc/nsf.

[34] (1985) Crim LR 318.

[35] It had been recommended by the Franks Committee.

[36] David Shayler's allegations of a conspiracy to assassinate President Qaddifi would be an example.

[37] See *The Observer and the Guardian* v *United Kingdom* (1992) 14 EHRR 153, paragraph 63.

government concern. Such persons now have access to an independent staff counsellor whose function has been supported by the Intelligence and Security Committee. In *R v Shayler* (2002)[38] the lack of a public interest defence in the Act was confirmed by the House of Lords and no incompatability with Article 10 was found. Shayler's prosecution was, in the circumstances, a proportionate restriction on the freedom of expression of security service agents. It was proportionate because authorised disclosures can be made to various officials such as the staff counsellor or to the Metropolitan Police; if those officials do not act, agents can seek lawful authority from their superiors and, if that is unreasonably refused, judicial review is available and, through the test of proportionality, it provides a hard look at such matters.[39]

There has been speculation that the common law defence of necessity is available in respect of a prosecution under the Act. Despite Court of Appeal approval in principle, the issue is undecided.[40]

Damage
With the exception of security and intelligence officers disclosing matters relating to security and intelligence, the Act provides that only disclosures which are damaging can be the basis of a criminal prosecution. The specific type of damage is defined in relation to each of the different categories of information to which the Act applies.

16.4.2 Security and intelligence information

1 Security and intelligence
(1) A person who is or has been –
    (a) a member of the security and intelligence services; or
    (b) a person notified that he is subject to the provisions of this subsection,
    is guilty of an offence if without lawful authority he discloses any information, document or other article relating to security or intelligence which is or has been in his possession by virtue of his position as a member of any of those services or in the course of his work while the notification is or was in force.

Section 1(1) creates a strict offence, based on disclosure, for current and past members of the security and intelligence services; there is no need to prove that the disclosures are damaging. It reflects the lifelong duty of confidentiality that members of the security and intelligence services place themselves under. Security and intelligence services are not defined in the Act but presumably the subsection is confined to members of the services defined by the Security Service Act 1989 and the Intelligence Services Act 1994.[41] Any other person can be brought within the reach of the strict offence by notification; this has been done, for example, to members of the Intelligence and Security Committee, a

---

[38] [2002] UKHL 11; [2002] 2 All ER 477 HL.
[39] *R v Shayler* [2002] 2 All ER 477 HL, paragraph 27.
[40] Court of Appeal: *R v Shayler* [2001] EWCA Crim 1977; [2001] 1 WLR 2206; not followed by the House of Lords on the necessity point.
[41] Special Branch, a service concerned with gathering intelligence on national security matters, is, arguably, within the reach of s.1(1) – see Stone, *op. cit.*, p. 181.

body which includes Members of Parliament. A number of intelligence officers, including David Shayler, have sought to write memoirs in which they make serious allegations of wrongdoing. The absence of a public interest defence, mentioned above, makes it very difficult for them to avoid prosecution under the Act

Other Crown servants or government contractors can be prosecuted under section 1(3) for unauthorised disclosure of security and intelligence matters. The central difference with the section 1(1) offence is that not only must there be proof of unauthorised disclosure but the disclosure must be shown to be damaging to security and intelligence matters.

> **[1. Security and intelligence]**
> (3) A person who is or has been a Crown servant or government contractor is guilty of an offence if without lawful authority he makes damaging disclosure of any information, document or other article relating to security or intelligence which is or has been in his possession by virtue of his position as such but otherwise than as mentioned in subsection (1) above.
> (4) For the purposes of subsection (3) above a disclosure is damaging if –
> (a) it causes damage to the work of, or of any part of, the security and intelligence services; or
> (b) it is of information or a document or other article which is such that its unauthorised disclosure would be likely to cause such damage or which falls within a class or description of information, documents or articles the unauthorised disclosure of which would be likely to have that effect.

It is not clear how effective the 'damage' requirement will be in restraining prosecutions under the Act. There is no general requirement that the damage be serious; damage can be shown on the basis of something likely to happen, proof that damage has occurred is not required, and the likelihood of damage can be based not on the content but on the class, the type, of any information or document, and on the assumption that the disclosure of any information or document of that class, no matter how harmless in itself, is damaging. The court may be reluctant to examine in any detail the precise way that damage may occur and find damage in the mere fact that the matter affected security and intelligence matters

16.4.3 Defence

Disclosure by Crown servants or government contractors of matters relating to defence is an offence under section 2 if it is 'damaging'. Damage is given an extensive and exclusive definition.

> **[2. Defence]**
> (2) For the purposes of subsection (1) above a disclosure is damaging if –
> (a) it damages the capability of, or of any part of, the armed forces of the Crown to carry out their tasks or leads to loss of life or injury to members of those forces or serious damage to the equipment or installations of those forces; or
> (b) otherwise than as mentioned in paragraph (a) above, it endangers the interests of the United Kingdom abroad, seriously obstructs the promotion

or protection by the United Kingdom of those interests or endangers the safety of British citizens abroad; or

(c) it is information or a document or article which is such that its unauthorised disclosure would be likely to have any of those effects.

This definition includes, under (2)(c), disclosure which not only causes damage but which is likely to do so. There is no reference to classes of information or document. Damage relating to defence must be shown from the contents of what is disclosed and not just from the fact that disclosure affects defence.

The Act defines 'defence'. This approach, giving an exclusive definition of the terms used, is preferable and more in line with the Convention requirement of legality than leaving the words undefined and subject to the *ex post* claims of the Crown and the discretion of the judiciary.

(4) In this section 'defence' means–
   (a) the size, shape, organisation, logistics, order of battle, deployment, operations, state of readiness and training of the armed forces of the Crown;
   (b) the weapons, stores or other equipment of those forces and the invention, development, production and operation of such equipment and research relating to it;
   (c) defence policy and strategy and military planning and intelligence;
   (d) plans and measures for the maintenance of essential supplies and services that are or would be needed in time of war.

16.4.4 International relations

Section 3 makes it an offence for a Crown servant or government contractor to make a damaging disclosure of any information, document or other article relating to international relations or of confidential information or documents obtained from a foreign state or international organisation.

[3. International relations]
(2) For the purposes of subsection (1) above a disclosure is damaging if–
   (a) it endangers the interests of the United Kingdom abroad, seriously obstructs the promotion or protection by the United Kingdom of those interests or endangers the safety of British citizens abroad; or
   (b) it is of information or of a document or article which is such that its unauthorised disclosure would be likely to have any of those effects . . .
(5) In this section 'international relations' means the relations between States, between international organisations or between one or more States and one or more such organisations and includes any matter relating to a State other than the United Kingdom or to an international organisation which is capable of affecting the relations of the United Kingdom with another State or with an international organisation.

As with defence matters, the definition includes, under 3(2)(b), a disclosure which is likely cause damage, but there is no reference to classes of information or document and so it is arguable that damage must be shown from the contents of what is disclosed.

The definition of damage might authorise restrictions on freedom of expression which do not fit easily with the legitimate aims of such restriction permitted under Article 10(2). In particular the 'interests of the United Kingdom abroad' could include economic interests which are purposefully not listed in Article 10(2). It may be that the term will need a restrictive interpretation in order, as far as is possible, for any conviction to be compatible with Convention Rights.

16.4.5 Criminal matters

Persons who are or have been Crown servants or government contractors commit an offence if they disclose any information, document or other article with specified effects on crime and the criminal justice process.

> **[4. Crime and special investigation powers]**
> (2) This section applies to any information, document or other article–
>   (a) the disclosure of which–
>   (i)   results in the commission of an offence; or
>   (ii) facilitates an escape from legal custody or the doing of any other act prejudicial to the safekeeping of persons in legal custody; or
>   (iii) impedes the prevention or detection of offences or the apprehension or prosecution of suspected offenders; or
>   (b) which is such that its unauthorised disclosure would be likely to have any of those effects.

It is a defence for a person charged under section 4(2)(a) to prove they did not know, at the time the offence was committed, and had no reasonable cause to know, that the disclosure would have any of the effects listed in section 4(2)(a)(i)–(iii).

Section 4(3) deals with information obtained by various forms of surveillance. The subsection refers to 'any' information and is not expressly confined to matters pertaining to crime. There is no requirement that disclosures be damaging. Certain disclosures of information obtained by warranted interceptions under the Regulation of Investigatory Powers Act 2000, the Security Service Act 1989 and the Intelligence Services Act 1994 are offences. However, section 4 does not refer to all forms of authorised surveillance. Disclosure under Part II of the Regulation of Investigatory Powers Act 2000 or under Part III of the Police Act 1997, for example, is not an offence under those Acts or under section 4 of the Official Secrets Act 1989. Such disclosures might, however, form the basis of a complaint that could be made to the Tribunal established under Part IV of the Regulation of Investigatory Powers Act 2000.[42]

16.4.6 Third-party disclosures and the media

The Official Secrets Act 1989 covers not only primary disclosure by officials but it also extends to the further disclosure of information by any person, including by the media.

---

[42] See Chapter 7.

Section 5(6) of the Official Secrets Act 1989 relates to the spying provisions of the 1911 Act. It is an offence for a person (a newspaper editor for example) to 'disclose any information, etc., which he knows or has reasonable cause to believe, to have come into his possession as a result of contravention of section 1 of the Official Secrets Act 1911'. This offence applies whether such disclosure is or is not damaging though the public interest defence inherent in section 1 of the 1911 Act (that the original obtaining of the information was not done for 'any purpose prejudicial to the safety or interests of the State') will apply.

Different considerations apply where the Official Secrets Act 1989 may have been breached. Further disclosure, by the media for example, of information obtained in breach of the Act, is not an offence under sections 1–4. Such further disclosure is an offence, under section 5 of the 1989 Act, if the following conditions apply. The person making the further disclosure (e.g. an editor) must know or have reasonable cause to believe that the information etc. is protected from disclosure by the 1989 Act and that it came into his or her possession on the basis of a breach of the Act by someone or was so entrusted to him or her on the basis of confidentiality. If the information etc. relates to security and intelligence, defence or international relations then the editor only commits an offence if the further disclosure (e.g. the broadcasting or publication in a newspaper) is damaging and it is made knowing or having reasonable cause to believe that it would be so damaging. The test for damage is the same as for the primary disclosure offences. Thus the strict offence applied to members of the security and intelligence services disclosing matters relating to security and intelligence does not apply to those, such as in the media, who obtain and pass on their disclosures.[43]

In the case of information relating to crime protected from disclosure by section 4, there is no need to prove that the further disclosure is damaging; the fact that the person making the disclosure knew or had cause to know how it came into his or her possession and that it was protected from disclosure is enough to ground an offence under section 5. Section 6 of the Official Secrets Act 1989 creates an additional offence if further damaging disclosure of information, protected by sections 1–3 of the Act, was information supplied in confidence by the United Kingdom to a foreign state or international organisation.

Media freedom is, of course, highly weighted under the European Convention on Human Rights and section 12 of the Human Rights Act 1998 provides that special care must be taken by the courts when asked to restrain press freedom. The absence of a public interest defence under sections 5 and 6 may raise a Convention issue in so far as it makes it difficult for the media to argue that the further publication of protected information is reasonable and a prosecution under the Act is disproportionate.

16.5 Breach of confidence

The Official Secrets Act 1989 creates criminal offences to protect official secrets from disclosure. Such secrets can also be protected by the use of the civil law,

---

[43] See to the same effect *Lord Advocate* v *The Scotsman Publications Ltd and others* [1990] 1 AC 812.

specifically by the government seeking injunctions to prevent direct disclosure by Crown servants or indirect disclosure by the press. A general reluctance to use the criminal law, especially if matters of conscience are involved, has meant that the use of such injunctions has not been uncommon since the 1980s.

The courts will grant an injunction on the grounds of a breach of confidence (or, perhaps, to protect simple privacy) if, on a weighing of relevant considerations, the public interest in maintaining secrecy outweighs the public interest in disclosure (see Chapter 11). Such injunctions have traditionally been available to protect personal or private matters invested with confidentiality such as domestic and matrimonial privacy, commercial secrets and medical records.

Since the mid-1970s, a relationship of confidentiality, sufficient to ground an injunction, has also been found in the political arena. In *Attorney General* v *Jonathan Cape Ltd* (1976) it was accepted that the views of individual Cabinet members were, against the background of collective Cabinet responsibility, confidential and capable of protection by injunctive relief.[44] The most dramatic extension of breach of confidence into the political arena occurred with the *Spycatcher* litigation. This long and much reported saga[45] involved the British government's attempt, both at home and abroad, to prevent the publication of memoirs by Peter Wright, a one-time member of the security services. The memoirs contained allegations of criminal and improper activity by the security services, some of it aimed at senior figures in the Labour Party and government. The focus of the issue was whether the press could be stopped from publishing excerpts from the book or articles about the book or descriptions of court cases in other countries, especially Australia, in which the allegations were aired. Broadly speaking the government succeeded in obtaining temporary injunctions against the press[46] but failed to sustain these as permanent injunctions.[47]

The *Spycatcher* judgments confirm that a member of the security services is under a lifelong duty of confidentiality which the law will uphold against him or her directly. Section 1(1) of the Official Secrets Act 1989 gives effect to this in the criminal law. The duty of confidentiality is also seen as creating a private law, contractual and fiduciary relationship with the Crown which may, in exceptional circumstances, entitle the Crown to more than the usual remedies for breach of contract; for example, it may be entitled to receive profits made from unauthorised disclosures.[48]

16.5.1 The public interest

The *Spycatcher* litigation is predominantly about whether there are public interest reasons which outweigh the reasons for secrecy and which should

---

[44] In the case an injunction was refused because, by passage of time, confidentiality, as a matter of substance, was lost and the court did not accept that the public interest demanded perpetual protection based upon the class or type of document involved.

[45] Bailey, Harris, and Jones, *op. cit.*, pp. 411–16, 474–88, 829–32; Ewing and Gearty, *op. cit.*, pp. 152–69.

[46] *Attorney General* v *Guardian Newspapers Ltd and others and related appeals* [1987] 3 All ER 316.

[47] *Attorney General* v *Guardian Newspapers Ltd and others (No. 2)* [1988] 3 All ER 545.

[48] *Attorney General* v *Blake (Jonathan Cape Ltd, third party)* [2000] 4 All ER 385.

permit disclosure to go ahead. The burden is on the Crown to show not only that the issue is touched with confidentiality, but also that the public interest requires publication to be restrained and there is no overriding public interest consideration favouring publication.[49] In the national security context, the public interest issue applies particularly to the possibility of restraining public disclosures by the media. An injunction will be available directly against the officer or his or her agent (e.g. their publisher). Different considerations apply to the media if it comes into possession of what it knows to be confidential information or wishes to comment when such information has been disclosed elsewhere such as in court proceedings or in a book published overseas.[50] The courts may refuse the government an injunction against the media in the absence of evidence that publication would be damaging (in this respect the civil law on injunctions is in line with section 5 of the Official Secrets Act 1989). Damage may be based on the nature of the information disclosed. In *Lord Advocate* v *The Scotsman Publications Ltd and others* (1990)[51] the Crown sought an injunction to restrain *The Scotsman* from publishing extracts from the memoirs of a member of the security services. Small numbers of the memoirs had been privately printed and distributed. The Crown conceded that the information in the memoirs was not damaging to national security.

The Crown will also find it hard to establish that further publication of confidential matter in the media is damaging if the information has already been widely and publicly disseminated. In *Spycatcher* the injunctions were discharged at the full trial. The book had been widely published, including in the United States, and consequently all possible damage had been done and could not be increased by further publication. There was, therefore, no point is continuing the ban.[52] In earlier proceedings the interlocutory injunctions had been maintained by the House of Lords, despite publication in the USA, on the grounds that the Crown had other reasons for seeking to prevent publication which would be rendered nugatory if the injunctions were granted at the full trial. These other reasons were: maintaining the morale of the security services and its reputation and asserting the importance of lifelong confidentiality against any other security services personnel who might be tempted to follow Peter Wright's example. At the full trial such reasons were not sufficient to provide a public interest reason to refuse publication.

Where, however, there has been no concession from the Crown that publication would not be damaging and no previous publication, then the media is likely to be under the same restraint as the member of the security services. In the *Spycatcher* litigation, it was accepted by the courts that the original injunctions, granted before widespread publication, were properly made.[53]

---

[49] *Attorney General* v *Guardian Newspapers Ltd and others (No. 2)* [1988] 3 All ER 545, 640 per Lord Keith following *Attorney General* v *Jonathan Cape Ltd* [1976] QB 752.
[50] *Lord Advocate* v *The Scotsman Publications Ltd and others* [1990] 1 AC 812, 822.
[51] [1990] 1 AC 812.
[52] *Attorney General* v *Guardian Newspapers Ltd and others (No. 2)* (1988) 3 All ER 545.
[53] *Attorney General* v *Guardian Newspapers Ltd and others (No. 2)* (1988) 3 All ER 545; *Lord Advocate* v *The Scotsman Publications Ltd and others* [1990] 1 AC 812.

As we have seen, the criminal law, in the form of the Official Secrets Act 1989, does not provide for a 'public interest' defence. We have also seen that the partial public interest defence under section 1 of the Official Secrets Act 1911 is very difficult to establish against a government counterclaim of the public interest. To the contrary, at the heart of an application for a breach of confidence injunction is an argument about the public interest. The public interest may require disclosure of, for example, well founded allegations of criminal action or infamous deeds.[54] The fact of a well founded allegation of wrongdoing will not, necessarily, lead to the refusal of an injunction and publication. In a national security context, the courts may still decide that confidentiality should be retained. As is clear from the *Spycatcher* litigation and, more recently, *R v Shayler* (2002),[55] the existence of internal mechanisms for hearing security officers' concerns and allegations and a sense that accusations of criminal behaviour should be made to the police rather than the media increases the likelihood that injunctions against the media will still be granted in respect of national security matters which have retained their confidentiality, even when serious malpractice by the security services is in issue.[56] The problem, of course, is that it is impossible to tell whether the courts' trust in the internal mechanisms is well placed.

16.5.2 Breach of confidence and Article 10

The impact of Article 10 ECHR, through the Human Rights Act 1998, on breach of confidence injunctions in the context of national security is hard to judge. The interlocutory injunctions in the *Spycatcher* litigation were upheld by the Strasbourg court.[57] They were 'prescribed by law' and for a legitimate purpose: that of maintaining the authority of the judiciary; final injunctions can be for 'national security'. The court also accepted the compatibility with the Convention of the injunctions up until widespread publication destroyed confidentiality. From that point there was no confidentiality left and continuing the temporary injunctions was a violation of Article 10. One of the primary purposes of Article 10 is to keep open channels of political debate and information and, consequently, the presence of allegations of political misconduct should now weigh more heavily with British courts than heretofore. The Strasbourg court's judgment permits injunctions to maintain confidentiality, including the lifelong duty of confidentiality owed by the security services, even, it seems, despite allegations of serious criminal misconduct. Once confidentiality is lost, however, it seems that the other arguments for secrecy, such as those going to the morale and reputation of the security services, will be outweighed by the public interest in knowing about allegations of wrongdoing.

---

[54] See Chapter 11.
[55] [2002] UKHL 11; [2002] 2 All ER 477 HL; discussed above.
[56] See *Attorney General v Punch Ltd and another* [2001] EWCA Civ 403; [2001] 2 All ER 655, discussed in Chapter 12.
[57] *Guardian Newspapers v United Kingdom* (1992) 14 EHRR 229; *The Observer and the Guardian v United Kingdom* (1992) 14 EHRR 153.

16.6 Defence Advisory Notices

Freedom of expression, specifically freedom of the press, can also be affected by the system of 'Defence Advisory Notices'. Since 1912 there has been a system by which the government advises the press and media on matters which ought not to be published for national security reasons and the expectation is that the media will comply with this advice. The system has been based on a committee on which both government and media are represented. The system was replaced by direct censorship during the Second World War but revived afterwards. The current system derives from changes introduced in 1993 and reflects the end of the 'cold war' and the climate of greater openness in government that is found.[58]

The current name for the committee is the Defence, Press and Broadcasting Advisory Committee. It has four members representing government and up to 13 representing the media. It is chaired by the Permanent Under Secretary of State at the Ministry of Defence, has a vice-chairman representing the press, three senior officials from the Home Office, Ministry of Defence and the Foreign and Commonwealth Office and up to 12 other senior figures from the national and local media nominated by the major media organisations. A central role is played by the Secretary and Deputy Secretary to the Committee who are, by custom, senior retired naval officers. Since 1971 the system has avoided ad hoc notices dealing with specific issues and preferred to issue standing notices (Defence Advisory Notices) which identify certain general areas touching on national security in respect of which publication or broadcasting needs careful consideration. When a particular story comes within the terms of a standing notice, editors, producers, etc. are encouraged to seek the guidance of the Secretary. There are currently five standing Defence Advisory Notices which relate to highly classified information in the following areas: 1 'Military Operations, Plans and Capabilities'; 2 'Nuclear and Non-Nuclear Weapons and Equipment'; 3 'Ciphers and Secure Communications'; 4. 'Sensitive Installations and Home Adresses'; 5 'United Kingdom Security and Intelligence Services and Special Forces'. The Secretary may also issue general advice about specific issues. In 1999, for example, he advised editors not to publish information found on a website which purported to give the names and addresses of secret service personnel and has also advised against publishing the address of David Shayler's website.[59] In the context of the 'war on terrorism' and the possible use of the armed forces, the Secretary has advised against an overuse by the media of well informed, recently retired officers whose speculation may be near to the truth.

The DA Notice system is a form of self-regulation. The system is not based on statute and the Committee has no powers directly to enforce its notices. In particular compliance with a Notice and accepting and following the Secretary's advice is not a defence to a prosecution under the Official Secrets Acts nor to an action for an injunction. In 1987, for example, injunctions were

---

[58] The basic information about the system is found on the website, http://www.dnotice.org.uk/, from which much of the following paragraph is taken.
[59] *R* v *Central Criminal Court ex parte Bright* [2001] 2 All ER 244, paragraph 12.

obtained to prevent the broadcasting of a radio programme, *My Country Right or Wrong*, which contained interviews with past and current members of the security services. The Secretary gave advice that, in respect of the content of the programme, no issue of national security was raised. The injunctions were, nevertheless, granted perhaps on the (now doubtful) grounds of maintaining the formal duty of confidentiality of security service members rather than the content of what was said.[60] The DA Notice system is, in effect, a restraint on freedom of expression. Though the government side is outnumbered on the Committee it is clear that the media representatives are generally willing to accept their advice. Though the Committee may have a useful function, its lack of any recognisable legal basis means it probably fails the 'prescribed by law' requirement of Article 10 ECHR and it is unlikely that it could, lawfully, impose any direct or indirect sanction against the media.

---

[60] But see Fairly, D. (1990) 'D Notices, Official Secrets and the Law', 10 *OJLS* 430 for a sceptical view of this.

17

Public order and political action

17.1 The context

This chapter is about the law relating to politically motivated meetings, marches, demonstrations, protests and acts of disruption.[1] Such political activity is a recurring feature of British political life,[2] has raised significant problems of public order and sometimes has been violent.[3] Major political gains in the twentieth century, female suffrage in particular, were obtained only after sustained campaigns of extra-Parliamentary action. Trade unions have felt the need to pursue the interests of their members and of trade unionism in general through strikes, picketing and demonstrations and some of these, such as the miners' strike 1984–85,[4] have had serious violent episodes. Popular opposition to government policy, particularly where the policy was supported by a Parliamentary consensus among the major parties, has frequently manifested itself through protest. Major examples include: opposition to the Vietnam War in the 1960s, the campaign against nuclear weapons which began in the 1950s with CND and revived in the 1980s with, for example, the women's peace camp at Greenham Common; the anti-roads and other environmental campaigns of the 1990s; the movement against the Community Charge or poll tax of the early 1990s; opposition by students to cuts in grants and the imposition of fees; assertions of their rights by gay and lesbian groups; and protests against fuel tax. Racist political parties such as the National Front or the British National Party have pursued their objectives by marching and demonstrating and have been met by counter-demonstrations such as those by the Anti-Nazi League in the 1980s. Race discrimination in the context of inner-city deprivation has been part of the explanation of major urban riots, particularly in Brixton, the West Midlands and Merseyside during the 1980s, and may explain some forms of opposition to asylum seekers that emerged in the late 1990s. Some protest has been aimed less at government policy and more at inhibiting lawful but, for the demonstrators, morally unconscionable activities of others. Campaigns against hunting with dogs, the

---

[1] For a detailed survey of the law relating to public order see Card, R. (2000) *Public Order Law*. Bristol: Jordan Publishing.

[2] See Waddington, P.A.J. (1994) *Liberty and Order*. London: UCL Press, chapter 1, esp. pp. 14–24.

[3] For identification and discussion of issues and the public order problems they gave rise to from a police point of view, see the annual reports of HM Chief Inspector of Constabulary (London: HMSO/TSO) or of the Commissioner of Police of the Metropolis (London: Metropolitan Police).

[4] See McCabe, S. *et al.* (1988) *The Police, Public Order and Civil Liberties: Legacies of the Miners' Strike*. London: Routledge.

treatment of animals used for experimentation and the export of livestock are examples from the 1990s; anti-free trade and, more generally, anti-capitalism is emerging as a cause of demonstration and disorder in the early twenty-first century as, perhaps, is a new, conservative 'countryside' agenda. In the mid-1990s HM Inspector of Constabulary was reporting a more settled public order environment than previously, though an increase in disorder was reported in 1995. An important theme of Inspectors' reports is the random, unpredictable nature of public order problems and it cannot be assumed that less confrontational state politics, if such there be when the 1980s are contrasted with the later 1990s, goes along with a more peaceful civil society. Indeed the reverse may the case since consensus state politics excludes and marginalises the radical opposition. The extent to which the 'war on terrorism' will generate extra-Parliamentary opposition is, at the time of writing, hard to predict. More than a million people marched against the Iraq war in February 2003.

17.2 The police

Political protest raises issues about the role and powers of the police. The police have, in the past, been viewed as a party to the disorder rather than an impartial power seeking a just balance of interests between demonstrators and others affected by the demonstration. They have been accused, for example, of a disproportionate resort to violence against demonstrators, which has the effect of preventing the expression of serious, legitimate grievances.[5] On occasions, such as the National Front meeting at Southall in which a demonstrator died, the inner-city riots of the early 1980s and the miners' strike in the mid-1980s, the police themselves became a target for demonstrators and a source of continuing grievance comparable to the original grievance behind the demonstration. Waddington,[6] on the other hand, writing about the late 1980s and early 1990s, suggests a subtle and complex set of factors which determine police policies and attitudes towards public order which cannot be reduced to the simple assertion of aggressive, authoritarian policing by a force indifferent to the rights and values of protestors. A matter of concern is the absence of a full independent inquiry into allegations of disproportionate violence.[7] Policing methods cause continuing controversy. There is an ongoing development in the type of equipment and organisational techniques used by the police in the context of public order.[8] The use of riot equipment such as shields, helmets and long batons; the forming of elite squads with a public order remit; gathering evidence by means of surveillance cameras and hospital interrogation teams; and the arrangements for mutual aid between forces which have indicated to some the emergence, in effect, of a national police force – have all been matters of controversy. As indicated in Chapter 4 it is

---

[5] For example, Hewitt, P. (1982) *The Abuse of Power: Civil Liberties in the United Kingdom*. London: Martin Robinson, pp. 138–41.

[6] Waddington, *op. cit.*

[7] Robertson, G. (1993) *Freedom, the Individual and the Law* Harmondsworth: Penguin Books, pp. 92–5.

[8] See Bailey, S.H., Harris, D.J. and Jones, B.L. (1995) *Civil Liberties Cases and Materials*, 4th edn. London: Butterworths, p. 175.

very difficult to challenge the exercise of policy discretion by the police even at the behest of a Police Authority[9] with elected members.

17.3 Convention rights

17.3.1 Article 11

The right to peaceful assembly is found in Article 11 ECHR which, unlike the equivalent provision in the ICCPR,[10] brings rights to assembly and association together. This chapter is confined to assembly. The text of Article 11 is found in Chapter 2.

Article 11 protects the freedom to march and to hold meetings.[11] Its focus is on assemblies which are more or less organised and which aim at the promulgation of information and ideas to the public. Private gatherings for private purposes may be protected by other provisions, such as Article 8. In *Anderson* v *UK*[12] the Commission of Human Rights denied that Article 11 guaranteed a right simply to be about in public places for purely social purposes.

The right to peaceful assembly, as with free expression, is fundamental to, and a foundation of, a democratic society. As such, it extends to assemblies which seek to promote purposes which may 'offend, shock or disturb the state or any section of the population'; in so doing, the Article embodies the 'pluralism, tolerance and broadmindedness without which there is no 'democratic society'.[13] Freedom of expression under Article 10(1) is an additional ground on which the freedom to protest and demonstrate could be asserted though there is likely to be little difference in effect.

To enjoy the protection of Article 11, assemblies must be 'peaceful'. This refers to the conduct of the meeting rather than the content of what is said. It excludes from the protection of the Article meetings in which the organisers and participants 'have violent intentions which result in public disorder'.[14] While there is no right to hold a meeting at which persons are physically attacked or threatened, a peaceful meeting where, for example, future acts of race hatred were encouraged would be within Article 11(1) and any restrictions on such a meeting would need to be justified under Article 11(2) – though Article 17 might prevent the organisers from asserting their Convention rights.[15] The importance of protest in a democracy requires a tolerant

---

[9] See Chapter 4 and, in particular, *R* v *Home Secretary ex parte Northumbria Police Authority* [1989] QB 26; [1988] 1 All ER 556.

[10] See also Article 21, ICCPR: 'The right of peaceful assembly shall be recognized. No restrictions may be placed on the exercise of this right other than those imposed in conformity with the law and which are necessary in a democratic society in the interests of national security or public safety, public order [*ordre public*], the protection of public health or morals or the protection of the rights and freedoms of others.' Discussed in Nowak, M. (1993) *UN Covenant on Civil and Political Rights. CCPR Commentary.* Kehl: N. P. Engel, pp. 370–82.

[11] *Christians against Racism and Fascism* v *UK* Ap. 8440/78; 21 D&R 138, 148.

[12] Ap. 33689/96, 27 October 1997.

[13] *Rassemblement Jurassien et Unité Jurassienne* v *Switzerland* Ap. 8191/78; 17 D&R 93, 119, quoting *Handyside* v *UK* (1979–80) 1 EHRR 737, paragraph 49.

[14] *MC* v *Federal Republic of Germany* Ap. 13079/87.

[15] See Chapter 14.

interpretation of 'peaceful' and actions which intentionally but non-violently interfere with the rights of others, such as sit-ins or obstructions of the highway, are likely to be within the protection of Article 11(1).

> MC participated in a demonstration in front of US military barracks. The demonstrators blocked the road for twelve minutes every hour and required the military and the police to close the road.
>   HELD (the European Commission of Human Rights): the prosecution of the demonstrators was an interference with their right to peaceful assembly which could only be justified on the grounds provided for by Article 11(2). The interference was so justified.
>   *MC* v *Germany* (1989) Ap. 13079/87

17.3.2 The 'opposition veto'

The state's first duty is to maintain public order. On that ground the law may permit restrictions on an otherwise lawful and peaceful meeting because it may provoke the violent reaction of opponents. This approach penalises the law abiding because of threats of unlawful violence by their opponents who choose to be provoked. As discussed below, the approach has been found in United Kingdom law. Article 11 requires states to take positive measures to try and protect assemblies from violent counter-demonstrations. This is only a duty to do what can reasonably be done; it is not a duty to protect the right to demonstrate come what may.[16] Without these positive duties, political assemblies could be restricted by the state on account of the violence of others and without regard to the requirements of the second paragraph of Article 11.[17]

17.3.3 'Prescribed by law'

Article 11(2) requires restrictions on peaceful assemblies to be 'necessary in a democratic society' and proportionate in respect of furthering the stated purposes (which include 'the prevention of disorder') and no others. Any restrictions must also be 'prescribed by law'.[18] A criticism made of public order law in the United Kingdom is that it grants too wide a discretion to the police and the executive so that the scope of the freedom to demonstrate cannot be known on the basis of reasonably clear and followable rules, but depends overmuch on the goodwill and individual judgments of the authorities.[19] It should be noted, however, that the 'prescribed by law' test is wide enough to include highly discretionary enabling powers, such as those under Article 39.2 of the Berne Convention[20] or the general disciplinary powers of a professional body.[21]

---

[16] *Platform Ärtze für das Leben* v *Austria* (1988) 13 EHRR 204.
[17] *Christians against Racism and Fascism* v *UK* Ap. 8440/78; 21 D&R 138, 148.
[18] See Chapter 2.
[19] For example, Klug, F., Starmer, K. and Weir, S. (1996) *The Three Pillars of Liberty*. London: Routledge, p. 201.
[20] 'In order to ward off imminent danger [the Executive Council] may temporarily call upon the armed forces, issue orders and prohibitions subject to penalties': *Rassemblement Jurassien et Unité Jurassienne* v *Switzerland* Ap. 8191/78; 17 D&R 93, 119.

17.4 General legal framework

17.4.1 Legislation

The disturbances of the late 1970s and early 1980s stimulated a range of reports and inquiries which resulted in the Public Order Act 1986.[22] This is a comprehensive piece of legislation which provides a national, statutory scheme, complementing common law powers, covering the control of marches and meetings and providing a range of offences relating to behaviour of differing degrees of seriousness. The overall effect of this controversial legislation is hard to judge. For critics it represented a dangerous and unnecessary increase in police powers on which could be founded the claim that the governance of Britain was becoming more authoritarian and less tolerant of reasonable dissent.[23] For supporters, it provided a framework within which proper balancing of the interests of demonstrators and the public interest in order. The Conservative government of the 1990s felt the powers in the Public Order Act 1986 were ineffective in respect of disruptive activities by groups such as hunt saboteurs, motorway protestors, 'travellers' and others, where a central aspect of the activities involved trespass. Police powers, particularly over trespassers, were increased by the Criminal Justice and Public Order Act 1994.[24] These two Acts remain at the centre of public order law. They complement highly discretionary common law powers.

17.4.2 Police powers and breach of the peace

General powers
Meetings, marches and demonstrations may become disorderly or violent. The police can deal with this by arresting and detaining those who they reasonably suspect have committed one of a number of public order offences for which there is a statutory power of arrest, or who have committed an 'arrestable' offence under section 24 of the Police and Criminal Evidence Act 1984 or a non-arrestable offence where the 'general arrest conditions', in section 25 of the Act, apply.

The police are also under a general duty to uphold the peace and, with that authority, can take discretionary, appropriate actions to control meetings, marches and demonstrations (see Chapter 4). Such action can be a discretionary alternative to arrest and prosecution, or, of great importance, it can be the taking of coercive measures against persons who are acting lawfully or against whom there are no grounds for suspecting that an arrestable offence has been

---

[21] *Ezelin v France* Ap. 11800/85; (1991) 14 EHRR 362.

[22] The Home Affairs Committee, *Fifth Report: The Law Relating to Public Order*, HC Papers 756-I, 756-II, Parliamentary Papers 1979–80, xlviii; Lord Scarman (1981) *The Brixton Disorders*, Cm 8427; The Law Commission Report No. 123 (1983) *Offences Relating to Public Order*, HC Papers 85; Home Office (1985) *Review of Public Order* (White Paper), Cm. 9510.

[23] Critics are summarised by Waddington, P.A.J. (1994) *Liberty and Order*. London UCL Press, p. 25, who argues that the Act does not represent a significant increase on the already wide and discretionary powers of the police.

[24] For its passage through Parliament see Klug, F., Starmer, K. and Weir, S. (1994) 'Civil Liberties and the Parliamentary Watchdog: The Passage of the Criminal Justice and Public Order Act 1994', 49 *Parliamentary Affairs* 4, 536–49.

committed, but who are provoking others to disorder. Keeping the peace is a police duty, and so a person who refuses to act as required or who physically resists may be liable for obstructing or assaulting the police in the exercise of their duty.[25] Though in themselves these offences are not arrestable, the general arrest conditions in section 25 of the Police and Criminal Evidence Act may be made out.[26]

Arrest for breach of the peace

If the general arrest conditions do not apply, or if, in the circumstances, the police prefer to avoid taking actions which threaten criminal penalties, then the common law recognises a power to arrest or detain without arrest[27] for a breach of the peace. In *R v Howell*[28] it was said that this power of arrest can be exercised in respect of an action committed in the presence of the person making the arrest, or on the basis of a reasonable belief by the arrestor that such an action will be committed in the immediate future or where a breach of the peace has been committed and it is reasonably believed that a renewal of it is threatened. The power to arrest or detain for breach of the peace can be exercised by anyone, not just a police officer.[29]

Breach of the peace in this context is not a criminal offence. The arrest and detention may continue, it seems, for as long as is necessary to meet the immediate problem. Alternatively the person detained can be brought before a magistrate to be bound over to keep the peace or to be of good behaviour and to face imprisonment if he or she refuses. In *Steel and others* v. *United Kingdom*,[30] the applicant was detained for 44 hours, though she was eventually charged with an offence. The legality of the detentions was not tested in the United Kingdom courts.[31] Detention under powers in the Police and Criminal Evidence Act 1984 relates to those suspected of committing offences; this is not necessarily the case in respect of breach of the peace. Article 5 ECHR is relevant and, unless there is a serious gap in the law, there is a strong argument that the PACE 1984 provisions should be treated as applying to breach of the peace detentions. In the case of a person who refuses to stop the activities in question, the answer is to get them before a magistrate as soon as possible for the issue of binding over to be decided.[32]

The police duty to act in respect of breaches of the peace has been widely criticised on the grounds that it allows a wide discretion to junior police officers which is not sufficiently guided by clear legal principles so as to provide a basis on which the freedom to meet, march and protest can be established. Partly under the influence of the 'legality' provisions in the ECHR,

---

[25] See Chapter 4.
[26] See Chapter 5.
[27] *Albert v Lavin* [1982] AC 547.
[28] [1981] 3 All ER 383.
[29] *Albert v Lavin* [1982] AC 547.
[30] (1998) 28 EHRR 603.
[31] The first applicant was eventually charged with a public order offence and convicted, the second applicant was bound over and the third, fourth and fifth applicants had their cases dropped.
[32] Though some commentators doubt that clarity has been achieved: Kerrigan, K. (1997) 'Breach of the Peace and Binding Over – Continuing Confusion', 2 *Journal of Civil Liberties* 1, 30.

the courts, in recent years, have sought to clarify important issues and to lay down some basic principles to govern the exercise of police discretion.

First, it has been established that a breach of the peace requires actual or threatened violence, even if slight.[33] The suggestion, in a case involving environmental protestors, that a breach of the peace could be found where demonstrators prevented, non-violently but effectively, contractors from doing their job,[34] has not been followed in other political cases[35] and was not accepted by the Court of Appeal in summarising the current state of breach of the peace law for both political and non-political purposes.[36]

Second, the police officer's actions must be reasonable and the test for this is objective. The court must be satisfied that, in the light of contemporaneous knowledge, it was reasonable for the officer to fear a breach of the peace. The good faith of the arresting officer is not enough.[37]

Thirdly, the courts now accept that the legality of an arrest for breach of the peace must take into account the reasonableness of the defendant's conduct and of those who are provoked. The notorious case of *Duncan* v *Jones*[38] seemed to permit the 'opposition veto' in English law. The Divisional Court upheld Duncan's conviction for obstruction of the police in the execution of their duty. She had attempted to address a street meeting which a police inspector had banned. There was no allegation that Duncan had committed, incited or provoked a breach of the peace. The reason for the ban was that, at a similar meeting ten months earlier, there had been disorder, again not incited or provoked by Duncan. A late nineteenth-century case, *Beatty* v *Gillbanks*,[39] was not followed. In *Beatty* the Queens Bench Division held that it was unlawful to ban a march by the Salvation Army on the grounds that it might provoke the Skeleton Army, their enemies, to violence. An otherwise peaceful assembly cannot be rendered unlawful on the sufficient ground that others will oppose it with violence.[40]

Recent English cases suggest that the principles underlying *Beatty* may now better reflect the law. In *Nicol and Selvanayagam* v *DPP*[41] the appellants had engaged in non-violent disruption of an angling competition. Simon Brown LJ held that breach of the peace, on provocation grounds, required proof that the defendant had acted unreasonably in the circumstances.[42] The deliberate interference with the rights and liberties of others (e.g. interrupting hunting or motorway building) is likely to be thought unreasonable. But unreasonable behaviour is not enough. In *R* v *Morpeth Justices ex parte Ward*,[43] a case

---

[33] *R* v *Howell* [1981] 3 All ER 383.
[34] *R* v *Chief Constable of Devon and Cornwall ex parte Central Electricity Generating Board* [1982] 1 QB 458.
[35] *Percy* v *DPP* [1995] 3 ALL ER 124 QBD; *Nicol and Selvanayagam* v *DPP* (1996) 160 JP 155, and *Redmond-Bate* v *DPP* (2000) 163 JP 789.
[36] *Bibby* v *Chief Constable of Essex* (2000) 164 JP 297.
[37] *Redmond-Bate* v *DPP* (2000) 163 JP 789, 791, Sedley LJ.
[38] [1935] All ER Rep 711 KBD; for the political context of the case see Ewing, K. and Gearty, C. (2000) *The Struggle for Civil Liberties*. Oxford: Oxford University Press.
[39] (1882) 15 Cox CC 138 QBD.
[40] But see Glanville Williams (1954) 'Arrest for Breach of the Peace', *Crim LR* 578, 581 for a different perspective on the Salvationist's behaviour.
[41] (1996) 160 JP 155
[42] See also *Redmond-Bate* v *DPP* (2000) 163 JP 789 QBD, Sedley LJ.

involving the disruption of a pheasant shoot, it was held that there would be a breach of the peace if the activities of the defendant 'would have the natural consequence of provoking others to violence'. Cases since *Morpeth* suggest that provocation to violence is only a 'natural consequence' if the reaction of those provoked, though probably unlawful, would not be 'entirely unreasonable'.[44] In *Percy* v *DPP* (1995)[45] magistrates bound over a peaceful protester who regularly climbed fences into a military base. The Divisional Court held it was 'highly improbable that the non-violent acts of trespass committed by the appellant would provoke trained personnel to violent reaction'[46] and in *Nicol and Selvanayagam* v *DPP* (1996)[47] Simon Brown LJ suggested that a violent reaction would be wholly unreasonable if people were provoked to violence by actions which did not significantly interfere with other people's rights, or if the defendant was doing no more than 'properly exercising his own basic rights, whether of assembly, demonstration or free speech'.[48]

If the breach of the peace is anticipated rather than happening at the time of arrest, the question of its proximity arises. Most definitions of breach of the peace require the anticipated violence to be imminent in terms both of time and place.[49] This requirement sits uneasily with a well known case from the 1984–85 miners' strike, *Moss* v *McLachlan* (1985).[50] Striking miners were stopped at a motorway junction several miles from collieries where other miners were working. In all the circumstances of the strike and the widespread violence that had been reported in the media and, accurately or not, attributed to the picketing miners, the Divisional Court held that those who had sought to push through the police barrier were rightly convicted for obstruction of the police in the execution of their duty. The police view, that a breach of the peace was likely if the miners got through to the collieries, could, in the circumstances, be reasonable. No breach of the peace was imminent and so, given recent clarifications of the law, the case might be decided differently today.

Breach of the peace and Convention rights

The European Court of Human Rights has found that, in the light of the restatement of the law in the cases discussed above, the general law on breach of the peace is compatible with both Article 5 and Article 10 ECHR.

> The first applicant was arrested when she attempted to obstruct a grouse shoot by walking in front of a gun; the second applicant was arrested for obstructing the building of a motorway; the third, fourth and fifth applicants were arrested for handing out protest leaflets and holding up banners at an arms fair. The first and second applicants were bound over; the third, fourth and fifth had their cases dismissed when the prosecution offered no evidence.

[43] (1992) 96 Cr App Rep 215 QBD.
[44] *Redmond-Bate* v *DPP* (2000) 163 JP 789, 797; see also *Nicol and Selvanayagam* v *DPP* (1996) 160 JP 155, 163.
[45] [1995] 3 All ER 124.
[46] [1995] 3 All ER 124, 133.
[47] (1996) 160 JP 155.
[48] (1996) 160 JP 155, 163.
[49] *Bibby* v *Chief Constable of Essex* (2000) 164 JP 297; *Foulkes* v *Chief Constable of the Merseyside Police* [1998] 3 All ER 705 CA.
[50] [1985] IRLR 77.

HELD (ECHR): Article 5 and Article 10 were violated in respect of the third, fourth and fifth applicants but not in respect of the first and second applicants.
Steel and others v *UK* (1998) 28 EHRR 603

Individual applications of the law can still violate the Convention. Thus, in respect of the third, fourth and fifth defendants, the Court held that the arrests could not be explained on the grounds that the defendants' behaviour had the natural consequence of reasonably provoking others to violence.

In both recent domestic law and under the Convention there is an emerging distinction between protest and disruption. The former aims to present arguments and reasons against a particular activity but, although the presentations may be hard to avoid, does not coercively interfere with the activity; the latter is a direct attempt to prevent or make more difficult a lawful activity. It is against the latter rather than the former that the law on breach of the peace is aimed.

17.5 Meetings

Meetings can take place on roads, in halls, in open spaces, or wherever the requirements of the assembly dictate. These places may be owned or controlled by public authorities or they may be in private hands; they may be places which are customarily the site of assemblies or they may be land used for wholly other purposes, industrial, recreational or whatever.

17.5.1 Private owners

Permission is needed from the person or company in possession of 'private' land. Without it a tort action, such as for trespass, can be brought with the aim of damages or an injunction. An owner is entitled to use reasonable force to remove a trespasser. Where the use of such force may give rise to a breach of the peace, the police may exercise their discretion to assist such self-help measures.[51]

Private owners or occupiers are free to refuse or revoke any licence or permission they give, and may do so without giving reasons; it is an incident of property rights. This seems to apply even in respect of places, like shopping malls or leisure centres, which are widely used by the public and which may be part of a thoroughfare or occupy a large part of a city centre. A withdrawal of permission must be consistent with the general law and within the terms of any lease or other private right the owner or occupier has, but otherwise can be imposed for any purpose. Withdrawal of permission would then make lawful the forcible removal of the persons affected.

CIN P leased a town shopping centre from the local authority. The centre occupies about three-fifths of the town centre. The lease required them to allow full pedestrian

---

[51] See *R* v *Chief Constable of the Devon and Cornwall Constabulary ex parte CEGB* [1981] 3 All ER 826, discussed below. Section 10 of the Criminal Law Act 1977 makes it an arrestable offence to resist or obstruct intentionally a court officer executing process for enforcing a court order for the recovery of premises.

access to the common parts of the premises. CIN P formed the view that R and other young black men were committing nuisances and sought to ban them from the centre.

HELD (CA): members of the public had no equitable right to use the common parts of the centre and so CIN P had the right to determine the defendants' licences subject only to any restraints in the general law such as the Race Relations Act.

CIN Properties v *Rawlins and others* (1995) TLR 9.2.95[52]

On this approach, commercial organisations would be able to restrict peaceful public assemblies on land to which the public have apparently open access. Any restrictions can simply promote the interests of the organisation and need not take into account any fundamental rights to freedom of speech or assembly enjoyed by the public. Scheduled Convention rights are not directly binding on a commercial company. It is arguable that where the company, as part of its lease, has agreed to give public access, it is, in that regard, exercising a 'public function' and so, by virtue of section 6(3) of the Human Rights Act 1998, counts as a 'public authority' and must act compatibly with Convention rights. Perhaps, also, a local council which grants a lease providing for public access would act unlawfully unless Convention rights, including Article 11, were express or implied conditions to the lease.

17.5.2 Public authorities

Public authorities, often local authorities, can occupy land or have other statutory authority to control the use of land and premises that organisers may want to use for meetings. It is more than likely that the prime sites, the central pedestrian precincts, the biggest halls and the parks, will be so controlled. As with private owners, public authorities can uphold their legal rights by, for example, bringing actions in tort,[53] including injunctions,[54] and they can also be supported by the police on the same grounds as with private owners.[55] Public authorities are likely to have additional statutory powers and remedies which they can exercise when making decisions on the use of land and premises.

Public authorities need to be distinguished from private owners. They are subject to the ordinary principles of administrative law which means that they do not have private landlords' freedoms to act in their own interest for any reason. They must act to promote their conception of the public interest and can only do things that they have express or implied authority to do.

SCC purported to ban deer hunting over an area of common land. The relevant statute, section 120(1)(b) of the Local Government Act 1972, allowed councils to acquire and manage land for the 'benefit, improvement or development of their area'.

HELD (CA): in making its decision the councillors had acted on the basis of their personal views on hunting. They had not considered their statutory powers and

---

[52] See, further, *Anderson* v *UK* Ap. 33689/96, 27 October 1997.

[53] For example, under section 222 of the Local Government Act 1972; see Bailey, S.H. (1997) *Cross on Principles of Local Government Law*, 2nd edn. London: Sweet & Maxwell, chapter 10.65.

[54] For example, *Burnley* v *England* (1977) 76 LGR 393; 77 LGR 227.

[55] The CEGB was, of course, a public authority: *R* v *Chief Constable of the Devon and Cornwall Constabulary ex parte CEGB* [1981] 3 All ER 826.

whether the ban was beneficial to their area but had acted as if they had the freedom of private land owners. The decision to ban hunting was quashed.
R v Somerset County Council ex parte Fewings [1995] 3 All ER 20

Public authorities, when taking decisions relating to meetings, marches and demonstrations, may also have a general duty to consider and safeguard the rights of others in going about their lawful business. In *R v Coventry City Council ex parte Phoenix Aviation*[56] the High Court ordered the resumption of flights and shipments of livestock which had been banned by airport and port authorities in order to prevent disruption by animal rights protesters. The authorities controlled the docks or airports on the basis of statutory powers which required access to all persons and business on equal terms. This meant that, other than in emergency situations, fear of disruption by demonstrators was not a ground for distinguishing between different lawful trades. Such a rule could apply to a privatised company exercising similar statutory powers. The court also held that public authorities had an additional duty to uphold the rule of law and not surrender to the dictates of unlawful protest.[57] A similar position applies to states in respect of the enforcement of Community law.[58]

Decisions by public authorities are challengeable in the courts by way of judicial review. Prior to the Human Rights Act 1998, decisions which involved human rights, such as freedom of expression and freedom of assembly, were subject to closer, more demanding, scrutiny by the courts than some other decisions.[59] The Act takes this further and makes it unlawful for an authority to act incompatibly with Convention rights and requires judges to interpret and give effect to the legislation, including the byelaws, under which the authority purports to act, so far as is possible, for compatibility with Convention rights.

The public have no general right to use public open spaces for meetings. This includes, for example, areas that have traditionally been so used, 'common land',[60] land controlled by public authorities including the beach and sea shore[61] or sites controlled by English Heritage.[62] Usually the land in question is subject to byelaws. These may restrict the holding of meetings or give the authority the right to grant or refuse permission for meeting and assemblies. Breach of a valid byelaw may be a criminal offence. Byelaws can be challenged on the grounds that they are made without proper authority. Famously, byelaws, passed to try and turn the trespassing activities of peace protestors outside military bases into criminal offences were successfully

[56] [1995] 3 All ER 37.
[57] [1995] 3 All ER 37, 62.
[58] *Cullet v Centre Leclerc Toulouse* [1985] ECR 305; *Commission v France* [1997] ECRI-6959; cf. *R v Chief Constable of Sussex ex parte International Traders' Ferry Ltd* [1999] 1 All ER 129. Discussed in Baker, E. (2000) 'Policing, Protest and Free Trade: Challenging Police Discretion under Community Law', *Crim LR* 95.
[59] For example, *R v Lord Saville and others ex parte A and others* [1999] 4 All ER 860.
[60] *De Morgan v the Metropolitan Board of Works* (1879–80) v QBD 155, DC.
[61] *Mayor of Brighton v Packham* (1907–08) xxiv TLR 603.
[62] *R v The Commission of English Heritage ex parte Firsoff* (unreported), 19 June 1991, cited in Bailey, Harris and Jones, *op. cit.*, 194.

challenged on this ground.[63] Byelaws can also be challenged on the grounds of being repugnant to the general law, uncertain and unreasonable.[64] The courts have usually upheld byelaws which restrict the holding of public meetings[65] but they will prevent byelaws being used for disproportionate bans on political activity,[66] a view which the Human Rights Act 1998 encourages.

In London the traditional meeting places have been regulated by statute. The courts have denied a basic public right to use Hyde Park[67] or Trafalgar Square[68] for assemblies. Permission is required on the basis of regulations. The regulations governing Hyde Park[69] require written permission to be sought from the Department of Culture, Media and Sport before any public meeting or procession etc. can be held,[70] other than at Speakers' Corner in Hyde Park. Here speeches can be made without permission though a police order to move must be complied with.[71] Trafalgar Square, not being a Crown Property, is subject to the permission and control of the Mayor of London.[72] The Mayor, acting alone, though on behalf of the Authority, may make byelaws for 'securing the proper management', the 'preservation of order' and the 'prevention of abuses' of the areas. The Mayor is required to have regard to any guidance issued by the Secretary of State.[73] Trafalgar Square is, however, a highway and, in so far as the public have a right to hold meetings on the highway,[74] these are permissible in Trafalgar Square without the Mayor's permission.

Any refusal of permission is subject to judicial review both on the ordinary principles of administrative law and under the Human Rights Act 1998. Unlike the powers of the police to seek a ban on a march (see below), a refusal of permission for a meeting may be in respect of a particular meeting rather than a general ban. Political bias in the granting or withholding of permission would be a ground of review. As noted above, under the Human Rights Act 1998 there is a positive right to hold peaceful assemblies and this narrows the discretion of public authorities to refuse.[75] A refusal must be for one of the

---

[63] *DPP v Hutchinson* [1990] 2 AC 783. See also (on different grounds) *Bugg v DPP, Percy v DPP* [1993] 2 All ER 815; cf. *Percy v Hall* [1996] 4 All ER 523.

[64] *Halsbury's Laws of England*, 4th edn, vol. 29(1) *Local Government* (2001), paragraphs 430–5.

[65] For example, *Slee v Meadows* (1911) 105 LT 127 DC.

[66] *R v Barnet London Borough Council* (1991) 89 LGR 581 (QBD).

[67] *Bailey v Williamson* (1872–73) viii LR QBC 118.

[68] *Ex parte Lewis* (1888) 21 QBD 191, DC; see also *R v Cunninghame Graham and Burns* (1888) 16 Cox CC 420.

[69] There are common regulations for the Royal Parks and other parks and areas controlled, now, by the Secretary State for Culture, Media and Sport. These are the Royal Parks and Other Open Spaces Regulations 1997, SI 1997/1639. The regulations are made under the Parks Regulation (Amendment) Act 1926, s. 2(1).

[70] The Royal Parks and Other Open Spaces Regulations 1997, SI 1997/1639, 4(15) and (17).

[71] The Royal Parks and Other Open Spaces Regulations 1997, SI 1997/1639, 3(14).

[72] Greater London Authority Act, s. 383(3) and s. 384(8).

[73] Sections 385–6, Greater London Authority Act 1999.

[74] See below.

[75] The European Commission of Human Rights seems to take a tolerant view of executive refusals of permission, for example, *Rai, Allmond and Negotiate Now v The United Kingdom* (1995) 19 EHRR CD 93; Ap 25522/94, where the Department of National Heritage refused permission to use Trafalgar Square even though the police were satisfied there was no danger to public order. The Commission found the ban to be proportionate because of the prominence of the location and because it was not a blanket ban.

legitimate purposes listed Article 11(2), must be based on law and be proportionate to the achievement of the purpose. A refusal could be based on a well-founded fear that the meeting will be used to violate the rights of others in the sense identified in Article 17. Public authorities and police may need to take reasonable steps to protect such meetings from the disruption of counter-demonstrators but it is unclear how far this positive duty goes. The non-discrimination provisions on the Convention require equal treatment of applicants.

Local councils may have a duty to provide at least some suitable premises for the holding of peaceful assemblies.[76] The extent of any such duty is unclear. As discussed in Chapter 13, there is a positive duty on local councils, under the Representation of the People Act 1983, to provide for election meetings. Apart from that, there is little evidence of a legally enforceable duty to provide meeting places. Where a public authority has a contractual obligation to provide a hall for a political meeting the court may enforce the contract by specific performance if freedom of expression is in issue.[77] The strongest assertion of a positive duty is in respect of universities and institutions of higher or further education which are under a legal duty to secure freedom of expression for students, staff and visiting speakers.[78]

17.5.3 Highways

Meetings, marches and demonstrations often take place on the highway. The point about the highway is that the public may use it as of right, without needing the permission of private landowner or public authority; if the right is exceeded, civil actions, trespass, for example, can be brought by those whose land abuts or is crossed by the highway; similarly, criminal offences may be committed. The fact that such activities have been tolerated does not create a right to them.

Civil liability
The basic right of the public on a highway is the right of passage and re-passage.[79] Using the highway for other purposes may make a person vulnerable to civil action by the occupier of land over which the highway goes. Disrupting a grouse shoot[80] or observing the condition of race horses[81] are famous examples of highway uses which were held to be outside the scope of the right of passage. Both cases contain authority for the view that the right to use the highway extends beyond mere passage and re-passage. The question is whether other activities can be done, as of right, only when they are incidental to a basic intention to pass or re-pass (e.g. stopping to talk to a friend), or whether they can extend, as a matter of right, to activities (e.g.

---

[76] As advocated, in respect of the law prior to the Act, by Robertson, G. (1993) *Freedom, the Individual and the Law*, 7th edn. Harmondsworth: Penguin, pp 66–7, following Street, H.S. (1977) *Freedom, the Individual and the Law*, 4th edn. Harmondsworth: Penguin, p 49.

[77] *Verrall* v *Great Yarmouth* [1981] 1 QB 202.

[78] Section 43, Education Act (No. 2) 1986; *R* v *University of Liverpool ex parte Caesar-Gordon* [1990] 3 All ER 821.

[79] For example, *R* v *Pratt* (1855) 4 E&B 860; 119 ER 319.

[80] *Harrison* v *Duke of Rutland* [1893] 1 QB 143 CA.

[81] *Hickman* v *Maisey* [1900] 1 QB 752 CA.

busking) which are not necessarily linked to passage. Any such extra rights must not be inconsistent with the basic right by obstructing or interfering with the rights of others to pass and re-pass.

A non-obstructive march or procession is likely to be consistent with the right of passage.[82] The problem arises in respect of a meeting or demonstration which, being stationary, is not ancillary to the right of passage. The issue was considered by the House of Lords in *DPP v Jones*.

> Section 14A of the Public Order Act 1986 authorises the prohibition, by order, of 'trespassory assemblies'. These are assemblies of 20 or more persons held, *inter alia*, on land to which the public has only a 'limited right of access' where the assembly exceeds that right of access. Section 14A(9) expressly recognises a highway as conferring only a limited right of access. J was a member of a group of more than 20 gathered on the grass verge of a highway as part of an ongoing protest concerning the right to use Stonehenge. The area was subject to a section 14A order. They were arrested and convicted for taking part in a trespassory assembly. The courts accepted as a matter of fact that the assembly was peaceful and non-obstructive.
>
> HELD (HL): peaceful, non-obstructive meetings on the highway are capable of being within the public's right of access to the highway and J and others, in this particular case, had not exceeded their right of access on the highway.
> *DPP v Jones* [1999] 2 All ER 257 (HL)

Different views were taken and the extent to which the highway can be used for political gatherings as of right remains unclear. Two of their lordships dissented, and upheld the traditional view that the right to use the highway is confined to passage and re-passage. The majority, however, accepted that the highway could be used, as of right, for some non-obstructive purposes which were not incidental to passage. These could include the holding of political meetings. Of the majority, however, only two, Lord Irvine LC and Lord Hutton, grounded their judgment, though in different ways, on the need to adjust the law so as to uphold a positive right of assembly compatible with Article 11 ECHR.

Criminal liability

Meetings, marches and demonstrations on the highway may give rise to arrests for breach of the peace or to criminal liability.[83] Breach of the peace and the public order offences in the Public Order Act 1986 can all be committed on the highway and involve a power of arrest. Conversely, for some public order offences such as aggravated trespass, activity on the highway is expressly excluded from the definition of the offence.[84]

The principal statutory offence is wilful obstruction of the highway, currently found at section 137 of the Highways Act 1980.[85]

---

[82] For example, *Jones v DPP* [1999] 2 All ER 257, 286.

[83] *Burden v Rigler* [1910] 1 KB 337 – the offence of disrupting a 'lawful' meeting under the Public Meetings Act 1908 could apply to a public meeting on the highway.

[84] Section 61, Criminal Justice and Public Order Act 1994, referred to by section 68(5).

[85] For discussion of cases relating to predecessor legislation see annotations to section 137 by Cross, C.A. and Sauvian, S.J. (1981) *Current Law Statutes Annotated 1980*, Vol. 2. London: W. Green & Son, c.66/137.

137 Penalty for wilful obstruction

If a person without lawful authority or excuse, in any way wilfully obstructs the free passage along a highway he is guilty of an offence and liable to a fine not exceeding level 3 on the standard scale

Similarly, 'causing an unlawful obstruction of the highway' is one of the conditions justifying arrest for an otherwise non-arrestable offence under section 25 of the Police and Criminal Evidence Act 1984.[86] The offence can be committed even though there is no complete obstruction of the highway and traffic and pedestrians still have a restricted right of passage.[87] There need be no intention to obstruct, merely an intention to do the activities which actually cause the obstruction.[88]

In *Hirst and Agu* v *Chief Constable of West Yorkshire* (1987)[89] (a case involving the prosecution of anti-fur trade protestors who had picketed a furrier) it was held that a component of the offence, which the prosecution must prove, is that the obstruction was without lawful authority and was not a 'reasonable' use of the highway. This brought the offence of obstruction in line with the common law offence of public nuisance.[90] Reasonableness is a highly contested concept and the prosecution's success in proving unreasonable use may depend on the personal constitutional morality of magistrates. In *Hirst and Agu* Otton J, agreeing with Glidewell LJ, related the possible reasonableness of an obstructive use of the highway to the right of free speech and protest. This view can only be strengthened by the Human Rights Act 1998. Schedule 1, Article 11 arguably establishes a presumption of lawful authority in respect of a peaceful assembly even on the highway,[91] and any restrictions, such as those grounded on wilful obstruction, need to be compatible with Article 11(2). *Hirst and Agu* does not prevent the conviction of demonstrators who create significant obstruction of roads and pavements. The more significant the obstruction the less likely it will even engage Article 11.[92]

17.5.4 Power of police to enter meetings

The police have a power to enter and remain on private premises to deal with an actually occurring breach of the peace[93] and can do this even if the persons in control of the meeting object. The power to arrest for breach of the peace

---

[86] Section 25 (3)(d)(v), Police and Criminal Evidence Act 1984.

[87] *Homer* v *Cadman* (1885–86) II TLR 407.

[88] *Arrowsmith* v *Jenkins* [1963] 2 QB 561.

[89] (1987) 85 Cr App R 143 (QBD).

[90] *R* v *Clark (No. 2)* [1964] 2 QB 315 CCA: the conviction of the secretary of CND, who had urged a crowd of demonstrators to move behind a police cordon thereby causing an obstruction of the highway, of inciting persons to commit a public nuisance, was set aside on the grounds that the question of the reasonableness of the demonstrators' use of the highway had not been put to the jury.

[91] In *DPP* v *Jones* [1999] 2 All ER 257, 267 Lord Irvine suggested that Article 11 means that the law must start with the assumption that assembly on the highway will not necessarily be unlawful.

[92] For example, *Birch* v *DPP* [2000] Crim LR 301.

[93] For example, *R* v *Marsden* (1868) LR 1 CCR 131; *Robson and another* v *Hallett* [1967] 2 QB 939. The power is assumed rather than expressly asserted.

can be exercised on private land[94] as can, it would seem to follow, less draconian common law powers such as imposing conditions on an assembly. More controversially, the courts have upheld the power of the police to enter a peaceful meeting, against the wishes of the organisers, in anticipation of a future breach of the peace. The fear here is that the police presence may be intimidatory, particularly if it is the behaviour of the police themselves that is the subject of the meeting.

> There was a private hiring of a hall in a library to hold a meeting, widely advertised to the public, to protest against the Incitement to Disaffection Bill and to demand the resignation of the Chief Constable of Glamorgan. Between 500 and 700 people attended. The police officers were refused entry; nevertheless they sat in the front row and refused to leave when asked. The organiser attempted to eject them and alleged assault and battery against the police when they resisted his efforts. Magistrates held that the police had acted with a reasonable apprehension of a breach of the peace.
>   HELD: there was ample authority from which it could be inferred that police had the power, as part of their preventative duties, to enter private premises to deal with apprehended breaches of the peace.
>   *Thomas* v *Sawkins* [1935] 2 KB 249

The existence of the power is contentious.[95] It might be confined to meetings that the police could, in any case, attend as members of the public. Nevertheless, the general principle has been confirmed in *McLeod* v *Commissioner of Police for the Metropolis*,[96] a non-political case. The power was said to have been recognised by Parliament in section 17(6) of the Police and Criminal Evidence Act 1984, though all section 17(6) does is to retain 'any power of entry to deal with or prevent a breach of the peace', it does not create any new powers. In *McLeod* it is stressed, by the Court of Appeal, that the power to enter private premises against the wishes of the owner or occupier to prevent an apprehended breach of the peace should be exercised with great care and discretion and exists only where the police, on reasonable grounds, believe there is a 'real and imminent' risk of a breach of the peace.

In *McLeod* v *United Kingdom*[97] the power of the police to enter private premises to deal with a breach of the peace was upheld in general terms as a restriction on private life capable of authorisation under Article 8(2) (the particular exercise of the power in the case was held to have been disproportionate). Political meetings will place in issue the rights to private life, to freedom of expression and to freedom of assembly. Given the Strasbourg court's recognition of the importance of political expression in maintaining the

---

[94] *McConnell* v *Chief Constable of the Greater Manchester Police* [1990] 1 All ER 423 CA which cites, as an example, *R* v *Chief Constable of Devon and Cornwall Constabulary ex parte Central Electricity Generating Board* [1981] 3 All ER 826.

[95] Clayton, R. and Tomlinson, H. (1992) *Civil Actions against the Police*. London: Sweet & Maxwell, p. 242; Feldman, D. (1986) *The Law Relating to Entry, Search and Seizure*. London: Butterworth, pp. 324–5; Goodhart, A.L. (1936–38) '*Thomas* v *Sawkins*: A Constitutional Innovation', CLJ 22; Feldman, D. (2002) *Civil Liberties and Human Rights in England and Wales*, 2nd edn. Oxford: Oxford University Press, pp. 1075–9.

[96] [1994] 4 All ER 553.

[97] *McLeod* v *UK* (1999) 27 EHRR 493.

democratic context in which human rights flourish, the threshold of a proportionate response by the police should be set high in terms, at least, of the imminence and seriousness of the apprehended breach of the peace.

The police also have their general powers to enter premises without a warrant.[98] Section 17 of the Police and Criminal Evidence Act 1984, in particular, authorises a police constable to enter (and search) premises without a warrant for the purpose, among others, of arresting a person for an arrestable offence. Not all public order offences are arrestable offences, and section 17 also specifically identifies offences such as section 4 of the Public Order Act 1986 (fear or provocation of violence) as offences for which this power of entry in order to arrest applies.

17.5.5 Power to impose conditions on certain meetings in the open air

The common law duty to maintain the peace authorises the police to issue appropriate instructions to organisers of and participants in public meetings. As we have seen, failure to abide by these instructions could be a ground for arrest or its could amount to the offence of obstruction of the police in the exercise of their duty under section 89 of the Police Act 1996.

Section 14 the Public Order Act 1986
Section 14 of the Public Order Act 1986 gives the police powers to impose conditions on 'public assemblies'. These powers are in additional to common law powers. They are more precise and have the authority of Parliament behind them. Conditions may relate to place, duration or to the number of persons permitted to be present and they can be imposed either in advance of, or during, the meeting. Public assemblies are of '20 or more persons in a public place which is wholly or partly in the open air'.[99] A 'public place' is defined to include a privately organised public meeting such as the meeting in *Thomas v Sawkins*, had it been partially in the open air. An organiser of, or a participant in, a meeting who knowingly fails to comply with a condition imposed under section 14 commits an offence, but either organiser or participant can establish a defence that non-compliance arose from circumstances beyond their control. The detail of the conditions must be clearly communicated to the defendants.[100]

The powers can only be exercised on the basis of a reasonable belief of a senior police officer, who may be simply the most senior present if the conditions are imposed during a meeting, that one of the 'triggers' exists. These are that the public assembly may result in (a) serious public disorder, (b) serious damage to property, (c) serious disruption to the life of the community, or (d) the purpose of the persons organising it is the intimidation of others with a view to compelling them not to do an act they have a right to do, or to do an act they have a right not to do. These triggers are also necessary for the exercise of other police powers which will be referred to below.

---

[98] See Chapter 6.
[99] Section 16, Public Order Act 1986.
[100] *Brickley and Kitson v Police* (1988) *Legal Action*, July, p. 21.

The 'triggers' and Convention rights

The exercise of the powers under section 14 are subject to 'ordinary' judicial review and also to review under the Human Rights Act 1998. Restrictions on freedom of expression and assembly authorised by section 14 and aimed at stopping violence or threats to property are likely to be accepted as being for a legitimate purpose as identified in Article 10(2) or Article 11(2). However, the third trigger, 'serious disruption to the life of the community', may not, in general terms, be compatible with those purposes. The trigger may include non-violent behaviour and so be even more wide ranging than a breach of the peace. This openness of the trigger may be incompatible with the 'prescribed by law' requirement for restrictions on the freedoms of expression and association permitted under the second paragraphs of Article 10 and 11. Furthermore, preventing 'disruption' to people's lives is not a listed purpose under the second paragraphs. It may be that any restriction based on this trigger must justify itself as being for the protection of 'rights of others' – a term which usually excludes behaviour which is merely offensive.

Section 14 does not requires the police, when deciding whether or not to impose conditions, to take the source of any serious threat to public order, property or the life of the community into account. Thus section 14 does not inhibit the police in imposing conditions on an entirely lawful meeting which others may wish to disrupt. Yet both common law, in the recent cases involving breach of the peace[101] and the Convention, particularly in *Platform Ärtze für das Leben* v *Austria*[102] are sensitive to the danger of the 'opposition veto', discussed above: opponents of an assembly should not, by threatening disorder, be able to force the police to take action against the otherwise reasonable activity of the organisers or participants. This issue is not mentioned in the statute but may now be relevant to the compatibility of the section with Convention rights and on the proportionality of any particular exercise of the power.

There is no statutory power to ban a public assembly although such a step is, as an extreme measure, possible under the breach of the peace powers discussed above. Section 14A of the Public Order Act 1986 gives the police authority to seek a ban on a trespassory assembly. This power is discussed below.

17.5.6 Offences involving the disruption of meetings

Disorder at public meetings it can be dealt with under the breach of the peace powers or through the imposition of conditions under section 14 of the Public Order Act 1986. The police may arrest in respect of offences for which the power of arrest exists. The Public Meeting Act 1908 makes it an offence to act, or incite others to act, in a disorderly manner at a 'lawful public meeting'. There is no power of arrest though the general arrest conditions under section 25 of the Police and Criminal Evidence Act 1984 apply. The Act can apply to meetings on the highway,[103] but not to election meetings although there are

---

[101] For example, *Redmond-Bate* v *DPP* (2000) 163 JP 789 QBD.
[102] (1988) 13 EHRR 204.
[103] *Burden* v *Rigler* [1910] 1 KB 337.

equivalent provisions under section 97 of the Representation of the People Act 1983. Disrupters of lawful meetings held in the open air can, if they are trespassers, be arrested and prosecuted for 'aggravated trespass'; the offence is discussed later in the chapter.

17.6 Marches and processions

A procession is not defined by statute but in *Flockhart v Robinson*[104] it was held to be a 'body of persons moving along a route'. Some degree of physical coherence uniting the body of persons is necessary. A loose grouping of like-minded persons moving in the same direction will not be a procession until a sufficient, though hard to define, degree of coherence is obtained.[105] As with meetings and assemblies, so with marches and processions: marchers will be trespassers unless they have the legal right to be on the route they are moving along and this may require the express or implied permission of those in possession of the land. A procession on the highway is, unlike a meeting, likely to be the exercise of the right of passage and this is an uncontroversial incident of the public's right of access to the highway. However the mere fact that a person is moving on the highway does not in itself mean that the right of passage is being exercised and, depending on the circumstances, a body of persons moving along a route could, nevertheless, be a use of the highway going beyond the right of passage.[106] Police can regulate marches and processions under their general powers relating to breach of the peace. Criminal offences including public order offences, discussed below, can be committed during marches as much as during meetings and, as has been noted, the police will usually have the power of arrest for these.

17.6.1 Notice – section 11, Public Order Act 1986

The Public Order Act 1986 contains provisions related particularly to processions and these involve an increase in and greater specification of the regulatory powers contained in the Public Order Act 1936 which it replaced. Under section 11 there is a provision that was not in the 1936 Act requiring notice of a non-traditional, political or commemorative march to be given to the police by the organisers. Six days' notice should be given unless this is not reasonably practicable; in that case advance notice still needs to be delivered as soon as it is reasonably practicable. Organisers of a march are guilty of an offence for failing to give notice as required, though it is a defence for defendants to prove that they neither knew of nor suspected that the requirement to give notice existed.

Section 11 is a requirement of notice to the police; it is emphatically not a requirement that the police give permission for marches. Its justification is to allow time for the police to negotiate on times and routes etc. with organisers and, if they, the police, think necessary, to impose conditions or even seek

---

[104] [1950] 2 KB 498.
[105] *Flockhart v Robinson* [1950] 2 KB 498.
[106] As in *Hickman v Maisey* [1900] 1 QB 752 CA and *Hubbard v Pitt* [1976] 1 QB 142 CA.

banning orders under powers in sections 12 and 13, discussed below. Of course, in effect, that may seem very like permission. A notice provision is generally compatible with the right to freedom of assembly under Article 11. It can help to ensure the peaceful nature of a procession and can be instrumental in assisting the police to take reasonable positive measures to protect marchers and others from intimidation and counter-demonstration.[107]

17.6.2 Conditions – section 12, Public Order Act 1986

Section 12 of the Public Order Act 1986 authorises the police to impose conditions, in advance or at the time, on a political or commemorative procession. These conditions can include stipulations as to the route to be taken. The power is triggered on the same basis as the power to impose conditions on public assemblies: a reasonable belief by the police that serious public disorder, serious damage to property, serious disruption to the life of the community or intimidation will otherwise result. The conditions imposed are limited to those the police believe to be necessary to prevent the feared disorder, damage, disruption or intimidation. Offences are committed by the organisers of and participants in marches who knowingly fail to comply with any conditions unless their failure to comply arose from circumstances beyond their control. The issues and the case law relevant to public assemblies applies with equal force to processions, if only because a single political event will often consist of both and it may not always be clear when the one begins and the other ends. Other legislation, in particular section 21 of the Town Police Clauses Act 1847, which applies widely throughout the country, gives additional powers to the police to control the route and conduct of a procession. Though expressed in general terms, these powers can apply to political marches and assemblies which are taking place on the highway. The powers are additional to those under the Public Order Act 1986 though in controversial situations the police are likely to feel that the latter Act gives more specific and more recent authority.

In the London area, where many political meetings and marches take place, powers are given to the Commissioner of Police under section 52 of the Metropolitan Police Act 1839 and section 22 the City of London Police Act 1839.

The Metropolitan Police Act 1839, section 52
It shall be lawful for the commissioners of police, from time to time, and as the occasion shall require, to make regulations for the route to be observed by all carts, carriages, horses, and persons, and for preventing obstruction of the streets and thoroughfares within the Metropolitan Police District, in all times of public processions, public rejoicings, or illuminations, and also to give directions to the constables for keeping order and for preventing any obstruction of the thoroughfares in the immediate neighbourhood of Her Majesty's palaces and the public offices, the High Court of Parliament, the courts of law and equity, the police courts, the theatres, and other places of public resort, and in any case when the streets or thoroughfares may be thronged or may be liable to be obstructed.

---

[107] *Rassemblement Jurassien and Unité Jurassienne v Switzerland* Ap. 8191/78; 17 D&R 93. For the position under the ICCPR, see Nowak, *op. cit.*, p. 381.

An offence is committed by a person who wilfully disregards such regulations and directions after they have been made known to him or her. It is triggered by police anticipation of the need to prevent or control obstruction of the highway and to keep order and so is, for the police, a much easier power to use than section 12 of the Public Order Act 1986.

Section 52 is used by the police to give effect to a sessional order made by the House of Commons on the day that the Parliamentary session commences: 'the passages through the streets leading to the Houses of Parliament shall be kept free and open and no obstruction shall be permitted to hinder the passage of members to and from the Houses of Parliament and no disorder shall be allowed in Westminster Hall or any passages leading to the Houses of Parliament during the sitting of Parliament and there shall be no annoyance therein or thereabouts'.[108] Thus the police can seek to control lobbies of Parliament and protests concerned with Parliament's activities. In *Papworth v Coventry*[109] (1967), a case involving anti-Vietnam war protest on the corner of Whitehall and Downing Street, it was held that regulations and directions made under the Act expressly to give effect to the sessional order would be *ultra vires* if they sought to control areas outside the 'immediate neighbourhood of the Houses of Parliament' or if they sought to authorise police actions that went beyond the prevention of obstruction or 'disorder, [or] annoyance of the kind itself likely to lead to a breach of the peace'. The linkage of 'annoyance' to breach of the peace is important since restricting freedom of speech or assembly to prevent mere annoyance is unlikely to be compatible with Convention rights. The greater specification of breach of the peace, particularly the focus on the source of possible violence and the reasonableness of a defendant's activities,[110] will also be significant in limiting the wide discretion police enjoy under the Act.[111]

17.6.3 Banning marches – section 13, Public Order Act 1986

If, in the reasonable view of the police, the imposition of conditions is insufficient to prevent a procession resulting in serious public disorder, the police may seek a banning order. The order is made by the local council, to whom the police apply, and the consent of the Secretary of State is required. Organisers and participants in public processions which they know to be banned are guilty of an offence, as are those who incite them. Uniformed police have the power to arrest. The punishment for those who organise or incite is a fine or a maximum of three months' imprisonment or both; participants can only be fined.

The ban is for a period that does not exceed three months and is limited to a definite geographical area. There is no power to ban a single march. Only all marches or a class of marches can be banned. This requirement is explained

---

[108] The sessional order is not 'law'; its direct impact is confined to the precincts of Parliament. The law does not require the police to give the order effect, though they do.

[109] [1967] 1 WLR 663.

[110] Discussed above.

[111] For examples of the enforcement of sessional orders against political groups and for police attitudes thereto see Waddington, P.A.J. (1994) *Liberty and Order*. London: UCL Press, p. 64.

by the need for the police to be able to demonstrate political impartiality which, it is feared, might be compromised if they could request bans in respect of particular marches.

The local authority, not the police, imposes the ban (in London, the Mayor). The local authority is unlikely to substitute its own views for that of the police, though an authority which fettered its discretion by automatically accepting applications from chief officers would be acting unlawfully. Conversely, local authorities have no right to require chief constables to seek bans against their, the chief constables', contrary judgments and this, in the past, has been a source of tension. The exercise of the banning power requires a careful balancing of competing interests and rights. The involvement of the unelected chief constable (deciding whether there is a risk to order), the elected councillors (deciding that the risk justifies a ban in the local circumstances) and the Home Secretary, responsible to Parliament, who confirms and may modify the ban, is, perhaps, the proper balance of decision-taking forces.

The banning power is harder to trigger than the power to impose conditions. It is confined to a reasonable belief by the police that the imposition of conditions is insufficient to prevent serious public disorder. Failure to prevent serious or long-term disruption to the community will not in itself justify a ban. The wish, for example, by an ethnic minority community to be spared an offensive march by racists does not of itself give the police power to seek a ban.

A ban is challengeable by way of judicial review, although its lawfulness could also be raised as a defence to criminal proceedings. In *Kent* v *Metropolitan Police Commissioner* (1981)[112] ordinary administrative law principles were applied which meant that the Commissioner had to meet a low threshold of legality: the ban would be lawful so long as he took relevant matters into account. Since that case, emphatically since the Human Rights Act 1998 was brought into effect, the courts subject the reasons of officials to a closer, more demanding scrutiny when human rights, such as free speech and freedom of assembly, are in issue. Schedule 1, Article 11 will be directly in issue and any ban must be in accordance with Article 11(2). In *Christians against Racism and Fascism* v *United Kingdom* (1978)[113] the Human Rights Commission found that a ban imposed over the whole of the London area in respect of a National Front march in a district of London was compatible with Article 11. In all the circumstances, the ban was reasonable and proportionate. The principal issue is the need, under the Act, to ban all marches, or marches of a class, not just the march in respect of which there is the fear of disorder. It is doubtful, however, if a general ban on all marches can be compatible with the Convention if it is imposed merely for the sake of the appearance of police impartiality rather than being justified by a real danger to order. It has been suggested that the power should be recast to be confined to marches concerned with the same political issue[114] (e.g. fear of violence in respect of a loyalist march relating to Northern Ireland would also, within the three-month period,

---

[112] (1981) *The Times*, 13 May.
[113] Ap. 8440/78; 21 D&R 138.
[114] See Fenwick, H. (1998) *Civil Liberties*. London: Cavendish, p. 296.

require the banning of a republican march, even if peaceful, but not of a march opposing war in the Middle East).

The banning power is a draconian restriction on political freedom and is usually controversial. It was widely used before, during and after the Second World War,[115] and again in early 1980s.[116] Since the later 1990s the power has been rarely used although there may be signs of a revival in the context of the 'war against terrorism'. The decline in the use of the banning power results partly from a reduction in violent political protest but also from the police sense that the legal criteria for a ban are difficult to establish, particularly given the need, under the Human Rights Act 1998 to meet the criteria in Article 11(2), that bans may be ineffective and difficult to enforce, that seeking a ban may cause more trouble, in terms of the politics of policing, than it is worth and that the public order objectives can be best fulfilled by negotiation with demonstrators and the imposition of conditions.[117]

17.7 Demonstrations

A political demonstration, as understood here, involves something more than a march or assembly; it involves actions taken to coerce or prevent others doing what they are lawfully entitled to do. Using Convention language, a demonstration aims to undermine the rights of others in respect of the activities to which the demonstrators object. It is a form of civil disobedience in which laws are broken in order to pursue a cause which, at least in the views of the demonstrators, is of such fundamental importance that the constitutional processes of law, government and opposition must be overridden. Some of the most important gains for democracy, votes for women for example, have been obtained partly at least through coercive pressure of this kind. The rights of the unborn, the protection of the environment, animal welfare and the cause of peace and disarmament are current examples of causes in respect of which demonstration, in this sense, is undertaken. In the early years of the twenty-first century, the price of petrol and the freedoms of country dwellers are causes for which some people feel they are entitled to demonstrate. Liberal political theory seeks to make a principled distinction between causes that deal with fundamental matters which are outside the proper remit of any legislature to ignore (the basic right to vote or to equality before the law, for example) and other causes which simply reflect the normal clash of interests in a country. Demonstration and civil disobedience may be justifiable in respect of the former, less so in respect of the latter. Whether such a principled approach will satisfy anyone who has not already accepted the liberal constitutional agenda must be doubted.[118]

---

[115] Parliamentary Written Answer 10.3.78, cited *Christians against Racism and Fascism* v *UK* Ap. 8440/78; 21 D&R 138.

[116] *Report of HM Chief Inspector of Constabulary for 1981* (1981–82) HC 463, paragraph 8.6.

[117] Waddington, *op. cit.*, p. 59.

[118] See in particular Rawls, J. (1972) *A Theory of Justice*. Oxford: Oxford University Press, chapter VI, sections 55–9; Dworkin, R. (1986) *A Matter of Principle*. Oxford: Clarendon Press, chapter 4.

17.7.1 General powers

Demonstrations, as defined above, are likely to involve meetings and marches and so the law discussed above, both common law, such as breach of the peace, and statute, such as police powers under the Public Order Act 1986, will be relevant. Other powers, of particular significance in respect of demonstrations, also exist.

17.7.2 Civil remedies for occupiers

The courts are willing to issue injunctions to protect those in possession of land from serious continuing trespass. These can have a significant deterrent effect on demonstrators' willingness to maintain a protest. Injunctions may also be issued where there is interference, by unlawful means, with the carrying on of business or works on land, where there is 'watching and besetting' or where there has been a private nuisance. Such injunctions are available in a political context such as against anti-road demonstrators who try to prevent construction work continuing.[119] Civil injunctions are generally not directly enforceable by the police. As discussed above, the police have duties to prevent actual or reasonably apprehended breaches of the peace and this duty may authorise them to act in support of the landowner.[120] The creation of the offence of 'aggravated trespass' by the Criminal Justice and Public Order Act 1994 (discussed below), which includes a power of arrest, may make such injunctions unnecessary.

A landowner may be able to obtain an interlocutory or temporary injunction. This is a holding measure which will require the ending of a protest until the courts are able to make a final judgment. In practice it will bring a protest to an end. A central question for the courts is not where the rights of the matter lie (that is for the full injunction) but what the balance of convenience is:[121] who stands to lose most if, at the holding stage, they are prevented from doing that which, at the final stage, it is determined they have a right to do. If the claimant's business is losing significant profit as a consequence of a demonstration and the demonstrators are simply losing an opportunity which in theory, if not in practice, can be revived, the balance of convenience is likely to lie with the claimant. This was the approach of the majority in *Hubbard* v *Pitt* (1976)[122] when an estate agent obtained a temporary injunction against the organisers of a street picket who were objecting to the estate agent's policies of selling properties for redevelopment.

In *Hubbard* v *Pitt* (1976) Lord Denning, in a much quoted dissent, argued that the issue of remedies in such a situation should give proper weight to fundamental political rights such as to freedom of expression and assembly.[123] This position is now strengthened by the general requirements of the Human

---

[119] *Department of Transport and others* v *Williams* (1993) TLR 627.
[120] See *R* v *Chief Constable of the Devon and Cornwall Constabulary ex parte CEGB* [1981] 3 All ER 826.
[121] *American Cyanamid Co.* v *Ethicon* [1975] AC 396 HL; [1975] 1 All ER 504 HL.
[122] [1976] 1 QB 142 CA.
[123] See also *Verrall* v *Great Yarmouth* [1981] 1 QB 202, above.

Rights Act 1998 and, in so far as freedom of expression is in issue, section 12.[124] Of course Schedule 1, Article 11 will only be in issue if the assembly is 'peaceful' as understood in Convention jurisprudence[125] and while some degree of obstruction of the highway is acceptable, a full-scale interference with the lawful activities of others may go outside the protection of the Article. In *The Observer and the Guardian* v *United Kingdom*[126] the Court of Human Rights accepted the balance of convenience test for a temporary injunction even where fundamental rights were at stake.[127] Nevertheless, as regards a peaceful demonstration, the demonstrators' rights to assembly should now be given greater weight in assessing the balance of convenience and, if free speech is in issue, section 12 of the Human Rights Act 1998 requires the likely outcome of the full trial to be assessed.

17.7.3 Harassment

The Protection from Harassment Act 1997 creates both a civil remedy and criminal offences in respect of 'harassment'. Harassment is not defined in the Act but involves a course of conduct, not just a single occurrence. The more serious of the criminal offences involves making the victim fear the use of violence. The Act is primarily designed for use against stalkers, bad neighbours or racial abusers. It has been held, in the context of a campaign against an animal experiment company, that the Act should not be used against those exercising the right to protest and who make this the basis of the defence of 'reasonableness' under section 1(3).[128] There is, of course, no fundamental right to non-peaceful assembly and where harassment is established then the fact that it is also a form of political protest is not sufficient to establish the defence.[129] Menacing phone calls and letters, and the abuse of customers, for example, of furriers, can lead to injunctions if not criminal penalties under the Act.[130]

17.7.4 Disruption offences

As noted above, the police have legal authority to enter private land to deal with an occurring or a reasonably anticipated breach of the peace. In so doing they have appeared, in effect, to be acting for a landowner in pursuit of a civil injunction. Police authority in this area has been clarified by section 68 of the Criminal Justice and Public Order Act 1994 which created the offence of 'aggravated trespass',[131] an offence which applies in relation to wide-scale, disruptive, trespassory protests in the open air such as those by hunt saboteurs or anti-road building campaigners.

---

[124] See Chapter 11.
[125] See above.
[126] (1992) 14 EHRR 153.
[127] (1992) 14 EHRR 153, paragraph 63.
[128] *Huntingdon Life Sciences* v *Curtin* (1997) *The Times*, 11 December.
[129] *DPP* v *Moseley (Joanna)* (1999) *The Times*, 3 June.
[130] See *The Independent*, 23 October 2001.
[131] Card, R. and Ward, R. (1994) *The Criminal Justice and Public Order Act 1994*. Bristol: Jordan Publishing.

Section 68 Offence of aggravated trespass

(1) A person commits the offence of aggravated trespass if he trespasses on land in the open air and, in relation to any lawful activity which persons are engaging in or are about to engage in on that or adjoining land in the open air, does there anything which is intended by him to have the effect –

   (a) of intimidating those persons or any of them so as to deter them or any of them from engaging in that activity,

   (b) of obstructing that activity, or

   (c) of disrupting that activity.

Aggravated trespass cannot be committed by activity taking place on a highway.[132] There is a power of arrest by a constable in uniform; it is a summary offence for which a person can be sentenced for up to three months in prison or a fine, or both.

The main components of aggravated trespass have been summarised in *Winder and others* v *DPP*[133] where it was successfully used against hunt saboteurs. The defendant must have been a trespasser, as defined by ordinary law, on open-air land at the time the offence was alleged. The defendant must have done a distinct and overt act which was intended to deter the lawful acts of others through intimidation, or to disrupt or to obstruct; unintended disruption is not an offence.[134] Merely trespassing – standing around, for example – is not enough. There must be evidence of additional activities intended to deter lawful activity, etc.[135] Observing the activities of others, such as huntsmen, does not necessarily deter the huntsmen and so may not establish the offence.[136] The person intimidated, disrupted or obstructed must be engaging in an activity that they can lawfully do on the land, so disrupting unlawful acts, like the digging for badgers or of a hunt which is itself trespassing, is not within the offence.[137] Under section 69 of the Criminal Justice and Public Order Act 1994 police have a linked power to direct those they believe, on reasonable grounds, to be committing or intending to commit aggravated trespass to leave the land. Failure to leave is an offence.[138]

The intention to intimidate or disrupt may mean that an assembly is not 'peaceful' and so Article 11 will not be engaged. However, protests involving limited obstruction could both be caught by the Criminal Justice and Public Order Act 1994 and need to be measured against Article 11.[139] Protecting the rights of others, such as the occupiers of land and contractors, is a legitimate purpose under Article 11(2) but any restriction will need to be proportionate and this will not necessarily be established by the simple fact that the defendants have been or will be trespassers.

---

[132] Section 68(5)(a), Criminal Justice and Public Order Act 1994.

[133] (1966) 160 JPR 713; followed in *DPP* v *Barnard and others* [2000] Crim LR 371.

[134] Thus trespassing huntsmen whose presence may be highly intimidating or disruptive are unlikely to have committed the offence: Card and Ward, *op. cit.*, pp. 53–4.

[135] *DPP* v *Barnard and others* [2000] Crim LR 371 where the evidence only disclosed trespass but not a further overt act of occupation of an open-cast mining site.

[136] *Capon* v *DPP* [1988] Crim LR 870.

[137] Card and Ward, *op. cit.*, p. 52.

[138] *Capon* v *DPP* [1998] Crim LR 870.

[139] As in *MC* v *Germany* (1989) Ap. 13079/87, discussed above, though the 'coercion' here took place on a road.

17.7.5 Trespassory assemblies

The Criminal Justice and Public Order Act 1994 introduces sections 14A–C into the Public Order Act 1986. These give the police power to seek a ban of certain trespassory assemblies. This power relates to the police's ability to intervene, albeit unintentionally, on behalf of private landowners and contractors. (The power also needs to be considered in the light of general powers over marches and meetings, discussed above.) Under these provisions the police may seek an order from the local authority to ban any trespassory assembly. The power to seek a ban is triggered by a belief that 'serious disruption to the life of the community' may result from the meeting or that a historical monument may be significantly damaged. A trespassory assembly is an assembly, in the open air, of 20 or more persons[140] held on land without the permission of the occupier of the land or held on land to which the public have a right of access (like a highway) but in a manner that exceeds the limits of that right. The local authority, acting with the consent of the Secretary of State, may then make an order banning all such trespassory assemblies (not just the meeting that caused the original concern) for a period of up to four days and within a five-mile radius of a specified place. It in an offence knowingly to take part, organise or incite others to take part. A police constable in uniform has a power of arrest. The ban can only relate to assemblies involving trespass and, as we have seen, this may not necessarily apply to a non-obstructive assembly taking place on the highway.[141] It can include, however, much land regulated by byelaws if the holding of a meeting would transgress those byelaws.

Compatability of such bans with Schedule 1, Article 11 raises a number of issues. It is triggered by the chief constable's reasonable belief that 'serious disruption to the life of the community' may result if the meeting goes ahead. As discussed above, this may not be a precise enough term to enable people to know what behaviour is or is not prohibited to meet the 'prescribed by law' test in Article 11(2). It may authorise wider restrictions than those aimed at preventing violence or damage to property and this may be outside the range of purposes for which the non-trespassory right to assembly can be restricted under the 1986 Act The ban extends to all trespassory assemblies, even peaceful ones. Any particular order must meet the proportionality test inherent in Article 11(2). The Commission of Human Rights has accepted that an order, made because of previous damage to Stonehenge by New Age travellers, which prevented the holding of peaceful Druidic ceremonies near to the monument during the summer solstice was proportionate.[142]

Demonstrators who enter premises as trespassers may commit an arrestable offence under section 6 the Criminal Law Act 1977. The offence is to threaten violence without lawful authority for the purpose of securing entry into any premises were there is 'someone present on those premises at the time who is opposed to the entry which the violence is intended to secure, and the person using or threatening the violence knows that that is the case'. Premises is defined in relation to buildings and land related to buildings and is not

---

[140] Section 14A(9), Public Order Act 1986.
[141] *Jones* v *DPP* [1999] 2 All ER 257 HL, discussed below.
[142] *Arthur U. Pendragon* v *United Kingdom* Ap. 31416/95; application inadmissible.

confined to open-air land. The violence can be directed against the person or against property and need not be to acquire possession. Damage to against property and, perhaps, even minimal violence against the person can still be within the concept of 'peaceful' assembly. If so, Article 11 ECHR is engaged and though section 6 is a prescription of the law and pursues a legitimate purpose, any particular restriction on assembly imposed under it will need to be proportionate.

More problematic in respect of Article 11 ECHR is the offence under section 9 of the Criminal Law Act 1977 of trespassing on premises of a foreign mission. This is an offence that demonstrators protesting against the policy of a foreign government may commit. The offence is committed by merely entering as a trespasser premises which are within the definition of a diplomatic mission found in the Vienna Convention on Diplomatic Relations.[143] Such an action can clearly be 'peaceful' and so any prosecution, which can only be brought with the consent of the Attorney General, will need to be for a legitimate purpose and proportionate.

Under the Criminal Justice and Public Order Act 1994, the police have a range of other powers to deal with trespassing groups or groups creating a nuisance on open land. Sections 61–2 and 67 provide a power to remove trespassers who are intending to reside on the land and sections 63–7 give a power to remove persons who are preparing for, awaiting or attending certain 'raves'.

17.7.6 Damage to property

Protestors who damage property in order to make a political point may commit criminal damage in breach of the Criminal Damage Act 1971. Section 5 provides a defence for a defendant with an honest belief that the property was in need of immediate protection and that the means of protection adopted were reasonable in the circumstances. Reasonableness has been an attempted defence in a number of political cases involving peace protestors. However, although the Act states that the reasonableness of the defendant's honest belief should not be in issue, the courts have put barriers in the way of the defence. In cases involving peace protesters who intended to cut the perimeter wire of military bases, a jury was instructed to convict in one case[144] and prevented from considering the defence in another.[145] There is, nevertheless, some evidence that putting the reasonableness of the defendant's action to a jury may still lead to acquittal or at least to comment by the jury. A jury accepted

---

[143] Cm 2565.

[144] *R v Hill; R v Hall* [1989] Crim LR 136, and critical comment by J.C. Smith at 138–9. See also *Hipperson v DPP* (unreported), 3 July 1996 (breaking into AWE Aldermaston with the honest but mistaken intention of helping to prevent offences under the Genocide Act 1969). The claim by a vicar that he acted on God's authority, who owned all property, when he wrote a biblical quotation on a concrete pillar outside Parliament was rejected as being incapable of meeting the s. 5 defence in *Blake v DPP* [1993] Crim LR 586, with less sympathetic comments by J.C. Smith.

[145] *R v Ashford and Smith* [1988] Crim LR 682, critical comment by J.C. Smith at 683–4. See Ewing, K. and Gearty, C. (1990) *Freedom under Thatcher*. London: Fontana, pp. 100–3. The defendants were convicted of possession of an article but acquitted of attempting to damage the wire.

a political or moral justification and acquitted defendants who had damaged a jet fighter to prevent its possible use by the Indonesian government in East Timor,[146] and a jury held that a protester who had painted anti-nuclear graffiti at Westminster, though convicted, had reasonable cause for her behaviour.[147] Juries have also been prepared to acquit environmental campaigners accused of both criminal damage and theft after damaging genetically modified crops in order to subvert experimental plantings.[148]

17.7.7 'Watching and besetting, etc.'

Under section 241 of the Trade Union and Labour Relations (Consolidation) Act 1992[149] offences are committed when a person does one of a range of activities 'with a view to compelling' another person not to do or to do an act which the person compelled has a legal right to do or not to do. The forbidden activities include: using violence, intimidating, persistently following, hiding or depriving persons of their property, hindering, watching or besetting and following. These offences are not confined to activities committed in the context of strikes or other forms of industrial action[150] and have been used, for example, against an anti-roads protester who chained himself to a crane thus hindering the driver in his work[151] and (unsuccessfully) against anti-abortionists picketing an abortion clinic.[152] There must be evidence that the activity, the watching and besetting etc., must have been done to compel, not merely to persuade, another from acting in a way they are legally entitled to do.[153] These are arrestable offences.

17.7.8 Remedies

Binding over
An alternative to arrest in order to prosecute for an offence is that demonstrators may be arrested and brought before magistrates to be bound over to keep the peace or be of good behaviour for a period of time. The person must consent to being bound over and may (though need not) be secured by a sum of money paid into court which is forfeit if the order is breached. A person who refuses to consent to a binding over order can be imprisoned as can a person who fails to comply with the terms of the order. As mentioned above, a person who is arrested or detained by police for breach of the peace will often be then brought before a magistrate to be bound over. The power is found in the Magistrates' Courts Act 1980, section 115. Magistrates have an

---

[146] See *The Times*, 31 July 1996, 1. For a controversial Scottish case, which was overturned on appeal, see *HM Advocate v Zelter* (unreported) 21 October 1999.
[147] Helen John's case, see Carter, H. (1999) 'A Jury Backs Granny's Anti-nuclear Graffitti', *The Guardian*, 18 December, p. 11.
[148] Stallworthy, M. (2000) 'Damage to Crops – Part 1 and Part 2, *New Law Journal*, 19 May, pp. 728–9, 26 May, 801–2.
[149] This provision was formerly section 7 of the Conspiracy and Protection of Property Act 1875.
[150] *DPP v Todd* (1995) *The Independent*, 5 May.
[151] *DPP v Todd* (1995) *The Independent*, 5 May.
[152] *DPP v Fidler* [1992] 1 WLR 91.
[153] *DPP v Fidler* [1992] 1 WLR 91.

additional power under the Justice of the Peace Act 1361 and also, it is believed, under common law powers from time immemorial to bind over for the same purposes any person who is before them. The power has been frequently used in the context of political demonstrations such as anti-hunt or anti-arms trade demonstrations.

As we have seen, clarifications in the law relating to breach of the peace enabled the Court of Human Rights to find that the general principle of binding over to keep the peace was compatible with Convention rights. In a hunt saboteur case, *Hashman and Harrup v United Kingdom* (1999),[154] the Court of Human Rights held that binding over for good behaviour (as distinct from preventing a breach of the peace) was incompatible with Article 10. 'Good behaviour' was not certain enough, too much within the discretion of magistrates, for a person to be able to foresee what behaviour was or was not going to be acceptable to the authorities. The 'prescribed by law' test was failed. Such orders should not now be made. It is worth noting that the 'prescribed by law' requirement, in this context, is not enormously demanding. In *Chorherr v Austria* (1993)[155] an arrest in Austria of an anti-arms trade demonstrator for a breach of the peace 'likely to cause annoyance' was held to be well defined and coherent.

Bail conditions

People arrested and charged enjoy, under both the Bail Act 1976 and Article 6 of the Convention, a presumption that they should be bailed. In granting bail, magistrates may impose conditions. Political demonstrators, accused of public order offences, may be prevented from continuing with the protest while on bail where there is a real risk that, by rejoining the protest, they will commit further offences. Bail conditions can seem like a punishment without conviction. Dissatisfaction is all the greater since the imposition of conditions in the first place and decisions on whether to remand a defendant for breach of a condition can be done by magistrates on the basis of their general understanding of the situation rather than on the basis of specific, cross-examinable evidence against the individuals concerned. This can lead to a sense of grievance and a feeling of guilt by association.[156]

17.8 Public order offences

17.8.1 Harassment, alarm or distress

The Public Order Act 1986 replaced the public order offences in the Public Order Act 1936 and in doing so extended the reach of the criminal law. In particular section 5 created offences in relation to behaviour which previously had not been criminal.

---

[154] Ap. 25594/94.
[155] Ap. 13308/87, A266-B; (1993) 17 EHRR 358.
[156] See, in the context of the miners' strike *R v Mansfield Justices ex parte Starkey* [1985] 1 QB 613; on the decision to remand in a non-political case, see *R (DPP) v Havering Magistrates Court* [2001] 3 All ER 997.

5. Harassment, alarm or distress

(1) A person is guilty of an offence if he –

  (a) uses threatening, abusive or insulting words or behaviour, or disorderly behaviour, or

  (b) displays any writing, sign or other visible representation which is threatening, abusive or insulting,

within the hearing or sight of a person likely to be caused harassment, alarm or distress.

Police have a power of arrest without a warrant but only after a warning has been given and ignored.[157] Persons convicted can be punished by a fine.

The declared aim of the section was to deal with hooligan activity but it has been used, not always successfully, against political demonstrators. Persons who, for example, picket abortion clinics, shout at those entering, display plastic foetuses and pictures of dead foetuses[158] or who prevent people entering abortion clinics[159] can be committing the offence as can those who try to prevent road builders doing their work by interfering with the work of surveyors and others.[160]

This is not a single offence but a range of different offences since the terms used are to be read disjunctively.[161] It is necessary to prove both conduct (insulting etc.) and effect (likelihood that a person be caused harassment, alarm or distress).

Of great importance is that an offence can be committed without the use or threat of violence and without a person being coerced in any way or put in fear for their own personal safety. The display of an insulting sign which, in the opinion of a court, is likely to cause a person distress can be an offence under the section.

Whether behaviour is threatening, abusive, insulting or disorderly is to be determined by giving these words their ordinary meaning and courts should not redraft, as it were, the statute by seeking synonyms. This was the view of the House of Lords in *Brutus* v *Cozens* (1973)[162] when they upheld the acquittal of anti-apartheid demonstrators who had interrupted a tennis match at Wimbledon. However, the case is also authority for the view that certain behaviour is not capable of being insulting. Thus affronting people or showing contempt or disrespect for them or annoying them, or being merely rude and offensive, are different from being insulting and not within the ambit of the offence.[163] Likewise behaviour which is annoying to others is not, thereby, insulting.[164] In *Vigon* v *DPP*[165] the secret filming of customers trying on

---

[157] The arresting constable need not be the constable who gave the warning (Public Order (Amendment) Act 1996); the conduct which occurs after the warning must amount, at least, to an offence under section 5 but need not be the same conduct as triggered the warning: s. 5(4), Public Order Act 1986.

[158] *DPP* v *Fidler* (1992) 1 WLR 91.

[159] *Morrow, Geach and Thomas* v *DPP and others* [1994] Crim LR 58.

[160] *Chambers and Edwards* v *DPP* [1995] Crim LR 896 (QBD).

[161] *Chambers and Edwards* v *DPP* [1995] Crim LR 896 (QBD).

[162] [1973] AC 854 HL.

[163] *Ambrose* (1973) 57 Cr Ap Rep.

[164] *Bryan* v *Robinson* [1960] 2 All ER 173 DC.

[165] (1988) 162 JP 115.

swimwear was said to be insulting, in the ordinary sense of the word, because it was an affront to dignity and modesty.

Under section 6(4) of the Act a person cannot be guilty of an offence under section 5 unless he or she intends or is aware that his words etc. are threatening etc. In *DPP* v *Clarke*[166] (1991), where anti-abortion demonstrators had protested outside a clinic by carrying photographs of aborted foetuses, it was held that the test for intention or awareness of the character of the defendant's words or actions was subjective and the required intention or awareness could not be attributed to the defendants merely because their action could cause alarm or distress. Section 5(3) provides a defence that the defendant had no reason to believe that any person within hearing or sight was likely to be caused harassment, alarm or distress. If a person does act with the intention of causing harassment, alarm and distress, they may be guilty of more serious offences under section 4A of the Public Order Act 1986 which was inserted by the Criminal Justice and Public Order Act 1994. The offence was introduced to combat racist activity but is couched in general terms and can, in principle, be used against any political activist aiming to inhibit a lawful activity (such as animal testing, for example) by harassing, alarming or distressing those involved).

Under section 5(3)(c) it is a defence to a prosecution under section 5(1) that the defendant's conduct was reasonable. The test is objective: that in the circumstances the conduct was, in the view of the court, reasonable.[167]

> Anti-abortion demonstrators protested outside a clinic. They shouted slogans, waived banners and prevented staff and patients from entering the clinic. Some patients became distressed. On being prosecuted under section 5, M, G and T defended themselves on the grounds that their conduct was reasonable and also they had done no more than use reasonable force in the prevention of crime as permitted by section 3 of the Criminal Law Act 1967. The allegation underlying their defence was an honest belief that unlawful abortions were being performed in the clinic.
>
> HELD: the reasonableness of a defendant's actions should be assessed on the basis of the circumstances as the defendant honestly believed them to be. Here, regarding section 5(3)(c) of the Public Order Act 1986, the defendant's behaviour could not be thought as a reasonable reaction to the facts as they understood them; nor, regarding section 3 of the Criminal Law Act 1967, could they be reasonably preventing the commission of any crimes that they honestly believed were being committed since their actions were incapable of distinguishing between lawful and unlawful abortions.
>
> *Morrow, Geach and Thomas* v *DPP and others* [1994] Crim LR 58

The reasonableness of political protest may be established in so far as persons are exercising their rights to freedom of speech, assembly and association. However, action which seriously interferes with the rights of others has little if any support in Convention rights.

---

[166] (1991) 94 Cr App R 359.
[167] The objective test was approved in *DPP* v *Clarke* (1991) 94 Cr App R 359.

17.8.2 Fear or provocation of violence

Section 4 of the Public Order Act 1986 creates an offence of fear or provocation of violence. This is where behaviour which is threatening, abusive or insulting is intended to cause another to believe that violence is likely or intended to provoke another to violence. Terms such as 'insulting' have the same meaning as under section 5. A person convicted of such an offence can be punished by imprisonment of not more than six months or a fine or both. A police officer in uniform can arrest a person suspected of committing the offence.

Unlike the section 5 offence, there must be a link established between threatening etc. behaviour and a fear of violence. There must be an intention to cause another, by words or actions, to believe immediate violence is likely, or an intention to provoke another to immediate violence.[168] The link with the likelihood of or provoking of immediate violence means that, from a civil liberties and human rights perspective, this offence is less problematic than section 5. There is no human right to non-peaceful assembly and rights of free expression can be properly restricted to protect the rights of others from violence. In *R v Horseferry Road Magistrates Court ex parte Siadatan*[169] an attempt was made to invoke the offence against the publishers of *The Satanic Verses* by Salman Rushdie. The allegation was that the work was abusive and insulting writing whereby it was likely that unlawful violence would be provoked. The court held that, at most, any violence would be provoked a considerable time after the distribution by the publisher of the writing. The violence need not be an instantaneous response to the provoking act but the term 'immediate' in the section required a restricted time period.[170]

Section 4 includes the provocation of violence in the offence. The cases on provocation in the context of breach of the peace, discussed above, imply that the reasonableness of the alleged provoker's actions and the unreasonableness of the persons provoked should be taken into account. This would permit proper weight to be given to the exercise by the alleged provoker of the right of freedom of expression.

17.8.3 Offences of violence

The Public Order Act 1986 also includes offences dealing with the threat or use of violence. Section 1 defines 'riot', an offence which involves the use or threat of violence by 12 persons or more acting for a common purpose and the use or threat of violence is to such a degree that a 'person of reasonable firmness present at the scene' would be caused 'to fear for his personal safety'. Section 2 defines 'violent disorder' where three or more persons, not necessarily with a common purpose, threaten or use violence to the same degree. Section 3 defines 'affray', the least serious of these offences, which can be committed by one person threatening or using violence to the same degree.

These offences create many problems in criminal law but fewer in the context of human rights and civil liberties. The threat or use of violence to the

---

[168] *Winn v DPP* (1992) 142 NLJ 527.
[169] [1990] 3 WLR 1006, DC.
[170] See also *Valentine v DPOP* [1997] COD 339.

degree that someone reasonably fears for their safety is unlikely to be justifiable in human rights terms. These are serious offences and their use, particularly riot, in a public order context can be controversial. It was, for example, alleged that, in the context of the miners' strike 1984–85, prosecutions for riot (under the law prior to the 1986 Act) were used as a deterrent and punishment since charges were dropped in a number of instances when the cases came for trial.

18
Terrorism and law

18.1 Introduction: special powers

Serious violence used with the intention of terrorising civilian populations, and through them, governments, into acceding to political demands has now become one of the most pressing problems facing governments throughout the world. Bombings in Moscow attributed to Chechen rebels, the attacks in New York and Washington of 11 September 2001, the continuing violence in Israel/Palestine, killings in India and Pakistan connected with Kashmir and religious issues and the bombings of tourists in Bali in October 2002 are some of the more serious examples of this problem. The reaction of states to this violence raises its own problems, including allegations of disproportionate responses that, by leading to many civilian deaths, equate to the use of terror.

Civil liberties issues arise in respect of the action of governments towards their own populations. Terrorist actions will be criminal offences, subject to the normal procedures of investigation, prosecution and trial of suspects and, on conviction, punishment. The issue for governments, including the United Kingdom's, is whether there is a need for special powers, over and above the ordinary criminal law. Such special powers can, for example, create new criminal offences for activities connected with terrorism and they can introduce new measures to facilitate the prevention of terrorist action and the investigation and trial of suspects. Special powers, however, are likely to diminish the personal and, above all, the political freedom of individuals, groups and associations.[1]

Radical political groups, operating outside the constitutional consensus, may be disproportionately affected. For example, political radicals opposed to the arms trade or who are acting in pursuit of various environmental objectives may commit serious crimes against property. It is not obvious that the danger they create justifies the use of special powers over and above the criminal law. Similarly, people may espouse the cause of radical or revolutionary politics because they support the ends being pursued or wish to associate with a cause. It does not follow that they are necessarily supporting the use of violent means. Special powers may create a form of guilt by association: by which supporters of a particular cause, say that of a Palestinian state, are stigmatised and, perhaps, arrested and questioned, because of the violent acts of other supporters.

---

[1] See Fenwick, H. (2000) *Civil Rights, New Labour, Freedom and Human Rights*. Harlow: Longman, pp. 60–4.

Special powers may diminish conventional and traditional protections built into the fair trial process. For example, they may allow unusually long periods for the detention and questioning of suspects. Ministers argue that, at times of such emergency, normal civil liberties can properly be restricted given the overwhelming need for public protection. The contrary argument is perfectly reasonable: that it is precisely those 'civil liberties' which relate to the fairness of the trial process and to the detention and treatment of suspects which should be carefully protected at times when there is strong political and social pressure on police and the courts to bring perpetrators to justice. There is no point to the protection offered by civil liberties and human rights law if it can be set aside or diminished at times of crisis when they are most needed.[2]

Special powers can raise difficult questions relating to freedom of speech, of the press and of assembly. There may be a strong mood among the majority in society of hostility to the perpetrators of the attacks and majority support for the government's response. Questioning this mood may be seen as supporting, or being ambivalent about, terrorism or denying to society and to the government the support it deserves in difficult times. Yet, at the heart of freedom of speech, is the protection of offensive and unpopular opinion. The extent to which this is undermined by special powers needs to be considered. Again, state reactions to terrorism can be highly controversial. One view is that, at times of crisis, the main institutions of civil society, including the media, should rally to the national cause as defined by the government and not print stories or take action that might undermine the national effort. The alternative is that it is precisely at such times, when special powers may be used and when military action may be being taken, that government should be most carefully scrutinised.[3]

The use of special powers in the context of terrorist outrage needs to be carefully scrutinised in respect of its impact on civil liberties and human rights. Fenwick, for example, argues that special powers are justified only as a proportionate response to a historically and socially specific and active threat. Special powers should wax and wane in proportion to the degree of violence in a particular situation, Northern Ireland for example, rather than just being generally available to the police and other agencies against a perceived but speculative future possibility.[4]

Of equal importance is to remind ourselves that a commitment to human rights does not permit the supporters and perpetrators of acts of terror to hide behind the norms of a rights-orientated, albeit imperfect, democratic society. Indiscriminate violence against civilians makes democratic politics impossible,

---

[2] A point often made by senior judges, for example comments by the Lord Chief Justice in a British Academy lecture (*The Guardian*, 16 October 2002). The Home Secretary, on the other hand, has suggested that the right to life, threatened by terrorism, should take priority over other liberties (see, *The Independent*, 29 September 2001).

[3] On 15 October 2001, the government called a meeting of broadcasters to discuss the use of material supplied by Al Jezeerah, a Middle East based news TV channel. The government's concern was that coded messages to terrorists might be being broadcast. Against that concern is the point that the channel with access to opposition or enemy views is a convincing countervailing source to the official spokespersons on the issue of civilian casualties and the impact of the war: *The Independent*, 16 October 2001.

[4] Stressed by Fenwick, *op. cit.*

or at least something that only disproportionately brave people will engage in. To assert the importance of civil liberties and human rights in the context of anti-terrorist special powers implies the acceptance of special measures which are, truly and proportionately, necessary to protect political and private freedom, and are reasonable actions for the state to take. It is not consistent to defend the civil liberties and human rights position without accepting that point.

Such a point is, of course, embedded in human rights law. Articles 10(2) and 11(2) of the European Convention on Human Rights permit the proportionate and necessary restriction of freedoms of expression and association for purposes including the protection of the rights of others, the interests of national security and public safety and the prevention of crime and disorder. Article 17[5] prevents states, groups or persons from using their Convention rights in order to destroy the rights of others; political and private freedom is not to be exploited by those who would destroy that freedom. In addition, in a '. . . time of war or other public emergency threatening the life of the nation' Article 15 permits states to make specific acts of derogation from most Convention rights, including the right to a fair trial and personal freedom. The detail of the Convention position is given below.

18.2 United Kingdom law

18.2.1 Northern Ireland

Terrorism has been an issue in the United Kingdom for many years. Between the late 1960s and late 1990s about 3,300 people died in Northern Ireland and a further 121 in Great Britain directly as a result of political violence relating to the constitutional settlement in Northern Ireland.[6] As well as the ordinary criminal law and process, the government's response was to use special powers. Northern Ireland (Emergency Provisions) Acts applied to actions in Northern Ireland while the Prevention of Terrorism Acts applied throughout the United Kingdom. The kinds of powers found in the legislation included: the proscription of organisations with related offences of membership etc.; internal exile; enhanced powers of the police over the investigation of offences, and the use of special courts. Internment, detention without trial, was an emergency power but it was repealed in 1998. The powers were introduced incrementally by a series of Acts of Parliament and amendments over the years. They were aimed at meeting a progressively worsening or increasingly intractable situation in Northern Ireland and to that extent represented a graded, proportionate response.[7] The powers were temporary or subject to annual renewal and also to annual review. Initially they were confined to Northern Ireland's affairs although, from 1989, the Prevention of Terrorism Acts applied to terrorism relating to non-British international conflicts.

---

[5] See Chapter 2.
[6] Home Office and Northern Ireland Office (1998) *Legislation Against Terrorism: A Consultation Paper*, Cm 4178, paragraph 2.2.
[7] Fenwick, *op. cit.*

18.3 Anti-terrorist legislation

18.3.1 The Terrorism Act 2000

Political violence connected with Northern Ireland is now significantly reduced. The response of the government was not been to wind down emergency legislation but, rather, to introduce a single, permanent, anti-terrorist statute of general application. The Terrorism Act 2000 continues a regime of special powers but these powers are explicitly not confined to Northern Ireland. They apply to both international and 'domestic' terrorism. It was based upon *Legislating Against Terrorism: A Consultation Paper*[8] which was a response to a report by Lord Lloyd of Berwick.[9] The bill was subject to close, lengthy scrutiny in Parliament. The 2000 Act is permanent and not subject to annual re-enactment or review. The Home Secretary must, however, make an annual report to Parliament on it workings.[10]

18.3.2 The Anti-terrorism, Crime and Security Act 2001

Religious-based international terrorism was identified as one of the threats justifying the provisions in the 2000 Act. Following the 11 September attacks, however, the government had Parliament enact additional legislation, the Anti-terrorism, Crime and Security Act 2001. This is a long and complicated Act. It is highly controversial for two principal reasons. First, it contains some severe anti-terrorist powers which may be disproportionate to the actual threat facing the United Kingdom. Second, it contains many provisions that increase the general powers of the police and other state agencies but with no restraint that such increased powers are confined to anti-terrorism activities.[11] It was as if the immediate emergency was used to push through a major expansion of powers which would not otherwise have been acceptable to Parliament. The Bill received short, intense, sometimes influential, Parliamentary scrutiny.[12] It leaves most of the Terrorism Act 2000 intact.

18.3.3 The threats

Despite the ceasefire in Northern Ireland of the major paramilitaries, the government took the view that there was a continuing threat of terrorism which warranted special legislative powers. The Consultation Paper identified three main sources of continuing political violence[13] which, in the govern-

---

[8] Secretary of State for the Home Department and Secretary of State for Northern Ireland (1998) Cm 4178.

[9] Home Office and Northern Ireland Office (1998) *Legislating Against Terrorism: A Consultation Paper*, Cm 4178. The consultation paper was a response to the report by Lord Lloyd of Berwick (1996) Cm 3420 and its main provisions were enacted as the Terrorism Act 2000.

[10] Section 126, Terrorism Act 2000.

[11] Tomkins, A. (2002) 'Legislating against terror: The Anti-terrorism, Crime and Security Act 2001', *Public Law* 205 (Summer).

[12] Zander, M. (2001) 'The Anti-Terrorism Bill – What Happened?' 151 *NLJ* 1880.

[13] Home Office and Northern Ireland Office (1998) *Legislating Against Terrorism: A Consultation Paper*, Cm 4178, chapter 2.

ment's view , constituted a 'clear and present terrorist threat to the United Kingdom from a number of fronts . . .'[14]

First is the continuing threat in Northern Ireland. While many paramilitary groups are maintaining the ceasefire, smaller, breakaway groups are not and they pose a clear and present threat of which the Omagh bomb is the most terrible example. Given these uncertainties, Part VII of the Terrorism Act preserves a separate set of anti-terrorist measures for a period of five years in respect of Northern Ireland.

Second, the new legislation applies to international terrorism, that is to say actions taken in the United Kingdom in relation to political, religious or ideological struggles in foreign countries. This is not a new extension of anti-terrorism legislation since, in 1984, many of the provisions of the Prevention of Terrorism Act (though not proscription) were extended to include acts done in the United Kingdom relating to political conflicts abroad. Prior to the 2000 Act it was already an offence to conspire to commit an offence abroad where the substantive act is an offence under both the law of the foreign country and the law of the United Kingdom.[15] Given that some of the most serious terrorist outrages concern the relationship between 'western' and 'Islamic' worlds, this aspect of the law is hard to challenge. Human rights embody universal values and so there is nothing offensive, in principle, about suppressing in one country actions that will seriously undermine human rights in another. The concern is that these provisions may be used against those supporting the overthrow of oppressive regimes, a situation in which the morality of political violence may be complex. The Act could be used selectively in a manner that reflects foreign policy assessments of the time being with no action against those plotting to overthrow foreign regimes the current government does not like, Iraq (pre-2003) perhaps, but with prosecutions of those plotting against more favoured regimes.[16]

The most controversial extension of anti-terrorist legislation made by the Terrorism Act 2000 was to 'domestic terrorism'. The threat was identified in the Consultation Paper as coming mainly from militant animal rights activists and from nationalist extremists, and, for the future, from other groups, such as anti-abortion protestors, who have used violence in the United States. It is easy to think of other groups, such as anti-environment protestors, those opposing the arms trade, anti-nuclear activists and anti-capitalist and anti-free trade groups who have participated in serious violence against property and could apparently come within the definition of terrorist groups. The grave danger is that the Terrorism Act 2000 will have a chilling and disproportionate effect on radical politics in the United Kingdom, particularly where a clear distinction is made between damage to property and violence against persons. Acts of violence or damage to property are already caught by the criminal law. The reach of the Terrorism Act 2000 includes supporters and sympathisers who may support the cause but have an ambiguous and troubled relationship with the methods used.

[14] *Ibid.*, paragraph 2.7.
[15] Section 1A of the Criminal Law Act 1977 introduced by the Criminal Justice (Terrorism and Conspiracy) Act 1998.
[16] The consent of the Attorney General is required for some prosecutions: s. 117(3), Terrorism Act 2000.

A particular type of threat, the chaos that malicious computer hacking could cause, was also identified.

18.4 Definition of terrorism

Section 1 of the Terrorism Act 2000 contains the definition of terrorism to which the other provisions of the Act relate. The definition has two strands involving the use or threat of action. First, action must be undertaken to achieve a certain kind of objective.

> 1(1) (b)   the use or threat is designed to influence the government or to intimidate the public or a section of the public, and
>   (c)   the use or threat is made for the purpose of advancing a political, religious or ideological cause.

The second strand relates to the consequences of the action.

> 1(2)   Action falls within this subsection if it–
>   (a)   involves serious violence against a person,
>   (b)   involves serious damage to property,
>   (c)   endangers a person's life, other than that of the person committing the action,
>   (d)   creates a serious risk to the health or safety of the public or a section of the public, or
>   (e)   is designed seriously to interfere with or seriously to disrupt an electronic system

Terrorism is defined in general terms; what are, in effect, special powers, over and above the ordinary criminal law, are no longer justified by reference to a specific political dispute. Under the Prevention of Terrorism Act 1989 terrorism was defined as 'the use of violence for political ends' which included 'any use of violence for the purpose of putting the public, or any section of the public in fear'. The new definition is more restricted in that it includes only 'serious' violence. In other ways it is less restrictive. It includes serious damage to property; yet it is by no means clear that damage to property, which raises different moral issues from violence, warrants special powers in addition to the general law. 'Serious' is not defined. It is not at all clear that damaging war planes or uprooting genetically modified crops or even burning down an empty animal laboratory, etc. is sufficiently similar to bombing a public place as to justify the application of these powers. Similarly, the malicious use of computers, for hacking or planting viruses, can be hugely damaging,[17] but it does not follow that such threats justify general anti-terrorist legislation rather than specific, focused Acts of Parliament. The definition is also more extensive than under the 1989 Act in that it includes 'religious and ideological' causes as well as political ones. Obviously such terms fade into each other but their

---

[17] Seen by some as the most pressing threat to the modern military (*The Independent*, Friday, 30 March 2001).

inclusion recognises the expressed religious context within which political violence, especially internationally, takes place. Nothing in the definition restricts terrorism to acts undertaken against a more or less democratic state (democratic, for example, in the terms of the European Convention) and so the Act could be used against opponents of oppressive regimes. Conversely the definition could be applied to states oppressing part of their population. It is not clear that this was intended and any prosecutions, particularly where they require the Attorney General's consent, would, no doubt, need to be compatible with United Kingdom foreign policy.

18.5 General issues

18.5.1 Summary

The Terrorism Act 2000 and the Anti-terrorism Crime and Security Act 2001 are major pieces of legislation. There is only space here to deal with some of the major issues. The Terrorism Act 2000 provides the basic framework. It allows for the proscription of organisations, creates offences relating to the use of property for terrorist purposes and permits confiscation and forfeiture of such property; it increases the powers of the police in respect of the investigation of terrorist offences and the actions that may be taken against terrorist suspects; it increases police powers in respect of port and border controls, and it creates a range of offences connected with acts of terrorism both at home and overseas. The Act also continues additional emergency powers in Northern Ireland at least for five years.

18.5.2 Use of force

The Act significantly increases police powers in a number of terrorist contexts and it is made clear that these powers are additional to the other common law or statutory powers the police may have. A terrorist investigation is likely to be a combination of 'ordinary' and Terrorism Act powers. Reasonable force can be used, subject, of course, to the general limits of the Human Rights Act 1998, Schedule 1, Articles 2 and 3.[18] Article 3 cannot be subject to a general derogation under Article 15 but Article 2 can be derogated from in respect of 'deaths resulting from lawful acts of war'. It is unlikely that 'the war' against terrorism meets this definition.

18.5.3 Proof and reverse onus offences

The Terrorism Act 2000 creates a number of new offences, some involving long imprisonment. Proof of terrorist intentions can be hard to establish and the government, despite the unhappy record of wrongful convictions for terrorist offences in the 1970s, has been tempted to lessen the burden of proof in certain circumstances. Offences under the Terrorism Act 2000 will have to be proved by the prosecution with evidence establishing the case beyond a reasonable

---

[18] See Chapter 4.

doubt. However, for some offences, the law allows assumptions to be made by the court (at its discretion) with a burden then passing to the defendant to prove that this assumption is false. An example is that the possession of an article for terrorist purposes can be assumed if it is proved that the article was on premises at the same time as the accused.[19] Other offences allow a defence to the effect that an otherwise criminal state of affairs (e.g. collecting information of use to terrorists) is open to an innocent or reasonable explanation. Again, proof is for the defence. Putting the burden, or onus, of displacing a presumption or proving a defence is known as a 'reverse onus' defence.

Reverse onus provisions raise an issue of compatibility with the presumption of innocence expressed in Article 6(2) ECHR. In *R v DPP ex parte Kebilene* (1999),[20] in which the House of Lords disagreed with the Court of Appeal, it was held that such reverse onus provisions are unlikely to violate Article 6 so long as the overall burden of proof remains with the prosecution. The Strasbourg jurisprudence seems to support this position.[21]

Section 118 of the Terrorism Act 2000 aims to give effect to the Convention position. Where it applies, a defendant need only to introduce evidence which is 'sufficient to raise an issue' relevant to the matters in terms of which an assumption of guilt may be displaced or a defence established. Once the issue is raised the court must take the defence as being made out and acquit. The burden then shifts back to the prosecution to disprove, beyond a reasonable doubt, the evidence by which the issue was raised. In this way, it is likely to be argued, it can be said that the overall burden of proof remains with the prosecution and Article 6(2) not violated.

18.6 Proscription

Prior to the Terrorism Act 2000 there had been no general power to ban political organisations. The Public Order Act 1936, enacted in the context of the rise of the British Union of Fascists in the early 1930s,[22] creates general offences which are still in force. Section 1 relates to the wearing of political uniforms in public places[23] and section 2 to the organisation, management, training or equipping of political groupings whose purposes are either the usurpation of the functions of the armed forces or police or to display physical force in the promotion of a political object. The Act has not been widely used though there have been successful prosecutions against Spearhead, a neo-Nazi group, and the Free Wales Army.[24]

---

[19] Terrorism Act 2000, s. 57.

[20] [1999] 4 All ER 801 HL. See also *R v Benjafield* (2000) *The Times*, 28 December.

[21] See in particular *AP v Switzerland* (1998) 26 EHRR 541 and *Salabiaku v France* (1991) 13 EHRR 379, paragraph 28.

[22] See Ewing, K.D and Gearty, C. (2000) *The Struggle for Civil Liberties*. Oxford: Oxford University Press, ch. 6.

[23] The Act was applied to Irish republicans in *O'Moran and others v Director of Public Prosecutions* [1975] QB 864.

[24] See cases cited by Bailey, S.H., Harris, D.J. and Jones, B.L. (1995) *Civil Liberties Cases and Materials*, 4th edn. London: Butterworths, p. 181.

Proscription – banning – was introduced in the context of Northern Ireland and is continued by the Terrorism Act 2000. There is a debate about the effectiveness of the power to proscribe. The arguments ultimately accepted by the government are that, through proscription, it is easier to prove various terrorist offences and restrict fund-raising activities. Proscription also symbolises social abhorrence of terrorist activity and can deter groups and, by driving them underground, make it harder for them to promote themselves. It is nevertheless accepted that proscription may have little direct impact on the level of violence since banned groups may simply reconstitute themselves under a different name.[25] In Northern Ireland there have been very few prosecutions for proscription offences.

Section 3 of the Terrorism Act 2000 gives powers to the Secretary of State to proscribe terrorist organisations which he or she believes to be 'concerned in' terrorism. 'Concerned in' is a very broad concept made all the broader by the wide definition of terrorism mentioned above.

> . . . an organisation is concerned in terrorism if it –
>   (a)   commits or participates in acts of terrorism,
>   (b)   prepares for terrorism,
>   (c)   promotes or encourages terrorism, or
>   (d)   is otherwise concerned in terrorism.

'Otherwise concerned in terrorism' is obviously question-begging. The phrase could cover organisations which support a cause but which dissent from or have a morally complex attitude towards the terrorist activities of others. It is such a vague and uncertain phrase that it makes the circumstances in which a ban might be considered unforeseeable and hence, perhaps, incompatible with the 'legality' provisions in the Convention rights, including Article 11, discussed below.

Schedule 2 of the Act identifies 14 organisations involved in Northern Ireland politics which were and remain proscribed. The Secretary of State may add to or remove organisations from the list. In March 2000 the Home Secretary added a further 21 organisations. These were all foreign organisations involved in Greek, Middle East, Sri Lankan, Basque, Kashmiri and Turkish politics. They included Al-Qa'ida and other expressedly Islamic groups.[26] A further four Islamic groups were added in November 2002.

Article 11 and Article 17 offer ample justification for the Court of Human Rights to uphold bans on political parties and organisations which use violence or which, in power, would introduce widespread and systematic violation of Convention Rights and Freedoms. Restrictions must meet the Convention test for legality and be 'necessary in a democratic society' in the sense of being proportionate means of protecting public safety, or national security, the 'the rights and freedoms of others' or any other purpose listed in Article 11(2).

---

[25] Chapter 4, Consultation Document. See also Lord Jellicoe's review of the Prevention of Terrorism Act 1983 for similar points.

[26] Terrorism Act 2000 (Proscribed Organisations) (Amendment) Order 2001 (Draft) (prepared 15 March 2001): for example, Egyptian Islamic Jihad, Al-Gama'at al-Islamiya, Armed Islamic Group, Palestinian Islamic Jihad-Shaqiqi, Islamic Army of Aden.

The Convention offers more protection to an organisation which pursues a radical agenda in a climate of violence without being a direct advocate or perpetrator of the violence. The Convention, as interpreted by the Court, gives a very high weighting to politically inspired speech and action in the way it interprets freedom of expression and association. States must show they are responding to genuine threats to the democratic conduct of politics.

> The Communist Party of Turkey was dissolved by state action before it was able to start acting as an association. In particular support for separatism and other values held to be inconsistent with the Turkish constitution was alleged against the party.
>   HELD (ECHR): there was a violation of Article 11. The Communist Party had been banned because of its name and programme not its actions and the ban was disproportionate to the aim pursued.
>   *United Communist Party of Turkey and others* v *Turkey* (1998) 26 EHRR 121

The Court recognised that states could take action to protect major institutions of the state. It would not concede, however, that this removed the protection of Article 11 from political parties which challenged the existing constitutional structure, even when doing so, as in the Turkish case, against a background of violence.[27] The case contains a strong affirmation of pluralism (which is necessary to democracy and hence to the protection of human rights). It follows that the restrictions in Article 11(2) must be strictly interpreted. The case speaks of the need to compromise between protecting constitutional institutions on the one hand and pluralism, but it is hard to read the case other than making it very difficult for a state to interfere with the Article 11(1) freedoms of parties seeking constitutional change. Nothing in the judgment requires a state to tolerate organisations which directly use violence and, under Article 17, groups that might use their political freedom to undermine the rights and freedoms of others cannot protect that freedom through the Court.[28] The banning of the Republican Clubs in the early 1970s might, without a direct link to violence, now be incompatible with Convention rights.[29]

18.6.1 Deproscription

Prior to the Terrorism Act 2000 a political organisation could only challenge proscription by judicial review and the courts were unlikely to find against a reasoned decision of the Secretary of State.[30] The Terrorism Act provides for a process for 'deproscription'. A proscribed organisation can apply to the Secretary of State and, if that is turned down, it can appeal to a body, the Proscribed Organisations Appeal Commission, which the Act creates.[31] The Commission may order the organisation to be removed from the list of proscribed organisations. The Commission must apply ordinary judicial review principles or, under rules made by the Secretary of State, it can deal

---

[27] See also *Sidiropoulos and others* v *Greece* (1998) Ap. 57/1997/841/1047.
[28] *KPD* v *Federal Republic of Germany* (1957) Ap. 250/57; 1 Yearbook 222 – but no longer good law?
[29] *McEldowney* v *Forde* [1971] AC 632.
[30] See the Republican Clubs case: *McEldowney* v *Forde* [1971] AC 632.
[31] Sections 4–9, Terrorism Act 2000.

with a direct complaint under the Human Rights Act 1998. In either case the Commission will have to decide on the purpose and the proportionality[32] of the Secretary of State's decision.

The procedure before the Commission is in Schedule 3 of the Act. The Commission is expressly permitted to use material intercepted by telephone tapping and other means. Such material must not be disclosed to the proscribed organisation, a prohibition that may put the proscribed organisation at a disadvantage and deny it 'equality of arms' under Article 6 of the Convention, if it applies.[33] A further question is whether the Commission is sufficiently independent of the executive to meet the requirements of Article 6 since its officers are appointed by the Lord Chancellor.[34]

Commission decisions are subject to appeal to the Court of Appeal by any party, including the Secretary of State.[35] An appeal is confined to questions of law and requires the permission of the Commission or the Court.

18.6.2 Offences involving proscribed organisations

A range of offences are created by the Terrorism Act 2000, sections 11–13 which apply only in respect of proscribed organisations. They continue offences found in the replaced prevention of terrorism legislation. It is, first, an offence to belong to or profess to belong to a proscribed organisation; second, it is an offence to invite support for a proscribed organisation generally or by specific activities such as organising or addressing meetings, and, third (a less serious matter), it is an offence to wear clothing or display articles 'in such a way or in such circumstances as to arouse reasonable suspicion that he is a member or supporter of a proscribed organisation'.

These offences are widely drawn. For example, the point of addressing a meeting in support of a proscribed organisation may have been to advance the goals of the organisation without, necessarily, endorsing the violent means that the organisation is associated with. Yet such an address could be an offence under section 12. The organiser of a private meeting has a reverse onus defence if he or she can prove that there was no reasonable cause to believe that a speech given at the meeting would be in support of a proscribed organisation. Section 118 applies and so the burden on the organiser is to raise an issue about what it was reasonable to believe about the content of the speeches.

These offences clearly involve the right of freedom of association and freedom of expression under Articles 11(1) and 10(1) of the scheduled Convention rights. They are, however, likely to be acceptable restrictions under the second paragraph of those Articles in terms of the legitimacy of their purpose. They will, therefore, be compatible with the Convention so long as a court accepts, in any particular case, that there has been a proportionate response to a pressing social need. 'Belonging to' a proscribed organisation

---

[32] *R v Secretary of State for the Home Department ex parte Daly* [2001] UKHL 26; [2001] 3 All ER 433.

[33] Since a number of offences turn on whether an organisation is proscribed, the Commission can be taken to be involved in the 'determination of . . . any criminal charge, and hence bound by Article 6.

[34] On this and other procedural disadvantages see Fenwick, *op. cit.*, pp. 94–5.

[35] Section 6, Terrorism Act 2000.

may be too imprecise a term for a person to foresee what is or is not a prohibited relationship. If so, the offence is vulnerable to the 'prescribed by law' provision in Article 11(2).

18.7 Terrorist property

A range of provisions in anti-terrorism legislation are concerned to starve terrorist organisations of their financial and other resources. The Terrorism Act 2000, Part III, enhanced by the Anti-terrorism, Crime and Security Act 2001, maintains and extends earlier provisions concerned with 'terrorist property': property likely to be used for terrorist activity or which is the proceeds of terrorist activity. It includes but is not confined to the property of proscribed organisations. The provisions make criminal offences of various financial transactions which, without the terrorist link, would be perfectly lawful. The offences relate to fund-raising activities, using property for terrorist purposes, entering into funding arrangements through which money becomes available for terrorist purposes and money laundering and other forms of the legal concealment of property.[36] There are also powers in the Terrorism Act 2000 which permit the courts to order the forfeiture of money or other property which is implicated in the offences relating to terrorist property mentioned above. Police and customs have a power to seize cash which, they suspect, is to be used for terrorist activities or by a proscribed terrorist organisation or is the result of terrorist activities. Seizure can be ordered independently of any prosecution for terrorist offences. Permanent forfeiture can be ordered by magistrates on application by the authorities. The Anti-terrorism, Crime and Security Act 2001 also introduces a 'freezing order'.[37] This can be made by the Treasury and freezes the assets of persons and governments outside the United Kingdom who, the Treasury believe, are acting to the economic detriment of the United Kingdom or who are threatening life and property. This power is not confined to terrorism.

Not all of these provision require proof that an offence, let alone a terrorist offence, has been committed. The orders do not require proof of a terrorist intention to a criminal law standard. There is a danger that property of those uninvolved in terrorism may be affected (though such a person can be heard by magistrates in respect of forfeiture). Convention rights, such as the right to peaceful enjoyment of possessions under Protocol 1, Article 1 and, in respect of the procedures, Article 6 may be in issue though Strasbourg case law suggests the authorities may have considerable freedom.[38]

18.8 Terrorist offences

The Terrorism Act 2000 creates a range of new terrorist offences taken over from Northern Ireland emergency legislation and applied generally to the United Kingdom.

---

[36] Sections 14 (definition of terrorist property) and 15–18 (the offences), Terrorism Act 2000.
[37] Part II.
[38] See *AGOSI* v *United Kingdom* (1987) 9 EHRR 1 and *Air Canada* v *United Kingdom* (1995) 20 EHRR 150.

Giving or receiving weapons training, such as in the use of firearms or explosives, is an offence under section 54. The definition of the offence makes no reference to terrorism and so, on its face, the offence can be committed by those using weapons and explosives for policing or commercial purposes. Relief for those involved in such legitimate forms of training is found in section 54(5) which makes it a defence for a person to prove that their involvement was wholly for non-terrorist purposes. Section 118 applies, and so such a defendant is merely required to raise the issue of legitimate training leaving the burden of proving a terrorist purpose beyond a reasonable doubt to the prosecution. These offences may place a burden of care on anyone offering weapons or explosives training to satisfy themselves as to the legitimate motives of those they offer the training to. The criminalisation of legitimate activities subject to a defence is, to say the least, an odd approach to this matter.

Directing a terrorist organisation, at any level, is an offence under section 56. The organisations to which this section applies are not confined to proscribed organisations. They can include any bodies which undertake terrorist activities as defined by section 1 of the Act. Section 121 defines 'acts' as including omissions, so directors of organisations which do nothing about members who may be planning terrorism could, perhaps, be vulnerable to this offence.

Possession of an article in circumstances which give rise to a reasonable suspicion of a connection with terrorism is an offence under section 57. It takes over section 16A of the Prevention of Terrorism Act 1989.[39] If the prosecution can prove that the circumstances in which an article was possessed give rise to a reasonable suspicion of a connection with terrorism it is open to the defendant to prove that this suspicion in not well founded. Section 118 applies and so the defendant need only raise an issue related to the defence which the court must accept unless the prosecution can disprove it beyond a reasonable doubt. Section 57(3) allows the court to assume that the defendant was in possession of the article if it was on premises at the same time as the accused or if he was the occupier or a habitual user of the premises. This assumption can be set aside if the accused can prove that he or she did not know the article was on the premises or that they had no control over the article. Again section 118 expressly applies and so the burden of proof shifts back to the prosecution if the defendant can produce sufficient evidence to raise an issue on which the defence can be founded. The circumstances in which the court may make this assumption need to be clarified in case law. Arguably, the jury should be directed to the effect that, even if the defendant is unable to prove the innocence of his or her possession of the article, there must still be sufficient evidence for a conviction beyond a reasonable doubt.[40]

18.9 International terrorism

The international nature of the 'terrorist threat' is apparent from the attacks of 11 September and the bombings in Bali. It was apparent at the time of the

---

[39] Discussed *R v DPP ex parte Kebilene* [1999] 4 All ER 801 HL.
[40] *R v Killen* [1974] NI 220.

enactment of the Terrorism Act 2000 and fully recognised in the consultation paper from which the Act stemmed.

18.9.1 Border controls

The Terrorism Act 2000 increases port and border controls. These include wide powers for designated officials to stop, detain and question anyone entering the United Kingdom in order to discover whether they are connected with terrorism.[41] Detention for reasonable suspicion that an offence has been committed or that it is necessary to prevent the commission of an offence or that it is necessary to prevent an unauthorised entry into the country are, if proportionate, compatible with Article 5 ECHR. An objective basis for the suspicion is necessary. In *R (Saadi and others) ex parte Secretary of State for the Home Department*[42] the Court of Appeal took a deferential attitude towards government national security assessments, and this is likely to assist customs and police in any human rights challenge.

18.9.2 Inciting terrorism overseas

An offence of inciting acts of terrorism overseas is created by section 59 of the Terrorism Act 2000.[43] The essence of the offence is the incitement of an act overseas which is within the definition of terrorism in section 1 of the Act and also one of the serious offences, such as murder, listed in the section. The meaning of incitement under the Act is unclear. It will require some degree of direct and proximate encouragement of violence to be committed overseas. The distinction between the legitimate support for a cause and an incitement to violence will need to be worked out. The offence can be committed by citizens or aliens and it can be recalled that Article 16 ECHR, a 'convention right' under the Human Rights Act 1998, removes the application of Articles 10, 11 and 14 from restrictions on the political activities of aliens. The section may criminalise those who actively support insurrection and civil war in other countries where the conditions in those other countries justify the war or insurrection. The section makes no discrimination between just and unjust causes for political violence and it is hard to imagine that it could without involving British judges in impossible evaluations. The consent of the DPP is required for a prosecution and it is likely that, through this, government views of the just and the unjust cause will be significant.[44] If the definition of terrorism required war crimes or attacks on civilians, attacks aimed at undermining the civil institutions of a reasonable democracy, this problem would be lessened.

---

[41] The legal basis is in Schedule 7 and Schedule 8 identifies various rights and the circumstances in which they may be postponed.

[42] [2001] EWCA Civ 670; [2001] 4 All ER 961.

[43] Similar offences apply, with necessary changes, in respect of Scotland and Northern Ireland.

[44] The obvious example, at the time of writing, is the 'Northern Alliance' in Afghanistan which, it seems, is being incited to attack the Taliban by special forces from the UK. Crown servants are exempted from liability under the Act.

18.9.3 Deportation

The Home Secretary may deport someone, who is not a citizen, on the grounds that their presence in the United Kingdom is not conducive to the public good.[45] This can clearly extend to deportations to protect national security and against terrorism. 'Ordinary' deportations are subject to a (circumscribed) right of appeal to the Immigration Appeal Tribunal which operates on normal procedures. Deportations, or other immigration action, on public good grounds cannot be appealed to a tribunal but may be taken to the Special Immigration Appeals Commission (SIAC) established under the Special Immigration Appeals Commission Act 1997. The Commission has a closed procedure with only limited rights of the defence though, in human rights terms, it has a surer basis than the informal 'three wise men' procedure it replaces.[46] The grounds of appeal include not only that the decision was made unlawfully but also that 'the discretion should have been exercised different-ly'.[47] A further appeal to the Court of Appeal is possible, including by the Secretary of State. The extent to which SIAC is able to be an effective bulwark against possibly oppressive actions by the Home Secretary has, perhaps, been limited by *Secretary of State for the Home Department* v *Rehman*[48] It was accepted that the Home Secretary could act on a wide range of information available to him, much of it inadmissible in court, and that it was not necessary for there to be a direct and immediate threat to the safety of the United Kingdom. The House of Lords accepted a deferential attitude to the executive as necessary not only because the executive has access to information but also, for Lord Hoffman, in order to ensure democratic accountability in respect of the difficult, political decisions that will have to be made. Critics will point out that such deference can involve the withdrawal of intense judicial scrutiny precisely in those times when it is most needed.

18.9.4 Detention without trial

The Anti-terrorism, Crime and Security Act 2001 permits the detention without trial of non-citizens, mainly when they would otherwise be subject to deportation on national security grounds.

In *Chahal* v *United Kingdom*[49] the Court of Human Rights confirmed that it violates Article 3 ECHR to deport a person to a country in which they might suffer torture or inhuman or degrading treatment or punishment even though the country to which they are deported is not a signatory of the ECHR. The deportation of terrorist suspects is likely in many cases to be incompatible with Convention rights. The question for the executive is what should be done with such people. The Anti-terrorism, Crime and Security Act 2001, Part IV, permits the Secretary of State to issue a certificate to the effect that a person's presence

---

[45] Immigration Act 1971, s. 3(5)(a) (as amended). There are, of course, other grounds for deportation.
[46] Which was held to be incompatible with Article 13 ECHR, the right to a remedy, *Chahal* v *United Kingdom* (1997) 23 EHRR 413.
[47] Section 4, Special Immigration Appeal Commission Act 1997.
[48] [2001] UKHL 47; [2002] 1 All ER 122.
[49] (1997) 23 EHRR 413.

in the United Kingdom is a risk to national security and that the person is a terrorist, as defined by the Terrorism Act 2000. If the person cannot be deported because of a 'point of law relating to an international agreement' (i.e. because they might suffer torture etc.) or because of a 'practical consideration' (examples given in Parliament were that travel documents could not be obtained) then, under section 23 of the 2001 Act, the person can be detained indefinitely pending deportation. The person may leave voluntarily.

This legislation is highly controversial. There is a right of appeal to SIAC, given High Court powers by the Act. It may cancel the Secretary of State's certificate. The Commission is prepared to assert its independence and, in its first case, held that the power to detain without trial was fundamentally flawed: by applying only to foreign nationals and not to British citizens who might be believed to be equally dangerous, the legislation related to Article 5 ECHR in a discriminatory way which was incompatible with Article 14 ECHR.[50] The SIAC position was overruled by the Court of Appeal which agreed with the government that there was an objective basis for treating foreigners differently.[51] Despite the outcome of particular cases, appeal to SIAC remains unsatisfactory from the point of view of the detainee since the rights of the defence are severely curtailed and detainees are not able to know and attempt to answer for themselves the evidence alleged against them.

Detention without trial is obnoxious. The government does not believe that the detentions can be brought within Article 5(1)(f) (which permits detention of a person 'against whom action is being taken with a view to deportation . . .') and has derogated from this Convention right, as it may seek to do under Article 15 ECHR. The condition for proper derogation under the Convention is that there is a state of 'war or other public emergency threatening the life of the nation'. The Court of Appeal has held that SIAC is entitled to conclude that the threat from extreme Islamic, anti-western terrorism is such a public emergency.[52] The Court of Human Rights gives a wide margin of appreciation to national governments on the assessment of such threats, though the outcome of a challenge is hard to predict. In *Brannigan and McBride* v *United Kingdom* (1993)[53] the Northern Ireland situation was considered a sufficient 'public emergency' to justify derogation.

There is a dilemma here. The government could deport the suspects to a safe country where their Article 3 rights would not be compromised. Such countries may be reluctant to accept them; furthermore, the United Kingdom government can reasonably consider it would be avoiding its responsibilities if it deported someone to a country so that they can continue there with what the government in the United Kingdom believes to be terrorist activities. The alternative, canvassed by critics,[54] is a prosecution for an offence under the

---

[50] *A and others* v *Secretary of State for the Home Department* (2002) (SIAC).
[51] *A and others* v *Secretary of State for the Home Department* [2002] EWCA Civ 1502; *The Times*, 29 October.
[52] *A and others* v *Secretary of State for the Home Department* [2002] EWCA Civ 1502; *The Times*, 29 October.
[53] (1993) 17 EHRR 539. See *Lawless* v *Ireland* (1961) 1 EHRR 15.
[54] For example, Tomkins, A. (2002) 'Legislating against terror: The Anti-terrorism, Crime and Security Act 2001', *Public Law* 205 (Summer).

Terrorism Act 2000 including for inciting terrorism under section 59. This is attractive, but has two drawbacks. First, a prosecution requires a higher standard of proof than that required for deportation; second, it may be that the information on which the Secretary of State has formed his or her judgment has been gained from surveillance activities and some of it is not admissible in court or, even if admissible, would compromise intelligence-gathering. On the other hand, people who may be innocent of any connection with terrorism are detained indefinitely in conditions which make it very difficult for them to establish their innocence. These provisions will need to be renewed after 15 months.

18.10 The investigation of terrorist offences

Parts IV and V of the Terrorism Act 2000 increase the powers of the police over the investigation of terrorist offences. These powers are over and above police officers' ordinary powers in the Police and Criminal Evidence Act 1984.[55]

Part IV identifies major police powers which are triggered in respect of a 'terrorist investigation'. This term is defined by section 32.

Terrorist investigation
32 In this Act 'terrorist investigation' means an investigation of –
(a)   the commission, preparation or instigation of acts of terrorism,
(b)   an act which appears to have been done for the purposes of terrorism,
(c)   the resources of a proscribed organisation,
(d)   the possibility of making an order under section 3(3) [a proscription order] or
(e)   the commission, preparation or instigation of an offence under this Act.

This wide definition can trigger some very significant police powers. Terrorist acts are likely to involve serious crimes, but an act of terrorism, as such, is not a crime. The scope of a terrorist investigation is likely to be wider, less confined by the definition of any particular crime, than an ordinary criminal investigation. Section 32(b), for example, requires only the appearance of a terrorist act. The section makes no reference to the degree of evidence necessary to ground such an appearance or whether it is an objective matter or simply based on the good faith judgment of a police officer. Sections 32(a) and (e) refer to the 'commission, preparation or instigation' of terrorist acts or offences. 'Preparation' and, perhaps, 'instigation' clearly go beyond 'incitement', which is the normal basis for criminal liability and will, therefore, permit significant powers of investigation to be used against those whose actions may be too remote to justify criminal liability.[56] The width and subjective nature of its definition means that a police claim that a terrorist investigation is going on is likely to be hard to challenge in the courts, though, as the act of public officials, the exercise of any power must be proportionate in the circumstances.

---

[55] See Chapters 4–6.
[56] Of course many of the offences created by the Act, such as those connected with terrorist property or those dealing with training and direction of terrorism, are, clearly, capable of being preparatory to acts of terrorism.

18.10.1 Cordon: restricting access and stop and search

A 'terrorist investigation' authorises considerable police powers which can be used in respect of the public at large as well as those suspected of terrorism.

Sections 33–6, and section 37, allow the police to cordon off an area and exercise certain powers within it.[57] This can be done if a senior police officer, or in an emergency any police officer, considers it 'expedient for the purposes of a terrorist investigation'. A bomb scare is the obvious situation when the power might be used but it is by no means confined to that. A cordon can, with renewals, last for 28 days. The power is solely within the discretion of the police and does not require judicial supervision. In so far as Convention rights are in issue, such as the right to a home under Article 8 or the use of property under Article 1 of the First Protocol, the lack of judicial supervision may be a problem if the Convention test of legality is not met.

The cordon permits the police to order people and drivers to leave an area and to restrict access to it by pedestrians and vehicles. Failure to comply with such directions is a summary offence. Under Schedule 5, the declaration of a cordon can also trigger extensive powers of entry, search of premises, the seizure of items and the superficial search of persons.[58] If there is a cordon, the normal requirement for judicial supervision through the process of applying for a warrant is suspended. The powers are based on a police judgment that such powers are 'expedient' for a terrorist investigation. Nothing in the Act prevents the designation of an area subject to cordon in order to undertake the entry, search and seizure power.

18.10.2 Stop and search

Even in the absence of a cordon, the police have a power to stop and search drivers and pedestrians in order to look for 'articles connected with terrorism'. This power mirrors section 60 of the Criminal Justice and Public Order Act 1994. It is based on the designation of an area by a senior police officer within which it is then permissible to stop and search anyone in the area without there needing to be (as there must be under Part I of PACE 1984) any grounds of suspicion, particularly against the individuals being searched. The authorisation can last for up to 28 days.[59] There is no judicial supervision of the power although the Home Secretary must be informed of and confirm the authorisation. The procedures in Part I PACE 1984 and Code A must be followed in the way the search is conducted. The police officer designating the area must believe the stop and search power is 'expedient for the prevention of acts of terrorism'. A judgment of 'expediency' is hard to challenge. However, it also may lack sufficient precision to enable a person to foresee when the stop and search power might be used. If so the exercise of the power may be inconsistent with the legality provisions of Article 5 ECHR.

---

[57] Sections 48–52 of the Terrorism Act 2000 allow the police to prohibit car parking in certain areas if this is considered expedient to prevent terrorism. The declaration of a cordon is not required.

[58] Terrorism Act 2000, Schedule 5, paragraph 3.

[59] Compare the 24 hours under s. 60, Criminal Justice and Public Order Act 1994.

18.10.3 Entry, search and seizure

Under section 37 and Schedule 5 of the Terrorism Act 2000, a 'terrorist investigation' authorises the police to seek a warrant, from a magistrate, to enter and search premises for material that will be of substantial value to a 'terrorist investigation' and seize it in order to prevent it being 'concealed, lost, damaged, altered or destroyed'. A 'terrorist investigation' does not require evidence of a specific offence, so that, once a terrorist context is established, a warrant should be easy to obtain. There must be a reasonable belief (by the constable applying) and a satisfaction (by the magistrate) that the material sought will be of substantial value to a terrorist investigation and that there are reasonable grounds for believing the material is on the premises. Where residential premises are to be entered the warrant must be 'necessary' in all the circumstances. It is hard to imagine a search not being necessary if there is a well founded suspicion that matters of substantial value to a terrorist investigation will be found. There is, at least, some form of judicial supervision of the exercise of these powers; they are not solely dependent on police discretion. In times of great emergency, however, the Act permits that judicial supervision can be dispensed with.

Schedule 5 authorises the police to apply to a circuit judge for an order requiring the production of excluded or special procedure material, but not legally privileged material.[60] The former two include journalistic material and so are of particular interest in a civil liberties context. The power is similar to that in the Police and Criminal Evidence Act 1984, discussed in Chapter 6. The judge has discretion to make the order if, first, the material to which the order relates is sought for the purposes of a terrorist investigation and is likely to be of substantial value to that investigation, and, second, it is in the public interest that the order should be made. As under PACE 1984, the focus of the public interest test is less on whether the grounds for an order are made out and more on whether, given this, the judge should exercise his or her discretion to make the order. It is on that point that arguments about freedom of the press in terrorist circumstances can be made.[61] The need for a free and vigorous press is, it is suggested, as strong as ever even in respect of terrorism and a terrorist context should not be used to inhibit proper investigation of alleged wrongdoing. The circumstances in *DPP* v *Channel 4 Television Co. and another*,[62] where the broadcaster was eventually fined for being in breach of a production order, was an investigation into allegations of collusions between the police in Northern Ireland and protestant paramilitary gangs.

There is a power, with no equivalent in PACE 1984, to require an explanation to be given in respect of material produced under a warrant or a production order.[63] Legally privileged material is excluded. There is a danger here that a person can be compelled to incriminate themselves in breach of both Article 6 ECHR and the common law. The explanation, however, cannot be used as evidence in court for any offence, including a terrorist offence. It is

---

[60] See Chapter 6 for the definitions of these terms.
[61] *R* v *Central Criminal Court ex parte Bright* [2001] 2 All ER 244 – see Chapter 6.
[62] [1993] 2 All ER 517.
[63] Schedule 5, paragraphs 13–14.

admissible only as evidence of the specific offence of making a misleading explanation. Journalists have no special protection from these requirements which, again, could have an inhibiting impact on the media.

18.10.4 Obtaining customer information

Section 38 brings Schedule 6 into effect. The police may apply to a judge for an order requiring financial institutions to provide general information about their customers' accounts. These are accounts relevant to a terrorist investigation. The Anti-terrorism Crime and Security Act 2001 introduces new monitoring procedures. There is no power under Schedule 6 to inspect the accounts which, without the bank's consent, would require a production order under Schedule 5.

18.11 Suspected terrorists

The powers discussed in the previous section can be exercised because to do so is expedient, or of substantial value to, a terrorist investigation. There is no need for reasonable suspicion of crime or terrorism against the persons involved. Where, however, a person is suspected on reasonable grounds of involvement in terrorism, the Terrorism Act 2000 has significantly increased the powers of the police to arrest and detain persons and search premises over those they have in respect of non-terrorist crime under PACE 1984.

Section 40 defines a 'terrorist' for the purposes of the Act.

Terrorist: interpretation

40 (1) In this Part 'terrorist' means a person who –
    (a) has committed an offence under any of sections 11, 12, 15 to 18, 54 and 56 to 63, or
    (b) is or has been concerned in the commission, preparation or instigation of acts of terrorism.
  (2) The reference in subsection (1)(b) to a person who has been concerned in the commission, preparation or instigation of acts of terrorism includes a reference to a person who has been, whether before or after the passing of this Act, concerned in the commission, preparation or instigation of acts of terrorism within the meaning given by section 1.

This definition includes most of the offences created by the Terrorism Act 2000 (involving proscribed organisations, terrorist property, terrorist offences, inciting terrorism overseas, etc.). It extends to actions of commission, preparation and instigation of terrorism even though these may be outside the normal relationship of proximity required for the offences of conspiracy or incitement. It operates retrospectively in that persons can be treated as terrorists in respects of actions done before the Act came into force. It is important to note, therefore, that being a terrorist or performing a terrorist act is not in itself a criminal offence. If it were, the offence would be vulnerable under ECHR not only because the various uncertainties of the definition might be inconsistent with the legality principle but also because subsection 2 raises an issue under

Article 7 ECHR which prohibits retrospective offences for other than the most heinous and uncivilised acts.

18.11.1 Arrest and detention

Section 41 and Schedule 8
The definition of a 'terrorist' triggers police powers of arrest, detention, questioning and search. Section 41 continues powers that were in the Prevention of Terrorism Act 1989 and applies them throughout the United Kingdom. The section permits arrest without a warrant of a person against whom there is reasonable suspicion that he or she is a terrorist. The arrest can be to obtain information about matters of which the person is believed to have knowledge. The detention under section 41 is for a maximum of 48 hours although it can be extended up to seven days.

The arrest of a person under section 41 brings the rights and duties found in schedule 8 of the Act into effect. The schedule deals with matters such as place of detention, tape recording and videoing of interviews, fingerprinting and so on.[64] These are complex powers which, as regards fingerprinting, have been enhanced under the Anti-terrorism, Crime and Security Act 2001.

Schedule 8 stipulates the rights enjoyed by a person detained under section 41. As under PACE 1984, detainees have the right to have a named person informed, and a right to consult a solicitor. As under PACE 1984, a senior police officer may authorise a postponement in the exercise of either of these rights. The delay can be for up to 48 hours. Where, under PACE 1984, postponement is confined to serious arrestable offences, under the Terrorism Act 2000, the grounds can include a reasonable belief that the immediate exercise of the right would interfere in various ways with the investigation or prevention of the commission, preparation or instigation of acts of terrorism. Police also have the power to insist that any consultation with a solicitor must be in the presence of the police. This implies the belief that, through contact with legal advisors, information of use to terrorists can sometimes be communicated.

As with non-terrorist crime there is a review procedure for persons detained under section 41 of the Terrorism Act 2000. Its purpose is to ensure that the grounds for detention continue to exist and it should be conducted by an officer independent of the investigation. A detained person has the right, in person or by a solicitor, to make representations to the review officer.

Under PACE 1984, detention prior to charge can be for a maximum of four days, and any period after 36 hours must be authorised by a magistrate. Under the Terrorism Act 2000 the maximum period is seven days. Previous anti-terrorist legislation allowed an extended period of detention to be authorised by the Secretary of State. In *Brogan* v *United Kingdom*[65] the Court of Human Rights held that this violated Article 5(1)(c) ECHR, the requirement that a detained person must be brought 'promptly' before a 'competent legal authority' who has the power to order release. Schedule 8 of the Terrorism Act

---

[64] Terrorism Act 2000, Schedule 8, paragraphs 1 (place of detention), 2 (identity), 3 and 4 (audio and video recording), 10–14 (fingerprints and samples).
[65] (1988) 11 EHRR 117.

2000 permits police detention for up to 48 hours. Any period beyond, to the maximum of seven days, needs the authorisation of, in England and Wales, a district judge. The grounds for an extension are that the judicial authority is satisfied further detention is necessary to obtain or preserve relevant evidence, that the detained person is a terrorist as defined by section 40 and that the investigation is being conducted diligently.[66] The detainee or his or her representative may be excluded from any hearing, and the court may order that some or all of the information on which the application is based be similarly withheld.[67] The protection for the detainee lies in Code C, made under the Police and Criminal Evidence Act 1984, which applies to Terrorism Act detainees. The Code has provisions for custody records, discretionary visits, interviews, etc.

Convention rights
These provisions raise a number of questions regarding compatibility with Article 5 ECHR, scheduled under the Human Rights Act 1998.

The first concerns the purpose of detention. Under Article 5(1)(c) a person can be detained '. . . on reasonable suspicion of having committed an offence or when it is reasonably considered necessary to prevent his committing an offence . . .' Detention under section 41 and Schedule 8 of the Terrorism Act 2000 is authorised not only of those suspected of terrorist offences but also, under section 40(1)(b), of persons suspected of being concerned in the 'commission, preparation or instigation of acts of terrorism' and this, by no means, is confined to criminal offences. However, in *Brogan* v *United Kingdom* (1988)[68] (a terrorism case) and *Steel and others* v *United Kingdom* (1998)[69] (involving breach of the peace) the Court adopts an autonomous, Convention-specific meaning to the word 'offence'. In *Brogan* the Court found that the acts connoted by the word 'terrorism' were 'well in keeping with the [Convention] idea of an offence'.[70] In *Steel* the Court stressed the need for precision in defining the grounds for arrest and detention and it is certainly arguable the Terrorism Act's definitions of terrorist purposes and actions meet the rather lose Convention criteria of precision. There is, however, room for doubt. The facts in *Brogan* v *United Kingdom*, which were material for the Court, were that the detainees, though arrested on suspicion of terrorism, were in fact immediately questioned for specific offences. This would not necessarily be the case in respect of persons arrested under section 40(1)(b) of the Terrorism Act 2000.

The difficulty of seeking compatibility with Article 5 is exacerbated by the requirement that, for a detention on suspicion of an offence to be compatible with Article 5(1)(c), it must have as its purpose the bringing of a person before the court on a charge. A detention under section 41which was intended merely to obtain information from a person who was not believed to have committed an offence might not be compatible with the Convention.

---

[66] Terrorism Act 2000, Schedule 8, paragraph 32.
[67] Terrorism Act 2000, Schedule 8, paragraph 34.
[68] (1988) 11 EHRR 117.
[69] (1998) 28 EHRR 603.
[70] *Ireland* v *United Kingdom* (1979–80) 2 EHRR 25, paragraph 196, quoted in *Brogan* v *United Kingdom* (1988) 11 EHRR 117, paragraph 51.

A second area of difficulty deals with the right to a fair trial under Article 6. The fairness of a trial under Article 6 can be determined in relation to pre-trial events. A person subject to a criminal charge, on the basis of information obtained by detention under section 41 of the the Terrorism Act 2000, might have grounds for complaint under Article 6. Although section 41 deals with investigation and not trial, the lack of equality of arms in the investigation stage may be of importance. In particular, the defendant can be denied access to the information on which a district judge decides whether or not to extend detention for up to a week. The Court of Human Rights, and United Kingdom courts, recognise the particular difficulties and importance of terrorist investigations. Nevertheless this is not a green light for the authorities to do as they please and the courts must be sure that the essence of the fair trial rights in issue are not compromised.[71] The government believes that section 41 is compatible with the Convention, and it made, at the enactment stage, a declaration to that effect under section 19 of the Human Rights Act 1998. Schedule 8 reproduces rules used in Northern Ireland which, apart from the need for detainees to be brought promptly before a competent legal authority, did not fall foul of the Convention.

18.11.2 Search

Section 42 allows a magistrate to issue a warrant to permit police to enter specified premises to search for a person reasonably suspected of falling with section 40(1)(b) (concerned in the commission, preparation or instigation of acts of terrorism). A constable executing such a warrant will be lawfully on the premises and so be able to seize any item which is evidence of an offence under section 19 of the Police and Criminal Evidence Act 1984. A suspected terrorist may also be stopped and searched anywhere and items seized.[72]

18.12 Disclosure offences and media freedom

The definition of terrorism, terrorist actions and the state response to terrorism are politically charged matters. State responses to terrorism are likely to diminish, or at least threaten, the political and private liberties of citizens, and there will be claims that the authorities should be given a free hand and that opposition is in some way wrong and tolerant of violence. In this context there is a 'watchdog' role for the media and for serious investigative and critical journalism. At the same time the authorities are entitled to take measures, proportionate to the risk, to deny groups that might be planning atrocities against civilians access to information that could be helpful to them.

One issue is whether terrorist groups themselves (e.g. proscribed organisations) can be denied access to the media. This was tried in respect of Northern Ireland groups in the middle 1980s. A media ban on the direct broadcasting

---

[71] See *Murray* v *United Kingdom* (1996) 22 EHRR 29, though, following the Youth Justice and Criminal Evidence Act 1999, the issue of access to a solicitor is no longer significant in respect of a fair trial (see Chapter 5).

[72] Section 43, Terrorism Act 2000.

by representatives of alleged terrorist groups was imposed under powers in the Broadcasting Act 1990.[73] Justification for such a ban is to remove the fear and apprehension that such broadcasts can cause in potential targets and to deny such groups the 'oxygen of publicity'. The main objection is that such a ban makes it harder to understand the motive and political context of terrorist actions. The ban was upheld in the United Kingdom courts in *R v Home Secretary ex parte Brind* (1991)[74] but was dealt with under ordinary principles of administrative law and was not fully measured against Article 10 ECHR. Media bans are not authorisable by the Terrorism Act 2000. It is not an offence for a member of a proscribed organisation to broadcast although the media will need to take care that their activities cannot be construed as an offence connected with organising meetings promoting proscribed organisations under section 12 of the Terrorism Act 2000. Limitations on the media are principally achieved through the regulatory system and Codes of Practice. Any restrictions will now need to be compatible with Schedule 1, Article 10 of the Human Rights Act 1998.

Offences

The Terrorism Act 2000 includes offences relating to the disclosure of information. These offences apply to all persons. They have no special application to the media and, indeed, are likely to have their main impact on financial institutions. However, potentially, they have a restrictive impact on investigative reporting in a terrorist context.

Section 19 the Terrorism Act 2000[75] makes it an offence to fail to inform the police of a suspicion that a person has committed one of the offences relating to terrorist property in Part III of the Act (e.g. fund-raising and money laundering). The offence is limited to suspicion that arises on the basis of information obtained in the course of a trade, profession, business or employment.[76] The offence is intended to place duties, in particular, on financial institutions to report their suspicions to the police, but clearly such suspicions may easily occur to a journalist. Matters subject to legal privilege need not be disclosed by lawyers. Information concerning terrorism can be disclosed even if other statutes, such as the Data Protection Act 1998, might otherwise to broken.[77]

Section 39 of the Terrorism Act 2000 makes it an offence to disclose to another that a terrorist investigation (as defined by section 32, above) is taking place if to do so would be likely to prejudice the investigation or create an interference with material likely to be relevant to the investigation. This could have serious and restricting implications for the media and journalists reporting on terrorist situations. An interference can, for example, include the destruction of material, such as when a newspaper destroys information sent to it rather than handing it on to the police. Prosecutions require the consent of the DPP.[78]

---

[73] See Chapter 11.
[74] [1991] 1 AC 696.
[75] The section reproduces s. 18A, Prevention of Terrorism Act 1989.
[76] Section 18, Prevention of Terrorism Act 1989 also related to suspicions arising from home and family life but has not been repeated in the 2000 Act.
[77] Section 20, Terrorism Act 2000.

Section 58 makes the collecting or recording of information useful to terrorists, or possessing a document or record with such information on it, an offence. This offence clearly has implications for journalists, academics and others who may be investigating terrorist activity.

These offences may have an inhibiting effect upon journalists investigating terrorism and terrorist organisations. They may commit offences if they do not disclose their suspicions, or if they publish their stories or keep records and pieces of information to themselves.

Reasonable excuse

The offences do not require the prosecution to prove an intention to promote terrorism.[79] In respect to all three offences the Act provides a defence of 'reasonable excuse'.[80] Whether, and to what extent, the fact that the defendant was involved in bona fide investigative journalism will satisfy this defence is a matter of speculation. The Act makes no reference to the media or to any public interest that might be invoked. The courts, through the common law and on the basis of Schedule 1, Article 10 of the Human Rights Act 1998 fully recognise the importance of freedom of expression and a free media even in the context of national security issues.[81] Previous cases suggest the courts will be cautious. In *DPP* v *Channel 4 Television Co. and another* (1993)[82] (decided under the Prevention of Terrorism Act 1989) the public interest in investigative reporting did not prevent the courts from fining a broadcaster for failing to disclose the sources of a story that alleged serious malpractice by the authorities in a terrorist context. The current 'war against terrorism' may be thought as increasing, not decreasing, the likelihood that the courts will find that the needs of the authorities in the investigation of terrorism outweigh the public interest in a free press.

In relation to section 39 (disclosing information about terrorist investigations) and section 58 (having information useful to terrorists), section 118 applies. This means that a defendant journalist need only raise investigative journalism as an issue of reasonableness. If the court accepts this, the burden then shifts back to the prosecution to disprove the reasonableness of the journalistic defence at least in the particular case. As regards section 19 (failing to disclose suspicions about terrorist finances), however, section 118 does not apply and so the burden of proving the reasonableness remains with the media organisations. The development of these matters must await case law.

---

[78] Section 117, Terrorism Act 2000.
[79] Contrast the offence of disclosing information prejudicing safety at nuclear installations under s. 79, Anti-Terrorism Crime and Security Act 2001.
[80] See ss. 19(3), 39(5)(b), 58(3).
[81] For example, *R* v *Central Criminal Court ex parte Bright* [2001] 2 All ER 244.
[82] [1993] 2 All ER 517.

Part V
Private life

19

The protection of personal information

19.1 Introduction

This chapter, and the chapters that follow, deal with different aspects of privacy. The concept of privacy was introduced in Chapter 1 and it is a feature of other areas already dealt with such as media law. Article 8 of the European Convention on Human Rights provides a right to privacy. Its detailed provisions are dealt with in context.

Respect for privacy requires legal protection against the misuse of personal information. This means ensuring that, where personal information is given with consent, it is only used within the terms of that consent, and that where it is obtained compulsorily, covertly or otherwise without the knowledge of the person, it is only used for legitimate purposes. An important feature of privacy is the right of individuals to have some control over the use that others make of personal information about them, in particular to prevent the misuse of personal data that has been collected for legitimate purposes. Those in possession of personal information may seek to profit from it or they may make decisions based upon it. Privacy is engaged both in terms of controlling the use that is made of a person's name by others and also in terms of giving some degree of protection from unasked for, mistaken or improper intrusions by others. Regulating the uses of personal information is not merely a private matter. The control of data may be of political significance: police or security service's information held about political groups, for example, may include personal data; information on trade unionists may be held by employer associations.

Modern society, through its public and private institutions, has an enormous need for personal information. Technological developments, particularly the computer, has hugely enhanced the capacity to obtain and use such information. Commercial businesses, banks, retailers, utility providers, etc., obtain masses of information about their customers. The obtaining and use of such information will be largely based on contract. Improper use of such information can be a breach of the particular terms of the contract. Similarly there are a number of general legal remedies that can apply to the improper use of such information. Two examples are that disclosure or publication of defamatory personal information can be the basis of an action for damages and, secondly, that the courts will protect certain confidential personal information through the issuing of an injunction.[1] Of course, it is common for people to consent to wide uses of some of the personal information that they give to commercial organisations, for further advertising purposes, for example.

A mass of information is also held by a range of public authorities. This is information that the authority may need or be required to hold in order to perform its functions. The information may be compulsorily obtained, such as by the Inland Revenue, or be obtained as a consequence of a decision by a person to receive a service, as by Health Authorities and NHS Trusts. Information is held by public authorities on the basis of specific statutory powers. These Acts, characteristically, will determine the purposes for which the information can be obtained and the limits on the power of the authority to disclose the information. Section 50 of the Race Relations Act 1976, for example, empowers the Commission for Racial Equality to obtain information for the purpose of an investigation and section 52 makes it an offence to disclose such information except under certain circumstances. The police and security services have wide powers, discussed in earlier chapters, to obtain personal information. This can be obtained through the normal powers of investigation (Chapter 6) or through surveillance (Chapter 7). The holding of information by public authorities is subject not only to the restraints and conditions in the relevant statutes, but also to the general law such as defamation and breach of confidence. Public authorities which make otherwise unauthorised disclosures on the basis of a strong public interest, may enjoy a qualified privilege and so be exempt from action.[2] The position of many public authorities regarding the disclosure of information has been transformed by provisions in the Anti-terrorism, Crime and Security Act 2001, discussed below.

Media organisations and journalists employed by them are also likely to be in possession of personal information about individuals. This information may be obtained in the course of journalistic investigations and is not held on any contractual or statutory basis. The law recognises a strong public interest in a free press. Not only may media organisations be able to assert a qualified privilege in respect of defamation proceedings and to press for a justifying public interest in respect of breach of confidence, but also, as we shall see below, the media enjoy considerable exemptions under the provisions of data protection legislation.

19.2 Convention rights

There is no express right to have access to personal information in the Convention rights in Schedule 1 of the Human Rights Act 1998. The right to receive information in Article 10 has been confined to information that someone is prepared to give. The government does not have a positive obligation to provide access to the personal information it retains or to compel

---

[1] For further details see Chapter 11 on the media and Chapter 16 on national security.
[2] For example, *R v Chief Constable of North Wales ex parte AB* [1998] 3 All ER 310, where it was in the public interest for the police to disclose to the owner of a caravan park the fact that a husband and wife staying there had child abuse convictions.

private businesses (who are not directly bound by the Convention) to do so in respect of the information they keep.[3]

Article 8, respect for private and family life, provides the basis for at least some claims in respect of private information. In *Gaskin* v *United Kingdom* (1989)[4] the Court of Human Rights declined to take a view on whether Article 8(1) might, in general, provide a right of access to personal data. If this were the case, each and every refusal of access would need justification under the terms of Article 8(2). The Court accepted that there could be a positive duty on a state to give access to personal information where there were vital interests, connected to a person's sense of identity, to which the information related. In *Gaskin* the information involved the applicant's childhood in care, and the records were the main means of having knowledge of his past. Even then the Court recognised that there might be overwhelming and reasonable issues of confidentiality which were capable of displacing any duty to disclose. In *X* v *United Kingdom* (1982)[5] the Commission of Human Rights accepted that information on gender, marital status and place of birth could come within the protection of Article 8. Information in health records was accepted as covered by the Article in *X* v *Finland* (1998).[6] Medical evidence, in exceptional circumstances, could be disclosed in closed court but the state had a duty to ensure that confidentiality was maintained; a ten-year ban on reporting was insufficient. Disclosure of personal information, for purposes other than for which it was obtained, may be incompatible with Article 8(1);[7] if so, any such disclosures will need justification under Article 8(2).

In the context of criminal investigations, the Court of Human Rights has tended to uphold the right of police and security services to obtain and retain personal information and to take and retain fingerprints and photographs of suspects, even if they are not eventually charged with or convicted of an offence. The principal cases relate to anti-terrorism where, on the issue of proportionality, the Court is prepared to grant a wide margin of appreciation to the authorities.[8] The extent to which the extension of powers on these matters in the Anti-terrorism, Crime and Security Act 2001 are compatible with Article 8 under the Human Rights Act 1998 will remain to be seen. In the context of terrorism the courts may be prepared to defer to official judgments on the risk and the need for special measures; however, it is not clear that such tolerance will apply to the prevention of non-terrorist crime.

The Data Protection Act 1998 and other relevant legislation will need to be interpreted for compatibility with the scheduled Convention rights. The relative paucity of Strasbourg law directly in this area means that United Kingdom courts will develop their own sense of the importance of, in particular, Article 8.

---

[3] *Leander* v *Sweden* (1987) 9 EHRR 433; see Chapter 15 for further discussion and case law.
[4] (1989) 12 EHRR 36.
[5] (1982) 30 D&R 239.
[6] (1998) 25 EHRR.
[7] See *TV* v *Finland* (1994) Ap 21780/93, 76A D&R 140, cited in Harris, D., O'Boyle, M. and Warbrick, C. (1995) *Law of the European Convention on Human Rights*. London: Butterworths, p. 348.
[8] *Murray and others* v *United Kingdom* (1995) 19 EHRR 193; *McVeigh, O'Neill and Evans* v *United Kingdom* (1983) 5 EHRR 71.

19.3 Specific legislation

From the 1980s strong pressure on successive governments led to the enactment of a number of statutes that grant rights of access by individuals to personal information held about them by public bodies. This legislative trend can be linked with the trend to greater openness in government and the moves in the direction of permitting access to non-personal information about government services and policies which has been discussed in Chapter 15.

The Data Protection Act 1984 gave rights of access and control in respect of personal information held on computers. It applied to most public agencies as well as to private individuals and companies. It is now repealed and its provisions taken over and expanded by the Data Protection Act 1998, discussed below. The Access to Personal Files Act 1987 allowed the Secretary of State to make regulations for allowing rights of access to personal information held by public authorities. The Act was, under government pressure, narrowed so that regulations could only be made in respect of personal files relating to social services[9] and housing.[10] It was repealed by the Data Protection Act 1998. The Access to Medical Reports Act 1988 is still in force and provides a right of access by individuals to medical reports made about them for insurance and employment purposes. Likewise the Access to Health Records Act 1990 remains in force and provides for a person's access, subject to various exclusions, to his or her medical records compiled after 1 November 1991.

19.4 Data Protection Act 1998

The Data Protection Act 1998 is the principal instrument through which a person can have various rights of control over the personal information that others, official, commercial or otherwise, hold about her or him. It creates a comprehensive and exclusive legislative code on the processing or personal data and its jurisdiction is retained by the Freedom of Information Act 2000. Requests for personal information are explicitly exempted from the scope of the latter Act.

The Act is the legislative response of the United Kingdom to the European Communities Data Protection Directive (1995).[11] The Directive has direct effect and so not only must the Act be interpreted for conformity with the Directive but breach by a public authority can be the basis of an action.[12]

19.4.1 The scope of the Act

The Act regulates the processing of information relating to individuals. In its terms it regulates the processing of 'personal data' about a 'data subject' by a

---

[9] Access to Personal Files (Social Services) Regulations 1989, SI 1989 No. 206.
[10] Access to Personal Files (Housing) Regulations 1989, SI 1989 No. 503.
[11] *Directive on the Processing of Personal Data*, Directive 95/46/EC. This Directive is complemented by a range of other instruments including, from July 2002, the *Directive on Privacy and Electronic Communications*, Directive 2002/58/EC.
[12] For example, *R (Robertson)* v *Wakefield Metropolitan District Council* [2001] EWHC Admin 915; [2002] 2 WLR 889.

'data processor' on behalf of a 'data controller'. These terms are defined in section 1.

The Act is concerned with 'data'. This involves not only information held on, and retrievable by, means of a computer but also manual records in so far as they are part of a filing system which is structured to facilitate access to information about individuals, or are health, education and public records of certain kinds.[13] Under the Freedom of Information Act 2000, all personal information recorded and held by public authorities (as identified by the 2000 Act) will be included whether or not it is on a record or filing system, though the data subject's rights in respect of this additional information are limited.

The Act is concerned only with 'personal' data: this is data from which a living individual can be identified. It includes not only facts about a person but also statements of opinions about them and intentions towards them. The 'data subject' is the person identifiable from the data. A data subject is defined in terms of individuals, not associations or companies.

Data is 'processed' when various things are done such as being obtained, recorded, altered, disclosed and so on. The 'data processor' processes data on behalf of the 'data controller' who is the person or organisation which determines the purposes for which data is processed. The Act is binding on the Crown but is emphatically not confined to public authorities. Individuals, public bodies, commercial enterprises, all manner of associations, etc. can be data controllers and are covered directly by the Act if they are established in or operating through the United Kingdom.[14]

19.4.2 The data principles

Personal data must only be processed according to the 'Data Protection Principles' These are identified in Schedule 1 of the Act and must be interpreted in accordance with Schedule 2[15].

First Principle and Schedule 2
Principle 1 states:

> Personal data shall be processed fairly and lawfully and, in particular, shall not be processed unless –
> (a) at least one of the conditions in Schedule 2 is met and,
> (b) in the case of sensitive personal data, at least one of the conditions in Schedule 3 is also met.

Thus, for ordinary data, at least one of the very broad conditions in Schedule 2 must be satisfied. These conditions are that: the process is with the consent of the data subject, or is necessary for the performance of a contract with the data subject, or is necessary for compliance with another legal obligation on the data subject, or is necessary to protect the 'vital interests' (undefined) of the data subject. Schedule 2 also permits data processing to facilitate the

---

[13] As defined by s. 68 and Schedules 11 and 12.
[14] Section 5, Data Protection Act 1998.
[15] Section 4(4), Data Protection Act 1998.

performance of public functions by the government or any person; this includes the administration of justice. Data can also be processed in order to further the legitimate interests of the data controller. The Secretary of State can, by order, produce other conditions.

Sensitive personal data: Section 2 and Schedule 3
'Sensitive personal data', defined in section 2, is information on a range of matters which are considered to be particularly private and in need of additional protection. It includes information on: racial or ethnic origin, political opinions, religious beliefs, trade union membership, physical or mental health, sexual life, the commission of offences and information about criminal proceedings. It is noticeable that economic interests, such as earnings or investments, are excluded. The list is less extensive than the range of personal matters that receive legal protection in other contexts. The grounds for prohibited discrimination under Article 14 ECHR or the private and family matters protected from unreasonable interference under Article 8(1) ECHR include more than is covered by 'sensitive personal data'.

Schedule 3 lists a range of conditions at least one of which must be met in order to satisfy the first data protection principles in respect of sensitive personal data. Condition 1 is that processing sensitive personal data will satisfy the first data protection principle only if it has the 'explicit' consent of the subject. Many of the other conditions in Schedule 3 mirror Schedule 2 but with more precise specification and additional safeguards. Schedule 3 also imposes conditions in new areas. Thus information on racial or ethnic origins can only be processed, without the explicit consent of the subject, in order to further racial equality and with adequate protections for the rights of others.[16] Paragraph 4 of Schedule 3 allows political parties, without explicit consent, to process information about the political opinions of their members and others connected with them, but not of the general public.[17] Paragraph 10 authorises the Secretary of State to identify further circumstances in which the processing of personal data may take place. This has been done.[18] Canvassing at election times, for example, which involves sensitive personal data obtained from the general public and so is not covered by paragraph 4 of Schedule 3, is protected by the Secretary of State's regulations. These permit canvassing or political opinions by registered political parties so long as any processing of the data does not cause substantial damage or distress to the data subject of another person.[19]

The other data protection principles
As well as satisfying the First Principle, processing both sensitive and non-sensitive data can only be lawful if the other seven data protection principles and followed. These are: (2) that information should be kept only for certain specified and lawful purposes and not for others; (3) that the

---

[16] Data Protection Act 1998, Schedule 3, paragraph 9.
[17] Data Protection Act 1998, Schedule 3, paragraph 4.
[18] The Data Protection (Processing of Sensitive Personal Data) Order 2000, SI 2000 No. 417.
[19] The Data Protection (Processing of Sensitive Personal Data) Order 2000, SI 2000 No. 417, paragraph 8.

information obtained should be proportionate to its purposes; (4) information should be accurate and kept up to date; (5) it should not be kept longer than is required by the purpose or purposes; (6) it should be processed in accordance with the rights of data subjects (as identified in the Act); (7) that appropriate measures are to be taken to avoid unauthorised or unlawful processing or against accidental loss or destruction or damage; and (8) that the information is not transferred to a country outside the European Economic Area unless that country has adequate data protection. These principles are identified in Schedule 1, Part 1 and are to be interpreted in the light of Part 2. Schedule 4 identifies situations where data can be transferred outside the EEA, the Eighth Principle not withstanding.

19.4.3 Enforcement

The compliance of data controllers with the Data Protection Principles is enforced through the office of Information Commissioner (renamed from Data Protection Commissioner when given responsibilities under the Freedom of Information Act 2000). The decisions of the Commissioner can be appealed to the Information Tribunal. Data controllers must register with the Commissioner.[20]

The Commissioner's jurisdiction is concerned with whether the Data Protection Principles have been complied with. This is done through the Commissioner's extensive duties and powers to publish general guidance on the application of the principles in a range of areas[21] and through significant enforcement powers in individual cases.

Information notices and enforcement notices
On application, under section 42, from a data subject, the Commissioner has powers to investigate an alleged breach of the Data Protection Principles. The Commissioner may issue an information notice to obtain access to relevant information. If the Commissioner finds that the Data Protection Principles have not been complied with, an enforcement notice may be issued to the data controller. An enforcement notice requires remedial steps to be taken or that the controller desist from further processing. Failure by a data controller to comply is a criminal offence.[22] The Act permits the defence of due diligence to comply with the principles.

An investigation can also be undertaken on the basis of the Commissioner's own suspicions or concerns, whether or not an individual has complained.

The Information Tribunal
The person on whom an enforcement notice has been served has a right of appeal to the Information Tribunal against the issuing of the notice or the Commissioner's refusal to cancel it. The data subject does not have an

---

[20] Data Protection Act 1998, s.17.
[21] For example, the Code of Practice on the 'Promotion of a political party: the use of direct mail', telephone and e-mail. For a full list see the Information Commissioner's website: www.dataprotection.gov.uk.
[22] Data Protection Act 1998, s. 47.

equivalent right of appeal against the Commissioner's refusal to issue a notice. The Tribunal's jurisdiction is wide: the appeal can be both on the grounds that the notice or refusal to cancel was not 'in accordance with the law' or that the Commissioner should have exercised his or her discretion over the matter differently. The Tribunal can review the determination of facts. Its remedies are to allow the appeal (i.e. cancel the notice), substitute a different decision from the range that the Commissioner could have made, or dismiss the appeal. There is a further right of appeal from the Tribunal to the High Court on a point of law.

19.4.4 Legal rights of data subjects

As well as requiring data to be processed according to the Data Protection Principles, the Data Protection Act 1998 creates legal rights for data subjects. These are full legal rights which can be enforced directly by a court. These rights are also within the Commissioner's jurisdiction, since the Sixth Data Protection Principle requires that personal data 'be processed in accordance with the rights of data subjects under this Act'. These rights are found in Part II of the Act. They include the right of a data subject to be informed promptly of and given information about data processing by any data controller and to receive the data from the data controller including information about its source.[23] Data subjects have the right to a court order stopping uses of data which are likely to cause them substantial damage or distress.[24] There is also a right to a court order requiring a data controller to rectify, in various ways, any errors in the personal data held.[25] Compensation can be ordered, under section 13, but only where loss is caused to the person (not necessarily the data subject) seeking the compensation. Mere distress is not sufficient for compensation.

The Act also creates a criminal offence of obtaining or disclosing personal data knowing that the data controller, who is legitimately in possession of the information, has not given consent to disclosure.[26] There are numerous exemptions covering the purposes for which data can legitimately be obtained.

The Directive on which the Act is based has direct effect. Thus it can be argued, on judicial review for example, that the Act, and regulations under it, though followed by a data controller, do not give proper effect to the Directive. The High Court must then interpret the Act so far as possible to give effect to the Directive.[27] The Act, its regulations and other related statutes must, of course, also be interpreted for compatibility with the Convention rights scheduled in the Human Rights Act 1998. Judicial review is likely to generate only a declaratory remedy. The Act should be used directly for damages, rectification, etc.

---

[23] Data Protection Act 1998, s. 7.
[24] Data Protection Act 1998, s. 10.
[25] Data Protection Act 1998, s. 14.
[26] Data Protection Act 1998, s. 55.
[27] *R (Robertson)* v *Wakefield Metropolitan District Council* [2001] EWHC Admin 915; [2002] 2 WLR 889.

19.4.5 Exemptions

The Act provides for exemptions. The way in which the exemptions are interpreted by the Commissioner, Tribunal and court is very important for the effectiveness of the Act. Exemptions should be restrictively interpreted in line with their purpose. As under the Freedom of Information Act 2000, the exemptions do not have standard form but are complex and individuated. Different, specified classes of information are subject to different degrees of exemption from all or some of the Data Protection Principles (and hence from the jurisdiction of the Commissioner and Tribunal) and from all or some of the legal rights of subjects in Part II of the Act.

National security

Any information whose non-disclosure is necessary for safeguarding national security is fully exempt from both the Data Protection Principles (the domain of the Commissioner) and the legal rights of subjects (the domain of the Commissioner and the court). A ministerial certificate is conclusive evidence of the needs of national security although the reasonableness of the minister's grounds for a certificate can be challenged before the Tribunal.

Other exemptions

The other exemptions are mainly limited to the subject access provisions (i.e. the right of a person to know of, receive, correct and prevent misuse of personal data). They do not exempt data controllers from processing data according to the Data Protection Principles or from other legal duties such as paying compensation. The exemption in respect of the prevention of crime and the assessment of taxes is limited to most of the First Data Protection Principle and to the subject access rights of section 7. Subject access to health, education and social work can, on orders made by the Secretary of State, be limited. Section 31 allows exemptions in respect of subject access provisions for personal data processed for a range of regulatory functions and the activities of various Ombudsmen. There are exemptions in relation to research, history and statistics.

The Secretary of State can exempt, from subject access provisions, personal data whose disclosure is prohibited by other statutes or where exemption is necessary to protect the rights and freedoms of others.[28]

Journalistic, literary and artistic purposes

Personal information held for journalistic, literary or artistic purposes ('special purposes') receives exempting treatment under section 32 of the Data Protection Act 1998. The processing of personal information for such purposes is exempt from the Data Protection Principles (except the seventh, which deals with taking measures to avoid improper processing) and from the subject access and most of the other legal rights established in Part II of the Act. The exemption depends upon the reasonable belief of the data controller (e.g. a newspaper) that 'having regard in particular to the special importance of the

---

[28] Data Protection Act 1998, s. 7 and s. 38.

public interest in freedom of expression, publication would be in the public interest'. In coming to such a judgment, the data controller may have regard to any designated code of practice, such as that issued by the Press Complaints Commission. In other words, personal information can be disclosed by the media on the grounds of a reasonable belief by the press or broadcasters that it is in the public interest so to disclose. This is a huge breach of the idea that persons should be able to control the use of personal information that others hold of them and is said to be justified in terms of the importance of freedom of expression. The public interest is a very broad term which can include, simply, matters the public are interested in.[29] By relying on the reasonable belief of the data controller, the balance of the Act comes down in favour of freedom of the press over privacy.

> Naomi Campbell sought damages under section 13 of the Data Protection Act 1998 in respect of a story, published in the *Daily Mirror,* that gave details of the treatment she was obtaining for drug addiction.
>   HELD: section 32 gave exemption from an action for damages to the publication of stories in breach of the Act
> *Campbell* v *Mirror Group Newspapers* [2002] EWCA Civ 1373

The Court of Appeal rejected the newspaper's argument that they were not covered by the Data Protection Act 1998 at all, but then accepted their view, against prevailing academic opinion, that the media were protected by section 32 not only in respect of prior restraints, such as 'gagging' injunctions, but also in respect of final publication.

The data subject may still complain to the Commissioner or the court. The Commissioner can seek information, through a special information notice, from the controller, e.g. a media organisation. The Commissioner cannot, however, serve an enforcement notice on the controller unless satisfied that the personal information is not being processed exclusively for journalistic, literary or artistic purposes. If it is being processed for these special purposes but not exclusively so, an enforcement order can only be issued if the breach of the Data Protection Principles is of substantial public importance. The Act, therefore, provides no direct protection for privacy when personal information is used exclusively for journalistic, artistic or literary purposes.[30] The data subject still has whatever remedies are available from the general law, such as an action for breach of confidence or, in respect of the media, the relevant regulatory regime and its Code of Practice. In other words, the Act upholds media self-regulation.

Exemptions for exclusively journalistic, artistic and literary uses are permitted by Article 9 of the European Directive. However the Directive permits such exemptions only if they are 'necessary to reconcile the right to privacy with the rules governing freedom of expression'. The exemptions in the Act, however, seem to give priority to media freedom rather than a balancing of the two interests which the word 'reconcile' might be thought to imply.

---

[29] See, for example, *A* v *B Plc* [2002] 2 All ER 543, paragraph 48.
[30] Data Protection Act 1998, ss. 45 and 46.

19.5 Disclosure of information held by public authorities

Public authorities hold vast amounts of personal information about individuals and companies. The Freedom of Information Act 2000 requires that all personal information held by public authorities be subject to the Data Protection Act 1998 Act even if the same kinds and forms of information, if held by others, would not be covered by the Act. However, the subject access rights to this additional personal information held by public authorities are limited.

Characteristically public authorities hold the information on the basis of specific statutory powers which specify the purposes for which the information can be used and restrict the purposes for which it can be disclosed and the agencies to whom it can be disclosed. The fact that a health authority has information about you does not mean that the information can be disclosed by the authority to the police or to an insurance company. This principle is in addition to the rules and principles of data protection described in this chapter.

The principle, that public authorities should only hold personal information for their own purposes, has now been significantly breached. Schedule 4 of the Anti-terrorism, Crime and Security Act 2001 identifies many statutory provisions which permit disclosure of personal information by public authorities. Characteristically, these powers are severely limited and offences committed if they are breached. Section 17 of the 2001 Act, however, authorises the disclosure of such information to anyone, such as the police, for the purposes of a criminal investigation. Only public authorities which come within the definition in section 6 of the Human Rights Act 1998 are covered by the Act, which is likely to be a more restricted list than those identified under the Freedom of Information Act 2000. The Anti-terrorism, Crime and Security Act 2001, it should be stressed, enables but does not compel these disclosures. There is no guidance on the circumstances in which authorities should disclose or to whom, although the Act does require that the authorities must be satisfied that such disclosures are proportionate. 'Processing' includes disclosure of information.[31] Therefore these provisions could violate the Second Data Protection Principle which prevents the processing of information in a manner incompatible with the purpose for which it was obtained. Processing information for the prevention of crime is exempt from the second principle, but the exemption only applies where non-disclosure would 'be likely to prejudice' the prevention or detention of crime etc.[32] It may not be difficult to persuade a public authority that the exemption applies. Nevertheless, section 17 needs to be interpreted, and if necessary given a strained interpretation, to ensure that directly effective rights under the Data Protection Directive are maintained[33] and, under section 3 of the Human Rights Act 1998, be interpreted for compatability with Article 8 ECHR. Similar provisions, relating to the retention of communications data, are found in the 2001 Act and are discussed in Chapter 7.

---

[31] Section 1(1), Data Protection Act 1998.
[32] Sections 29(3) and 27(4)(b), Data Protection Act 1998.
[33] *R (Robertson)* v *Wakefield Metropolitan District Council* [2001] EWHC Admin 915; [2002] 2 WLR 889.

20
Bodily integrity

20.1 Introduction

Privacy means little unless it includes the idea of a person's right to control what happens to his or her own body. A person's body cannot, by right, be touched, beaten, cut, entered, etc. by another without consent. Conversely, a person, by right, controls the uses to which his or her body is put. No one, by right, can be compelled, for example, to procreate, to use or not use contraception, to have an abortion, etc.

We can properly speak of bodily integrity as a matter of 'right'. It is central to the conception of personhood upon which fundamental rights are predicated. The freedoms inherent in the notion of bodily integrity are inherent in the meaning of being a 'person' or in the concept of human 'dignity'.

Bodily integrity receives its principal protection through the general law in a range of contexts which are outside the scope of this book. The criminal law prohibits all but the most trivial interferences. Similarly, interferences with bodily integrity can be the subject of a tort action aiming at damages or an injunction. 'Interference, however slight, with a person's elementary civil right to security of the person, and self-determination in relation to his own body, constitutes trespass to the person'.[1] Carelessness towards the person of others can be the basis of a negligence action.

No crime or tort is committed if the interference has lawful authority. In Chapter 4 we have already considered the extent of lawful authority enjoyed by police, military and other state agents to use force, including lethal force, in the execution of their duties. The rights of other groups, such as parents or doctors, to interfere with bodily integrity forms much of the content of this chapter.

Crimes and torts may not be committed if a person properly consents to an interference which would otherwise be unlawful. In relation to both crime[2] and tort,[3] the effect of consent can raise complex issues. It is clear that, especially regarding the commission of crimes, the granting of express consent, though covering the activities and risks in issue, may be insufficient to override the public purposes that justify the illegality of the activity in the first

---

[1] Brazier, M.R. (1995) *Clerk and Lindsell on Torts*, 17th edn. London: Sweet & Maxwell, chapter 12, p. 583. The passage cites *Collins* v *Willcox* [1984] 3 All ER 374, 378, which contains further references.
[2] See Ashworth, A. (1999) *Principles of Criminal Law*. Oxford: Oxford University Press, pp. 330–7.
[3] See Brazier, *op. cit.*, chapter 3.33 *et seq.*

place. In particular the general power of consent to excuse or nullify otherwise criminal acts is limited to assault and battery but does not, subject to important exceptions,[4] extend to more serious offences.

20.2 Physical punishments

The state, by definition, enjoys the monopoly of legitimate violence in society. This is asserted, ultimately, by the capacity of the state to punish those who transgress its rules. The predominant punishments today involve financial penalties, work in the community or imprisonment. Physical punishment by the state, is no longer practised in the United Kingdom. Such punishments interfere with bodily integrity. Their unacceptability remains controversial, especially as regards the death penalty. It is hard to identify basic common ground on which the protagonists might agree. Physical punishment may be justified as a deterrent, though there can be disagreement over whether physical punishments in fact deter. For opponents of physical punishments, the issue of deterrence is irrelevant. Any punishment must be morally acceptable before there is any point in assessing its deterrent value. Physical punishments are alleged to be morally unacceptable on various grounds such as that they violate background rights to life (in the case of the death penalty) or not to suffer cruel or humiliating punishments (as in birching, for example). Proponents of physical punishments, on the other hand, assert the moral value of physical punishments. Such punishments balance the wrong done by a violent criminal and so provide a sense of justice for the victim, and they are unambiguously forms of punishment rather than reform, and as such are more effective in asserting the revulsion of society towards the crimes committed. Proponents doubt the moral claims made by opponents since, conventionally, institutionalised versions of the right to life exclude the death penalty and a punishment, by definition is humiliating and degrading.

General principles of law and the law of England and Wales seem to be hostile to the more severe forms of physical punishment.

20.2.1 The death penalty

Both Article 6 ICCPR and Article 2 ECHR, which specify the right to life within their different institutional settings, expressly permit the death penalty. Article 6(2) ICCPR expressly limits the death penalty to 'the most serious crimes in accordance with the law in force at the time of the commission of the crime' and prevents the punishment from being carried out on persons under 18 years of age or on pregnant women. The jurisprudence and General Comments of the Human Rights Committee indicate a tendency towards abolition[5] and the Second Optional Protocol[6] requires the abolition of the death penalty

---

[4] *R v Brown and other appeals* [1993] 2 All ER 75; the issue is discussed in more detail in Chapter 21.
[5] Nowak, M. (1993) *U.N. Covenant on Civil and Political Rights. CCPR Commentary.* Kehl: N.P. Engel, pp. 113–16.
[6] Second Optional Protocol to the International Covenant on Civil and Political Rights Aiming at the Abolition of the Death Penalty, 15 December 1989.

by signatories and recognises the general desirability of opposition. Among states, the international tendency is, with significant exceptions, towards abolition.[7]

Protocol 6 of the European Convention, expressing a 'general tendency in favour of abolition of the death penalty', requires abolition by signatory states although there is an exception in respect of acts committed in time of war or imminent threat of war. This Protocol is a 'convention right' under the Human Rights Act 1998.

Article 3 ECHR cannot be read as abolishing the death penalty[8] but the manner and the circumstances in which a death sentence is imposed can come within its terms. Article 3 bars signatory states from extraditing or otherwise removing persons to countries where they may suffer torture or inhuman or degrading treatment or punishment, even though the country concerned is not a signatory of the Convention. In *Soering* v *United Kingdom* (1989)[9] the Court of Human Rights held that the anguish and tension of being on death row for many years (while the appeals process was exhausted) along with the applicant's age at the time of the offences and his mental state meant that extradition would be incompatible with the Convention.[10]

In the United Kingdom the death penalty is no longer an available punishment for any offence. It was abolished for murder by the Murder (Abolition of the Death Penalty) Act 1965, section 1(1). This left treason and piracy with attempted murder as the only civilian offences carrying a death sentence and this possibility was ended by section 36(4) and (5) of the Crime and Disorder Act 1998. A range of military offences such as misconduct in action and mutiny[11] used to be punishable by death when committed by military personnel in wartime or to assist the enemy. The death penalty for these offences was abolished by section 21(5) of the Human Rights Act 1998.

Protocol 6 ECHR (mentioned above) will limit the effectiveness of any purported reintroduction of the death penalty. Reintroduction for military offences in wartime would not be incompatible with convention rights since Article 2, Protocol 6 permits a death sentence (for anyone) in time of war or imminent threat of war. In peacetime, for both civilians and the military, any purported reintroduction would have to be non-discretionary since a discretionary sentence, given section 6 of the Human Rights Act 1998, would need to be exercised compatibly with Convention rights. A mandatory sentence could still be legally effective by virtue of section 6(2)(a) of the Act on the grounds that, because of primary legislation reintroducing capital punishment, the court could not have acted differently; an appropriate court could make a

---

[7] For a full discussion of the moral, political and legal issues, discussed in an an international context, see the case in which South Africa's Constitutional Court was a cruel punishment which violated the Constitution: *The State* v *Makwanyane and Mchunu* (1995) CCT/3/94; (3) SA 391.

[8] *Ibid.*, paragraph 103.

[9] (1989) 11 EHRR 439.

[10] The principle has been applied to an intended removal to face possible death or torture at the hands of factions in the Indian police (*Chahal* v *United Kingdom* Ap. 22414/93; (1997) 23 EHRR 413) and in respect of a man dying of Aids who was to be removed to a country with inadequate medical facilities (*D* v *United Kingdom* Ap. 30240/96; (1997) 24 EHRR 423).

[11] For example, ss. 24–26, 36, Army Act 1955.

declaration of incompatibility.[12] The scheduling of Articles 1 and 2 of Protocol 6 is also likely to prevent extradition or other forms of removal of a person from the United Kingdom to a country where he or she is in danger of suffering death. No longer will it be necessary to rely on surrounding circumstances such as the 'death row phenomena' so as to prevent such removals under Article 3.

20.2.2 Corporal punishment: as a criminal punishment

Corporal punishments for criminal offences and for prisoners have been removed from English law.[13] An act of birching in the Isle of Man, where the punishment was retained, was held to violate Article 3 ECHR in *Tyrer v United Kingdom*.

> T, a 15-year-old Isle of Man resident, was sentenced to be birched. He had been convicted of assault occasioning actual bodily harm. After the sentence had been carried out he complained[14] to the European Court of Human Rights.
>
> HELD (ECHR): the birching amounted to degrading treatment and violated Article 3 ECHR.
>
> *Tyrer* v *United Kingdom* (1978) 2 EHRR 1

The Court held that the degree of degradation in birching went beyond that inherent in punishment generally; in this it was influenced by developing European standards. Whether a punishment violated Article 3 depended on an assessment of all the circumstances such as, in this case, the institutionalised nature of the punishment by which he was entirely under the direct physical control of those in authority, and the mental anguish of anticipating what was to be done to him. A punishment that violated Article 3 could not become acceptable by balancing the degradation against the strength of countervailing advantages such as, for example, any deterrent effects the punishment might have. *Tyrer* applies to corporal punishment generally.

20.2.3 Corporal punishment: parents and children

The freedom of parents and those with control of children to administer reasonable physical correction without either criminal or tort liability for assault or battery is preserved by section 1(7) of the Children and Young Persons Act 1933. Without the intention to punish, parents may be liable for a range of offences for physical neglect and abuse. The common law has long recognised this right of parents, and of teachers who may be *in loco parentis*, to 'for the purpose of correcting what is evil in the child inflict moderate and

---

[12] Which could trigger remedial action if the political will changed.

[13] Finally by s. 65, Criminal Justice Act 1967 which abolishes corporal punishment for prisoners.

[14] Tyrer sought to withdraw his application but the Court decided to continue with the case. Under the Strasbourg system, friendly settlements are common but raise the awkward point that the state is, in some circumstances, buying its way out of responsibility for a human rights violation.

reasonable corporal punishment, always, however, with this condition, that it is moderate and reasonable'.[15]

The doctrine of reasonable chastisement came under scrutiny for compatibility with Article 3 ECHR in *A* v *United Kingdom* (1999).

> A, a 9-year-old child, was regularly beaten by his stepfather with sufficient severity to cause bruising. The stepfather was prosecuted for causing actual bodily harm but acquitted by a jury on the basis of a 'reasonable chastisement' defence.
>
> HELD (ECtHR): there had been a violation of Article 3 ECHR. The injuries caused were, in all the circumstances, including the age of the victim, above the threshold level of severity required to establish inhuman and degrading punishment. The state, though not directly responsible for the stepfather's actions, was required to take measures to ensure that the provisions of Article 3 were met and the jury's acquittal meant it had failed in this regard.
>
> *A* v *United Kingdom* (1999) 27 EHRR 611

The state must do more than bring a prosecution. It has a positive duty to ensure that the application of the law is sufficient to deliver Article 3 rights for children. Article 3 requires a careful, structured consideration in which factors, such as age, sex, the instrument used and so on are properly weighed in the question of whether a punishment is lawful or not. Leaving the matter to the unstructured good sense of a jury creates a danger of arbitrariness and inequality in the protection offered by English law, and this is not compatible with Article 3. The Strasbourg case law does not require an outright ban on corporal punishment. The government continues to permit smacking of children by parents.[16]

20.2.4 Schools

Section 548 of the Education Act 1996, as amended in 1998, abolishes corporal punishment in all schools, whether fully or partially maintained or independent.[17] It bans corporal punishment (defined as any action which would otherwise constitute a battery) in so far as it is given in pursuit of any right such as, in particular, the common law right of reasonable chastisement of pupils by teachers. It is punishment that is banned and not the use of reasonable force to avert immediate personal danger or damage to property or disruption.[18]

Corporal punishment is defined in relation to the tort of battery and this includes the application of just a slight degree of force. The ban is more extensive than is necessary under Article 3 ECHR. In *Costello-Roberts* v *United*

---

[15] *R* v *Hopley* (1860) 2 F & F 202, 206; 175 ER 1024, 1026 (punctuation as in the original). Blackstone, nearly 100 years earlier, justified parents enjoying the freedom of reasonable correction on the grounds of the benefit to the child's education: Blackstone, W. (1765–69) *Commentaries on the Laws of England*, volume 1, chapter 16, p. 2.

[16] Department of Health (2000) *Protecting Children, Supporting Parents*. DoH.

[17] Corporal punishment had been banned in maintained and other public sector schools by the Education (No. 2) Act 1986, s. 47(1). This was re-enacted by the Education Act 1996 which s. 131 of the School Standards and Framework Act 1998 Act amended to include independent schools.

[18] Section 550A(1), Education Act 1996 inserted by s. 4, Education Act 1997.

Kingdom (1993)[19] there was, in all the circumstances, no violation of Article 3 when a 7-year-old boy at an independent boarding school was beaten, on his buttocks, through his shorts, three times with a rubber-soled gym shoe. There were no significant after effects. The Court accepted that the United Kingdom was responsible for providing the freedoms under Article 3 even though the punishment was administered in an independent school. The facts in the case can be compared with other cases such as *Warwick v United Kingdom* (1989) or *Y v United Kingdom* (1994)[20] where visible injuries were caused by the administration of corporal punishment to a 16-year-old girl and a 15-year-old boy respectively. In *Warwick* the Commission found the punishment to be, in all the circumstances, degrading; in *Y* a friendly settlement was reached to the expressed regret of a commissioner.

The interference with bodily integrity inherent in corporal punishment is capable of being an interference with a person's private life under Article 8(1)[21] and, if so, would need to be justified by the state under Article 8(2). The administration of punishment is not, in itself, a permissible ground for such interference.

Article 2 of Protocol 1 requires states to respect the religious and philosophical convictions of parents in relation to the educational functions that it, the state, undertakes. The power of teachers to punish seems to be based on delegated authority from parents. Despite this parents have found it difficult, in practice, to withdraw that authority without having to remove their children from schools which, in the context of compulsory education, can result in criminal penalty if alternative schools cannot be found. In *Campbell and Cosans v United Kingdom* (1982),[22] a challenge to the use of the tawse in Scottish state schools, the Court of Human Rights held that deeply held parental views on punishment could be thought of as philosophical convictions which the state needed to recognise. Such a line of argument might be a two-edged sword in that equally serious and cogent parental views in favour of mild corporal punishment might also need protection.[23] The Administrative Court in the United Kingdom, however, has distinguished a philosophical objection to corporal punishment from parental acceptance that corporal punishment is an effective means to good discipline. It denied the protection of Article 2 of the First Protocol to teachers and parents of certain Christian independent schools who were seeking to challenge the legal ban on corporal punishment.[24]

20.2.5 Children's homes

Corporal punishment is banned in children's homes under regulations produced by the Secretary of State which must be followed by local authorities

---

[19] (1995) 19 EHRR 112.
[20] (1989) 60 D&R 5; (1994) 17 EHRR 238.
[21] *Costello-Roberts v United Kingdom* (1995) 19 EHRR 112.
[22] (1982) 4 EHRR 293.
[23] For example, *Seven Individuals v Sweden* Ap. 8811/79; (1982) 29 D&R 104. The parent's case was held to be inadmissible because the ban on mild corporal punishment they objected to did not have the force of law.
[24] *R (Williamson) v Secretary of State for Education and Employment* [2001] EWHC Admin 960; [2002] 1 FLR 493. The Court of Appeal held that Article 2g Protocol 1 was engaged, though it dismissed the appeal. [2002] EWCA Civ 1820; [2003] 1 All ER 385.

and other bodies responsible for operating homes.[25] Regulations, produced by the Department of Health, ban 'physical punishments' in day nurseries, playgroups, children's centres and crèches, but, by amendments introduced in August 2000 by the Department of Health, permit smacking by childminders when permission has been given by parents. Previous guidance had suggested that a refusal by a potential childminder not to smack could be a significant ground for refusing to register her; however, a local authority that treated the refusal as an automatically sufficient ground for not registering, could be held to be acting unlawfully.[26]

20.3 Bodily integrity, the right to life and the right to consent to medical treatments

20.3.1 Suicide and euthanasia

Bodily integrity raises agonisingly difficult questions concerning the power a person has, lawfully, to choose to die. The issue is whether a person has a legal right, under domestic or human rights law, to die rather than to suffer in ways which are, to them, undignified and intolerable. In human rights terms, in issue is the right to life (Article 2 ECHR) and the right to private life (Article 8 ECHR).

A person may choose to kill themselves. Suicide, a willed act of self-destruction,[27] is not an offence under English law and, consequently, neither is attempting suicide.[28] Similarly, the right to life in international law has not been interpreted in a way that places a duty on states to make suicide an offence though, conversely, there are no express requirements that states withdraw the threat of criminal penalties from suicides. Prosecutions for attempted suicide are, arguably, interferences with the private life of the would-be suicide and so would require justification under the terms of Article 8(2) ECHR.

The problems for the law arise if a person of sound mind wishes to die but the acts or omissions of third parties, including medical professionals, are required for this to happen.

Doctors and other medical staff, by agreeing to care for their patients, take on a legal duty towards their patients. Deliberate, even if well intentioned, breach of that duty, if it leads to an outcome recognised by the criminal law such as death or severe injury, can be the basis of an offence. Actions intentionally causing death may justify a murder conviction; failing to discharge the duty by being recklessly or negligently indifferent to the fate of the patient could justify a manslaughter conviction.[29] Similarly, breach of the duty can be the basis of a private action for damages, a tort action in trespass for example.

---

[25] *The Children's Homes Regulations* 1991, SI 1991/1506, paragraph 8; the Children Act 1989, s. 63(11) and Schedule 6.

[26] *Sutton LBC v Davis* [1995] 1 All ER 53.

[27] *Clift v Schwabe* (1846) 3 CB 437; followed in *In re Davis, Decd* [1968] QB 72.

[28] Section 1, Suicide Act 1961.

[29] *R v Stone, R v Dobinson* [1977] 2 All ER 341, where the duty was attributed to an inadequate couple who had taken on the care of the man's sister.

The scope of the duty to treat is limited by the clear consent of the patient. Failure to give appropriate treatment when a patient of sound mind refuses consent will not be a breach of duty by a doctor.[30] The sense of personal autonomy, inherent in the notion of bodily integrity, means that an adult patient, who can give effective consent, must be respected in the choice they make even though relatives, professionals or others think that the result is against the patient's best interests and even if the outcome is the patient's death.[31]

The principle of personal autonomy is sufficiently strong to outweigh the wishes or interests of others such as dependent relatives. A foetus has no independent legal interest in respect of a mother's decision whether or not to have a caesarian birth; even if it did, it is doubtful whether such an interest could outweigh a mother's autonomy.[32] There is no evidence of a greater recognition of a foetus's rights under the ECHR than under English law. Consent of an apparently sensible adult has occasionally been set aside but normally on the grounds that, in the circumstances, an autonomous choice could not be exercised.[33]

This fundamental right to refuse treatment and accept death was given emphatic recognition, on the principle of autonomy, in *Re B (Consent to treatment: Capacity)* (2002).[34]

> A hospital trust refused the request of a patient who, though mentally competent, had a severe physical disability, that she should be able to decide when her life support apparatus should be switched off. In making such a choice she would be deciding the time of her own death.
>
> HELD: a declaration would be granted in favour of the patient. The personal autonomy of the patient, who was of sound mind, needed to be respected despite the consequences.
>
> *Re B (Consent to treatment: Capacity)* [2002] EWHC 429; [2002] 2 All ER 449

A state's duty to protect persons from degrading treatment, under Article 3 ECHR, may require respect for autonomy since whether a highly invasive treatment is, in all the circumstances, intolerably degrading may depend upon the judgment of the patient and be necessarily expressed through their granting or withholding of consent.

The 'living will' of a competent adult is likely to be accepted by the courts. This involves instructions as to treatment in circumstances that, at the time of the will, are foreseen and in which, when they occur, the patient will not be

---

[30] *R v Blaue* [1975] 1 WLR 1411.

[31] *Re JT (Adult: Refusal of Medical Treatment)* [1998] 1 FLR 48 (refusal of renal treatment); *Re C (Adult: Refusal of Medical Treatment)* [1994] 1 WLR 290 (refusal of amputation of gangrenous leg).

[32] *St George's Healthcare NHS Trust v S; R v Collins and others ex parte S* [1998] 3 All ER 673 and *Re MB* [1997] 8 Med LR 217.

[33] For example, *Re T (adult: refusal of medical treatment)* [1992] 4 All ER 649 CA (a lapsed Jehovah's Witness's refusal to accept a blood transfusion was based on the overbearing influence of her mother).

[34] [2002] EWHC 429; [2002] 2 All ER 449. The principle is clearly endorsed by the House of Lords in *Airedale NHS Trust v Bland* [1993] 1 All ER 821 (e.g. 859, per Lord Keith), although this case did not involve a mentally competent patient. See also *St George's Healthcare NHS Trust v S; R v Collins and others ex parte S* [1998] 3 All ER 673.

able to give or withdraw his or her consent.[35] The position of such 'advance directives' made in the absence of knowledge of any particular, developing, condition is much less certain.[36]

Where what the doctors 'do' involves not giving treatment in the first place or withdrawing treatment and allowing an illness to take its course, their actions are likely to be classified as 'omissions' in law and, if done with the free and specific consent of the patient, will not be unlawful either as a crime or a tort. The principle of 'double effect' is also recognised in law: where a doctor, as part of a treatment for which there is consent, properly prescribes drugs, usually for the relief of pain, which have the incidental, foreseeable effect of bringing about an outcome the law otherwise forbids, such as the patient's earlier death.[37] Legal acceptance of such 'passive euthanasia' is not inconsistent with Convention rights.[38]

However, if what the doctor 'does' is seen by the court as a positive act, best understood as hastening death, then there is the likelihood that a serious offence will have been committed. The patient's consent, even though given in sound mind and as a clear expression of their autonomy, is irrelevant. The policy of the law is that the consent of a victim is not a defence to serious crimes against the person such as murder or manslaughter.[39] Euthanasia based on positive actions is unlawful and it is irrelevant that the doctors and other professionals acted in good faith with the humanitarian motive of relieving acute suffering.[40] To kill someone in response to their request is likely to be murder under English law. Section 2 of the Suicide Act 1961 makes it an offence to aid, abet, counsel or procure the suicide or attempted suicide of another. The maximum sentence is 14 years imprisonment. The consent of the Director of Public Prosecutions is required for a prosecution.[41] The law on this has been recently affirmed by the House of Lords and agreed as being compatible with Convention rights.

> P suffered from motor neurone disease and wished to avoid the pain and indignity she would have to bear in the final stages of her illness. She was not dependent on a life-support machine. She was of sound mind but was physically incapable of ending her own life. She needed the assistance of her husband to help her commit suicide at an appropriate time. She sought a declaration from the DPP that her husband would not be prosecuted under section 2 of the Suicide Act 1961.
>   HELD:

---

[35] *Airedale NHS Trust* v *Bland* [1993] 1 All ER 821, 836, 859.

[36] Mason, J.K. and McCall Smith, R.A. (1999) *Law and Medical Ethics*, 5th edn. London: Butterworths, pp. 433–44.

[37] Recognised in *Airedale NHS Trust* v *Bland*; following *R* v *Adams* (1957) – see Palmer, H. (1957) 'Dr Adams' Trial for Murder', *Crim LR* 365; *R* v *Cox* (1992) 12 BMLR 38. See also: *R* v *Moor* [2000] Crim LR 31, discussed in Cooper, S. (2000) 'Summing up intention', 150 *NLJ* 6949, 1258.

[38] Harris, D., O'Boyle, M. and Warbrick, C. (1995) *Law of the European Convention on Human Rights*. London: Butterworths, p. 38.

[39] *R* v *Cox* (1992) 12 BMLR 38. See also *R* v *Brown and other appeals* [1993] 2 All ER 75, discussed in Chapter 21.

[40] *Airedale NHS Trust* v *Bland* 867, per Lord Goff.

[41] Participation in a suicide pact is, on the part of a survivor, likely to amount to the commission of an offence under s. 2 although the public interest is unlikely to require a prosecution (*Dunbar* v *Plant* [1998] Ch 412 CA).

(1) the Bill of Rights 1689 denied the DPP the power to make prospective promises to set the law aside in individual cases;
(2) Article 2 ECHR did not impose a positive duty on states to allow assisted suicide; and
(3) there was no breach of Article 3
   R (Pretty) v *DPP* [2001] UKHL 61; [2002] 1 AC 800

The House of Lord's view that Article 2 ECHR did not confer a right to die was agreed with by the Court of Human Rights. The Strasbourg court also found that there was no breach of a duty by the state, under Article 3, to prevent a person suffering degrading treatment. Article 8(1), on the other hand, was engaged. The 'essence' of the Convention is respect for dignity and freedom, and it is through the concept of private life that questions about the quality of life can be asked. However, the Court held that the state had satisfied the requirements of Article 8(2): the DPP's refusal was a proportionate application of a legal rule designed to protect the terminally ill from fraud and abuse and was, therefore, for a legitimate purpose.[42]

In so far as the argument about consensual killing turns on the distinction between acts and omissions there can be serious difficulties. There is an arbitrariness in the way matters are classified: the withdrawal of treatment, which clearly requires action by doctors, is, nevertheless, classed as an omission. It may be illogical, even cruel, to grant or withhold permission for a death to occur on the classification of what needs to be done, when it is the condition of the patient, the reasonableness of their desire for death, that should be in issue. A helpless would-be suicide is denied a freedom that he or she would otherwise have solely because of their helplessness and the need for another's assistance. Under Article 14 ECHR the Convention is violated if a matter covered by the Convention is dealt with in a manner which discriminates between different types of persons and which does not have a reasonable justification. In *Pretty* v *United Kingdom* (2002) the Court of Human Rights decided that the ban on assisted suicide, which included both those of sound and unsound mind, had a reasonable justification (protection of the terminally ill from abuse and fraud) and so did not violate Article 14. There is, of course, no moral consensus on the issue and for those who intuitively oppose euthanasia the discrimination point is absurd yet for those who support euthanasia it gives legal expression to a major reason for that support.

20.3.2 Child of sound mind

Autonomy, up to and including a refusal of treatment which will cause death, is limited in respect of children and young persons under 18 years old and of adults not of sound mind.

Regarding children, the law accepts that parents and those with parental responsibility can give consent on behalf of their children. The Family Law Reform Act 1969, section 8(1) gives minors between the ages of 16 and 18 the right to consent to medical treatment. A child under 16 may be able to give consent to treatment under the *Gillick* principle.

---

[42] *Pretty* v *United Kingdom* (Ap. 2346/02) [2002] 2 FLR 45.

A Department of Health circular asserted that a doctor could lawfully prescribe contraceptives to girls under the age of 16 (the age of consent) and, exceptionally, do so without their parent's consent. The health authority refused to give G an assurance that her daughter would not be given contraceptives or advice without her consent.

HELD (HL): that there was no absolute fixed rule that parents had the exclusive right to consent to their children's medical treatment. A child of sufficient understanding and intelligence who fully understood the treatment that was proposed and its consequences and who could make a well founded decision was capable of consenting to his or her own medical treatment.

Gillick v *West Norfolk and Wisbech Area Health Authority and Another* [1986] 1 AC 112

The significance of '*Gillick* competence' diminishes with the seriousness of the medical issues involved. Where there is the likelihood of death or irreversible damage resulting from a competent child's refusal of treatment, the principle may mean little more than the need to give serious consideration to the wishes of a child which will, nevertheless, be overridden on strong paternalistic grounds reflecting the court's understanding of the future quality of life probably available to the child. The courts have held that the expressed wishes of an otherwise competent child can be overreached by a court exercising its wardship or inherent jurisdiction or by parents or others exercising parental responsibility. Section 8 of the Family Law Reform Act 1969 does not extend to a refusal of consent and does not remove the rights others may have to give consent concurrently with that of a competent child.[43]

If intelligent understanding is the main criterion for consent, it is arbitrary for this to be determined by age: it is unreasonable to deny to someone under 18 and otherwise competent absolute control over their bodily integrity on grounds of age alone. Supporters of a modified *Gillick* position, which seems to reflect the current law, can deny the claim of arbitrariness on the grounds that it is good judgment, not just intelligence, that is in issue and good judgment is a matter of experience which is itself a function of age.

20.3.3 Incompetent child

A child may be incompetent when, because of age, development or some kind of mental incapacity, he or she is not capable of sufficient understanding to be able to give effective consent to medical treatment. In that case, consent can be given by parents or others with parental responsibility which may include local authorities with care responsibilities under the Children Act 1989. Consent can also be given by the court exercising its wardship jurisdiction or under its inherent powers over children within its jurisdiction. The wishes of children concerned are to be taken into account to an extent that reflects their intelligent perception but it is implicit in the law that these wishes can be overborn by those with (until the child is *Gillick* competent) the predominant power to consent.

---

[43] For example, *Re W (a minor) (medical treatment)* [1992] 4 All ER 627 – refusal by a 16-year-old girl of best interests treatment for anorexia nervosa; *Re R (a minor) (wardship: medical treatment)* [1991] 4 All ER 177 – refusal by a 15-year-old girl, ward of court, of best interests treatment for deteriorating mental health; *Re M (child: refusal of medical treatment)* [1999] 2 FLR 1097, where the court overrode a competent child's wish not to have a heart transplant.

The basic test used by the courts is the 'best interests' of the child. The views of doctors and other professionals are likely to be prominent and may, in appropriate cases, even overrule parental wishes. Parents may be simply negligent, in which case they are likely to have committed an offence under section 1 of the Children and Young Person's Act 1933.[44] Alternatively they may be motivated by a reason of belief or conscience to refuse consent to life-saving treatment. Here, again, a parent may be liable for the offence[45] and the conscientious nature of the refusal is no defence. Any right to freedom of thought, conscience and religion under Article 9 ECHR is subject to restriction in respect of protecting the rights of others, including the child. A court may be asked to order treatment on the basis, for example, of an application for the child to be made a ward by a local authority, discharging its duty, under the Children Act 1989, to safeguard and promote the welfare of children in their area.[46] On the basis of the best interests of the child the courts have been prepared to order treatment to be given to seriously ill children, despite their parents preference that the child should be allowed to die a natural death,[47] and have even, exceptionally, permitted doctors to withdraw treatment from very ill babies against the wishes of parents.[48] It is now no longer sufficient to consider only the 'best interests' of the child but also his or her Convention rights such as a 'right', inherent in Article 3, to dignity in death and perhaps, in respect of arguments about the quality of life, a child's limited right to private life under Article 8 ECHR.[49]

20.3.4 Incompetent adults

For patients detained under the Mental Health Act 1983 some treatments for the mental disorder can be given without consent.[50] Treatments not directly aimed at alleviating the mental disorder, however, require consent. The courts no longer have jurisdiction, *parens patriae*, to give consent in the patient's stead.[51] The court is competent to declare a course of treatment, chosen by doctors or carers but to which the adult is unable to consent, not unlawful so long as it is in the patient's best interests.[52] The best interests test is criticised for giving too much weight to the views of professionals, though the test is not confined to their views. A person with impaired mental capacity but who can, nevertheless, understand the purpose of proposed medical treatment, is entitled to the legal protection of his right to consent to treatment[53] or to refuse

---

[44] *R v Sheppard and another* [1980] 3 All ER 899.
[45] *R v Senior* [1899] 1 QB 283, as explained in *R v Sheppard and another* [1980] 3 All ER 899.
[46] In *Re R (Minor)* (1993) 15 BMLR 72 the court overrode the wishes of Jehovah Witness parents that their child should not receive blood products.
[47] *Re B (a minor) (wardship: medical treatment)* [1981] 1 WLR 1421.
[48] *A National Health Service Trust v D* [2000] 2 FLR 677.
[49] *Pretty v United Kingdom* (Ap. 2346/02) [2002] 2 FLR 45.
[50] Section 63, Mental Health Act 1983.
[51] *F v West Berkshire Health Authority and another (Mental Health Act Commission intervening)* [1989] 2 All ER 545 HL.
[52] *F v West Berkshire Health Authority and another (Mental Health Act Commission intervening)* [1989] 2 All ER 545 HL.
[53] *Re C (Adult: Refusal of Medical Treatment)* [1994] 1 WLR 290.

treatment even if may lead to death.[54] In *Airedale NHS Trust* v *Bland* (1993)[55] the House of Lords declared that it was appropriate for doctors to cease life-preserving treatment of a young man in a 'persistent vegitative state' on the test of the patient's best interests. There was no legal requirement that life, for itself, must be preserved despite the absence of any quality to the life. This approach is not incompatible with Article 2 ECHR. Any positive duties on the state were discharged by a properly made clinical decision based on a test of the patient's best interests.[56] Following *Pretty* v *United Kingdom*, it can be suggested that any contrary principle, asserting the value of life itself over an assessment of its quality, would be incompatible with Article 8.

20.4 Bodily integrity and non-therapeutic treatment

20.4.1 Non-therapeutic interventions

The courts can order, or uphold the rights of others to impose, non-therapeutic medical treatments on individuals, particularly children. These are physical interventions done, without or irrespective of consent, and the primary purpose is not to cure a disease but some other social or legal purpose. Courts have, for example, various powers to order medical examinations of children. These may be for purposes of assessment or to justify an emergency protection measure.[57] Such powers are exercised in the best interests of the child and are consistent with Convention rights in so far as they seek to protect the interests of children.[58] Similarly, blood tests, done to prove paternity, can be ordered by a court under powers in sections 20–23 of the Family Law Reform Act 1969. The consent of a person over 16 is required. In the case of small children, if such consent is not forthcoming from the person with care and control, the court can order a test in the best interests of the child.[59]

Parents can consent to non-therapeutic procedures of a relatively minor kind at least so long as they do not reach the level of severity of inhuman or degrading treatment implicit in Article 3 ECHR. Ear piercing of young children to satisfy parental vanity, perhaps to confirm gender to a wider world, is an example; it is unlikely to cause serious resentment when the child grows up. Some temptations for parents, or older children, are prohibited by law. Tattooing of a person under 18, other than for medical reasons, is an offence[60] and this is best explained by the permanency of the procedure.

20.4.2 Circumcision and cultural identity

Parents can consent to the ritual circumcision of their young sons.[61] Such an operation can be seen as in the child's best interests in so far as it is an

---

[54] *Re JT (Adult: Refusal of Medical Treatment)* [1998] 1 FLR 48.
[55] [1993] 1 All ER 821.
[56] *NHS Trust A* v *M/NHS Trust B* v *H* [2001] 1 All ER 801.
[57] For example, ss. 43 and 44, Children Act 1989.
[58] Also consistent with the basic principles of the United Nations Convention on the Rights of the Child.
[59] See *S* v *S* [1972] AC 24 for the common law approach.
[60] Tattooing of Minors Act 1969.
[61] As they can do when such a procedure is medically called for.

important feature in establishing the social, cultural and religious identity of the boy and his acceptance in, predominantly, the Moslem or Jewish community into which he has been born. Where parents agree it seems the circumcision is lawful. This was agreed *obiter* by the House of Lords in *R v Brown* (1994),[62] supported by the Law Commission[63] and expressly accepted by the Court of Appeal in *Re J (child's religious upbringing and circumcision)* (2000).[64] Where parents disagree, the issue is ultimately for the court to decide. Circumcision is one of a number of irreparable interventions, such as sterilisation, which require judicial authority. Again, permission is based on a judgment of the child's best interests and cannot be determined solely by those with parental responsibility.[65]

Parents cannot consent to the ritual circumcision of their daughters. Section 1 of the Prohibition of Female Circumcision Act 1985 makes the performance or the aiding, abetting, counselling or procuring of such a procedure, for non-therapeutic purposes, a serious criminal offence. Though the arguments for cultural identity and acceptance may be as strong as they are for male circumcision, female circumcision is distinguished on the grounds that it is 'undoubtedly a mutilation which is designed to control female sexuality'.[66] Male circumcision is seen as a more slight, normally harmless, intervention which cannot justify legal prohibition. There is a developing body of hostile medical opinion and some evidence that sexual pleasure is, in fact, diminished by the removal of the foreskin.[67] If the latter is the case to any significant degree then the ground of distinction with female circumcision is diminished and a case for abolition is made stronger.

In *Re J* (2000)[68] it was accepted that parents had rights under Article 9 ECHR to bring their children up within the tenets of their religion and this can include ritualistic practices such as circumcision. The problem is that such a right is limited, under Article 9(2), by reference to the rights of others. If medical evidence accumulates that male circumcision is harmful and if there are complaints from circumcised adults (secular Jews or Muslims, perhaps), the courts may have to rule on whether childhood, non-consensual circumcision is a violation of a person's right to private life. The courts could take a strong line and hold that parents can only give consent for their children in medical cases; alternatively, and most likely, they would maintain the 'best interests' test which, given the link to social acceptance, is likely to be met by circumcision where parent's agree.

---

[62] *R v Brown* [1994] 1 AC 212, 231.
[63] The Law Commission Consultation Papers Vol. 23, pp. 119–20.
[64] [2000] 1 FCR 307. See Vickers, J. and Board, J. (2000) 'Circumcision – the Unkindest Cut of All', *NLJ* 1694 (17 November).
[65] *Re J (child's religious upbringing and circumcision)* [2000] 1 FCR 307, paragraph 32, per Dame Elizabeth Butler-Sloss.
[66] *Re J (Specific Issue Orders Muslim Upbringing and Circumcision)* [1995] 2 FLR 678, 688. See *R v Adesanya* (1994) *The Times*, 16 and 17 July.
[67] Dr S's evidence as summarised in *Re J* [1995] 2 FLR 678.
[68] [2000] 1 FCR 307.

20.5 Abortion, life and privacy

English law does not recognise a foetus as having a legal right-bearing existence independently of the rights and interests of the mother.[69] Sections 58 and 59 of the Offences Against the Person Act 1861 create offences designed to prevent mothers intentionally procuring their miscarriage and section 1 of the Infant Life (Preservation) Act 1929 makes it an offence intentionally to cause the death of an unborn 'child' which is capable of being born alive. Twenty-eight weeks was stipulated as the period from which a child is presumed to be capable of being born alive.

These provisions are now subject to the Abortion Act 1967 as amended by the Human Fertilisation and Embryology Act 1990. All lawful abortions must be performed by a registered medical practitioner and be agreed to on the basis of opinions as to the permissible grounds formed by two registered medical practitioners acting in good faith.

One ground for permissible abortions is limited to pregnancies that have not exceeded their twenty-fourth week. This is where, under section 1(1)(a) of the Abortion Act 1967:

> ... the continuance of the pregnancy would involve risk, greater than if the pregnancy were terminated, of injury to the physical or mental health of the pregnant woman or any existing children of her family.

Section 1(2) permits medical practitioners to take 'the pregnant woman's actual or reasonably foreseeable environment' into account in the assessment of risk.

This is a controversial ground of abortion. Critics allege that, given the high level of safety of abortion methods, there will always be a greater risk of injury to a pregnant woman's health from continuing with a pregnancy than from early termination. The Act says nothing about the reasons a woman must have for seeking an abortion and so, critics say, the Act provides 'abortion on demand'. The Act, it should be noted, removes from medical practitioners a criminal liability which would otherwise exist. Nothing in the Act gives a woman the right to insist upon an abortion even if the grounds exist. Doctors are under no duties to perform an abortion but may do so for any legal reason so long as the grounds exist. The law is silent on the reasons for performing abortions and this is left to the medical agencies, NHS, commercial and charitable.

The controversial nature of abortion and its obvious bearing on fundamental issues of respect for life explain the provision under section 4 of the Abortion Act 1967. This allows a person to refuse on grounds of conscience what would otherwise be a contractual or statutory duty to participate in any treatment, other than a life-saving treatment, authorised by the Act. The burden of proof lies with the conscientious objector. Conscientious objection may only be tolerable so long as it has no impact on the achievement of publicly agreed

---

[69] For example, *In Re F (in utero)* [1988] Fam 122; *Paton v BPAST* [1979] QB 276, 279; *C v S* [1988] QB 135, 140; and see *St George's Healthcare NHS Trust v S; R v Collins and others ex parte S* [1998] 3 All ER 673 and *Re MB* [1997] 8 Med LR 217.

purposes. It is wrong that a personal judgment of conscience can veto the implementation of a collectively agreed good. The conscientious objection of a senior doctor could, for example, limit abortion provision in a particular area of the NHS. If there is no legal duty to provide abortion services, then no legal problems arise. However, regarding the NHS, there is likely to be a general duty, founded in administrative law, for the distribution of services to be grounded on reasonable, egalitarian grounds and the conscience clause could mean that the availability of abortion is limited by the arbitrary factor of the presence in key posts of conscientious objectors. Conscientious objection is limited to those directly involved in the medical activity of an abortion. It does not extend to ancillary workers, such a medical secretaries or referring GPs.[70]

Abortion is permitted on three other grounds. These are less controversial since they embody purposes for which medical treatment would normally be expected. They are:

Abortion Act 1967, section 1(1)

(b) that the termination is necessary to prevent grave permanent injury to the physical or mental health of the pregnant woman; or

(c) that the continuance of the pregnancy would involve risk to the life of the pregnant woman, greater than if the pregnancy were terminated; or

(d) that there is a substantial risk that if the child were born it would suffer from such physical or mental abnormalities as to be seriously handicapped.

The pregnant woman's 'actual or reasonably foreseeable environment' can be taken into account in the risk assessment under (b). Abortion performed under these three grounds is not time limited nor linked to the Infant Life (Preservation) Act 1929 and so can, in theory, be performed on a 'child capable of being born alive'.

The European Convention on Human Rights has not provided the basis for strong guidance on the laws that states ought to have in respect of abortion. Women likely to have standing under Article 34 will usually be complaining about too restrictive abortion laws, though restrictive regimes, such Ireland's, have not been directly challenged. A ban on abortion which applied not withstanding a significant threat to a woman's life or health would be hard to justify under Article 2 ECHR which, arguably, imposes a duty to permit life-saving abortions in such extreme and restricted circumstances. The Commission has held that abortion is not simply a matter of private life[71] and hence states do not have to justify their abortion laws in terms of Article 8(2) ECHR. There have been challenges to liberal abortion regimes. The father may have standing under Article 34 to bring a Strasbourg case, but has few substantive rights to prevent an abortion which is otherwise lawful under the domestic law.[72] In *RH* v *Norway*[73] the Commission accepted a rule permitting early abortion where having a child would 'place [the mother] in a difficult situation in life'. The basic issue of whether a foetus has a right to life under

[70] *Janaway* v *Salford AHA* [1988] 2 WLR 1350 HL.
[71] *Brüggemann and Scheuten* v *FRG* (1978) 10 D&R 100.
[72] *Paton* v *United Kingdom* (1981) 3 EHRR 408.
[73] Hudoc. Ap. 17004/90.

Article 2 ECHR has been left undecided by the Court.[74] But the Court is also clear that, even if the foetus does have such a right, there remains an implied limitation to protect the life and health of the mother which can be given effect by an abortion law.

[74] *Paton v United Kingdom* (1981) 3 EHRR 408.

21
Sexual freedom

21.1 Introduction

Few would contest that the sexual drive, in its direct non-sublimated form, is one of the most powerful and determining of the features through which the human person is defined. Sexuality and sexual activity are significant components of any description of a human individual. It deals with the most intimate and personal aspects of a life and with the involvement with others. Sexuality is essentially linked to the concept of a person as a private individual. From this perspective there are no questions of the common good or the public interest that relate to sexuality and any role for the law is doubtful. The law should not delimit sexual practices or partners; in particular it should not restrict the freedom to marry and have children with whom one wants.

Indeed, sexual freedom, or aspects of it, may be asserted as a fundamental human right. Natural law thinkers, for example, commonly assert that a right to procreative freedom, the freedom to have children, is self-evidently fundamental; the justification for such rights is derived from reasoning about human nature and the general circumstances of humanity.[1] If sexual freedom is justified only by the self-evident good of procreation, however, the full range of sexual practices, such as masturbation, felatio and buggery and homosexual practices of any kind, will fall outside the scope of a fundamental right to sexual freedom. A different philosophical position might assert that the pursuit of pleasure is the underlying point to life. This would, of course, justify a right to the full range of sexual practices but, unlike procreation, it is hard to see why such a right should be fundamental and outweigh claims about the public interest, the common good or the power of morality.[2] A right to sexual freedom, which is not limited to procreative activities but extends to the full range of sexual activity, is, therefore, best understood as an incident of the more general right to privacy. On this view, and apart from procreative sexual activity, the right to sexual activity can reasonably be restricted on the same grounds as any other aspect of privacy, no less than but also, more controversially, no more than.

---

[1] For example, Finnis, J. (1980) *Natural Law and Natural Rights*. Oxford: Oxford University Press, for whom procreative freedom is a basic good.

[2] One of the earliest defences in English of homosexuality, on utilitarian grounds, is by Jeremy Bentham – see Bentham, J. (1978). 'Offences Against Oneself: Paederasty', in *Journal of Homosexuality*, Summer–Fall, published by Hawarth Press.

The power of sexual passion, however, makes it an area of life that is open to abuse and this is one reason why the law is used to regulate it. Sexual activity may be imposed upon another, including through violence or the threat of violence, and most societies have special offences such as, in England and Wales, rape and indecent assault, to try and deal with this. Usually such offences are committed by men against women but are not confined to such. Despite the absence of violence or its threat, sexual activity may be imposed upon another through the exploitation of a relationship of trust.

Controversially, however, sexuality is linked to morality and to socio-cultural ideas of right and proper behaviour. Many societies have sought to limit certain sexual practices and to punish them even if undertaken on the basis of consent. Male homosexuality generally and buggery, both heterosexual and homosexual, have been prime targets. Though consented to by those involved, they are seen as undermining the moral values of the majority or of an idea of society as a whole, and therefore worthy of suppression. Similarly, societies have, through their legal systems, sometimes tried to promote marriage as the primary context for sexual activity. A Freudian explanation for such moral thinking is based on the fear of the pleasure principle, of the destructive impact of unbridled and unsublimated sexuality on the progress of civilisation.[3] A more economic approach explains such moral thinking in terms of the social need to control the fecundity of women. This may be rooted in a man's alleged need to be confident in the legitimacy of his heirs and thus the security of his property[4] and discloses itself in partriarchy, the need and opportunity of men to exert power and possession over women. Through contraception and through economic and social change, women are now more able than ever before to inhabit primary economic, social and political roles that, previously, have been preserved for men. Given this, the economic explanation for general moral restriction on sexual practices is severely weakened and, with it, we find society today finding fewer and fewer morally based reasons for limiting sexual activity by consenting adults.

In *The Enforcement of Morals*[5] Patrick Devlin argued that the state had a legitimate interest in upholding strongly felt moral values in society and could, in reference to the issue of the day, enforce criminal sanctions against consensual homosexual practices on these grounds. The test for what was or was not permissible was not a matter of majority opinion but could be left to the good sense of a randomly selected jury. The basis of the argument was that such moral discrimination is essential to the cohesiveness and integrity of a society; its identity as a whole is conditioned by moral values, and from this comes the legitimate interest of the state to suppress immoral behaviour. What was or was not permissible would change over time.

Objections to this view contest many of its assumptions: in particular that social cohesion really does depend upon upholding particular views of

---

[3] Freud, S. (1930) *Civilisation and its Discontents*. London: Hogarth Press.

[4] See David Hume's famous argument justifying the application of different moral standards to men and women on sexual matters; Hume, D. (1978) *A Treatise of Human Nature*. Oxford: Oxford University Press.

[5] Devlin, P. (1965) *The Enforcement of Morals*. Oxford: Oxford University Press.

acceptable sexual behaviour and, second, that, even if this were true, there is no test for identifying what those standards might be which is sufficiently rigorous to be a safe foundation for a criminal penalty.

Those opposed to the 'enforcement of morality' are also likely to uphold a liberal conception of law. This requires that, on matters of personal behaviour, the only test for legal intervention is whether harm to others will result. Behaviour which is harmless to others should not be subject to criminal sanction even if it harms those involved.[6] The difficulty with defining 'harm' is very great and for some political theorists it is a sufficient reason for discarding the approach. The argument from harm is at its strongest if 'harm' is defined as harm to another's interests; that is to say, an action is only harmful in the required sense if it prevents others doing something that, because it is in their interests, they would otherwise want to do. The point of the argument is to prevent an action being stopped simply because others, who may be the majority or an influential group, are offended or disgusted by knowing of the action. The fact that an action is thought to be offensive or disgusting is not in itself sufficient to justify legal constraint.

More recent, contractarian accounts of liberalism are also likely to oppose the 'enforcement of morality' by the law. At the heart of such accounts is the claim that the state should be 'neutral' as between different conceptions of the good. Individuals will have different views of what goes to make a worthwhile life for them, and the state has no business in promoting one view over another but should establish just conditions in which one person's freedom can be permitted as far as it is compatible with the equal degree of freedom for others.[7] Sexual activity and sexual identity are likely to figure significantly in many people's conceptions of what is good for them and, according to the theory, should be permitted so long as it does not prevent others acting in pursuit of their own interests. On this view a neutral state has a duty not to interfere with consensual choices on sexual activity.[8]

21.2 Reform of the law

The law in England and Wales is being reformed. In July 2000 the Home Office published a review of sexual offences, *Setting the Boundaries: Reforming the law on sex offences*[9] and many of its principles and proposals will be enacted in 2003.[10] For *Setting the Boundaries* any reform of the law should reflect the tolerance now found in social attitudes. The underlying principle is that the law should not invade sexual privacy unless there are strong reasons for doing so. Normally these will be based on lack of consent. The law should maintain and even expand criminal offences based upon the absence of consent.

---

[6] The argument is associated with John Stuart Mill: Mill, J.S. (1962) *On Liberty*. London: Fontana, chapter 1.

[7] See Rawls, J. (1972) *A Theory of Justice*. Oxford: Oxford University Press, and the tradition of political theory it has spawned.

[8] See, for example, Leader, S. (1990) 'The Right to Privacy, the Enforcement of Morals, and the Judicial Function: An Argument', *Current Legal Problems* 115–34.

[9] Home Office, July 2000.

[10] See: Sexual Offences Bill, 2002–3.

However, through properly defined offences, the law should continue to protect the vulnerable, in particular children, the mentally impaired and those in a relationship of trust, even if they may have given, or appear to have given, their consent. The law should not differentiate between rules applicable to men, to women and to homosexuals. It should only ever regulate consensual sex between competent adults for 'very good reason', which can include the protection of the family as an institution. The review contains a consideration of the law in the context of the Human Rights Act 1998 and the need for compatibility of English law with Convention rights.

21.3 Convention rights

Sexual activity and sexual identity are engaged by Article 8(1), the 'right to respect for private and family life', a scheduled Convention right in the Human Rights Act 1998. 'Private ... life' extends to the making of relationships with others, covers the 'emotional field, for the development and fulfilment of one's own personality' and includes the 'physical and moral integrity of the person' part of which is a person's sexual life.[11] Sexual activity in public, however, may fall outside the protection of Article 8(1).[12] Restrictions on sexual activity, therefore, must be justified in the terms of Article 8(2): they must be 'in accordance with the law', for one of the legitimate purposes listed, and each individual restrictive act must be proportionate and thus 'necessary'. Article 8(2) allows restrictions to be 'for the protection of health or morals or for the protection of the rights and freedoms of others' and these terms are likely to be sufficient for any reasonable legal restrictions. Where a restriction is based on the protection of morals, the Court of Human Rights tends to allow a wide margin of appreciation. The Convention also prohibits discrimination, less favourable treatment, in respect of a Convention-protected freedom.[13] Laws that distinguish between the treatment of heterosexuals and homosexuals may be in issue on this point. Less favourable treatment can be permitted in terms of a 'reasonable and objective justification', but widespread social dislike of another's sexual preferences is unlikely to meet this test.

The Court of Human Rights has held that, in some circumstances, Article 8 may impose a positive duty on states to take steps to ensure that Article 8 freedoms are protected. In particular the state may need to ensure that the law provides adequate protection for vulnerable people from sexual exploitation. Gaps in the law which leave vulnerable people exposed to risk to their private life may need to be filled.[14]

---

[11] See for example *Niemietz* v *Germany* (1992) 16 EHRR 97; *X* v *Iceland* (1976) 5 D&R 86; *X and Y* v *The Netherlands* (1985) 8 EHRR 235.

[12] Harris, D., O'Boyle, M. and Warbrick, C. (1995) *Law of the Convention on Human Rights*. London: Butterworths.

[13] Article 14 ECHR.

[14] *X and Y* v *The Netherlands* (1985) 8 EHRR 235: the Convention was breached because the law of The Netherlands prevented a child with a mental disorder from bringing a criminal action; in *Stubbings* v *United Kingdom* (1996) 23 EHRR 213, the Court of Human Rights emphasised the duty on states to protect children and the vulnerable from serious interference with their private life.

21.4 The limits of consent

Most sexual crime does not lead to major civil liberties issues. It is a matter of non-consensual sex forced on an adult or a child, usually by a male adult, sometimes by an older child. Such behaviour is punished by a range of offences, such as rape or indecent assault. From the perspective of this book the focus is on those forms of sexual relationship which are forbidden or restricted by the law irrespective of whether there is consent or not.

21.4.1 Children

The age of consent to sexual intercourse and sexual acts which, without consent, would be acts of indecency is 16, both for heterosexual and homosexual acts. Intercourse with a girl under 13[15] is a serious offence which can lead to life imprisonment; intercourse with a girl between 13 and 16, though still an offence, is less serious.[16] Consent is not in issue. Neither a girl nor a boy under the age of 16 is lawfully able to consent to a sexual act which would, in the absence of consent, be an indecent assault.[17] Even actual full consent, by a '*Gillick* competent' 15-year-old, does not prevent such offences being committed although the prosecution's discretion may prevent a case being brought. Such offences are not rape, there is actual consent, and the concept of statutory rape is not proposed by *Setting the Boundaries*. Rape retains its deep seriousness by being based on the absence of actual consent. The point of the law is that the state has a duty to protect children and young persons from exploitation or manipulation and from the consequences of their own poor judgment. *Setting the Boundaries* proposes to keep the age of consent at 16 for such reasons. The age of consent also gives young persons unlawfulness as a reason for refusing a sexual advance. A higher age of consent, 18, has been introduced by the Sexual Offences (Amendment) Act 2000. This relates to relationships where an adult is in a position of trust, such as between a social worker and a client-child in a children's home.

21.4.2 The mentally ill

Persons suffering from a mental illness are protected by the general law and offences of rape and indecent assault etc. apply to such persons equally as anyone else. Where an offence is based on lack of consent, such as rape, lack of an actual ability to give consent may establish the offence although the accused may be able to satisfy the court of the honesty of his belief in consent.

Persons with serious mental conditions and patients in institutions have additional protection under the law. It is justified by their vulnerability. Sexual intercourse by a man with a woman who is 'defective' or a sexual act by a man with another man suffering from a 'severe mental handicap' is an offence.[18]

---

[15] Section 5, Sexual Offences Act 1956.
[16] Section 6, Sexual Offences Act 1956.
[17] Sections 14 and 15, Sexual Offences Act 1956.
[18] Section 7, Sexual Offences Act 1956 and s. 1(3), Sexual Offences Act 1967 respectively.

'Defective' (an insulting term) and 'severe mental handicap' are defined in the same way to mean 'a person suffering from a state of arrested or incomplete development of mind which includes severe impairment of intelligence or social functioning'.[19] The legislation aims to protect those with severe mental impairment and does not extend to everyone in a mental institution or who has been diagnosed with a mental illness. Thus it can be declared lawful for carers and medical staff to require the sterilisation of a woman with mental impairment who is able to consent to a sex and, presumably, enjoy a lawful sexual relationship, albeit she is not capable of giving consent to a sterilisation operation[20] or cope with having children. A male member of staff in a mental institution commits an offence if he has sexual intercourse with a female patient or commits buggery or some other indecent act with a male patient. The basis of the offence is the breach of a relationship of trust and the offence applies irrespective of consent. *Setting the Boundaries* proposes extending and rationalising these offences into the general offence, no longer gender specific, of abusing a relationship of trust.

The problem of special law in this area is to permit proper protection for the vulnerable while avoiding intrusive, paternalist restriction on the sexual lives of mentally impaired people. *Setting the Boundaries* acknowledges the problem and seeks a clearer definition of the degree and nature of the mental impairment which prevents proper consent to sexual activity.

21.4.3 Family

Consent is irrelevant to sexual relations, specifically intercourse, within the immediate family. The general sexual offences and the rules on the age of consent apply but sections 10 and 11 of the Sexual Offences Act 1956 create offences of incest which apply even to consensual acts, should they occur. Incest involves sexual intercourse, specifically, involving a man or a woman and a person he or she knows to be his or her grandchild, child, sibling, half-sibling or parent. The purpose of the law of incest is the protection of children from abusive family relationships and adults from abusive relationships which may have started when they were children. More generally, it is to uphold the family as a place of trust and safety. *Setting the Boundaries* suggests widening the scope of the offence to include a fuller range of sexual activities and to include step-relations, unmarried parents and primary carers.

Since the protection of children is at the heart of the offence, it is not clear why the offence should be applied to the few cases of adult siblings pursuing a sexual relationship. *Setting the Boundaries* would maintain the offence in these circumstances on the ground that an adult relationship may have built on an exploitative childhood one. If there is genuine consent, begun or revived in adulthood, keeping the offence looks like outlawing consensual sex on the grounds of a moral objection, or even an argument from eugenics, rather than a proper concern for the safety of children within the family.

---

[19] Section 45, Sexual Offences Act 1956.
[20] For example, *F v West Berkshire Health Authority and another (Mental Health Act Commission intervening)* [1989] 2 All ER 545 HL.

21.4.4 Alleged wrongfulness

Some forms of entirely consensual sexual activity have been crimes or made subject to special constraints because, for various historically specific reasons, they have been thought to be morally wrong. They may, for example, be held to be unnatural, and thus (what does not follow) objectionable; or the majority, or a consensus of the powerful, may claim to be offended by the idea that they take place. The basic point is that the sexual activity is in some way restricted even though there is no question of rape or assault and even though the parties are adults about whose capacity to consent there is no question. The general arguments about such crimes, the question of the 'enforcement of morality', have been rehearsed earlier in this chapter. The main examples are male homosexuality, buggery and sado-masochism.

Homosexuality

Male homosexuality has always been highly controversial. Buggery, which can be committed between men, is an offence under section 12 of the Sexual Offences Act 1956 and section 13 creates the offence of 'gross indecency' between men. Gross indecency is not defined but includes acts such as mutual masturbation and oral sex. Homosexual acts in public, such as in public lavatories, have also been prosecuted as common law outrages of public decency.[21] The Sexual Offences (Amendment) Act 1967 removed criminal sanctions from both buggery and gross indecency if it took place between no more than two consenting adults, over 21 years of age, and in private.[22] Subsequent Acts have lowered the age of consent to such acts and now, by virtue of the Sexual Offences (Amendment) Act 2000, it is 16, the same as for heterosexual relations.[23]

'Private' is not defined in the 1967 Act, although it stipulates that an act is not private if more than two persons take part or are present or if the act takes place in a public lavatory. Restricting privacy to no more than two men has been successfully challenged before the European Court of Human Rights.

ADT was convicted of gross indecency under section 13 of the Sexual Offences Act 1956. His private dwelling had been searched by police. Police had removed videos which showed up to four men taking part in homosexual acts in the dwelling.

HELD (ECHR): Article 8 had been violated. ADT's private life had been interfered with; he was prosecuted solely because more than two men had been involved in the acts. There was no likelihood that the videos would be made public. The state had not shown that the prosecution was necessary for the protection of morals.

ADT v *United Kingdom* Ap. 35765/97

---

[21] For example, *R* v *Mayling* [1963] 2 QB 717.

[22] Maintaining the criminal illegality of private homosexual acts is likely to be incompatible with Article 8 ECHR: *Dudgeon* v *United Kingdom* (1982) 4 EHRR 149; *Norris* v *Ireland* (1991) 13 EHRR 186.

[23] In *Sutherland* v *United Kingdom* Ap. 25186/94 (2001) *The Times*, 13 April the Commission of Human Rights found that to have different ages of consent between male and female homosexuals violated Article 8 ECHR when taken together with Article 14.

The Court accepted that the state had a genuine interest in limiting public sexual acts, but here the acts were entirely private and the prosecution was based on the numbers involved alone.

The Court in *ADT v United Kingdom* could have gone on to consider whether Article 14, 'prohibition of discrimination', might apply. Only male homosexuals, unlike female homosexuals or heterosexuals, are barred from group sex in otherwise private circumstances. Similarly, sexual activity by heterosexuals in a public lavatory will not necessarily be an offence and, in the past at least, it is clear that male homosexuals have been much more likely to be prosecuted for public displays of sexual desire than heterosexual couples and, perhaps, lesbians.[24] There is no offence of gross indecency between women. A girl under 16 cannot consent to an act which would otherwise be a sexual assault and that is the principal legal rule relating to lesbians. *Sutherland v United Kingdom*[25] suggests that discrimination against male homosexuals in comparison with female homosexuals will, in the absence of good reason, be likely to violate Article 14 taken with Article 8. Social disapproval of male homosexuality is unlikely to be a sufficient reason. The discriminatory features of the law are hard to justify, given the general lack of credence for any kind of 'enforcement of morals' position. *Setting the Boundaries* suggests the repeal of section 13 of the Sexual Offences Act 1956 for consenting adults.

Buggery

Consensual buggery, anal intercourse, is treated differently from vaginal intercourse. Section 12 of the Sexual Offences Act 1956 makes it an offence for a man to commit buggery with any person, a man or a woman. The reform of the law since 1967, mentioned above, extends to buggery by a man on a woman and so no offence is committed by consenting persons over the age of 16 in private. 'In private' is defined the same as for indecent acts between men and so there is the same incompatability with Article 8 ECHR. *Setting the Boundaries* suggests repeal of section 12 and a focus more on preventing non-consensual acts and protecting the young and vulnerable.

Sado-masochism

In one area of consensual sexual activity, the policy of the law is still in favour of criminality, at least as regards its most serious manifestations. This is sado-masochism, through which consenting adults get pleasure from doing painful or dangerous things to each other. What is done is sufficiently serious to be a criminal offence and the courts have denied that the consent of those involved is a full defence.

A group of sado-masochist male homosexuals willingly participated, in private, in various forms of genital torture and other actions. They all took pleasure in giving and receiving pain. They were prosecuted for malicious wounding and assault occasioning actual bodily harm under the Offences Against the Person Act 1861.

---

[24] For example, *Masterson v Holden* [1986] 3 All ER 39 where two men were convicted of insulting behaviour for kissing in the street (cited in Harris, O'Boyle and Warbrick, *op. cit.*, p. 312).
[25] Ap. 25186/94 [1998] EHRLR.

HELD (HL): public policy required criminal sanctions in these, extreme, circumstances. There was both the danger of proselytisation and corruption of others as well as the potential for the infliction of serious injury.
R v Brown and other appeals [1993] 2 All ER 75

Lord Mustill, who dissented, was the only one to argue that a right to sexual freedom and privacy was the central issue. Lord Slynn, also dissenting, took the view that it was for Parliament and not the courts to determine what specific forms of consensual sexual activity were to be banned.

The decision was upheld by the European Court of Human Rights in *Laskey, Jaggard and Brown v United Kingdom* (1997).[26] The Court accepted, though with some doubts, that the activities concerned were sufficiently in private to engage Article 8. It focused on whether such criminal penalties were necessary in a democratic society. Article 8 and the Convention generally allows states to penalise actions which involve the affliction of harm. The proper purpose of such laws can be to uphold health and also as part of the prevention of crime. The criminal penalty in the case was for a legitimate purpose. On the issue of necessity, states had a margin of appreciation and the extreme nature of the practices in *Brown* meant that the convictions in question were proportionate.

The decision in *Brown* does not mean that consent can never be a defence in such matters. Actions which would otherwise be criminal can be consented to so long as a threshold of seriousness is not crossed. In *R v Wilson*[27] consent was a full defence for a husband who branded his wife's buttocks with his initials; in contrast the conviction in *R v Emmett* (1999)[28] was upheld against a man who had taken part in sexual activities involving the partial asphyxiation and burning of his partner. The partner fully consented but required medical treatment and both parties accepted the potential dangers of what they did.

This area of law remains an example of the criminalisation of private sexual activity between consenting adults and it is not clear what public interest is served by its suppression. In *R v Brown* the House of Lords suggested that there was the danger of the corruption of others. On such a view a court is asked to make a moral judgment about what is or is not morally acceptable private behaviour and this is a position it is increasingly difficult to justify. There is clearly a case for the law in this area to be reviewed and reconsidered as a matter of sexual privacy. *Setting the Boundaries*, however, does not deal with the issue.

21.4.5 Public activity

Consent between adults may be thought to justify sexual practices but only in so far as they are conducted in private. Activities which are acceptable in private can become criminal when conducted in public. Consent, this time of the public, remains the underlying issue: the public are legitimately protected from the actions they do not want or choose to experience.

---

[26] Ap. 21627/93; (1997) 24 EHRR 39.
[27] [1997] QB 47.
[28] (1999) *The Times*, 15 October.

A narrow definition of 'private' has been applied in respect of indecency between men and buggery, one which excludes activity in a private place of more than two persons, though, as we have seen, following *ADT* v *United Kingdom*, this may now be hard to sustain. 'Private', in respect of these offences, also expressly excludes public lavatories. Sexual acts in public are also dealt with under general legislation. Section 5 of the Public Order Act 1986 covers the use of 'insulting' or 'disorderly' behaviour within the hearing or sight of a person likely to be caused 'harassment, alarm or distress' thereby. The common law offence of 'outraging public decency' is also used.[29] The courts must decide whether an act in public is of such a 'lewd, obscene or disgusting nature as to amount to an outrage to public decency'.[30]

Setting the Boundaries endorses two strong principles which should guide the law in this area. Unfortunately they may work against each other. First, the law should not discriminate between heterosexual and homosexual acts. Second, the law should concern itself with public order matters and aim to protect the public from harassment, alarm and distress. Under this, second, public order principle, the fact that an activity takes place in a public place does not necessarily imply that an offence is committed (courting couples in deserted lay-bys are protected from the law). It also means that different standards may apply in different places reflecting the likely expectations of the public (different standards may be acceptable in a red light district than in a shopping mall). The problem is that the public order standard, being caused harassment, alarm or distress by sex in public, is not necessarily neutral as between different types of sexual activity. The public may continue to have significant homophobic elements among it and some parents may be more worried that their children should witness homosexual rather than heterosexual acts. If so, the public order principle may generate more prosecutions of homosexual than of heterosexual public displays thus undermining the first principle. The policy of the law will need to decide whether the principle of neutrality has priority over the public order principle. The Human Rights Act 1998 is unlikely to help. There is no Convention right to sexual activity in public to which freedom from discrimination under Article 14 can apply. The principle of equality under the law, enshrined in the common law, requires that any 'harassment, alarm or distress' alleged by members of the public should be discounted to the extent that it flows from the sexual orientation of those involved. This, by implication, is the position in *Setting the Boundaries*.[31]

21.5 Transsexuals

Sexuality is linked to a person's sense of his or her identity and to their sense of self-worth. A significant number of people change their sexual identity from that determined by parents and medical staff at birth and so registered. It is a highly complex issue reflecting a range of physical conditions, psychological dispositions, social practices and medical interventions only loosely covered

---

[29] There are about 60 prosecutions each year.
[30] See Chapter 22 for a fuller discussion of the case law.
[31] Implied from section 8.4.

by the term 'transsexual'. A significant civil liberties issue has developed regarding those who seek legal and official recognition of their change of gender. It may be a change of birth certificate or other official document that is required and the purpose can be just to achieve full social and administrative recognition of what has occurred or it may be for a more specific purpose such as to get married or divorced. A state's refusal to amend a birth certificate can make married family life for a transsexual person difficult to achieve. Inability to have other documentation, such as a driving licence or a national insurance card, changed can make life difficult in employment. Underlying it is the sense that unless such official recognition is obtained, transsexual persons will not be fully and equally recognised as citizens and will suffer unjustified discrimination and embarrassment at the hands of officials, work colleagues and others.

United Kingdom law has continued to uphold the position that, for matrimonial causes, the courts will not recognise a gender reassignment.[32] The position was recently confirmed in *Bellinger* v *Bellinger* (2001).[33] The Court of Appeal recognised that there have been major changes in medical understanding and in moral attitudes but held that important questions of public status and recognition are involved when it comes to the registration of birth, adoption, marriage, divorce, nullity and death. These are not matters that should be reduced to the subjective will of the parties. It was for Parliament to determine the preconditions for the registration of gender.[34]

There is very little to prevent the government from seeking changes in the law to make it compatible with the gigantic advances in medical understanding and practices that have occurred since the 1970s. If no change occurs when, in reality, the factual position of a transsexual is very similar in all but history to a person with unchanged gender, any failure to change will take on the appearance of moral disapproval and would be hard for a government to sustain. Change is on the way. This was recognised by an interdepartmental working party which reported, with options for change, to Parliament in July 2000.

Pressure on the government to regularise all legal and administrative disadvantages for transsexuals is now much greater following the change in its position by the European Court of Human Rights. In issue are Articles 8 and 12 and also 14. In earlier cases, such as *Rees* v *United Kingdom* (1986),[35] followed by *Cossey* v *United Kingdom* (1991),[36] the Court had refused to declare that a refusal to change a birth certificate, even though it clearly led to discrimination is respect of the matrimonial rights of the parties, violated the Convention. The general position was maintained in *Sheffield and Horsham* v *United Kingdom* (1999)[37] but in this case the Court recognised that the

---

[32] *Corbett* v *Corbett (otherwise Ashley)* [1970] 2 All ER 33.
[33] [2001] EWCA Civ 1140; [2002] 1 All ER.
[34] A strong dissent by Thorpe LJ stresses the medical and moral changes and developments in Europe, and claims that Parliament, on issues such as these, has given the court more room for coming to its own conclusions than the majority recognise.
[35] (1986) 9 EHRR 56.
[36] (1991) 13 EHRR 622.
[37] (1999) 27 EHRR 163.

Convention position is evolving to reflect a more tolerant and inclusive sensibility and therefore the situation needed to be kept under review.[38] In *Goodwin* v *United Kingdom* (2002) and *I* v *United Kingdom* (2002)[39] the Court has finally changed its position. It has held that refusing to give full legal and administrative acknowledgment of a person's gender reassignment, including changing a birth certificate, was a direct violation of Article 8 and Article 12. The Court acknowledged its previous case law but asserted the need to maintain a 'dynamic and evolutive' approach to the Convention. The Court notices both the gradual change in official opinion in the United Kingdom which mirrored the international tendency. To refuse to take appropriate administrative and legal steps is no longer within the margin of appreciation of the United Kingdom. At the time of writing it was not clear what steps the United Kingdom government would take to meet the requirements of these decisions.

---

[38] *B* v *France* (1993) 16 EHRR 1.
[39] Ap. 28957/95 and 25680/94 respectively; on the law, the judgments have the same text.

22

Obscenity and indecency

22.1 Introduction

Many people gain considerable and obsessive pleasure from pictures, books, films, video, Internet sites, etc. which are sexually explicit or very violent or combine both. Historically, these matters have never been left to individual taste and to the market. States, including the United Kingdom, acting through secular or ecclesiastical processes, have often tried to restrict the availability of such material measured against a standard of social acceptability. The standard changes over time and has apparently been getting more liberal over the last half century. The standard changes not only in relation to what people feel is tolerable but also in relation to the kinds of images that are made available. Currently pornographic and violent material is restricted by regulatory powers (e.g. in broadcasting), by the criminal law (e.g. the power of the courts to punish for obscene publication), by administrative powers, such as of seizure and forfeiture, even in the absence of a criminal conviction (e.g. the powers of Customs and Excise) and by other methods such as planning law (e.g. opening sex shops).[1]

22.2 Harm

The most compelling argument for laws which make the distribution of pornography a criminal offence is that pornography causes harm to others. John Stuart Mill's basic point[2] was that a proper acceptance of the liberty of the individual in a free society, a society devoted to the greatest happiness of its members, means that the state ought not to restrict tastes and pursuits on the sufficient grounds that they are immoral or bad for the people involved. The only ground necessary and sufficient for restricting a person's freedom is that his or her activities cause harm to others.[3] 'Harm' is a term that can mean almost anything. Unless it is to be a principle of such vagueness as to be capable of justifying just about any degree of restriction, it needs to be confined. The most compelling restriction is to require the person alleging

---

[1] See generally Robertson, G. (1979) *Obscenity*. London: Weidenfeld & Nicolson.
[2] Mill, J.S., *On Liberty*, chapter 1, in Mill, John Stuart (1968) *Utilitasianism, Liberty and Representative Government*. London: Dent.
[3] The 'harm' principle was the working assumption, only occasionally departed from, of the Williams Committee (1979) which investigated the United Kingdom's laws on obscenity and film censorship.

they are harmed to show that, in some reasonably proximate way, they have been harmed in their interests: they are no longer able to pursue their own tastes and pursuits because, for example, they have been physically injured or emotionally damaged, their property taken away or their liberty restricted.

There is some evidence of an apparent link of pornography with violent crime but this is controversial and challenged and it is not clear whether the pornography causes the violence or whether people who like violent pornography are also likely to be violent men. It is also unclear whether there is sufficient proximity between looking at the pornography and the harmful actions to justify intervention. Feminist theory has also suggested various forms of harm derived from pornography.[4] One argument is that pornography explains and causes violence to women. This is a straightforward argument from harm but which is subject to the general difficulties with the idea outlined above. Other feminist arguments are to do with projection and promotion of a particular view of women as defined through the experiences of men, as sexual objects and as socially subordinate. This may be an argument in its own account or it may also be a version of the argument from moral welfare, outrage and, in particular, corruption discussed below. It is not an argument about 'harm' in the narrow stipulated sense.

The actual legal regulation of pornography is based on principles and assumptions that go beyond restricting harmful activities in the stipulated sense. We find in the law three different but interrelated concepts. The state may prosecute: first, in order to uphold moral values; second, to protect the public from being outraged; and third, to protect persons from being depraved or corrupted. We will be exploring these three different but interrelated concepts in this chapter.

A tendency to 'deprave and corrupt' is the basis of obscenity. Section 2(4) of the Obscene Publications Act 1959 prohibits common law proceedings against publications which such a tendency. The common law offence of obscene libel has, therefore, been rendered inoperative. The common law does, however, retain its bite in respect of upholding morality and preserving the public from outrage since those concepts do not, necessarily, involve depravity and corruption.

22.3 Public good

The publication of works with sexual or violent themes may deal with matters of public concern. They may, like D.H. Lawrence's *Lady Chatterley's Lover*, be driven by a political desire to raise social awareness and promote discussion on sexual matters; they may wish to make a political or religious[5] point by graphic and distressing images aimed at shocking the public out of its complacency; they may claim the justification of art as images with a

---

[4] For example, Russell, D.E.H. (ed.) (1993) *Making Violence Sexy: Feminist Views on Pornography.* Buckingham: Open University Press.

[5] *R v Hicklin* (1868) LR 3 QB 360, the case which defines 'obscenity' for legal purposes, involved an anti-Papist pamphlet.

fascination and tendency to delight, or they may claim to promote the public good by providing a virtual reality by which undesirable tendencies, say to sexual or other violence, are relieved. Without a doubt such works can set going significant social debate on the nature of society and the values it may or may not possess. Claims to know what is or is not acceptable are often controversial, reflecting both different theories of the relationship of the law and morality but also, perhaps, the interests of different age groups, of men and women or of ethnic or religious groups. Arguments about moral standards are often arguments about who has power in society rather than a politically innocent argument about morals. An important legal question, which will come up in what follows, is the extent to which the law permits arguments about the public good of the works that would otherwise be punished as obscene or indecent.

22.4 Human rights

Obscenity and pornography is likely to engage the right to freedom of expression found, in particular, under Article 10(1) ECHR, a scheduled Convention right under the Human Rights Act 1998. Any prosecution will need justification in terms of Article 10(2). On one view, pornography, a mere form of pleasure, ought not to have a human rights defence at all. Legal regulation should be left to the view of the majority as expressed through representative institutions and there is no good reason why the morally important language of human rights, which describes those values which ought to trump the collective will, should apply to the provision of pornography. Of course such an argument does not apply where there is an alleged public good to the work.

The Convention issue is likely to be whether a prosecution or regulatory restriction can be authorised by Article 10(2). Prosecutors need to show, first, that the law under which the case is brought meets the Convention standard of legality. Concepts such as 'moral welfare' or 'indecency' are potentially open to the claim that they do not describe matters with sufficient precision to enable people to regulate their actions. Second, the prosecution or restriction must serve a legitimate purpose. Article 10(2) accepts the 'protection of . . . morals' as a legitimate purpose for restricting expression and this will cover most prosecutions. Third, a prosecution must be 'necessary in a democratic society'. The Convention gives a very high value to expression which engages with political and social issues, broadly defined,[6] and which will include the sexual morality of society. Article 10 protects speech which can 'offend, shock or disturb the State or any section of the population'.[7] These points suggest that state actions against sexual or violent works can be incompatible with Article 10, particularly if the works have credible claims to political or artistic significance. On the other hand the Court of Human Rights has tended to assert that nation states enjoy a wide margin of appreciation on moral

---

[6] *Lingens* v *Austria* (1986) 8 EHRR 407.
[7] *Handyside* v *United Kingdom* (1979) 1 EHRR 737.

questions including those involving indecency,[8] obscenity[9] and blasphemy,[10] the Court's view being that moral standards are neither certain nor common throughout Europe and that state authorities are best placed to decide what is or is not acceptable. Much depends, therefore, on how a work is presented to the Court – as being merely pornographic or whether it has political or artistic significance. It follows that domestic court proceedings should allow the argument for political or social significance to be made.

22.5 Moral welfare

One basis for legal restriction of pornography is to protect the 'moral welfare of the state'. This implies the existences of certain minimum standards of proper behaviour in the preservation of which the state has an interest. The assumption must be that these standards are necessary for the coherence and identity of the state; perhaps they are one of the conditions under which the allegiance of people can be required. In any event the state is entitled to uphold the standards and to criminalise not only a breach of the standards but also its advocacy.[11]

22.5.1 Conspiracy to corrupt public morals

There is no offence of corrupting public morals. Any such offence would be so uncertain that individuals would find it hard to know whether their actions were criminal or not thus violating the principle of 'legality'.[12] Conspiring to corrupt public morals, however, remains an offence. It consists in an agreement with others to do an act which undermines the moral welfare of the state. The Criminal Law Act 1977 abolished offences of conspiracy unless the actions to be performed on the basis of the agreement would be criminal. However, a conspiracy to corrupt public morals was retained as one of three exceptions to this general rule.[13] The offence escapes redundancy under section 2(4) of the Obscene Publications Act 1959 because an act which corrupts public morals need not necessarily have obscenity (depravity and corruption of those affected) as its essence and also because the offence can be committed on the basis of an agreement to publish a work promoting immorality, even if, in the end, no publication, takes place.

The main point of the offence is to prevent the promotion or advocacy of actions or states of affairs which undermine morality even if those actions or states of affairs are not unlawful. The offence was declared in *Shaw v DPP* (1962)[14] where the House of Lords upheld the conviction of a man for publishing a contact magazine for prostitutes. It is for the jury, properly directed, to decide whether an agreement would lead to corruption of moral

---

[8] *S and G v United Kingdom* (1991) Ap. 17634/91.
[9] For example, *Muller v Switzerland* (1991) 13 EHRR 212.
[10] See Chapter 23.
[11] See the discussion of the 'enforcement of morals' in Chapter 21.
[12] In *Hashman and Harrup v the United Kingdom* (1999) Ap. 25594/94 the concept of 'good behaviour' was held to be too imprecise to justify a binding over power by magistrates.
[13] A conspiracy to outrage public decency and to defraud are also retained.
[14] [1962] AC 220; confirmed in *Knuller v DPP* [1973] AC 435.

welfare. The offence is open to all the objections concerning the enforcement of morals: whether there is a coherent morality inherent in the state; if there is, how is it identified and is its protection by the state necessary?[15]

Schedule 1, Article 10 of the Human Rights Act 1998 is engaged. Any restriction of freedom of expression must, under Article 10(2), satisfy the test of legality. The offence does have a basis in law, since it has been confirmed twice by the House of Lords, but there must remain an issue about whether the activities caught by the offence are defined with sufficient precision to meet the requirement that a person must be able to predict, with reasonable certainty, whether his or her actions are within the law. Though the offence pursues one of the legitimate aims in Article 10(2) (it is for the 'protection of ... morals'), any prosecution would need to be 'necessary in a democratic society': meeting a pressing social need by a proportionate action. Of significance here is that there is no explicit public interest defence and its absence limits the ability of the defendant to challenge the need for the prosecution. Given the liberalisation of values in contemporary society, the strong sense that moral values are relative to time, place and culture, and given the strong opposition in the courts to censorship, it is perhaps unlikely that, in the foreseeable future, prosecutions will take place.

22.6 Outraging public decency

The essence of this idea is that the public are entitled to be protected from sights and sounds which induce in them a sense of outrage. There is no need to show that a person is harmed in their interests – the point of any offence is not that anyone has been injured, their property removed or their freedoms curtailed. The offence aims to protect people's feelings rather than some alleged set of moral values inherent in society. What is protected is the alleged right of the public not to be offended, shocked or disturbed by what is available to them. Liberal theory tends to deny that the state has any right to suppress an activity merely because other people are offended or shocked, even deeply, by the knowledge that it is going on. The absence of harm to others' interests is sufficient to cause doubt on whether this is properly within the scope of the criminal law. The offence that people feel is, as it were, for them to deal with, it does not justify the suppression of the freedom of others. To allow the outraged feelings of some to dictate what others can or cannot do gives a particular group unequal power to veto and control the lives of others. Furthermore, the sense of outrage is a feeling; it is validated by the sense of self of the person outraged and does not need further reasoning or justification on principled grounds, it is a mere assertion of power. Of course it is possible to argue that harm of a psychological kind is done to others by their being offended. But, as suggested above, this argument weakens the justificatory power of the 'harm' principle since it merges all types of objection to the material involved. Moral objection or objection on the grounds of causing outrage in others is simply seen as a version of harm, and so 'harm to

---

[15] See Chapter 21 in which these matters are discussed.

others' can no longer play a useful role is distinguishing appropriate from inappropriate grounds for the intervention of the law.

Liberal theory justifies offences of outraging public decency in so far as the point of any prosecution is less the sense of outrage and more the need that members of the public are entitled to go about their own business, particularly in public places, without being shocked or offended by the activities of others. Then the point of the offence is to protect the public space for the public. The freedom of the public is curtailed if they are unable to avoid experiences, sights and sounds they would rather not have. Liberal political theory has always recognised that different standards can apply in relation to what is tolerated in public and what is tolerated in private. The distinction can be found in respect of sexual offences and it also goes some way to justify the strict controls exercised by regulators over broadcast media and advertising. Conversely, it may also explain why cinemas and theatres are exempted from prosecution for outraging the public.[16] If it is the public nature of acts which is the burden of the offence it should be reflected in the way the offence is proved and it should make the offence difficult to establish in respect of actions done only in the presence of a consenting and informed audience.

22.6.1 Conspiracy to outrage public decency and outraging public decency

Outraging public decency is a common law offence; it is also an offence to conspire with another to do the same. The Criminal Law Act 1977 retains the latter offence. The offence was given House of Lords approval in *Shaw v DPP* and *Knuller v DPP*. Male homosexual encounters in public lavatories, simulated sexual intercourse and nude bathing are examples of common targets of the offence, and not necessarily in the past. It is currently used against brothel-keepers and owners of pubs and clubs putting on sex shows of various kinds.[17] The offence is not confined to sexual actions[18] and can be used in a context which raises issues of freedom of expression.

> G, an artist, exhibited in the second defendant's art gallery. The exhibits included freeze dried foetuses attached as earrings to model's heads. The exhibition was open to the public and G had undertaken some promotional activities. G was convicted of outraging public decency.
> HELD: G's conviction was upheld.
> *R v Gibson* [1991] 1 All ER 439 CA

In *Gibson* the Court of Appeal recognised the offence and that it could still be prosecuted where the essence of the offence was not obscenity. The act must be in public with at least two non-participants present.[19] There should be evidence that those who witnessed the act were in fact outraged; without this

---

[16] Section 2(4A), Obscene Publications Act 1959; s. 2(4)(a), Theatres Act 1968.
[17] For a recent case, in which the prosecution failed for other reasons, see *R v Paul McManus and Andrew Cross* [2001] EWCA Crim 2455.
[18] For example, *R v Lynn* (1788) 2 Tem Rep 733, disinterring a corpse.
[19] *R v Walker* [1996] 1 Cr App Rep 111.

evidence there is a danger is that the offence will be refocused as an offence protecting the moral welfare of society rather than protecting the public from outrage. There must be evidence of a highly indecent act (or of an agreement to perform an act) from which a sense of outrage is likely to flow. In *Knuller v DPP* Lord Simon defined indecency as going 'beyond offending the susceptibilities of, or even shocking, reasonable people. Recognised minimum standards of decency ... are likely to vary from time to time ... the jury should be invited, where appropriate, to remember that they live in a plural society, with a tradition of tolerance towards minorities, and this atmosphere of toleration is itself part of public decency'.[20] The *mens rea* of the offence is intending to do an act which, a jury finds, outrages public decency; it does not require proof of an intention to outrage. There is no 'public interest' defence allowed. Such a defence has been brought in for obscene acts and it would seem to be arbitrary, though clearly accepted by the courts,[21] that Parliament confined the defence to obscenity alone.[22]

Despite the absence of a public interest defence, Gibson's prosecution and the offence in general terms, was upheld by the Commission for Human Rights in *S and G v United Kingdom* (1991).[23] The prosecution was a restriction on freedom of expression which met the various requirements of Article 10(2): it was prescribed by law, for a legitimate purpose and it was proportionate to a pressing social need. The authority of the case is not great since much of it turns on the doctrine of the margin of appreciation, and this doctrine does not apply in domestic law. United Kingdom courts, deciding cases under the Human Rights Act 1998, must decide for themselves whether the absence of a public interest defence means that the issues under Article 10(2) cannot be properly explored. Outraging public decency is distinguished from statutory obscenity on this point; it also needs to be distinguished from the statutory offence under section 5 of the Public Order Act 1986, of causing 'harassment, alarm or distress' by using or displaying insulting words or visual representations.[24] Section 5(3) permits the defence that the conduct was 'reasonable'.

It has been argued by the Law Commission that the offence should be abolished but at the present time abolition is not proposed.[25]

22.7 Tending to deprave and corrupt

The third focus of the law is the idea that individuals can be protected from a form of harm: being depraved and corrupted by sights and sounds. It is not harm to interests in the narrow sense of harm but, perhaps, a species of psychological harm. As such it is subject to the accusation of over-

---

[20] *Knuller v DPP* [1973] AC 435, 495, per Lord Simon.
[21] *R v Gibson* [1991] 1 All ER 439, CA.
[22] Section 2(4), Theatres Act 1968 and s. 2(4A), Obscene Publications Act 1959 also exempt the theatre and cinemas (film exhibitors) from prosecutions for indecency, thus confining the criminal law to obscenity and so making available the public interest offence to prosecutions.
[23] (1991) Ap. 17634/91.
[24] Section 5, Public Order Act 1986, discussed in Chapter 17.
[25] See also Feldman, D. (2002) *Civil Liberties and Human Rights in England and Wales*, 2nd edn. Oxford: Oxford University Press, pp. 933–8.

inclusiveness: too broad a concept of harm loses it power to justify legal restriction. The law appears as a form of paternalism which seeks to protect individuals from themselves. It suffers from the main defect of paternalism which is that adult persons, who ought to be able to decide for themselves what is good for them, are being denied what they want because others believe it is bad for them. It benefits from the main point of paternalism which is the protection of children and the vulnerable. It is different in principle from either the idea of upholding society's alleged moral values (it claims not to be protecting society but protecting individuals from a form of self-harm) or protecting the public from things that they think are offensive (a socially recognised standard of depravity and corruption is not necessarily the same thing as people's opinions about what is offensive).

22.7.1 Obscene Publications Act 1959

The offence relating to depravity and corruption is in the Obscene Publications Act 1959 which provides the basis for the law against pornography. Section 2(4) of the Act outlaws common law offences of obscenity.

> **1 Test of obscenity**
> (1) For the purposes of this Act an article shall be deemed to be obscene if its effect or (where the article comprises two or more distinct items) the effect of any one of its items is, if taken as a whole, such as to tend to deprave and corrupt persons who are likely, having regard to all relevant circumstances, to read, see or hear the matter contained or embodied in it.

The offence is the publication of an obscene article whether or not for gain and the possession of an obscene article with a view to its publication for gain.[26] Possession of an obscene article for pleasure is not an offence under the Act.

Publication is widely defined to include selling, distributing and lending, for example, and also, for films, showing. Articles covered by the Act include books, magazines, newspapers, CDs, tapes, pictures and pornography supplied directly through the Internet.[27] Films, videos, newspapers, advertisements and broadcast programmes are also included though, for these, the Act is a last line of defence. These media are also subject to the various regulatory regimes, statutory and voluntary, that apply to them.[28] Plays and other theatrical productions are not covered by the definition of 'article' in the Act but equivalent provisions, including a public good defence, are found in the Theatres Act 1968.

Deprave and corrupt
There is no definition of depravity and corruption.[29] These are for the good sense and ordinary experience of the jury. Nor is it a matter for expert

---

[26] Section 1, Obscene Publications Act 1964 makes the possession of an obscene article with a view to its publication for gain an offence.
[27] The last words of s. 1(3)(b) were introduced under the Criminal Justice and Public Order Act 1994. Difficulties of enforcing the laws in a practical way are considerable.
[28] See Chapter 11.
[29] The statutory definition follows the common law definition in *R v Hicklin* (1868) LR 3 QB 360.

opinion.[30] A belief in the judgment of the jury is important for the credibility of the offence. There are difficulties, however. First, different juries may have different standards and this will lead to inconsistency in the application of the criminal law throughout the country. Secondly, the offence can be tried summarily in which case the test for corruption is for magistrates, by no means a cross section of ordinary sensibility.

A jury must be satisfied that the work is more than in bad taste or undesirable[31] and something more than repulsive, loathsome[32] or lewd or indecent.[33] In the trial of D.H. Lawrence's *Lady Chatterley's Lover* Mr Justice Byrne defined the terms: 'to deprave means to make morally bad, to pervert, to debase, or corrupt morally. The words "to corrupt" mean to render morally unsound or rotten, to destroy the moral purity or chastity of, to pervert, to ruin a good quality, to debase, to defile . . .' Whether these definitions assist a jury is doubtful; the words used are contestable and depend upon different individuals' understandings. Nevertheless it is clear that obscenity is at the high end of the scale. By leaving the test to the jury, defenders of the law will say it allows the standard to change with changing social values. Opponents will argue that it makes the test impossibly uncertain and unpredictable with criminal liability depending on the unchallengeable prejudices of different members of the jury. The difficulty for any jury is compounded by the fact that depravity and corruption is a state of mind which is to be assumed from the experience of the article in question and does not need to be proved in terms of bad or perverted consequential actions. There may be evidence that sexual crime may be linked to pornography but such evidence is not essential to any prosecution for obscene publication. There must be evidence that a significant proportion of those who experience the article have been corrupted. Evidence that the main witnesses were police officers, who are unlikely to be depraved and corrupted by what they experience, may mean that no offence is committed.[34] However, the argument that those most likely to experience the publication, visitors to sex shops or cinemas, are depraved and corrupted before they see or read the work in question, failed.[35] The lack of the need for such external proof implies the issue is not harm to others. Linking this with the impossibility of proving a state of mind, and what emerges is an offence whose essence is the saving of individuals from themselves and what others see as a shameful and pointless activity.

Public good
The capacity for the prosecution authorities to use obscenity law against works of artistic importance or of political significance led to the most important innovation in the 1959 Act: the public good defence under section 4.

---

[30] *R* v *Anderson* [1972] 3 All ER 1152.
[31] *R* v *Secker and Warburg* [1954] 2 All ER 687.
[32] *R* v *Anderson* [1972] 3 All ER 1152.
[33] *R* v *Anderson* [1972] 3 All ER 1152.
[34] *R* v *Clayton and Halsey* (1963) 1 QB 163.
[35] *DPP* v *Whyte* [1972] AC 849.

4 Defence of public good
Subject to subsection (1A) of this section a person shall not be convicted of an offence against section 2 of this Act, and an order for forfeiture shall not be made under the foregoing section, if it is proved that publication of the article in question is justified as being for the public good on the ground that it is in the interests of science, literature, art or learning, or of other objects of general concern.

'Other objects of general concern' may include works with an underlying political purpose, such as obscene caricatures; educational purposes may also come within the general category, though these may also be within the 'interests of science'. This public good defence is more narrowly defined in respect of films. Subsection 1A, relating specifically to films or soundtracks, permits the public good defence only in respect of the interests of 'drama, opera, ballet or any other art, or of literature or learning' and excludes the general category. Given the importance of the film media this is an important constraint which appears to make entirely arbitrary distinctions between different media. Prosecution of films, unlike other media, require the consent of the DPP.

Public good is a matter for the jury. Unlike the test for obscenity, it can be proved on the basis of expert evidence. Obscenity trials, like that of *Lady Chatterley's Lover*, have been famous for the procession of notable people speaking up in defence of serious works of art. The job for the jury is to decide, first, whether the article is obscene, second whether publication would be for the public good and, third, whether the public good is sufficiently strong to justify the publication of an otherwise obscene work.[36] It is a strange judgment to make: that a book has both a tendency to deprave and corrupt yet it is in the public good it should be published. The public good defence clearly allows arguments about the need for, and proportionality of, a ban to be properly aired in court as is required under Article 10(2) ECHR.

Seizure and forfeiture
Section 3 of the Obscene Publications Act 1959 authorises a magistrate to issue a search warrant in respect of obscene articles being kept for sale. The warrant is issued to a police officer who can enter premises and remove articles that he or she reasonably believes are obscene. A magistrate can then order the articles to be forfeited. The test for obscenity is the same but, in respect of forfeiture, the sound sense of the jury is not available. The public good defence under section 4 applies and any interested party, including the 'owner, author or maker' of the articles' can challenge a forfeiture order.

22.8 Other provisions

Other statutes restrict the use of indecent or obscene articles. For example, the Indecent Displays (Control) Act 1981 prohibits the display of indecent matter in public places and includes a power of seizure. It is an offence to send obscene or indecent articles through the post or obscene or indecent messages

---

[36] *R v Calder and Boyars Ltd* [1969] 1 QB 15.

over the telephone.[37] These offences can all be tried summarily; again the alleged role of the jury in determining what are publicly acceptable standards is lost; similarly there is no express public good defence and so, to provide that, the Human Rights Act 1998 will need to be relied upon.

The importation of indecent or obscene articles is prohibited under section 42 of the Customs Consolidation Act 1876 and such goods, if seized, can be forfeited under the provisions of section 49 Customs and Excise Management Act 1979. Seizure by customs of obscene or indecent articles from a European Union country is likely to be a quantitative restriction on imports, unlawful under Article 28 EC Treaty. Article 30 permits such restrictions on grounds of 'public morality' but requires that such permitted restrictions 'must not constitute a means of arbitrary discrimination or disguised restriction on trade between member states'. Restrictions on material which would also be banned under the Obscene Publications Act 1959 are not arbitrary.[38] Since, under domestic law, confiscation and forfeiture is confined to obscene articles and not (in the absence of public display) indecent articles, a similar restriction should be read into section 49 governing Customs' seizures.[39]

22.9 The protection of children

Liberal theory permits paternalist restrictions on freedom of speech in order to protect the interests of children. The general argument about autonomy is compatible with restrictions aimed at protecting children from abuse, danger and undesirable temptation. In the context of pornography, the law creates a range of offences relating to indecent photographs of children.

The Protection of Children Act 1978 makes the taking, permitting to be taken, making, distributing, showing, possession with a view to distribution or showing or the advertising of indecent photographs of children an offence. Section 160 of the Criminal Justice Act 1988 makes the mere possession, for personal use, of such photographs an offence. Images downloaded from the Internet, and those opened from an e-mail attachment,[40] are included. Downloading has been held to be 'making' a photograph and within the scope of the more serious offence under the 1978 Act.[41] Whether a picture is indecent is for the judgment of jury or magistrate. There are provisions under the Act for search, seizure and forfeiture similar to those under the Obscene Publications Act. The penalty is severe with ten years' imprisonment under the 1978 Act and five years' under the 1988 Act as the maximum on trial by indictment.[42] Innocent possession or possession for a legitimate reason, such as research into pornography, is a defence.[43]

---

[37] Section 85(3), Postal Services Act 2000 and s. 43(1), Telecommunications Act 1984, to send indecent or obscene messages over the telephone.
[38] *R v Henn* [1981] AC 850.
[39] Feldman, *op. cit.*, p. 950.
[40] *R v Smith* [2002] EWCA Crim 683; *The Times* 23 April.
[41] *R v Bowden* [2000] 2 All ER 418.
[42] The penalties were increased to these maximums by s. 41, Criminal Justice and Court Services Act 2000 which made mere possession an indictable offence.
[43] Section 160(2), Criminal Justice Act 1988; *Atkins v DPP* [2000] 2 All ER 425.

The Criminal Justice and Public Order Act 1994 enlarged the reach of both Acts to include 'psuedo-photographs'. These are images, made by a computer, which appear to be photographs. They may, in fact, be one or more innocent photographs loaded onto a computer and altered into an indecent image.[44] Similarly a photograph is within the scope of the Acts if it appears to be, but is not, the photograph of a child. No child need, therefore, be harmed in the process of making these photographs and, of course, the offence is established without having to prove that any harm to others results from the possession etc. of the psuedo-photograph. Whether the protection of children is, in fact, served by this extension is unclear. Nevertheless the offences have been held, by the Court of Appeal, to be compatible with both Article 8 and, in particular, Article 10 ECHR, as being proportionate and necessary restrictions on freedom of expression for the prevention of crime and the protection of morals.[45]

22.10 Prior restraints

There is no censorship in the United Kingdom, using that term to mean the existence of a government office whose prior approval is necessary before anything can be published or broadcast. Many of the various media through which sexual or violent images and ideas are conveyed are subject not to censorship but to regulation. Usually the regulation will be by a body more of less independent of government which will have been either established by the government by statute or by self-regulation as an alternative to government action. Chapter 11, on the media, describes the system of regulation and focuses mainly on regulation pertaining to political impartiality and privacy. The same regulation also deals with obscenity and indecency.

22.10.1 The theatre

Neither subsidised nor commercial theatre is subject to regulation. Censorship by the Lord Chamberlain's office was abolished by the Theatres Act 1968. The Obscene Publications Act 1959 does not apply to the theatre but there are equivalent provisions in the Theatres Act 1968. By section 2(4)(a) of that Act, an obscenity charge cannot be circumvented by the charge of outraging public decency. In this way freedom of expression in the theatre is protected against moralising opposition at least to the extent that those who seek the closure of a play must meet the higher obscenity standard. A 'public good' defence, similar to section 4 of the Obscene Publications Act 1959, is available to defendants in an obscenity prosecution. As well as obscenity, it is an offence to put on a play which was intended to provoke a breach of the peace or (more

---

[44] '... it is possible on a computer screen to take the picture of a child's face from a Kays or Grattons catalogue, transpose it onto the pornographic image of an adult, alter the size of the breasts, the pubic hair and other parts of the anatomy, and make it appear that the indecent photograph is that of a child.' Mr Mike O'Brien MP, HC Committee Co. 742 (quoted in Card, R. and Ward, R. (1994) *The Criminal Justice and Public Order Act 1994*. Bristol: Jordan Publishing, p. 109).
[45] *R v Smethurst* [2002] 1 Cr App Rep 6.

controversially) was likely to have that effect.[46] Similarly, a play which is likely to stir up racial hatred is an offence.[47]

22.10.2 Press

As discussed in Chapter 11, the press is subject to voluntary self-regulation by the Press Complaints Commission which operates on the basis of a Code of Practice. The Code does not have specific sections on indecency and so the portrayal of sex and violence, absent some other feature such as privacy or the treatment of children, cannot be the basis of a complaint. The Commission is satisfied with the standard of obscenity and indecency set by the general law and which applies to the press.

22.10.3 Advertising

Advertising is subject to strict regulation either (for press, poster or magazines) on a voluntary basis, through the Advertising Standards Authority, or (for broadcast advertising) through the statutory powers of the Independent Television Authority (to be replaced by Ofcom). Both authorities regulate on the basis of Codes of Practice and restrict portrayals of sexual and violent activity. The Advertising Standards Authority requires advertisements to be 'decent' and, specifically, paragraph 5.1 of the Code requires advertisers to avoid serious or widespread offence on the grounds of sex. Paragraph 11.1 prohibits advertisers from condoning or provoking violence – which is not the same thing as prohibiting violent imagery.[48] The Independent Television Commission's Code has similar provisions.

22.10.4 Film

Films are subject to the Obscene Publications Act 1959, which includes a public good defence. Under section 2(4A) that defence cannot be circumvented by a prosecution for outraging decency or conspiracy to corrupt public morals. Film prosecutions require the consent of the Director of Public Prosecutions.

Local authorities license cinemas and do so 'on such terms and conditions and subject to such restrictions . . . as they think fit', although they have a duty to prohibit children from attending unsuitable films.[49] Invariably local authorities license on the basis of category certification by the British Board of Film Classification though, on general principles of administrative law, they must retain their discretion and be willing, in particular instances, to make their own judgment about a particular film. Local authorities have additional powers only to license sex shops and sex cinemas in certain areas and to refuse a licence in others.[50]

---

[46] Section 6, Theatres Act 1968.
[47] Section 20, Public Order Act 1986.
[48] Paragraph 13.
[49] Section 1, Cinemas Act 1985.
[50] Section 2, Local Government (Miscellaneous Provisions) Act 1982.

The British Board of Film Classification reviews all films and videos which are to be shown or made available to the public and gives them a classification: U for unclassified, PG that the film should only be seen by children on the basis of parental guidance, and the classifications of 12, 15 and 18 which mean that the film is unsuitable to be seen by children and young persons younger than the specified age. 12A permits a film to be seen by a child under 12 so long as accompanied by an adult. The category R18 applies to videos to be sold through sex shops. The Board operates on the basis of general principles and on guidelines which describe the general standards appropriate to each classification and the matters of concern such as drugs or the portrayal of children, which classifiers will bear in mind. The principles are that adults should be free to view a film provided it is lawful and not potentially harmful, that films should be able to reach their widest appropriate audience, that the context of sexual and violent images is important and that the classification guidelines should be regularly reviewed to reflect changes in public taste, attitudes and concerns.[51]

The Board's work can be controversial. Through the link with cinema licensing by local authorities, classification is, in effect, censorship.[52] The Board can, in effect, prevent adults from seeing films or scenes even though these do not reach the 'deprave or corrupt' standard of the criminal law. Currently the Board's central concern is with the protection of children though even here the Board's most recent classification, 12A, permits young children to see films the Board thinks are unsuitable for them so long as they are accompanied by an adult. Some argue that the role of the Board should be advisory, to give consumer advice assisting parents and adults to make informed choices about the films they wish to see.[53]

22.11 Videos

Like films, videos are subject to the Obscene Publications Act 1959. Videos are seen at home, not in public places. There is and has been great concern that children and parents, in particular, need, at the least, information about the content and suitability of videos they are purchasing or borrowing. The Video Recordings Act 1984[54] introduced a system by which all videos are to be classified by the British Board of Film Classification. Various offences are created for the supply or possession for purposes of supply of unclassified videos. Videos classified R18 are for supply through sex shops only. The Act requires that there be an independent appeals process and the Video Appeals Committee has been established for that purpose.

Section 4A identified matters to which the Board must have regard.

---

[51] Guidelines can be found under 'policy' on the Board's website: www.bbfc.co.uk/.
[52] The Board's original name was British Board of Film Censors.
[53] This move has been predicted by Andreas Whittam Smith when he retired as chairman of the Board in 2002.
[54] Amended by the Video Recordings Act 1993.

Video Recordings Act 1984

4A ... special regard to harm to potential viewers or, through their behaviour, to society, by the manner in which the work deals with:

(a)   cruel behaviour

(b)   illegal drugs

(c)   violent behaviour or incidents

(d)   horrific behaviour in incidents

(e)   human sexual activity.

In the Board's view these statute-based standards merely embody its existing principles but require it to be more explicit and open in the way they are applied.

Under the Human Rights Act 1998 the requirement that any restriction on freedom of expression must be proscribed by law is likely to be met since the grounds of restriction are clarified both in the Act and statements of guidance. The mere fact that discretion is handed to a body such as the BBFC does not itself offend against the principle of legality.[55] There is a legitimate purpose to such classification, namely the protection of morals. The major question is proportionality. The margin of appreciation does not apply to domestic courts. Judicial deference to a body established by Parliament specifically to make the judgments involved is proper but of no assistance if two such bodies disagree. In *R v Video Appeals Committee of the British Board of Film Classification ex parte the British Board of Film Classification*[56] the courts upheld the view of the Video Appeals Committee that, contrary to the view of the Board, proportionality under Article 10 ECHR required certain sexually explicit and violent videos to be given an R18 classification and made available. The Board's 'principles' required it to take into account 'potential' harm and it had refused classification until the potential risks of the videos in question could, if at all, be quantified. The Video Appeals Committee's view was that unquantified potential harm was too speculative to be given much weight as a ground of restriction in a proportionate judgment about classification. As regards R18 videos it also should be accepted that, in the absence of evidence to the contrary, the risks of children viewing the videos was slight. As a consequence of this case, the Board has reconsidered its guidelines on the R18 category in the direction of tolerance for adult entertainment on the basis of informative classification

22.12 Broadcasting

The Obscene Publications Act 1959 applies to broadcast matter. However the primary way in which violent and sexually explicit matter is dealt with is through the regulatory system for television and radio which has been described in Chapter 11. The primary duty is on the broadcasters to ensure that programmes do not offend against 'good taste and decency'.[57] These

---

[55] *Wingrove* v *United Kingdom* (1996) 24 EHRR 1, paragraph 40.

[56] [2000] EMLR 850.

[57] Section 6, Broadcasting Act 1990; paragraph 5.1(d) in the BBC's Agreement with the government.

standards are further developed in the Independent Television Commission's Programme Code and the BBC's Producer Guidelines. The Broadcasting Standards Commission's Code of Standards for broadcasting (discussed in Chapter 11) includes detailed discussion of what is acceptable regarding the portrayal of sexual or violent conduct. The authority the Commission claims for its adjudications, based on the Code, is that of social opinion, derived from research rather than just the paternalistic instincts of the great and the good. Of particular importance for the Commission is to protect children through the concept of a timed 'watershed' before which portrayals of sex and violence should be limited. However, some matters, such as the portrayal of actual rather than simulated intercourse, remain improper in the Commission's view even if shown very late at night.

Much but not all satellite television is regulated by the ITC. That which is not is still subject to the Obscene Publications Act 1959 and to a further power of the Secretary of State to proscribe a foreign satellite service – a television or radio service provided by a person not under United Kingdom jurisdiction who is providing a satellite service received in the United Kingdom. It is an offence to support a proscribed service by ways such as by advertising on it or supplying it with services of various kinds.[58] Any order must be in the public interest and compatible with the United Kingdom's international obligations. European satellite stations may be protected by European Community law. A directive 'Television without Frontiers'[59] permits restrictions on cross-frontier broadcasts in order to prevent 'impairment to the physical, mental or moral development of minors', not on general 'good taste and decency' grounds. Nevertheless the Court of Appeal has upheld the view that the proscribing of a Danish satellite station broadcasting adult pornography was compatible with the Directive.[60]

22.13 Internet[61]

The Internet is the major source of easily available pornography and much of it meets the test for obscenity under the law. Child pornography, in particular, seems to be widely available.

The Obscene Publications Act 1959 and the common law offences can apply to words and images on the Internet, though it must be possible to identify a person responsible. Maintaining a commercial website selling hardcore images directly or, more usually, by linking it back to an overseas site which is outside the jurisdiction, can come within the concept of 'publication' in the Act.[62] Direct enforcement under the Act remains difficult and requires cooperation at international level between governments and police forces. As we have seen,

---

[58] Sections 177 and 178, Broadcasting Act 1990.

[59] Directive 97/36.

[60] *R v Secretary of State for Culture, Media and Sport ex parte Danish Satellite Television* [1999] CLY 3916 QBD; [1999] 3 CMLR 919 CA. See also *Erotica Rendez-Vous* [2001] All ER (EC) 577.

[61] Akdeniz, Y., Walker, C. and Wall, D. (2000) *The Internet, Law and Society*. London: Pearson Education, chapters 9 and 10, on which this section is based.

[62] *R v Perrin (Stephanie Laurent)* [2002] EWCA Crim 747; *R v Waddon* (Graham) [1999] ITCLR 422, affirmed CA 6 April 2000 (2000 WL 491456).

the downloading and storage of a pornographic 'pseudo-photograph' of a child is an offence.

There is pressure for more intense regulation. The defenders of the Internet, on the other hand, wish to see it as an area of freedom, available to all, which should not be regulated, and emphatically not to the very strict standards of terrestrial television. Attempts at regulation by Act of Parliament will need to be compatible with Article 10 ECHR.

An alternative is self-regulation by using rating and filtering systems. These are electronic devices, introduced to the distribution process, such as by an ISP (rating) or adopted by the receiving computer (filtering), used to inhibit the introduction of violent or sexually explicit images. These devices are widely used but are open to objections, first, generally to the principle of censorship and, second, to the claim that they filter out matter that ought not to be censored because, for example, it reflects the interests of unpopular sexual minorities. It also enables the authorities to take or encourage action against websites without it having to be proved that they meet the test of illegality.[63] This is censorship by commercial organisations and it may be difficult to raise free speech objections on the basis of Article 10 ECHR. Conversely, rating and filtering may create a false sense of security.

Internet Watch Foundation (www.IWF.org.uk) is an industry-based self-regulatory body, established in 1996 with the support of the United Kingdom government. Funded by the industry it also enjoys some assistance from the European Union. It aims to monitor the Internet, receive complaints from the public, and liaise with police and ISPs. The criteria on which it acts is 'potential' illegality. It can encourage the rating of a site without proof of obscenity. Its principal target is pornography involving children.

---

[63] Letter from Metropolitan Police to ISPs in 1996 listing alleged pornographic sites; cited in Akdeniz *et al.*, p. 223.

23

Religious freedom and blasphemy

23.1 Introduction

It is fundamental to modern liberalism that individuals should enjoy religious freedom and that the state should not promote a particular religion or denomination as a requirement for its citizens or officials. Religion affects individuals' personal and spiritual relationships to God but also deals with ethical and moral questions about right behaviour in various areas often involving sexual and family life. As such, religion can have political overtones. Organised religion may influence behaviour and contribute to the question of what the law should or should not permit. Through this social and moral influence, but also through the proselytising tendency of many religions, religious people and their churches may seek to affect the lives of others, and sometimes to limit their liberty – over sexual behaviour, for example. From the liberal point of view, therefore, it is reasonable to restrict religious freedom in order to protect the rights and freedoms of others.

The liberal position is challenged. For many, some form of religious identity is not only a basic good for individuals but also a perfectly reasonable foundation on which a state can be built. Some states such, as Ireland, recognise God in their constitution or, like the United Kingdom, have an established church. In practice, such provisions are not necessarily incompatible with religious tolerance. The problem arises when, on the basis of this religious connection, certain requirements are imposed on, for example, the education system or religious tests are imposed for those who may serve the state in an official capacity. The claim is that the integrity, coherence and decency of a society requires this kind of religious identity and that the state is thereby entitled to enforce, by law, both the moral and theological precepts of the religion.

23.2 Discrimination law

Religious freedom, the freedom to adhere to a religion's beliefs and practise its tenets, is protected in various ways in different circumstances and subject to different conditions, by common law and statute.[1] There is, however, no

[1] See Hamilton, C. (1995) *Family Law and Religion*. London: Sweet & Maxwell.

express statutory equivalent to the provisions of the Race Relations Act 1976 or the Sex Discrimination Act 1975,[2] although some religious groups may also be ethnic groups and hence within the protection of the 1976 Acts.[3] Under the EC's Framework Directive on discrimination, measures to outlaw religious discrimination in the workplace must be in effect by the end of 2003.[4] The Anti-terrorism, Crime and Security Act 2001 amends the Crime and Disorder Act 1998 to make religiously aggravated offences like racially aggravated offences and capable of more severe punishment than the non-aggravated form of the offence.

23.3 Human rights

Under the Human Rights Act 1998, United Kingdom courts must interpret statutory provisions and evaluate the actions of public authorities against the standards of Article 9 ECHR, which protects freedom of thought, conscience and religion. The text is quoted in Chapter 2. The Article gives absolute protection to a person's freedom to adhere to a religious doctrine but permits legal restrictions on the activities by which such belief may be manifested. These restrictions are limited in ways broadly similar to those by which privacy, freedom of expression and freedom of association may be limited.[5] Restrictions must be on the basis of law for one of the legitimate purposes and any restriction must be a proportionate response to a pressing social need.

Freedom of thought, conscience and religion is understood by the Court of Human Rights as one of the foundations of a democratic and pluralist society.[6] Article 9 protects a wide range of beliefs, by no means confined to the major religions or to beliefs which encompass the notion of man's relation with a deity.[7] There is no absolute protection for manifestations of belief. An action which is motivated by religion but which is not in itself a requirement of religious observance, will not generally be protected under Article 9(2).[8] Similarly, the Court has not been sympathetic to claims based on a tension between duties owed to an employer under a contract of employment and religious observance.[9] The pluralism which justifies religious freedom entails the possibility of restrictions on the manifestation of that freedom in order to

---

[2] Northern Ireland's law does have express provisions outlawing various forms of religious discrimination. These reflect the particular circumstances of the conflict there.

[3] *Mandla* v *Dowell Lee* [1983] 2 AC 548, referring to Sikhs; *Tower Hamlets LBC* v *Rabin* [1989] ICR 693, referring to Jews

[4] Framework Directive 2000/78/EC. Other forms of discrimination have longer before they need to be brought into effect.

[5] *Church of X* v *United Kingdom* (1968) 12 YB 306. The restriction in the interests of the economic well-being of the country is only found in relation to privacy.

[6] *Kokkinakis* v *Greece* (1993) 17 EHRR 397.

[7] Freedom of thought and conscience is a 'precious asset for atheists, agnostics, sceptics and the unconcerned'. Narrow political beliefs are excluded: *McFeely* v *United Kingdom* (1981) 3 EHRR 161.

[8] For example: a religious-based refusal to pay a proportion of taxation equivalent to expenditure on nuclear weapons. Conscientious objectors to military service have also generally failed to obtain the protection of the Court. Advertisements will not enjoy Article 9 protection just because they are placed in a religious context (*X* v *Sweden* (1976) 16 DR 44).

[9] *Ahmed* v *United Kingdom* (1981) 22 DR 27; *Stedman* v *United Kingdom* [1997] EHRLR 545.

ensure that everybody else's beliefs are protected.[10] Article 9 may impose positive obligations on states to provide laws and remedies to protect religious people from improper attacks on their religion[11] or from other actions, including in the context of private employment, which violate the freedom protected by Article 9.[12]

Other Articles of the Convention may be relevant to religious belief, including Article 14 which prevents, among others, religious discrimination in respect of a person's exercise of any of the Convention rights and freedoms and Article 10, freedom of expression, or Article 8, the right to respect for private and family life. Even rights to property, under Article 1 of the First Protocol, can be involved, when planning questions for religious building arise, for example.[13]

Section 13 of the Human Rights Act 1998 appears to give extra weight to religious claims under the Act. It was agreed to by the government as a concession to religious organisations who feared that provisions in the Convention, in particular the non-discrimination provisions, under Article 14, might require schools and other institutions to take steps that would undermine their religious identity.

13 Freedom of thought, conscience and religion

(1) If a court's determination of any question arising under this Act might affect the exercise by a religious organisation (itself or its members collectively) of the Convention right to freedom of thought, conscience and religion, it must have particular regard to the importance of that right.

(2) In this section 'court' includes a tribunal.

It is hard to see how this measure has much of substance in it since a court can hardly do anything else than have 'particular regard' to Article 9, if Article 9 is in issue in a case.

23.4 Common law

Though it may have been once, Christianity is not part of the common law in the sense that non-Christian or even anti-Christian purposes will, if otherwise lawful, be supported by the law. In *Bowman* v *Secular Society Ltd* (1917)[14] a gift to the Secular Society was upheld by the House of Lords against a claim that it was unlawful because the Society sought to deny the truth of Christianity. Lord Parker could find no basis in statute, general criminal law or public policy for holding the gift invalid.[15] Apart from the exclusion of Roman Catholics from the Crown,[16] statutory religious tests have been abolished in

---

[10] *Kokkinakis* v *Greece* (1993) 17 EHRR 397, paragraph 33.
[11] *Dubowska and Skup* v *Poland* (1997) 24 EHRR CD 75.
[12] The implication of *Stedman* v *United Kingdom* [1997] EHRLR 545; Mrs Stedman's complaint, that her private employer made her work on the Sabbath, was unsuccessful on its merits not because no state interest was engaged.
[13] *ISKCON* v *United Kingdom* (1994) 18 EHRR CD 133 where it was argued, unsuccessfully, that the Court should permit a narrower margin of appreciation in respect of religious-based planning applications.
[14] [1917] AC 406.
[15] *Bowman* v *Secular Society Ltd* [1917] AC 406, 434.
[16] Act of Settlement 1700, s. 2.

respect of public functions, though religious organisations, such as faith schools, seem to be able to discriminate in respect of who they employ. Such discrimination, in respect of public office, might be incompatible with Article 14, as a Convention right, measured with Article 9. The Oaths Act 1978 provides a form of oath for Christians and Jews and allows others to choose to affirm.[17]

Private dispositions of property in favour of one religion and withdrawn from others, such as through a charitable donation or in a will, are valid despite their discriminatory quality. Donative and testamentary freedom outweighs religious discrimination.[18] Section 34 of the Race Relations Act 1976 outlaws discrimination on grounds of colour for charitable donations but has not, despite suggestions, been extended to include religious discrimination. Whether such donative and testamentary discrimination is incompatible with Convention rights is not clear. Any engagement of Convention rights would require positive duties on states to impose non-discriminatory rules in the private sphere generally, and not confine them to employment. Such dispositions are a clear and strong manifestation of religious belief[19] and may give sufficient grounds for the kind of 'reasonable and objective' justification for differences in treatment that are permitted under the jurisprudence relating to Article 14 ECHR.[20]

23.5 Religious exemptions

The law may promote religious freedom by providing exceptions to the general law in order to protect the necessities of religious observance.[21] For example, single-sex ministry is permitted as one of the exceptions in the Sex Discrimination Act 1975, overseas polygamous marriages, which may have a religious justification, are recognised, and male followers of the Sikh religion, who must wear turbans, have exemption from legal requirements to wear crash hats[22] or safety helmets.[23]

Such exemptions as these are justified as being necessary for believers if basic tenets and manifestations of belief are to be upheld. They also have little, if any, impact on others. Where manifestations of religious belief have an impact on a person's ability to work as directed by an employer, the courts have been much less sympathetic and have generally not allowed claims by employees for exemption from contractual duties in order to pursue religious observance, even where there is a general statutory duty on an employer not

---

[17] Oaths Act 1978, s. 5. No provision for an Islamic oath has been made.
[18] *Blathwayt* v *Baron Cawley* [1976] AC 397; *Re Lysaght* [1966] Ch 191; *Re Tuck's Settlement Trust* [1976] Ch 99.
[19] See Lord Cross in *Blathwayt*.
[20] *Belgian Linguistics Case* (1979–80) 1 EHRR 784.
[21] See, for example, Bailey, S.H., Harris, D.J. and Jones, B.L. (1995) *Civil Liberties Cases and Materials*, 4th edn. London: Butterworths, pp. 599–601.
[22] The Road Traffic Act 1988, s. 16(2).
[23] Employment Act 1989, ss. 11 and 12.

to discriminate on religious grounds.[24] Employees' claims have been rejected by the Court of Human Rights.[25]

The law does not normally permit conscientious objection, even if motivated by religious belief, to relieve persons from the burdens of the law such as the payment of tax for the purchase of armaments by Quaker pacifists.[26] In such cases what is in issue is not the direct requirements of religious observation but the moral perspective that a religious belief may engender. Fundamental to the rule of law in a democracy is that all are bound, even by the laws they oppose. Nor can conscientious, religion-based belief act as a defence to what would otherwise be crimes.[27] There are some areas in which conscientious objection, including religious based, is accepted. Section 4 of the Abortion Act 1967 is a good example which, given that it could lead to very unequal provision of abortion services in particular areas, illustrates both the virtue and the difficulty of conscientious objection provisions.[28]

23.6 The promotion of religion

Aspects of the law promote or give advantages to religion, particularly Christianity. The Church of England, the established church, enjoys certain advantages at the cost of some state interference in its internal affairs.[29] Although the leaders of other religions may be appointed to the House of Lords none of them enjoy the right *ex officio* to sit in the House of Lords. Legal recognition of Sunday, the Christian Sabbath, as a special day is greatly reduced and most restraints in the areas of entertainments and shopping have now been lifted,[30] though the extent to which the rights of employees who wish not to work on Sunday have been protected is questionable.

Traditionally, the legal promotion of Christianity has been through the state maintained education system. The long-standing requirement for Christian worship in state schools (community or grant maintained) is now lessened. Community schools are required to have a compulsory act of worship that must have a broadly Christian character.[31] Parents have individual rights to withdraw their children from this.[32] By section 394 of the Education Act 1996 a school can seek permission from the local education authority to be exempt from the requirement for Christian worship on grounds which include the family background of many of their pupils. Permission requires the approval

---

[24] *Ahmad* v *ILEA* [1978] 1 All ER 574, CA, in which a Muslim teacher missed 45 minutes of his teaching duties in order to attend Friday prayers. Section 30, Education Act 1944 prevented religious discrimination in the recruitment of teachers or requiring teachers to give religious instruction.

[25] See above, note 9.

[26] As in *Cheney* v *Conn* [1968] 1 All ER 779, dealing with a challenge to the validity of an Act of Parliament. The general position is upheld under ECHR in *C* v *United Kingdom* (1983) 37 DR 142.

[27] *Blake* v *DPP* [1993] Crim LR 586; *R* v *Senior* [1899] 1 QB 283.

[28] See comments in Chapter 21.

[29] *Halsbury's Laws of England*, 4th edn. vol. 14 'Ecclesiastical Law' (1975), paragraphs 345–60.

[30] Sunday Trading Act 1994, which allows large shops to open on Sundays for six hours; access to entertainment is extended by the Cinemas Act 1985.

[31] Section 70, School Standards and Framework Act 1998, and Schedule 20.

[32] Section 71, School Standards and Framework Act 1998.

of the education authority's Standing Advisory Council of Religious Education. The acts of worship can then be non-denominational or can be distinctive
of another faith. A child who is not withdrawn by his or her parents can still
be compelled to worship in one religion or another. These exemptions are
explained by Article 2, Protocol 1 ECHR, the 'right to education', which
requires states to give effect to a right of parents that their children be educated
in line with their, the parents', religious and philosophical convictions.[33]

The New Labour government promoted 'faith-based' schools. The link
between religion and morality and ethics makes such proposals controversial.
Difficult questions about sex education, the equality of the educational
provision for girls and the degree of acceptance and awareness of other faiths
are likely to arise in this context.

Religion is also promoted by religious organisations being able to benefit
from charitable status. This can bring significant tax advantages, although it
also brings limits on, for example, the pursuit of political purposes,[34] and it
brings supervision by the Charity Commissioners. It is in the context of groups
claiming such advantages that the courts have had to deal with the question
of what is a 'religion' and whether groups such as the Church of Scientology
or the Moonies count as religions or whether the Exclusive Brethren, though
religious, can be charitable.[35]

23.7 The protection of religion: blasphemy

The issue of blasphemy is whether religion, distinctively, should enjoy the
protection of the law from criticism and attack. Blasphemy involves a tension
between a claim that religious belief is of such fundamental significance for
persons that it needs the special protection of the law and, on the other hand,
the denial that the special claims of religion exist or are sufficiently strong to
override the rights of others to freedom of expression.

Criticisms of the Church and Christianity which fell short of heresy were, in
the pre and early-modern world, understood to be the concern of ecclesiastical
courts rather than the common law. By the end of the seventeenth century, the
state began to replace the Church as the punisher of morally unacceptable
behaviour[36] and blasphemous libel was accepted as a common law offence in
Attwoods' Case (1617).[37] The basis of common law jurisdiction was partly the
protection of morality but, more significantly, an attack on religion, specifically
Christianity, undermined the authority of the laws generally. 'If religion is a
cheat the body politic is threatened; the oaths, contracts and obligations are
meaningless . . . Christianity is a parcel of the laws of England'.[38] A century

---

[33] The reservation entered into by the United Kingdom in respect of the parental rights provision
of Article 2 relates to the maintenance of efficient instruction and training and the avoidance of
unreasonable public expenditure. It is retained under the Human Rights Act 1998.
[34] Davis, H. (2000) *Political Freedom*. London: Continuum, chapter 4.
[35] Bailey, Harris and Jones, *op. cit.*, p. 580.
[36] Unsworth, C. (1995) 'Blasphemy, Cultural Divergence and Legal Relativism', 58 *MLR* 5, 658.
[37] (1617) Cro Jac 421, 79 ER 359. For a review of the case law see *R v Chief Metropolitan Stipendiary
Magistrate ex parte Choudhury* [1991] 1 All ER 306.
[38] *Taylor's Case* (1676) Vent 293, 86 ER 189.

later, during the repression aimed at limiting the influence of the French Revolution, blasphemous libel was used against political opponents of the established order; again, an attack on Christianity was seen as an attack on the state and the laws.[39] Blasphemous libel, on this view, includes within the reach of the offence reasoned scepticism about, or refutation of, the truths of Christianity. During the politically calmer and more scientifically aware nineteenth century an apparent shift in *actus reus* seems to have occurred. Honest and sober disagreements between reasonable persons about the truth or otherwise of Christian doctrine are acceptable. Instead, blasphemy is found in the tone, the insulting spirit, of any attack.[40] This position was eventually given House of Lords authority in *Bowman* v *Secular Society* (1917).[41] Denying the truth of Christianity is not sufficient. There must be an attack and it must have a 'scurrilous, ribald or contumelious' tone. A scurrilous tone is one of buffoon-like jocularity, coarseness and indecency; a ribald tone is obscene or involves coarse language or is abusive and low; a contumelious tone involves insolent abuse or is insulting or contemptuous or illustrates scornful rudeness, tending to humiliation.[42] There were few reported decisions and the offence went into decline.[43]

The law was revived in *R* v *Lemon* (1979).[44] Its origins were in a successful prosecution of the publication in *Gay News*, edited by Lemon, of a poem by James Kirkup, an established poet who wrote on gay themes. 'The poem purports to describe in explicit detail acts of sodomy and fellatio with the body of Christ immediately after His death and to ascribe to Him during his lifetime promiscuous homosexual practices with the Apostles and with other men'.[45] The appeal to the House of Lords was on the *mens rea* of the offence which was held to be strict in the sense that no intention to blaspheme need be proved, only an intention to publish what is, objectively, a blasphemy. The case involves a shift in the general burden of the offence. It is the offensiveness to others that comes to the fore, the capacity of the work in issue to outrage religious feeling. This capacity to offend can be found in serious works, in poems, films and novels, which would not normally be thought of as 'scurrilous, ribald or contumelious'.

Offensiveness to others has been accepted by the Commission and Court of Human Rights as being an acceptable ground for a blasphemy law. The Strasbourg institutions have allowed bans of blasphemous works as being within the margin of appreciation of signatory states[46] so long as the denial of religious truth is not in itself a criminal offence and criminality is triggered by a high degree of offensiveness.[47] A law on blasphemy is compatible with

---

[39] *R* v *Williams* (1797) Howell's State Trials, volume 26, 656: the prosecution of the publisher of Thomas Paine, *The Age of Reason*.
[40] *R* v *Hetherington* (1841) 9 State Trials (NS) 563; *Ramsay* v *Foote* (1883) 15 Cox CC 231 which refers to *R* v *Waddington* (1822) 1 State Trials (NS), 107 ER 11.
[41] [1917] AC 406.
[42] These definitions are taken from the *Shorter Oxford English Dictionary*.
[43] Few if any cases were reported after *R* v *Gott* (1922) 16 Cr App Rep 87.
[44] [1979] AC 617.
[45] *R* v *Lemon* [1979] AC 617, 632, per Lord Diplock.
[46] A wide margin of appreciation is commonly allowed on 'moral' issues such as blasphemy or obscenity.
[47] *Wingrove* v *United Kingdom* Ap. 17419/90; (1997) 24 EHRR 1.

Article 10(2) ECHR (freedom of expression) as being to protect the rights of others. The right others are said to enjoy is to be protected from a high level of insult and outrage to religious sensibility.[48] The level of insult must be high since there is ample Strasbourg authority that free speech under the Convention protects offensive and unpopular speech.[49] In *Choudhury* v *United Kingdom* (1991)[50] the Commission denied that states had a positive duty to protect this right by positive measures which would apply equally for all religions. However, more recently, in *Dubowska and Skup* v *Poland* (1997),[51] the Commission suggested that there might be a positive duty on states to protect people from being disturbed in their worship by 'the manner in which religious beliefs or doctrines are opposed'.

In the United Kingdom, blasphemous libel is confined to serious insult to the Christian religion alone of the world's religions if it is a body of general beliefs that is attacked. Arguably, if the attack is on a church and its doctrines, the offence is limited to Anglicanism. In *R* v *Chief Metropolitan Stipendiary Magistrate ex parte Choudhury* (1991)[52] the Court of Appeal declined to extend the offence to other religions and this was accepted by the Commission of Human Rights in Strasbourg. Once the point of the crime shifted from upholding the authority of the laws and the established order to guarding against offensiveness to individual religious sensibility, confining it to one religion became arbitrary, a historical anomaly. In a multi-faith society there is no good reason why followers of only one of the faiths should enjoy this kind of protection. Such arbitrariness led to calls for reform; either the offence should be abolished or extended to all religions. The Law Commission in its review of the topic[53] argued for the abolition of the offence and its replacement by offences of incitement to religious hatred.[54]

The matter is highly controversial. If there is a need in modern society for a law of blasphemy, then it should be applied to all religions. This is a perfectly creditable position, rooted in equality under the law. A general argument for a law of blasphemy has as its target the liberal assumption that the state has no place in promoting or giving special protection to religion. Critics of liberal theory argue that its basic premises about persons and societies are over-individualistic and that, as a theory, it fails to give sufficient credence to the way any person's sense of self-hood, well-being and self-respect is rooted in community and collective understanding.[55] The profundities of faith can be central to well-being and self-respect in a way that rationally based political beliefs or moral rules are not. On this view it is justifiable for the law to protect

---

[48] See in particular *Lemon* v *United Kingdom* (1982) 5 EHRR 123; *Otto Preminger Institute* v *Austria* (1995) 19 EHRR 34; *Wingrove* v *United Kingdom* Ap. 17419/90; (1997) 24 EHRR 1.
[49] *Handyside* v *United Kingdom* (1979) 1 EHRR 737, paragraph 49.
[50] Ap. 17439/90; (1991) HRLJ 172.
[51] (1997) 24 EHRR CD 75.
[52] [1991] 1 All ER 306.
[53] The Law Commission (1981) *Criminal Law: Offences against Religion and Public Worship*, Working Paper 79; Report 145 (1985).
[54] A minority of the Commission argued for an extension to cover all religions and denominations.
[55] See, for example, Sandel, M. (1982) *Liberalism and the Limits of Justice*. Cambridge: Cambridge University Press. For sensitivity to the issue from within a liberal perspective see Kymlicka, W. (1989) *Liberalism, Community and Culture*. Oxford: Clarendon Press.

religious sensibility from the cruder and more vicious forms of attack. The argument is particularly strong in respect of a multi-cultural society, such as Great Britain, where adherents to minority faiths in particular may feel particularly vulnerable.

The arguments against a law of blasphemy, and hence against its universal application, are particularly strong given that the crime deals with highly offensive rather than directly harmful[56] words. The liberal position rejects the idea that a person can reasonably be punished merely for offending others. No harm is done to those who are offended: their interests are not harmed since the alleged blasphemy does not prevent them from worship. Free speech means little unless it permits speech which is unpopular and offensive. Opponents of a law of blasphemy also point out that it gives an advantage to the religious in any argument. It is like a trump card which those of a religious sensibility can play to stop argument and criticism of beliefs and practices. Religious-based morality and practices may need reform; they can be highly illiberal[57] and can sometimes appear to justify unlawful violence.[58] J.S. Mill's famous defence of freedom of speech contains the idea that social progress can result from the criticism of established views and beliefs and criticisms of religion are likely to be highly offensive particularly in their first appearances. There are also political objections to a law of blasphemy. The revival of the law of blasphemy in the 1980s, and its continued significance today, has been associated with the rise of the right wing in British politics and with the authoritarianism that that brought.[59] The extension of blasphemy to all religions would also raise a range of formal problems. In particular is the difficult job of defining a religion. Even if it is possible to confine religion to mankind's relations with God, as distinct from 'ethics' which deals with mankind's relations to man,[60] there will always be a range of claims to religious sensibility from outside the confines of the main world religions. These would need to be decided by courts which may not be competent to make the judgment involved. Minority and eccentric views would be given an unmerited protection. A further difficulty has been suggested: that different religious groups may expect different degrees of protection from offensive words and conduct.[61] It may, for example, be much easier to commit a blasphemy against Islam than against Christianity. Such differential treatment, which may be necessary to meet the aspirations of those seeking to protect their religions, will be difficult to defend given that equality under the law is the reason for extending blasphemy to all religions in the first place.

The alternative to a general law of blasphemy is the creation of offences of incitement to religious hatred. The New Labour government has been

---

[56] There is some authority for the view that blasphemous libel requires an anticipated breach of the peace. This would narrow the offence to situations in which violence is a foreseeable, proximate reaction to the alleged blasphemous act. The offence goes wider than this.

[57] In relation to homosexuals and to the position of women, for example.

[58] The 'fatwa' against Salman Rushdie is an obvious example; the alleged involvement of the Archbishop in Rwanda in the genocide of the Tutsi by the Hutu may be another.

[59] The argument relates particularly to the period of the Conservative government after 1979. On the link to blasphemy See Unsworth, *op. cit.*

[60] *Re South Place Ethical Society* [1980] 1 WLR 1565.

[61] See Unsworth, *op. cit.*

sympathetic to this approach, although its attempt to attach such an offence to the Anti-terrorism, Crime and Security Act 2001 failed in Parliament. The crucial issue is to ensure that such offences do not simply amount to a law against blasphemy by another name. One way is to ensure that, under any new offences, it will be necessary for the state to prove an intention to cause unreasonable hatred of religion which is likely to lead to violence. The government may relate such provisions with the provisions dealing with religious discrimination in employment that they must bring in during 2003.

Bibliography of works cited

Akdeniz, Y. Walker, C. and Wall, D. (2000) *The Internet, Law and Society*. London: Pearson Education.

Arblaster, A. (1994) *Democracy*, 2nd edn. Buckingham: Buckingham University Press.

Ashworth, A. (1999) *Principles of Criminal Law*. Oxford: Oxford University Press.

Bailey, S.H. (1997) *Cross on Principles of Local Government Law*, 2nd edn. London: Sweet & Maxwell.

Bailey, S.H., Harris, D.J. and Jones, B.L. (1995) *Civil Liberties Cases and Materials*, 4th edn. London: Butterworths.

Baker, E. (2000) 'Policing, Protest and Free Trade: Challenging Police Discretion under Community Law', *Crim LR* 95.

Barber, B. (1994) *Strong Democracy: Participatory Politics for a New Age*. Berkeley, CA: University of California Press.

Barendt, E. (1987) *Freedom of Speech*. Oxford: Clarendon Press.

Barendt, E. (1998) 'Judging the Media: Impartiality and Broadcasting', in Sector, J. (ed.), *Politics and the Media Harlots and Prerogatives at the Turn of the Millenium*. London: Blackwell.

Barry, B. (1995) *Justice as Impartiality*. Oxford: Clarendon Press.

Bayne, P. (1994) 'Freedom of Information and Political Free Speech', in Campbell, T. and Sadurski, W. (eds), *Freedom of Communication*. Aldershot: Dartmouth.

BBC (1989) *Annual Report and Handbook 1989*. London: BBC.

Bentham, J. (1978) 'Offences Against Oneself: Paederasty', *Journal of Homosexuality*, Summer–Fall.

Betten, L. and Grief, N. (1998) *EU Law and Human Rights*. London: Longman.

Bingham, T.H. (1993) 'The European Convention on Human Rights: Time to Incorporate', 109 *LQR* 390.

Birkinshaw, P. (1990) *Government and Information: The Law Relating to Access, Disclosure and Regulation*. London: Butterworths.

Blackstone, W. (1765–69) *Commentaries on the Laws of England*.

Blackstone's Criminal Practice (1999) London: Blackstone Press.

Boyle, A. (1983) 'Freedom of Expression as a Public Interest in English Law', *Public Law* 574.

Boyle, A. (1986) 'Political Broadcasting, Fairness and Administrative Law', *Public Law* 562.

Bradley, A. and Ewing, K. (2002) *Constitutional and Administrative Law*, 13th edn. London: Longmans.

Brazier, M.R. (1995) *Clerk & Lindsell on Torts*, 17th edn. London: Sweet & Maxwell.

Browne-Wilkinson, Rt Hon. Lord (1992) 'The Infiltration of a Bill of Rights', *PL* 397.

Brownlie, I. (ed.) *Basic Documents on Human Rights*, 3rd edn. Oxford: Clarendon Press.

Burrow, J. (2000) 'Bail and the Human Rights Act 1998–1', *NLJ* 677.

Burrow, J. (2000) 'Bail and the Human Rights Act 1998–2', *NLJ* 736.

Campbell, T. (1983) *The Left and the Rights: A Conceptual Analysis of the Idea of Socialist Rights*. London: Routledge.

Campbell, T. and Sadurski, W. (eds) (1994) *Freedom of Communication*. Aldershot: Dartmouth.

Card, R. (2000) *Public Order Law*. Bristol: Jordan Publishing.

Card, R. and Ward, R (1994) *The Criminal Justice and Public Order Act 1994*. Bristol: Jordan Publishing.

Carter, A. and Stokes, G. (1998) *Liberal Democracy and Its Critics*. Cambridge: Polity Press.

Carter, H. (1999) 'A Jury Backs Granny's Anti-nuclear Graffiti', *The Guardian*, 18 December, p. 11.

Clayton, R. and Tomlinson, H. (1992) *Civil Actions Against the Police*. London: Sweet & Maxwell.

Colvin, M. (1999) 'Surveillance and the Human Rights Act', in The University of Cambridge Centre for Public Law, *The Human Rights Act and the Criminal Justice Regulatory Process*. Oxford: Hart Publishing.

Commissioner of Police of the Metropolis (various) *Annual Reports*. London: Metropolitan Police.

Cooper, S. (2000) 'Summing up Intention', 150 *NLJ* 6949, 1258.

Craig, P. (1990) *Public Law and Democracy in the United Kingdom and the United States of America*. Oxford: Clarendon Press.

Craig, P. (1994) *Administrative Law*. London: Sweet and Maxwell.

Craig, P. and de Búrca, G. (2003) *EC Law, Text Cases and Materials*, 3rd edn. Oxford: Oxford University Press. Oxford: Clarendon Press.

Cross, C.A. and Sauvian, S.J. (1981) annotations, in *Current Law Statutes Annotated 1980*, Vol. 2, *The Highways Act 1980 c. 66*. London: Sweet & Maxwell.

Crown, G. (1997) 'Judicial Review and Press Complaints', 147 *NLJ* 8.

Curran, J. and Seaton, J. (1997) *Power without Responsibility*, 5th edn. London: Routledge.

Davis, H. (1988) '*Bowman* v *United Kingdom* – A Case for the Human Rights Act?', *Public Law* 592.

Davis, H. (1999) 'Constitutional Law Reform in the United Kingdom and the Right to Free and Fair Elections', *EHRLR*, 4, 411.

Davis, H. (2000) *Political Freedom*. London: Continuum.

Devlin, P. (1965) *The Enforcement of Morals*. Oxford: Oxford University Press.

Dicey, A.V. (1885) *Introduction to the Study of the Law of the Constitution*. Indianapolis, IN: Liberty Classics.

Drewry, G. (2002) 'What Happened to the Citizen's Charter?', *Public Law* 9 (Autumn).

Dworkin, R. (1977) *The Philosophy of Law*. Oxford: Oxford University Press.

Dworkin, R. (1977) *Taking Rights Seriously*. London: Duckworth.

Dworkin, R. (1986) *A Matter of Principle*. Oxford: Clarendon Press.

Dworkin, R. (1990) *A Bill of Rights for Britain*. London: Chatto & Windus.

Electoral Commission (2001) *Party Political Broadcasting 2001–02*, Discussion Paper. London: Electoral Commission.

Electoral Commission (2002) *Party Political Broadcasts Consultation Paper*. Electoral Commission.

Enright, S. (2000) 'Crime Brief', *NLJ* 14 July 1047.

Evans, M.D. and Morgan, R. (1998) *Preventing Torture: A Study of the European Convention for the Prevention of Torture and Inhuman or Degrading Treatment or Punishment*. Oxford: Oxford University Press.

Ewing, K. (1993) 'New Constitutional Constraints in Australia', *Public Law* 256.

Ewing, K. (1996) 'Human Rights, Social Democracy and Constitutional Reform', in Gearty, C. and Tomkins, A. (eds), *Understanding Human Rights*. London: Mansell.

Ewing, K. and Gearty, C. (1990) *Freedom under Thatcher. Civil Liberties in Modern Britain*. Oxford: Clarendon Press.

Ewing, K. and Gearty, C. (2000) *The Struggle for Civil Liberties*. Oxford: Oxford University Press.

Fairly, D. (1990) 'D Notices, Official Secrets and the Law' 10 *OJLS* 430.

Feldman, D. (1986) *The Law Relating to Entry, Search and Seizure*. London: Butterworth

Feldman, D. (2002) *Civil Liberties and Human Rights in England and Wales*, 2nd edn. Oxford: Oxford University Press.

Feldman, D. (2002) 'Parliamentary Scrutiny of Legislation and Human Rights', *Public Law* 323.

Fenwick, H. (1998) *Civil Liberties*. London: Cavendish.

Fenwick, H. (2000) *Civil Rights, New Labour, Freedom and the Human Rights Act*. Harlow: Longman.

Finnis, J. (1980) *Natural Law and Natural Rights*. Oxford: Oxford University Press.

Foster, S. (2001) 'Inhuman and Degrading Prison Conditions', *NLJ* 1222.

Fottrell, D. (2001) 'Developing Human Rights Protection beyond the Human Rights Act', 151 7008 *NLJ* 1688.

Freud, S. (1930) *Civilisation and its Discontents*. London: Hogarth Press.

Gearty, C. and Tomkins, A. (eds) (1996) *Understanding Human Rights*. London: Mansell.

Gibbons, T. (1998) *Regulating the Media*, 2nd edn. London: Sweet & Maxwell.

Goldberg, D., Prosser, T. and Verhulst, S. (eds) (1998) *Regulating the Changing Media: A Comparative Study*. Oxford: Clarendon Press.

Goodhart, A.L. (1936–7) '*Thomas* v *Sawkins*' A Constitutional Innovation *CLJ* 22.

Griffith, J.A.G. (1979) 'The Political Constitution', 42 1 *MLR* 1.

Griffith, J.A.G. (1981) *The Politics of the Judiciary*, 2nd edn. London: Fontana.

Griffith, J.A.G. (1985) 'Judicial Decision-Making in the Law', *Public Law* 564.

Halsbury's Laws of England, 4th edn and reissues (1973–). London: Butterworths.

Hamilton, C. (1995) *Family Law and Religion*. London: Sweet & Maxwell.

Harris, D., O'Boyle, M. and Warbrick, C. (1995) *Law of the European Convention on Human Rights*. London: Butterworths.

Hewitt, P. (1982) *The Abuse of Power: Civil Liberties in the United Kingdom*. London: Martin Robinson.

Hirst, P. (1994) *Associative Democracy*. London: Polity Press.

HM Chief Inspector of Constabulary (various) *Annual Reports*. London: HMSO/TSO.

Home Affairs Committee (1979–80) 'Fifth Report: The Law Relating to Public Order', *Parliamentary Papers 1979–1980*, HC Papers 756-I, 756-II, xlviii.

Home Office (1994) *Guidelines on Special Branch Work in Great Britain*, reproduced at http://www.Scotland.gov.uk/hmic/docs/fpeo-12.asp.

Hume, D. (1978) *A Treatise of Human Nature*. Oxford: Oxford University Press.

Hunt, M. (1997) *Using Human Rights Law in English Courts*. Oxford: Hart Publishing.

Information Commissioner (2000) *Code of Practice for Users of Closed Circuit Television*. Wilmslow: Information Commissioner.

Information Commissioner (2001) *Promotion of a Political Party: The Use of Direct Mail, Telephone and E-mail*. Wilmslow: Information Commissioner.

Jones, P. (1994) *Rights*. London: Macmillan Press.

Jones, T.H. (1995) 'The Devaluation of Human Rights Under the European Convention', *Public Law* 430.

Jowell, J. and Oliver, D. (eds) (1989) *The Changing Constitution*, 2nd edn. Oxford: Clarendon Press.

JUSTICE (1998) *Under Surveillance – Covert Policing and Human Rights Standards*. London: JUSTICE.

Kerrigan, K. (1997) 'Breach of the Peace and Binding Over – Continuing Confusion', 2 *Journal of Civil Liberties* 1, 30.

Klug, F., Starmer, K. and Weir, S. (1994) 'Civil Liberties and the Parliamentary Watchdog: The Passage of the Criminal Justice and Public Order Act 1994', 49 *Parliamentary Affairs* 4, 536–49.

Klug, F., Starmer, K. and Weir, S. (1996) *The Three Pillars of Liberty*. London: Routledge.

Kymlicka, W. (1989) *Liberalism, Community and Culture*. Oxford: Clarendon Press.

Lakoff, S. (1996) *Democracy. History, Theory and Practice*. Oxford: Westview Press.

Law Commission (1983) *Offences Relating to Public Order*, Law Commission Report No. 123, HC Papers 85.

Lawson, R. (2001) 'Challenging the Advertising Standards Authority', *NLJ* 13 April, 526–7.

Leader, S. (1990) 'The Right to Privacy, the Enforcement of Morals, and the Judicial Function: An Argument', *Current Legal Problems* 115–34.

Leader, S. (1992) *Freedom of Association*. New Haven, CT: Yale University Press.

Lester of Herne Hill, Lord (2002) 'Thirty Years on: The East African Asians Case Revisited', *Public Law* 52, Spring.

Lester of Herne Hill, Lord and Pannick, D. (eds) (1999) *Human Rights Law and Practice*. London: Butterworths.

Lively, J. (1975) *Democracy*. Oxford: Blackwell.

Livingstone, S. and Owen, T. (1999) *Prison Law*, 2nd edn. Oxford: Oxford University Press.

Loughlin, M. (1992) *Public Law and Political Theory*. Oxford: Oxford University Press.

Loveday, B. (1986) 'Central Co-ordination, Police Authorities and the Miners' Strike', 60 *PQ* 68.

Loveland, I. (ed.) (1988) *Incorporating the First Amendment*. Oxford: Hart Publishing.

McCabe, S. *et al.* (1988) *The Police, Public Order and Civil Liberties: Legacies of the Miners' Strike*. London: Routledge.

McClusky, J.H. (Lord) (1986) *Law, Justice and Democracy*. London: Sweet & Maxwell.

MacFarlane, L.J. (1981) *The Right to Strike*. Harmondsworth: Penguin.

McNair, B. (1996) *News and Journalism in the U.K.*, 2nd edn. London: Routledge.

Macpherson of Cluny, Sir William (1999) *The Stephen Lawrence Inquiry. Report*, CM 4262-I. London: Stationery Office.

Markesinis, B. (ed.) (1999) *Protecting Privacy*. Oxford: Oxford University Press.

Mason, J.K. and McCall Smith, R.A. (1999) *Law and Medical Ethics*, 5th edn. London: Butterworths.

Meiklejohn, A. (1961) 'The First Amendment is an Absolute', *Supreme Court Review*, 245.

Miers, D. (1999) 'Deregulation Procedure: An Expanding Role', *Public Law* 477.

Mill, John Stuart (1909) *Principles of Political Economy* [1848]. London: Longman, Green & Co.

Mill, John Stuart (1968) *Utilitarianism, Liberty and Representative Government*. London: Dent.

Morris, G.S. (1998a) 'Political Activities of Public Servants and Freedom of Expression', in Loveland, I. (ed.), *Incorporating the First Amendment*. Oxford: Hart Publishing.

Morris G.S. (1998b) 'Local Government Workers and Rights of Political Participation: Time for a Change', *Public Law* 25.

Morris, G. (1999) 'The Political Activities of Local Government Workers and the European Convention on Human Rights', *Public Law* 211.

Mowbray, A. (1999) 'The Role of the European Court of Human Rights in the Promotion of Democracy', *Public Law* 703.

Mulhall, S. and Swift, A. (1996) *Liberals and Communitarians*, 2nd edn. Oxford: Blackwell.

Munro, C. (1996) '*SNP* v *BBC* round two', 146 *NLJ* 143.

Munro, C. (1996) 'The Banned Broadcasting Corporation', 146 *NLJ* 1433.

Nowak, M (1993) *U.N. Covenant on Civil and Political Rights. CCPR Commentary*. Kehl am Rhein: N.P. Engel.

O'Higgins, P. (1996) annotations, in *Current Law Statutes 1996*, Vol. 2, *Security Service Act 1996 c. 35*. London: Sweet & Maxwell.

Oakeshott, M. (1991) *Rationalism in Politics and Other Essays*. Indianapolis, IN: Liberty Press.

Oliver, D. (2000) 'The Frontiers of the State: Public Authorities and Public Functions under the Human Rights Act 1998', *Public Law* 476.

Palmer, H. (1957) 'Dr Adams' Trial for Murder', *Crim LR* 365.

Pannick, D. (1998) 'Principles of Interpretation of Convention Rights under the Human Rights Act and the Discretionary Area of Judgment', *PL* 545 (Winter), pp. 546–48.

Parpworth, N. (2000) 'The Citizen's Power of Arrest', *Justice of the Peace*, 3 June.

Parpworth, N. (2000) 'Section 28 of PACE and Unlawful Arrest', *Justice of the Peace*, 1 July.

Paul, E.F. *et al.* (2000) *The Right to Privacy*. Cambridge: Cambridge University Press.

Pitt, G. (2000) *Employment Law*, 4th edn. London: Sweet & Maxwell.

Rawlings, H.F. (1988) *Law and the Electoral Process*. London: Sweet & Maxwell.

Rawls, J. (1972) *A Theory of Justice*. Oxford: Oxford University Press.

Robertson, G. (1979) *Obscenity*. London: Weidenfeld & Nicolson.

Robertson, G. (1993) *Freedom, the Individual and the Law*. Harmondsworth: Penguin Books.

Robertson, G. and Nicol, A. (1992) *Media Law*, 3rd edn. Harmondsworth: Penguin.

Rodley, N.S. (1998) *The Treatment of Prisoners under International Law*, 2nd edn. Oxford: Oxford University Press.

Russell, D.E.H. (ed.) (1993) *Making Violence Sexy: Feminist Views on Pornography*. Buckingham: Open University Press.

Ryan, A. (1986) *Property and Political Theory*. Oxford: Blackwell.

Sandel, M.J. (1996) *Liberalism and the Limits of Justice*. 2nd edn. Cambridge: Cambridge University Press.

Scanlon, T. (1972) 'A Theory of Freedom of Expression', in Dworkin, R. (ed.), *The Philosophy of Law*. Oxford: Oxford University Press.

Scarman, Lord (1974) *English Law – the New Dimension*. London: Stevens.

Schauer, F. (1982) *Freedom of Speech: A Philosophical Inquiry*. Cambridge: Cambridge University Press.

Schumpeter, J. (1982) *Capitalism, Socialism and Demcracy*. London: Routledge.

Scrutton, R. (2000) *The Meaning of Conservatism*, 3rd edn. London: Palgrave.

Sector, J. (1998) *Politics and the Media: Harlots and Prerogatives at the Turn of the Millenium*. London: Blackwell.

Stallworthy, M. (2000) 'Damage to Crops – Part 1 and Part 2', 150 *NLJ* 728, 801.

Stanley, P. (2000) annotations, in *Current Law Statutes 2000*, Vol. 2, *Freedom of Information Act 2000 c. 36*. London: Sweet & Maxwell.

Starmer, K. (1999) *European Human Rights Law*. London: LAG.

Steiner, H. (1988) 'Political Participation as a Human Right', 1 *Harvard Human Rights Yearbook*, 77.

Stephen, Sir James (1883) *A History of the Criminal Law*. London: Macmillan.

Stevens, J. and Feldman, D. (1997) 'Broadcasting Advertisements by Bodies with Political Objectives, Judicial Review and the Influence of Charities Law', *Public Law* 615.

Steyn, Rt Hon. Lord (1997) 'The Weakest and Least Dangerous Department of Government', *PL* 84.

Stone, R. (2000) *Textbook on Civil Liberties*. London: Blackstone Press.

Street, H.S. (1977) *Freedom, the Indicdual and the Law*, 4th edn. Harmondsworth: Penguin.

Supperstone, M. and Coppell, J. (1997) 'A New Approach to Public Interest Immunity', *PL* 211.

Tomkins, A. (2002) 'Legislating Against Terror: the Anti-terrorism, Crime and Security Act 2001', *Public Law* 205 (Summer).

Turpin, C. (1989) 'Ministerial Responsibility – Myth or Reality', in Jowell, J. and Oliver, D. (eds), *The Changing Constitution*, 2nd edn. Oxford: Clarendon Press.

Unsworth, C. (1995) 'Blasphemy, Cultural Divergence and Legal Relativism', 58 *MLR* 5, 658.

Vickers, J. and Board, J. (2000) 'Circumcision – the Unkindest Cut of All', *NLJ* 1694 (17 November).

Wacks, R. (1995) *Privacy and Press Freedom*. London: Blackstone Press.

Waddington, P.A.J. (1994) *Liberty and Order*. London: UCL Press.

Wade, E.C.S. (1948) 'Seditious Libel and the Press', 64 *LQR* 203.

Wade, Sir William and Forsyth, C.F. (2000) *Administrative Law*, 8th edn. Oxford: Oxford University Press.

Wadham, J. (2000) 'Remedies for Unlawful CCTV Surveillance – Part 1', *NLJ* 4 August, 1173.

Wadham, J. (2000) 'Remedies for Unlawful CCTV Surveillance – Part 2', *NLJ* 11 August, 1236.

Wadham, J. (2001) 'The Human Rights Act: Sufficient Protection?', *NLJ* 1411.

Waldron, J. (1993) 'A Right-Based Critique of Constitutional Rights', 13 *OJLS* 18.

Wicks, E. (2000) 'The United Kingdom's Government's Perception of the European Convention on Human Rights at the Time of Entry' *Public Law* (Autumn) 438.

Williams, G.L. (1954) 'Arrest for Breach of the Peace', *Crim LR* 578.

Weale, A. (1999) *Democracy*. London: Macmillan.

Woolf, Rt Hon. Lord (1995) 'Droit Public – English Style', *Public Law* 57.

Woolf, L.J. and Tumim J. (1991) *Prison Disturbances: April 1990*, Cm 1456. London: Stationery Office.

Zander, M. (2002) 'The Revised PACE Codes', 152 7039 *NLJ* 1035.

Zander, M. (2001) 'The Anti-Terrorism Bill – What Happened?', 151 *NLJ* 1880.

Zander, M. (2002) 'The Police Reform Act 2002, Part 2', 152 *NLJ* 1387.

Index